Untangling Smart Cities

From Utopian Dreams to Innovation Systems for a Technology-Enabled Urban Sustainability

Untangling Smart Cities

From Utopian Dreams to Innovation Systems for a Technology-Enabled Urban Sustainability

Luca Mora

Mark Deakin

ELSEVIER

Elsevier
Radarweg 29, PO Box 211, 1000 AE Amsterdam, Netherlands
The Boulevard, Langford Lane, Kidlington, Oxford OX5 1GB, United Kingdom
50 Hampshire Street, 5th Floor, Cambridge, MA 02139, United States

Notices

Knowledge and best practice in this field are constantly changing. As new research and experience broaden our understanding, changes in research methods, professional practices, or medical treatment may become necessary.

Practitioners and researchers must always rely on their own experience and knowledge in evaluating and using any information, methods, compounds, or experiments described herein. In using such information or methods they should be mindful of their own safety and the safety of others, including parties for whom they have a professional responsibility.

To the fullest extent of the law, neither the Publisher nor the authors, contributors, or editors, assume any liability for any injury and/or damage to persons or property as a matter of products liability, negligence or otherwise, or from any use or operation of any methods, products, instructions, or ideas contained in the material herein.

Library of Congress Cataloging-in-Publication Data
A catalog record for this book is available from the Library of Congress

British Library Cataloguing-in-Publication Data
A catalogue record for this book is available from the British Library

ISBN 978-0-12-815477-9

Publisher: Joe Hayton
Acquisition Editor: Brian Romer
Editorial Project Manager: Andrae Akeh
Production Project Manager: Nirmala Arumugam
Cover Designer: Christian J. Bilbow

Typeset by SPi Global, India

Contents

Foreword: The landscape of smart cities

Smart cities are a product of the continued scaling down of computers and the all pervasiveness of ever faster communication systems enabling these technologies to be embedded into the very fabric of the built environment all around us. Since the invention of the smart phone, most people now have devices that enable them to connect up with anyone, anywhere, any time, so that they might avail themselves of the social and economic benefits of such instant communications. Passive sensors linked to one another are being quickly built into the physical environment, while our own use of mobile devices is enabling us to connect up with these sensors and to link ourselves to the streams of real-time data gushing from these new reservoirs. The prospect of making the city smarter through the use of these technologies to control and manage ourselves more effectively appears to promise new ways of thinking about how we might make cities more efficient, more equitable, and more sustainable.

This then is the prospect that new technologies that are being invented more and more rapidly can be implemented so that many functions in the city can be automated to provide a basis for a much improved quality of life in cities. This seems appealing if it were not for the fact that most discussions of smart city technologies take place in a theoretical vacuum. The corporate and IT sectors that are wedded to the hype that computers and sensors everywhere will instantly provide us with a better life. They have no real context other than their longstanding uncritical belief that automation is good for its own sake. The notion is that it has been good so far and will always be good in the future. But cities are not machines; they are more like biological organisms that grow from the bottom up and cannot be planned from the top down. Cities develop incrementally, and good cities are able to continually modify and adapt their technologies to realize a better quality of life, and as such, they are few and far between. Our experience in planning the future city so far has not been good, and the worry is that with this great wave of smart city euphoria sweeping over us, the quest for better planning will be drowned in corporate hype, unthinking applications of new IT, and an ever more problematic morass of disconnected systems.

There is little doubt that when you first attempt to understand what has been written about the smart city and what the main applications and demonstrators are about, the morass of material is bewildering. For a start, because cities have become "hot" in the last 20 years, many people from many walks of life are writing about them and making suggestions for how they might be improved.

Into this pot has come the notion of the smart city and many are now writing about cities in general terms but using the term smart city. In retrospect of course, the city is no more smart than it ever has been because what makes it smart is its citizens, ourselves that is. I am not saying that all cities or citizens rather are smart and have always been smart for there are many differences between people and places, but we need to take the term with a pinch of salt and qualify it in ways that make it intelligible.

What Luca Mora and Mark Deakin do in this book is broach the literature and the experience of smart cities head-on. This is the first book of which I am aware that tries to unpick all the elements of the smart city and cast them in the wider context of using new information technologies to improve the city—to raise the quality of life in cities for all of us. Their aim is to think of smart cities and the technologies involved as part of a wider quest to think of future cities as more sustainable. To this end, they allude to the Sustainable Development Goals (SDG) as set out by the United Nations in its General Assembly in 2015 for the year 2030. What is particularly key to their approach is that in their first chapter, Mora and Deakin review the heritage of those who have proposed future cities in the past, ideal cities really that have dominated urban planning from classical times to about the middle of the last century. To an extent, urban planning is still dominated by ideas about the ideal city that is more a city of geometry where form follows function than a city of economic and social processes, but the smart city focus blows all this open. In the last 50 years, our idea of the optimal future city has changed, and it is much more now one of processes that need to be improved so that cities can grow more sustainability from the bottom up. The challenge of smart cities that the authors pose in this book is to define the context in which this can take place.

In Chapter 1, they sketch the context as to how smart technologies can engineer the smart city. Chapter 2 describes a series of trends in information technologies that show how populations are connecting up and developing living environments that enable a variety of goals involving resource management, food security, waste management, and such like physical processes to be controlled sustainably. This sets the focus for Chapter 3 where they sketch the development of smart cities over the last 20 years from the time when the word smart cities was first used. They do this by undertaking a bibliometric analysis that is focused on contributions to academic approaches in Europe to more corporate applications of the smart city idea in North America. This provides a broad canvas on which to begin to fill in the big picture. What has emerged at this point is that the field is confused but that the authors are able to track how various literatures define the field, thus making sense of what we know so far. In the next chapter, they extend their bibliometric analysis by identifying the overall structure of how the literature—where they use "literature" in a very broad sense including formal papers to the "grayer literature" of the corporate world—divides up into clusters and themes. In particular the main development paths of the smart city movement are identified, and this indicates how the field is organized in terms of its divisions in approach that have emerged over the last 20 years.

In Chapter 4, four themes are pulled from the analysis in the previous chapter, dichotomies that are defined as technology-led development or more holistic characterizations of the field; different models of innovation based on the helical structure of how organization, government, and so on combine and interact; top-down versus bottom-up approaches; and, last but not least, monodimensional or integrated intervention logics. This is a strong policy focus, and rather than defining smart cities in terms of software and hardware, the policy context takes hold in this book. The authors then illustrate these ideas in Chapters 5 and 6 where they draw examples from European cities, four in all, and then from North America, mainly New York City. They conclude with the major lessons that their analysis provides for the key stakeholders in progressing the idea of smart cities.

Most books on smart cities focus on hardware and software as well as applications of these technologies to particular places. Unlike this book, few focus on how smart cities enter the wider policy debate about the future city. The particular strength of the ideas presented here is that they focus on policy, on how new technologies can be organized into forms that will apply to realizing the sustainable development goals. Some of the big questions pertaining to the next 50 years are noted: climate change, pollution and waste management, aging and differential urban growth within an envelope of continuing developments of information technologies that will be embedded not only into the city but also into ourselves and much else as well. It is impossible to know what cities built of information technologies will look like in this future. But what we can be certain about, which is the message of the first chapter, is that they will look nothing like the ideal cities of the future proposed a century or more ago by Wright, Corbusier, Howard, and before them Leonardo during the Renaissance in Europe and Plato in classical times. The focus on policy rather than form and function is to be welcomed, and this book makes a real contribution to our understanding of the great morass of ideas about the smart city, which are increasingly pervading our world.

Michael Batty
Centre for Advanced Spatial Analysis, University College London, London, United Kingdom

Chapter 1

Moving beyond the smart city utopia

Chapter Outline

1.1 Utopian urbanism

Dreaming about the future of cities and conceiving new visionary schemes for improving the sustainability of urban development has a long tradition. In these schemes, the deficiencies of the present translate into stimuli for shaping alternative urban systems in which a new set of rules and standards, that society is expected to adhere to, become the assurance of an improved sustainability. However, despite being built on a genuine intent to improve the human condition, some of these alternative solutions have resulted in urban utopias: unrealistically perfect spatial imaginaries whose highly symbolic rendering of the future is flawed due to the tendency for the visions that they embody to be based on stereotypical ideas misrepresenting reality.

One of the first utopias was created in Ancient Greece, when Plato introduced his totalitarian philosophy of the city. Plato images cities as economic independent and self-sufficient entities in which the community is divided into three classes. For Plato, discipline, perfect obedience, and control over each single member of community are the key components of a perfect society, and they can be secured by combining stringent authority and coercion. As Mumford explains in his analysis of historical utopias, this Greek utopia stands on principles that relate to an historical era whereby survival is based on the capacity that society has to be prepared for war (Mumford, 1922, 1965).

Following Plato's urban imaginary, a significant amount of utopian thinking has emerged in which the stringent authority and coercion have been replaced with less militaristic set of principles. For example, Thomas More's Utopia, a fictional island society in the New World, represents one of the most famous spatial imaginaries produced so far. Conceived in the framework of the urban challenges affecting England in the early 16th century, Utopia manifests itself

Untangling Smart Cities. https://doi.org/10.1016/B978-0-12-815477-9.00001-3

as a future state of affairs that stands in opposition to war, oppression, and injustice, by proposing a new social structure based on common ownership (Goodey, 1970; Wilde, 2017). Utopia's ambition to end social inequalities is also shared by Edward Bellamy and the blueprint of the perfect society that he introduces in *Looking Backward: 2000–1887*. In his vision, which is conceived 300 years after Utopia, Bellamy portrays the stresses of the 19th century industrial society of the United States, that is, violent class conflicts, the end of the frontier and antiimmigrant xenophobia, the labor movement, poor working conditions, poverty, and hunger. The solution that Bellamy offers is for society to replace the competitive economic system with a utopia that promotes universal employment and total equality (Bellamy, 1888).

Utopian visions of the future city can also be found into the work of some of the most influential modern architects and planners, who provided an invaluable contribution to urban development theory and practice. For example, the English town planner Ebenezer Howard is known for initiating the garden city movement. Shaped in the idea of progress and as a reaction to the overpopulation, inequalities, and pollution of industrial cities, garden cities were intended as new compact towns surrounded by rolling green belts and populated by self-contained and self-sufficient communities. These new towns were expected to grow outside large metropolitan agglomerations, on large areas of agricultural land, and to combine the desirable features of both the city and the countryside. Howard believed this connection between urban and rural would have set the ground for a new civilization and more sustainable urban planning policies and improved living arrangements capable of ending urban poverty (Howard, 1898).

Howard's utopian thinking was greatly influenced by *Looking Backward*, and his work represents an attempt to put forward a practical approach for testing Bellamy's utopian conceptions of future cities in a real-world setting (Howard, 1965; MacFadyen, 1970). However, the garden city experiments failed to meet the expectations. Research by Sharifi (2016) and Hügel (2017) demonstrates that garden cities have proved unsuccessful in building self-sufficient communities and addressing the needs of low-wage workers. In addition, their financial model, which was unsuitable to attract the investments of the banking sector, forced Howard to accept the trade-off between equitable development on the one hand and market support on the other hand (Williamson et al., 2002; Gillette, 2010; Edwards, 1914; Falk, 2017).

Despite its limitations, the essence of the garden city movement has maintained an enduring influence and produced long-lasting effects that still resonate in urban development studies (Hardy, 1992). The principles embedded in the garden city idea have become an inspirational source for colonial planning in sub-Saharan Africa and new residential areas in Brazil (Bigon, 2013; Rego, 2014). Yeo (2019) describes the cross agency initiatives that are contributing to introduce the garden city idea into the high-density urban context of Singapore, whose environmental policy exposes its ambition to become a model green city (Han, 2017). Hou (2018) reports on the outcomes of the "Garden City Initiative" that the city government of Taipei has launched to expand urban gardens, exposing the connection between the garden city movement and urban planning practice in Taiwan. The garden city movement has also influenced the Scottish housing reform and town planning practice of the 20th century, leading to significant changes in the approach to construction of working-class housing developments (Rosenburg, 2016). In addition, there is also evidence of a new garden city idea whose functionality has been recently tested out in York and Oxford. This 21st century version of the garden city builds on Howard's ideology and is proposed as a possible solution to the housing crisis affecting the United Kingdom (Falk, 2017).

The deep preoccupation for the future of cities and civilization that stimulates Howard's utopian thinking is also shared by Frank Lloyd Wright and Charles Edouard Jeanneret, better known as Le Corbusier. As Fishman (1977: 12) states in his presentation of the ideal cities pictured by these three visionary urban planners, all of them "hated the cities of their time with an overwhelming passion" and the urban environments in which they were living represented "the hell that inspired their heavens." The unrealized masterplan of the *Ville Radiouse* (Radiant City), designed by Le Corbusier in the 1920s, encompasses his utopian vision of the future city. The Radiant City is created by following the modernist understanding of tradition, which is perceived as a barrier to progress, and suggests building a new generation of urban environments on the ashes of 19th-century cities. According to Le Corbusier, nothing could solve the inefficiencies of cities and their unsustainable development patterns but demolishing and rebuilding cities infused with strict order, symmetry, and standardization. These are the main features of the Radiant City, which rises from a regular layout and a highly organized zoning system composed of the following parallel areas: satellite towns for hosting special functions, such as government buildings; the business center; railroad station and air terminal; hotels and embassies; housing areas segregated by income, which are split between middle-class apartments in monolithic skyscrapers for luxury high-density living arrangements and six-story buildings and modest accommodations for lower-income residents; factories; warehouses; and heavy industry (Hall, 1988). In addition, in the Radiant City, all the areas are connected through an intricate network of high-speed traffic roads and parking lots exposing an autocentric design that was expected to satisfy both the needs of a fast-emerging modern transport system and the never-ending obsession of the Swiss-French modernist architect for automobiles (Jacobs, 1961), the same obsession that inspired his architectural work (Amado, 2011). As Le Corbusier explains in his manifesto for modern architecture, the mass-production principles and standardized manufacturing process of the automotive industry should have been considered as an inspiration for the construction sector. In his vision, building houses by applying the same level of standardization was the only way to reach a new spirit, whose elevated aesthetic of perfection would in turn lead to the rebirth of architecture (Le Corbusier, 1986).

The standardization and strict order that Le Corbusier suggests are also the driving forces behind his utopian view of modern cities and society that is supposed to live such spaces. As Le Corbusier explains while describing his plan and idea of modern city planning, "the city of today is dying because it is not constructed geometrically. To build on a clear site is to replace the accidental layout of the ground, the only one that exists today, by the formal layout. Otherwise nothing can save us. And the consequence of geometrical plans is repetition and mass-production. And as a consequence of repetition, the standard is created, and so perfection" (Le Corbusier, 1987: 220).

Chandigarh, the capital city of the northern Indian states of Punjab and Haryana, gives a tangible form to the utopian vision that the Radiant City stands for. Immediately after the British voluntarily granted India its independence, India and Pakistan became two different geographic entities. As a consequence of the partition, Punjab was split into two independent countries, and this division left the Indian Punjab without a capital city. Rather than granting the status of capital to an existing city, the prime minister of the Indian Punjab decided to authorize the construction of Chandigarh, a new city that was expected to embody the faith of the nation in a new beginning. In the 1950s, a team of modern architects that included Le Corbusier, his cousin Pierre Jeanneret, Maxwell Fry, and Jane Drew was invited to implement the master plan for Chandigarh, a master plan that the American architect and planner Albert Mayer was commissioned to oversee the design of. However, instead of collaborating in giving expression to Mayer's plan, which was already approved, Le Corbusier took the leadership and used this opportunity to test his strict zoning system and idea of a perfect form of urbanism on a greenfield site (Chalana, 2015; Chalana and Sprague, 2013; Fitting, 2002; Hall, 1988; Prakash, 2002).

The in-depth examination of the Chandigarh experience conducted by Hall (1988) and Sarin (1982) in the 1980s, which pictures the city as an incubator of poverty and injustice, uncovers the limitations of the utopian vision proposed by Le Corbusier. This vision has been harshly criticized for being affected by a "profound misunderstanding of human nature" (Fitting, 2002: 80) and a lack of concern for the lifestyle habits of people (Jacobs, 1961), who were expected to accept an imposed one-size-fits-all design that was nothing but incapable of meeting everyone's needs (Hall, 1988). The failure lays in the monumental dimension of an unrealistic vision, which has proved to be distant from the citizens of Chandigarh, and also the strong belief of Le Corbusier in the triumph of industrial standardization and mass-production methods in the architecture of future cities (Fitting, 2002; Hall, 1988; Jacobs, 1961; Mumford, 1961).

Fixing the modern city by using a new code was also the ambition of the American Architect Frank Lloyd Wright and Broadacre City, his utopian vision of a decentralized urbanity. With Broadacre City, Wright attempts to reconcile the progressive power of technological development with the magnificence of nature, two forces that have been drastically separated in the cities of the industrial age. Wright believed that modern technologies were offering society with the opportunity to escape the pitfalls of the industrial city and to embrace improved living arrangements hosted in rural lower-density settlements surrounded by the beauty of nature but without renouncing urban conveniences. In this vision, Broadacre City was conceived as the means for reestablishing the symbiotic relationship between human beings and natural environment (Wright, 1931, 1932), a relationship that Howard, Le Corbusier, and Wright all considered fundamental for individual fulfillment and societal progress.

Wright started conceiving Broadacre City in the 1924, and his vision aligns with some of the philosophical principles underlying the garden city vision proposed by Howard. Wright's utopian thinking shares the same: "rejection of the big city (and high population density), the same populist antipathy to finance capital and landlordism, the same anarchist rejection of big government, the same reliance on the liberating effects of new technologies, and the same belief in the homesteading principle and the return to the land" (Hall, 1988: 312). However, unlike Howard, Wright does not want the countryside to absorb the life of cities to facilitate community planning, but to give every citizen a place for living as free individuals (Wright, 1932).

As Levine (2008: XI) describes, Broadacre City was meant "to offer all the advantages of modern technology without any of the disadvantages of the urban congestion and blight that many recognized at the time as a major consequence of modernity." Wright envisions a democratized society "that would be technologically advanced in practice but agrarian in organization and values" (Shaw, 2009: IV), where each family is assigned an acre, that is, the democratic minimum of land. In addition, this vision for a sustainable urban future was also meant to become the antithesis of what Wright considered as "the superficial suggestions of the machine-made utopia" (Levine, 2008: I) of Le Corbusier and the total loss in human culture this utopia was leading to (Wright, 1931), by imposing verticalization and "the tyranny of the skyscraper" (Wright, 1943: 323).

Unlike Le Corbusier, Wright never had the opportunity to build Broadacre City. However, the fast-expanding trend toward exurbanization, which the United States started registering in the 1940s, caused the massive move that Wright was dreaming about. Cities were gradually depopulating in favor of the countryside, where decentralized forms of communities began growing. Year by year, Wright's utopian vision was becoming reality (Hall, 1988), but rather than producing the beneficial transformations that he was strongly believing in, this trend made it possible to expose the limitations of the visionary scheme driving his "experiment in civilization" (Wright, 1932: 29).

The 1940s was a period in which the growth in the demand for and supply of rural residential developments began acting as a force of change in the urban development dynamics of North American countries (Davis et al., 1994; Dueker et al., 1983; Nelson, 1990, 1992, 1995; Newburn and Berck, 2006). This change has generated exurbanization, a process of urban sprawl that "occurs when people move from central cities and suburbs into the countryside" (Davis et al., 1994: 45), and it resulted in a new low-density and noncontiguous form of urbanization that has irreversibly modified the North American rural landscape. Nelson and Dueker (1990: 93) estimated that during the period between 1960 and 1985, "exurban counties accounted for nearly a third of the share of continental US growth," and they also expanded "faster than all other counties in both nominal and share-of-growth terms."

This migration pattern from urban to rural was triggered by a combination of multiple factors. On the one hand, there are socioeconomic and political conditions. The living arrangements offered by suburban and urban areas were unsustainable, especially when seeking for affordable real estate (Sutton et al., 2006), and the urban policy promoted by the federal government was undoubtedly favoring "new construction over rehabilitation or reuse of buildings, highways over public transit, converting open space to urban uses over leaving it alone, construction of single-family (owner occupied) over multiple-family (renter) housing, growing areas over depressed ones, and new locations over old ones" (Nelson and Dueker, 1990: 91). On the other hand, new telecommunication technologies (radio, telephone, and telegraph) and modern mobility, combined with the advent of flextime, decentralized working, and manageable commuting costs, were offering the possibility to benefit of urban conveniences but from the natural setting of rural areas (Nelson and Dueker, 1989).

Over the last five decades, urban sprawl has drastically changed land-use dynamics and the spatial distribution of population in US countries, and it has generated a number of sustainability challenges affecting the agrarian landscape. A large number of new rural developments have resulted from this decentralization process in which the land consumed per unit of housing is higher than urban and suburban developments (Nelson, 1992; Newburn and Berck, 2006; Heimlich and Anderson, 2001; Theobald, 2001; Sutton et al., 2006; Nelson and Dueker, 1989). This phenomenon has caused a high level of land fragmentation that is found responsible for:

- altering natural habitats by disrupting wildlife, hydrologic systems, energy flows, and biodiversity (Alberti and Marzluff, 2004; Dale et al., 2005; Chalfoun et al., 2002; Grimm et al., 2008; Hansen et al., 2005; Newburn and Berck, 2006; Merenlender et al., 2009);
- decreasing agricultural and forest productivity (Hasse and Lathrop, 2003; Carsjens and van der Knaap, 2002);
- increasing the costs for public service provision and the overinvestment in the construction of transport infrastructure (Brueckner, 2000; Hasse and Lathrop, 2003; Zhao, 2010; Kunstler, 1993);
- the disappearance of culturally relevant open spaces and natural amenities (Deller et al., 2001; Schipper, 2008; Swensen and Jerpåsen, 2008).

What is more, among the negative externalities documented over the years in relation to sprawl dynamics, Frumkin (2002), Ewing et al. (2003) and Lopez (2004) have also included the adverse impacts on public health. Their research demonstrates that "the adverse impacts of sprawl do not fall equally across the population" (Frumkin, 2002: 212), but residents of sprawling areas tend to exercise less, weigh more, and have greater prevalence of hypertension than residents of compact urban areas (Lopez, 2004; Ewing et al., 2003).

Once again, this demonstrates that sustainable urban development, which utopian visionaries like Wright, Howard, and Le Corbusier were so passionately trying to reach, cannot materialize through simplistic sets of universal rules and standards, because they will always fall short of understanding the complexity of urban life. No perfect code or design for cities exists that can remedy all societal problems, improve the human condition, and instill the fundamental principles of sustainability and democracy that modern society seems to have partially lost over the years. For as many commenters suggest, approaching sustainable urban development by using autocratic and top-down visionary schemes can produce nothing but the illusion of a universal panacea for urban problems (Mumford, 1956; Grabow, 1977; Hollands, 2015; Jones, 1966; Sassen, 1991).

1.2 Smart cities and the new utopia

In recent studies, Hügel (2017), Townsend (2013), and Datta (2015b) draw a parallel between the weaknesses of Ebenezer Howard, Frank Lloyd Wright, and Le Corbusier's utopian visions and those shortcomings related to the development of smart cities. This alignment is significant, because it exposes what a growing number of commenters studying these developments agree about: smart cities represent a new chapter in the context of utopian urbanism, which is serving nothing but the interests of corporations operating in the information and communications technology (ICT) industry. These commenters describe smart cities as a techno-led urban imaginary that is not "driven [...] by visionary architects and planners, but rather by the corporate sector" (Datta, 2015b: 8) and a development rooted in the same utopian conceptions of future cities that have emerged in the past (see Hollands, 2015; Söderström et al., 2014; Wiig and Wyly, 2016; Klauser et al., 2014; March, 2018; Watson, 2015; Cugurullo, 2013; Datta, 2015a; Marvin et al., 2016; Wiig, 2015, 2016, 2018; Bunnell, 2015; Valdez et al., 2018; Grossi and Pianezzi, 2017).

According to this literature, the development of smart cities is controlled by the corporate sector, and a new panacea is growing from the narrative they promote. This narrative brings ICT corporations in close collaboration with local and national governments and suggests that the massive uptake of high-tech fixes can cure all the imperfections that limit the sustainability of urban environments. By sourcing evidence from a number of smart city experiences that failed to meet the expectations of adopting a smart city approach to urban sustainability, such as Dholera (Datta, 2015b), Masdar (Cugurullo, 2013), Milton Keynes (Valdez et al., 2018), Philadelphia (Wiig, 2015, 2016), Camden (Wiig, 2018), and Genoa (Grossi and Pianezzi, 2017), this literature exposes the limitations of a standard recipe, which oversimplifies the complexity of urban dynamics. In addition, it raises important questions about the contradictory nature of smart urbanism, which is accused of promoting urban development by means of technological determinism ideologies generating nothing but "elite enclaves, gated communities and other exclusive zones that exacerbate existing social divides and create new spaces for the 'digerati', corporate executives and other elites" (Moser, 2015: 33).

For example, Datta (2015b) examines the attempt made by Dholera to enable the smart city approach to urban sustainability. The findings indicate that the local government has adopted an approach that builds on the same premises as Chandigarh. As Datta points out, Dholera's pathway toward becoming smart was affected by the same lack of consideration for the diversity of local sociocultural landscapes and authoritarianism emerging from Le Corbusier's unequal top-down logic, and this in turn led to a technocratic mode of governance responsible for (1) benefitting the political elite, middle classes, and a few corporations interested in expanding the global market for smart city technologies in India and (2) overshadowing interests of public value and the principles of justice and social equality.

The similarity between earlier utopian experiments and smart city developments continues being explored in research by Townsend (2013), where the attention shifts from Dholera to Songdo International Business District (IBD), a new business district built from scratch by using about 600 ha of land reclaimed from the Yellow Sea of Incheon (Strickland, 2011). "Much as Broadacre City reimagined a thoroughly suburbanized America around the capabilities of the automobile, Songdo would reimagine the Korean metropolis around the potential of ubiquitous computing" (Townsend, 2013: 26). Songdo IBD has emerged from the collaboration between real estate developers, institutional investors, and the national government and industry, which decided to combine their different expectations. In this collaboration, the national government decided to build Songdo in order to showcase Korea as a world leader in smart city development. Cisco, as the technological partner leading the joint venture, saw this initiative as a 47 million dollar investment for acquiring the leadership in the smart city market by building one of the first urban operating systems and the world's first urban environment in which everything would have been interconnected and automated.

Songdo probably succeeded in becoming "the most wired city on Earth" (Strickland, 2011: 11). However, a number of commentators agree in suggesting that this smart city development has failed to display a sustainable blueprint for future cities (Yoo, 2017), because of its incapability to turn into something more than an experimental testbed for new technological solutions (Datta, 2015a; Townsend, 2013). Despite the technological advancement that is generated by the testing of innovative ubiquitous technologies, Songdo IBD's approach to smart city development is criticized for being an example of technical transformation that nurtures inequalities (Nguyen and Davidson, 2017; Huston et al., 2015; Carvalho, 2015) and is powered by elite coalitions and the "marketing rhetoric of the big technology companies" (Shelton et al., 2015: 21). Therefore, as feared by the United Nations Environment Programme, this approach to smart city development can "reinforce the stark techno-apartheid that is splintering cities around the world" rather than deploying technological innovation for creating "the basis for greater equity, reduced levels of poverty, and greater opportunities to build" sustainable communities (UNEP, 2013: 46).

1.3 Making sense of smart cities: Aim and structure of this book

"Isolation, stratification, fixation, regimentation, standardization, militarization," rigidity, and authoritarianism are the main attributes entering into the conception of utopian cities and the unrealistic one-size-fits-all urban sustainability schemes they bring forward (Mumford, 1965: 277). These attributes cannot cope with the complexity of urban dynamics and the organic nature of cities (Batty, 2005a,b). However, despite their autocratic and top-down approach to urban development, utopian dreams are also rooted in a genuine and firmly held belief in progress. When seeking more sustainable urban development paths, the challenge is to find the right balance between this unquestionable confidence in progress, local development needs, and the sense of continuity and authenticity of urban environments, that is, their "genius loci" (Norberg-Schulz, 1980). This claim finds support in the comprehensive view of urban development dynamics that Michael Batty offers in the framework of complex system theories (see Batty, 1976, 2005a,b, 2008; Batty et al., 1999; Batty and Longley, 1994; Batty and Torrens, 2005; Batty and Xie, 1994). His work is remarkable in showing that bottom-up and top-down forces are not mutually exclusive of each other, but complementary in nature, possessing the capacity to instigate evolutionary processes that sustain urban development.

However, as history teaches, first there are the utopias (Foucault, 1984) and then the struggling in realizing where the balance is and extracting the possible from what seems impossible (Lefebvre, 1970). Nobody can deny that utopian visions are far from desirable models, because they attempt to impose universal values, which the world is supposed to be shaped by, and they can be "charged with dangerous authoritarianism" (Pinder, 2015: 30). However, despite these limitations, utopianism plays an important role in urban development dynamics and the bettering of such processes. This search for alternative futures has the potential to boost creative thinking, experimentation and invention, and the capacity to combine contemporary challenges with new radical solutions (Fernando et al., 2018; Lefebvre, 1970; Sargisson, 2000; Vanolo, 2016). Visionary schemes can act as sources of motivation and trigger beneficial transformative changes in society (Levitas, 1990, 2007, 2008).

As well explained by Pinder (2015: 43) while exploring Henri Lefebvre's attempt to prove the usefulness of utopia in urban studies, "the utopian gesture is the gesture which changes the coordinates of the possible. Rather than 'idle dreaming about ideal society in total abstraction from real life,' utopia is 'a matter of innermost urgency' when it is no longer possible to go on within the parameters of the possible." This explains what Levitas (2007) describes as the "necessity of utopia" and its relevance in the evolutionary theory of cities (Batty and Marshall, 2009; Marshall, 2009).

When looking at the smart city concept, the criticism emerging from the failures of the utopian corporate interpretation does nothing but generating doubts on the real potential for innovation embedded in the ICT-driven approach to urban sustainability that smart cities represent. However, these failures cannot be considered as a justification for reaching the conclusion that smart cities are simply a false dawn. Instead, they should arouse interest in looking beyond the urban utopia by developing that "critical understanding of smart urbanism" (Luque-Ayala and Marvin, 2015: 2113) that is necessary to shape a more progressive and human vision of smart city development (Hollands, 2008; Caragliu et al., 2011; Hollands, 2015). The challenge is to (1) avoid the hype and misleading information surrounding the utopia, which offers little more than a fuzzy vision of smart city development and (2) find genuine and effective approaches that "make sense of smart cities" (Kitchin, 2015: 131) and offer a knowledge platform to build them in real-life environments.

This book prepares the foundations of this knowledge platform. By adopting a progressive and constructivist perspective, it first clarifies the meaning of the smart city concept and its potential to sustain sustainable urban development. Subsequently, it exposes the theoretical and practical limitations affecting the development of smart cities, which are tackled by (1) analyzing the successful approach that a group of European and North American cities have adopted to engage with smart city development and enable the ICT-driven approach to urban sustainability this development stands on, (2) codifying the knowledge that these best practices offer to share in the form of recommendations and strategic principles for other cities to follow, and (3) orienting future research on smart city development in the light of the results that this book reports on.

This aim is achieved by conducting a multistage investigation in which a mixed-method research strategy is adopted that combines bibliometric techniques and case study research. Each stage of the investigation has been assigned a chapter, which reports on the results of the analytic process. The following paragraphs offer a comprehensive overview of the book's structure and a brief description of what each chapter contains.[1]

Chapter 2: Smart city development as an ICT-driven approach to urban sustainability

Helping cities enable smart city development has become one of the key commitments for academia, industry, local and national governments, and civil society organizations, which all recognize the important role that ICTs play in making urban environments sustainable. Chapter 2 demonstrates the validity of

1. This book builds on and expands the line of enquiry started with a group of publications that the authors produced between 2015 and 2019 (Bolici and Mora, 2015; Komninos and Mora, 2018; Mora and Bolici, 2016, 2017; Mora et al., 2017, 2018a,b, 2019a,b,c).

such a conviction by reporting on a series of smart city projects that showcase how ICT solutions can be instrumental in tackling the global issues that affect urban environments. After providing an overview of the emerging technological trends which have paved the way for a smart city approach to sustainable urban development, a comprehensive account is offered of (1) the smart city projects that have been selected, which are here deployed as descriptive case studies, (2) the urban challenges that these projects have tackled, and (3) the benefits that they have produced. The analysis concludes with a critical reflection upon the current debate on smart city development. This last activity aims to call attention to the research gaps and questions that this book focuses attention on.

Chapter 3: The first two decades of research on smart city development
This chapter reports on a bibliometric analysis of the smart city literature published between 1992 and 2012, that is, the first two decades of research on smart city development. The analysis shows that smart city research is fragmented, lacks cohesion, and promotes two main development paths for smart cities. The first path is based on the peer-reviewed publications produced by European universities and those who support a holistic perspective on smart cities. In contrast, the second path stands on the gray literature produced by the American business community and relates to a technocentric understanding of the subject. Divided along such paths, the analysis suggests future development of this new and promising field of research risks being undermined.

Chapter 4: Revealing the main development paths of smart cities.
This chapter reports on a second bibliometric analysis in which two hybrid techniques are combined, which allow clusters of related documents obtained from a co-citation analysis to be labeled using textual data. The aim of this bibliometric study, which continues the analysis of the first two decades of research on smart city development, is to (1) visualize the network of publications shaping the overall intellectual structure of the smart city research field by considering the period between 1992 and 2012, (2) map the clusters of thematically related publications, and (3) reveal the emerging development paths that each thematic cluster represents and strategic principles that they embody. The findings demonstrate that the emerging development paths of smart cities are not only two but five. The development paths that this second analysis uncovers and the strategic principles each of them stands on are then compared by reviewing the most recent literature on smart city development. Overall, this chapter offers a systematic review of the smart city research produced between 1992 and 2018, and it serves to further expose the division within its intellectual structure. A division is caused by the dichotomous nature of the development paths that each thematic cluster relates to.

Chapter 5: Smart city development in Europe
The bibliometric analyses and extensive literature review presented in the previous chapters demonstrate the presence of a deep-rooted division in the research on smart cities, which surfaces as a set of dichotomies questioning whether smart city development should be based on a (1) technology-led or holistic strategy,

(2) double- or quadruple-helix model of collaboration, (3) top-down or bottom-up approach, and (4) monodimensional or integrated intervention logic. These dichotomies suggest divergent hypotheses on what principles need to be considered when implementing strategies for enabling smart city development. This generates a critical knowledge gap that this chapter starts filling by reporting on the findings of a multiple case study analysis conducted into European best practices. The validity of the hypotheses emerging from each dichotomy is tested by analyzing four European cities considered to be leaders in the field of smart city development. The results of this best practice analysis offer critical insight into what strategic principles drive smart city development in Europe and generate scientific knowledge that helps to start overcoming the dichotomous nature of smart city research.

Chapter 6: Smart city development in North America
The previous best practice analysis offers a series of critical insights into the complex architecture of smart cities, revealing their building blocks and the strategic principles driving their assembling process. The investigation this chapter reports on demonstrates that the validity of this insight extends beyond Europe and into the development of North American smart cities. The evidence needed to support this broader generalization is drawn from the results of a best practice analysis that reveals the approach that New York City has adopted to enable smart city development and the ICT-driven approach to urban sustainability this stands on. The additional evidence that is produced by this investigation further highlights the strong correlation that the previous chapter started to uncover between successful smart city developments and the strategic deployment of specific programs of activities.

Chapter 7: The social shaping of smart cities
This last chapter concludes the investigation by summing up the key lessons and recommendations that this book can offer to the community of stakeholders involved in smart city research, policy, and practice. The series of complementary analyses which the previous chapters report on demonstrate that, when untangled from the technocentric urban utopia pictured by the corporate sector, smart cities have the potential to develop into innovation systems which set the stage for a technology-enabled approach to urban sustainability. But realizing this opportunity requires to move beyond traditional boundaries, separate the hype from reality, and strengthen the focus on the social shaping of smart cities. The investigation demonstrates that, in order for such a social shaping perspective to develop, the design of smart cities needs to be understood as a collective action in which two complementary forces are combined. On the one hand, the faith in the technological advancement exposed in the utopian thinking. On the other, the knowledge, skills, and interests of a quadruple-helix collaborative environment where the need for technological innovation in response to urban sustainability goals is not shaped by the corporate sector and its technocentric and market-oriented logic, but an open community whose actions serve the public interest and are based on a holistic interpretation of smart city development.

References

Alberti, M., Marzluff, J.M., 2004. Ecological resilience in urban ecosystems: linking urban patterns to human and ecological functions. Urban Ecosyst. 7 (3), 241–265.

Amado, A., 2011. Voiture Minimum: Le Corbusier and the Automobile. MIT Press, Cambridge, MA.

Batty, M., 1976. Urban Modelling: Algorithms, Calibrations, Predictions. Cambridge University Press, Cambridge.

Batty, M., 2005a. Agents, cells, and cities: new representational models for simulating multiscale urban dynamics. Environ. Plann. A: Econ. Space 37 (8), 1373–1394.

Batty, M., 2005b. Cities and Complexity: Understanding Cities with Cellular Automata, Agent-Based Models, and Fractals. MIT Press, Cambridge, MA.

Batty, M., 2008. The size, scale, and shape of cities. Science 319 (5864), 769–771.

Batty, M., Longley, P., 1994. Fractal Cities: A Geometry of Form and Function. Academic Press, San Diego, CA.

Batty, M., Marshall, S., 2009. The evolution of cities: Geddes, Abercrombie and the New Physicalism. Town Plann. Rev. 80 (6), 551–574.

Batty, M., Torrens, P.M., 2005. Modelling and prediction in a complex world. Futures 37 (7), 745–766.

Batty, M., Xie, Y., 1994. From cells to cities. Environ. Plann. B: Urban Anal. City Sci. 21, S31–S48.

Batty, M., Xie, Y., Sun, Z., 1999. Modeling urban dynamics through GIS-based cellular automata. Comput. Environ. Urban. Syst. 23 (3), 205–233.

Bellamy, E., 1888. Looking Backward: 2000–1887. Ticknor and Company, Boston, MA.

Bigon, L., 2013. Garden cities in colonial Africa: a note on historiography. Plan. Perspect. 28 (3), 477–485.

Bolici, R., Mora, L., 2015. Urban regeneration in the digital era: how to develop smart city strategies in large European cities. TECHNE: J.Technol. Architect. Environ. 5 (2), 110–119.

Brueckner, J.K., 2000. Urban sprawl: diagnosis and remedies. Int. Reg. Sci. Rev. 23 (2), 160–171.

Bunnell, T., 2015. Smart City returns. Dialogues Hum. Geogr. 5 (1), 45–48.

Caragliu, A., Del Bo, C., Nijkamp, P., 2011. Smart cities in Europe. J. Urban Technol. 18 (2), 65–82.

Carsjens, G.J., van der Knaap, W., 2002. Strategic land-use allocation: dealing with spatial relationships and fragmentation of agriculture. Landsc. Urban Plan. 58 (2–4), 171–179.

Carvalho, L., 2015. Smart cities from scratch? A socio-technical perspective. Camb. J. Reg. Econ. Soc. 8 (1), 43–60.

Chalana, M., 2015. Chandigarh: city and periphery. J. Plan. Hist. 14 (1), 62–84.

Chalana, M., Sprague, T.S., 2013. Beyond Le Corbusier and the Modernist City: reframing Chandigarh's 'world heritage' legacy. Plan. Perspect. 28 (2), 199–222.

Chalfoun, A.D., Ratnaswamy, M., Thompson, F.R., 2002. Songbird nest predators in forest-pasture edge and forest interior in a fragmented landscape. Ecol. Appl. 12 (3), 858–867.

Cugurullo, F., 2013. How to build a sandcastle: an analysis of the genesis and development of Masdar City. J. Urban Technol. 20 (1), 23–37.

Dale, V., Archer, S., Chang, M., Ojima, D., 2005. Ecological impacts and mitigation strategies for rural land management. Ecol. Appl. 15 (6), 1879–1892.

Datta, A., 2015a. A 100 smart cities, a 100 utopias. Dialogues Hum. Geogr. 5 (1), 49–53.

Datta, A., 2015b. New urban utopias of postcolonial India: Entrepreneurial urbanization in Dholera Smart City, Gujarat. Dialogues Hum. Geogr. 5 (1), 3–22.

Davis, J.S., Nelson, A.C., Dueker, K.J., 1994. The new' burbs the exurbs and their implications for planning policy. J. Am. Plan. Assoc. 60 (1), 45–59.

Deller, S.C., Tsai, T., Marcouiller, D.W., English, D.B.K., 2001. The role of amenities and quality of life in rural economic growth. Am. J. Agric. Econ. 83 (2), 352–365.

Dueker, K.J., Strathman, J.G., Levin, I.P., Phipps, A.G., 1983. Rural residential development within metropolitan areas. Comput. Environ. Urban. Syst. 8 (2), 121–129.

Edwards, T., 1914. A further criticism of the Garden City movement. Town Plan. Rev. 4 (4), 312–318.

Ewing, R., Schmid, T., Killingsworth, R., Zlot, A., Raudenbush, S., 2003. Relationship between urban sprawl and physical activity, obesity, and morbidity. Am. J. Health Promot. 18 (1), 47–57.

Falk, N., 2017. Garden cities for the twenty-first century. Urban Des. Int. 22 (1), 91–110.

Fernando, J.W., Burden, N., Ferguson, A., O'Brien, L.V., Judge, M., Kashima, Y., 2018. Functions of utopia: how utopian thinking motivates societal engagement. Personal. Soc. Psychol. Bull. 44 (5), 779–792.

Fishman, R., 1977. Urban Utopias in the Twentieth Century. MIT Press, Cambridge, MA.

Fitting, P., 2002. Urban planning/utopian dreaming: Le Corbusier's Chandigarh today. Utop. Stud. 13 (1), 69–93.

Foucault, M., 1984. Des Espace Autre. Architecture, Mouvement, Continuité 5, 46–49.

Frumkin, H., 2002. Urban sprawl and public health. Public Health Rep. 117 (3), 201–217.

Gillette, H., 2010. Civitas by Design: Building Better Communities, from the Garden City to the New Urbanism. University of Pennsylvania Press, Philadelphia, PA.

Goodey, B.R., 1970. Mapping "utopia": A comment on the geography of sir Thomas more. Geogr. Rev. 60 (1), 15–30.

Grabow, S., 1977. Frank Lloyd Wright and the American City: the Broadacres debate. J. Am. Plan. Assoc. 43 (2), 115–124.

Grimm, N.B., Faeth, S.H., Golubiewski, N.E., Redman, C.L., Wu, J., Bai, X., Briggs, J.M., 2008. Global change and the ecology of cities. Science 319 (5864), 756–760.

Grossi, G., Pianezzi, D., 2017. Smart cities: utopia or neoliberal ideology? Cities: Int. J. Urban Policy Plann. 69, 79–85.

Hall, P., 1988. Cities of Tomorrow: An Intellectual History of Urban Planning and Design, fourth ed. Blackwell Publishing, Oxford.

Han, H., 2017. Singapore, a Garden City: Authoritarian environmentalism in a developmental state. J. Environ. Dev.t 26 (1), 3–24.

Hansen, A.J., Knight, R.L., Marzluff, J.M., Powell, S., Brown, K., Gude, P.H., Jones, K., 2005. Effects of exurban development on biodiversity: patterns, mechanisms, and research needs. Ecol. Appl. 15 (6), 1893–1905.

Hardy, D., 1992. The Garden City campaign: an overview. In: Ward, S.V. (Ed.), The Garden City: Past, Present, and Future. Spoon Press, Abingdon, pp. 187–209.

Hasse, J.E., Lathrop, R.G., 2003. Land resource impact indicators of urban sprawl. Appl. Geogr. 23 (2–3), 159–175.

Heimlich, R.E., Anderson, W.D., 2001. Development at the Urban Fringe and beyond: Impacts on Agriculture and Rural Land. Agricultural Economic Report No. 803, United States Department of Agriculture. https://ageconsearch.umn.edu/bitstream/33943/1/ae010803.pdf. (Accessed February 20, 2018).

Hollands, R.G., 2008. Will the real smart city please stand up? City: Anal. Urban Trends Culture Theory Policy Action 12 (3), 303–320.

Hollands, R.G., 2015. Critical interventions into the corporate smart city. Camb. J. Reg. Econ. Soc. 8 (1), 61–77.

Hou, J., 2018. Governing urban gardens for resilient cities: examining the 'Garden City initiative' in Taipei. Urban Stud. https://doi.org/10.1177/0042098018778671.

Howard, E., 1898. To-Morrow: A Peaceful Path to Real Reform. William Swan Sonnenschein, London.

Howard, E., 1965. Garden Cities of To-Morrow. MIT Press, Cambridge, MA.

Hügel, S., 2017. From the Garden City to the smart city. Urban Plann. 2 (3), 1–4.
Huston, S., Rahimzad, R., Parsa, A., 2015. 'Smart' sustainable urban regeneration: Institutions, quality and financial innovation. Cities: Int. J. Urban Policy Plann. 48, 66–75.
Jacobs, J., 1961. The Death and Life of Great American Cities. Random House, New York City, NY.
Jones, B., 1966. Design from knowledge, not belief. In: Whiffen, M. (Ed.), The Architect and the City. MIT Press, Cambridge, MA.
Kitchin, R., 2015. Making sense of smart cities: addressing present shortcomings. Camb. J. Reg. Econ. Soc. 8 (1), 131–136.
Klauser, F., Paasche, T., Soderstrom, O., 2014. Michel Foucault and the Smart City: power dynamics inherent in contemporary governing through code. Environ. Plann. D: Soc. Space 32 (5), 869–885.
Komninos, N., Mora, L., 2018. Exploring the big picture of smart city research. Scienze Regionali: Ital. J. Region. Sci. 1 (2018), 15–38.
Kunstler, J.H., 1993. The Geography of Nowhere: The Rise and Decline of America's Man-Made Landscape. Simon & Schuster, New York City, NY.
Le Corbusier, 1986. Towards a New Architecture. Dover Publications, New York City, NY.
Le Corbusier, 1987. The City of Tomorrow and Its Planning, eighth ed. Dover Publications, New York City, NY.
Lefebvre, H., 1970. La Révolution Urbaine. Éditions Gallimard, Paris.
Levine, N., 2008. Introduction. In: Wright, F.L. (Ed.), Modern Architecture. Princeton University Press, Princeton, NJ.
Levitas, R., 1990. The Concept of Utopia. Philip Allan, London.
Levitas, R., 2007. Looking for the blue: The necessity of utopia. J. Polit. Ideol. 12 (3), 289–306.
Levitas, R., 2008. Pragmatism, utopia and anti-utopia. Crit. Horiz. 9 (1), 42–59.
Lopez, R., 2004. Urban sprawl and risk for being overweight or obese. Am. J. Public Health 94 (9), 1574–1579.
Luque-Ayala, A., Marvin, S., 2015. Developing a critical understanding of smart urbanism? Urban Stud. 52 (12), 2105–2116.
MacFadyen, D., 1970. Sir Ebenezer Howard and the Town Planning Movement. MIT Press, Cambridge, MA.
March, H., 2018. The smart city and other ICT-led techno-imaginaries: any room for dialogue with degrowth? J. Clean. Prod. 197, 1694–1703.
Marshall, S., 2009. Cities, Design and Evolution. Routledge, London.
Marvin, S., Luque-Ayala, A., McFarlane, C. (Eds.), 2016. Smart Urbanism: Utopian Vision or False Dawn? Routledge, New York City, NY.
Merenlender, A.M., Reed, S.E., Heise, K.L., 2009. Exurban development influences woodland bird composition. Landsc. Urban Plan. 92 (3–4), 255–263.
Mora, L., Bolici, R., 2016. The development process of smart city strategies: the case of Barcelona. In: Rajaniemi, J. (Ed.), Re-City: Future City – Combining Disciplines. Juvenes Print, Tampere, pp. 155–181.
Mora, L., Bolici, R., 2017. How to become a smart city: learning from Amsterdam. In: Bisello, A., Vettorato, D., Stephens, R., Elisei, P. (Eds.), Smart and Sustainable Planning for Cities and Regions: Results of SSPCR 2015. Springer, Cham, pp. 251–266.
Mora, L., Bolici, R., Deakin, M., 2017. The first two decades of smart-city research: a bibliometric analysis. J. Urban Technol. 24 (1), 3–27.
Mora, L., Deakin, M., Aina, Y.A., Appio, F.P., 2019a. Smart City development: ICT innovation for urban sustainability. In: Leal Filho, W., Azul, A.M., Brandli, L., Özuyar, P.G., Wall, T. (Eds.), Encyclopedia of the UN Sustainable Development Goals: Sustainable Cities and Communities. Springer, Cham.

Mora, L., Deakin, M., Reid, A., 2019b. Combining co-citation clustering and text-based analysis to reveal the main development paths of smart cities. Technol. Forecast. Soc. Change 142, 56–69. https://doi.org/10.1016/j.techfore.2018.07.019.

Mora, L., Deakin, M., Reid, A., 2019c. Strategic principles for smart city development: a multiple case study analysis of European best practices. Technol. Forecast. Soc. Change 142, 70–97. https://doi.org/10.1016/j.techfore.2018.07.035.

Mora, L., Deakin, M., Reid, A., 2018a. Smart city development paths: insights from the first two decades of research. In: Bisello, A., Vettorato, D., Laconte, P., Costa, S. (Eds.), Smart and Sustainable Planning for Cities and Region: Results of SSPCR 2017. Springer, Cham, pp. 403–427.

Mora, L., Deakin, M., Reid, A., Angelidou, M., 2018b. How to overcome the dichotomous nature of Smart City research: proposed methodology and results of a pilot study. J. Urban Technol. https://doi.org/10.1080/10630732.2018.1525265.

Moser, S., 2015. New cities: old wine in new bottles? Dialogues Hum. Geogr. 5 (1), 31–35.

Mumford, L., 1922. The Story of Utopias. Boni & Liverigh, New York City, NY.

Mumford, L., 1956. The Urban Prospect. Harcourt Brace & World, New York City, NY.

Mumford, L., 1961. The City in History: Its Origins, Its Transformations, and Its Prospects. Harcourt, New York City, NY.

Mumford, L., 1965. Utopia, the city and the machine. Daedalus 94 (2), 271–292.

Nelson, A.C., 1990. Regional patterns of exurban industrialization: results of a preliminary investigation. Econ. Dev. Q. 4 (4), 320–333.

Nelson, A.C., 1992. Characterizing exurbia. J. Plan. Lit. 6 (4), 350–368.

Nelson, A.C., 1995. The planning of exurban America: lessons from frank Lloyd Wright's Broadacre City. J. Architect. Plann. Res. 12 (4), 337–356.

Nelson, A.C., Dueker, K.J., 1989. Exurban living using improved water and wastewater technology. J. Urban Plann. Dev. 115 (3), 101–113.

Nelson, A.C., Dueker, K.J., 1990. The exurbanization of America and its planning policy implications. J. Plann. Educ. Res. 9 (2), 91–100.

Newburn, D.A., Berck, P., 2006. Modeling suburban and rural-residential development beyond the urban fringe. Land Econ. 82 (4), 481–499.

Nguyen, T.M.P., Davidson, K., 2017. Contesting green technology in the city: techno- apartheid or equitable modernisation? Int. Plan. Stud. 22 (4), 400–414.

Norberg-Schulz, C., 1980. Genius Loci: Towards a Phenomenology of Architecture. Rizzoli, New York City, NY.

Pinder, D., 2015. Reconstituting the possible: Lefebvre, utopia and the urban question. Int. J. Urban Reg. Res. 39 (1), 28–45.

Prakash, V., 2002. Chandigarh's Le Corbusier: The Struggle for Modernity in Postcolonial India. University of Washington Press, Seattle, WA.

Rego, R.L., 2014. Brazilian garden cities and suburbs: accommodating urban modernity and foreign ideals. J. Plan. Hist. 13 (4), 276–295.

Rosenburg, L., 2016. Scotland's Homes Fit for Heroes: Garden City Influences on the Development of Scottish Working-Class Housing 1900 to 1939. The World bank, Washington, DC.

Sargisson, L., 2000. Utopian Bodies and the Politics of Transgression. Routledge, New York City, NY.

Sarin, M., 1982. Urban Planning in the Third World: The Chandigarh Experience. Mansell Publishing, London.

Sassen, S., 1991. The Global City: New York, London, Tokyo. Princeton University Press, Princeton, NJ.

Schipper, J., 2008. Disappearing Desert: The Growth of Phoenix and the Culture of Sprawl. University of Oklahoma Press, Norman, OK.

Sharifi, A., 2016. From Garden City to eco-urbanism: the quest for sustainable neighborhood development. Sustain. Cities Soc. 20, 1–16.

Shaw, W.R., 2009. Broadacre City: American Fable and Technological Society. University of Oregon. https://scholarsbank.uoregon.edu/xmlui/bitstream/handle/1794/10177/Shaw_William_R_ma2009fa.pdf;sequence=1. (Accessed February 10, 2019).

Shelton, T., Zook, M., Wiig, A., 2015. The 'actually existing smart city'. Camb. J. Reg. Econ. Soc. 8 (1), 13–25.

Söderström, O., Paasche, T., Klauser, F., 2014. Smart cities as corporate storytelling. City: Anal. Urban Trends Culture Theory Policy Action 18 (3), 307–320.

Strickland, E., 2011. Cisco bets on south Korean Smart City. IEEE Spectr. 48 (8), 11–12.

Sutton, P.C., Cova, T.J., Elvidge, C.D., 2006. Mapping "exurbia" in the conterminous United States using nighttime satellite imagery. Geocarto Int. 21 (2), 39–45.

Swensen, G., Jerpåsen, G.B., 2008. Cultural heritage in suburban landscape planning: a case study in southern Norway. Landsc. Urban Plan. 87 (4), 289–300.

Theobald, D.M., 2001. Land-use dynamics beyond the American urban fringe. Geogr. Rev. 91 (3), 544–564.

Townsend, A., 2013. Smart Cities: Big Data, Civic Hackers, and the Quest for a New Utopia. W.W. Norton & Company Ltd, New York City, NY.

UNEP, 2013. City-Level Decoupling: Urban Resource Flows and the Governance of Infrastructure Transitions. United Nations Environment Programme. http://wedocs.unep.org/handle/20.500.11822/8488. (Accessed January 20, 2019).

Valdez, A., Cook, M., Potter, S., 2018. Roadmaps to utopia: tales of the smart city. Urban Stud. 55 (15), 3385–3403.

Vanolo, A., 2016. Is there anybody out there? The place and role of citizens in tomorrow's smart cities. Futures 82, 26–36.

Watson, V., 2015. The allure of 'smart city' rhetoric: India and Africa. Dialogues Hum. Geogr. 5 (1), 36–39.

Wiig, A., 2015. IBM's Smart City as techno-utopian policy mobility. City: Anal. Urban Trends Culture Theory Policy Action 19 (2–3), 258–273.

Wiig, A., 2016. The empty rhetoric of the smart city: from digital inclusion to economic promotion in Philadelphia. Urban Geogr. 37 (4), 535–553.

Wiig, A., 2018. Secure the city, revitalize the zone: smart urbanization in Camden, New Jersey. Environ. Plann. C: Polit. Space 36 (3), 403–422.

Wiig, A., Wyly, E., 2016. Introduction: thinking through the politics of the smart city. Urban Geogr. 37 (4), 485–493.

Wilde, L., 2017. Thomas More's Utopia: Arguing for Social Justice. Routledge, New York City, NY.

Williamson, T., Imbroscio, D., Alperovitz, G., 2002. Making a Place for Community: Local Democracy in a Global Era. Routledge, New York City, NY.

Wright, F.L., 1931. Modern Architecture. Princeton University Press, Princeton, NJ.

Wright, F.L., 1932. The Disappearing City. William Farquhar Payson, New York City, NY.

Wright, F.L., 1943. Frank Lloyd Wright: An Autobiography. Duell, Sloan and Pierce, New York City, NY.

Yeo, M.T., 2019. From garden city to city in a garden and beyond. In: Schröpfer, T., Menz, S. (Eds.), Dense and Green Building Typologies: Research, Policy and Practice Perspectives. Springer, Singapore, pp. 21–25.

Yoo, S., 2017. Songdo: The Hype and Decline of World's First Smart City. In: Caprotti, F., Yu, L. (Eds.), Sustainable Cities in Asia. Routledge, New York City, NY, pp. 146–160.

Zhao, P., 2010. Sustainable urban expansion and transportation in a growing megacity: consequences of urban sprawl for mobility on the urban fringe of Beijing. Habitat Int. 34 (2), 236–243.

Chapter 2

Smart city development as an ICT-driven approach to urban sustainability

Chapter Outline

2.1 Introduction

Smart cities are those cities[1] in which a platform of ICT solutions is deployed to meet urban sustainability priorities. Making cities smart by helping them activate this ICT-driven approach to sustainable urban development has become a key commitment for academia, industry, governments, and civil society organizations, which all agree in suggesting that ICTs play an extremely important role in making urban environments more sustainable.

1. This book uses the term "city" to refer to any types of urban areas, irrespective of their population size.

Untangling Smart Cities. https://doi.org/10.1016/B978-0-12-815477-9.00002-5

New purpose-built labs and research centers designed for supporting academic researchers in examining smart city development are now active in some of the world's leading research institutions. The Massachusetts Institute of Technology (MIT) has recently set up the City Science Lab and the Senseable City Lab, which focus on the application of smart technologies in the field of architecture, personal mobility vehicles, and urban and regional planning. The research activity they have conducted to date shows that both labs are taking on the challenge of developing innovative decision support systems and visualization tools for optimizing the management of city-scale interventions. These systems and tools are expected to analyze large streams of information, which current advancements in the ICT sector have made available, and reveal how urban environments work. The knowledge produced with these advanced urban analytic systems can help local governments embrace a data-driven and evidence-based approach to urban design and planning.

Technology-enabled urban analytics is also explored at the Centre for Advanced Spatial Analysis of University College London, and additional examples of university-led research centers focusing attention on smart city development include the following: the Data Science Institute's Smart Cities Center at Columbia University, in New York City; the University of Cambridge's Centre for Smart Infrastructure and Construction; Smart City Research at the Oxford Internet Institute; the Future Cities Laboratory, which is led by ETH Zurich and the National Research Foundation of Singapore; and the Smart Cities Institute at Swinburne University of Technology, in Australia.[2]

Solution providers and consultancy firms working in the ICT sector are now trying to enter the market of urban technologies by specializing in smart city development. For example, the International Data Corporation (IDC) provides city and national governments with a research advisory service that helps them leverage digital technology to improve urban operations and public service delivery. The International Business Machines Corporation (IBM) and Cisco Systems offer the very same advisory service, along with the platforms of ICT solutions they have respectively designed for supporting smart city development. IBM has also been running the Smarter Cities Technology Centre since 2010, a European-based laboratory in which an interdisciplinary team of researchers is dedicated to the study of smart technologies and their impact (IDC, 2018a; Palmisano, 2008; IBM Corporation, 2010; Cisco Systems, 2017; Paroutis et al., 2014).

---

2. See the following websites for additional information: MIT City Science Lab, https://www.media.mit.edu; MIT Senseable City Lab, http://senseable.mit.edu; UCL Centre for Advanced Spatial Analysis, https://www.ucl.ac.uk/bartlett/casa; Columbia University, Smart Cities Center, http://datascience.columbia.edu/smart-cities; University of Cambridge, Centre for Smart Infrastructure and Construction, https://www-smartinfrastructure.eng.cam.ac.uk; University of Oxford, Smart City Research, http://smartcities.oii.ox.ac.uk; Singapore-ETH Centre, Future Cities Laboratory, http://www.fcl.ethz.ch; and Swinburne University of Technology, Smart Cities Research Institute, http://www.swinburne.edu.au/research/our-research/institutes/smart-cities.

Additional examples of multinational companies delivering smart city services globally are Microsoft, Hitachi, and Huawei, which have strengthen their collaboration by joining the Smart Cities Council, an industry-led network that is acting as a trusted and expert advisor in smart city transitions. A similar service is offered by the Institute of Electrical and Electronics Engineers (IEEE), the world's largest professional organization supporting the advancement of technology. IEEE has set up a new division whose objective is to raise awareness of the benefits and downsides of smart city development and to guide cities towards adopting a smart city approach to urban sustainability.[3]

In Africa, smart city development is at the heart of the national agenda for socioeconomic development. The 55 member states of The African Union Commission (2015), which represents almost the entire continent, have committed to leveraging ICTs to promote sustainable urban development. The same interest emerges in the United States, where The White House (2015) has invested over 160 million dollars in smart city initiatives aiming at harnessing ICT to tackle local communities' challenges, such as reducing traffic congestion, fostering economic growth, fighting crime and climate change, and improving the delivery of public services. This choice is aligned with the results of the trend analysis conducted by the National Intelligence Council (NIC), a center for long-term strategic thinking that reports directly to the president of the United States. While investigating the global trends that will shape the world out to 2030, the National Intelligence Council (2012: IX) has forecasted that "information technology-based solutions to maximize citizens' economic productivity and quality of life while minimizing resource consumption and environmental degradation will be critical to ensuring the viability of megacities."

Even Europe is already aware of the critical role that ICT is playing in urban sustainability. To help citizens and businesses to get the most out of digital technologies, the European Union and its 28 member states have launched the Digital Agenda for Europe. This policy document suggests Europe must exploit ICTs to help address many of the global challenges that modern society is currently facing and to make cities more sustainable. In the 2014–15 budget of the Horizon 2020 Research and Innovation program, the European Commission made available about 200 million Euro to accelerate progress in the field of smart cities and communities and enlarge the scale of rollout of ICT solutions for urban sustainability issues (European Commission, 2010b, 2014).

Europe's efforts to embrace an ICT-driven approach to urban sustainability are part of its contribution to implementing the 2030 Agenda for Sustainable Development and the New Urban Agenda, two policy documents in which the United Nations (UN) point out what transformative actions are urgently needed to make the world more inclusive, safe, resilient, and sustainable. The New Urban Agenda clearly states that supporting cities in enabling smart

3. See: Smart Cities Council, https://smartcitiescouncil.com, and IEEE Smart Cities, https://smartcities.ieee.org.

city development has become one of the key commitments for the 193 member states of the United Nations, which suggest dealing with urban challenges by deploying ICT-related innovations is key to (1) cultivate environmentally friendly, resource-efficient, safe, inclusive, and accessible urban environments, (2) sustain an economic growth based on the principles of environmental sustainability and inclusive prosperity, and (3) provide equal access for all to public goods and high-quality services (European Commission, 2017; United Nations, 2015, 2017a).

All these institutions share the very same conviction that digital technologies will help drive cities towards new sustainable development paths. This chapter demonstrates the validity of such a firmly held belief by reporting on a series of smart city projects that showcase how ICT solutions can be instrumental in tackling the global issues affecting urban environments. In these projects, which are here deployed as descriptive case studies, ICT contributes to supporting the realization of the transformative commitments that the United Nations have included in the New Urban Agenda (United Nations, 2017a).

This chapter is split in three main sections. The first section offers a detailed overview of the technological trends that have underpinned the development of the smart city concept and the ICT-driven approach to urban sustainability that this concept stands for (Section 2.2). This overview is followed by comprehensive accounts of the smart city initiatives that have been selected. For each initiative, attention will be focused on (1) the urban challenges that have been faced by means of a smart city approach to urban sustainability, (2) the ICT solutions that have been deployed, and (3) the benefits that such solutions have contributed to generate (Section 2.3). The chapter concludes with a critical reflection upon the current debate on smart city development, which is instrumental in calling attention on the research gaps and questions that this book aims to address (Section 2.4).

2.2 Cities in the digital era: Emerging technological trends

By 2007, for the first time in human history, the population living in urban areas outnumbered the inhabitants of rural areas (see Fig. 2.1).[4] This massive demographic change reversed the picture of majority rural populations that has characterized human history, and as shown in Fig. 2.2, it took place with astonishing rapidity. A massive rural-urban migration began in the 1950s, with urban environments exerting an increasingly strong pull due to the concentration of cultural, social, professional, economic, and personal opportunities that they offer. By 2014, 54% of the world's population was urban dwellers (United Nations, 2014, 2017b).

4. According to the North Carolina State University (2007) and University of Georgia's hypothesis, the population shift happened on May 23 2007.

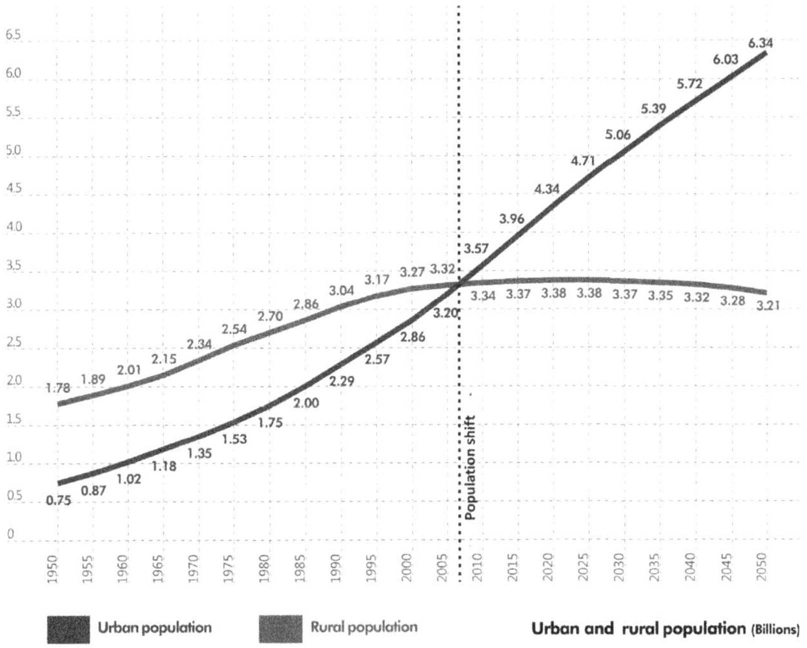

FIG. 2.1 Urban and rural population worldwide. *(Data source: United Nations, 2017b. World Population Prospects: The 2017 Revision, Key Findings and Advance Tables. ESA/P/WP/248. United Nations. https://esa.un.org/unpd/wpp/publications/Files/WPP2017_KeyFindings.pdf. Accessed 10.12.2017.)*

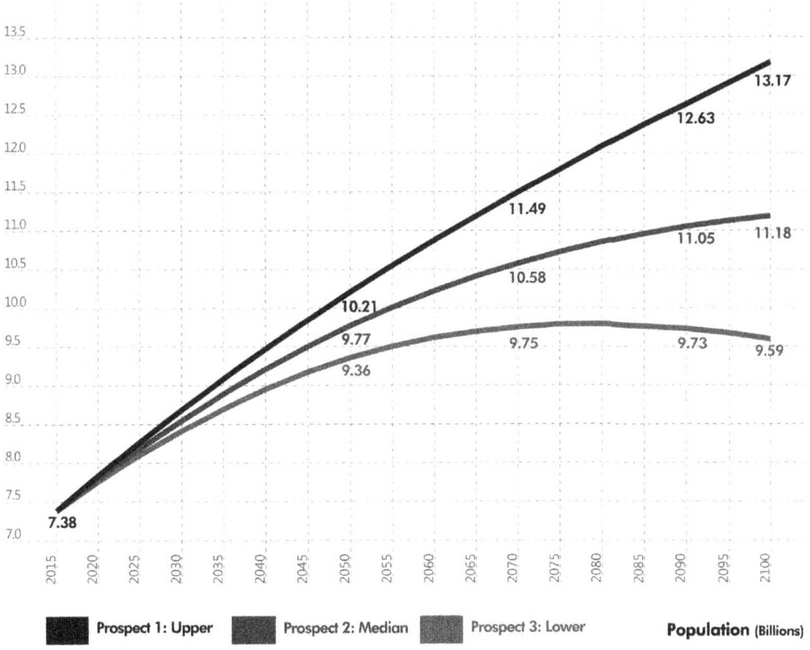

FIG. 2.2 UN World population prospects. *(Data source: United Nations, 2017b. World Population Prospects: The 2017 Revision, Key Findings and Advance Tables. ESA/P/WP/248. United Nations. https://esa.un.org/unpd/wpp/publications/Files/WPP2017_KeyFindings.pdf. Accessed 10.12.2017.)*

In addition, this global trend is expected to continue. Both the world's population and the proportion of it living in urban areas are forecast to rise considerably over the coming decades. The United Nations has predicted that the global population will stand at between 9.6 and 13.2 billion by 2100 (as opposed to 7.4 billion in 2015), which is an increase of between 30% and 78%. It is also predicted that cities in the developing world will account for 80% of this population growth, bringing developing countries closer to the 75%–25% urban-rural breakdown that already characterizes the member states of the European Union (European Commission, 2010a; United Nations, 2014, 2017b).

Such an enormous rise in world population poses considerable challenges to urban environments, which have proved incapable of meeting the needs of a continuously growing demand in a sustainable way. This demographic transition has resulted in inefficiency levels that are growing hand in hand with the urban population and calls for a redesign of sustainable urban development strategies. New approaches to urban sustainability are required and unlocking the potential for accelerating urban sustainability that is embedded in the technological advancements of the digital revolution will be crucial in achieving this objective.

Technological advance has always been key throughout the history of urban development. The technological innovations of the Neolithic era favored the initial transition from nomadic groups of hunter-gatherers to the first agricultural settlements and early civilization. Leaping forwards to the 18th century, the industrial revolution introduced new combinations of buildings, transport systems, and telecommunication networks, triggering a radical transformation of the urban landscape and making cities become a promise for a better quality of life (Benevolo, 1993).

The latest period of technological innovation has seen the cities of the industrial revolution being rapidly transformed by the products of the digital revolution. As a result of this process of change, new ICT devices and infrastructure have absorbed a wide range of functions in urbanized areas and have led to radical transformations in urban development dynamics. The modern society is witnessing "a rapid and silent revolution" (Mitchell, 1995), which has opened up a new opportunity for supporting sustainable urban development: using information and communication technologies to solve the issues limiting urban sustainability. The challenge is to learn how to harness the technological trends that the digital revolution has brought about and to exploit the possibilities that these trends offer to realize the social, economic, and environmental improvements needed for an urban development that is sustainable. Some of these technological trends are discussed in the following paragraphs.

2.2.1 Faster, cheaper, smaller: The evolutionary process in the ICT sector

The fast-paced advancements in the ICT sector have been triggering innovation processes in other product and service areas. A good example that clearly exemplifies this synergy can be seen in the evolution of the automobile industry, which has been analyzed by Bjarke Ingels Group (BIG), a US- and Danish-based architecture firm. In 2011 BIG took part in the annual Audi Urban Future Awards contest. Their proposal for a reprogrammable digital street surface was informed by a very detailed mapping exercise that put together the major technological breakthroughs that contributed to revolutionize automobile manufacture (see Fig. 2.3). BIG worked across a large historical canvas, charting the evolution of the automobile since the invention of the wheel. Three major points emerged from their presentation: (1) There have always been bursts of technological progress, but the timeframe dividing these bursts has become exponentially shorter through history; (2) the last decade, between 2001 and 2011, had seen more technological breakthroughs than any previous period; and (3) the reason for this clustering of advancements lay with the digital revolution and rapid evolution of the ICT sector.

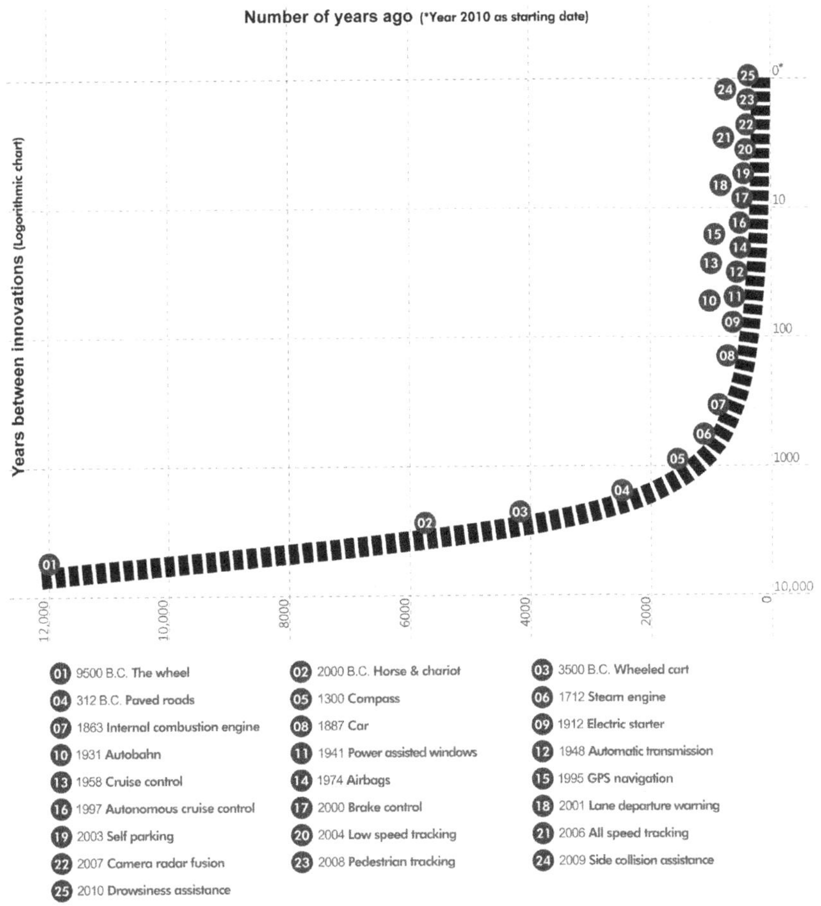

FIG. 2.3 The technological evolution of the car. *(Data source: Jordana, S., 2010. BIG's Proposal for the Audi Urban Future Award. Online article. ArchDaily. http://www.archdaily.com/77103/bigs-proposal-for-the-audi-urban-future-award/. Accessed 08.03.2014.)*

The never-ending growth of the ICT sector has been triggered by the invention of both the planar transistor and integrated circuit. It is the merging of these two components that unleashed "the potential for extending the cost and operating benefits of transistors to every mass-produced electronic circuit, including the microprocessors that control computer operations" (Schaller, 1997: 53). These two components have prompted the manufacturing and distribution of technological products that help people manage complex computational activities and continually augment their analytical skills.

As for human beings, even technological products are subject to constant evolutionary change. The pace of this change was predicted in the 1960s by Gordon Moore, inventor of the integrated circuit, ICT pioneer, and cofounder of Intel. Moore estimated that manufacturers would have doubled the number of transistors per integrated circuit approximately every 18 months, resulting in circuits running twice as fast at regular intervals. This prediction, which has proven correct, is known as Moore's Law, and the continuous upgrading process it captures explains the astonishing speed with which technological devices with a continuously augmented computational power become available (Moore, 1965; Schaller, 1997).

However, while the processing ability of digital devices with computational power has been dramatically increasing, their relative costs have been progressively decreasing. This second trend, which is analyzed in research by Raymond Kurzweil, Director of Engineering at Google, has made electronic devices pervasive because more affordable to a greater number of people. After observing the speed in instructions per unit cost of 49 famous calculators and computers spanning the entire 20th century, Kurzweil (2004, 389) concludes by pointing out that the "computer speed (per unit cost) doubled every three years between 1910 and 1950, doubled every two years between 1950 and 1966, and is now doubling every year."

However, technological development is not only speeding up the computation power of ICT devices but also bringing down manufacturing costs. It is also reducing selling prices and enabling ever smaller, more portable versions of such devices to be brought to market. This trend is captured in research by Eyre and Bier (1998), Mitchell (1995, 1999), and Mack (2011), who suggest the ability to produce smaller, faster, and cheaper electronic devices has powered new markets to grow and triggered the mass diffusion of modern computing technology across the globe. The billions of smartphones in use worldwide are a case in point, as shown in Fig. 2.4. Subscription data recorded by the smartphone manufacturer Ericsson shows that the global number of smartphone subscriptions has grown significantly since 2010, moving from 0.5 billion devices to the 3.9 of 2016, and is expected to reach around 6.8 billion by the end of 2022.

2.2.2 Intangible: The virtual image of cities

Although published nearly 60 years ago, "The Image of the City" (Lynch, 1960) remains among the most influential contribution to large-scale urban design

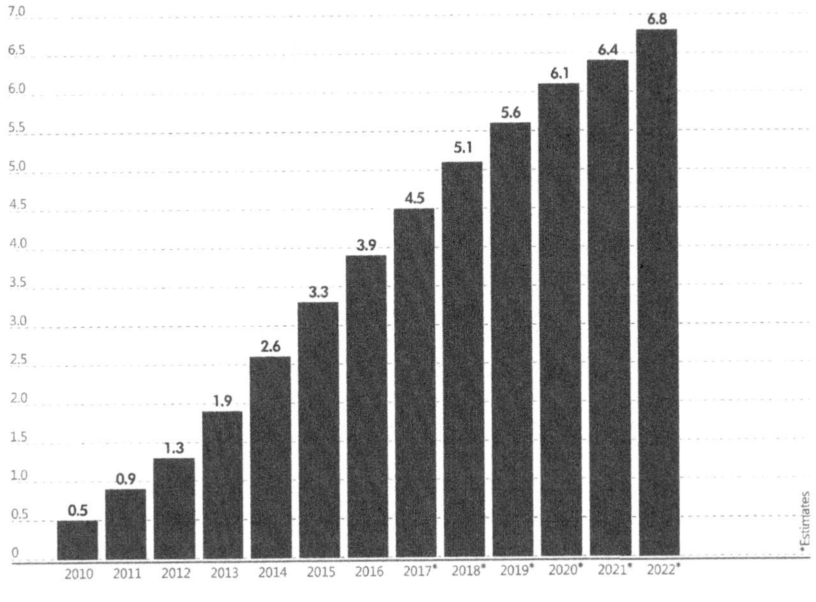

FIG. 2.4 Number of smartphone subscriptions in the world by year. *(Data source: Ericsson, 2013. Ericsson Mobility Report: On the Pulse of the Networked Society. Ericsson. http://www.ericsson.com/res/docs/2013/ericsson-mobility-report-november-2013.pdf. Accessed 10.06.2014; Ericsson, 2014. Ericsson Mobility Report: On the Pulse of the Networked Society. November 2014. Ericsson. https://www.ericsson.com/assets/local/mobility-report/documents/2014/ericsson-mobility-report-november-2014.pdf. Accessed 13.01.2018; Ericsson, 2015. Ericsson Mobility Report: On the Pulse of the Networked Society. November 2015. Ericsson. https://www.ericsson.com/assets/local/mobility-report/documents/2015/ericsson-mobility-report-nov-2015.pdf. Accessed 13.01.2018; Ericsson, 2016. Ericsson Mobility Report: On the Pulse of the Networked Society. November 2016. Ericsson. https://www.ericsson.com/assets/local/mobility-report/documents/2016/ericsson-mobility-report-november-2016.pdf. Accessed 13.01.2018; Ericsson, 2017. Ericsson Mobility Report: On the Pulse of the Networked Society. June 2017. Ericsson. https://www.ericsson.com/assets/local/mobility-report/documents/2017/ericsson-mobility-report-june-2017.pdf. Accessed 13.01.2018.)*

theory. This book was written by Kevin Lynch, American urban planner and emeritus professor of city planning of the Massachusetts Institute of Technology (MIT), and its contents are still providing a valid theory answering the following research questions: (1) How do large groups of individuals formulate the environmental image of the city in which they live? (2) What are the main elements composing this common mental picture? (3) What can city planners do to make such environmental images more legible, more distinctive, and able to offer emotional security?

The theoretical contribution that Lynch offers surfaces from a multiple case study analysis of three North American cities. Working over a 5-year period in Boston, Jersey City, and Los Angeles, he elicited information from groups of citizens about how they understood and experienced their cities visually and then correlated his findings to identify common themes and structures. The study demonstrates that the majority of urban dwellers work within the same multielement mental framework, which suggests the image of a city can be broken down into five type-element classes of tangible components:

- Paths: channels along which people move throughout the city, such as streets, walkways, and railroads.
- Edges: elements, like walls, that close one part of the city off from others.
- Districts: medium-to-large sections of the city in which common physically or culturally related features are perceived.
- Nodes: polarizing spots that can be either junctions of paths or concentrations gathering people together, like squares.
- Landmarks: objects that are significant and easily identifiable and help observers orient in the complexity of the urban landscape.

Lynch's investigation yielded one possible theory explaining how city users elaborate the images of cities and what basic elements tend to populate such images. This theory has offered new insights into the collective perception of the urban landscape and suggests cities can be decomposed into a group of interconnected physical elements. What all these elements have in common is that they are tangible. But when considering cities in the information age, this theory seems incomplete. The digital revolution has augmented the complexity of cities by leading to the growth of their intangible counterparts, which relate not to physical assets but the immateriality of urban environments. These new components cannot be perceived visually, but nevertheless affect how cities function and contribute to the transformation of the physical elements that Lynch captured.

As Mitchell (1995, 2003) and Castells (1996) explain, each urban environment has an intangible counterpart, whose structures exhibit common distinct features. These spaces are (1) virtual, because hosted in the immateriality of the Internet, (2) built of fast-expanding data streams, and (3) home to the network society, that is, a society composed of people who can enter such intangible environments via their technological devices and communicate through online networks (Fig. 2.5). As Mitchell (2004, 127) explains, physical cities and their virtual counterparts are strictly interrelated, with each influencing how the other functions. "At one end of the spectrum are completely traditional, place-based communities composed entirely of physical spaces, organized around traditional types of public spaces, and held together by physical circulation through streets and transportation networks. At the other end of the spectrum are fully virtual communities."

Created in the 1990s, this invention has allowed any person who owns a technological device with Internet-access capacity to share data across and through physical borders and become part of the network society (Ryan, 2010). According to the International Telecommunication Union (ITU), Internet users

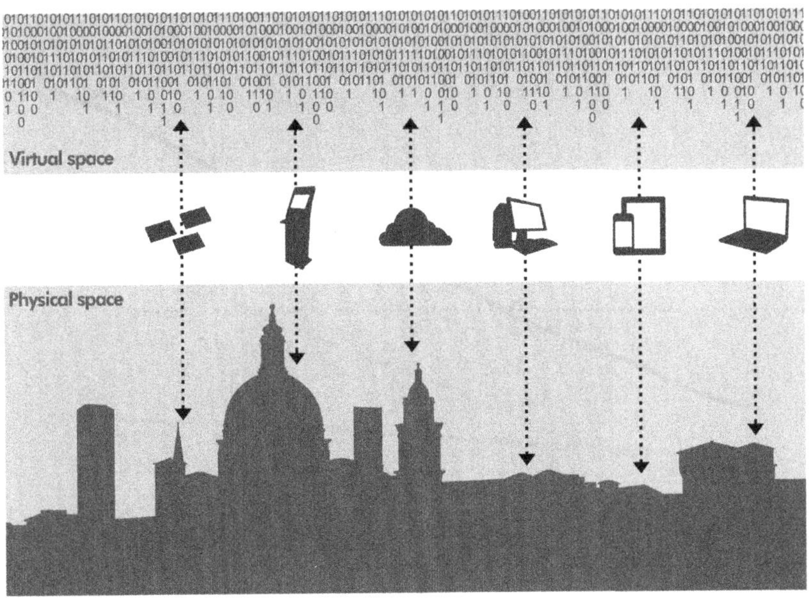

FIG. 2.5 The image of cities.

have massively increased in number in both developing and developed areas of the world. As shown in Fig. 2.6 the period 2005–16 saw an increase from 1.02 billion individual users to 3.4 billion. This indicates that nearly 47% of the global population is now connected to the Internet and is contributing to shaping the intangible counterparts of physical cities (ITU and UNESCO, 2016). The network society, distinct from societies based around physical locations, is therefore growing rapidly all over the world.

2.2.3 Everywhere: Mobility, ubiquity, and the Internet of Things

By inventing the telegraph, Guglielmo Marconi marked the beginning of the wireless world. His telegraph, for the first time in history, made it possible to send signals between two different locations without any physical carriers. In discussing Marconi's wireless system and the effects that this invention has produced, Mitchell (2003) introduces mobility, ubiquity, and the Internet of Things (IoT), three additional global trends that have radically changed urban environments and society.

The development of wireless technologies, such as Bluetooth, Wi-Fi, cellular data networks and radio-frequency identification (RFID) technology, is allowing billions of electronic devices to connect to the Internet while on the move, rather than having to remain "plugged in" to specific locations. The devices that can use such wireless technologies have been freed from the constraints

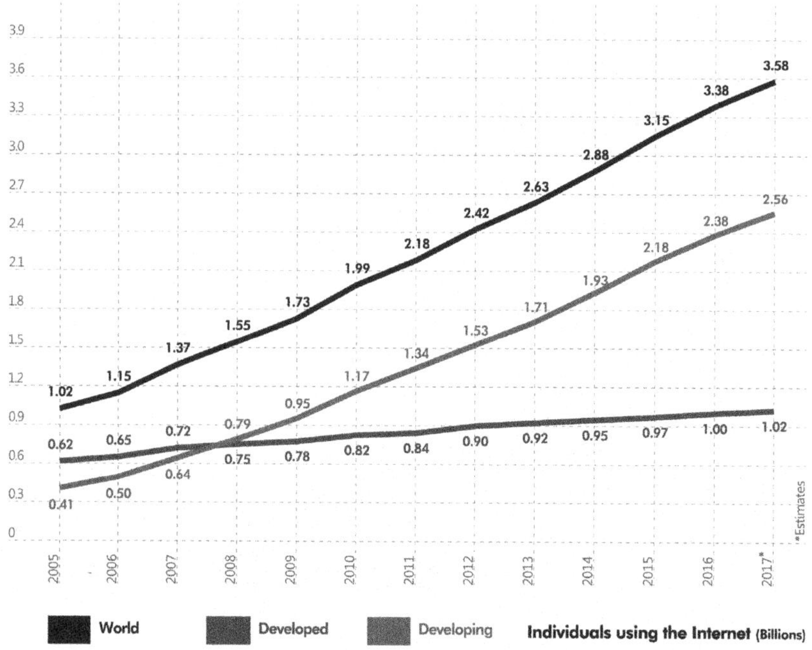

FIG. 2.6 Number of individuals using the Internet. *(Data Source: ITU, 2014. Global ICT Developments. Dataset. International Telecommunication Union. http://www.itu.int/en/ITU-D/Statistics/Documents/statistics/2014/stat_page_all_charts_2014.xls. Accessed 10.04.2014; ITU, 2016. Key ICT Indicators for Developed and Developing Countries and the World (Totals and Penetration Rates). Dataset. International Telecommunication Union. https://www.itu.int/en/ITU-D/Statistics/Documents/statistics/2017/ITU_Key_2005-2017_ICT_data.xls. Accessed 20.01.2018.)*

of a fixed location, and as it can be seen from the data shown in Fig. 2.7, their popularity and usage have significantly grown over time. Over the past 13 years, according to the data released by ITU, mobile-broadband subscriptions have far outstripped fixed-broadband subscriptions, to the point that, by 2016, the former accounted for 81% of active broadband subscriptions in the world. This growth trend clearly manifests the preference expressed by Internet users for mobile networks and mobile devices.

In addition, many commenters suggest these numbers will continue to rise. While the urban population was outnumbering the population living in rural areas, the number of electronic devices with Internet-connection capacity exceeded the number of inhabitants on the planet. This second epoch-making change is exposed by Cisco Internet Business Solutions Group (IBSG), whose analysis is presented in Fig. 2.8. In addition to suggesting that the shift took place between 2003 and 2010, Cisco IBSG predicts that the gap between the number of Internet-connected objects will continue to rise exponentially. Fifty billion devices connected to the Internet by 2020 are forecasted, and the ratio of people to devices is expected to become 1–7 (Evans, 2011). Although there are

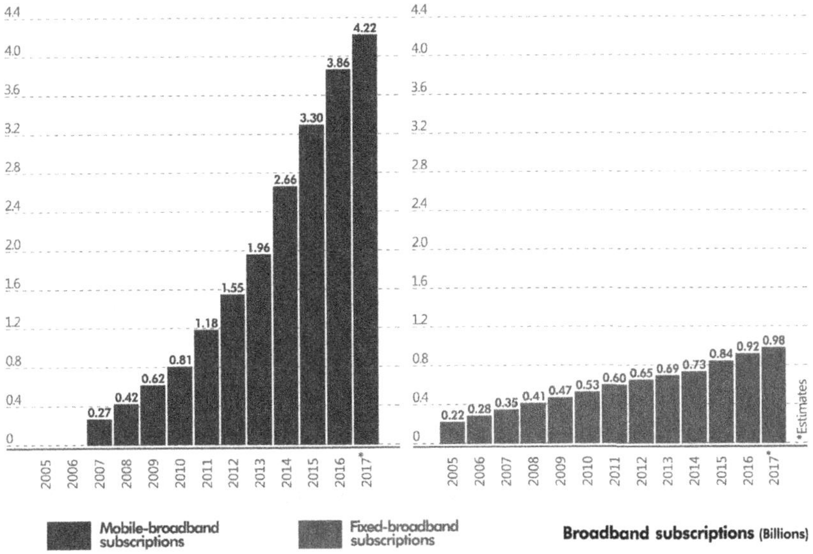

FIG. 2.7 Number of broadband subscriptions in the world by type. *(Data Source: ITU, 2014. Global ICT Developments. Dataset. International Telecommunication Union. http://www.itu.int/en/ITU-D/Statistics/Documents/statistics/2014/stat_page_all_charts_2014.xls. Accessed 10.04.2014; ITU, 2016. Key ICT Indicators for Developed and Developing Countries and the World (Totals and Penetration Rates). Dataset. International Telecommunication Union. https://www.itu.int/en/ITU-D/Statistics/Documents/statistics/2017/ITU_Key_2005-2017_ICT_data.xls. Accessed 20.01.2018.)*

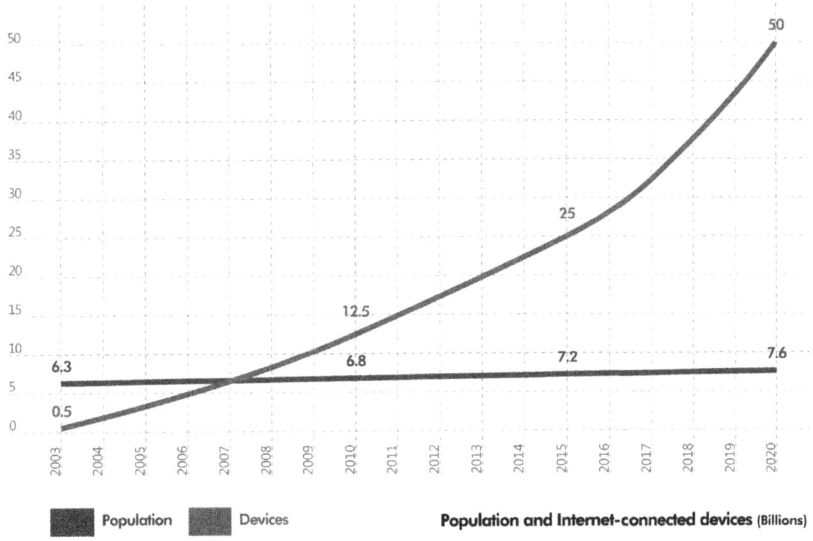

FIG. 2.8 Growth in the world's population and number of Internet-connected devices according to Cisco IBSG.

differences in the figures they propose, this growth trend is also forecasted by Gartner, ABI Research, and Ericsson. By 2020, ABI Research (2013) expects 30 billion devices connected to the Internet, while Gartner (2013) and Ericsson (2015) both forecast a figure of 26 billion.

All this data pictures an expanding ecosystem of constantly improving technological devices, which are becoming increasingly available to a mass consumer base. Mobile-broadband users are expected to connect 15 billion smartphones, tablets, laptops, and PCs to the Internet by the end of 2020. However, considering an expected growth scenario between of 26 and 30 billion Internet-connected objects, this only accounts for about 50% of the total. The other 50% will be composed of networks of sensors embedded in the build environment, which are expected to populate the Internet with a huge amount of autonomously produced data (Ericsson, 2015).

As Mitchell pointed out, the advent of wireless technologies has changed thing-to-thing relationships. "Many things that might benefit from network connections never got them because it was just too difficult to run the wires. By the dawn of the twenty-first century, though, inexpensive, ubiquitous wireless connections were linking whole new classes of things into networks. Very tiny things, very numerous things, very isolated things, highly mobile things, things deeply embedded in other things, and things that were jammed into tight and inaccessible places" (Mitchell, 2003: 3). This leaves the Internet populated by both human users and a growing number of networks made of physical objects that can sense the external environment and communicate with it.

This wave of Internet-connected devices has enabled the IoT, a new paradigm that is made possible by the pervasive presence of a large variety of sensor-type technologies able to link the physical environment in which they are embedded, to the virtual world. These objects can automatically communicate to each other and provide services and applications characterized by a high degree of autonomous data capture, data transfer, network connectivity, and interoperability. The IoT is expected to lead towards the most disruptive technological revolution since the advent of the Internet, with massive potential to bring about positive technical, social, economic, and political transformational changes. A huge range of policy domains have already benefitted from deploying IoT solutions, with more expected to harness their potential in the near future, especially for urban sustainability purposes (Atzori et al., 2010; Holler et al., 2014; Tselentis et al., 2009).

2.2.4 Volume, velocity, and variety: Data production in the digital era

The increasingly widespread deployment of electronic devices with Internet-connection capability is one of the major factors behind the expansion of the network society. These tools allow anyone to access the Internet and either access a wide range of information items and services or contribute to the creation and diffusion of new ones, fueling the continued growth of data streams and digital applications that the global network has to offer. This collective data production process has made the Internet become a fast-expanding information-rich environment.

The estimates released by IDC give an idea of the staggering growth in the volume of digital data available. In 2007 this was estimated to be 281 exabytes, and by 2011 it exceeded 1843 exabytes (Gantz et al., 2008; Gantz and Reinsel, 2011). What is more, the growth in the volume of data being uploaded onto the digital universe seems to be exponential and unstoppable because, as of 2012, "about 2.5 exabytes of data are created each day, and the number is doubling approximately every 40 months or so. More data are produced every second than was stored in the entire Internet just 20 years ago" (McAfee and Brynjolfsson, 2012: 62). However, far less of this information is created *by* Internet users than is created *about* them by the ever-increasing number of objects with Internet-connection capacity (Gantz and Reinsel, 2011). Physical objects and people have become members of a single, large community and are both actively involved in the production of the huge stream of data shaping the digital universe.

Fig. 2.9 renders the explosive growth in data availability more comprehensible by using books as a unit of measurement. Considering that one exabyte amounts to 4803 billion 200-page books, the information stored digitally in 2011 was the equivalent of approximately 9000 trillion books. This growth has led to the big-data era, a term that is mainly used to describe enormous datasets composed of large masses of unstructured and heterogeneous data. In the era of big data, the rate of data production speeds up, so does the velocity with which analysts can process the increasing amounts of data gathered, which is collected from an ever-greater variety of sources.

This newfound velocity of processing, the unprecedented variety of data sources, and the ever-increasing volume of data available are the main trends in today's knowledge production processes. However, although progress is constantly made to keep up with big data-related trends, innovative methodological models and technologies enabling high-speed collection, aggregation, processing, and discovery are required to capture the benefits that transforming large volumes of raw data into knowledge can offer to sustainable urban development (Boyd and Crawford, 2012; Chen et al., 2014; McAfee and Brynjolfsson, 2012).

2.3 Smart stories: Deploying ICT to boost urban sustainability

This section aims to showcase how urban environments can benefit from the emerging technological trends previously described and use ICT solutions to accelerate urban sustainability. In doing so, a selection of smart city initiatives will be introduced as descriptive case studies and presented thematically, by considering the urban transformative commitments for urban sustainability that each initiative has helped achieve. These commitments, which are defined by

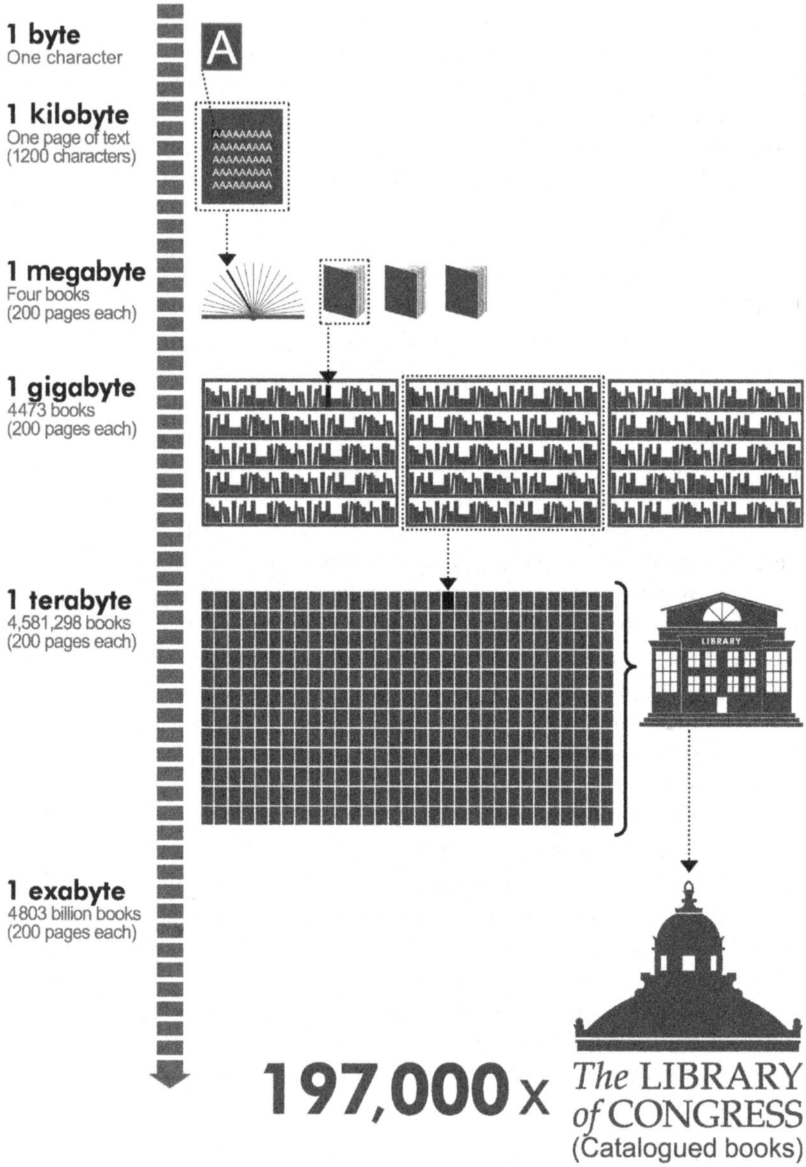

FIG. 2.9 From bytes to books: understanding data production in the digital era. (*Adapted from Piedmont-Palladino, S.C., 2011. Intelligent Cities. National Building Museum, Washington, DC. Values from Computer Hope (http://computerhope.com) and The Library of Congress (https://loc.gov).*)

the United Nations (2017a) and listed in their New Urban Agenda, include: (1) facilitating the sustainable management of natural resources, (2) ensuring equal access to basic services and infrastructures, (3) improving food security, (4) promoting environmentally sound waste management and reducing waste generation, and (5) improving the resilience of cities to natural disasters.

2.3.1 Facilitating the sustainable management of natural resources

With an enormous quantity of digital information being generated across the world, researchers have been tasked with structuring this data in a meaningful way to improve the functionality and quality of urban environments. One such approach has seen the deployment of big-data analytics in an attempt to understand the collective behavior of city users. This insight can be used to raise collective awareness in relation to specific issues affecting urban environments and support informed policy-making, helping city governments to tailor responses that meet the needs of their citizens.

For example, the HubCab project (www.hubcab.org) is emblematic of how big-data analytics can become a tool for fostering the sustainable management of natural resources (see Badger, 2014; Santi et al., 2014; Stertz, 2014; Szell and Groß, 2014). The overarching aim of this project was to help reduce air pollution in New York City by encouraging its users to share taxis. This project made it possible to (1) reveal the positive impact of large-scale taxi sharing on environmental sustainability and service cost reduction, (2) stimulate behavioral changes in personal mobility patterns involving taxi trips, and (3) inform local policy-makers about the feasibility and effectiveness of activating a new taxi-sharing system or program for New York City.

HubCab results from a collaboration between researchers at the Senseable City Lab of Massachusetts Institute of Technology, the German automobile manufacturer Audi, and the multinational conglomerate company General Electric. Together, these three partners mapped an entire year of taxi trips originating and ending in Manhattan. This mapping exercise was performed by putting together the 172 million trips that the taxicabs operating in New York City officially registered in 2011. The data describing each trip was captured by using the Global Positioning System (GPS) trackers that all the New York City taxis have been mandated to install since 2008. This included nearly 14,000 vehicles. The data obtained from the GPS trackers was included in a single, massive dataset in which every trip is connected to the vehicle ID, the travel time, and the GPS coordinates of both the pickup and drop-off locations.

The data was processed using a mathematical model to visualize the results in the form of an interactive map, which is shown in Figs. 2.10 and 2.11. The taxi pickup and drop-off points are represented on the map as yellow and blue dots, respectively, whereas the thickness of the street segment is proportional to the level of taxi activity. In selecting a pickup point and destination on the

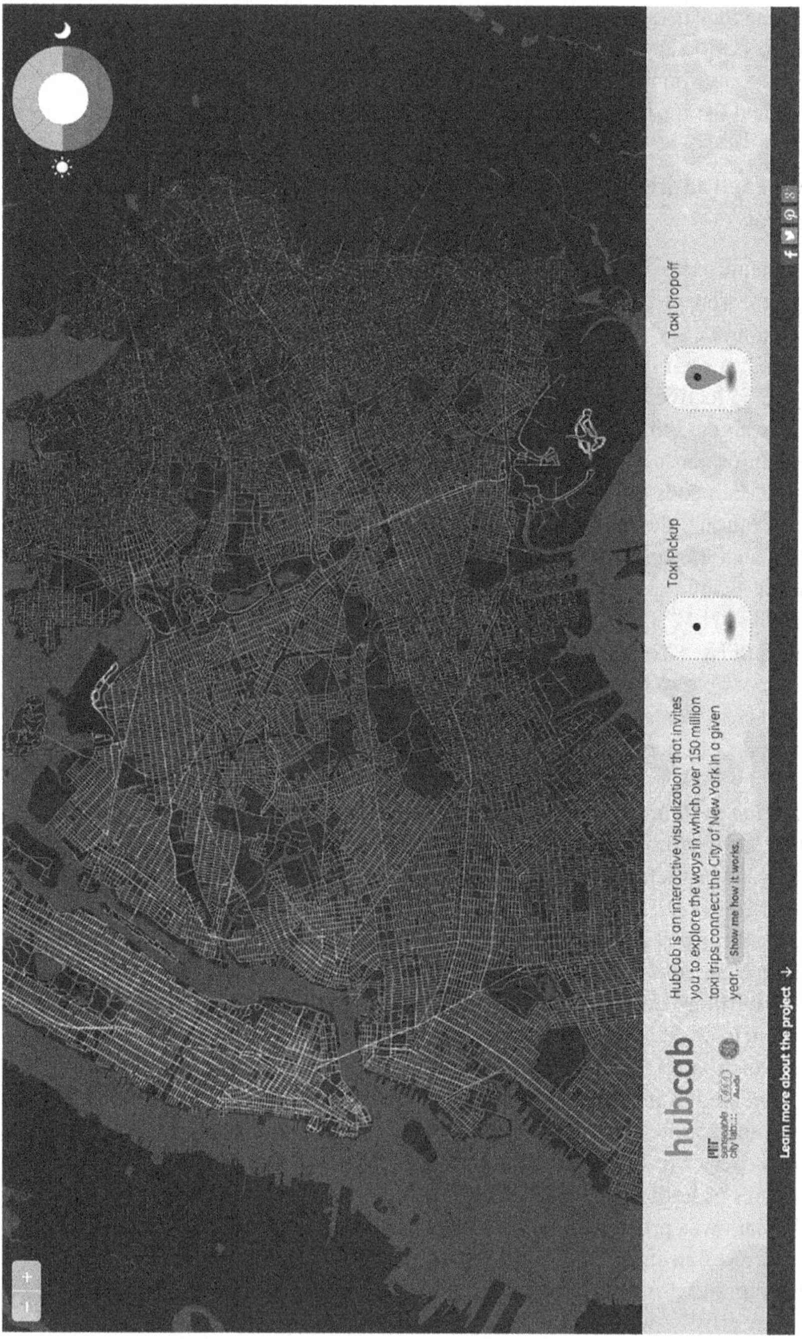

FIG. 2.10 Screenshot of the HubCab visualization map, showing pickup and drop-off locations of all 170 million taxi trips. *(Copyright MIT Senseable City Lab.)*

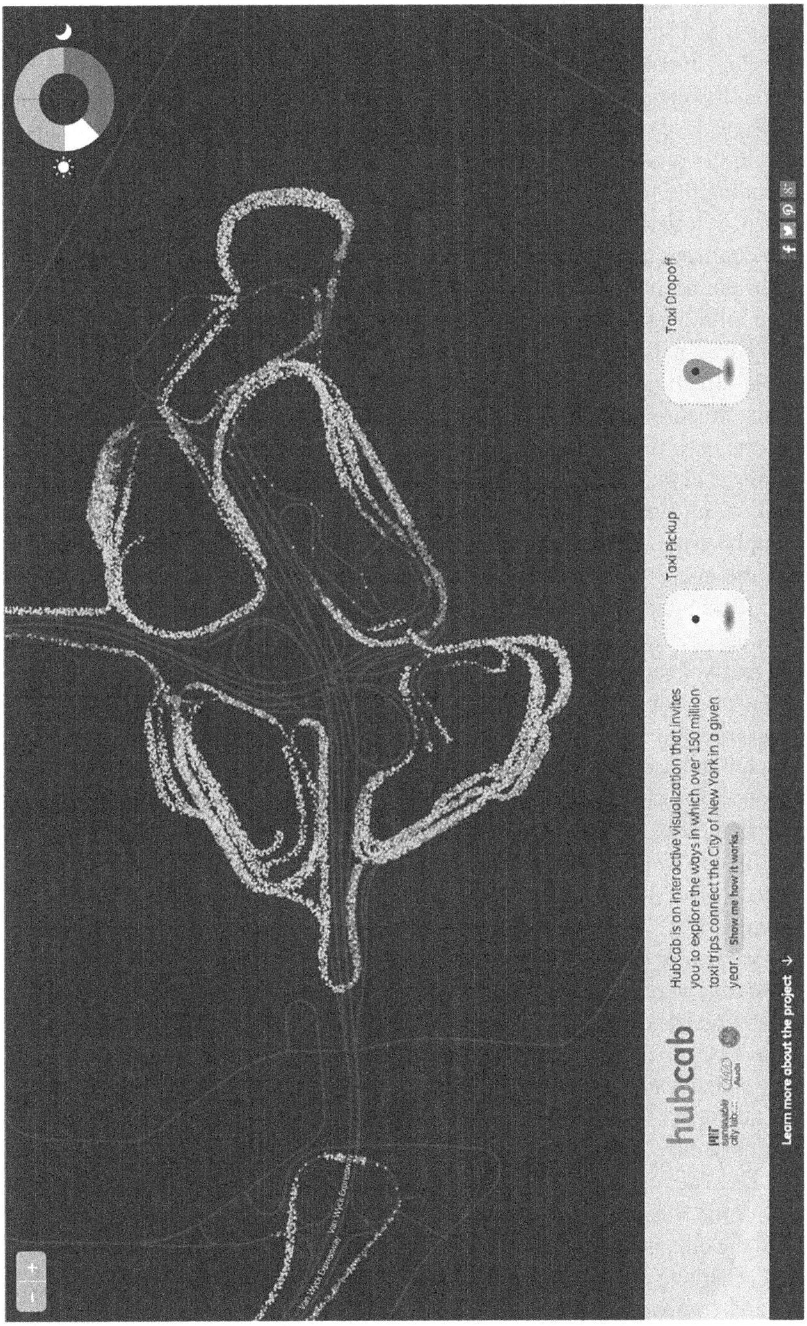

FIG. 2.11 Screenshot of the HubCab visualization map, showing all taxi pickups and drop offs at JFK airport daily between 3 a.m. and 6 a.m. *(Copyright MIT Senseable City Lab.)*

HubCab map, users can access information about the frequency of trips between these two points at different times of the day. This information allowed the project team to calculate the potential benefits of taxi sharing, which include the following: financial savings for the customer, reduced traffic congestion, and carbon dioxide savings.

The HubCab project demonstrates that the integration of wireless sensor networks in the urban environment, which are driving the big-data movement and expanding the IoT, is making it possible to obtain representations of complex urban dynamics and trigger urban sustainability practices. Additional evidence confirming the benefits of using big-data analytics for boosting sustainable urban development can be sourced from the following literature that reports on initiatives in which sensor-generated information has been deployed to identify free parking areas (Jeffrey et al., 2012); monitor road conditions and enable effective maintenance interventions (Collotta et al., 2012); detect emergency situations, such as wild fires, flash flooding, and earthquakes, and improve response times (Bouabdellah et al., 2013; Castillo-Effen et al., 2004; Díaz-Ramírez et al., 2012; Faulkner et al., 2011; Fischer et al., 2013); assess and monitor the structural conditions of buildings and bridges (Plessi et al., 2007); improve the efficiency of farming operations (Pierce and Elliott, 2008); optimize the energy management of residential buildings (Erol-Kantarci and Mouftah, 2011); improve access to health care and promote healthy living (Kulkarni and Sathe, 2014); and measure both indoor and outdoor air quality (Hejlová and Voženílek, 2013).

The faster-cheaper-smaller trend generated by the continuous technological advancement is leading to the large-scale diffusion of sensing networks, including home-based sensing kits. This low-cost and easy-to-use technological equipment allows citizens to collect local environmental data in real time and share this knowledge by using crowdsourced maps, which help update the information provided by professional sensing networks (Saunders and Baeck, 2015). The Smart Citizen Kit (https://smartcitizen.me) is an example of these home-based sensing kits, which targets the nonprofessional market and aims at supporting participatory collection and sharing processes of environmental data.

The Smart Citizen Kit is the output of a project launched in 2012, which included Fab Lab Barcelona, the Institute for Advanced Architecture of Catalonia, and Geoteo as project partners. The Smart Citizen Kit is a tiny piece of hardware that consists of a set of environmental sensors, a data-processing board, a battery, and a Wi-Fi antenna. The sensors can measure air composition, temperature, humidity, light intensity, solar radiation, wavelength exposure, and sound levels. The real-time information captured by this sensing device is then streamed to the Smart Citizen online platform, where all the kits are georeferenced and the data is displayed on an interactive map. The map is accessible via a weblink, enabling citizens to examine the environmental integrity of a specific location and compare different geographic areas (Balestrini et al., 2014; Diez and Posada, 2013; Saunders and Baeck, 2015).

Pachube is an additional example of online platform for crowdsourcing user-generated environmental data. As the Smart Citizen platform, Pachube enables any types of Internet-connected devices to stream real-time environmental data, which is stored in a cloud-based system and visualized on an interactive map. This platform offers people an open, online monitoring service that everybody can help to expand and acquire information from. During the Fukushima's earthquake and nuclear emergency, Pachube became the main integrating and sharing point of crowdsourced radiation data and helped to diffuse critical environmental information across the country (Courtland, 2011; Salim and Haque, 2015; Schenkman, 2011).

2.3.2 Ensuring equal access to basic services and infrastructures

Online platforms that pool crowd-generated data are not only helping cities monitor environmental quality but also making urban spaces more accessible. For example, "pervasive computing technology can enhance quality of life for those with disabilities by providing access to timely information and helping them to navigate their environment independently" (Rector, 2018: 9).

In 2010, the nonprofit organization Social Heroes launched Wheelmap (https://wheelmap.org), an online map for wheelchair accessible places identification. The information provided by Wheelmap is generated using a Wikipedia approach. Users share their knowledge with other users in relation to the wheelchair accessibility of the locations they have visited. Anyone can access the map and contribute to its development by (1) marking public places around the world, (2) rating their level of accessibility for individuals with mobility impairments, (3) changing details in the information related to any places, and (4) uploading photographs. At present, Wheelmap provides data on more than 840,000 public places and is available in 25 languages. This data helps people with reduced mobility to make informed travel plans and contribute to make owners of wheelchair-inaccessible public places aware of the issue.

The accessibility application called Project Sidewalk (http://sidewalk.umiacs.umd.edu) shares the same ambition as Wheelmap. This application has been developed by the University of Washington and University of Maryland, and its aim is to transform how information about accessibility is produced, collected, and visualized by relying upon contributions from volunteers. Project Sidewalk makes it possible to virtually explore the streets of a city by using Google Street View. In doing so, users can identify and label the accessibility issues that sidewalks are affected by, such as obstacles, missing curb ramps, and damaged surfaces. The information that is collectively produced is expected to improve city planning processes by informing governmental authorities of the problems limiting wheelchair accessibility within the city. The application was successfully piloted in Washington D.C. in September 2016 (Saha et al., 2017).

2.3.3 Improving food security

The global food system is one of the world's largest consumers of land, water, and energy, and it is also one of the most wasteful, with around one-third of all food globally produced that is lost along the food supply chain. This suggests the current food system is being mismanaged and food security is under threat. The United Nations confirm this threat by reporting on the effects that the global food system is having on health and well-being. As the estimates released by the United Nations reveal, malnutrition is on the rise and has become a global issue: 12.5% of the world's population is undernourished, 26% of the world's children experience stunted growth, and 2 billion people suffer from micronutrient deficiencies (FAO, 2013; FAO et al., 2015a, b; Pinstrup-Andersen et al., 2014; Pullman and Wu, 2012; WHO, 2016).

FoodCloud (https://food.cloud) is an example of how information and communication technology can help end hunger and tackle food waste. Operating in the United Kingdom and Ireland, FoodCloud is an online food-sharing service that alerts charities and community organizations when surplus food is available for donation. The surplus food is donated via retail partners, which include some of the largest chain of Irish and British supermarkets. When retail partners have surplus food, they can upload a description of the items onto the FoodCloud warehousing system by using in-store scanners or the FoodCloud mobile application. As soon as a donation request is completed, it reaches the local charities and community organizations partnering with FoodCloud, which are instantly alerted via a notification from the app. The notification asks to confirm the acceptance of the food and to proceed with the collection process. At present, FoodCloud supports a network of more than 11,500 organizations of which about 7,500 are charities and community groups (Fox, 2016; Holmes, 2018).

Similarly, the food-sharing app Olio (https://olioex.com) allows food to be shared between people and local businesses, to minimize the amount of waste. Anyone with surplus food only needs to (1) upload a picture and a description of the food upon Olio, (2) select the time and location for the pickup, and (3) wait for a notification reporting on someone's interest in having the product. According to the statistics published in Olio's official website, this digital service is currently active in 32 countries and has more than 600,000 registered users, who have helped to save nearly 1,200,000 portions of food from being wasted. What is more, in addition to reducing global food waste, Olio is also helping to provide free food to those who cannot afford to feed themselves (Clay, 2016; Harris, 2017; Lei Win, 2017; McEachran, 2016).

2.3.4 Promoting environmentally sound waste management and reducing waste generation

The United Nations are working alongside the Chinese company Baidu, who specialize in Internet-related services and products, to improve the electronic waste management systems that China has been deploying. With China

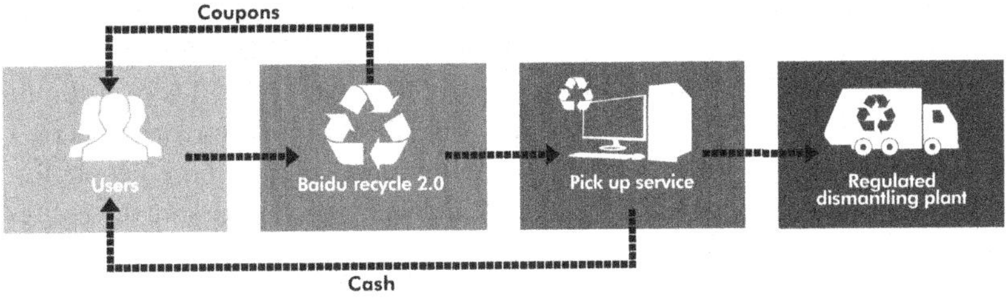

FIG. 2.12 Baidu Recycle: transaction flow chart.

contributing an estimated 70% of the world's annual 500 million tons of e-waste, Baidu and the United Nations have developed a mobile app for supporting e-waste recycling. The result of this collaboration is the Baidu Recycle smartphone application, which was launched in August 2014.

Now available in 22 cities across China, the Baidu Recycle app has led to the safe disposal of 5,900 electronic items per month on average. This app seeks to simplify the recycling process and effectively connect consumers, qualified dismantling companies, and manufactures. Fig. 2.12 provides an overview of the transaction flow. After selecting the type of appliance to recycle, the user can upload a picture of the obsolete electronic device, and in return, Baidu Recycle provides an estimated value. The user is then asked to complete a pickup request, which the application automatically forwards to the nearby legally certified e-waste disposal companies. Finally, any company interested in proceeding with the safe disposal and recycling of the device can contact the user and arrange the collection of the appliance. The Baidu Recycle app helps streamline the recycling process and cut down on any informal recycling stations, offering an additional example of how information technology and circular economy can be successfully linked (UNDP, 2015, 2016a, b).

iRecycle (https://earth911.com/irecycle) is another example of a free mobile application that aims to improve the recycling process. However, unlike Baidu Recycle, all types of general waste are included, not only obsolete electronic devices. This application offers easy access to one of North America's most extensive databases of plant locations, where private consumers and commercial organizations can recycle their waste. The database is composed of over 100,000 recycling venues, which are georeferenced on an interactive map. By clicking on a single venue, the following information is provided: the full address of the location, the opening hours, and the types of materials that are accepted. Overall, the venues included in the database make it possible to recycle more than 350 materials.

2.3.5 Improving the resilience of cities to natural disasters

Natural disasters, like floods, hurricanes, and earthquakes, produce large-scale shocks and lead to tragic human losses, displaced people, complete destruction of infrastructure, disrupted livelihoods, and impending costs of recovery and reconstruction. According to the data published by the United Nations and the Centre for Research on the Epidemiology of Disasters (CRED) of Catholic University of Leuven, 1.35 million people were killed by natural disasters over the 20 years between 1996 and 2015, and more than half of those people lost their lives during earthquakes and the resulting tsunamis. In addition, the figures describing the year 2016 show that 445 million people were affected by natural disasters and the global economic losses were about 140 billion dollars (CRED and UNISDR, 2016; United Nations, 2017c).

ICT can help protect developed and developing countries from the growing threat of natural disasters and reduce the number of losses. For example, despite some limitations, early warning systems based on real-time and automated analysis of ground motion are an effective technological advancement for mitigating the effects of dangerous seismic activities. These predictive systems allow to constantly collect data describing the moving of the earth's surface in a geographic area and understand whether a dangerous seismic activity is imminent. Where these real-time seismic monitoring facilities are in place, it is possible to predict when an earthquake or a tsunami will occur and alert populated areas before the catastrophic event happens. This early warning capability makes it possible to reduce the damages produced by the seismic activity, in particular the number of deaths (Minson et al., 2018; Nakamura et al., 2011; Hsiao et al., 2011; Peng et al., 2013; Zambrano et al., 2017).

Early warning systems that are either already operating or under development can be found in many regions of the world. Yamamoto and Tomori (2013) introduce the earthquake early warning system operated by JR-EAST, one of the major railway companies in Japan. The system was effective in securing 27 trains that were running at a speed of approximately 270 km/h during a strong earthquake that occurred in March 2011. Satriano et al. (2011) and Zollo et al. (2014) report on the testing phase of a free and open-source software platform that integrates algorithms for real-time earthquake location, magnitude estimation, and damage assessment. In addition, while Espinosa-Aranda et al. (2009) evaluate the seismic alert system that is monitoring the Mexican coastline, Allen and Kanamori (2003) demonstrate the feasibility of ElarmS, an innovative earthquake alarm system for mitigating seismic hazard in southern California.

2.4 The smart city movement is worldwide

A global movement has developed around embracing ICT solutions for enabling a smart city approach to urban sustainability, and such a movement is pushing a new technology market that is expected to grow exponentially. IDC (2018b) forecasts the worldwide spending on technological solutions for smart cities will hit 80 billion dollars in 2018 and 135 billion dollars in 2021, while the market intelligence released by the consulting firms ARUP, BCC Research, Research and Markets, and Frost & Sullivan provide even more optimistic figures. By combining their forecasts, the smart city technology market will be equivalent to 408 billion dollars by 2020 and 775 billion dollars in 2021. Then, it will reach between 2000 and 3600 billion dollars in 2025 (Sullivan, 2017; ARUP, 2013b; Research and Markets, 2017; Frost and Sullivan, 2018).

Despite significant differences in the global forecasts through 2025, a common agreement emerges: as a result of an increasing demand for ICT solutions for urban sustainability, the global market of technologies for smart cities will grow significantly in the next few years and at a rapid pace. This increasing demand can be captured by comparing the data provided by Frost & Sullivan, Yonsei University, and RAND Corporation. In 2010, according to Frost & Sullivan, only 41 cities across the world were trying to enable smart city development (Singh, 2010). However, when this mapping exercise was repeated by Yonsei University in 2012, the figure had significantly changed. In two years, the number of cities increased from 41 to 143 (Lee and Hancock, 2012), and most of the cases were found in Europe, Asia, and North America. This growth trend was also confirmed in 2014 by RAND Corporation, with a study conducted on behalf of the European Parliament. By limiting the search for smart city cases to the European Union's member states, about 500 cities were found in the process of assembling smart city development strategies (Manville et al., 2014).

Strategies for smart city development can be found all over the world, and researchers have made significant efforts in investigating their design and implementation processes, particularly in Europe, America, and Asia. By focusing attention on European cities, for example, Pokrić et al. (2014) present the attempts of Novi Sad to integrate augmented reality in public transports, while Walravens (2015) provides an overview of the mobile services and applications that the city of Brussels offers to its citizens. Palomo-Navarro and Navío-Marco (2017) and Vaquero-García et al. (2017) introduce the Spanish Network of Smart Cities (RECI), which was set up in June 2012 and currently counts over 75 partner cities. Since its establishment, RECI has sponsored smart city development at the national level. This network includes Santander and Barcelona, whose strategy for adopting a smart city approach to urban sustainability is analyzed by Sanchez et al. (2014) and Mora and Bolici (2016), respectively. The latter study compares the smart city transformation process undertaken by Amsterdam and Barcelona. The investigation into the Amsterdam's smart city development strategy continues with van Winden and van den Buuse (2017), who examine a group of smart city pilot projects launched by the capital city of the Netherlands. These projects, which made it possible for Amsterdam to test the technical feasibility of a set of ICT solutions for urban sustainability, have been instrumental in providing new insights into the upscaling processes.

The European approach to smart city development is further analyzed by Cowley et al. (2018) and Deakin and Reid (2016), who focus attention on the United Kingdom, in particular, the cities of Bristol, Glasgow, London, Manchester, Milton Keynes, and Peterborough. In addition, (1) Mora et al. (2018)

assemble a new research methodology for conducting multiple case study analyses of smart cities and test its practical feasibility, effectiveness, and logistics on Vienna; (2) Vanolo (2014) describes the commitment of Italy to smart city development and provides some theoretical reflections on the approach adopted by the cities of Bari, Bologna, Turin, Genoa, Milan, and Naples; (3) Grossi and Pianezzi (2017) extend the analysis of Genoa; and (4) Hielkema and Hongisto (2013) show how Helsinki is using the Living Lab methodology to accelerate smart city development.

The efforts made by North and South American cities to enable smart city development start being captured by Alawadhi et al. (2012), whose interviews with government officials and managers clarify how Philadelphia, Seattle, Quebec City, and Mexico City are managing their smart city transition process. Philadelphia's approach to smart city development is also investigated by Wiig (2015a, b), who expresses doubts in relation to its effectiveness in addressing urban inequalities. The analysis of North American smart cities continues with Lee et al. (2014) and Ylizaliturri-Salcedo et al. (2016). The former compares the smart city development strategies of San Francisco and Seoul, while the latter investigates how developing regions are progressing in the field of smart cities by introducing the case of Tijuana, a Mexican border city that is located south of California. In addition, Lee et al. (2016b) introduce Orlando and describe the set of ICT solutions that the city government has put in place to improve urban mobility, public safety, waste and water management, and energy efficiently.

Schreiner (2016) and Amar Flórez (2016) shift the focus from North America to South America and analyze Rio de Janeiro and the Colombian city of Medellin respectively. The approach to smart city development of Rio de Janeiro is also examined by Viale Pereira et al. (2017a), Kitchin (2014), and Berger Bernardes et al. (2017). They all report on the Rio Operations Center, which has been established after an extensive collaboration between IBM and the city government. This center is meant to optimize city functioning and improve public safety by deploying a new surveillance system and big-data analytics. In continuing their line of enquiry into smart city development in South America, Viale Pereira et al. (2017b) also develop a methodology for assessing the cities belonging to the Brazilian Network of Smart and Human Cities (RBCIH). RBCIH is a national network that brings together the 350 largest cities of the country and supports smart city development by stimulating the sharing of good practices among its partner cities and evaluating the effectiveness of their smart city-related activities.

Asian smart city developments have become objects of scientific enquiry in the studies conducted by Fietkiewicz and Stock (2015) and Alvin Yau et al. (2016). The first study questions the Japanese approach to smart city development after analyzing the activities that Tokyo, Yokohama, Osaka, and Kyoto have implemented to become smart. The second describes the ambition of Kuala Lumpur to extend smart city development at the metropolitan level by working closely with its surrounding municipalities on a shared strategy. Additional insight into the Asian experience of smart city development is also provided by Lee et al. (2016a, c, d, e), who focus attention on Anyang, Namyangju, and Pangyo, three cities located in the Republic of Korea and Singapore. This extends the assessment of Korea's smart city development cases started by Shin (2007, 2009), Shin and Kim, 2010, Shwayri (2013), and Yigitcanlar and Lee (2014).

Ghosseini (2017) contributes to this extensive analysis of smart city cases by inviting to reflect on the approach towards a smart city adopted by Baakline, a town of the Lebanese Republic. In addition, Datta (2015), Yu et al. (2016), Gupta and Hall (2017), Praharaj et al. (2017), Sharma and Rajput (2017), and Bansal et al. (2017) all reflect upon the Indian approach to smart city development.

Additional examples of smart city development strategies can also be found in the following publications, in which efforts are made to cut across the geographical borders and compare smart city cases in different continents:

- Leydesdorff and Deakin (2011) analyze the smart city development strategies of Montreal and Edinburgh.
- Alcatel-Lucent compares more than 50 smart city cases, covering Europe, North and South America, Australia, Asia, and Africa (Anderson et al., 2012).
- In a report commissioned by the Government of the United Kingdom, ARUP (2013a) compares Chicago, Rio de Janeiro, Boston, Stockholm, Barcelona, and Hong Kong.
- Angelidou (2017) compares smart city development practices in Europe, Africa, Asia, and both North and South America by focusing on the experiences of Amsterdam, Barcelona, Cyberjaya, King Abdullah Economic City, Konza, London, Masdar, PlanIT Valley, Rio de Janeiro, Singapore, Skolkovo, Songdo, and Stockholm.

Altogether, this literature demonstrates the existence of a worldwide movement towards smart city development and the ICT-driven approach to urban sustainability that such a development promotes. Cities of both the developed and developing countries are pushing the smart city movement forward, making it visible their increasing interest in exploiting ICT in the fight against the current unsustainable urban development paths. However, this literature also exposes the uncertainty, confusion, and division around smart city development, a complex and interdisciplinary subject that the research produced to date has not been able to untangle yet.

As revealed with the two bibliometric analyses that Chapters 3 and 4 present, despite three decades of research dealing with smart city development, the knowledge that such a research offers falls short of providing the strategic, organizational, and technological insights needed for the community of stakeholders working on smart city development to make it become an effective approach to urban sustainability. For the ambiguity that surrounds smart cities still leaves many gaps in what is understood about these developments and how the

ICT-driven approach lying at the center of any such transformation can be deployed to deliver urban sustainability (Ahvenniemi et al., 2017; Alkandari et al., 2012; Chourabi et al., 2012; Colding and Barthel, 2017; Deakin and Reid, 2016; Kitchin, 2015; Grossi and Pianezzi, 2017; Hollands, 2008; Meijer and Bolivar, 2016; Yigitcanlar and Kamruzzaman, 2018).

References

ABI Research (2013). More Than 30 Billion Devices Will Wirelessly Connect to the Internet of Everything in 2020. Press release. ABI Research. https://www.abiresearch.com/press/more-than-30-billion-devices-will-wirelessly-conne. Accessed 09.05.2013.

Ahvenniemi, H., Huovila, A., Pinto-Seppä, I., Airaksinen, M., 2017. What are the differences between sustainable and smart cities? Cities: Int. J. Urban Policy Plan. 60, 234–245.

Alawadhi, S., Aldama-Nalda, A., Chourabi, H., Gil-Garcia, R.J., Leung, S., Mellouli, S., Nam, T., Pardo, T.A., Scholl, H.J., Walker, S., 2012. Building understanding of smart city initiatives. In: Scholl, H.J., Janssen, M., Wimmer, M.A., Moe, C.E., Flak, L.S. (Eds.), Electronic Government: 11th IFIP WG 8.5 International Conference, EGOV 2012, Kristiansand, Norway, September 3–6, 2012, Proceedings. Springer, Berlin, pp. 40–53.

Alkandari, A., Alnasheet, M., Alshekhly, I.F., 2012. Smart cities: survey. J. Adv. Comput. Sci. Technol. Res. 2 (2), 79–90.

Allen, R.M., Kanamori, H., 2003. The potential for earthquake early warning in Southern California. Science 300 (5620), 786–789.

Alvin Yau, K., Lau, S., Chua, H.N., Ling, M.H., Iranmanesh, V., Charis Kwan, S.C., 2016. Greater Kuala Lumpur as a smart city: a case study on technology opportunities. In: 2016 8th International Conference on Knowledge and Smart Technology (KST), Chiangmai, 3–6 February 2016. Institute of Electrical and Electronics Engineers (IEEE), Piscataway, NJ, pp. 96–101.

Amar Flórez, D. (2016). International Case Studies of Smart Cities: Medellin, Colombia. Discussion Paper IDB-DP-443. Inter-American Development Bank. https://publications.iadb.org/handle/11319/7716. Accessed 15.07.2017.

Anderson, J., Fisher, D., and Witters, L. (2012). Getting Smart About Smart Cities: Understanding the Market Opportunity in the Cities of Tomorrow. Alcatel-Lucent. http://www2.alcatel-lucent.com/knowledge-center/admin/mci-files-1a2c3f/ma/Smart_Cities_Market_opportunity_MarketAnalysis.pdf. Accessed 01.01.2013.

Angelidou, M., 2017. The role of smart city characteristics in the plans of fifteen cities. J. Urban Technol. 24 (4), 3–28.

ARUP (2013a). Global Innovators: International Case Studies on Smart Cities. BIS Research Paper n°135. Government of the United Kingdom - Department for Business, Innovation and Skills. https://www.gov.uk/government/uploads/system/uploads/attachment_data/file/249397/bis-13-1216-global-innovators-international-smart-cities.pdf. Accessed 08.09.2016.

ARUP (2013b). The Smart City Market: Opportunities for the UK. BIS Research Paper n°136. Government of the United Kingdom - Department for Business, Innovation and Skills. https://www.gov.uk/government/uploads/system/uploads/attachment_data/file/249423/bis-13-1217-smart-city-market-opportunties-uk.pdf. Accessed 23.01.2014.

Atzori, L., Iera, A., Morabito, G., 2010. The Internet of Things: a survey. Comput. Netw. 54 (15), 2787–2805.

Badger, E. (2014). How a System for Shared Taxi Rides Could Transform New York City. CityLab. http://www.citylab.com/cityfixer/2014/03/how-system-shared-taxi-rides-could-transform-new-york-city/8530/. Accessed 10.05.2015.

Balestrini, M., Marshall, P., Diez, T., 2014. Beyond boundaries: the home as city infrastructure for smart citizens. In: Proceedings of the 2014 ACM International Joint Conference on Pervasive and Ubiquitous Computing, Seattle, WA, 13–17 September 2014. ACM Press, New York, NY, pp. 987–990.

Bansal, S., Pandey, V., Sen, J., 2017. Redefining and exploring the smart city concept in indian perspective: case study of Varanasi. In: Seta, F., Sen, J., Biswas, A., Khare, A. (Eds.), From Poverty, Inequality to Smart City: Proceedings of the National Conference on Sustainable Built Environment 2015. Springer, Singapore, pp. 93–107.

Benevolo, L., 1993. The European City. Blackwell Publishing Ltd, Oxford.

Berger Bernardes, M., Mazzilly S. de Souza, R., Pacheco de Andrade, F., and Novais, P. (2017). The Rio De Janeiro, Brazil, experience using digital initiatives for the co-production of the public good: the case of the operations centre. In A. Rocha, A. M. Correia, H. Adeli, L. P. Reis, and S. Costanzo (Eds.), WorldCIST: World Conference on Information Systems and Technologies. Recent Advances in Information Systems and Technologies, vol. 1, pp. 18-27. Cham: Springer.

Bouabdellah, K., Noureddine, H., Larbi, S., 2013. Using wireless sensor networks for reliable forest fires detection. Procedia Comput. Sci. 19, 794–801.

Boyd, D., Crawford, K., 2012. Critical questions for big data: provocations for a cultural, technological, and scholarly phenomenon. Inf. Commun. Soc. 15 (5), 662–679.

Castells, M., 1996. The Rise of the Network Society. Blackwell Publishing Ltd, Oxford.

Castillo-Effen, M., Quintela, D.H., Jordan, R., Westhoff, W., Moreno, W., 2004. Wireless sensor networks for flash-flood alerting. In: Proceedings of the Fifth IEEE International Caracas Conference on Devices, Circuits and Systems, 2004, Punta Cana, 3–5 November 2004. Institute of Electrical and Electronics Engineers (IEEE), Piscataway, NJ, pp. 142–146.

Chen, M., Mao, S., Liu, Y., 2014. Big data: a survey. Mobile Netw. Applicat. 19 (2), 171–209.

Chourabi, H., Nam, T., Walker, S., Gil-Garcia, R.J., Mellouli, S., Nahon, K., Pardo, T.A., Scholl, H.J., 2012. Understanding smart cities: an integrative framework. In: Sprague, R.H. (Ed.), Proceedings of the 45th Hawaii International Conference on System Sciences (HICSS), Maui, HI, 04–07 January 2012. Institute of Electrical and Electronics Engineers (IEEE), Piscataway, NJ, pp. 2289–2297.

Cisco Systems (2017). Digitising Local Government: For Smarter Businesses, Smarter Services and Smarter Cities. Cisco Systems. https://www.cisco.com/c/dam/assets/global/UK/public_sector/cisco_in_government/pdf/local_government_digitising.pdf. Accessed 07.03.2018.

Clay, X. (2016). Feed Thy Neighbour? There's an App for That - Xanthe Clay Tried Out Food-sharing App Olio. The Telegraph. https://www.telegraph.co.uk/food-and-drink/features/feed-thy-neighbour-theres-an-app-for-that---xanthe-clay-tried-ou/. Accessed 10.11.2017.

Colding, J., Barthel, S., 2017. An urban ecology critique on the "smart city" model. J. Clean. Prod. 164, 95–101.

Collotta, M., Pau, G., Salerno, V., Scatá, G., 2012. Wireless sensor networks to improve road monitoring. In: Matin, M. (Ed.), Wireless Sensor Networks: Technology and Applications. InTech, Rijeka, pp. 323–346.

Courtland, R. (2011). Radiation Monitoring in Japan Goes DIY. IEEE. https://spectrum.ieee.org/tech-talk/energy/.../radiation-monitoring-in-japan-goes-diy. Accessed 10.10.2013.

Cowley, R., Joss, S., Dayot, Y., 2018. The smart city and its publics: insights from across six UK cities. Urban Res. Pract. 11 (1), 53–77.

CRED and UNISDR. (2016). Poverty & Death: Disaster Mortality, 1996–2015. Centre for Research on the Epidemiology of Disasters and United Nations Office for Disaster Risk Reduction. http://www.unisdr.org/files/50589_creddisastermortalityallfinalpdf.pdf. Accessed 02.03.2018.

Datta, A., 2015. New urban utopias of postcolonial India: entrepreneurial urbanization in Dholera Smart City, Gujarat. Dialog. Hum. Geogr. 5 (1), 3–22.

Deakin, M., Reid, A., 2016. Smart cities: under-gridding the sustainability of city-districts as energy efficient-low carbon zones. J. Clean. Prod. 173, 39–48.

Díaz-Ramírez, A., Tafoya, L.A., Atempa, J.A., Mejía-Alvarez, P., 2012. Wireless sensor networks and fusion information methods for forest fire detection. Procedia Technol. 3, 69–79.

Diez, T., Posada, A., 2013. The Fab and the Smart City: the use of machines and technology for the city production by its citizens. In: Proceedings of the 7th International Conference on Tangible, Embedded and Embodied Interaction, Barcelona, 10–13 February 2013. ACM Press, New York City, NY, pp. 447–454.

Ericsson (2013). Ericsson Mobility Report: On the Pulse of the Networked Society. Ericsson. http://www.ericsson.com/res/docs/2013/ericsson-mobility-report-november-2013.pdf. Accessed 10.06.2014.

Ericsson (2014). Ericsson Mobility Report: On the Pulse of the Networked Society. November 2014. Ericsson. https://www.ericsson.com/assets/local/mobility-report/documents/2014/ericsson-mobility-report-november-2014.pdf. Accessed 13.01.2018.

Ericsson (2015). Ericsson Mobility Report: On the Pulse of the Networked Society. November 2015. Ericsson. https://www.ericsson.com/assets/local/mobility-report/documents/2015/ericsson-mobility-report-nov-2015.pdf. Accessed 13.01.2018.

Ericsson (2016). Ericsson Mobility Report: On the Pulse of the Networked Society. November 2016. Ericsson. https://www.ericsson.com/assets/local/mobility-report/documents/2016/ericsson-mobility-report-november-2016.pdf. Accessed 13.01.2018.

Ericsson (2017). Ericsson Mobility Report: On the Pulse of the Networked Society. June 2017. Ericsson. https://www.ericsson.com/assets/local/mobility-report/documents/2017/ericsson-mobility-report-june-2017.pdf. Accessed 13.01.2018.

Erol-Kantarci, M., Mouftah, H.T., 2011. Wireless sensor networks for cost-efficient residential energy management in the smart grid. IEEE Trans. Smart Grid 2 (2), 314–325.

Espinosa-Aranda, J., Cuellar, A., Garcia, A., Ibarrola, G., Islas, R., Maldonado, S., Rodriguez, F., 2009. Evolution of the Mexican Seismic Alert System (SASMEX). Seismol. Res. Lett. 80 (5), 694–706.

European Commission (2010a). A Commitment Towards Europe's Energy and Climate Policy. Brochure. European Commission. http://www.eumayors.eu/IMG/pdf/com_brochure_en.pdf. Accessed 05.06.2014.

European Commission (2010b). Communication from the Commission to the European Parliament, the Council, the European Economic and Social Committee and the Committee of the Regions. A Digital Agenda for Europe. COM(2010) 245 final. European Commission. http://eur-lex.europa.eu/legal-content/IT/TXT/PDF/?uri=CELEX:52010DC0245R(01)&from=EN. Accessed 02.02.2014.

European Commission, 2014. Digital Agenda for Europe. Publications Office of the European Union, Luxembourg.

European Commission (2017). Horizon 2020 Work Programme 2018-2020: 10. Secure, Clean and Efficient Energy. European Commission Decision C(2017)7124. European Commission. http://ec.europa.eu/research/participants/data/ref/h2020/wp/2018-2020/main/h2020-wp1820-energy_en.pdf. Accessed 20.01.2018.

Evans, D. (2011). The Internet of Things: How the Next Evolution of the Internet Is Changing Everything. White paper. Cisco Systems. http://www.cisco.com/web/about/ac79/docs/innov/IoT_IBSG_0411FINAL.pdf. Accessed 14.06.2014.

Eyre, J., Bier, J., 1998. DSP processors hit the mainstream. Computer 31 (8), 51–59.

FAO, 2013. The State of Food and Agriculture: Food Systems for Better Nutrition. Food and Agriculture Organization of the United Nations, Rome.

FAO, IFAD, WFP, 2015a. Achieving Zero Hunger: The Critical Role of Investments in Social Protection and Agriculture. Food and Agriculture Organization of the United Nations, Rome.

FAO, IFAD, WFP, 2015b. The State of Food Insecurity in the World: Meeting the 2015 International Hunger Targets: Taking Stock of Uneven Progress. Food and Agriculture Organization of the United Nations, Rome.

Faulkner, M., Olson, M., Chandy, R., Krause, J., Chandy, K.M., Krause, A., 2011. The next big one: detecting earthquakes and other rare events from community-based sensors. In: 2011 10th International Conference on Information Processing in Sensor Networks (IPSN), Chicago, IL, 12–14 April 2011. Institute of Electrical and Electronics Engineers (IEEE), Piscataway, NJ, pp. 13–24.

Fietkiewicz, K.J., Stock, W.G., 2015. How smart are Japanese cities? An empirical investigation of infrastructures and governmental programs in Tokyo, Yokohama, Osaka and Kyoto. In: T. X. Bui, and R. H. Sprague (Eds.), Proceedings of the 48th Hawaii International Conference on System Sciences (HICSS), Kauai, HI, 5–8 January 2015. Institute of Electrical and Electronics Engineers (IEEE), Piscataway, NJ, pp. 2345–2354.

Fischer, J., Redlich, J., Scheuermann, B., Schiller, J., Gunes, M., Nagel, K., Wagner, P., Scheidgen, M., Zubow, A., Eveslage, I., Sombrutzki, R., Juraschek, F., 2013. From Earthquake detection to traffic surveillance: about information and communication infrastructures for smart cities. In: Haugen, Ø., Reed, R., Gotzhein, R. (Eds.), System Analysis and Modeling: Theory and Practice. 7th International Workshop, SAM 2012, Innsbruck, Austria, October 1–2, 2012. Revised Selected Papers. Springer, Berlin, pp. 121–141.

Fox, K. (2016). FoodCloud: New App Proves a Nourishing Idea for Wasted Food. The Guardian. https://www.theguardian.com/environment/2016/dec/04/new-app-proves-a-nourishing-idea-for-wasted-food-foodcloud. Accessed 10.08.2017.

Frost & Sullivan (2018). Frost & Sullivan Experts Announce Global Smart Cities to Raise a Market of Over $2 Trillion by 2025. Press Release. Frost & Sullivan. https://ww2.frost.com/news/press-releases/frost-sullivan-experts-announce-global-smart-cities-raise-market-over-2-trillion-2025/. Accessed 13.04.2018.

Gantz, J. F., Chute, C., Manfrediz, A., Minton, S., Reinsel, D., Schlichting, W., and Toncheva, A. (2008). The Diverse and Exploding Digital Universe: An Updated Forecast of Worldwide Information Growth Through 2011. White Paper. IDC. https://www.ag.bka.gv.at/at.gv.bka.wiki-bka/img_auth.php/f/fe/Diverse-exploding-digital-universe.pdf. Accessed 10.03.2018.

Gantz, J., and Reinsel, D. (2011). Extracting Value from Chaos. Press Release. IDC. https://www.emc.com/collateral/analyst-reports/idc-extracting-value-from-chaos-ar.pdf. Accessed 10.03.2018.

Gartner (2013). Gartner Says the Internet of Things Installed Base Will Grow to 26 Billion Units by 2020. Press Release. Gartner. http://www.gartner.com/newsroom/id/2636073. Accessed 12.12.2013.

Ghosseini, N., 2017. Baakline: towards a smart city—leading change into Chouf Souayjani Region. In: Stratigea, A., Kyriakides, E., Nicolaides, C. (Eds.), Smart Cities in the Mediterranean: Coping with Sustainability Objectives in Small and Medium-sized Cities and Island Communities. Springer, Cham, pp. 59–84.

Grossi, G., Pianezzi, D., 2017. Smart cities: utopia or neoliberal ideology? Cities: Int. J. Urban Policy Plan. 69, 79–85.

Gupta, K., Hall, R.P., 2017. The Indian perspective of smart cities. In: Proceedings of the 2017 Smart City Symposium Prague (SCSP), Prague, 25–26 May 2017. Institute of Electrical and Electronics Engineers, Piscataway, NJ.

Harris, S. A. (2017). Food Waste App OLIO Has Become A Lifeline for Those Who Can't Afford to Feed Themselves. HuffPost. https://www.huffingtonpost.co.uk/entry/food-waste-app-olio-hidden-hunger_uk_595f4212e4b0d5b458e97c36. Accessed 05.03.2018.

Hejlová, V., Voženílek, V., 2013. Wireless sensor network components for air pollution monitoring in the urban environment: criteria and analysis for their selection. Wirel. Sens. Netw. 5 (12), 229–240.

Hielkema, H., Hongisto, P., 2013. Developing the Helsinki smart city: the role of competitions for open data applications. J. Knowl. Econ. 4 (2), 190–204.

Hollands, R.G., 2008. Will the real smart city please stand up? City: Anal. Urban Trends Cult. Theory Policy Action 12 (3), 303–320.

Holler, J., Tsiatsis, V., Avesand, S., Karnouskos, S., Boyle, D., 2014. From Machine-to-Machine to the Internet of Things: Introduction to a New Age of Intelligence. Elsevier, Oxford.

Holmes, H., 2018. New spaces, ordinary practices: circulating and sharing within diverse economies of provisioning. Geoforum 88, 138–147.

Hsiao, N., Wu, Y., Zhao, L., Chen, D., Huang, W., Kuo, K., Shin, T., Leu, P., 2011. A new prototype system for earthquake early warning in Taiwan. Soil Dyn. Earthq. Eng. 31 (2), 201–208.

IBM Corporation (2010). IBM Opens Smarter Cities Technology Centre in Ireland. Press Release. IBM Corporation. https://www-03.ibm.com/press/us/en/pressrelease/29745.wss. Accessed 05.12.2016.

IDC (2018a). IDC Government Insights Smart Cities Strategies: Working with Cities to Accelerate Transformation. International Data Corporation. https://www.idc.com/promo/ebook-smartcities. Accessed 01.03.2018.

IDC (2018b). Investments in Technologies Enabling Smart Cities Initiatives Are Forecast to Reach $80 Billion in 2018, According to a New IDC Spending Guide. Press Release. International Data Corporation. https://www.idc.com/getdoc.jsp?containerId=prUS43576718. Accessed 20.04.2018.

ITU (2014). Global ICT Developments. Dataset. International Telecommunication Union. http://www.itu.int/en/ITU-D/Statistics/Documents/statistics/2014/stat_page_all_charts_2014.xls. Accessed 10.04.2014.

ITU (2016). Key ICT Indicators for Developed and Developing Countries and the World (Totals and Penetration Rates). Dataset. International Telecommunication Union. https://www.itu.int/en/ITU-D/Statistics/Documents/statistics/2017/ITU_Key_2005-2017_ICT_data.xls. Accessed 20.01.2018.

ITU and UNESCO (2016). The State of Broadband: Broadband Catalyzing Sustainable Development. September 2016. International Telecommunication Union and UNESCO. https://www.itu.int/dms_pub/itu-s/opb/pol/S-POL-BROADBAND.17-2016-PDF-E.pdf. Accessed 27.03.2018.

Jeffrey, J., Patil, R.G., Kaipu Narahari, S.K., Didagi, Y., Bapat, J., Das, D., 2012. Smart parking service based on wireless sensor networks. In: IECON 2012 - 38th Annual Conference on IEEE Industrial Electronics Society, Montreal, 25-28 October 2012. Institute of Electrical and Electronics Engineers (IEEE), Piscataway, NJ, pp. 6029–6034.

Jordana, S. (2010). BIG's Proposal for the Audi Urban Future Award. Online article. ArchDaily. http://www.archdaily.com/77103/bigs-proposal-for-the-audi-urban-future-award/. Accessed 08.03.2014.

Kitchin, R., 2014. The real-time city? Big data and smart urbanism. GeoJournal 79 (1), 1–14.

Kitchin, R., 2015. Making sense of smart cities: addrfessing present shortcomings. Camb. J. Reg. Econ. Soc. 8 (1), 131–136.

Kulkarni, A., Sathe, S., 2014. Healthcare applications of the Internet of Things: a review. Int. J. Comput. Sci. Inform. Technol. 5 (5), 6229–6232.

Kurzweil, R., 2004. The law of accelerating returns. In: Teuscher, C. (Ed.), Alan Turing: Life and Legacy of a Great Thinker. Springer, Berlin, pp. 381–416.

Lee, J., and Hancock, M. G. (2012). Toward a Framework for Smart Cities: A Comparison of Seoul, San Francisco and Amsterdam. Presentation. Yonsei University and Stanford University. http://iis-db.stanford.edu/evnts/7239/Jung_Hoon_Lee_final.pdf. (Accessed 12.06.2014).

Lee, J., Hancock, M.G., Hu, M., 2014. Towards an effective framework for building smart cities: lessons from seoul and San Francisco. Technol. Forecast. Soc. Chang. 89, 80–99.

Lee, S.K., Kwon, H.R., Cho, H., Kim, J., Lee, D., 2016a. International Case Studies of Smart Cities: Namyangju, Republic of Korea. Discussion Paper IDB-DP-459. Inter-American Development Bank. https://publications.iadb.org/handle/11319/7724. (Accessed July 15, 2017).

Lee, S.K., Kwon, H.R., Cho, H., Kim, J., Lee, D., 2016b. International Case Studies of Smart Cities: Orlando, United States of America. Discussion Paper IDB-DP-460. Inter-American Development Bank. https://publications.iadb.org/handle/11319/7725?locale-attribute=es. (Accessed July 15, 2017).

Lee, S.K., Kwon, H.R., Cho, H., Kim, J., Lee, D., 2016c. International Case Studies of Smart Cities: Pangyo, Republic of Korea. Discussion Paper IDB-DP-461. Inter-American Development Bank. https://publications.iadb.org/handle/11319/7720. (Accessed July 15, 2017).

Lee, S.K., Kwon, H.R., Cho, H., Kim, J., Lee, D., 2016d. International Case Studies of Smart Cities: Singapore, Republic of Singapore. Discussion Paper IDB-DP-462. Inter-American Development Bank. https://publications.iadb.org/handle/11319/7723. (Accessed July 15, 2017).

Lee, S.K., Kwon, H.R., Cho, H., Kim, J., Lee, D., 2016e. International Case Studies of Smart Cities: Songdo, Republic of Korea. Discussion Paper IDB-DP-463. Inter-American Development Bank. https://publications.iadb.org/handle/11319/7721. (Accessed July 15, 2017).

Lei Win, T. (2017). There Is Now 'Tinder for Food' and It Could Help Save the Environment. The Independent. https://www.independent.co.uk/news/business/news/tinder-food-waste-olio-help-save-environment-a8113091.html. (Accessed 03.03.2018).

Leydesdorff, L., Deakin, M., 2011. The triple-helix model of smart cities: a neo-evolutionary perspective. J. Urban Technol. 18 (2), 53–63.

Lynch, K., 1960. The Image of the City. The MIT Press, Cambridge, MA.

Mack, C., 2011. Fifty years of Moore's law. IEEE Trans. Semicond. Manuf. 24 (2), 202–207.

Manville, C., Cochrane, G., Cave, J., Millard, J., Pederson, J. K., Thaarup, R. K., Liebe, A., Wissner, M., Massink, R., and Kotterink, B. (2014). Mapping Smart City in the EU. Research Report. European Parliament—Directorate-General for Internal Policies. http://www.europarl.europa.eu/RegData/etudes/etudes/join/2014/507480/IPOL-ITRE_ET(2014)507480_EN.pdf. Accessed 05.02.2014.

McAfee, A., Brynjolfsson, E., 2012. Big data: the management revolution. Harv. Bus. Rev. 90 (10), 60–68.

McEachran, R. (2016). Can a Craigslist for Cucumbers Tackle the UK's Food Waste?. The Guardian. https://www.theguardian.com/media-network/2016/may/12/craigslist-uk-food-waste-sharing-economy-apps. Accessed 05.06.2017.

Meijer, A., Bolivar, M.P.R., 2016. Governing the smart city: a review of the literature on smart urban governance. Int. Rev. Adm. Sci. 82 (2), 392–408.

Minson, S.E., Meier, M., Baltay, A.S., Hanks, T.C., Cochran, E.S., 2018. The limits of earthquake early warning: timeliness of ground motion estimates. Sci. Adv. 4 (3), 1–10.

Mitchell, W.J., 1995. The City of Bits: Space, Place, and the Infobahn. The MIT Press, Cambridge, MA.

Mitchell, W.J., 1999. E-topia: Urban Life, Jim—But Not as We Know It. The MIT Press, Cambridge, MA.

Mitchell, W.J., 2003. Me++: The Cyborg Self and the Networked City. The MIT Press, Cambridge, MA.

Mitchell, W.J., 2004. The city of bits hypotesis. In: Graham, S. (Ed.), The Cybercities Reader. Routledge, New York City, NY, pp. 123–128.

Moore, G., 1965. Cramming more components onto integrated circuits. Electronics 38 (8), 1–4.

Mora, L., Bolici, R., 2016. The development process of smart city strategies: the case of Barcelona. In: Rajaniemi, J. (Ed.), Re-city: Future City—Combining Disciplines. Juvenes Print, Tampere, pp. 155–181.

Mora, L., Deakin, M., Reid, A., Angelidou, M., 2018. How to overcome the dichotomous nature of smart city research: proposed methodology and results of a pilot study. J. Urban Technol. https://doi.org/10.1080/10630732.2018.1525265.

Nakamura, Y., Saita, J., Sato, T., 2011. On an earthquake early warning system (EEW) and its applications. Soil Dyn. Earthq. Eng. 31 (2), 127–136.

National Intelligence Council, 2012. Global Trends 2030: Alternative Worlds. National Intelligence Council, Washington, DC.

North Carolina State University (2007). Mayday 23: World Population Becomes More Urban Than Rural. ScienceDaily. http://www.sciencedaily.com/releases/2007/05/070525000642.htm. Accessed 05.06.2014.

Palmisano, S. J. (2008). A Smarter Planet: The Next Leadership Agenda. IBM Corporation. https://www.ibm.com/ibm/cioleadershipexchange/us/en/pdfs/SJP_Smarter_Planet.pdf. Accessed 03.03.2011.

Palomo-Navarro, Á., Navío-Marco, J., 2017. Smart city networks' governance: the Spanish smart city network case study. Telecommun. Policy https://doi.org/10.1016/j.telpol.2017.10.002.

Paroutis, S., Bennett, M., Heracleous, L., 2014. A strategic view on smart city technology: the case of IBM smarter cities during a recession. Technol. Forecast. Soc. Chang. 89, 262–272.

Peng, C., Zhu, X., Yang, J., Xue, B., Chen, Y., 2013. Development of an integrated onsite earthquake early warning system and test deployment in Zhaotong, China. Comput. Geosci. 56, 170–177.

Piedmont-Palladino, S.C., 2011. Intelligent Cities. National Building Museum, Washington, DC.

Pierce, F.J., Elliott, T.V., 2008. Regional and on-farm wireless sensor networks for agricultural systems in Eastern Washington. Comput. Electron. Agric. 61 (1), 32–43.

Pinstrup-Andersen, P., Rahmanian, M., Allahoury, A., Guillou, M., Hendriks, S., Hewitt, J., Iwanaga, M., Kalafatic, C., Kliksberg, B., Maluf, R., Murphy, S., Oniang'o, R., Pimbert, M., Sepúlveda, M., Tang, H., Prakash, V., Ambuko, J., Belik, W., Huang, J., Timmermans, A., and Gitz, V. (2014). Food Losses and Waste in the Context of Sustainable Food Systems. Report. High Level Panel of Experts on Food Security and Nutrition (HLPE). http://www.un.org/en/zerohunger/pdfs/HLPE_FLW_Report-8_EN.pdf. Accessed 05.10.2016.

Plessi, V., Bastianini, F., Sedigh, S., 2007. A wireless system for real-time environmental and structural monitoring. In: Obermaisser, R., Nah, Y., Puschner, P., Rammig, F.J. (Eds.), Software Technologies for Embedded and Ubiquitous Systems: 5th IFIP WG 10.2 International Workshop, SEUS 2007, Santorini Island, Greece, May 2007. Revised Papers. Springer, Berlin, pp. 456–465.

Pokrić, B., Krčo, S., Pokrić, M., 2014. Augmented reality based smart city services using secure IoT infrastructure. In: Barolli, L., Li, K.F., Enokido, T., Xhafa, F., Takizawa, M. (Eds.), 2014 28th International Conference on Advanced Information Networking and Applications Workshops (WAINA), Victoria, 13-16 May 2014. Institute of Electrical and Electronics Engineers (IEEE), Piscataway, NJ.

Praharaj, S., Han, J.H., Hawken, S., 2017. Urban innovation through policy integration: critical perspectives from 100 smart cities mission in India. City Cult. Soc. 12, 35–43.

Pullman, M., Wu, Z., 2012. Food Supply Chain Management: Economic, Social and Environmental Perspectives. Routledge, New York City, NY.

Rector, K., 2018. Enhancing accessibility and engagement for those with disabilities. IEEE Pervasive Comput. 17 (1), 9–12.

Research and Markets (2017). Smart City Market to 2025—Global Analysis and Forecast by Industry Verticals. Report. Research and Markets. https://www.researchandmarkets.com/research/2w8qht/smart_city_market. Accessed 04.03.2018.

Ryan, J., 2010. A History of the Internet and the Digital Future. Reaktion Books Ltd., London.

Saha, M., Hara, K., Behnezhad, S., Li, A., Saugstad, M., Maddali, H., Chen, S., Froehlich, J.E., 2017. A pilot deployment of an online tool for large-scale virtual auditing of urban accessibility. In: ASSETS'17: Proceedings of the 19th International ACM SIGACCESS Conference on Computers and Accessibility, Baltimore, MD, 29 October—01 November 2017. ACM Press, New York City, NY, pp. 305–306.

Salim, F., Haque, U., 2015. Urban computing in the wild: a survey on large scale participation and citizen engagement with ubiquitous computing, cyber physical systems, and Internet of Things. Int. J. Hum.-Comput. Stud. 81 (1), 31–48.

Sanchez, L., Muñoz, L., Galache, J.A., Sotres, P., Santana, J.R., Gutierrez, V., Ramdhany, R., Gluhak, A., Krco, S., Theodoridis, E., Pfisterer, D., 2014. SmartSantander: IoT experimentation over a smart city testbed. Comput. Netw. 61, 217–238.

Santi, P., Resta, G., Szell, M., Sobolevsky, S., Strogatz, S., Ratti, C., 2014. Quantifying the benefits of vehicle pooling with shareability networks. PNAS 111 (37), 13290–13294.

Satriano, C., Elia, L., Martino, C., Lancieri, M., Zollo, A., Iannaccone, G., 2011. PRESTo, the earthquake early warning system for southern Italy: concepts, capabilities and future perspectives. Soil Dyn. Earthq. Eng. 31 (2), 137–153.

Saunders, T., and Baeck, P. (2015). Rethinking Smart Cities from the Ground Up. Research Report. Nesta. http://www.nesta.org.uk/sites/default/files/rethinking_smart_cities_from_the_ground_up_2015.pdf. Accessed 02.11.2015.

Schaller, R.R., 1997. Moore's law: past, present, and future. IEEE Spectr. 34 (6), 52–59.

Schenkman, L. (2011). Japan Radiation Map Roundup. Science. http://www.sciencemag.org/news/2011/03/japan-radiation-map-roundup. Accessed 01.04.2017.

Schreiner, C. (2016). International Case Studies of Smart Cities: Rio De Janeiro, Brazil. Discussion Paper IDB-DP-447. Inter-American Development Bank. https://publications.iadb.org/handle/11319/7727. Accessed 15.07.2017.

Sharma, P., Rajput, S. (Eds.), 2017. Sustainable Smart Cities in India: Challenges and Future Perspectives. Springer, Cham.

Shin, D., 2007. A critique of Korean National Information Strategy: case of National Information Infrastructures. Gov. Inf. Q. 24 (3), 624–645.

Shin, D., 2009. Ubiquitous city: urban technologies, urban infrastructure and urban informatics. J. Inf. Sci. 35 (5), 515–526.

Shin, D., Kim, T., 2010. Large-scale ICT innovation and policy. In: Kocaoglu, D.F., Anderson, T.R., Daim, T.U., Jetter, A., Weber, C.M. (Eds.), PICMET 2010 Proceedings: Technology Management for Global Economic Growth, Seoul, 18-22 July 2010. Institute of Electrical and Electronics Engineers (IEEE), Piscataway, NJ, pp. 148–161.

Shwayri, S.T., 2013. A model Korean ubiquitous eco-city? The politics of making Songdo. J. Urban Technol. 20 (1), 39–55.

Singh, S. (2010). Top 20 Mega Trends and Their Impact on Business, Cultures and Society. Frost & Sullivan. http://www.frost.com/prod/servlet/cpo/213016007. Accessed 25.11.2017.

Stertz, B. (2014). MIT, Audi Launch HubCab Project in New York City. Press Release. AUDI. https://www.audiusa.com/newsroom/news/press-releases/2014/03/mit-audi-hubcab-project-new-york-city. Accessed 05.05.2015.

Sullivan, M. (2017). Smart Cities: Growing New IT Markets. BCC Research. https://www.bccresearch.com/market-research/information-technology/smart-cities-growing-new-markets-report-ift115b.html. Accessed 20.01.2018.

Szell, M., Groß, B., 2014. HubCab—exploring the benefits of shared taxi services. In: Offenhuber, D., Ratti, C. (Eds.), Decoding the City: How Big Data Can Change Urbanism. Birkhäuser, Basel, pp. 28–39.

Taylor, C. (2013). Three Enormous Problems Big Data Tech Solves. Wired. http://www.wired.com/2013/08/three-enormous-problems-big-data-tech-solves/. Accessed 12.01.2014.

The African Union Commission (2015). Agenda 2063: The Africa We Want. Framework Document. The African Union Commission. http://www.un.org/en/africa/osaa/pdf/au/agenda2063-framework.pdf. Accessed 04.04.2018.

The White House (2015). Administration Announces New "Smart Cities" Initiative to Help Communities Tackle Local Challenges and Improve City Services. Press Release. The White House. https://obamawhitehouse.archives.gov/the-press-office/2015/09/14/fact-sheet-administration-announces-new-smart-cities-initiative-help. Accessed 03.02.2018.

Tselentis, G., Domingue, J., Galis, A., Gavras, A., Hausheer, D., Krco, H., Lotz, V., Zahariadis, T. (Eds.), 2009. Towards the Future Internet: A European Research Perspective. IOS Press, Amsterdam.

UNDP (2015). Smartphone App to Turn E-trash Into Hard Cash in China Is Among Winning Innovations at Global Solutions Summit. United Nations Development Programme. http://www.asia-pacific.undp.org/content/rbap/en/home/presscenter/pressreleases/2015/09/29/smartphone-app-to-turn-e-trash-into-hard-cash-in-china-is-among-winning-innovations-at-global-solutions-summit.html. Accessed 10.03.2018.

UNDP (2016a). China: Turning E-Trash into Cash. United Nations Development Programme. http://www.asia-pacific.undp.org/content/rbap/en/home/ourwork/development-impact/innovation/projects/china-ewaste.html. Accessed 10.03.2018.

UNDP (2016b). China's E-waste Recycling App Goes Global. United Nations Development Programme. http://www.asia-pacific.undp.org/content/rbap/en/home/presscenter/pressreleases/2016/06/02/china-s-e-waste-recycling-app-goes-global-.html. Accessed 10.03.2018.

United Nations (2014). World Urbanization Prospects: The 2014 Revision. ST/ESA/SER.A/352. United Nations. https://esa.un.org/unpd/wup/publications/files/wup2014-highlights.pdf. Accessed 31.02.2017.

United Nations (2015). Transforming Our World: The 2030 Agenda for Sustainable Development. A/RES/70/1. United Nations. https://sustainabledevelopment.un.org/content/documents/21252030%20Agenda%20for%20Sustainable%20Development%20web.pdf. Accessed 10.12.2017.

United Nations (2017a). New Urban Agenda. A/RES/71/256. United Nations. http://habitat3.org/wp-content/uploads/NUA-English.pdf. Accessed 10.12.2017.

United Nations (2017b). World Population Prospects: The 2017 Revision, Key Findings and Advance Tables. ESA/P/WP/248. United Nations. https://esa.un.org/unpd/wpp/publications/Files/WPP2017_KeyFindings.pdf. Accessed 10.12.2017.

United Nations (2017c). With Focus on Natural Disasters, UN Risk Reduction Forum Opens in Mexico. United Nations. https://news.un.org/en/story/2017/05/558182-focus-natural-disasters-un-risk-reduction-forum-opens-mexico. Accessed 05.04.2018.

van Winden, W., van den Buuse, D., 2017. Smart city pilot projects: exploring the dimensions and conditions of scaling up. J. Urban Technol. 24 (4), 51–72.

Vanolo, A., 2014. Smartmentality: the smart city as disciplinary strategy. Urban Stud. 51 (5), 883–898.

Vaquero-García, A., Álvarez-García, J., Peris-Ortiz, M., 2017. Urban models of sustainable development from the economic perspective: smart cities. In: Peris-Ortiz, M., Bennett, D., Pérez-Bustamante Yábar, D. (Eds.), Sustainable Smart Cities: Creating Spaces for Technological, Social and Business Development. Springer, Cham, pp. 15–29.

Viale Pereira, G.V., Macadar, M.A., Luciano, E.M., Testa, M.G., 2017a. Delivering public value through open government data initiatives in a smart city context. Inf. Syst. Front. 19 (2), 213–229.

Viale Pereira, G., Berger Bernardes, M., Bernardini, F., Cappelli, C., Gomyde, A., 2017b. Building a reference model and an evaluation method for cities of the Brazilian network of smart and human cities. In: Dg.o '17: Proceedings of the 18th Annual International Conference on Digital Government Research, New York City, NY, 07-09 June 2017. ACM Press, New York City, NY.

Walravens, N., 2015. Mobile city applications for Brussels citizens: smart city trends, challenges and a reality check. Telematics Inform. 32 (2), 282–299.

WHO, 2016. World Health Statistics 2016: Monitoring Health for the SDGs. World Health Organization, Geneva.

Wiig, A., 2015a. IBM's smart city as techno-utopian policy mobility. City: Anal. Urban Trends Cult. Theory Policy Actio 19 (2-3), 258–273.

Wiig, A., 2015b. The empty rhetoric of the smart city: from digital inclusion to economic promotion in Philadelphia. Urban Geogr. 37 (4), 535–553.

Yamamoto, S., Tomori, M., 2013. Earthquake early warning system for railways and its performance. J. JSCE 1 (1), 322–328.

Yigitcanlar, T., Kamruzzaman, M., 2018. Does smart city policy lead to sustainability of cities? Land Use Policy 73, 49–58.

Yigitcanlar, T., Lee, S.H., 2014. Korean ubiquitous-eco-city: a smart-sustainable urban form or a branding hoax? Technol. Forecast. Soc. Change 89, 100–114.

Ylizaliturri-Salcedo, M.Á., García-Macías, J.A., Cardenas-Osuna, R., Aguilar-Noriega, L., 2016. Smart cities for the rest of us. In: Sucar, E., Mayora, O., Munoz de Cote, E. (Eds.), Applications for Future Internet. International Summit, AFI 2016, Puebla, Mexico, May 25–28, 2016, Revised Selected Papers. Springer, Cham, pp. 8–11.

Yu, J., Shannon, H., Baumann, A., Schwartz, L., Bhatt, M., 2016. Slum upgrading programs and disaster resilience: a case study of an Indian 'smart city'. Procedia Environ. Sci. 36, 154–161.

Zambrano, A., Perez, I., Palau, C., Esteve, M., 2017. Technologies of Internet of Things applied to an earthquake early warning system. Futur. Gener. Comput. Syst. 75, 206–215.

Zollo, A., Colombelli, S., Elia, L., Emolo, A., Festa, G., Iannaccone, G., Martino, C., Gasparini, P., 2014. An integrated regional and on-site earthquake early warning system for southern Italy: concepts, methodologies and performances. In: Wenzel, F., Zschau, J. (Eds.), Early Warning for Geological Disasters. Springer, Berlin, pp. 117–137.

Chapter 3

The first two decades of research on smart city development

Chapter Outline

3.1 Introduction

The science of complexity and modern theories of urban dynamics have completely changed the way in which the functioning of cities and their evolutionary process are understood. Cities are now perceived as complex systems whose structure is shaped by a multitude of heterogeneous and apparently disconnected bottom-up activities that give rise to an internal order. This order is extremely sensitive and subject to continuous changes, which trigger an endless process of evolution (Batty, 2005, 2013; Batty and Marshall, 2009; Jacobs, 1961). Dealing with this never-ending evolution is a challenge whose complexity has required researchers operating in many different academic disciplines to join forces and pool their knowledge (Benevolo, 1993; Secchi, 2011). This collective understanding of cities has resulted in a unique knowledge domain which is known as urban studies (Liu, 2005), a domain that Kamalski and Kirby (2012: S3) consider to be "one of the longest established interdisciplinary fields within the modern academy."

Computer science is one of the academic disciplines that has become part of this large interdisciplinary field of study. The interest of computer science in the urban landscape and its development dynamics began at the end of the 20th century, when the digital revolution was on the verge of transforming cities "into a constellation of computers" (Batty, 1997: 155) and large networks of electronic devices started to be embedded into the built environment (Mitchell, 1995). Despite being only in its early stages of development, this transformative process immediately attracted the attention of academic environments, in which

Untangling Smart Cities. https://doi.org/10.1016/B978-0-12-815477-9.00003-7

researchers were either concerned with the potential consequences on society or interested in better understanding the opportunities opened up by such a far-reaching change. This interest resulted in a widespread perception that is well explained by Alessandro Aurigi in a briefing paper written in 2003 to introduce a series of seminars on virtual and cyber cities: in the mid 1990s, by looking at the diffusion of ICT devices, many researchers suggested the new frontier of ICTs was to provide spatial, social, economic and environmental challenges with a solution, and "cities looked like the ideal arena where this revolution would test and show itself, changing economic development, services, and above all, community life" (Firmino, 2003).

The relationship between ICTs and the development of urban systems started being analyzed with Graham and Marvin's book "Telecommunications and the City: Electronic Spaces, Urban Places" (Graham and Marvin, 1996). Their research activity, along with the work published by Castells (1989, 1996, 2004) and Mitchell (1995, 1999, 2000, 2003), has allowed this new knowledge area to take shape and grow. This knowledge production process has resulted in the publication of a large body of academic literature (see Graham and Marvin, 1996, 1999, 2001, 2004; Graham, 1997, 2000, 2001, 2002, 2004). Many of these publications can now be considered as some of the key intellectual resources exploring the complex and still poorly understood relationship linking the sustainable development of urban environments to the deployment of information and communication technology (Graham and Marvin, 1996).

Smart city development is part of this knowledge domain and the research investigating this new concept started in 1992 with the book entitled "The Technopolis Phenomenon: Smart Cities, Fast Systems, Global Networks" (Gibson et al., 1992). Over the years, smart cities have become the symbol of ICT-driven urban sustainability and have received growing attention from many researchers working not only in the academia, but also for governmental organizations, industry, and civil society organizations. Thanks to the interest expressed by such researchers, smart city research has been growing sharply since 1992.

Evidence of this trend emerges when analyzing the data offered by Google Scholar. Following a keyword search aiming at identifying the literature produced between 1992 and 2017 where the term smart city is used, either the singular or plural form, Google Scholar sources 73,239 documents.[1] The data collected during the search, which is shown in the bar chart of Fig. 3.1, demonstrates that the annual volume of publications dealing with smart city development has increased by approximately 650 times within 26 years, moving from 26 in 1992 to 16,700 in 2017.

The study reported on in this chapter aims to (1) provide an overall and detailed picture of what happened during the first two decades of research on

1. The keyword search was conducted in April 2018 using the following search query: "smart city" OR "smart cities" (Time span: 1992–2017).

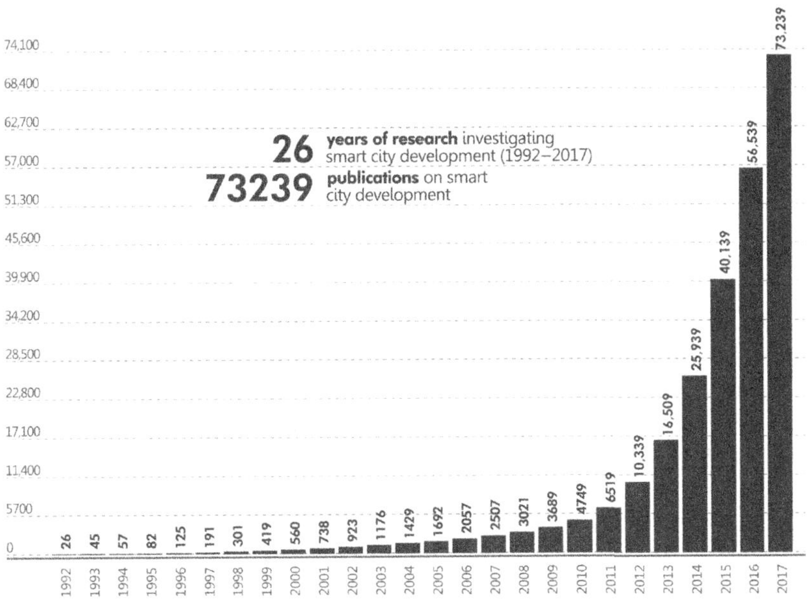

FIG. 3.1 Annual production of smart city literature from 1992 to 2017.

smart city development and (2) lead to an improved understanding of this research field. This aim is met by answering the following questions:

- What are the main characteristics of the literature on smart cities that is produced between 1992 and 2012?
- How large is the scientific community researching this subject?
- What are the productivity levels of the researchers within this community?
- What organizations do members of this research community belong to?
- What are the interpretations of smart city development that emerge from this literature?
- What are the main factors that have influenced the production of literature during the first two decades of smart city research?

To answer these questions, bibliometrics is used to analyze both (1) the literature on smart city development published between 1992 and 2012 and (2) the community of researchers involved in this process of knowledge production. The methodology adopted to conduct this analysis is presented in Section 3.2, which is followed by a comprehensive account of the findings (see Section 3.3). The analysis will shed light on the first 21 years of research into smart cities and will start to uncover the division that such a research has produced. Sections 3.4 and 3.5 discuss the relevance of the findings in the framework of the literature on smart city development produced subsequent to the period under investigation.

3.2 Bibliometrics and the analysis of knowledge domains

Bibliometrics helps analyze the formal properties of knowledge domains by using statistical methods (Broadus, 1987; De Bellis, 2009; Ding et al., 2001; Godin, 2006; Pritchard, 1969). The interest in applying bibliometric methods and techniques to explore the developments of smart city research has grown considerably over the years, and it has resulted in the production of a series of bibliometric analyses that this study builds on.

The first investigations were conducted by Tregua et al. (2015) and Ricciardi and Za (2015). The former examines the relationship between smart cities and sustainable cities by considering 367 books and journal articles indexed in Web of Science. The latter analyzes approximately 100 conference papers stored in the websites of two international conferences on smart cities. The aim of the study proposed by Ricciardi and Za (2015: 163) was "to define the boundaries of smart city research and to draw a map of [its] interdisciplinary community." One year later, Ojo et al. (2016) sought to map this interdisciplinary community by using the Scopus-indexed journal articles and conference papers on smart cities and intelligent cities, two terms that the authors consider as equivalent to one another. In addition, de Jong et al. (2015) identify the conceptual differences between twelve dominant city categories: sustainable city, eco city, low carbon city, livable city, green city, digital city, ubiquitous city, intelligent city, information city, knowledge city, resilient city, and smart city. These differences are captured by way of a bibliometric analysis in which the academic literature retrieved from both Web of Science and Scopus is considered. Finally, Durán-Sánchez et al. (2017) deploy bibliometrics to compare the Web of Science and Scopus' literature on smart cities, sustainability and life quality and to provide an overview of the mechanisms of scientific knowledge production related to these thematic areas.[2]

These investigations expose a common tendency that limits their effectiveness. Rather than capturing the overall picture of the research dealing with smart city development, they either focus attention on single aspects of such a research, or compare smart cities to other different city categories. In addition, it should be noted that the findings of these studies result from bibliometric analyses that are conducted by using a limited number of publications or databases in which grey literature is not indexed (Hutton, 2009). Therefore, as this bibliometric analysis will demonstrate, some relevant source documents[3] have been missed.

---

2. Web of Science (https://clarivate.com/products/web-of-science) and Scopus (https://www.scopus.com) are two of the largest databases of peer-reviewed literature. Web of Science and Scopus are managed by Clarivate Analytics and Elsevier respectively.

3. As De Bellis (2009) and Small and Griffith (1974) suggest, a field of research can be envisioned as a mosaic or puzzle of publications, which are clustered together by way of subject-related repositories, like journals, and produced through the research activities carried out by a community of scholars. These publications are considered as source documents in bibliometric analyses, because they represent the output of the research conducted into a specific field of study. In addition, they are used to collect the raw data that are needed to perform the analyses (Casillas and Acedo, 2007;Ingwersen et al., 2014;Schneider et al., 2009;Shiau and Dwivedi, 2013;Small and Crane, 1979).

The bibliometric analysis reported in this chapter overcomes these limitations by: (1) focusing attention only on the smart city research field; (2) expanding the number of databases used to source documents; and (3) including both academic publications and grey literature, which represents a component of considerable significance in knowledge production processes (Schopfel and Farace, 2010). Grey literature represents the literature that is "produced on all levels of government, academics, business and industry in print and electronic formats, but [...] not controlled by commercial publishers, i.e., where publishing is not the primary activity of the producing body" (Schopfel, 2010: 12).

This bibliometric study was carried out by using 1,067 source documents, which were identified thought a series of keyword searchers conducted in eight scholarly databases: Web of Science, Scopus, Google Scholar, IEEE Xplore, SpringerLink, Engineering Village, ScienceDirect, and Taylor and Francis Online. The use of multiple databases made it possible to conduct a comprehensive interdisciplinary search and avoid the risk of building an incomplete representation of the smart city research field, a common issue that research by Jacobsen et al. (2013) and Zhao et al. (2009) reports on, and that can surface due to the exclusion of relevant publications or the analysis of a too limited amount of literature.

The source documents that were selected to conduct the bibliometric analysis represent all the English-language literature on smart city development published between 1992 and 2012, in which the terms "smart city" and "smart cities" were found in at least one of the following sections: title, abstract, keyword list, or body of the text. To analyze such a literature, this study deployed citation analysis, which made it possible to measure the degree of connection between source documents, and citation and publication counts, the two most basic bibliometric measures (Colledge and Verlinde, 2014; Martin and Daim, 2008; Tijssen and van Leeuwen, 2003).

Along with smart cities, many other new categories of cities have recently entered the debate linking ICT to urban sustainability, for example, green cities (Beatley, 2012), digital cities (Fraser, 2015), intelligent cities (Komninos, 2014), information cities (Curwell et al., 2005), virtual cities (Aurigi and Graham, 1997, 2000), cyber cities (Arribas-Bel et al., 2015), knowledge cities (Yigitcanlar et al., 2008), ubiquitous cities (Shen et al., 2017), resilient cities (Desouza and Flanery, 2013), eco cities (Chang and Sheppard, 2013), low-carbon cities (Voytenko et al., 2016), livable cities (Marsal-Llacuna et al., 2015), low-carbon eco-cities (Zhou et al., 2015), and ubiquitous eco-cities (Yigitcanlar and Lee, 2014). Despite being characterized by conceptual and practical differences, these categories of cities are frequently used interchangeably in the literature on smart cities (de Jong et al., 2015), and this tendency has generated the terminological confusion that Hollands (2008), Deakin and Al Wear (2011), and Nam and Pardo (2011a, b) describe in their research.

After taking these differences into account and mindful of the specific focus of this study on smart city development, a decision was taken to set the keyword search of this bibliometric analysis on the smart city category only. No varying

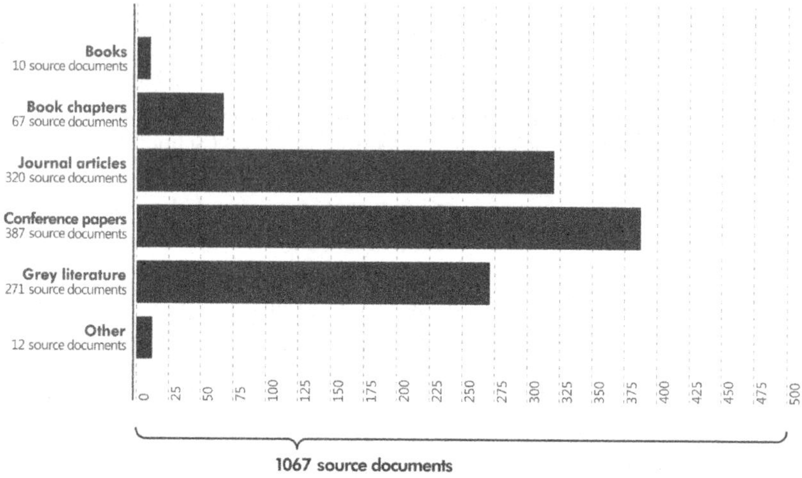

FIG. 3.2 Source documents by type.

or related terms were considered during the search for the knowledge objects to include in the analytical process. This approach made it possible to avoid the risk of adversely affecting the study by including literature not directly connected to the subject under investigation.

To build a comprehensive list of all the available source documents, the publications identified during the keyword searches were included in a single dataset. This list was then checked to identify and correct typographical errors in the titles, names of authors, and publication dates. This check phase was also instrumental in removing the presence of duplicate documents. Finally, the title, abstract, keyword list, and body of the text of each of the remaining publications were then read, so as to verify the presence of the keyword. Any documents showing the results of this search to be negative were subsequently removed from the dataset.

After completing the search phase and the cleaning process, 1067 source documents remained, which were grouped by type. The following six categories were considered in this classification process: books, book chapters, journal articles, conference papers,[4] grey literature,[5] and others. The last category includes abstracts, editorials, book reviews, and books' forewords and introductions. The breakdown by type of document is shown in Fig. 3.2.

All source documents were then associated with their authors, who were referenced by their full names and the organizations they represent. Details on the organizations were sourced from their official websites, the databases used

4. In this study, following the definition proposed by Schopfel (2010), only conference papers included in repositories controlled by commercial publishers are not considered as grey literature.
5. Most of the grey literature was extracted from Google Scholar, a database particularly recommended for identifying this type of publications (Hutton, 2009).

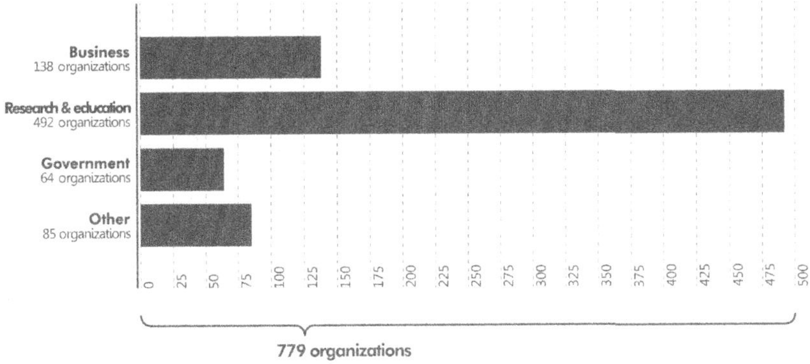

FIG. 3.3 Organizations by type.

during the keyword searches, and the source documents. During this activity, the data on both the type and location of each organization was also collected[6] (see Fig. 3.3). Four main categories were identified:

- Research and education: universities, academies and colleges.
- Business: private companies operating in the ICT sector that are involved in research activities, consultancy, and/or in the distribution of goods and services.
- Government: public authorities and their research institutes.
- Others.

As part of this analysis, citation data was extracted from the list of references included in each source document. This activity was conducted manually. In addition, after being extracted, all the citations were tested for correctness and completeness, so as to guarantee the highest degree of reliability. This check was carried out because, as Adam (2002) points out, citation data often contains errors that can lead to significant variations in the results of bibliometric analysis. In total, 22,137 citations were collected, of which 957 were attributed to source documents and 21,180 to nonsource documents. To complete this first bibliometric analysis, only the citations to source documents were considered.

The intellectual structure of research fields is composed of two different types of resources: (1) source documents, which are the publication output resulting from the research activities carried out into a specific field of study, and (2) nonsource documents, the literature that is not part of the field of study, but that researchers cite to transfer intellectual work from other research areas to their own field. This book's investigation into the intellectual structure of the smart city research field begins with this bibliometric analysis, which was conducted by only considering source documents. The overall intellectual structure

6. In cases where the organizations operate in multiple locations, the main headquarters were selected.

will be then analyzed in the following chapter, which reports on the findings of a second bibliometric study whereby source and nonsource documents are brought together.

3.3 The first two decades of smart-city research

The data processing phase made it possible to obtain a detailed overview of the first two decades of research on smart city development and to capture some initial insights into the ambiguity and division surrounding this new field of study.

3.3.1 New and fast-growing

Smart city research establishes itself as a new field of scientific enquiry in 2009 and has grown steadily over the years, arousing interest from an expanding community of knowledge producers. This growth becomes particularly noticeable when looking at the production of source documents, which continues to progress over the 21 years under investigation. The same trend can also be seen when observing the growth in the number of researchers involved in the production of this literature (Fig. 3.4). Initially, with less than 20 source documents published during the first decade of research, the smart city research field appears significantly restricted in size. The production of source documents starts increasing between 2002 and 2009. During these eight years, an average of about 17 source documents per year is produced. But the most relevant time frame is from 2010

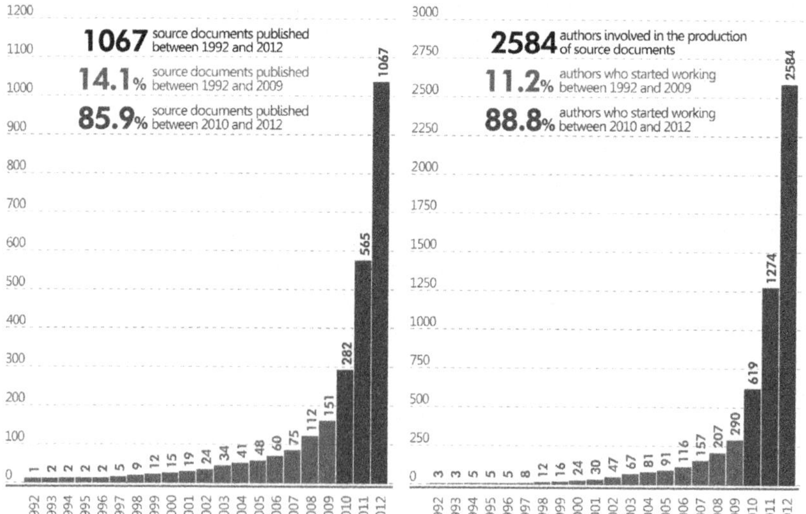

FIG. 3.4 Cumulative growth of source documents and authors.

to 2012, which is characterized by an impressive growth. More than 900 source documents are produced in just three years and these publications account for roughly 86% of all the literature on smart city development published during the first two decades of research.

3.3.2 Lack of cohesion

Research fields comprise large groups of interconnected publications, and their structure can be assembled and visualized by way of mapping techniques. These techniques make it possible to obtain knowledge maps showing the big picture of any research field (Moya-Anegon et al., 2004), that is, "a spatial representation of the relationship among [...] individual documents as reflected in some formal, strictly quantifiable properties of scientific literature at a given time" (De Bellis, 2009: 142). In these maps, the publications are connected through a network of citations, "a type of symbolic currency that signals intellectual influences" and can be used to measure the significance of scientific documents (Jacobsen et al., 2013: 226). By means of citations, researchers can incorporate the intellectual work of others into their own studies and collaborate with them in the construction of a research field (Garfield, 1970; Small, 1973, 1978).

The use of these mapping techniques was instrumental in visualizing the smart city research field resulting from the first 21 years of research on smart city development. The research field is represented by a network of undirected and unweighted links in which the 1067 source documents are nodes and the 957 citations referring to them are the connecting elements. This graph, which is illustrated in Fig. 3.5, was built by using Gephi, an open-source network analysis and visualization software, and its Fruchterman and Reingold (1991)'s layout algorithm. In this network, the source documents are represented as circles with a diameter directly proportional to the number of citations that they have received. Therefore, the greater number of citations, the larger the circle. In addition, the source documents without citations are colored grey, whereas those with at least one citation are shown in blue.

Looking at the composition of the network, it is clear that the intellectual structure of the smart city research field is fragmentated due to the lack of connections between the source documents. Despite being small, the core of the network is well-articulated and compact, due to the existence of citations, which provide evidence of active knowledge exchange, but when looking at the external boundaries, the organization of the network changes radically. The source documents are either not connected or combined in very small groups of publications detached from the central core. This means that the growth of available literature previously observed develops in tandem with the absence of any cohesion among the researchers engaged in the knowledge production process. As a consequence, smart city research is divided into a growing multitude of publications that are disconnected from one another.

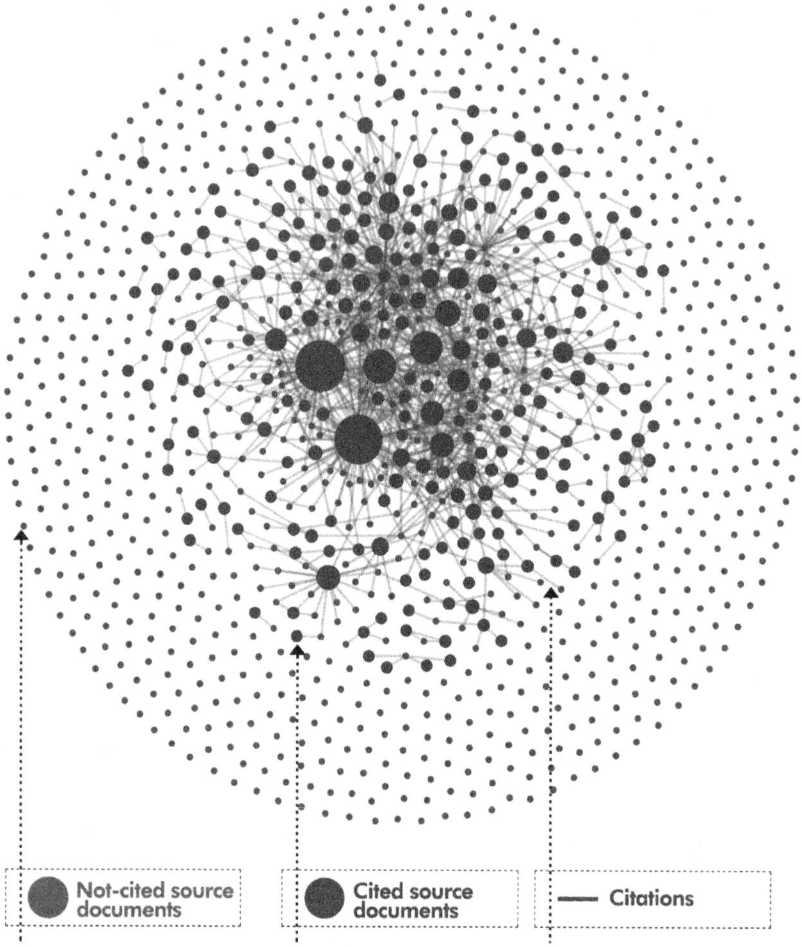

FIG. 3.5 The smart city research field (1992–2012).

3.3.3 Divergent roots

The limited intellectual exchange, lack of cohesion, and divergence become even more pronounced when attempting to extract a commonly accepted definition of the smart city concept from the source literature. The absence of such a definition is pointed out in a number of source documents, in particular those from Alkandari et al. (2012), Chourabi et al. (2012), Hollands (2008), and Paskaleva (2011). Many attempts to provide a definition of the smart city concept can be found, but they expose a tendency to mark themselves out from each other, making it difficult to acquire a common agreement as to what smart city means. Some of these definitions, which have been extracted from the source documents to illustrate this trend, are listed in Fig. 3.6.

Hall et al. (2000: 1)	The smart city is "the urban center of the future, made safe, secure environmentally green, and efficient because all structures [...] are designed, constructed, and maintained making use of advanced, integrated materials, sensors, electronics, and networks which are interfaced with computerized systems comprised of databases, tracking, and decision-making algorithms"
Brisbane City Council (2001, in Partridge 2004: 4)	"A smart city is [a city that] where technology makes easier for people to have their say, gain access to services and to stay in touch with what is happening around them, simply and cheaply"
Odendaal (2003: 586)	"A smart city [...] is one that capitalizes on the opportunities presented by Information and Communication Technology (ICT) in promoting its prosperity and influence"
Paskaleva (2009: 406)	"In the context of the present study, the smart city is defined as one that takes advantages of the opportunities offered by ICT in increasing local prosperity and competitiveness—an approach that implies integrated urban development involving multi-actor, multi-sector and multi-level perspectives"
Vassilaras and Yovanof (2010: 378)	"Building upon the foundations of a digital city infrastructure, an entire city can be designed and programmed to function as an intelligent/smart-city ecosystem which is able to acquire and apply knowledge about an environment and its inhabitants in order to improve their experience in that environment"
Ballon et al. (2011: 1)	"Smart cities collectively tend to suggest the use of innovative ICT-based technologies such as the Internet of Things (IOT) and Web 2.0 to deliver more effective and efficient public services that improve living and working conditions and create more sustainable urban environments that are associated with the provision and consumption of intelligent public services"
Hernandez-Munoz et al. (2011: 452)	"Smart Cities can represent an extraordinary rich ecosystem to promote the generation of massive deployments of city-scale applications and services for a large number of activity sectors"
Lu (2011: 117)	"Smart City means that, in the process of urban development, in order to perform the duties of economic regulation, market supervision, social management and public services, local governments make full use of information and communication technologies [...] to smartly perceive, analyze and integrate city's environment, resources, infrastructure, public safety, city services, public utilities, city participants' operational state and their demand for government functions, and further make the appropriate government action"
Oliver (2011: 16)	"Smart cities [...] focuses on improving the quality of life of an urban environment by understanding the city dynamics through the data provided by ubiquitous technologies"
Alkandari et al. (2012: 79)	"A smart city is one that uses a smart system characterized by the interaction between infrastructure, capital, behaviours and cultures, achieved through their integration"
Lazaroiu and Roscia (2012: 326)	"A new city model, called 'the smart city', which represents a community of average technology size, interconnected and sustainable, comfortable, attractive and secure"
Schaffers et al. (2012: 57)	"The smart city [...] is a future scenario (what to achieve), even more it is an urban development strategy (how to achieve it). It focuses on how (Internet-related) technologies enhance the lives of citizens [...] The smart city is about how people are empowered, through using technology, for contributing to urban change and realizing their ambitions. The smart city [...] is an urban laboratory, an urban innovation ecosystem, a living lab, an agent of change"

FIG. 3.6 Multiple definitions of the smart city concept.

In this confused scenario, researchers seem to agree in picturing the smart city as an urban environment in which an ICT-driven approach to urban sustainability is activated. However, when trying to understand what needs to be done in order to manage smart city development, divergent opinions can be identified. In particular, two divergent development paths emerge from the analysis of the relationship among the 10 most cited source documents (see Fig. 3.7) and

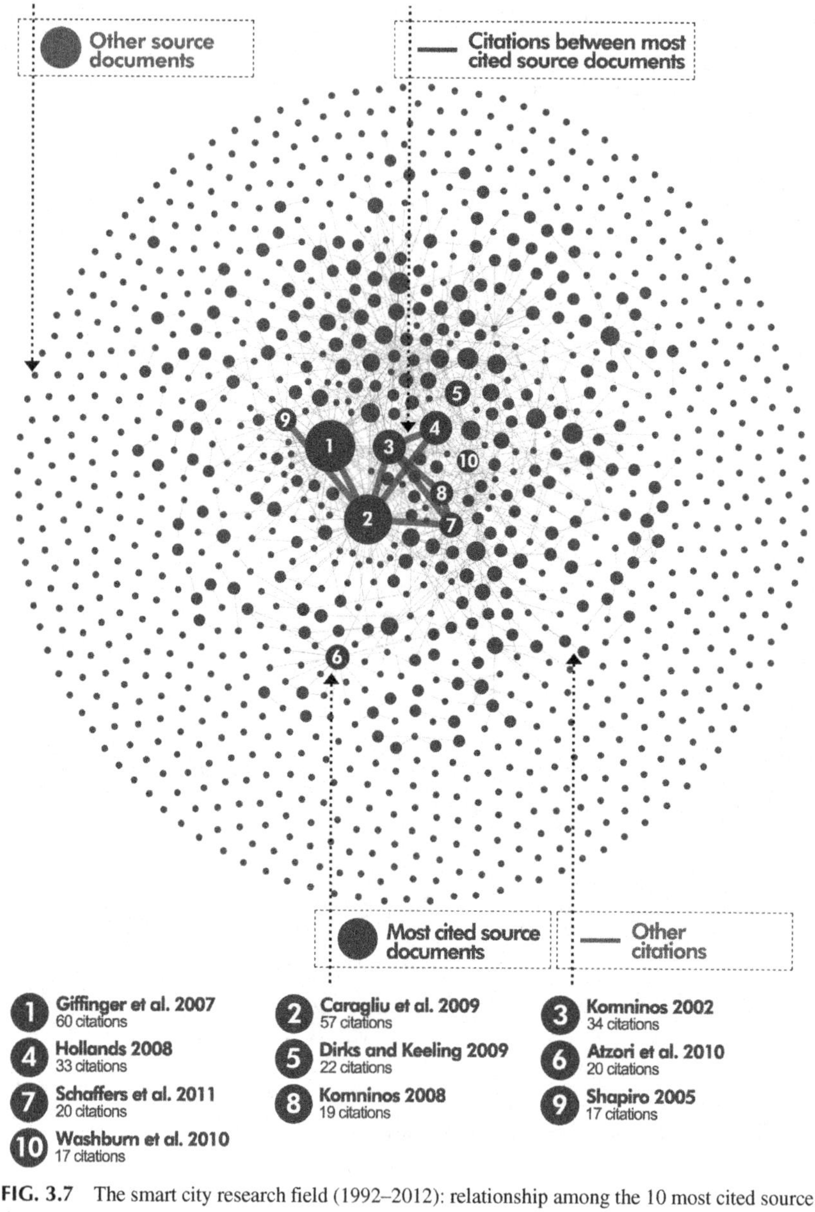

FIG. 3.7 The smart city research field (1992–2012): relationship among the 10 most cited source documents.

their content. Based on the development path of smart cities that they each support, these publications can be split in two different groups.

The first group of publications is connected by a single network of citations, which provide evidence of an active exchange of knowledge among their authors. These publications promote a development path that can be defined as holistic. This path describes smart city development as the result of the balanced combination of human, social, cultural, economic, environmental and technological factors, which stand alongside one another. In contrast, the second group of publications is composed of source documents that are disconnected, but provide the same techno-centric understanding of smart city development.

The holistic path starts developing the research published by Giffinger et al. (2007). This publication is the most influential source document produced between 1992 and 2012, and it represents one of the first attempts to move the smart city concept away from an excessively techno-centric perspective by offering a human-related reading of the subject. In this representation, smart cities are not only pictured as spaces with a greater availability of ICT solutions, but also urban environments "well performing in [...] six characteristics [economy, people, governance, mobility, environment and living], built on the 'smart' combination of endowments and activities of self-decisive, independent and aware citizens." Caragliu et al. (2009, 2011) make a significant contribution to this vision by suggesting that "a city [is] smart when investments in human and social capital and traditional (transport) and modern (ICT) communication infrastructure fuel sustainable economic growth and a high quality of life, with a wise management of natural resources, through participatory governance" (Caragliu et al., 2011: 70).

This holistic interpretation, which is also supported by Schaffers et al. (2011), responds to the request made by Hollands (2008: 315) for a more progressive view of smart cities, which "must seriously start with people and the human capital side of the equation, rather than blindly believing that IT itself can automatically transform and improve cities." This point also surfaces in the research conducted by Komninos (2006), quoted in Hollands, 2008), where the smart city concept is merged with the notion of intelligent cities. In his work, the latter are defined as: "territories with high capacity for learning and innovation, which is built-in to the creativity of their population, their institutions of knowledge creation, and their digital infrastructure for communication and knowledge management" (Komninos, 2006: 13). In the interpretation that Komninos provides, smart cities are urban areas in which ICT-related infrastructures become a means to generate new knowledge of urban issues and to increase the capability of local communities to solve them (Komninos, 2002, 2008).

In direct contrast to this interpretation, the smart city conceived by Dirks and Keeling (2009) at the International Business Machines Corporation (IBM) is an urban environment in which all physical infrastructures are interconnected by way of information technologies. In this case, attention focuses almost exclusively on the role that ICT has in supporting the assembling of one-size-fits-all platforms of digital services and applications whose integration in the built environment is expected to automatically enable smart city development. This is the same interpretation of smart cities provided by Forrester Research, an American market research company. According to this interpretation, "what makes a [city] smart is the combined use of software systems, server infrastructure, network infrastructure, and client devices [...] to better connect seven critical city infrastructure components and services: city administration, education, healthcare, public safety, real estate, transportation, and utilities" (Washburn et al., 2010: 2).

Both IBM and Forrester suggest this transformation process is made possible by the continuous and rapid diffusion of electronic devices that are capable of retrieving and transmitting data. These devices mainly include smartphones and sensor networks, and have supported the growth of the Internet of Things (IoT) (see Atzori et al., 2010).

3.3.4 Two leading knowledge hubs

Between 1992 and 2012, the scientific community working in the field of smart city development is composed of 2584 researchers. These researchers are divided among 779 organizations, which are located in 434 cities and 69 countries. To measure and compare the productivity and influence at any level of aggregation (authors, organizations, countries, and continents), a calculation has been made to determine the quantity of source documents produced by each author and the number of citations they have acquired. For publications produced by two or more authors, the unit value of the document and the number of citations it has acquired have been divided by the total number of authors involved, so each can be assigned an equal share. This allowed individual researchers to become the basic elements for conducting a multi-level analysis which is based on the counting process explained in Fig. 3.8.

The results of the counting process show that research on smart city development starts in Australia and North America. They also indicate that: (1) interest in this

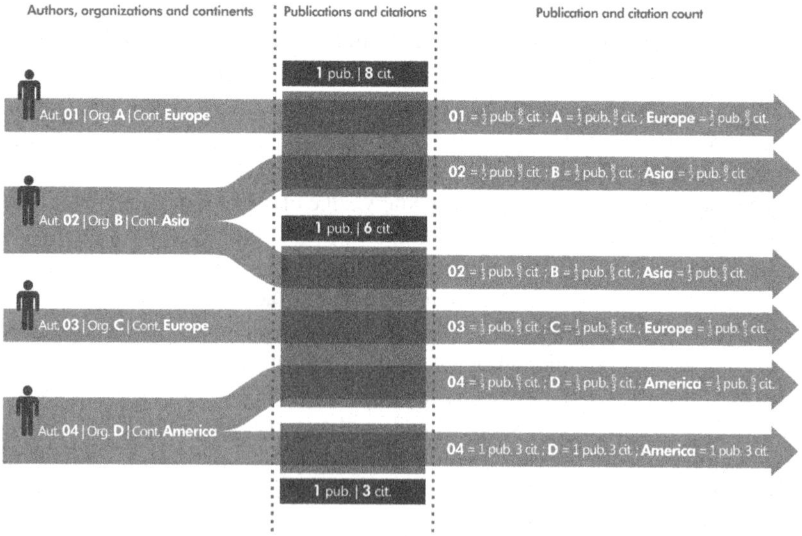

FIG. 3.8 Counting process for measuring and comparing the productivity and influence of authors, organizations, countries, and continents.

TABLE 3.1 Growth in the number of authors by continent

	Number of authors (annual growth/cumulative growth)					
Year	Africa	Asia	Australia	Europe	North America	South America
1992	0 (0)	0 (0)	0 (0)	0 (0)	+3 (3)	0 (0)
1993	0 (0)	0 (0)	0 (0)	0 (0)	0 (3)	0 (0)
1994	0 (0)	0 (0)	+2 (2)	0 (0)	0 (3)	0 (0)
1995	0 (0)	0 (0)	0 (2)	0 (0)	0 (3)	0 (0)
1996	0 (0)	0 (0)	0 (2)	0 (0)	0 (3)	0 (0)
1997	0 (0)	0 (0)	0 (2)	+3 (3)	0 (3)	0 (0)
1998	0 (0)	+1 (1)	0 (2)	0 (3)	+3 (6)	0 (0)
1999	0 (0)	+1 (2)	+3 (5)	0 (3)	0 (6)	0 (0)
2000	+1 (1)	0 (2)	0 (5)	+1 (4)	+6 (12)	0 (0)
2001	0 (1)	0 (2)	+1 (6)	+1 (5)	+4 (16)	0 (0)
2002	0 (1)	0 (2)	+5 (11)	+12 (17)	0 (16)	0 (0)
2003	+1 (2)	0 (2)	+2 (13)	+14 (31)	+3 (19)	0 (0)
2004	+2 (4)	+2 (4)	+3 (16)	+1 (32)	+6 (25)	0 (0)
2005	+3 (7)	0 (4)	+5 (21)	0 (32)	+2 (27)	0 (0)
2006	+1 (8)	+3 (7)	0 (21)	+19 (51)	+2 (29)	0 (0)
2007	+1 (9)	+16 (23)	+6 (27)	+9 (60)	+9 (38)	0 (0)
2008	+7 (16)	+12 (35)	+5 (32)	+20 (80)	+6 (44)	0 (0)
2009	+1 (17)	+25 (60)	+2 (34)	+34 (114)	+21 (65)	0 (0)
2010	0 (17)	+81 (141)	+11 (45)	+148 (262)	+84 (149)	+5 (5)
2011	+9 (26)	+152 (293)	+24 (69)	+351 (613)	+119 (268)	0 (5)
2012	+19 (45)	+374 (667)	+31 (100)	+714 (1327)	+162 (430)	+10 (15)

subject begins to grow between 1997 and 2000 across Europe, Asia, and Africa, and by 2010, this also covers South America; and (2) at the beginning of the knowledge production process, it is North America which maintains the highest number of both authors and publications, but this condition changes between 2002 and 2012, as the number of European authors increases from 17 to more than 1300 (see Table 3.1). These authors represent 51.4% of the global scientific community conducting research on smart city development during the 21 years under investigation. The rest of this community is located in the remaining continents, especially Asia, where 667 researchers have been identified (25.8%).

From the results, it is evident that Europe is also the largest contributor to the growth of smart city research and the region that has the greatest influence over this fast-expanding field of study. This occurs because the majority of the source documents are produced by European organizations (52%) and these have the greatest overall impact. The situation is also positive in North America, where researchers have published 16.6% of the source documents and account for 24% of the citations. However, the relationship between production and influence is negative in Asia, where the overall impact is much smaller (10.3%), despite a greater share of source documents (23.3%). This data is shown in Fig. 3.9.

The data demonstrates that Europe and North America are the main knowledge hubs in the field of smart city development, but it also exposes three relevant differences which characterize their approach to knowledge production. Table 3.2 and Figs. 3.10, 3.11 provide the information needed to analyze the first of these differences. In this instance, the data suggests European research

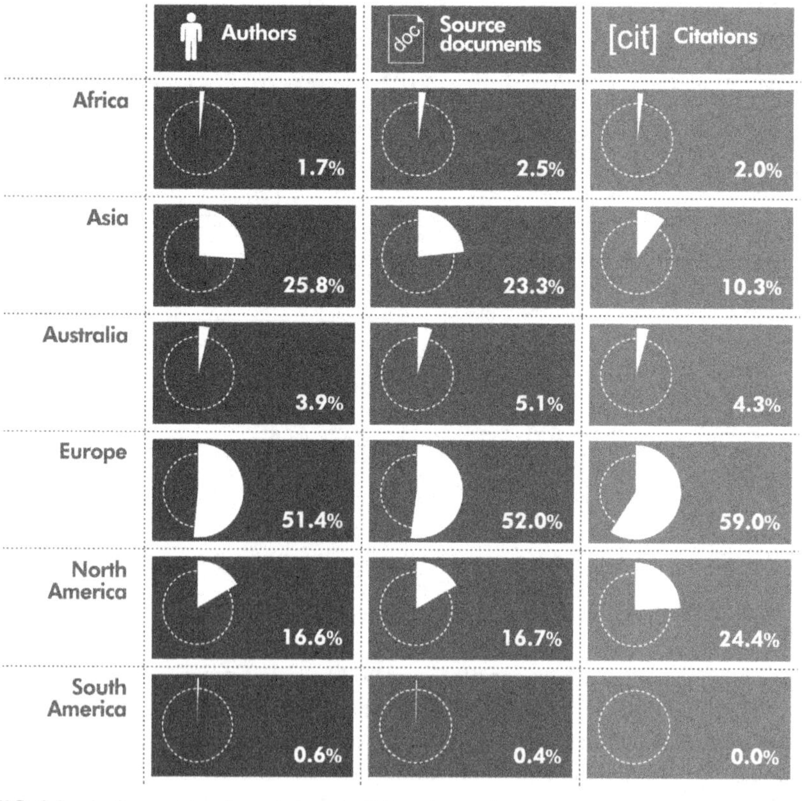

FIG. 3.9 Authors, source documents, and citations by continent.

TABLE 3.2 Percentage of authors, source documents, and citations by country, continent and organization type

Continents and countries	% authors in total					% source docs in total					% citations in total				
	B	R	G	O	Tot	B	R	G	O	Tot	B	R	G	O	Tot
Africa	**0.0**	**0.8**	**0.7**	**0.3**	**1.7**	**0.0**	**1.4**	**0.7**	**0.5**	**2.5**	**0.0**	**1.7**	**0.1**	**0.2**	**2.0**
South Africa	0.0	0.5	0.4	0.3	1.1	0.0	1.1	0.5	0.5	2.1	0.0	1.7	0.1	0.2	2.0
Others	0.0	0.4	0.3	0.0	0.7	0.0	0.2	0.2	0.0	0.4	0.0	0.0	0.0	0.0	0.0
Asia	**5.8**	**17.8**	**1.5**	**0.7**	**25.8**	**5.0**	**16.3**	**1.3**	**0.6**	**23.3**	**2.2**	**7.6**	**0.2**	**0.3**	**10.3**
China	0.9	8.9	0.6	0.0	10.4	0.6	7.3	0.4	0.0	8.4	0.0	3.6	0.0	0.0	3.7
India	0.7	0.9	0.1	0.0	1.6	0.8	0.9	0.1	0.0	1.7	0.3	0.0	0.0	0.0	0.3
Japan	4.1	2.4	0.0	0.4	6.9	3.2	1.8	0.0	0.3	5.3	0.6	0.4	0.0	0.0	0.9
Korea	0.1	3.1	0.2	0.1	3.6	0.1	3.1	0.4	0.1	3.8	0.3	1.8	0.1	0.0	2.2
Malaysia	0.0	0.9	0.0	0.0	0.9	0.0	1.7	0.0	0.0	1.7	0.0	1.7	0.0	0.0	1.7
Taiwan	0.0	0.7	0.2	0.2	1.1	0.0	0.7	0.1	0.1	0.9	0.0	0.0	0.1	0.0	0.1
Others	0.1	0.9	0.4	0.1	1.4	0.3	0.9	0.2	0.1	1.5	1.0	0.1	0.0	0.3	1.4
Australia	**0.5**	**3.3**	**0.2**	**0.0**	**3.9**	**0.4**	**4.4**	**0.3**	**0.0**	**5.1**	**0.3**	**3.9**	**0.1**	**0.0**	**4.3**
Australia	0.5	3.0	0.2	0.0	3.6	0.4	4.1	0.3	0.0	4.8	0.3	3.9	0.1	0.0	4.3
Others	0.0	0.2	0.0	0.0	0.2	0.0	0.3	0.0	0.0	0.3	0.0	0.0	0.0	0.0	0.0
Europe	**9.4**	**33.6**	**3.5**	**5.0**	**51.4**	**8.6**	**35.4**	**2.8**	**5.3**	**52.0**	**7.8**	**42.4**	**3.1**	**5.7**	**59.0**

Continued

TABLE 3.2 Percentage of authors, source documents, and citations by country, continent and organization type—cont'd

Continents and	% authors in total					% source docs in total					% citations in total				
countries	B	R	G	O	Tot	B	R	G	O	Tot	B	R	G	O	Tot
Austria	0.9	1.0	0.0	0.1	2.0	0.8	0.9	0.0	0.1	1.8	0.2	5.0	0.0	0.0	5.2
Belgium	0.2	1.3	0.7	0.3	2.6	0.2	0.9	0.8	0.2	2.1	0.0	0.3	1.0	0.1	1.5
France	1.1	1.9	0.8	0.2	4.0	0.9	1.7	0.8	0.2	3.5	0.6	0.6	1.4	0.4	2.9
Germany	2.1	3.2	0.3	0.6	6.2	2.4	3.0	0.1	0.8	6.2	3.6	0.9	0.0	0.5	5.0
Greece	0.3	2.4	0.2	0.5	3.4	0.1	2.6	0.1	0.6	3.4	0.0	8.8	0.1	0.9	9.8
Italy	0.9	6.3	0.5	0.8	8.5	0.6	6.1	0.4	1.0	8.0	0.4	7.7	0.0	1.7	9.8
The Netherlands	0.1	1.2	0.0	0.0	1.4	0.1	1.5	0.0	0.0	1.6	0.0	3.4	0.0	0.0	3.4
Spain	1.0	3.6	0.3	0.4	5.3	0.8	3.0	0.1	0.4	4.3	0.8	2.7	0.2	0.0	3.7
The United Kingdom	1.1	5.3	0.2	0.6	7.2	1.4	6.4	0.1	0.8	8.7	1.0	8.2	0.0	1.7	10.9
Others	1.7	7.5	0.5	1.5	11.1	1.3	9.4	0.5	1.3	12.5	1.2	4.7	0.5	0.4	6.8
North America	**6.7**	**8.0**	**0.9**	**1.0**	**16.6**	**6.0**	**8.8**	**0.6**	**1.3**	**16.7**	**12.7**	**9.9**	**0.8**	**1.0**	**24.4**
The United States	6.7	6.7	0.8	0.9	15.2	6.0	7.3	0.4	1.2	14.9	12.7	8.3	0.8	1.0	22.8
Other	0.0	1.2	0.1	0.1	1.4	0.0	1.5	0.2	0.1	1.8	0.0	1.5	0.0	0.0	1.5
South America	**0.1**	**0.5**	**0.0**	**0.0**	**0.6**	**0.1**	**0.3**	**0.0**	**0.0**	**0.4**	**0.0**	**0.0**	**0.0**	**0.0**	**0.0**

Organization types: business (B); research and education (R); government (G); and others (O).

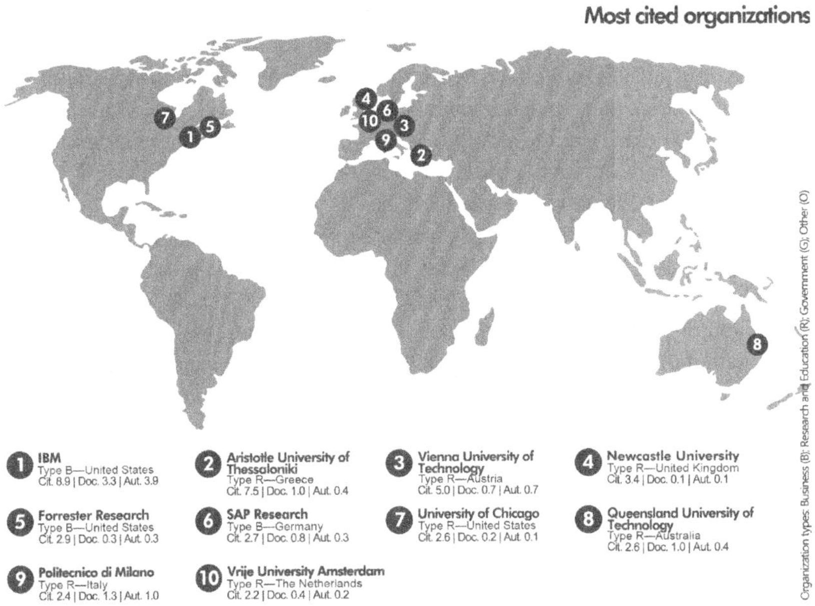

FIG. 3.10 The 10 most cited organizations in the world. Organization types: business (B); research and education (R); government (G); and others (O).

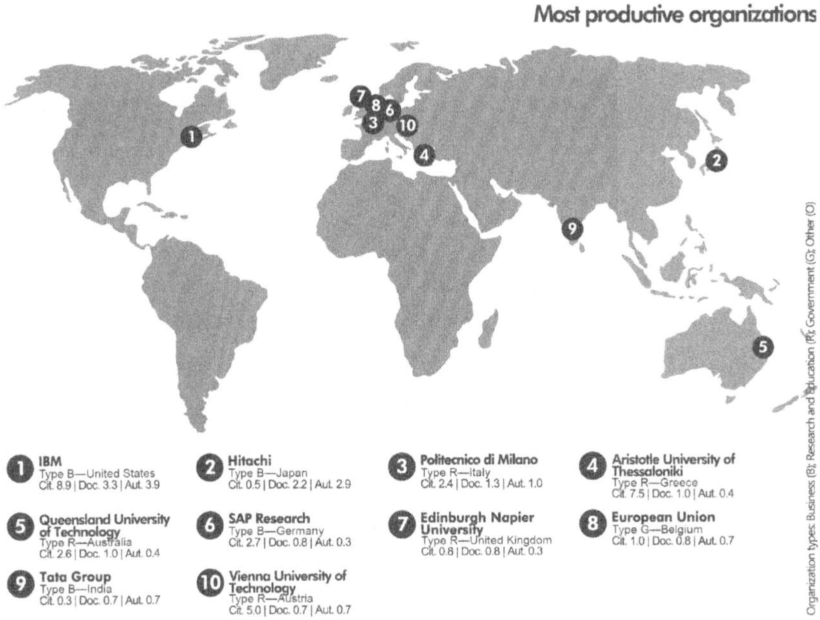

FIG. 3.11 The 10 most productive organizations in the world.

on smart cities is mainly conducted in universities, which have the greatest impact and highest level of productivity. In addition, it shows that the majority of the European authors are from academia, and these in turn account for 68% of the European source documents and approximately 72% of all the citations. In North America, the situation is far different, as the highest productivity is derived from universities and businesses operating within the ICT sector. However, the latter knowledge producer has a dominant role, thanks mainly to the work carried out by IBM and Forrester Research. Together, these two companies account for about 50% of all the citations that North American organizations have acquired during the first two decades of research on smart cities and approximately 70% of the source documents. In addition, with 100 researchers investigating this subject, at the end of 2012, IBM was the world's leading organization for number authors, productivity, and influence over the development of the smart city research field.

The remaining two differences relate to: (1) the divergent development paths of smart cities that each knowledge hub supports and (2) the approach that is used by researchers to produce and diffuse the literature reporting on these development paths. These differences can be observed by comparing the most cited source documents produced in Europe (Fig. 3.12) and North America (Fig. 3.13). The European knowledge hub supports the holistic

Source documents	Organizations	Type	Citations
Giffinger et al. (2007)	Delft University of Technology (R); University of Ljubljana (R); Vienna University of Technology (R)	GR	60
Caragliu et al. (2009)	Politecnico di Milano (R); University of Milan (R); Vrije University Amsterdam (R)	GR	57
Komninos (2002)	Aristotle University of Thessaloniki (R)	BO	34
Hollands (2008)	Newcastle University (R)	AR	33
Atzori et al. (2010)	Mediterranea University of Reggio Calabria (R); University of Catania (R); University of Cagliari (R)	AR	20
Schaffers et al. (2011)	INRIA (G); Aristotle University of Thessaloniki (R); ESoCE Net (O); Alfamicro (B); Lulea University of Technology (R)	CH	20
Komninos (2008)	Aristotle University of Thessaloniki (R)	BO	19
Paskaleva (2009)	University of Manchester (R)	AR	15
The Climate Group (2008)	The Climate Group (O)	GR	14
Karnouskos and Nass de Holanda (2009)	SAP Research (B)	CO	12
Hernández-Muñoz et al. (2011)	Alexandra Institute (B); University of Cantabria (R); Polytechnic University of Madrid (R); Telefonica (B); Luléa University of Technology (R)	CH	12

FIG. 3.12 The 10 most cited source documents produced by European organizations. Publication types: book (BO); book chapter (CH); journal article (AR); conference paper (CO); grey literature (GR); other (OT). Organization types: business (B); research and education (R); government (G); and others (O).

Source documents	Organizations	Type	Citations
Dirks and Keeling (2009)	IBM (B)	GR	22
Shapiro (2005)	University of Chicago (R)	GR	17
Washburn et al. (2010)	Forrester Research (B)	GR	17
Naphade et al. (2011)	IBM (B)	AR	13
Coe et al. (2001)	University of Ottawa (R)	AR	12
Moss Kanter and Litow (2009)	Harvard University (R); IBM (B)	GR	12
Dirks et al. (2009)	IBM (B)	GR	11
Dirks et al. (2010)	IBM (B)	GR	11
Belissent et al. (2010)	Forrester Research (B)	GR	10
Hall et al. (2000)	Brookhaven National Laboratory (G)	GR	8

FIG. 3.13 The 10 most cited source documents produced by North American organizations. Publication types: book (BO); book chapter (CH); journal article (AR); conference paper (CO); grey literature (GR); other (OT). Organization types: business (B); research and education (R); government (G); and others (O).

development path. This path initially stems from grey literature (Caragliu et al., 2009; Giffinger et al., 2007), but over the years, it has been progressively consolidated within the peer-reviewed literature (Hollands, 2008; Komninos, 2002, 2008; Paskaleva, 2009; Schaffers et al., 2011). In contrast to this, North American businesses promote a techno-centric development path, whose theoretical foundations are built on publications passing through the informal channels of grey literature (Belissent et al., 2010; Dirks and Keeling, 2009; Dirks et al., 2009, 2010; Hall et al., 2000; Moss Kanter and Litow, 2009; Washburn et al., 2010).

This data also suggests African and Asian organizations have not significantly influenced the development of the smart city research field during the first two decades of investigations. This situation reflects the limited volume of literature produced and small number of researchers working in the African continent. However, this is not the case in Asia, because some of the most productive organizations are located in India and Japan, for example, Hitachi and the Tata Group, which have produced almost 4% of the total source documents, thanks to the work of 92 researchers. These numbers are matched only by IBM. However, the American company has maintained a greater influence, with 9% of the total citations, whereas only 0.8% can be attributed to the two Asian companies.

3.4 A promising but divided research field

This bibliometric analysis offers a comprehensive picture of the first 21 years of research on smart city development. The findings demonstrate that the sum of literature shaping this new knowledge domain has increased significantly over the initial two decades of research, in particular starting from 2009. However, the limited intellectual exchange and the absence of cohesion that this in turn generates, reveals a tendency for smart city researchers to work in isolation from one another. As a consequence of this condition, the publications such researchers produce remain divided along lines of enquiry, which do not seem to converge.

In addition, the findings also suggest the knowledge exchange currently taking place on the defining features of smart cities lies at the intersection between two competing development paths. The first one is based on the peer-reviewed publications produced by European universities and those researchers who support a holistic interpretation of smart cities (holistic path). The second path, in contrast, stands on the grey literature produced by the American corporate sector, which endorses a techno-centric understanding of the smart city subject (corporate path).

The corporate path, which suggests smart cities deploy ICT solutions for urban sustainability purposes (Paroutis et al., 2014), has now been embraced by several large companies, who have all decided to follow IBM's lead and push this approach to smart city development, for example, Cisco Systems (Amato et al., 2012), ABB (2013) and Fujitsu (Tamai, 2014). However, this path is currently criticized for its incapability to account for the social and cultural challenges that smart city development poses in anything but technological terms. This is because in the corporate path, smart cities are assumed to arise from: (1) the concentration and interconnection of a one-size-fits-all platform of technological fixes, which are supposed to capture and manage large amounts of data and (2) computing models and algorithms that use such a data to resolve the inefficiencies that cities otherwise exhibit as service providers (Hollands, 2015, 2016; Soderstrom et al., 2014; Townsend, 2013).

The holistic path is based on a progressive and human-centric perspective on smart city development and the ICT-driven approach to urban sustainability that smart cities stand for. The holistic path suggests smart city development requires to link technological advancement with human, social, cultural, environmental and economic factors (Angelidou, 2014; Christopoulou et al., 2014; Concilio and Rizzo, 2016; Hemment and Townsend, 2013; Hollands, 2015, 2016; Komninos, 2014; Townsend, 2013). However, as reported by Lee et al. (2014: 80), the research supporting this vision of smart cities still "remains at a preliminary stage", because the knowledge gap between theory and practice has not yet been filled. "What elements go into making up a smart city" (Hollands, 2015: 62) and how to both design and implement strategies capable of enabling smart city development continue to be relevant subject-matters of investigation (Bolici and Mora, 2015; Deakin, 2014; Deakin and Leydesdorff, 2014; Komninos, 2014; Lazaroiu and Roscia, 2012; Mora and Bolici, 2016, 2017; Mora et al., 2018; Zygiaris, 2013).

As Lee et al. (2014: 80) also go on to state: "discussions in academic literature of relevant [theories] or frameworks are few [and the] analysis lags behind the actual practice of how different cities [...] are moving toward transforming themselves into a smart [...] city [...]. Even though actual practice often remains fragmented, real world implementation still generally outstrips any discussion in academic literature capable of generalization." As a result, the knowledge necessary to understand the process of building effective smart cities in the real world has not yet been produced, and neither are the tools for supporting the actors involved in this activity.

3.5 The need to act in concert

This bibliometric analysis only relates to developments taking place between 1992 and 2012, but it nevertheless serves to start revealing the division that still preoccupies many of the ongoing enquiries. This is because, while academics in the field continue to characterize smart cities as a new and promising research topic, a consistent and clear understanding of this concept is still missing. The work of defining and conceptualizing smart city development is still in progress and, as a consequence, smart city research remains divided and researchers are still looking for interpretations capable of overcoming the fragmentation that the first two decades of knowledge production have generated (Albino et al., 2015; Chourabi et al., 2012; Cocchia and Dameri, 2016; Fernandez-Anez, 2016; Meijer and Bolivar, 2016; Ojo et al., 2016).[7]

The results of this first bibliometric analysis indicate the main reasons for the confusion surrounding the scientific status of smart city research rest with:

- The lack of intellectual exchange among those conducting research in the field of smart city development, which emerges as one of the main terms of reference for ICT-driven urban sustainability.
- The tendency of smart city researchers to be subjective and follow personal research paths in isolation from one another.
- The division that this approach to knowledge production opens up in the scientific community.
- The struggle that the community has to find any common currency in the knowledge which smart city research produces.

This situation leaves smart city research fragmented, and in a position whereby its future development is put at risk. While this bibliometric analysis and data drawn from Google Scholar both indicate that smart cities are

7. Some examples can be found in research by Kitchin (2014), Townsend (2013), Greco and Cresta (2015), Urzaiz et al. (2014), and Christopoulou et al. (2014).

emerging as a fast-growing field of study, much of the knowledge that is generated about them is singularly technological in nature. It lacks the social intelligence, cultural artifacts, and environmental attributes which are needed in order to champion the ICT-driven approach to urban sustainability that such a research promotes the development of.

To address the challenge that this situation poses, the intellectual exchange between those members of the scientific community researching smart cities needs to increase. Rather than running the risk of becoming entrenched along the lines of division reported on in this chapter, researchers should instead begin to search out the grounds available to transcend them by "acting in concert." What is more, smart city researchers need to achieve this by integrating the respective fields of specialization into a mode or model of scientific enquiry that not only manages to bridge the structural division that is highlighted in this chapter, but also does this in a form whose content adds up to more than the "sum of the parts" it relates to. This will support the construction of the collaborative and interdisciplinary environment that is necessary to generate a possible agreement concerning the way of conceptualizing and enabling smart city development.

References

ABB (2013). ABB Power and Automation: Solid Foundations for Smart Cities. White Paper. ABB. http://new.abb.com/docs/default-source/smart-grids-library/abb_smart_grids_white_paper_2013.pdf?sfvrsn=2. Accessed 05.04.2014.

Adam, D., 2002. The Counting House. Nature 415 (6873), 726–729.

Albino, V., Berardi, U., Dangelico, R.M., 2015. Smart cities: definitions, dimensions, performance, and initiatives. J. Urban Technol. 22 (1), 3–21.

Alkandari, A., Alnasheet, M., Alshekhly, I.F., 2012. Smart cities: survey. J. Adv. Comput. Sci. Technol. Res. 2 (2), 79–90.

Amato, V., Bloomer, L., Holmes, A., and Kondepudi, S. (2012). Using ICT to Deliver Benefits to Cities by Enabling Smart+Connected Communities. White Paper. Cisco Systems. http://www.smartconnectedcommunities.org/docs/DOC-2150. Accessed 04.01.2013.

Angelidou, M., 2014. Smart city policies: a spatial approach. Cities: Int. J. Urban Policy Plan. 41 (Supplement 1), S3–S11.

Arribas-Bel, D., Kourtit, K., Nijkamp, P., Steenbruggen, J., 2015. Cyber cities: social media as a tool for understanding cities. Appl. Spat. Anal. Policy 8 (3), 231–247.

Atzori, L., Iera, A., Morabito, G., 2010. The Internet of Things: a survey. Comput. Netw. 54 (15), 2787–2805.

Aurigi, A., Graham, S., 1997. Virtual cities, social polarisation and the crisis in urban public space. J. Urban Technol. 4 (1), 19–52.

Aurigi, A., Graham, S., 2000. Cyberspace and the city: the "virtual city" in Europe. In: Bridge, G., Watson, S. (Eds.), A Companion to the City. Blackwell Publishing, Malden, MA, pp. 489–502.

Ballon, P., Glidden, J., Kranas, P., Menychtas, A., Ruston, S., Van der Graaf, S., 2011. Is there a need for a cloud platform for European smart cities? In: Cunningham, P., Cunningham, M. (Eds.), EChallenges E-2011 Conference Proceedings, Florence, 26–28 October 2011. International Information Management Corporation (IIMC), Dublin, pp. 1–7.

Batty, M., 1997. Virtual geography. Futures 29 (4/5), 337–352.

Batty, M., 2005. Cities and Complexity: Understanding Cities with Cellular Automata, Agent-Based Models, and Fractals. MIT Press, Cambridge, MA.

Batty, M., 2013. The New Science of Cities. The MIT Press, Cambridge, MA.

Batty, M., Marshall, S., 2009. The evolution of cities: geddes, abercrombie and the new physicalism. Town Plan. Rev. 80 (6), 551–574.

Beatley, T. (Ed.), 2012. Green Cities of Europe: Global Lessons on Green Urbanism. Island Press, Washington, DC.

Belissent, J., Mines, C., Radcliffe, E., and Darashkevich, Y. (2010). Getting Clever About Smart Cities: New Opportunities Require New Business Models. White Paper. Forrester Research. http://www.forrester.com/Getting+Clever+About+Smart+Cities+New+Opportunities+Require+New+Business+Models/fulltext/-/E-RES56701. Accessed 30.03.2012.

Benevolo, L., 1993. The European City. Blackwell Publishing Ltd, Oxford.

Bolici, R., Mora, L., 2015. Urban regeneration in the digital era: how to develop smart city strategies in large European cities. TECHNE: J. Technol. Archit. Environ. 5 (2), 110–119.

Brisbane City Council, 2001. Living in Brisbane 2010. Brisbane City Council. http: //www.birsbane.qld.gov.au/council_at_work/planning/brisbane_2010/index.shtml. (Accessed October 7, 2002).

Broadus, R., 1987. Toward a definition of bibliometrics. Scientometrics 12 (5–6), 373–379.

Caragliu, A., Del Bo, C., and Nijkamp, P. (2009). Smart Cities in Europe. Paper presented at 3rd Central European Conference in Regional Science, Kosice, 7-9 October 2009. http://www.inta-aivn.org/images/cc/Urbanism/background%20documents/01_03_Nijkamp.pdf. Accessed 29.12.2012.

Caragliu, A., Del Bo, C., Nijkamp, P., 2011. Smart cities in Europe. J. Urban Technol. 18 (2), 65–82.

Casillas, J., Acedo, F., 2007. Evolution of the intellectual structure of family business literature: a bibliometric study of FBR. Fam. Bus. Rev. 20 (2), 141–162.

Castells, J., 2004. Space of flows, space of places: materials for a theory of urbanism in the information age. In: Graham, S. (Ed.), The Cybercities Reader. Routledge, New York, United States, pp. 82–93.

Castells, M., 1989. The Informational City: Economic Restructuring and Urban Development. Balckwell Publishing Ltd, Oxford, United Kingdom.

Castells, M., 1996. The Rise of the Network Society. Blackwell Publishing Ltd, Oxford.

Chang, I.C., Sheppard, E., 2013. China's eco-cities as variegated urban sustainability: Dongtan eco-city and chongming eco-island. J. Urban Technol. 20 (1), 57–75.

Chourabi, H., Nam, T., Walker, S., Gil-Garcia, R.J., Mellouli, S., Nahon, K., Pardo, T.A., Scholl, H.J., 2012. Understanding smart cities: an integrative framework. In: Sprague, R.H. (Ed.), Proceedings of the 45th Hawaii International Conference on System Sciences (HICSS), Maui, HI, 04–07 January 2012. Institute of Electrical and Electronics Engineers (IEEE), Piscataway, NJ, pp. 2289–2297.

Christopoulou, E., Ringas, D., Garofalakis, J., 2014. The vision of the sociable smart city. In: Streitz, N., Markopoulos, P. (Eds.), Distributed, Ambient, and Pervasive Interactions: Second International Conference, DAPI 2014, Held as Part of HCI International 2014, Heraklion, Crete, Greece, June 22–27, 2014. Proceedings. Springer, Berlin, pp. 545–554.

Cocchia, A., Dameri, P., 2016. Exploring smart city vision by university, industry and government. In: D'Ascenzo, F., Magni, M., Lazazzara, A., Za, S. (Eds.), Blurring the Boundaries Through Digital Innovation: Individual, Organizational, and Societal Challenges. Springer, Berlin, pp. 259–270.

Coe, A., Paquet, G., Roy, J., 2001. E-governance and smart communities: a social learning challenge. Soc. Sci. Comput. Rev. 19 (1), 80–93.

Colledge, L., Verlinde, R., 2014. SciVal Metrics Guidebook. Elsevier. https://www.elsevier.com/__data/assets/pdf_file/0020/53327/scival-metrics-guidebook-v1_01-february2014.pdf. (Accessed January 15, 2017).

Concilio, G., Rizzo, F. (Eds.), 2016. Human Smart Cities: Rethinking the Interplay Between Design and Planning. Springer, Cham.

Curwell, S., Deakin, M., Cooper, I., Paskaleva, K., Ravetz, J., Babicki, D., 2005. Citizens' expectations of information cities: implications for urban planning and design. Build. Res. Inf. 33 (1), 55–66.

De Bellis, N., 2009. Bibliometrics and Citation Analysis: From the Science Citation Index to Cybermetrics. The Scarecrow Press, Lanham, MD.

de Jong, M., Joss, S., Schraven, D., Zhan, C., Weijnen, M., 2015. Sustainable-smart-resilient-low carbon-eco-knowledge cities; making sense of a multitude of concepts promoting sustainable urbanization. J. Clean. Prod. 109, 25–38.

Deakin, M. (Ed.), 2014. Smart Cities: Governing, Modelling and Analysing the Transition. Routledge, New York City, NY.

Deakin, M., Al Wear, H., 2011. From intelligent to smart cities. Intell. Build. Int. 3 (3), 140–152.

Deakin, M., Leydesdorff, L., 2014. The triple helix model of smart cities: a neo-evolutionary perspective. In: Deakin, M. (Ed.), Smart Cities: Governing, Modelling and Analyzing the Transition. Routledge, New York, NY, pp. 134–149.

Desouza, K.C., Flanery, T.H., 2013. Designing, planning, and managing resilient cities: a conceptual framework. Cities: Int. J. Urban Policy Plan. 35, 89–99.

Ding, Y., Chowdhury, G.G., Foo, S., 2001. Bibliometric cartography of information retrieval research by using co-word analysis. Inf. Process. Manag. 37 (6), 817–842.

Dirks, S., and Keeling, M. (2009). A Vision of Smarter Cities: How Cities Can Lead the Way Into a Prosperous and Sustainable Future. Executive Report. IBM Corporation. http://www-03.ibm.com/press/attachments/IBV_Smarter_Cities_-_Final.pdf. Accessed 03.02.2012.

Dirks, S., Gurdgiev, C., and Keeling, M. (2010). Smarter Cities for Smarter Growth: How Cities Can Optimize Their Systems for the Talent-based Economy. Executive Report. IBM Corporation. http://public.dhe.ibm.com/common/ssi/ecm/en/gbe03348usen/GBE03348USEN.PDF. Accessed 03.02.2012.

Dirks, S., Keeling, M., and Dencik, J. (2009). How Smart Is Your City: Helping Cities Measure Progress. Executive Report. IBM Corporation. http://public.dhe.ibm.com/common/ssi/ecm/en/gbe03248usen/GBE03248USEN.PDF. Accessed 06.06.2014.

Durán-Sánchez, A., de la Cruz del Río-Rama, M., Sereno-Ramírez, A., Bredis, K., 2017. Sustainability and quality of life in smart cities: analysis of scientific production. In: Peris-Ortiz, M., Bennett, D.R., Pérez-Bustamante Yábar, D. (Eds.), Sustainable Smart Cities: Creating Spaces for Technological, Social and Business Development. Springer, Cham, pp. 159–181.

Fernandez-Anez, V., 2016. Stakeholders approach to smart cities: a survey on smart city definitions. In: Alba, E., Chicano, F., Luque, G. (Eds.), Smart Cities. First International Conference, Smart-CT 2016, Málaga, Spain, June 15–17, 2016, Proceedings. Springer, Berlin, pp. 157–167.

Firmino, R. J. (2003). Defining and Understanding the Virtual Cities Phenomenon: Briefing Document. Briefing Document. University of Salford. https://www.academia.edu/977988/Defining_and_understanding_the_virtual_cities_phenomenon_Briefing_document. Accessed 03.10.2012.

Fraser, B., 2015. Digital Cities: The Interdisciplinary Future of the Urban Geo-Humanities. Palgrave Macmillan, Basingstoke.

Fruchterman, T.M.J., Reingold, E.M., 1991. Graph drawing by force-directed placement. Softw. Pract. Exp. 21 (11), 1129–1164.

Garfield, E., 1970. Citation indexing for studying science. Inf. Sci. 1 (15), 133–138.

Gibson, D.V., Kozmetsky, G., Smilor, R.W. (Eds.), 1992. The Technopolis Phenomenon: Smart Cities, Fast Systems, Global Networks. Rowman & Littlefield Publishers, Lanham, MD.

Giffinger, R., Ferter, C., Kramar, H., Kalasek, R., Pichler-Milanović, N., and Meijers, E. (2007). Smart Cities: Ranking of European Medium-sized Cities. Research Report. Vienna University of Technology—Centre of Regional Science (SRF). http://www.smart-cities.eu/download/smart_cities_final_report.pdf. Accessed 09.05.2012.

Godin, B., 2006. On the origins of bibliometrics. Scientometrics 68 (1), 109–133.

Graham, S., 1997. Telecommunications and the future of cities: debunking the myths. Cities: Int. J. Urban Policy Plan. 14 (1), 21–29.

Graham, S., 2000. Introduction: cities and infrastructure networks. Int. J. Urban Reg. Res. 24 (1), 114–119.

Graham, S., 2001. Information technologies and reconfigurations of urban spaces. Int. J. Urban Reg. Res. 25 (2), 405–410.

Graham, S., 2002. Bridging urban digital divides? Urban polarisation and information and communications technologies (ICTs). Urban Stud. 39 (1), 33–56.

Graham, S. (Ed.), 2004. The Cybercities Reader. Routledge, New York City, NY.

Graham, S., Marvin, S., 1996. Telecommunications and the City: Electronic Spaces, Urban Places. Routledge, New York City, NY.

Graham, S., Marvin, S., 1999. Planning cyber-cities? integrating telecommunications into urban planning. Town Plan. Rev. 70 (1), 89–114.

Graham, S., Marvin, S., 2001. Splintering Urbanism: Networked Infrastructures, Technological Mobilities and the Urban Condition. Routledge, New York City, NY.

Graham, S., Marvin, S., 2004. Planning cyber-cities? Integrating telecommunications into urban planning. In: Graham, S. (Ed.), The Cybercities Reader. Routledge, New York City, NY, pp. 341–347.

Greco, I., Cresta, A., 2015. A smart planning for smart city: the concept of smart city as an opportunity to re-think the planning models of the contemporary city. In: Gervasi, O., Murgante, B., Misra, S., Gavrilova, M.L., Rocha, A.M.A.C., Torre, C., Taniar, D., Apduhan, B.O. (Eds.), Computational Science and Its Applications—ICCSA 2015: 15th International Conference, Banff, AB, Canada, June 22–25, 2015, Proceedings, Part II. Springer, Berlin, pp. 563–576.

Hall, R. E., Bowerman, B., Braverman, J., Taylor, J., Todosow, H., and von Wimmersperg, U. (2000). The Vision of a Smart City. Paper Presented at 2nd International Life Extension Technology Workshop, Paris, 28 September 2000. http://www.osti.gov/scitech/servlets/purl/773961. Accessed 16.10.2014.

Hemment, D., Townsend, A. (Eds.), 2013. Smart Citizens. FutureEverything, Manchester.

Hernández-Muñoz, J.M., Bernat Vercher, J., Muñoz, L., Galache, J.A., Presser, M., Hernández Gómez, L.A., Pettersson, J., 2011. Smart cities at the forefront of the future Internet. In: Domingue, J., Galis, A., Gavras, A., Zahariadis, T., Lambert, D., Cleary, F., Daras, P., Krco, S., Muller, H., Li, M., Schaffers, H., Lotz, V., Alvarez, F., Stiller, B., Karnouskos, S., Avessta, S., Nillson, M. (Eds.), The Future Internet. Future Internet Assembly 2011: Achievements and Technological Promises. Springer, Berlin, pp. 447–462.

Hollands, R.G., 2008. Will the real smart city please stand up? City: Anal. Urban Trends Cult. Theory Policy Action 12 (3), 303–320.

Hollands, R.G., 2015. Critical interventions into the corporate smart city. Camb. J. Reg. Econ. Soc. 8 (1), 61–77.

Hollands, R.G., 2016. Beyond the corporate smart city? Glimpses of other possibilities of smartness. In: Marvin, S., Luque-Ayala, A., McFarlane, C. (Eds.), Smart Urbanism: Utopian Vision or False Dawn? Routledge, New York City, NY, pp. 168–184.

Hutton, G. R. (2009). Scientific Grey Literature in a Digital Age: Measuring its Use and Influence in an Evolving Information Economy. Paper presented at 37th Annual Conference of the Canadian Association of Information Science & Inaugural Librarians' Research Institute Symposium. Mapping the 21st Century Information Landscape: Borders, Bridges and Byways, Ottawa, 28–30 May 2009. http://www.cais-acsi.ca/ojs/index.php/cais/article/viewFile/126/518. Accessed 19.11.2013.

Ingwersen, P., Larsen, B., Garcia-Zorita, J.C., Serrano-Lopez, A.E., Sanz-Casado, E., 2014. Influence of proceedings papers on citation impact in seven sub-fields of sustainable energy research 2005–2011. Scientometrics 101 (2), 1273–1292.

Jacobs, J., 1961. The Death and Life of Great American Cities. Random House, New York City, NY.

Jacobsen, T., Punzalan, R.L., Hedstrom, M.L., 2013. Invoking collective memory: mapping the emergence of a concept in archival science. Arch. Sci. 13 (2-3), 217–251.

Kamalski, J., Kirby, A., 2012. Bibliometrics and Urban Knowledge Transfer. Cities: Int. J. Urban Policy Plan. 29 (Supplement 2), S3–S8.

Karnouskos, S., Nass de Holanda, T., 2009. Simulation of a smart grid city with software agents. In: EMS '09: Third UKSim European Symposium on Computer Modeling and Simulation, Athens, 25-27 November 2009. Institute of Electrical and Electronics Engineers (IEEE), Piscataway, NJ, pp. 424–429.

Kitchin, R., 2014. The real-time city? Big data and smart urbanism. GeoJournal 79 (1), 1–14.

Komninos, N., 2002. Intelligent Cities: Innovation, Knowledge, Systems and Digital Spaces. Spon Press, New York City, NY.

Komninos, N., 2006. The architecture of intelligent cities: integrating human, collective and artificial intelligence to enhance knowledge. In: Proceedings of the 2nd IET International Conference on Intelligent Environments, Athens, 05–06 July 2006. Page Bros Ltd, Norwich, pp. 13–20.

Komninos, N., 2008. Intelligent Cities and Globalization of Innovation Networks. Routledge, New York City, NY.

Komninos, N., 2014. The Age of Intelligent Cities: Smart Environments and Innovation-For-All Strategies. Routledge, New York City, NY.

Lazaroiu, G.C., Roscia, M., 2012. Definition methodology for the smart cities model. Energy 47 (1), 326–332.

Lee, J., Hancock, M.G., Hu, M., 2014. Towards an effective framework for building smart cities: lessons from Seoul and San Francisco. Technol. Forecast. Soc. Chang. 89, 80–99.

Liu, Z., 2005. Visualizing the intellectual structure in urban studies: a journal co-citation analysis (1992–2002). Scientometrics 62 (3), 385–402.

Lu, S., 2011. The smart city's systematic application and implementation in China. In: 2011 International Conference on Business Management and Electronic Information (BMEI), Guangzhou, 13–15 May 2011. Institute of Electrical and Electronics Engineers (IEEE), Piscataway, NJ, pp. 116–120.

Marsal-Llacuna, M., Colomer-Llinàs, J., Meléndez-Frigola, J., 2015. Lessons in urban monitoring taken from sustainable and livable cities to better address the smart cities initiative. Technol. Forecast. Soc. Chang. 90, 611–622.

Martin, H., Daim, T., 2008. Technology roadmapping through intelligence analysis: case of nanotechnology. Int. J. Soc. Syst. Sci. 1 (1), 49–65.

Meijer, A., Bolivar, M.P.R., 2016. Governing the smart city: a review of the literature on smart urban governance. Int. Rev. Adm. Sci. 82 (2), 392–408.

Mitchell, W.J., 1995. The City of Bits: Space, Place, and the Infobahn. MIT Press, Cambridge, MA.

Mitchell, W.J., 1999. E-topia: Urban Life, Jim—But Not as We Know It. MIT Press, Cambridge, MA.

Mitchell, W.J., 2000. Designing the digital city. In: Ishida, T., Isbister, K. (Eds.), Digital Cities: Technologies, Experiences and Future Perspectives. Springer, Berlin, pp. 1–6.

Mitchell, W.J., 2003. Me++: The Cyborg Self and the Networked City. MIT Press, Cambridge, MA.

Mora, L., Bolici, R., 2016. The development process of smart city strategies: the case of Barcelona. In: Rajaniemi, J. (Ed.), Re-city: Future City—Combining Disciplines. Juvenes Print, Tampere, pp. 155–181.

Mora, L., Bolici, R., 2017. How to become a smart city: learning from Amsterdam. In: Bisello, A., Vettorato, D., Stephens, R., Elisei, P. (Eds.), Smart and Sustainable Planning for Cities and Regions: Results of SSPCR 2015. Springer, Cham, pp. 251–266.

Mora, L., Deakin, M., Reid, A., Angelidou, M., 2018. How to overcome the dichotomous nature of smart city research: proposed methodology and results of a pilot study. J. Urban Technol. https://doi.org/10.1080/10630732.2018.1525265.

Moss Kanter, R., and Litow, S. S. (2009). Informed and Interconnected: A Manifesto for Smarter Cities. Working Paper. Harvard Business School. http://www.hbs.edu/faculty/Publication%20 Files/09-141.pdf. Accessed 24.01.2012.

Moya-Anegon, F., Vargas-Quesada, B., Herrero-Solana, V., Chinchilla-Rodriguez, Z., Corera-Alvarez, E., Munoz-Fernandez, F.J., 2004. A new technique for building maps of large scientific domains based on the cocitation of classes and categories. Scientometrics 61 (1), 129–145.

Nam, T., Pardo, T.A., 2011a. Conceptualizing smart city with dimensions of technology, people and institutions. In: Bertot, J., Nahon, K., Chun, S.A., Luna-Reyes, L., Atluri, V. (Eds.), Proceedings of the 12th Annual International Conference on Digital Government Research: Digital Government Innovation in Challenging Times, College Park, MD, 12–15 June 2011. ACM Press, New York City, NY, pp. 282–291.

Nam, T., Pardo, T.A., 2011b. Smart city as urban innovation: focusing on management, policy, and context. In: Estevez, E., Janssen, M. (Eds.), Proceedings of the 5th International Conference on Theory and Practice of Electronic Governance (ICEGOV2011), Tallinn, 26–28 September 2011. ACM Press, New York City, NY, pp. 185–194.

Naphade, M., Banavar, G., Harrison, C., Paraszczak, J., Morris, R., 2011. Smarter cities and their innovation challenges. Computer 44 (6), 32–39.

Odendaal, N., 2003. Information and communication technology and local governance: understanding the difference between cities in developed and emerging economies. Comput. Environ. Urban. Syst. 27 (6), 585–607.

Ojo, A., Dzhusupova, Z., Curry, E., 2016. Exploring the nature of the smart cities research landscape. In: Gil-Garcia, J.R., Pardo, T.A., Nam, T. (Eds.), Smarter as the New Urban Agenda: A Comprehensive View of the 21st Century City. Springer, Cham, pp. 23–47.

Oliver, N., 2011. Urban computing and smart cities: opportunities and challenges in modelling large-scale aggregated human behavior. In: Salah, A.A., Lepri, B. (Eds.), Human Behavior Understanding: Second International Workshop, HBU 2011, Amsterdam, the Netherlands, November 16, 2011. Proceedings. Springer, Cham, pp. 16–17.

Paroutis, S., Bennett, M., Heracleous, L., 2014. A strategic view on smart city technology: the case of IBM smarter cities during a recession. Technol. Forecast. Soc. Chang. 89, 262–272.

Partridge, H. (2004). Developing a Human Perspective to the Digital Divide in the Smart City. Paper Presented at ALIA 2004 Biennial Conference: Challenging Ideas, Gold Coast, 21-24 September 2004. http://eprints.qut.edu.au/1299/1/partridge.h.2.paper.pdf. Accessed 16.09.2014.

Paskaleva, K.A., 2009. Enabling the smart city: the progress of city E-governance in Europe. Int. J. Innov. Reg. Dev. 1 (4), 405–422.

Paskaleva, K.A., 2011. The smart city: a Nexus for open innovation? Intell. Build. Int. 3 (3), 133–152.

Pritchard, A., 1969. Statistical bibliography or bibliometrics? J. Doc. 25 (4), 348–349.
Ricciardi, F., Za, S., 2015. Smart city research as an interdisciplinary crossroads: a challenge for management and organization studies. In: Mola, L., Pennarola, F., Za, S. (Eds.), From Information to Smart Society: Environment, Politics and Economics. Springer, Cham, pp. 163–171.
Schaffers, H., Komninos, N., Pallot, M., Aguas, M., Almirall, E., Bakici, T., Barroca, J., Carter, D., Corriou, M., Fernadez, J., Hielkema, H., Kivilehto, A., Nilsson, M., Oliveira, A., Posio, E., Sällström, A., Santoro, R., Senach, B., Torres, I., Tsarchopoulos, P., Trousse, B., Turkama, P., and Lopez Ventura, J. (2012). Smart Cities as Innovation Ecosystems Sustained by the Future Internet. White Paper. http://hal.archives-ouvertes.fr/docs/00/76/96/35/PDF/FIREBALL-White-Paper-Final2.pdf. Accessed 24.08.2011.
Schaffers, H., Komninos, N., Pallot, M., Trousse, B., Nilsson, M., Oliveira, A., 2011. Smart cities and the future Internet: towards cooperation frameworks for open innovation. In: Domingue, J., Galis, A., Gavras, A., Zahariadis, T., Lambert, D., Cleary, F., Daras, P., Krco, S., Muller, H., Li, M., Schaffers, H., Lotz, V., Alvarez, F., Stiller, B., Karnouskos, S., Avessta, S., Nillson, M. (Eds.), The Future Internet. Future Internet Assembly 2011: Achievements and Technological Promises. Springer, Berlin, pp. 431–446.
Schneider, J.W., Larsen, B., Ingwersen, P., 2009. A comparative study of first and all-author co-citation counting, and two different matrix generation approaches applied for author co-citation analyses. Scientometrics 80 (1), 1053–1320.
Schopfel, J., 2010. Towards a Prague definition of grey literature. In: Farace, D.J., Fratzen, J. (Eds.), Twelfth International Conference on Grey Literature: Transparency in Grey Literature. Grey Tech Approaches to High Tech Issues, Prague, 6–7 December 2010. TextRelease, Amsterdam, pp. 11–26.
Schopfel, J., Farace, D.J., 2010. Grey literature. In: Bates, M.J., Maack, M.N. (Eds.), Encyclopedia of Library and Information Sciences. Taylor & Francis, New York City, NY, pp. 2029–2039.
Secchi, B., 2011. La Città Del Ventesimo Secolo, fifth ed. Laterza, Bari.
Shapiro, J. M. (2005). Smart Cities: Quality of Life, Productivity, and the Growth Effects of Human Capital. Working Paper. National Bureau of Economic Research. http://www.nber.org/papers/w11615. Accessed 21.02.2011.
Shen, J., Liu, D., Shen, J., Liu, Q., Sun, X., 2017. A secure cloud-assisted urban data sharing framework for ubiquitous-cities. Pervasive Mob. Comput. 41, 219–230.
Shiau, W., Dwivedi, Y.K., 2013. Citation and co-citation analysis to identify core and emerging knowledge in electronic commerce research. Scientometrics 94 (3), 1317–1337.
Small, H.G., 1973. Co-citation in the scientific literature: a new measure of the relationship between two documents. J. Am. Soc. Inf. Sci. Technol. 24 (4), 265–269.
Small, H.G., 1978. Cited documents as concept symbols. Soc. Stud. Sci. 8 (3), 327–340.
Small, H.G., Crane, D., 1979. Specialties and disciplines in science and social science: an examination of their structure using citation indexes. Scientometrics 1 (5-6), 445–461.
Small, H.G., Griffith, B.C., 1974. The structure of scientific literature I: identifying and graphing specialties. Sci. Stud. 4 (1), 17–40.
Soderstrom, O., Paasche, T., Klauser, F., 2014. Smart cities as corporate storytelling. City: Anal. Urban Trends Cult. Theory Policy Action 18 (3), 307–320.
Tamai, H., 2014. Fujitsu's approach to smart cities. FUJITSU Sci. Techn. J. 50 (2), 3–10.
The Climate Group (2008). SMART 2020: Enabling the Low Carbon Economy in the Information Age. Report. The Climate Group. http://www.smart2020.org/_assets/files/02_Smart2020Report.pdf. Accessed 05.06.2014.

Tijssen, R. J. W., and van Leeuwen, T. N. (2003). Extended Technical Annex to Chapter 5 of the 'Third European Report on S&T Indicators': Bibliometric Analyses of World Science. Research Report. Leiden University. ftp://ftp.cordis.europa.eu/pub/indicators/docs/3rd_report_biblio_ext_methodology.pdf. Accessed 13.06.2014.

Townsend, A., 2013. Smart Cities: Big Data, Civic Hackers, and the Quest for a New Utopia. W.W. Norton & Company Ltd, New York City, NY.

Tregua, M., D'Auria, A., Bifulco, F., 2015. Comparing research streams on smart city and sustainable city. China-USA Bus. Rev. 14 (4), 203–215.

Urzaiz, G., Hervas, R., Fontecha, J., Bravo, J., 2014. A high-level model for a healthy smart city. In: Pecchia, L., Luke Chen, L., Nugent, C., Bravo, J. (Eds.), Ambient Assisted Living and Daily Activities: 6th International Work-Conference, IWAAL 2014, Belfast, UK, December 2–5, 2014. Proceedings. Springer, Berlin, pp. 386–389.

Vassilaras, S., Yovanof, G.S., 2010. Wireless innovations as enablers for complex & dynamic artificial systems. Wirel. Pers. Commun. 53 (3), 365–393.

Voytenko, Y., McCormick, K., Evans, J., Schliwa, G., 2016. Urban living labs for sustainability and low carbon cities in Europe: towards a research agenda. J. Clean. Prod. 123, 45–54.

Washburn, D., Usman, S., Balaouras, S., Dines, R. A., Hayes, N. M., and Nelson, L. E. (2010). Helping CIOs Understand "Smart City" Initiatives. White Paper. Forrester Research. http://www.forrester.com/Helping+CIOs+Understand+Smart+City+Initiatives/quickscan/-/E-RES55590. Accessed 20.03.2012.

Yigitcanlar, T., Lee, S.H., 2014. Korean ubiquitous-eco-city: a smart-sustainable urban form or a branding Hoax? Technol. Forecast. Soc. Change 89, 100–114.

Yigitcanlar, T., O'Connor, K., Westerman, C., 2008. The making of knowledge cities: melbourne's knowledge-based urban development experience. Cities 25 (2), 63–72.

Zhao, Y., Cui, L., Yang, H., 2009. Evaluating reliability of co-citation clustering analysis in representing the research history of subject. Scientometrics 80 (1), 91–102.

Zhou, N., He, G., Williams, C., Fridley, D., 2015. ELITE cities: a low-carbon eco-city evaluation tool for China. Ecol. Indic. 48, 448–456.

Zygiaris, S., 2013. Smart city reference model: assisting planners to conceptualize the building of smart city innovation ecosystems. J. Knowl. Econ. 4 (2), 217–231.

Chapter 4

Revealing the main development paths of smart cities

Chapter outline

4.1 Introduction

This chapter reports on a second bibliometric study in which two hybrid techniques combining citation link-based clustering and text-based analysis (Braam et al., 1991a,b; Glanzel and Czerwon, 1996; Glanzel and Thijs, 2011; Meyer et al., 2014) are deployed to capture the structural division affecting the smart city research field.[1] Such a division is discussed in research by Albino et al. (2015),

1. This chapter is reprinted from Technological Forecasting and Social Change, Volume 142, Mora, L., Deakin, M., and Reid, A., Combining co-citation clustering and text-based analysis to reveal the main development paths of smart cities, 56–69, 2019, with permission from Elsevier. The contents of the article have not been altered but adapted minimally to serve the purpose of this book.

Untangling Smart Cities. https://doi.org/10.1016/B978-0-12-815477-9.00004-9

Alkandari et al. (2012), Chourabi et al. (2012), Hollands (2008), Paskaleva (2011), Nam and Pardo (2011a,b), and Meijer and Bolivar (2016), who all point out the lack of agreement on what needs to be done in order to make a city smart. Evidence of this situation is also provided in the previous chapter, where the results of the first bibliometric analysis reveal that the disagreement in the ways of conceptualizing smart city development is caused by the lack of intellectual exchange among smart city researchers and their tendency to be subjective and follow personal trajectories in isolation from one another.

These subjective, personal, and isolated interpretations fall short in providing both a clear understanding of smart cities and the scientific knowledge that policymakers and practitioners require to deal effectively with their progressive development. In addition, as previously observed, this division is now so firmly established within the scientific community that has resulted in different development paths, which have grown in parallel. This bibliometric study aims at mapping and analyzing these paths, making them visible and understandable within the big picture of smart city research. This provides the community of smart city researchers with (1) a comprehensive and systematic view of how smart city development is understood and (2) the knowledge necessary to start building a possible agreement concerning the way of thinking about smart city development and enabling the ICT-driven approach to urban sustainability it promotes.

This aim is achieved by continue focusing attention on the first two decades of research on smart city development and the large body of literature produced during such a period, which is analyzed to (1) build and visualize the network of publications shaping the intellectual structure of the smart city research field, (2) map the clusters of thematically related publications, and (3) reveal the main development paths of smart cities that each thematic cluster supports and the strategic principles they embody.

The methodology applied to conduct the bibliometric analysis is illustrated in the third section of the chapter (Section 4.3), which is anticipated by a short description of the rationale that stands behind the two hybrid techniques that are used and the need for combining co-citation clustering and text-based analysis in bibliometric studies (Section 4.2). The analysis further reveals the division affecting the smart city research field and uncovers five main development paths, which are presented in Section 4.4. The main strategic principles describing how to approach smart city development that each path proposes are then compared in Section 4.5 by reviewing the literature on smart city development that has been produced during and after the period under investigation. Four main dichotomies emerge from this comparison, along with a set of unanswered research questions.

4.2 Hybrid techniques for thematic cluster analysis

As observed in the previous chapter, bibliometrics makes it possible to outline complex knowledge maps representing the intellectual structure of research fields and investigate their properties. These maps are complex networks in which large groups of individual words, authors, documents, journals, or subject categories become interconnected nodes[2] (Pritchard, 1969; De Bellis, 2009; Ding et al., 2001; Godin, 2006) and their analysis provides information on "how specific [...] research fields are conceptually, intellectually, and socially structured" (Cobo et al., 2011: 1382). The degree of connection between each couple of nodes depends upon their degree of similarity, which can be measured by using co-citation analysis or co-word analysis, two bibliometric techniques that involve counting the number of times certain elements co-occur in the group of publications composing the research field under investigation (He, 1999; Glanzel and Thijs, 2011).[3]

Co-citation analyses are based on the relevance of citations, a reliable indicator of scientific communication that can be used to measure the interaction and impact of authors, publications, institutions, subject areas, and academic disciplines. By means of citations, researchers can incorporate intellectual work from other studies into their own research (Garfield, 1970, 1979a,b; Small, 1973, 1978; Small and Griffith, 1974; Jacobsen et al., 2013; Gmur, 2003). When performing a co-citation analysis, different units of analysis can be considered: documents (Jacobsen et al., 2013; Zhao et al., 2009), authors (McCain, 1986, 1990; White, 1990), journals (Ding et al., 2000; Liu, 2005; McCain, 1991; Tsay et al., 2003), or subject categories (Leydesdorff and Rafols, 2009).

In a document co-citation analysis, starting from a group of scientific publications, a co-citation exists when two references appear together in the same publication. The number of co-citations defines the similarity between two documents in terms of cognitive proximity and contents (Gmur, 2003; Small, 1973). This means that the more co-citations two documents have in common, the higher their degree of similarity. By considering the proximity between each couple of publications belonging to the initial sample, different subgroups of scientific documents can be identified. These subgroups can be considered as thematic clusters and can be used to map out the relationship among the main subject areas and lines of discussion shaping the intellectual structure of a specific research field (Kovács et al., 2015; De Bellis, 2009).

The same outcome can be achieved by using co-word analysis, a content analysis technique in which the strength of interrelationship between scientific publications is measured by comparing the words included in their full text instead of the references they cite (Callon et al., 1983, 1986, 1991; He, 1999).

---

2. Examples of knowledge maps can be found in research by Ding et al. (2001), Leydesdorff and Rafols (2009), Zhao et al. (2009), Heersmink et al. (2011), Leydesdorff et al. (2011), Liu et al. (2012), Jacobsen et al. (2013), Hashem et al. (2016), Randhawa et al. (2016), Reyes-Gonzalez et al. (2016), Song et al. (2016), Wang et al. (2016), and Zhu and Hua (2017).

3. Co-citation analysis and co-word analysis have different theoretical foundations, and both of them have their own strengths and weaknesses, some of which are discussed in research by King (1987), MacRoberts and MacRoberts (1989), Leydesdorff (1997), Adam (2002), and Glanzel and Thijs (2011).

By measuring the co-occurrence of pairs of either single terms or phrases in publications representative of a research field, this technique makes it possible to define the proximity of these documents and divide them into thematic clusters. As with co-citations, each cluster contributes to identifying trends and emerging subject areas within a narrowly defined field of study (Ding et al., 2001; Heersmink et al., 2011; Liu et al., 2012).

Unfortunately, when compared with knowledge mapping techniques based on textual data, the co-citation analysis appears limited, because it "does not provide an immediate picture of the actual content of the research topics dealt with in the literature" belonging to a thematic cluster (Ding et al., 2001:818). In response to this limitation, two hybrid techniques have been developed and tested in which clusters obtained from a document co-citation analysis are labeled using textual components in order to describe research fields in both structural and semantic terms. The first technique is proposed by Braam et al. (1991a,b) and is based on the following assumption: "if publications sharing citations to documents within the same co-citation cluster [...] represent the current work of a research specialty, then these (citing) publications are cognitively related and, as a consequence, are expected to contain [...] the same content-related words. Thus, topics involved in a particular research specialty can be indicated by aggregating and listing these words, together with their frequency of occurrence for the set of citing publications of each cluster. In this way a cluster word profile can be constructed that represents the research topics involved in the current work of a specialty indicated by the cluster" (Braam et al., 1991a: 236). As Braam et al. (1991a,b) also note, the words needed to make up the profiles can be extracted from titles, lists of keywords, abstracts, full texts, indexed terms, and classification codes.

The second hybrid technique combining citation link-based clustering and text-based research is provided by Glanzel and Czerwon (1996) and is related to the concept of "core document" (Glanzel and Thijs, 2011). In a thematic cluster, core documents are the publications with the highest centrality, which is expressed by the number of connections that they have with other publications belonging to the same cluster (Glanzel and Thijs, 2011; Glanzel and Czerwon, 1996; Meyer et al., 2014). "Since core documents are, by definition, strongly linked with a large number of other documents," they can be considered as the most representative publications of a thematic cluster and "are expected to form the very cognitive nodes" (Meyer et al., 2014: 477). According to this technique, the content analysis of thematic clusters can be undertaken by conducting a document co-citation clustering analysis and then labeling the resulted thematic clusters by directly using bibliographic data extracted from their core documents. This includes, for example, their titles, list of keywords, authors' names, and abstracts (Glanzel and Czerwon, 1996; Glanzel and Thijs, 2011; Meyer et al., 2014; Chi and Young, 2013).

4.3 Research methodology and results of the data processing phase

This bibliometric study combines the two hybrid techniques previously described to (1) analyze the overall intellectual structure of the smart city research field, by considering the first two decades of research conducted into this subject, and (2) identify the main development paths of smart cities that such a research promotes. This structure is outlined, graphically visualized, and then split into subgroups of publications by conducting a document co-citation clustering analysis. The result is a co-citation network in which 2273 publications are divided into 18 thematic clusters. After tracing the network of relationships between these publications, a description of the development paths supported by the most representative thematic clusters is provided based on both the identification of their core literature and the construction of word profiles.

The data for conducting the co-citation analysis was collected by manually extracting the lists of cited references from the 1067 source documents used to run the first bibliometric study. Altogether, 22,137 citations were collected and used to build a frequency table showing the cited publications and the number of citations that each of them received. The total number of cited references is 17,574. A co-citation network was then built by considering only the references with at least two citations. The network is composed of 45,534 edges connecting 2273 nodes of which only 124 are source documents. The edges' weight was measured by using the CoCit-Score, which had been calculated according to the formula proposed by Allmayer and Winkler (2013) and Gmur (2003)[4]:

$$\mathbf{CoCit}_{AB} = \frac{\left(\text{Co-citation}_{AB}\right)^2}{\text{minimum}\left(\text{citation}_A;\text{citation}_B\right)\times\text{meanvalue}\left(\text{citation}_A;\text{citation}_B\right)}$$

The nodes and edges with their weight were then entered into the open source software Gephi, and the co-citation network was graphically visualized by using the OpenOrd layout algorithm (Bastian et al., 2009). The result was an undirected and weighted network that was subsequently split into thematic clusters by using Blondel et al.'s (2008) clustering algorithm. The thematic clusters represent groups of densely connected publications that support the different development paths of smart cities that this study aims to identify and compare.

4. Co-citation networks are composed of two elements: (1) the nodes, which correspond to the cited references extracted from the source documents, and (2) the edges connecting the references that are co-cited in the same source document. The weight of an edge linking two nodes depends on their degree of textual similarity. More often two documents are co-cited, more similar they are in terms of content and, therefore, the higher their level of proximity is. The weights can be calculated using several approaches, but research by Gmur (2003) shows that the CoCit-Score is the most suitable method for clustering references and analyzing the intellectual structure of research fields.

The results obtained through the data processing are summarized in Figs. 4.1 and 4.2, and displayed in Fig. 4.3, which provides a graphic representation of the co-citation network. Within the network, each publication is shown as a node whose size is proportional to its degree of centrality. This attribute was calculated by adding up the number of times the publication has been co-cited.

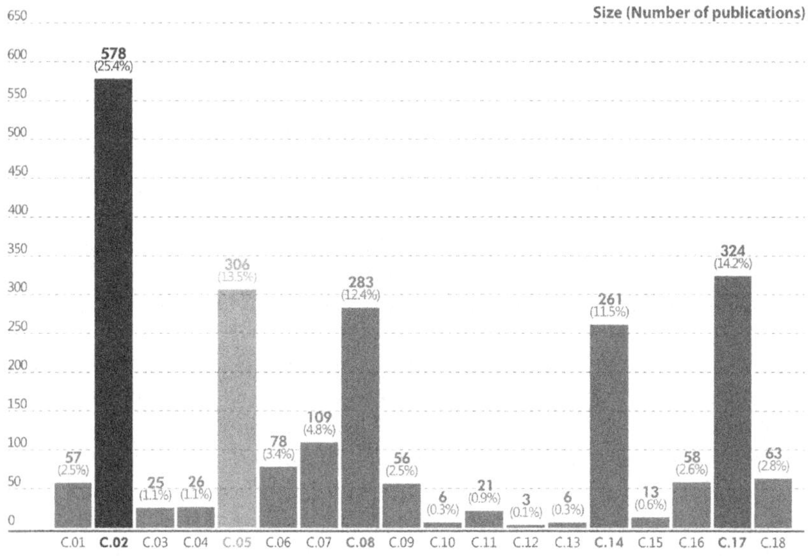

FIG. 4.1 Thematic clusters: size.

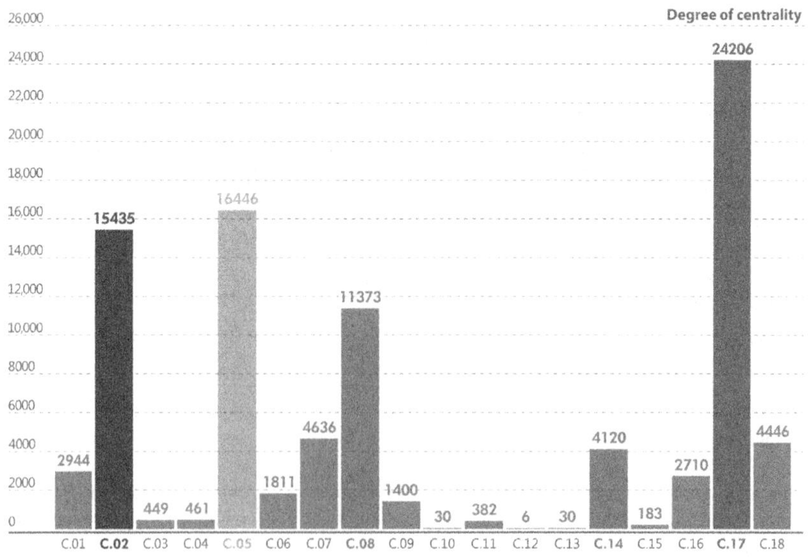

FIG. 4.2 Thematic clusters: degree of centrality.

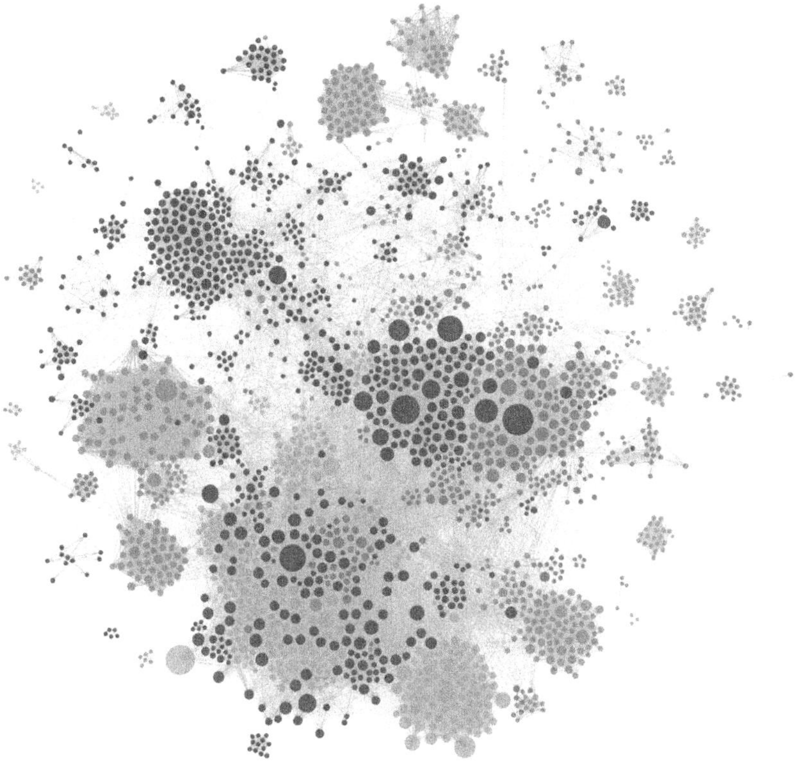

FIG. 4.3 Co-citation network: the intellectual structure of the smart city research field considering the period between 1992 and 2012.

The greater the quantity of co-citations associated with a node, the greater its number of links within the network and, consequently, its centrality in the whole system. The degree of centrality of the thematic clusters was defined by summing together the values related to their nodes.

The co-citation network is composed of 18 thematic clusters, which are labeled from C.01 to C.18, and their structure is described in Fig. 4.4. The clusters C.02, C.05, C.08, C.14, and C.17 can be considered as the main thematic clusters because, in addition to containing the largest number of publications, they also include most of the source documents. Given their dominant role in the co-citation network, these clusters were used to provide insight into the intellectual structure of the smart city research field. To achieve this aim, their content had been analyzed by combining the use of core documents and word profiles.

Five core documents for each cluster were selected by considering the in-degree measurement of the publications belonging to them. This attribute represents the sum of internal relationships that a document has with other publications

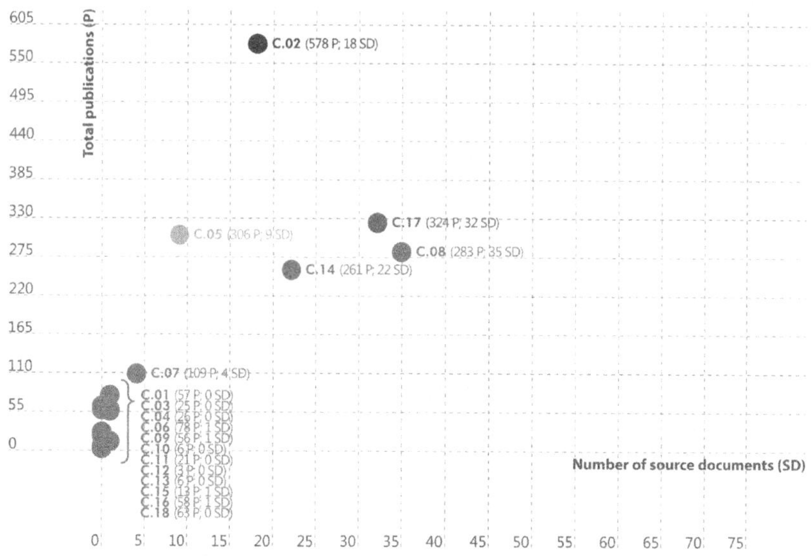

FIG. 4.4 Thematic clusters: composition.

in the same cluster and was used to measure their degree of centrality. Due to their high connectivity, these documents provided most of the information describing the content of the clusters (Gmur, 2003). A list of the core documents is presented in Table 4.1.

A word profile with 10 keywords was then built for each cluster by combining the full texts of its source documents. Five Rich Text Format (rtf) files with the textual data of each clusters' source documents were created and analyzed by using WordStat, a content analysis and text-mining software. During the production of the rtf files, each source document was searched to detect acronyms and abbreviations, which were converted to their extended form. In addition, bibliographic references and data concerning authors and their affiliations were eliminated because irrelevant to the content analysis and their presence risked generating unexplained variations in the results. All the words and phrases contained in the source documents were extracted with WordStat, which was also instrumental in calculating both their frequency and co-occurrence. The keywords selected for building the word profiles of each thematic cluster are the phrases with the highest frequency that were found in at least 30% of the source documents belonging to the cluster (Table 4.2). Word clouds were then built for each word profile to facilitate their reading and the comparative analysis. A word cloud is an image in which the keywords belonging to a word profile are grouped together and each of them is assigned a size that reflects its frequency. The higher the frequency, the greater the size of the word. The results obtained with this visual representation technique are shown in Fig. 4.5.

TABLE 4.1 Core documents

	Core document				
Cluster	**Reference**	**Title**	**Year**	**Type**	**In-degree**
C.02	Weiser (1991)	The computer for the 21st century	1991	AR	185
C.02	**Atzori et al. (2010)**	**The Internet of Things: a survey**	**2010**	**AR**	**100**
C.02	Polastre et al. (2004)	Versatile low-power media access for wireless sensor networks	2004	CO	97
C.02	ITU (2005)	ITU Internet Reports 2005: the Internet of Things	2005	GR	90
C.02	Sundmaeker et al. (2010)	Vision and challenges for realizing the Internet of Things	2010	BO	86
C.05	Florida (2002)	The rise of the creative class and how it's transforming work, leisure, community, and everyday life	2002	BO	157
C.05	Landry (2000)	The creative city: a toolkit for urban innovation	2000	BO	157
C.05	Yigitcanlar et al. (2008b)	Creative urban regions: harnessing urban technologies to support knowledge city initiatives	2008	BO	124
C.05	Yigitcanlar et al. (2008c)	Knowledge-based urban development: planning and applications in the information era	2008	BO	120
C.05	Florida (2005)	Cities and the creative class	2005	BO	106

Continued

TABLE 4.1 Core documents—cont'd

	Core document				
Cluster	Reference	Title	Year	Type	In-degree
C.08	**Dirks et al. (2010)**	**Smarter cities for smarter growth: how cities can optimize their systems for the talent-based economy**	**2010**	**GR**	**100**
C.08	**Moss Kanter and Litow (2009)**	**Informed and interconnected: a manifesto for smarter cities**	**2009**	**GR**	**90**
C.08	**Dirks and Keeling (2009)**	**A vision of smarter cities: how cities can lead the way into a prosperous and sustainable future**	**2009**	**GR**	**84**
C.08	**Harrison et al. (2010)**	**Foundations for smarter cities**	**2010**	**AR**	**81**
C.08	**Washburn et al. (2010)**	**Helping CIOs understand "Smart City" initiatives**	**2010**	**GR**	**80**
C.14	European Commission (2006)	European SmartGrids Technology Platform: vision for Europe's electricity networks of the future	2006	BO	47
C.14	US Department of Commerce – National Institute of Standards and Technology (2010)	NIST framework and roadmap for smart grid interoperability standards	2010	GR	37
C.14	**Karnouskos and Nass de Holanda (2009)**	**Simulation of a smart grid city with software agents**	**2009**	**CO**	**34**
C.14	**The Climate Group (2008)**	**SMART 2020: enabling the low-carbon economy in the information age**	**2008**	**GR**	**28**

TABLE 4.1 Core documents—cont'd

	Core document				
Cluster	Reference	Title	Year	Type	In-degree
C.14	**European Commission (2009a)**	**Communication from the Commission to the European Parliament, the Council, the European Economic and Social Committee and the Committee of the Regions. Investing in the development of low-carbon technologies (SET-Plan)**	**2009**	**GR**	**26**
C.17	**Komninos (2002)**	**Intelligent cities: innovation, knowledge, systems, and digital spaces**	**2002**	**BO**	**194**
C.17	**Caragliu et al. (2009)**	**Smart cities in Europe**	**2009**	**CO**	**180**
C.17	Ishida and Isbister (2000)	Digital cities: technologies, experiences, and future perspectives	2000	BO	170
C.17	Komninos (2006)	The architecture of intelligent cities: integrating human, collective, and artificial intelligence to enhance knowledge and innovation	2006	CO	162
C.17	Graham (2004b)	The cybercities reader	2004	BO	160

Source documents are in bold. Publication types: books (BO), journal articles (AR), conference papers (CO), and gray literature (GR).

4.4 Multiple smart city development paths

After completing the bibliometric analysis, word profiles and core documents are used to describe the main thematic clusters and present the development paths of smart cities each of them supports. The thematic clusters and their literature are discussed in the following subsections.

TABLE 4.2 Word profiles

Cluster	Word profile
C.02	Information technology (fr. 1998 - oc. 100,0%); Internet of Things (fr. 1433 - oc. 38,9%); ubiquitous computing (fr. 517 - oc. 38,9%); information and communication technology (fr. 494 - oc. 38,9%); sensor network (fr. 215 - oc. 61,1%); mobile device (fr. 175 - oc. 44,4%); mobile phone (fr. 171 - oc. 55,6%); rfid tag (fr. 136 - oc. 33,3%); smart city (fr. 128 - oc. 100,0%); wireless sensor (fr. 116 - oc. 61,1%)
C.05	Information technology (fr. 293 - oc. 100,0%); information and communication technology (fr. 157 - oc. 77,8%); knowledge city (fr. 73 - oc. 55,6%); urban development (fr. 55 - oc. 66,7%); local government (fr. 47 - oc. 66,7%); economic development (fr. 46 - oc. 66,7%); smart city (fr. 39 - oc. 100,0%); urban infrastructure (fr. 39 - oc. 44,4%); ubiquitous computing (fr. 27 - oc. 33,3%); knowledge economy (fr. 25 - oc. 55,6%)
C.08	Information technology (fr. 2265 - oc. 100,0%); smart city (fr. 838 - oc. 100,0%); information and communication technology (fr. 354 - oc. 62,9%); digital city (fr. 235 - oc. 34,3%); local government (fr. 87 - oc. 45,7%); quality of life (fr. 79 - oc. 48,6%); smarter city (fr. 68 - oc. 31,4%); city infrastructure (fr. 56 - oc. 31,4%); public service (fr. 55 - oc. 48,6%); urban development (fr. 50 - oc. 37,1%)
C.14	Information technology (fr. 642 - oc. 100,0%); information and communication technology (fr. 471 - oc. 73,9%); smart city (fr. 307 - oc. 100,0%); energy efficiency (fr. 129 - oc. 56,5%); smart grid (fr. 105 - oc. 52,2%); climate change (fr. 84 - oc. 34,8%); energy consumption (fr. 70 - oc. 60,9%); urban development (fr. 63 - oc. 30,4%); smart meter (fr. 55 - oc. 56,5%); renewable energy (fr. 51 - oc. 34,8%)
C.17	Information technology (fr. 2056 - oc. 96,9%); smart city (fr. 1148 - oc. 100,0%); intelligent city (fr. 586 - oc. 53,1%); information and communication technology (fr. 426 - oc. 78,1%); living lab (fr. 296 - oc. 46,9%); digital city (fr. 280 - oc. 37,5%); innovation system (fr. 273 - oc. 34,4%); Internet of Things (fr. 161 - oc. 31,3%); social capital (fr. 129 - oc. 40,6%); urban development (fr. 98 - oc. 59,4%)

Frequency (fr.): number of times the keyword appears in the cluster's source documents; Co-occurrence (oc.): percentage of cluster's source documents in which the keyword is included.

4.4.1 Experimental path (C.02): Smart cities as testbeds for IoT solutions

When comparing the clusters' word profiles, it becomes immediately evident that technology is one of the main drivers boosting the growth of smart city development as an object of enquiry, because information technology (IT) and ICT are always two of the keywords with the highest frequency and co-occurrence. Additional evidence is also provided by the content analysis of the thematic cluster C.02. With a structure composed of 578 publications, which corresponds

FIG. 4.5 Word clouds.

to 25.4% of the total 2273 publications, this is the largest thematic cluster of the co-citation network and its literature focuses attention on ICT devices and infrastructure components that have enabled ubiquitous computing and the Internet of Things (IoT). In addition, it stresses the potential contribution that these two concepts can offer in supporting urban sustainable development. Some of the devices and infrastructures discussed in the core documents are indeed part of the cluster's word profile. These include: sensor networks, radio-frequency identification (RFID) tags, mobile devices, mobile phones, and wireless sensors.

Ubiquitous computing is one of the key paradigms underlying the IoT (ITU, 2005) and originates from the work carried out by Mark Weiser and his group of researchers at the Computer Science Lab of Xerox PARC in Palo Alto, California. Ubiquitous computing is a technical vision based on the idea of making computers invisible to the user and spreading them ubiquitously throughout the physical environment. The ubiquitous computing philosophy suggests replacing the one-person/one-computer paradigm of the personal computing era with the one-person/many-computers paradigm. In the personal computing era, human being and machine communicate through the desktop and engage in a one-to-one relationship that aims to improve the cognitive skills of an individual. With the shift to the one-person/many-computers paradigm, computational power is embedded everywhere, and people can interact with computers any time and in any places, without necessarily having to sit in front of their personal computers (Weiser, 1991, 1993; Weiser et al., 1999).

According to the ubiquitous computing paradigm, which is formulated in the early 1990s, computers will be diffused in the real world and interconnected by ubiquitous networks. In addition, they will be able to control a countless range of functions in the physical space and work without human intervention, as autonomous and invisible agents. This vision becomes a reality with the advent of wireless technologies, which make it possible for physical objects containing embedded technology to populate the Internet and interact with the external environment in a completely independent way (Mitchell, 2003). This emerging wave of Internet-connected devices has enabled the IoT, a new concept that is rapidly growing within the debate on smart city development and the use of ICT to support urban sustainability. As already introduced in Chapter 2, the IoT refers to a global Internet-based network populated by smart objects that can (1) autonomously interact with each other, (2) collect and exchange data describing the environment in which they are located, and (3) collaborate in completing specific tasks. Smart objects are small computers equipped with a communication device and either a sensor or an actuator (Atzori et al., 2010; Sundmaeker et al., 2010).

The IoT, which can be considered as an extension of the existing Internet, has enabled a wide range of new digital services and applications (Atzori et al., 2010; ITU, 2005; Tselentis et al., 2009). The fields of application are many and include, for example, agriculture, building automation, factory monitoring, health management, education, smart grids, mobility, and, in a broader vision, smart cities (Holler et al., 2014; Sundmaeker et al., 2010). As Miorandi et al. (2012) point out, IoT technologies can find a large number of applications in smart city developments. The thematic cluster C.02 builds on this assumption and supports a vision of smart cities as urban environments characterized by a large deployment of IoT solutions. This is an interpretation in which cities become testbeds for experimenting IoT technologies and analyzing their functionality, relevance, and capability to improve urban sustainability.

Santander is an example of smart city resulting from the application of this development path. Located in the north coast of Spain, this small city has become an urban laboratory for the European research project SmartSantander, which is described in a number of publications belonging to this cluster. During the project, Santander and its surroundings have been equipped with more than 12,000 IoT devices (Sanchez et al., 2011) and transformed in "a European experimental test facility for [...] research and experimentation of architectures, key enabling technologies, services and applications for the loT in the context of a smart city" (Sanchez et al., 2013: 1). According to the consortium leading the project, this facility is expected to become "instrumental in fostering key enabling technologies for loT and providing the research community with a [...] platform for large scale loT experimentation and evaluation under realistic operational conditions" (Sanchez et al., 2013: 1).[5]

4.4.2 Ubiquitous path (C.05): The Korean experience of ubiquitous cities

In the thematic cluster C.05, smart city and ubiquitous city are considered as two equivalent terms and are described as a technical evolution of the knowledge city (Lee et al., 2008), a concept that is discussed in (1) a number of source documents belonging to this cluster (see Dvir and Pasher, 2004; Yigitcanlar et al., 2008a,d) and (2) the core documents published by Yigitcanlar et al. (2008b,c). Knowledge city is a term used to identify those cities that put knowledge production and dissemination at the core of their sustainable development strategy (Yigitcanlar et al., 2008d). Research by Yigitcanlar et al. (2008b) suggests the role of knowledge has become a crucial factor in wealth creation and urban sustainability, and local governments need to find new approaches able to harness the opportunities that a knowledge-based economy offers to boost sustainable growth and innovation in urban environments. This idea starts emerging in the early 2000s, with Landry (2000) and Florida (2002, 2005), who both highlight the growing importance of knowledge, creativity, and innovation in sustainable urban development processes, especially in terms of economic development and competitiveness.

Knowledge cities firmly encourage sustainable growth-oriented development paths based on the exploitation of information resources and knowledge ecosystems. As Lee et al. (2008) and Yigitcanlar et al. (2008a) explain, the possibility to achieve this aim by leveraging ICTs has marked the shift from the knowledge city to the ubiquitous city, linking Weiser's (1991) work on ubiquitous computing to the debate on infrastructure planning for sustainable cities. Ubiquitous cities are

5. Additional information on the SmartSantander's city-scale experimental research facility can be found on the project's official website: http://www.smartsantander.eu.

conceived as urban systems equipped with ubiquitous technologies that provide their users with access to real-time data describing the functionality of the city's infrastructure anywhere and anytime. These technologies include, for example, "broadband convergence networks, RFIDs, ubiquitous sensor networks, home networking, wireless broadband, digital multimedia broadcasting, telematics, geographic information systems, location-based systems and smart-card systems" (Shin and Kim, 2010: 148), and they are assembled to build a technological platform that links together all urban information systems and makes it possible for everyone to access them, anywhere and anytime (Shin, 2007, 2010; Shin and Kim, 2010; Lee et al., 2008).

Most of the attention that this concept has received comes from the Republic of Korea, where the national government launched a national program on ubiquitous cities in 2007. This program aimed at deploying state-of-the-art ubiquitous technologies to build the world's first ubiquitous society (Republic of Korea, 2007a,b). Only a few cities working on the ubiquitous city concept can be found outside the South Korean territory. Anthopoulos and Fitsilis (2010a,b), for example, introduce the work carried out by the Greek city of Trikala, while research by Gil-Castineira et al. (2011) and Shin and Lee (2011) reports on a number of projects that are implemented in Oulu, San Francisco, Philadelphia, Tokyo, Singapore, Hong Kong, Taiwan, and Malaysia.

The initiative of the South Korean government has encouraged many city governments to design ubiquitous city projects and strategies in an effort to deploy ubiquitous technologies for urban sustainability purposes. After 1 year into the program, 22 cities were already pursuing the construction of ubiquitous cities nationwide, and only 3 years later, they became 36, with a total of 53 ubiquitous city initiatives in progress throughout the country (Republic of Korea, 2007a; Tekes, 2011). Among the many projects developed under the ubiquitous city brand, Busan Green u-City and Songdo International Business District (IBD) are two of the most debated in the literature of this thematic cluster, in which both are presented by overlapping the terms smart city and ubiquitous city.

The Global System for Mobile Communications Association (GSMA) identifies Busan as an early example of a smart city. By leveraging an overall investment of 452 million dollars, the Busan Green u-City project aimed to implement a cloud-based infrastructure for hosting public services and commercial and industrial applications. Started in 2005 and based on a multistage development plan, this project was designed and implemented by a public–private consortium including the regional and local governments, the global technology supplier Cisco Systems, and KT Corporation, the largest telephone company operating in South Korea. With an additional investment of 47 million dollars, Cisco has also taken part in the construction of Songdo IBD, a new business district that has been built from scratch by using about 600 ha of land reclaimed from the Yellow Sea off Incheon. Songdo forms part of the Incheon Free Economic Zone, and according to its developers, it is one of the most Internet-connected and eco-friendly cities in the world (GSMA, 2012; Strickland, 2011; Juan et al., 2011).

The Korean experience of ubiquitous cities has been analyzed by Shin (2007, 2009, 2010), whose research demonstrates that this initiative is based on a top-down and centralized approach and "largely biased toward industrial and economic development, reflecting business providers' interests" rather than users' benefits (Shin, 2007: 636). According to Shin (2009, 2010), the South Korean's ubiquitous city developments are (1) designed primarily to increase the technological equipment and technical capability of cities, instead of supporting sustainable urban development purposes, and (2) driven by major ICT suppliers and industry's market perspectives and economic interests, instead of city users' needs.

4.4.3 Corporate path (C.08): IBM and the corporate smart city model

The technology-led vision of smart cities proposed in the cluster C.05 is the engine that fuels ICT multinational companies and their involvement in the market of smart cities technologies. Driven by the ambition to acquire a strong position in this new and promising market, companies such as Cisco Systems, Hitachi, and IBM have started operating within the domain of urban technology and have begun to actively participate in the debate on smart city development (Amato et al., 2012a,b,c; Kohno et al., 2011; Kurebayashi et al., 2011; Yoshikawa et al., 2011; Brech et al., 2011; Cosgrove et al., 2011; Kehoe et al., 2011; Katz and Ruano, 2011; Paul et al., 2011; Ruano et al., 2011; Schaefer et al., 2011; Chen-Ritzo et al., 2009; Harrison et al., 2010, 2011).

The literature produced by such companies has led to the growth of the corporate smart city model. This model conceives smart cities as urban environment that are equipped with a one-size-fits-all platform of interconnected sensing devices and digital solutions provided by ICT companies. IBM is one of the main supporters of this model, and its relevant role and influence in the smart city debate is demonstrated by the content analysis of this cluster, which further confirms the findings of the first bibliometric analysis (see Chapter 3). The thematic cluster C.08 promotes the interpretation of smart city development offered by the American multinational company. The most cited source documents of this cluster are produced by IBM researchers, and the degree of centrality of such publications is significantly high (see Moss Kanter and Litow, 2009; Dirks et al., 2009, 2010; Dirks and Keeling, 2009; Harrison et al., 2010). Four of the five core documents are indeed publications from IBM. What is more, the cluster's word profile contains the term "smarter city," a trademark officially registered by this company and used for its smart city campaign, which is driven by the following motto: "Building a Smarter Planet" (Palmisano, 2008).

The Smarter Planet initiative is a commercial venture that IBM launched at the end of 2008 and has positioned the company at the forefront of smart city development (Palmisano, 2008). This initiative suggests smart city development follows a standardized three-phase process (Harrison et al., 2010): (1) instrumentation, (2) interconnection, and (3) intelligence. This process is described by Dirks et al. (2009: 1): "Instrumentation enables cities to gather more high-quality data in a timely fashion than ever before. For example, utility meters and sensors that monitor the capacity of the power generation network can be used to continually gather data on supply and demand of electricity [...]. Interconnection creates links among data, systems and people [...], opening up new ways to gather and share information. Intelligence—in the form of new kinds of computing models and new algorithms—enables cities to generate predictive insights for informed decision making and action. Combined with advanced analytics and ever-increasing storage and computing power, these new models can turn the mountains of data generated into intelligence to create insight as a basis for action." According to IBM, this ICT-based transformation can automatically make any city smart and, consequently, more efficient, democratic, livable, attractive, environment-friendly, and economically prosperous (Dirks and Keeling, 2009).

From a review of this thematic cluster's literature emerges that one of the flagship projects falling within the Smarter Planet initiative was developed in Rio de Janeiro. By leveraging an investment of 14 million dollars, the city government worked with IBM to build the Rio Operations Center, an emergency response system that was inaugurated at the end of 2010. The center is based on a digital platform applying the analytic models developed by IBM, which are used to (1) obtain a holistic view of how the city is functioning and (2) predict possible emergency situations, in particular, the flood-related incidents that Rio de Janeiro frequently faces during the summer period due to intense rainfall. The data used for predicting emergency includes: real-time images captured by a surveillance system composed of 900 cameras located around the city; weather sensors; historical data series; and the messages sent by city users via phone, Internet, and radio (IBM Corporation, 2011; Naphade et al., 2011).

4.4.4 European path (C.14): Smart city for a low-carbon economy

The data released by both the United Nations and the American Association for the Advancement of Science (AAAS) suggests cities make a significant contribution to climate change, and their unsustainable development patterns are intensifying the environmental crisis. Considering both production- and consumption-based analyses, cities' overall allocation of responsibility for greenhouse gas (GHG) emissions is between 40% and 70%. In addition, cities also account for approximately 70% of the global energy consumption (AAAS, 2001; UN-Habitat, 2011). Fighting against climate change by modifying the functioning of urban environments has become a high-level priority for local and national governments, which are intervening with new sustainable energy policies and initiatives aimed to boost the progressive growth of a low-carbon future.

The core literature of the thematic cluster C.14 provides evidence of the decisive role played by ICT in helping governments to face this critical situation, in particular, the report "SMART 2020: Enabling the low-carbon economy in the information age." This report was published in 2008 by The Climate Group, an international nonprofit organization that supports leaders in government, business, and society to address climate risks and accelerate the transition to a low-carbon economy. This report demonstrates that the ICT industry is a key player in creating a low-carbon society, and the technological solutions that this sector offers can drastically unlock emissions reductions and energy saving. According to the report, "the biggest role ICTs could play is in helping to improve energy efficiency in power transmission and distribution (T&D), in buildings and factories that demand power and in the use of transportation to deliver goods" (The Climate Group, 2008: 9). The estimates suggest that, by acting on these five sectors, ICT can help save 15% of the global emissions by 2020 (The Climate Group, 2008).

This report and the other core documents make it clear that unlocking the potential of ICT is critical to win the challenge posed by climate change. In addition, they also suggest smart grids, the electricity networks of the future, are one of the most promising application domains (European Commission, 2006, 2009a; The Climate Group, 2008; Karnouskos and Nass de Holanda, 2009; US Department of Commerce – NIST, 2010). Smart grids improve the efficiency of current power transmission and distribution networks while responding to the new challenges and opportunities arising from the energy market. These networks make it possible to: manage flexible demand for energy, flexible storage, and highly variable prices; increase both power transfers and the degree of automation; reduce energy losses and cope with the issues imposed by traditional energy sources; apply efficient investments to replace aging infrastructure; develop strategies for local demand modulation and load control; increase social responsibility and sustainability by using smart meters and establishing a two-way flow of information between supplier and user; improve the long-distance transport and integration of renewable energy sources (microgeneration opportunities); and manage the integration of new products and services, such as electric vehicles (European Commission, 2006; The Climate Group, 2008; Karnouskos and Nass de Holanda, 2009).

The importance and urgency of modernizing the current electric power networks by transforming them into smart grids is widely recognized. For example, the Indian government has been developing policies to overcome barriers that limit the implementation of smart grid initiatives since 2001 (The Climate Group, 2008), while the European Commission has set up the SmartGrids Technology Platform, in which a large number of stakeholders representing the European energy sector have been tasked to design a joint vision for the European energy network of the future. The platform's vision is based on activating smart grid solutions across Europe (European Commission, 2006). The same aim is pursued by the government of the United States of America, where a set of interoperability standards and protocols for smart grid devices and systems have been established to accelerate their integration in the US territory (US Department of Commerce – NIST, 2010).

Mobilizing ICT to facilitate the transition to an energy-efficient and low-carbon economy has become a key ambition of the European Union's Member States, which have developed a group of measures focusing on what can be achieved "by fully exploiting the enabling capacity of ICTs in all sectors of society and the economy" (European Commission, 2009b: 2). These measures are published in 2009, along with the Strategic Energy Technology Plan (SET-Plan), a policy document that describes the strategy pursued by the European Union to accelerate innovation in cutting edge low-carbon technologies and their diffusion across its member states (European Commission, 2009a).

The European interpretation of smart city development, which is promoted by the thematic cluster C.14, has emerged from this growing interest in boosting a sustainable energy future. As reported in the SET-Plan, according to the European Commission, smart cities are those cities that "create the conditions to trigger the mass market take-up of energy efficiency technologies [by transforming] their buildings, energy networks and transport systems into those of the future, demonstrating transition concepts and strategies to a low-carbon economy" (European Commission, 2009a: 7). These cities are expected to be "the nuclei from which smart networks, a new generation of buildings and low-carbon transport solutions will develop into European wide realities that will transform [the] energy system" (European Commission, 2009a: 7). This interpretation is in line with the cluster's word profile, in which the smart city concept is strongly connected to keywords like energy efficiency, smart grids, climate change, energy consumption, smart meters, and renewable energy.

4.4.5 Holistic path (C.17): Digital, intelligent, smart

The thematic cluster C.17 is the second largest cluster of the co-citation network, and it also has the highest degree of centrality. In the literature belonging to this thematic cluster, the debate on smart city development is mainly connected to the scientific foundations of "urban ICT studies" (Graham, 2004a: 3), a subfield of urban studies in which researchers aim to investigate the relationship between ICTs and sustainable urban development. This knowledge area starts growing between the late 1990s and the early 2000s, and some of the publications that have provided a significant contribution in laying down its intellectual structure form part of this cluster (see Castells, 1996; Graham and Marvin, 1996, 2001; Mitchell, 1995, 1999, 2003), including the book "The Cybercities Reader" by Graham (2004b), which is one of the core documents.

While this literature started filling "the gap left by the long neglect of telecommunications in urban studies and policy-making" (Graham and Marvin, 1996: XII), cities all over the world began experimenting with the use of digital technologies for supporting urban sustainability by implementing projects and initiatives that have been called by using three main keywords: (1) digital city, (2) intelligent city, and (3) smart city. These keywords clearly emerge in both the word profile of this cluster and the core documents by Ishida and Isbister (2000), Komninos (2002, 2006), and Caragliu et al. (2009).

The term digital city dates back to the end of the 20th century and was used as a label for a number of projects launched by cities located in Europe, North America, and Asia.[6] These projects aimed to support social and economic development by building websites that were used to provide city users with access to digital services (Aurigi and Graham, 2000; Ishida and Isbister, 2000). In particular, research by Aurigi (2000) shows that these websites were developed mainly to (1) stimulate local economic development, (2) improve the visibility of the cities and their image, (3) widen access to the Internet and support community networking, (4) support the growth of online communities and democratic debates related to subjects of public interest, and (5) improve the management of cities' physical infrastructures.

At the beginning of the 21st century, while the world was experiencing the construction of digital cities, the term intelligent city emerged in research by Komninos (2002, 2006, 2008). As anticipated in Chapter 3, the definition of this concept is provided in a conference paper published in 2006: "intelligent cities [...] are territories with high capacity for learning and innovation, which is built-in to the creativity of their population, their institutions of knowledge creation, and their digital infrastructure for communication and knowledge management" (Komninos, 2006: 13). According to this interpretation, the distinguishing feature of intelligent cities is their capacity to exploit ICTs for increasing the problem-solving capability of urban communities and their ability to produce innovation within urban environments (Komninos, 2002). Consequently, intelligent cities and digital cities share the same interest for ICT-driven sustainable urban development. However, while the former focuses attention on facilitating some aspects of the social and economic life of urban systems, in the latter, ICT infrastructure and applications aim at strengthening the ability of cities to produce knowledge and innovation.

The transition from intelligent to smart seems to be the result of two different forces. On the one hand, there are the technological advancements in the ICT sector, which have resulted in the massive spread of smart objects fueling the growth of the Internet of Things' paradigm. This trend has

6. The digital city movement has been particularly active in Europe (Aurigi, 2000, 2003; Mino, 2000). Examples of successful experiences have been identified in Amsterdam (van den Besselaar, 2001), Helsinki (de Bruine, 2000), Antwerp, Newcastle upon Tyne (Peeters, 2000; Firmino, 2004), and Bologna and Bristol (Aurigi, 2003, 2005).

opened up new possibilities in addressing cities' issues and sustainable development priorities by deploying digital technologies (Komninos, 2011; Schaffers et al., 2011). On the other hand, there is a request for a more progressive, inclusive and human-centered approach to ICT-driven urban sustainability strategies. Such a request clearly emerges from the literature of this cluster (Caragliu et al., 2009; Hollands, 2008; Schaffers et al., 2011; Paskaleva, 2009; Ratti and Townsend, 2011; Townsend et al., 2011; Deakin and Al Wear, 2011) and was already highlighted in research previously undertaken by Aurigi (2005, 2006), Mino (2000), Graham and Marvin (1999), and Castells (1996).

The thematic cluster C.17 moves away from the technological determinism and top-down entrepreneurial-based business logic of the corporate smart city model and ubiquitous city experience, and it calls for a holistic interpretation of smart city development. An interpretation in which human, social, cultural, environmental, economic, and technological aspects stand alongside one another (Deakin and Al Wear, 2011; Leydesdorff and Deakin, 2011). In this cluster, smart cities are cities where ICT is adopted to meet local development needs, be they of either social, economic, or environmental nature, and the approach proposed for enabling smart city development is grounded in the collective intelligence of a bottom-up strategy and based upon participatory governance, open and user-driven innovation, and community-led urban development.

4.5 The dichotomous nature of smart city research

This bibliometric analysis reveals five main clusters that offer different interpretations of smart cities and the development paths that should be followed to activate the ICT-driven approach to urban sustainability they embed:

- Experimental path (C.02): smart cities are described as urban testbeds for experimenting IoT infrastructures and service applications for urban sustainability and analyzing their functioning, relevance, and potential impact in real-life environments.
- Ubiquitous path (C.05): smart cities and ubiquitous cities are considered as two equivalent categories of cities whereby data describing the functionality of the city is provided everywhere and anytime and their development is driven by corporate suppliers' financial interests, market perspectives, and economic impacts rather than public good.
- Corporate path (C.08): cities become smart when they are equipped with a one-size-fits-all platform of interconnected sensing devices and digital solutions provided by ICT consultancies.
- European path (C.14): smart cities are highly efficient urban systems in which digital technologies are used to develop a new generation of buildings, energy networks, and transport systems, which are instrumental in tackling environmental degradation and fighting climate change.

- Holistic path (C.17): smart cities are urban environments in which digital technologies are assembled to meet local development needs and their development process is grounded in collective intelligence, bottom-up actions, participatory governance, open and user-driven innovation, and community-led urban development.

These paths emerge from the literature on smart cities that is produced between 1992 and 2012, but the division that their presence generates still resonates in the publications that have surfaced since then. By comparing the strategic principles that each path stands on, four main dichotomies can be identified, and the knowledge gap that they open up still remains evident in the research produced during the period 2013–18, resulting in uncertainty on how smart city development should be approached. This is demonstrated by the comprehensive review of the smart city literature produced between 1992 and 2018, which this section reports on. The publications considered in this literature review, which are more than 100, are listed in Table 4.3.

4.5.1 Dichotomy 1: Technology-led or holistic?

All the development paths share the same notion of smart cities as being cities in which ICTs become a mean for supporting urban sustainability. However, the strategy that they suggest embracing for enabling smart city development represents one of the main points of divergence emerging from their comparison. Two competing visions can be identified, which are exposed in Chapter 3 of this book and research by Niaros (2016).

The experimental path, ubiquitous path, and corporate path agree to propose a technology-led and market-oriented approach to smart city development, which is mainly based on the following rationale: ICT and market perspectives represent the primary driving forces shaping smart cities, which are the result of a massive input of technological solutions in the built environment. The interest in this approach to smart city development is increasing, thanks to all the ICT companies, such as ABB, Fujitsu, and Siemens, which have decided to follow IBM and position themselves in the smart city market with their products. Additional evidence of this trend is provided by both Kitchin (2015) and Alizadeh (2017), who both report on the IBM's Smarter Planet initiative and its Smarter City Challenge (IBM Corporation, 2017a,b). This challenge promotes IBM's vision of smart city development and invites cities "to compete for [IBM's] consultancy, technical assistance and grants aimed at developing technological solutions" for urban development (Kitchin, 2015). The cities that have already been selected and included in this initiative exceed 130.

However, a large body of literature considers this technology-led theory of supply-push solutions to be inadequate and unable to deal with smart city development, because it promotes a utopian and technological deterministic interpretation that serves nothing but the interests of technology providers. In addition, this literature points out a group of concerns and tensions that

TABLE 4.3 Capturing the dichotomous nature of smart city research in the literature published between 1992 and 2018

	Dichotomy 1		Dichotomy 2		Dichotomy 3		Dichotomy 4	
Reference	**H1.1**	**H1.2**	**H2.1**	**H2.2**	**H3.1**	**H3.2**	**H4.1**	**H4.2**
ABB (2013)	X		X		X			
Alawadhi et al. (2012)				X				
Alizadeh (2017)								X
Amato et al. (2012a)	X		X		X			
Amato et al. (2012b)	X		X		X			
Amato et al. (2012c)	X		X		X			
Angelidou (2017)		X	X	X		X		
Angelidou and Psaltoglou (2017)		X						
Baccarne et al. (2014a)						X		
Baccarne et al. (2014b)						X		
Bergvall-Kåreborn et al. (2009)		X		X				
Bolici and Mora (2015)		X	X	X		X		
Brech et al. (2011)	X		X		X			
Breuer et al. (2014)			X	X				
Caragliu et al. (2011)		X						
Carvalho (2015)		X						

Chen-Ritzo et al. (2009)	X		X		X			
Christopoulou et al. (2014)		X						
Cisco Systems (2016a)								X
Cisco Systems (2016b)								X
Concilio and Rizzo (2016)		X						
Cosgrove et al. (2011)	X		X		X			
Cugurullo (2013)		X						
Cugurullo (2016)		X						
Dameri (2014)						X		
Dameri (2017)						X		
Deakin (2014a)		X				X		
Deakin (2014b)		X				X		
Deakin and Al Wear (2011)				X				
Deakin and Leydesdorff (2014)						X		
Dirks and Keeling (2009)	X		X		X			
Dirks et al. (2009)	X		X		X			
Dirks et al. (2010)	X		X		X			
Ersoy (2017)		X						
European Commission (2009a)							X	

Continued

TABLE 4.3 Capturing the dichotomous nature of smart city research in the literature published between 1992 and 2018—cont'd

	Dichotomy 1		Dichotomy 2		Dichotomy 3		Dichotomy 4	
Reference	**H1.1**	**H1.2**	**H2.1**	**H2.2**	**H3.1**	**H3.2**	**H4.1**	**H4.2**
European Commission (2012a)							X	
European Commission (2012b)							X	
European Commission (2016)							X	
European Innovation Partnership on Smart Cities and Communities (2013)							X	
Exner (2015)			X	X				
Gardner and Hespanhol (2018)						X		
Giffinger et al. (2007)								X
Gooch et al. (2015)				X				
Grossi and Pianezzi (2017)		X						
Harrison et al. (2010)	X		X		X			
Harrison et al. (2011)	X		X		X			
Hemment and Townsend (2013)		X		X				
Hollands (2008)		X						

Hollands (2015)		X						
Hollands (2016)		X						
IBM Corporation (2017a)	X		X		X			X
IBM Corporation (2017b)	X		X		X			X
Katz and Ruano (2011)	X		X		X			
Kehoe et al. (2011)	X		X		X			
Kitchin (2014)		X						
Kohno et al. (2011)	X		X		X			
Komninos (2014)		X		X		X		
Kourtit et al. (2014)		X				X		X
Kurebayashi et al. (2011)	X		X		X			
Lee and Hancock (2012)			X					
Lee et al. (2014)			X	X				
Leydesdorff and Deakin (2011)				X		X		
Lombardi et al. (2012a)		X						X
Lombardi et al. (2012b)		X						X
Luque-Ayala and Marvin (2015)		X						
Luque-Ayala et al. (2014)		X						
Manville et al. (2014)		X						X

Continued

TABLE 4.3 Capturing the dichotomous nature of smart city research in the literature published between 1992 and 2018—cont'd

	Dichotomy 1		Dichotomy 2		Dichotomy 3		Dichotomy 4	
Reference	**H1.1**	**H1.2**	**H2.1**	**H2.2**	**H3.1**	**H3.2**	**H4.1**	**H4.2**
McNeill (2016)		X						
Mora and Bolici (2016)		X	X	X		X		
Mora and Bolici (2017)		X	X	X		X		
Niaros (2016)		X						
Paul et al. (2011)	X		X		X			
Pollio (2016)		X						
Ratti and Townsend (2011)				X				
Reddy Kummitha and Crutzen (2017)		X						
Republic of Korea (2007a)	X		X		X			
Republic of Korea (2007b)	X		X		X			
Ruano et al. (2011)	X		X		X			
Schaefer et al. (2011)	X		X		X			
Schaffers et al. (2012)				X				
Schuurman et al. (2012)				X		X		
Schuurman et al. (2016)				X		X		

Scuotto et al. (2016)		X						
Selada (2017)		X				X		
Shin (2007)		X		X				
Shin (2009)		X		X				
Shin (2010)		X		X				
Siemens (2014)	X		X		X			
Soderstrom et al. (2014)		X				X		
Sujata et al. (2016)		X						
Tamai (2014)	X		X		X			
Townsend (2013)		X		X				
van Waart et al. (2016)						X		
van Winden and van den Buuse (2017)						X		
Viitanen and Kingston (2014)		X						
Yigitcanlar (2016)		X						
Yigitcanlar and Kamruzzaman (2018)		X						
Yigitcanlar and Lee (2014)		X						
Yoshikawa et al. (2011)	X		X		X			
Zygiaris (2013)		X						

Hypotheses: H1.1. Technology-led; H1.2. Holistic; H2.1. Top-down; H2.2. Bottom-up; H3.1. Double helix; H3.2. Quadruple helix; H4.1. Monodimensional; H4.2. Integrated.

the technology-led approach to smart city development is supposed to generate, which are related to privacy, democracy, security, and the importance of considering both "local diversity and the socio-political dimensions of cities" (Ersoy, 2017: 28).

The researchers raising objections to this technology-led and market-oriented vision call for a much more progressive and holistic vision that conceives smart cities not as technological fixes resulting from the agglomeration of ICT solutions in urban infrastructures, but as complex socio-technical systems in which technological development is aligned with human, social, cultural, economic, and environmental factors. This strategy is currently described as the most suitable for enabling smart city development and finds support in many recent studies. However, the research investigating the holistic path still remains at a preliminary stage and has not yet been able to provide the knowledge necessary to clearly understand how to move from theory to practice (Lee et al., 2014; Yigitcanlar and Kamruzzaman, 2018; Bolici and Mora, 2015; Mora and Bolici, 2016, 2017; Angelidou, 2017).

4.5.2 Dichotomy 2: Top-down or bottom-up?

Which is the most suitable approach for dealing with smart city development? Top-down and centralized, as promoted by the corporate path and ubiquitous path, or bottom-up, open, and diffused as suggested in the holistic path's vision? The distance between these two different approaches generates a second dichotomy. On the one hand, top-down smart cities originate from city governments, which assume a leadership role in designing and driving the implementation of a comprehensive strategy for enabling smart city development. Due to its high level of centralization, this approach is often characterized by limited opportunities for citizens to be engaged in the development process (Dameri, 2013; Cocchia, 2014). On the other hand, bottom-up smart city development stands on self-organization and grassroots efforts, which become more important than the presence of a comprehensive strategic framework (Ratti and Townsend, 2011).

The literature dealing with these two ideologically opposed approaches has generated diverging opinions concerning their effectiveness. Lee and Hancock (2012) and their model for measuring the maturity level of smart cities, for example, suggest a formalized and centralized top-down smart city development strategy aligned with the city's strategic priorities is preferable to a strategy based on a bottom-up approach. However, top-down smart cities are first criticized by Shin (2007, 2009, 2010) and more recently by Townsend (2013) and Gooch et al. (2015) for their incapability to effectively serve people and their needs, rather than "the demands of major corporate suppliers and industry" (Shin, 2009: 516).

Townsend (2013) describes smart cities as the result of bottom-up movements and suggests their development requires a radical shift from top-down innovation processes to open and bottom-up innovation (Schuurman et al., 2012, 2016). He also suggests "top-down visions ignore the enormous [and] innovative potential of grassroots efforts" and highlights the importance of maximizing the involvement of citizens and civic groups in the decision-making process leading to the integration of ICT solutions in the urban environment (Ratti and Townsend, 2011: 45). This line of thinking is aligned with previous research by Deakin and Al Wear (2011), Alawadhi et al. (2012), and Schaffers et al. (2012), who all recognize the importance of empowering citizens and providing them with the opportunity to become active actors of change in the development process of smart cities.

However, according to the alternative reading that is put forward by Breuer et al. (2014) and Exner (2015), top-down and bottom-up approaches are both affected by restrictions that can be overcome only by combing them together: "a purely top-down view on the smart city carries a danger of authoritarianism with it, while a bottom-up-only approach leans towards chaos and lack of long-term vision" (Breuer et al., 2014: 162). This opinion is also championed by Mora and Bolici (2016, 2017) and Lee et al. (2014: 95), with the latter suggesting either a dedicated organization or a cross departmental team is helpful during the early stages of the smart city development strategy, in particular, when setting up the governance structure, but needs to be replaced with an open governing system when the growth phase starts.

4.5.3 Dichotomy 3: Double or quadruple-helix?

The divergence between the holistic path and corporate path is also evident when comparing the collaborative models that they suggest considering in order to transform ordinary urban areas into smart cities. On the one hand, the corporate path's technology-driven, market-led, and top-down vision of smart city development has resulted in a new urbanism whereby IT solution providers try to persuade local governments in supporting sustainable urban development by adopting their smart technologies (Soderstrom et al., 2014; McNeill, 2016; Paroutis et al., 2014). The collaborative model characterizing this development path is based on a double-helix structure in which the interaction is only between (1) solution providers acting as consultants who offer their technological fixes and (2) city governments, which are persuaded to underpin smart city development by adopting such proprietary technologies. The double-helix structure of this collaborative model generates an entrepreneurial mode of governance where IT corporations working in the market of smart city services become "the main providers of solutions to urban problems" (Pollio, 2016: 515).

However, a large number of researchers suggest such a closed collaborative model does not provide the intellectual capital that is necessary to drive smart city development. Their studies call for a broader collaborative ecosystem in which the interests of governments, universities, and industry are combined (triple-helix structure), along with those expressed by citizens and civil society organizations (quadruple-helix structure).[7] According to this collaborative model, "different urban stakeholders (public, private, and civic) [need to] engage in coalitions and innovate together" in order for smart city development strategies to be successful (van Winden and van den Buuse, 2017: 68).

4.5.4 Dichotomy 4: Monodimensional or integrated?

The fourth dichotomy is related to the intervention logic. The European Commission's smart city development path focuses attention only on the energy sector, promoting a monodimensional vision of smart cities, which are described as low-carbon and resource-efficient urban environments committed to invest in smart transport solutions, smart buildings, and smart grids. The European Commission has been promoting and spreading this energy-driven interpretation of smart city development since 2009, by: (1) launching the Smart Cities and Communities Initiative (European Commission, 2009a); (2) activating the European Innovation Partnership on Smart Cities and Communities (2013), which involves a community of more than 3000 stakeholders representing public authorities, academic and research institutions, businesses, nongovernmental organizations, and private individuals[8] (European Commission, 2012b); and (3) continuing to launch calls for project proposals related to the Smart Cities and Communities topic, which have provided public and private actors with the financial support necessary to deliver new smart city solutions for facilitating cities' transition toward a low-carbon and resource-efficient economy (European Commission, 2011, 2012a, 2016).[9]

On the contrary, the holistic path, experimental path, ubiquitous path, and corporate path propose an integrated and multidimensional approach to smart city development. The multidimensional intervention logic is supported by IBM and Cisco Systems, which promote their operating systems for smart cities, that is, comprehensive ICT platforms that combine sets of digital solutions and applications to improve the management of urban systems, such as energy and

7. The triple-helix collaborative model is based on university-industry-government relations (Etzkowitz and Leydesdorff, 2000) and is embedded in the quadruple-helix model, where civil society organizations and citizens are added as fourth element of the collaborative ecosystem (Arnkil et al., 2010; Carayannis and Campbell, 2014; Cavallini et al., 2016). United Nations (1998), Food and Agriculture Organization (2013), World Economic Forum (2013), European Commission (2014), and London School of Economics (Hutter and O'Mahony, 2004) agree to define civil society organizations as a broad category that encompasses nongovernmental organizations (NGOs), community groups, charities, trusts, foundations, advocacy groups, faith-based organizations, and national and international nonstate associations.

8. This data is reported in the infographic that can be downloaded from the European Innovation Partnership on Smart Cities and Communities' website (http://ec.europa.eu/eip/smartcities).

9. More information about the European Commission's smart city vision can be found on the following online portals: (1) http://ec.europa.eu/eip/smartcities; (2) https://ec.europa.eu/inea/en/horizon-2020/smart-cities-communities; (3) https://eu-smartcities.eu; and (4) http://cordis.europa.eu.

utilities, parking, environment, safety and security, transportation, education, and health care.

This line of thinking can also be found in the ranking system for measuring the performance of medium-sized European smart cities that Vienna University of Technology, University of Ljubljana, and Delft University of Technology assembled in 2007. According to this ranking system, successful smart city development strategies cover six policy domains that are labeled using the following keywords: living, economy, people, environment, mobility, and governance (Giffinger et al., 2007). A similar assessment of smart city development strategies has been proposed in the evaluation studies conducted by Lombardi et al. (2012a,b), Kourtit et al. (2014), and Manville et al. (2014), who suggest a successful smart city development strategy covers all these application domains.

References

American Association for the Advancement of Science, 2001. AAAS Atlas of Population and Environment. University of California Press, Oakland, CA.

ABB, 2013. ABB Power and Automation: Solid Foundations for Smart Cities. White paper, ABB. http://new.abb.com/docs/default-source/smart-grids-library/abb_smart_grids_white_paper_2013.pdf?sfvrsn=2. (Accessed April 5, 2014).

Adam, D., 2002. The counting house. Nature 415 (6873), 726–729.

Alawadhi, S., Aldama-Nalda, A., Chourabi, H., Gil-Garcia, R.J., Leung, S., Mellouli, S., Nam, T., Pardo, T.A., Scholl, H.J., Walker, S., 2012. Building understanding of smart city initiatives. In: Scholl, H.J., Janssen, M., Wimmer, M.A., Moe, C.E., Flak, L.S. (Eds.), Electronic Government: 11th IFIP WG 8.5 International Conference, EGOV 2012, Kristiansand, Norway, September 3–6, 2012. Proceedings. Springer, Berlin, pp. 40–53.

Albino, V., Berardi, U., Dangelico, R.M., 2015. Smart cities: definitions, dimensions, performance, and initiatives. J. Urban Technol. 22 (1), 3–21.

Alizadeh, T., 2017. An investigation of IBM's smarter cites challenge: what do participating cities want? Cities: Int. J. Urban Policy Plann. 63, 70–80.

Alkandari, A., Alnasheet, M., Alshekhly, I.F., 2012. Smart cities: survey. J. Adv. Comput. Sci. Technol. Res. 2 (2), 79–90.

Allmayer, S., Winkler, H., 2013. Interface management research in supplier–customer relationships: findings from a citation analysis of international literature. J. Bus. Econ. 83 (9), 1015–1061.

Amato, V., Bloomer, L., Holmes, A., Kondepudi, S., 2012a. Using ICT to Deliver Benefits to Cities by Enabling Smart+Connected Communities. White paper, Cisco Systems. http://www.smartconnectedcommunities.org/docs/DOC-2150. (Accessed January 4, 2013).

Amato, V., Kondepudi, S., Holmes, A., 2012b. Transforming Communities with Smart+connected Services. White paper, Cisco Systems. http://www.smartconnectedcommunities.org/docs/DOC-2129. (Accessed January 4, 2013).

Amato, V., Bloomer, L., Holmes, A., Kondepudi, S., 2012c. Government Competitiveness Drives Smart+connected Communities Initiative. White paper, Cisco Systems. http://www.smartconnectedcommunities.org/docs/DOC-2174. (Accessed January 4, 2013).

Angelidou, M., 2017. The role of smart city characteristics in the plans of fifteen cities. J. Urban Technol. 24 (4), 3–28.

Angelidou, M., Psaltoglou, A., 2017. An empirical investigation of social innovation initiatives for sustainable urban development. Sustain. Cities Soc. 33, 113–125.

Anthopoulos, L., Fitsilis, P., 2010a. From digital to ubiquitous cities: defining a common architecture for urban development. In: Callaghan, V., Kameas, A., Egerton, S., Satoh, I., Weber, M. (Eds.), Proceedings 2010 Sixth International Conference on Intelligent Environments (IE), Kuala Lumpur, 19-21 July 2012. Institute of Electrical and Electronics Engineers (IEEE), Piscataway, NJ, pp. 301–306.

Anthopoulos, L., Fitsilis, P., 2010b. From online to ubiquitous cities: The technical transformation of virtual communities. In: Sideridis, A.B., Patrikakis, C.Z. (Eds.), Next Generation Society. Technological and Legal Issues: Third International Conference, E-Democracy 2009, Athens, Greece, September 23–25, 2009, Revised Selected Papers. Springer, Berlin, pp. 360–372.

Arnkil, R., Järvensivu, A., Koski, P., Piirainen, T., 2010. Exploring Quadruple Helix: Outlining User-oriented Innovation Models. Working paper, University of Tampere. https://tampub.uta.fi/bitstream/handle/10024/65758/978-951-44-8209-0.pdf?sequence=1. (Accessed July 10, 2016).

Atzori, L., Iera, A., Morabito, G., 2010. The internet of things: a survey. Comput. Netw. 54 (15), 2787–2805.

Aurigi, A., 2000. Digital city or urban simulator? In: Ishida, T., Isbister, K. (Eds.), Digital Cities: Technologies, Experiences and Future Perspectives. Springer, Berlin, pp. 33–44.

Aurigi, A., 2003. The First Steps of Digital Cities: Development of Social Shaping of Web-based Urban Cyberspace in Europe. Doctoral thesis, University of Newcastle upon Tyne. https://theses.ncl.ac.uk/dspace/handle/10443/506. (Accessed May 13, 2014).

Aurigi, A., 2005. Urban cyberspace as a social construction: non-technological factors in the shaping of digital Bristol. In: van den Besselaar, P., Koizumi, S. (Eds.), Digital Cities III. Information Technologies for Social Capital: Cross-Cultural Perspectives. Third International Digital Cities Workshop, Amsterdam, the Netherlands, September 18–19, 2003. Revised Selected Papers. Springer, Berlin, pp. 97–112.

Aurigi, A., 2006. New technologies, same dilemmas: policy and design issues for the augmented city. J. Urban Technol. 13 (3), 5–28.

Aurigi, A., Graham, S., 2000. Cyberspace and the City: The "virtual city" in Europe. In: Bridge, G., Watson, S. (Eds.), A Companion to the City. Blackwell Publishing, Malden, MA, pp. 489–502.

Baccarne, B., Mechant, P., Schuurman, D., 2014a. Empowered cities? An analysis of the structure and generated value of the smart city Ghent. In: Dameri, R.P., Rosenthal-Sabroux, C. (Eds.), Smart City: How to Create Public and Economic Value with High Technology in Urban Space. Springer, Cham, pp. 157–182.

Baccarne, B., Schuurman, D., Mechant, P., De Marez, L., 2014b. The role of urban living labs in a Smart City. In: XXV ISPIM Innovation Conference: Innovation for Sustainable Economy and Society, Dublin, 8–11 June 2014. International Society for Professional Innovation Management, Manchester.

Bastian, M., Heymann, S., Jacomy, M., 2009. Gephi: an open source software for exploring and manipulating networks. In: Adar, E., Hurst, M., Finin, T., Glance, N., Nicolov, N., Tseng, B. (Eds.), Proceedings of the Third International AAAI Conference on Weblogs and Social Media, San Jose, CA, 17–20 May 2009. AAAI Press, Menlo Park, CA, pp. 361–362.

Bergvall-Kåreborn, B., Ihlström Eriksson, C., Ståhlbröst, A., Svensson, J., 2009. A milieu for innovation – defining living labs. In: Proceedings of the 2nd ISPIM Innovation Symposium, New York City, NY, 6–9 December 2009. International Society for Professional Innovation Management (ISPIM), Manchester.

Blondel, V.D., Guillaume, J., Lambiotte, R., Lefebvre, E., 2008. Fast unfolding of communities in large networks. J. Stat. Mech. Theory Exp. 58 (10), 1–12.

Bolici, R., Mora, L., 2015. Urban regeneration in the digital era: how to develop smart city strategies in large European cities. TECHNE: J. Technol. Architect. Environ. 5 (2), 110–119.

Braam, R.R., Moed, H.F., van Raan, A.F.J., 1991a. Mapping of science by combined co-citation and word analysis. I: Structural aspects. J. Am. Soc. Inf. Sci. Technol. 42 (4), 233–251.

Braam, R.R., Moed, H.F., van Raan, A.F.J., 1991b. Mapping of science by combined co-citation and word analysis. II: Dynamical aspects. J. Am. Soc. Inf. Sci. Technol. 42 (4), 252–266.

Brech, B., Rajan, R., Fletcher, J., Harrison, C., Hayes, M., Hogan, J., Hopkins, L., Isom, P.K., Meegan, J., Penny, C., Snowdon, J.L., Wood, D.A., 2011. Smarter Cities Series: Understanding the IBM Approach to Efficient Buildings. IBM Corporation. http://www.redbooks.ibm.com/redpapers/pdfs/redp4735.pdf. (Accessed September 14, 2012).

Breuer, J., Walravens, N., Ballon, P., 2014. Beyond defining the smart city: meeting top-down and bottom-up approaches in the middle. TeMA: J. Land Use Mobil. Environ. 7, 153–164.

Callon, M., Courtial, J., Turner, W.A., Bauin, S., 1983. From translations to problematic networks: an introduction to co-word analysis. Soc. Sci. Inf. 22 (2), 191–235.

Callon, M., Law, J., Rip, A. (Eds.), 1986. Mapping the Dynamics of Science and Technology: Sociology of Science in the Real World. Macmillan, London.

Callon, M., Courtial, J.P., Laville, F., 1991. Co-word analysis as a tool for describing the network of interactions between basic and technological research: the case of polymer chemistry. Scientometrics 22 (1), 155–205.

Caragliu, A., Del Bo, C., Nijkamp, P., 2009. Smart cities in Europe. In: Paper presented at 3rd Central European Conference in Regional Science, Kosice, 7–9 October 2009. http://www.inta-aivn.org/images/cc/Urbanism/background%20documents/01_03_Nijkamp.pdf. (Accessed December 29, 2012).

Caragliu, A., Del Bo, C., Nijkamp, P., 2011. Smart cities in Europe. J. Urban Technol. 18 (2), 65–82.

Carayannis, E.G., Campbell, D., 2014. Developed democracies versus emerging autocracies: arts, democracy, and innovation in quadruple Helix innovation systems. J. Innov. Entrepreneurship 3 (12), 1–23.

Carvalho, L., 2015. Smart cities from scratch? a socio-technical perspective. Camb. J. Reg. Econ. Soc. 8 (1), 43–60.

Castells, M., 1996. The Rise of the Network Society. Blackwell Publishing Ltd., Oxford.

Cavallini, S., Soldi, R., Friedl, J., Volpe, M., 2016. Using the Quadruple Helix Approach to Accelerate the Transfer of Research and Innovation Results to Regional Growth. European Union - Committee of the Regions. http://cor.europa.eu/en/documentation/studies/Documents/quadruple-helix.pdf. (Accessed November 8, 2016).

Chen-Ritzo, C., Harrison, C., Paraszczak, J., Parr, F., 2009. Instrumenting the planet. IBM J. Res. Dev. 53 (3), 338–353.

Chi, R., Young, J., 2013. The interdisciplinary structure of research on intercultural relations: a co-citation network analysis study. Scientometrics 96 (1), 147–171.

Chourabi, H., Nam, T., Walker, S., Gil-Garcia, R.J., Mellouli, S., Nahon, K., Pardo, T.A., Scholl, H.J., 2012. Understanding smart cities: an integrative framework. In: Sprague, R.H. (Ed.), Proceedings of the 45th Hawaii International Conference on System Sciences (HICSS), Maui, HI, 04–07 January 2012. Institute of Electrical and Electronics Engineers (IEEE), Piscataway, NJ, pp. 2289–2297.

Christopoulou, E., Ringas, D., Garofalakis, J., 2014. The vision of the sociable smart city. In: Streitz, N., Markopoulos, P. (Eds.), Distributed, Ambient, and Pervasive Interactions: Second International Conference, DAPI 2014, Held as Part of HCI International 2014, Heraklion, Crete, Greece, June 22–27, 2014. Proceedings. Springer, Berlin, pp. 545–554.

Cisco Systems, 2016a. Cisco Smart+Connected Digital Platform: At-a-glance. Cisco Systems. http://www.cisco.com/c/dam/en_us/solutions/industries/docs/at-a-glance-c45-736521.pdf. (Accessed June 20, 2017).

Cisco Systems, 2016b. Cisco Smart+Connected Digital Platform: Data Sheet. Cisco Systems. http://www.cisco.com/c/dam/en_us/solutions/industries/docs/datasheet-c78-737127.pdf. (Accessed June 20, 2017).

Cobo, M., López-Herrera, A., Herrera-Viedma, E., Herrera, F., 2011. Science mapping software tools: review, analysis, and cooperative study among tools. J. Assoc. Inf. Sci. Technol. 62 (7), 1382–1402.

Cocchia, A., 2014. Smart and digital city: a systematic literature review. In: Dameri, R.P., Rosenthal-Sabroux, C. (Eds.), Smart City: How to Create Public and Economic Value with High Technology in Urban Space. Springer, Berlin, pp. 13–43.

Concilio, G., Rizzo, F. (Eds.), 2016. Human Smart Cities: Rethinking the Interplay between Design and Planning. Springer, Cham.

Cosgrove, M., Harthoorn, W., Hogan, J., Jabbar, R., Kehoe, M., Meegan, J., Nesbitt, P., 2011. Smarter Cities Series: Introducing the IBM City Operations and Management Solution. IBM Corporation. http://www.redbooks.ibm.com/redpapers/pdfs/redp4734.pdf. (Accessed September 14, 2012).

Cugurullo, F., 2013. How to build a sandcastle: an analysis of the genesis and development of Masdar City. J. Urban Technol. 20 (1), 23–37.

Cugurullo, F., 2016. Urban eco-modernisation and the policy context of new eco-city projects: where Masdar City fails and why. Urban Stud. 53 (11), 2417–2433.

Dameri, R.P., 2013. Searching for Smart City definition: a comprehensive proposal. Int. J. Comput. Technol. 11 (5), 2544–2551.

Dameri, R.P., 2014. Comparing smart and digital city: initiatives and strategies in Amsterdam and Genoa. Are they digital and/or smart? In: Dameri, R.P., Rosenthal-Sabroux, C. (Eds.), Smart City: How to Create Public and Economic Value with High Technology in Urban Space. Springer, Berlin, pp. 45–88.

Dameri, R.P., 2017. Smart City Implementation: Creating Economic and Public Value in Innovative Urban Systems. Springer, Cham.

de Bruine, A., 2000. Digital City Bristol: A case study. In: Ishida, T., Isbister, K. (Eds.), Digital Cities: Technologies, Experiences and Future Perspectives. Springer, Berlin, pp. 110–124.

De Bellis, N., 2009. Bibliometrics and Citation Analysis: From the Science Citation Index to Cybermetrics. The Scarecrow Press, Lanham, MD.

Deakin, M., 2014a. Smart cities: the state-of-the-art and governance challenge. Triple Helix 1 (7), 1–16.

Deakin, M. (Ed.), 2014b. Smart Cities: Governing, Modelling and Analysing the Transition. Routledge, New York City, NY.

Deakin, M., Al Wear, H., 2011. From intelligent to smart cities. Intell. Build. Int. 3 (3), 140–152.

Deakin, M., Leydesdorff, L., 2014. The triple helix model of smart cities: a neo-evolutionary perspective. In: Deakin, M. (Ed.), Smart Cities: Governing, Modelling and Analyzing the Transition. Routledge, New York, NY, pp. 134–149.

Ding, Y., Chowdhury, G.G., Foo, S., 2000. Journal as markers of intellectual space: Journal co-citation analysis of information retrieval area, 1987-1997. Scientometrics 47 (1), 55–73.

Ding, Y., Chowdhury, G.G., Foo, S., 2001. Bibliometric cartography of information retrieval research by using co-word analysis. Inf. Process. Manag. 37 (6), 817–842.

Dirks, S., Keeling, M., 2009. A Vision of Smarter Cities: how Cities Can Lead the Way Into a Prosperous and Sustainable Future. Executive report, IBM Corporation. http://www-03.ibm.com/press/attachments/IBV_Smarter_Cities_-_Final.pdf. (Accessed February 3, 2012).

Dirks, S., Keeling, M., Dencik, J., 2009. How Smart Is Your City: Helping Cities Measure Progress. Executive report, IBM Corporation. http://public.dhe.ibm.com/common/ssi/ecm/en/gbe03248usen/GBE03248USEN.PDF. (Accessed June 6, 2014).

Dirks, S., Gurdgiev, C., Keeling, M., 2010. Smarter Cities for Smarter Growth: How Cities Can Optimize Their Systems for the Talent-based Economy. Executive report IBM Corporation. http://public.dhe.ibm.com/common/ssi/ecm/en/gbe03348usen/GBE03348USEN.PDF. (Accessed February 3, 2012).

Dvir, R., Pasher, E., 2004. Innovation Engines for Knowledge Cities: an innovation ecology perspective. J. Knowl. Manag. 8 (5), 16–27.

Ersoy, A., 2017. Smart cities as a mechanism towards a broader understanding of infrastructure interdependencies. Region. Stud. Region. Sci. 4 (1), 1–6.

Etzkowitz, H., Leydesdorff, L., 2000. The dynamics of innovation: from national systems and "mode 2" to a triple helix of university-industry-government relations. Res. Policy 29 (2), 109–123.

European Commission, 2006. European SmartGrids Technology Platform: Vision for Europe's Electricity Networks of the Future. European Union, Brussels.

European Commission, 2009a. Communication from the Commission to the European Parliament, the Council, the European Economic and Social Committee and the Committee of the Regions. Investing in the Development of Low Carbon Technologies (SET-Plan). COM(2009) 519 final, European Commission. http://eur-lex.europa.eu/legal-content/IT/TXT/PDF/?uri=CELEX:52009DC0519&from=EN. (Accessed February 2, 2014).

European Commission, 2009b. Communication from the Commission to the European Parliament, the Council, the European Economic and Social Committee and the Committee of the Regions on Mobilising Information and Communication Technologies to Facilitate the Transition to An Energy Efficient, Low-carbon Economy. COM(2009) 111 final, European Commission. http://ec.europa.eu/information_society/activities/sustainable_growth/docs/com_2009_111/com2009-111-en.pdf. (Accessed February 2, 2014).

European Commission, 2011. Call FP7-ENERGY-SMARTCITIES-2012. Call fiche, European Commission. https://ec.europa.eu/research/participants/portal/doc/call/fp7/fp7-energy-smartcities-2012/31559-fiche_fp7-energy-2012-smartcities_en.pdf. (Accessed February 10, 2016).

European Commission, 2012a. Call FP7-SMARTCITIES-2013. European Commission. https://ec.europa.eu/research/participants/portal/doc/call/fp7/fp7-smartcities-2013/32801-call_fiche_fp7-smartcities-2013_en.pdf. (Accessed February 10, 2016).

European Commission, 2012b. Communication From the Commission: Smart Cities and Communities – European Innovation Partnership. C(2012) 4701 final, European Commission. http://eur-lex.europa.eu/legal-content/IT/TXT/PDF/?uri=CELEX:52009DC0519&from=EN. (Accessed February 2, 2014).

European Commission, 2014. National/Regional Innovation Strategies for Smart Specialisation (RIS3). European Commission. http://ec.europa.eu/regional_policy/sources/docgener/informat/2014/smart_specialisation_en.pdf. (Accessed February 2, 2014).

European Commission, 2016. Horizon 2020 Work Programme 2016–2017: Cross-cutting Activities (Focus Areas). European Commission Decision C(2016)4614, European Commission. http://ec.europa.eu/research/participants/data/ref/h2020/wp/2016_2017/main/h2020-wp1617-focus_en.pdf. (Accessed January 20, 2017).

European Innovation Partnership on Smart Cities and Communities, 2013. European Innovation Partnership on Smart Cities and Communities Strategic Implementation Plan. European Commission. http://ec.europa.eu/eip/smartcities/files/sip_final_en.pdf. (Accessed March 28, 2017).

Exner, J., 2015. Smart cities – field of application for planning support systems in the 21st century? In: Proceedings Computers in Urban Planning and Urban Management 2015, Cambridge, MA, 7–10 July 2015. Massachusetts Institute of Technology, Cambridge, MA.

Firmino, R.J., 2004. Building the Virtual City: The Dilemmas of Integrating Strategies for Urban and Electronic Spaces. PhD Dissertation, University of Newcastle upon Tyne. http://www.academia.edu/1112229/Building_the_virtual_city_the_dilemmas_of_integrating_strategies_for_urban_and_electronic_spaces. (Accessed September 1, 2014).

Florida, R., 2002. The Rise of the Creative Class: And How It's Transforming Work, Leisure, Community and Everyday Life. Basic Books, New York City, NY.

Florida, R., 2005. Cities and the Creative Class. Routledge, New York City, NY.

Food and Agriculture Organization, 2013. FAO Strategy for Partnerships with Civil Society Organizations. Food and Agriculture Organization. http://www.fao.org/3/a-i3443e.pdf. (Accessed May 27, 2017).

Gardner, N., Hespanhol, L., 2018. SMLXL: scaling the smart city, from metropolis to individual. City Cult. Soc. 12, 54–61.

Garfield, E., 1970. Citation indexing for studying science. Inf. Sci. 1 (15), 133–138.

Garfield, E., 1979a. Citation Indexing: Its Theory and Application in Science, Technology, and Humanities. John Wiley and Sons, New York City, NY.

Garfield, E., 1979b. Is citation analysis a legitimate evaluation tool? Scientometrics 1 (4), 359–375.

Giffinger, R., Ferter, C., Kramar, H., Kalasek, R., Pichler-Milanović, N., Meijers, E., 2007. Smart Cities: Ranking of European Medium-sized Cities. Research report, Vienna University of Technology – Centre of Regional Science (SRF). http://www.smart-cities.eu/download/smart_cities_final_report.pdf. (Accessed May 9, 2012).

Gil-Castineira, F., Costa-Montenegro, E., Gonzalez-Castano, F.J., Lopez-Bravo, C., Ojala, T., Bose, R., 2011. Experiences inside the ubiquitous Oulu Smart City. Computer 44 (6), 48–55.

Glanzel, W., Czerwon, H.J., 1996. A new methodological approach to bibliographic coupling and its application to the national, regional and institutional level. Scientometrics 37 (2), 195–221.

Glanzel, W., Thijs, B., 2011. Using 'core documents' for the representation of clusters and topics. Scientometrics 88 (1), 297–309.

Gmur, M., 2003. Co-citation analysis and the search for invisible colleges: a methodological evaluation. Scientometrics 57 (1), 27–57.

Godin, B., 2006. On the origins of bibliometrics. Scientometrics 68 (1), 109–133.

Gooch, D., Wolff, A., Kortuem, G., Brown, R., 2015. Reimagining the role of citizens in smart city projects (UbiComp/ISWC'15 Adjunct: Adjunct Proceedings of the 2015 ACM International Joint Conference on Pervasive and Ubiquitous Computing and Proceedings of the 2015 ACM International Symposium on Wearable Computers, Osaka, 7–11 September 2015). ACM Press, New York, NY, pp. 1587–1594.

Graham, S., 2004a. Introduction: From dreams of transcendence to the remediation of urban life. In: Graham, S. (Ed.), The Cybercities Reader. Routledge, New York, United States, pp. 1–29.

Graham, S. (Ed.), 2004b. The Cybercities Reader. Routledge, New York City, NY.

Graham, S., Marvin, S., 1996. Telecommunications and the City: Electronic Spaces, Urban Places. Routledge, New York City, NY.

Graham, S., Marvin, S., 1999. Planning cyber-cities? Integrating telecommunications into urban planning. Town Plan. Rev. 70 (1), 89–114.

Graham, S., Marvin, S., 2001. Splintering Urbanism: Networked Infrastructures, Technological Mobilities and the Urban Condition. Routledge, New York City, NY.

Grossi, G., Pianezzi, D., 2017. Smart cities: utopia or neoliberal ideology? Cities: Int. J. Urban Policy Plann. 69, 79–85.

GSMA, 2012. South Korea: Busan Green U-City. Report, GSMA. http://www.gsma.com/connectedliving/wp-content/uploads/2012/08/cl_busan_08_121.pdf. (Accessed June 20, 2013).

Harrison, C., Eckman, B., Hamilton, R., Hartswick, P., Kalagnanam, J., Paraszczak, J., Williams, P., 2010. Foundations for smarter cities. IBM J. Res. Dev. 54 (4), 1–16.
Harrison, C., Paraszczak, J., Williams, R.P., 2011. Preface: smarter cities. IBM J. Res. Dev. 55 (1–2), 1–5.
Hashem, I.A.T., Anuar, N.B., Gani, A., Yaqoob, I., Xia, F., Khan, S.U., 2016. MapReduce: review and open challenges. Scientometrics 109 (1), 389–422.
He, Q., 1999. Knowledge discovery through co-word analysis. Libr. Trends 48 (1), 133–159.
Heersmink, R., van den Hoven, J., van Eck, N.J., van den Berg, J., 2011. Bibliometric mapping of computer and information ethics. Ethics Inf. Technol. 13 (3), 241–249.
Hemment, D., Townsend, A. (Eds.), 2013. Smart Citizens. FutureEverything, Manchester.
Hollands, R.G., 2008. Will the real smart city please stand up? City: Anal. Urban Trends Culture Theory Policy Action 12 (3), 303–320.
Hollands, R.G., 2015. Critical interventions into the corporate smart city. Camb. J. Reg. Econ. Soc. 8 (1), 61–77.
Hollands, R.G., 2016. Beyond the corporate Smart City? Glimpses of other possibilities of smartness. In: Marvin, S., Luque-Ayala, A., McFarlane, C. (Eds.), Smart Urbanism: Utopian Vision or False Dawn? Routledge, New York City, NY, pp. 168–184.
Holler, J., Tsiatsis, V., Avesand, S., Karnouskos, S., Boyle, D., 2014. From Machine-To-Machine to the Internet of Things: Introduction to a New Age of Intelligence. Elsevier, Oxford.
Hutter, B.M., O'Mahony, J., 2004. The Role of Civil Society Organisations in Regulating Business. Discussion paper, London School of Economics and Political Science. http://www.lse.ac.uk/accounting/CARR/pdf/DPs/Disspaper26.pdf. (Accessed August 24, 2017).
IBM Corporation, 2011. City of Rio De Janeiro and IBM Collaborate to Advance Emergency Response System. Press release, IBM Corporation. http://www-03.ibm.com/press/us/en/pressrelease/35945.wss. (Accessed October 12, 2012).
IBM Corporation, 2017a. IBM Smarter Cities Challenge. Website, https://www.smartercitieschallenge.org. (Accessed March 20, 2017).
IBM Corporation, 2017b. IBM Smarter Planet. Website, http://www-03.ibm.com/ibm/history/ibm100/us/en/icons/smarterplanet/. (Accessed March 20, 2017).
Ishida, T., Isbister, K. (Eds.), 2000. Digital Cities: Technologies, Experiences and Future Perspectives. Springer, Berlin.
ITU, 2005. ITU Internet Reports 2005: The Internet of Things. Report, International Telecommunication Union. http://www.itu.int/osg/spu/publications/internetofthings/. (Accessed June 4, 2014).
Jacobsen, T., Punzalan, R.L., Hedstrom, M.L., 2013. Invoking collective memory: mapping the emergence of a concept in archival science. Arch. Sci. 13 (2–3), 217–251.
Juan, Y.K., Wang, L., Wang, J., Leckie, J., Li, K.M., 2011. A decision-support system for smarter city planning and management. IBM J. Res. Dev. 55 (1-2). 3:1–3:12.
Karnouskos, S., Nass de Holanda, T., 2009. Simulation of a smart grid city with software agents. In: EMS '09: Third UKSim European Symposium on Computer Modeling and Simulation, Athens, 25-27 November 2009. Institute of Electrical and Electronics Engineers (IEEE), Piscataway, NJ, pp. 424–429.
Katz, J.S., Ruano, J., 2011. Smarter Cities Series: Understanding the IBM Approach to Energy Innovation. IBM Corporation. http://www.redbooks.ibm.com/redpapers/pdfs/redp4739.pdf. (Accessed September 14, 2012).
Kehoe, M., Cosgrove, M., De Gennaro, S., Harrison, C., Harthoorn, W., Hogan, J., Meegan, J., Nesbitt, P., Peters, C., 2011. Smarter Cities Series: A Foundation for Understanding IBM Smarter Cities. IBM Corporation. http://www.redbooks.ibm.com/redpapers/pdfs/redp4733.pdf. (Accessed September 14, 2012).

King, J., 1987. A review of bibliometric and other science indicators and their role in research evaluation. J. Inf. Sci. 13 (5), 261–276.

Kitchin, R., 2014. The real-time city? Big data and smart urbanism. GeoJournal 79 (1), 1–14.

Kitchin, R., 2015. Making sense of smart cities: addressing present shortcomings. Camb. J. Reg. Econ. Soc. 8 (1), 131–136.

Kohno, M., Masuyama, Y., Kato, N., Tobe, A., 2011. Hitachi's smart city solutions for new era of urban development. Hitachi Rev. 60 (2), 79–88.

Komninos, N., 2002. Intelligent Cities: Innovation, Knowledge, Systems and Digital Spaces. Spon Press, New York City, NY.

Komninos, N., 2006. The architecture of intelligent cities: integrating human, collective and artificial intelligence to enhance knowledge. In: Proceedings of the 2nd IET International Conference on Intelligent Environments, Athens, 05–06 July 2006. Page Bros Ltd., Norwich, pp. 13–20.

Komninos, N., 2008. Intelligent Cities and Globalization of Innovation Networks. Routledge, New York City, NY.

Komninos, N., 2011. Intelligent cities: Variable geometries of spatial intelligence. Intell. Build. Int. 3 (3), 172–188.

Komninos, N., 2014. The Age of Intelligent Cities: Smart Environments and Innovation-For-All Strategies. Routledge, New York City, NY.

Kourtit, K., Deakin, M., Caragliu, A., Del Bo, C., Nijkamp, P., Lombardi, P., Giordano, S., 2014. An advanced triple helix network framework for smart cities performance. In: Deakin, M. (Ed.), Smart Cities: Governing, Modelling and Analyzing the Transition. Routledge, New York, NY, pp. 196–216.

Kovács, A., Van Looy, B., Cassiman, B., 2015. Exploring the scope of open innovation: a bibliometric review of a decade of research. Scientometrics 104 (3), 951–983.

Kurebayashi, T., Masuyama, Y., Morita, K., Taniguchi, N., Mizuki, F., 2011. Global initiatives for smart urban development. Hitachi Rev. 60 (2), 89–93.

Landry, C., 2000. The Creative City: A Toolkit for Urban Innovation. Earthscan, London.

Lee, J., Hancock, M.G., 2012. Toward a Framework for Smart Cities: A Comparison of Seoul, San Francisco and Amsterdam. Presentation, Yonsei University and Stanford University. http://iis-db.stanford.edu/evnts/7239/Jung_Hoon_Lee_final.pdf. (Accessed June 12, 2014).

Lee, S., Han, J., Leem, Y., Yigitcanlar, T., 2008. Towards ubiquitous city: concept, planning, and experiences in the Republic of Korea. In: Yigitcanlar, T., Velibeyoglu, K., Baum, S. (Eds.), Knowledge-Based Urban Development: Planning and Applications in the Information Era. IGI Global, Hershey, PA, pp. 148–169.

Lee, J., Hancock, M.G., Hu, M., 2014. Towards an effective framework for building smart cities: lessons from Seoul and San Francisco. Technol. Forecast. Soc. Chang. 89, 80–99.

Leydesdorff, L., 1997. Why words and co-words cannot map the development of the sciences. J. Am. Soc. Inf. Sci. Technol. 48 (5), 418–427.

Leydesdorff, L., Deakin, M., 2011. The triple-helix model of smart cities: a neo-evolutionary perspective. J. Urban Technol. 18 (2), 53–63.

Leydesdorff, L., Rafols, I., 2009. A global map of science based on the ISI subject categories. J. Am. Soc. Inf. Sci. Technol. 60 (2), 348–362.

Leydesdorff, L., Hammarfelt, B., Akdag Salah, A.A., 2011. The structure of the arts & humanities citation index: a mapping on the basis of aggregated citations among 1,157 journals. J. Am. Soc. Inf. Sci. Technol. 62 (12), 2414–2426.

Liu, Z., 2005. Visualizing the intellectual structure in urban studies: a journal co-citation analysis (1992-2002). Scientometrics 62 (3), 385–402.

Liu, G., Hu, J., Wang, H., 2012. A co-word analysis of digital library field in China. Scientometrics 91 (1), 203–217.

Lombardi, P., Giordano, S., Caragliu, A., Del Bo, C., Deakin, M., Nijkamp, P., Kourtit, K., Farouh, H., 2012a. An advanced triple helix network model for smart cities performance. In: Yalciner Ercoskun, O. (Ed.), Green and Ecological Technologies for Urban Planning: Creating Smart Cities. IGI Global, Hershey, PA, pp. 59–73.

Lombardi, P., Giordano, S., Farouh, H., Yousef, W., 2012b. Modelling the smart city performance. Innov. Eur. J. Soc. Sci. Res. 25 (2), 137–149.

Luque-Ayala, A., Marvin, S., 2015. Developing a critical understanding of smart urbanism? Urban Stud. 52 (12), 2105–2116.

Luque-Ayala, A., McFarlane, C., Marvin, S., 2014. Smart urbanism: cities, grids and alternatives? In: Hodson, M., Marvin, S. (Eds.), After Sustainable Cities? Routeldge, New York City, NY, pp. 74–90.

MacRoberts, M.H., MacRoberts, B.R., 1989. Problems of citation analysis: a critical review. J. Am. Soc. Inf. Sci. Technol. 40 (5), 342–349.

Manville, C., Cochrane, G., Cave, J., Millard, J., Pederson, J.K., Thaarup, R.K., Liebe, A., Wissner, M., Massink, R., Kotterink, B., 2014. Mapping Smart City in the EU. Research report, European Parliament – Directorate-General for Internal Policies. http://www.europarl.europa.eu/RegData/etudes/etudes/join/2014/507480/IPOL-ITRE_ET(2014)507480_EN.pdf. (Accessed February 5, 2014).

McCain, K.W., 1986. Cocited author mapping as a valid representation of intellectual structure. J. Am. Soc. Inf. Sci. Technol. 37 (3), 111–122.

McCain, K.W., 1990. Mapping authors in intellectual space: a technical overview. J. Am. Soc. Inf. Sci. Technol. 41 (6), 433–443.

McCain, K.W., 1991. Mapping economics through the journal literature: an experiment in journal cocitation analysis. J. Am. Soc. Inf. Sci. Technol. 42 (4), 290–296.

McNeill, D., 2016. IBM and the visual formation of smart cities. In: Marvin, S., Luque-Ayala, A., McFarlane, C. (Eds.), Smart Urbanism: Utopian Vision or False Dawn? Routledge, New York City, NY, pp. 34–51.

Meijer, A., Bolivar, M.P.R., 2016. Governing the smart city: a review of the literature on smart urban governance. Int. Rev. Adm. Sci. 82 (2), 392–408.

Meyer, M., Libaers, D., Thijs, B., Grant, K., Glanzel, W., Debackere, K., 2014. Origin and emergence of entrepreneurship as a research field. Scientometrics 98 (1), 473–485.

Mino, E., 2000. Experiences of European digital cities. In: Ishida, T., Isbister, K. (Eds.), Digital Cities: Technologies, Experiences and Future Perspectives. Springer, Berlin, pp. 58–72.

Miorandi, D., Sicari, S., De Pellegrini, F., Chlamtac, I., 2012. Internet of things: vision, applications and research challenges. Ad Hoc Netw. 10 (7), 1497–1516.

Mitchell, W.J., 1995. The City of Bits: Space, Place, and the Infobahn. MIT Press, Cambridge, MA.

Mitchell, W.J., 1999. E-Topia: Urban Life, Jim--But Not as We Know It. MIT Press, Cambridge, MA.

Mitchell, W.J., 2003. Me++: The Cyborg Self and the Networked City. MIT Press, Cambridge, MA.

Mora, L., Bolici, R., 2016. The development process of smart city strategies: the case of Barcelona. In: Rajaniemi, J. (Ed.), Re-City: Future City – Combining Disciplines. Juvenes Print, Tampere, pp. 155–181.

Mora, L., Bolici, R., 2017. How to become a smart city: learning from Amsterdam. In: Bisello, A., Vettorato, D., Stephens, R., Elisei, P. (Eds.), Smart and Sustainable Planning for Cities and Regions: Results of SSPCR 2015. Springer, Cham, pp. 251–266.

Moss Kanter, R., Litow, S.S., 2009. Informed and Interconnected: A Manifesto for Smarter Cities. Working paper Harvard Business School. http://www.hbs.edu/faculty/Publication%20Files/09-141.pdf. (Accessed January 24, 2012).

Nam, T., Pardo, T.A., 2011a. Conceptualizing smart city with dimensions of technology, people and institutions. In: Bertot, J., Nahon, K., Chun, S.A., Luna-Reyes, L., Atluri, V. (Eds.), Proceedings of the 12th Annual International Conference on Digital Government Research: Digital Government Innovation in Challenging Times, College Park, MD, 12–15 June 2011. ACM Press, New York City, NY, pp. 282–291.

Nam, T., Pardo, T.A., 2011b. Smart city as urban innovation: focusing on management, policy, and context. In: Estevez, E., Janssen, M. (Eds.), Proceedings of the 5th International Conference on Theory and Practice of Electronic Governance (ICEGOV2011), Tallinn, 26–28 September 2011. ACM Press, New York City, NY, pp. 185–194.

Naphade, M., Banavar, G., Harrison, C., Paraszczak, J., Morris, R., 2011. Smarter cities and their innovation challenges. Computer 44 (6), 32–39.

Niaros, V., 2016. Introducing a taxonomy of the "Smart City": towards a commons-oriented approach? tripleC 14 (1), 51–61.

Palmisano, S.J., 2008. A Smarter Planet: The Next Leadership Agenda. IBM Corporation. https://www.ibm.com/ibm/cioleadershipexchange/us/en/pdfs/SJP_Smarter_Planet.pdf. (Accessed March 3, 2011).

Paroutis, S., Bennett, M., Heracleous, L., 2014. A strategic view on smart city technology: the case of IBM smarter cities during a recession. Technol. Forecast. Soc. Chang. 89, 262–272.

Paskaleva, K.A., 2009. Enabling the smart city: the progress of city e-governance in Europe. Int. J. Innov. Region. Dev. 1 (4), 405–422.

Paskaleva, K.A., 2011. The smart city: a nexus for open innovation? Intell. Build. Int. 3 (3), 133–152.

Paul, A., Cleverley, M., Kerr, W., Marzolini, F., Reade, M., Russo, S., 2011. Smarter Cities Series: Understanding the IBM Approach to Public Safety. IBM Corporation. http://www.redbooks.ibm.com/redpapers/pdfs/redp4738.pdf. (Accessed September 14, 2012).

Peeters, B., 2000. The information society in the City of Antwerp. In: Ishida, T., Isbister, K. (Eds.), Digital Cities: Technologies, Experiences and Future Perspectives. Springer, Berlin, pp. 73–82.

Polastre, J., Hill, J., Culler, D., 2004. Versatile low power media access for wireless sensor networks. In: SenSys '04: Proceedings of the 2nd International Conference on Embedded Networked Sensor Systems, Baltimore, MD, 3–5 November 2004. ACM Press, New York City, NY, pp. 95–107.

Pollio, A., 2016. Technologies of austerity urbanism: the "smart city" agenda in Italy (2011–2013). Urban Geogr. 37 (4), 514–534.

Pritchard, A., 1969. Statistical bibliography or bibliometrics? J. Doc. 25 (4), 348–349.

Randhawa, K., Wilden, R., Hohberger, J., 2016. A bibliometric review of open innovation: setting a research agenda. J. Prod. Innov. Manag. 33 (6), 750–772.

Ratti, C., Townsend, A., 2011. The social nexus. Sci. Am. September. 2011, 42–48.

Reddy Kummitha, R.K., Crutzen, N., 2017. How do we understand smart cities? An evolutionary perspective. Cities: Int. J. Urban Policy Plann. 67, 43–52.

Republic of Korea, 2007a. U-city. Brochure, Republic of Korea. http://eng.nia.or.kr/english/bbs/download.asp?fullpathname=%5CData%5Cattach%5C201112221611231975%5Cu-City(2007).pdf&filename=u-City(2007).pdf. (Accessed September 6, 2014).

Republic of Korea, 2007b. U-Korea Master Plan: To Achieve the World First Ubiquitous Society. Republic of Korea. http://www.ipc.go.kr/servlet/download?pt=/ipceng/public&fn=u-KOREA+Master+Plan+.pdf. (Accessed September 6, 2014).

Reyes-Gonzalez, L., Gonzalez-Brambila, C.N., Veloso, F., 2016. Using co-authorship and citation analysis to identify research groups: a new way to assess performance. Scientometrics 108 (3), 1171–1191.

Ruano, J., Chao, T., Hartswick, P., Havers, B., Meegan, J., Wasserkrug, S., Williams, P., 2011. Smarter Cities Series: Understanding the IBM Approach to Water Management. IBM Corporation. http://www.redbooks.ibm.com/redpapers/pdfs/redp4736.pdf. (Accessed September 14, 2012).

Sanchez, L., Galache, J.A., Gutierrez, V., Hernandez, J.M., Bernat, J., Gluhak, A., Garcia, T., 2011. SmartSantander: the meeting point between future Internet research and experimentation and the smart cities. In: Cunningham, P., Cunningham, M. (Eds.), Future Network and Mobile Summit 2011 Conference Proceedings, Warsaw, 15-17 June 2011. Institute of Electrical and Electronics Engineers (IEEE), Piscataway, NJ, pp. 1–8.

Sanchez, L., Gutierrez, V., Galache, J.A., Sotres, P., Santana, J.R., Casanueva, J., Munoz, L., 2013. SmartSantander: experimentation and service provision in the Smart City. In: 2013 16th International Symposium on Wireless Personal Multimedia Communications (WPMC), Atlantic City, NJ, 24-27 June 2013. Institute of Electrical and Electronics Engineers (IEEE), Piscataway, NJ, pp. 1–6.

Schaefer, S., Harrison, C., Lamba, N., Srikanth, V., 2011. Smarter Cities Series: Understanding the IBM Approach to Traffic Management. IBM Corporation. http://www.redbooks.ibm.com/redpapers/pdfs/redp4737.pdf. (Accessed September 14, 2012).

Schaffers, H., Komninos, N., Pallot, M., Trousse, B., Nilsson, M., Oliveira, A., 2011. Smart cities and the future Internet: towards cooperation frameworks for open innovation. In: Domingue, J., Galis, A., Gavras, A., Zahariadis, T., Lambert, D., Cleary, F., Daras, P., Krco, S., Muller, H., Li, M., Schaffers, H., Lotz, V., Alvarez, F., Stiller, B., Karnouskos, S., Avessta, S., Nillson, M. (Eds.), The Future Internet. Future Internet Assembly 2011: Achievements and Technological Promises. Springer, Berlin, pp. 431–446.

Schaffers, H., Komninos, N., Pallot, M., Aguas, M., Almirall, E., Bakici, T., Barroca, J., Carter, D., Corriou, M., Fernadez, J., Hielkema, H., Kivilehto, A., Nilsson, M., Oliveira, A., Posio, E., Sällström, A., Santoro, R., Senach, B., Torres, I., Tsarchopoulos, P., Trousse, B., Turkama, P., Lopez Ventura, J., 2012. Smart Cities as Innovation Ecosystems Sustained by the Future Internet. White paper, http://hal.archives-ouvertes.fr/docs/00/76/96/35/PDF/FIREBALL-White-Paper-Final2.pdf. (Accessed August 24, 2011).

Schuurman, D., Baccarne, B., De Marez, L., Mechant, P., 2012. Smart ideas for smart cities: investigating crowdsourcing for generating and selecting ideas for ICT innovation in a City context. J. Theor. Appl. Electron. Commer. Res. 7 (3), 49–62.

Schuurman, D., De Marez, L., Ballon, P., 2016. The impact of living lab methodology on open innovation contributions and outcomes. Technol. Innov. Manage. Rev. 6 (1), 7–16.

Scuotto, V., Ferraris, A., Bresciani, S., 2016. Internet of things. Applications and challenges in smart cities: a case study of IBM smart city projects. Bus. Process. Manag. J. 22 (2), 357–367.

Selada, C., 2017. Smart cities and the quadruple helix innovation systems conceptual framework: the case of Portugal. In: Monteiro, S., Carayannis, E.G. (Eds.), The Quadruple Innovation Helix Nexus: A Smart Growth Model, Quantitative Empirical Validation and Operationalization for OECD Countries. Palgrave, New York City, NY, pp. 211–244.

Shin, D., 2007. A critique of Korean National Information Strategy: case of national information infrastructures. Gov. Inf. Q. 24 (3), 624–645.

Shin, D., 2009. Ubiquitous city: urban technologies, urban infrastructure and urban informatics. J. Inf. Sci. 35 (5), 515–526.

Shin, D., 2010. A realization of pervasive computing: ubiquitous city. In: Kocaoglu, D.F., Anderson, T.R., Daim, T.U. (Eds.), 2010 Proceedings of PICMET'10: Technology Management for Global Economic Growth, Seoul, 18–22 July 2010. Institute of Electrical and Electronics Engineers (IEEE), Piscataway, NJ, pp. 1–10.

Shin, D., Kim, T., 2010. Large-scale ICT innovation and policy. In: Kocaoglu, D.F., Anderson, T.R., Daim, T.U., Jetter, A., Weber, C.M. (Eds.), PICMET 2010 Proceedings: Technology Management for Global Economic Growth, Seoul, 18-22 July 2010. Institute of Electrical and Electronics Engineers (IEEE), Piscataway, NJ, pp. 148–161.

Shin, D., Lee, C., 2011. Disruptive innovation for social change: how technology innovation can be best managed in social context. Telematics Inform. 28 (2), 86–100.

Siemens, 2014. Our Future Depends on Intelligent Infrastructures. Siemens AG. https://www.siemens.com/digitalization/public/pdf/siemens-intelligent-infrastructure.pdf. (Accessed March 6, 2017).

Small, H.G., 1973. Co-citation in the scientific literature: a new measure of the relationship between two documents. J. Am. Soc. Inf. Sci. Technol. 24 (4), 265–269.

Small, H.G., 1978. Cited documents as concept symbols. Soc. Stud. Sci. 8 (3), 327–340.

Small, H.G., Griffith, B.C., 1974. The structure of scientific literature I: Identifying and graphing specialties. Sci. Stud. 4 (1), 17–40.

Soderstrom, O., Paasche, T., Klauser, F., 2014. Smart cities as corporate storytelling. City: Anal. Urban Trends Culture Theory Policy Action 18 (3), 307–320.

Song, J., Zhang, H., Dong, W., 2016. A review of emerging trends in global PPP research: analysis and visualization. Scientometrics 107 (3), 1111–1147.

Strickland, E., 2011. Cisco bets on south Korean Smart City. IEEE Spectr. 48 (8), 11–12.

Sujata, J., Saksham, S., Godbole, T., Shreya, 2016. Developing smart cities: an integrated framework. Procedia Comput. Sci. 93, 902–909.

Sundmaeker, H., Guillemin, P., Friess, P., Woelfflé, S. (Eds.), 2010. Vision and Challenges for Realising the Internet of Things. European Commission, Brussels.

Tamai, H., 2014. Fujitsu's approach to smart cities. FUJITSU Sci. Tech. J. 50 (2), 3–10.

Tekes, 2011. Ubiquitous City in Korea: Services and Enabling Technologies. Report, Tekes. https://www.tekes.fi/globalassets/global/ohjelmat-ja-palvelut/ohjelmat/ubicom/aineistot/raportit/korea/ubiquitouscityinkorea.pdf. (Accessed May 15, 2014).

The Climate Group, 2008. SMART 2020: Enabling the Low Carbon Economy in the Information Age. Report, The Climate Group. http://www.smart2020.org/_assets/files/02_Smart2020Report.pdf. (Accessed June 5, 2014).

Townsend, A., 2013. Smart Cities: Big Data, Civic Hackers, and the Quest for a New Utopia. W.W. Norton & Company Ltd., New York City, NY.

Townsend, A., Maguire, R., Liebhold, M., Crawford, M., 2011. A Planet of Civic Laboratories: The Future of Cities, Information and Inclusion. White paper, Institute for the Future. http://www.iftf.org/uploads/media/IFTF_Rockefeller_CivicLaboratoriesMap_01.pdf. (Accessed December 8, 2011).

Tsay, M., Xu, H., Wu, C., 2003. Journal co-citation analysis of semiconductor literature. Scientometrics 57 (1), 7–25.

Tselentis, G., Domingue, J., Galis, A., Gavras, A., Hausheer, D., Krco, H., Lotz, V., Zahariadis, T. (Eds.), 2009. Towards the Future Internet: A European Research Perspective. IOS Press, Amsterdam.

UN-Habitat, 2011. Cities and Climate Change: Global Report on Human Settlements 2011. Earthscan, London.

United Nations, 1998. Arrangements and Practices for the Interaction of Non-governmental Organizations in All Activities of the United Nations System. Report of the Secretary-General (A/53/170), United Nations - Department of Economic and Social Affairs. http://www.un.org/documents/ga/docs/53/plenary/a53-170.htm. (Accessed May 15, 2017).

US Department of Commerce - National Institute of Standards and Technology, 2010. NIST Framework and Roadmap for Smart Grid Interoperability Standards. Report, National Institute of

Standards and Technology - US Department of Commerce. http://www.nist.gov/public_affairs/releases/upload/smartgrid_interoperability_final.pdf. (Accessed September 30, 2014).

van den Besselaar, P., 2001. E-community versus E-commerce: the rise and decline of the Amsterdam Digital City. AI Soc. Knowl. Cult. Commun. 15 (3), 280–288.

van Waart, P., Mulder, I., de Bont, C., 2016. A participatory approach for envisioning a Smart City. Soc. Sci. Comput. Rev. 34 (6), 708–723.

van Winden, W., van den Buuse, D., 2017. Smart city pilot projects: Exploring the dimensions and conditions of scaling up. J. Urban Technol. 24 (4), 51–72.

Viitanen, J., Kingston, R., 2014. Smart cities and green growth: outsourcing democratic and environmental resilience to the global technology sector. Environ Plan A 46 (4), 803–819.

Wang, N., Liang, H., Jia, Y., Ge, S., Xue, Y., Wang, Z., 2016. Cloud computing research in the IS discipline: a citation/co-citation analysis. Decis. Support. Syst. 86, 35–47.

Washburn, D., Usman, S., Balaouras, S., Dines, R.A., Hayes, N.M., Nelson, L.E., 2010. Helping CIOs Understand "Smart City" Initiatives. White paper, Forrester Research. http://www.forrester.com/Helping+CIOs+Understand+Smart+City+Initiatives/quickscan/-/E-RES55590. (Accessed March 20, 2012).

Weiser, M., 1991. The computer for the 21st century. Mobile Comput. Commun. Rev. 3 (3), 3–11.

Weiser, M., 1993. Hot topics: ubiquitous computing. Computer 26 (10), 71–72.

Weiser, M., Gold, R., Brown, J.S., 1999. The origins of ubiquitous computing research at PARC in the late 1980s. IBM Syst. J. 38 (4), 693–696.

White, H.D., 1990. Author co-citation analysis: overview and defense. In: Borgman, C.L. (Ed.), Scholarly Communication and Bibliometrics. Sage Publications, Newbury Park, CA, pp. 84–106.

World Economic Forum, 2013. The Future Role of Civil Society. World Economic Forum. http://www3.weforum.org/docs/WEF_FutureRoleCivilSociety_Report_2013.pdf. (Accessed May 1, 2017).

Yigitcanlar, T., 2016. Technology and the City: Systems, Applications and Implications. Routledge, New York City, NY.

Yigitcanlar, T., Kamruzzaman, M., 2018. Does smart city policy lead to sustainability of cities? Land Use Policy 73, 49–58.

Yigitcanlar, T., Lee, S.H., 2014. Korean ubiquitous-eco-city: a smart-sustainable urban form or a branding hoax? Technol. Forecast. Soc. Change 89, 100–114.

Yigitcanlar, T., O'Connor, K., Westerman, C., 2008a. The making of knowledge cities: Melbourne's knowledge-based urban development experience. Cities 25 (2), 63–72.

Yigitcanlar, T., Velibeyoglu, K., Baum, S. (Eds.), 2008b. Creative Urban Regions: Harnessing Urban Technologies to Support Knowledge City Initiatives. IGI Global, Hershey, PA.

Yigitcanlar, T., Velibeyoglu, K., Baum, S. (Eds.), 2008c. Knowledge-Based Urban Development: Planning and Applications in the Information Era. IGI Global, Hershey, PA.

Yigitcanlar, T., Velibeyoglu, K., Martinez-Fernandez, C., 2008d. Rising knowledge cities: the role of urban knowledge precincts. J. Knowl. Manag. 12 (5), 8–20.

Yoshikawa, Y., Tada, K., Furuya, S., Koda, K., 2011. Actions for realizing next-generation smart cities. Hitachi Rev. 60 (6), 89–93.

Zhao, Y., Cui, L., Yang, H., 2009. Evaluating reliability of co-citation clustering analysis in representing the research history of subject. Scientometrics 80 (1), 91–102.

Zhu, J., Hua, W., 2017. Visualizing the knowledge domain of sustainable development research between 1987 and 2015: a bibliometric analysis. Scientometrics 110 (2), 893–914.

Zygiaris, S., 2013. Smart city reference model: assisting planners to conceptualize the building of smart city innovation ecosystems. J. Knowl. Econ. 4 (2), 217–231.

Chapter 5

Smart city development in Europe

Chapter outline

5.1 Introduction

Disagreements in smart city research were first reported on by Hollands (2008) after reviewing the scientific literature on smart cities that was published between 1990 and 2007. His research compares a number of attempts to explain what factors and conditions enable smart city development, and it captures both a lack of clarity and the absence of any agreement on how smart city

Untangling Smart Cities. https://doi.org/10.1016/B978-0-12-815477-9.00005-0

development is understood by the scientific community. According to Albino et al. (2015) and Meijer and Bolivar (2016), notwithstanding the growing interest in smart city development strategies and the increasing production of scientific literature investigating their design and implementation process, these disagreements on what smart city development represents are still firmly entrenched in smart city research. The validity of this claim is proved in the previous two chapters, which reveal the presence of a critical division in the intellectual structure of the smart city research field and uncover the contradictions that such a division has generated. These contradictions surface as four dichotomies questioning whether smart city development should be:

(1) Approached with a technology-led and market-oriented or holistic and human-centric strategy;
(2) Founded on either a double- or quadruple-helix model of collaboration;
(3) Based on a top-down or a bottom-up approach;
(4) Driven by a monodimensional or integrated intervention logic.

These dichotomies present divergent hypotheses on what strategic principles drive smart city development and the strategies assembled to enable it. As previously pointed out, such a division introduces uncertainty over the implementation of strategies for supporting smart city development. In addition, it reveals a critical knowledge gap that needs to be closed in order for smart cities to move forward as a set of urban innovation practices able to demonstrate the capacity that information and communication technology has to support urban sustainability.

This chapter reports on the findings of a deductive-based multiple case study analysis that helps to achieve this aim.[1] The validity of the hypotheses that each dichotomy puts forward to explain what strategic principles drive smart city development is tested in Europe. This task is accomplished by comparing four cities considered to be leading examples of smart cities. These hypotheses are listed in Table 5.1, and the cities selected for conducting the analysis are Amsterdam, Barcelona, Helsinki, and Vienna, which are respectively located in the Netherlands, Spain, Finland, and Austria (see Fig. 5.1).

The chapter is structured in four main sections. It begins by setting out the methodology used to conduct the multiple case study analysis (Section 5.2) and the results which were obtained, explaining how each city has approached smart city development in relation to the four dichotomies (Section 5.3). The results of this analysis make it possible to conclude with a number of recommendations that address: (1) which strategic principles European cities should take into consideration in order to support smart city development; and (2) how future

1. This chapter is reprinted from Technological Forecasting and Social Change, Volume 142, Mora, L., Deakin, M., and Reid, A., Strategic principles for smart city development: A multiple case study analysis of European best practices, 70–97, 2019, with permission from Elsevier. The contents of the article have not been altered but adapted minimally to serve the purpose of this book.

TABLE 5.1 Dichotomies and divergent hypotheses

Dichotomies	Hypotheses
Dichotomy 1: Technology-led or holistic strategy	*Hypothesis 1.1*: Technology-led strategy *Hypothesis 1.2*: Holistic strategy
Dichotomy 2: Double- or quadruple-helix model of collaboration	*Hypothesis 2.1*: Double-helix model of collaboration *Hypothesis 2.2*: Quadruple-helix model of collaboration
Dichotomy 3: Top-down or bottom-up approach	*Hypothesis 3.1*: Top-down approach *Hypothesis 3.2*: Bottom-up approach
Dichotomy 4: Monodimensional or integrated intervention logic	*Hypothesis 4.1*: Monodimensional intervention logic *Hypothesis 4.2*: Integrated intervention logic

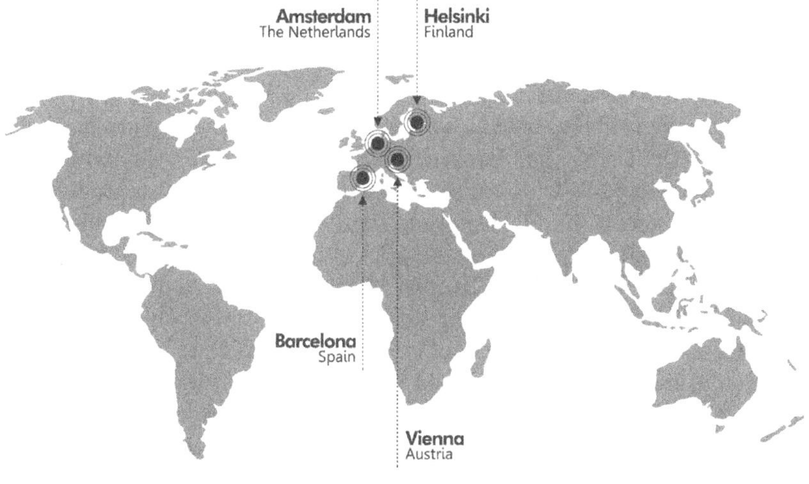

FIG. 5.1 The four smart city development strategies under investigation.

research on smart cities should continue to produce the scientific knowledge that is necessary to fully overcome the knowledge gap that the dichotomous nature of smart city research has generated. These recommendations are discussed in Sections 5.4 and 5.5, the two sections which conclude the chapter.

5.2 Hypothesis testing with case study research: Phase 1

This study reports on a multiple case study analysis which is conducted to start filling the knowledge gap generated by the dichotomous nature of smart city research and to generate insight into what strategic principles European cities should consider when approaching the design and implementation process of strategies for enabling smart city development. To meet this aim, the divergent hypotheses emerging from the dichotomies are tested by analyzing a group of outstanding examples of European smart cities, that is, cities in which smart city development strategies have been implemented and proved to be successful in serving sustainable urban development by adopting ICT-related solutions.

The sampling process was conducted by means of a theoretical approach, which led to the selection of Amsterdam, Barcelona, Helsinki, and Vienna. Therefore, the case studies that this investigation focused attention on were not randomly selected, but chosen as laboratory experiments, for their capability to offer theoretical insight (Eisenhardt and Graebner, 2007). These cities can be considered as extreme cases, that is, unusual manifestations of the smart city phenomenon which show outstanding success in approaching the ICT-driven approach to urban sustainability that smart cities promote (Eisenhardt, 1989; Patton, 2002; Eisenhardt and Graebner, 2007). Their success and international leadership in the field of smart cities are demonstrated by reviewing the literature reporting on (1) competitions in which these cities have been awarded for their smart city development strategies and (2) smart city rankings and comparative analyses of smart city cases in which one or more selected cities are shown to be as leading examples. The data resulting from this literature review is summarized in Table 5.2.

The investigation was conducted by adopting a literal replication logic[2] (Creswell, 2009; George and Bennett, 2005; Yin, 2009). This ensured that the selected cases were subject to the same analytic process, which started with the data collection phase. To establish what strategic principles have led these four cities toward becoming outstanding examples of smart city developments, two databases were built and analyzed. The first database classifies all the activities that each city has implemented to enable smart city development. The classification was managed by considering the four categories presented in Fig. 5.2. This system allowed the activities to be grouped according to the objectives and outcomes toward which efforts have been directed. The activities producing outcomes belonging to multiple categories were included in more than one group. The analysis of the percentage share related to each group made it possible to test the hypotheses related to Dichotomy 1 and Dichotomy 3 and to determine whether the smart city development strategies under investigation are (1) holistic or technology-led and (2) developed by means of a top-down or bottom-up approach.

The activities belonging to the category "C. Services and Applications" were then assigned to one or more application domains in order to investigate

2. When conducting multiple case study analyses, each case is subject to the same analytic process. This approach is called replication, which can be either literal or theoretical. The literal replication is used when the cases are chosen due to their similar settings, and their analysis is expected to provide similar results. On the contrary, the theoretical replication is adopted when the selected cases have different settings and variations are expected in the analysis' results. This happens when, for example, successful and unsuccessful cases are compared.

TABLE 5.2 The success of the selected cases in the field of smart cities: awards and positions in national and international ranking systems

Case study	Evidence of success
Amsterdam	2009: Amsterdam is included in the top 10 world's smart cities by Kotkin (2009)
	2009: Amsterdam is selected as "Benchmark of Excellence" by the European Commission, who describes the Amsterdam's smart city development strategy as a best practice to be replicated in other urban contexts (Velthausz, 2011)
	2011: Amsterdam is awarded the European City Star Award by the European Commission, which highlights the capability of its smart city development strategy to demonstrate how cities can make successful efforts in taking advantage of ICT technologies for urban development (Amsterdam Smart City, 2011)
	2012: Amsterdam wins the World Smart Cities Awards[a]
	2012: Amsterdam is one of the top 10 European smart cities according to Cohen's (2012b) evaluation system for smart cities
	2014: Amsterdam is among the top 10 European smart cities according to Cohen (2014)'s evaluation system for smart cities
	2014: Amsterdam is recognized by the European Parliament as one of six most successful smart cities in Europe and one of the most suitable cases for further in-depth analyses and benchmarking activities (Manville et al., 2014)
	2015: Amsterdam is among the finalists of the World Smart Cities Awards
	2015: Amsterdam is one of the top 5 cities in the world in policymaking for smart city development, urban innovation, and entrepreneurship according to the CITIE's assessment (Gibson et al., 2015)
Barcelona	2011: Barcelona is the second best smart city in Spain according to the International Data Corporation (IDC)'s Smart City Index Ranking (Achaerandio et al., 2011)
	2012: Barcelona is named Best Smart Community by the Intelligent Community Forum (ICF),[b] which recognizes the leading role of the Spanish city in supporting urban development and innovation by exploiting the potential offered by ICT solutions and infrastructures
	2012: Barcelona is among the top 10 smart cities in the world according to Cohen's (2012a) evaluation system for smart cities
	2014: Barcelona is one of the top 10 European smart cities according to Cohen's (2014) evaluation system for smart cities

Continued

TABLE 5.2 The success of the selected cases in the field of smart cities: awards and positions in national and international ranking systems—cont'd

Case study	Evidence of success
	2014: Barcelona is nominated European Capital of Innovation by the European Commission for its smart city development strategy (European Commission, 2014)
	2014: Barcelona is recognized by the European Parliament as one of six most successful smart cities in Europe and one of the most suitable cases for further in-depth analyses and benchmarking activities (Manville et al., 2014)
	2015: Barcelona is one of the top 5 cities in the world in policymaking for smart city development, urban innovation, and entrepreneurship according to the CITIE's assessment (Gibson et al., 2015)
	2015: Barcelona is among the finalists of the World Smart Cities Awards
Helsinki	2014: Helsinki is one of the top 10 European smart cities according to Cohen (2014)'s evaluation system for smart cities
	2014: Helsinki is recognized by the European Parliament as one of six most successful smart cities in Europe and one of the most suitable cases for further in-depth analyses and benchmarking activities (Manville et al., 2014)
	2015: Helsinki is one of the top 5 cities in the world in policymaking for smart city development, urban innovation, and entrepreneurship according to the CITIE's assessment (Gibson et al., 2015)
Vienna	2012: Vienna is ranked first in the world according to Cohen (2012a)'s evaluation system for smart cities
	2014: Vienna is one of the top 10 European smart cities according to Cohen (2014)'s evaluation system for smart cities
	2014: Vienna is recognized by the European Parliament as one of six most successful smart cities in Europe and one of the most suitable cases for further in-depth analyses and benchmarking activities (Manville et al., 2014)
	2016: Vienna wins the World Smart Cities Awards
	2016: Vienna is included among the most advanced smart city cases in Austria by IDC (2016)
	2017: Vienna heads the Smart City Strategy Index developed by the consulting firm Roland Berger (Zelt et al., 2017)

[a]*The World Smart Cities Awards is a competition that the Smart City Expo World Congress organizes annually to reward formally the most ambitious smart city development strategies and the most advanced smart city initiatives around the world. The complete lists of winners and finalists of each edition of the World Smart Cities Awards are available on the website of the Smart City Expo World Congress (http://www.smartcityexpo.com).*
[b]*The Intelligent Community Forum is an independent think tank based in New York City. All the information on its awards program and the winners of each edition can be found at http://www.intelligentcommunity.org.*

Categories	Description
Category A Community building	Activities making it possible to build the open and inclusive collaborative environment which is expected to support the design and implementation process of the smart city development strategy. This is done by: raising citizen engagement in the field of smart city development; stimulating user-driven innovation and community-led urban development; increasing public awareness and digital literacy; improving the level of understanding of the city's stakeholders about smart city development and the benefits it can generate as an ICT-driven approach to urban sustainability.
Category B Strategic framework	Activities aiming to develop the city's strategic framework for guiding and regulating smart city development. These activities produce: (1) action plans, programmes, guidelines, roadmaps, recommendations, governmental acts, and documents exposing the city government's commitment to enabling smart city development; (2) measures proposing standards, technical requirements and methods for evaluating both results and progress; and (3) workgroups that manage the general course of the smart city development strategy's operations.
Category C Services and applications	Activities allowing new ICT services and applications to be integrated within the city.
Category D Digital infrastructure	Activities aiming to develop the technological infrastructure necessary to use and benefit from the available ICT services and applications. Examples of activities include the integration of urban operating systems and the construction or extension of high-speed broadband networks and public Wi-Fi networks.

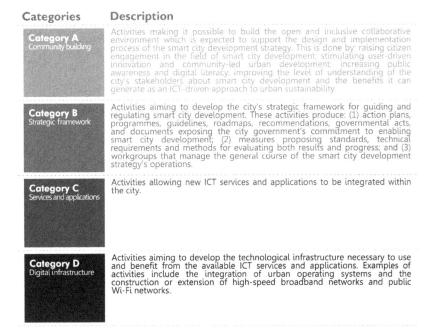

FIG. 5.2 Classification system 1.

the intervention logic of the four smart city development strategies, which is linked to Dichotomy 4. The matching of activities to application domains was conducted by deploying a second classification system, which divides such activities according to the type of technological solutions that they have integrated within the city. This system is composed of 11 application domains, which are listed in Fig. 5.3 and selected by merging the classification systems for smart city technologies developed to date (see Giffinger et al., 2007; Manville et al., 2014; Neirotti et al., 2014; Reviglio et al., 2013; Cisco Systems, 2016a,b; IBM Corporation, 2017). This typology made it possible to obtain a classification system as broad as possible.

The activities grouped in the first database were mapped and analyzed by cross-referencing the qualitative data extracted from multiple sources. Digital records reporting on the smart city developments under investigation and produced by the four city governments were considered as primary sources. These include the following data items: agendas; minutes of meetings; press releases; news and newsletters; conference presentations; conference speeches, which are obtained from either presentations' notes or videos of the events; reports; brochures; government documents; and webpages. Additional data was acquired from records produced by organizations that are either collaborating with the city governments in implementing the smart city development strategy of their cities or not directly involved but interested in providing data describing the programs of activities that have been undertaken. These sources were

Application domain	Description
C.01 Energy networks	To increase the efficiency and sustainability of either street lighting or networks for producing, storing and distributing energy.
C.02 Air	To ensure a better air quality in outdoor environments.
C.03 Water	To improve water resource management.
C.04 Waste	To improve waste management processes.
C.05 Mobility and transport	To provide city users with more sustainable and accessible transport systems and to address mobility issues.
C.06 Buildings and districts	To improve the efficiency, accessibility and management systems of buildings and districts.
C.07 Health and social inclusion	To improve the quality, accessibility and organization of health services and to support social inclusion and wellbeing.
C.08 Culture and recreation	To ensure a better protection of and access to both tangible and intangible cultural heritage and enhance their cultural value, and to help city users access recreational and cultural opportunities.
C.09 Education	To increase the quality of formal and informal teaching and learning processes.
C.10 Public security and justice	To ensure safety and security in urban spaces and to enhance criminal justice systems.
C.11 E-government	To apply ICT solutions to internal government functions and procedures with the purpose of enhancing their efficiency and to increase the accessibility and transparency of city data and information.
C.12 Other	ICT services and applications aiming at producing benefits different than those related to the previous application domains.

FIG. 5.3 Classification system 2.

considered as secondary and include reports produced by consultancy firms, news and articles published in online magazines, scientific literature, and research project deliverables.

This approach to data collection strengthened the quality of the analytic process because the multiple case study analysis was conducted by combining data that was extracted from multiple sources and provided by both internal and external observers. Overall, 2011 digital records in either written, audio, photographic, or video form were processed in this study.[3] These records were found between April and October 2016, by conducting a series of online searches in which Google's web search engine and multiple search strings were deployed. No restrictions for languages were set during the searches.

Coding was then used to organize the large volume of unstructured qualitative data sourced from the digital records and to facilitate both the identification

3. The breakdown of the digital records by city is: Amsterdam, 329; Barcelona, 1032; Helsinki, 165; and Vienna, 485.

of the activities and their progressive analysis.[4] The coding process was conducted by deploying the software Atlas.ti and following the procedure suggested by Eisenhardt (1989), Gibbs (2007), Robson (1993), and Strauss and Corbin (1990). After being uploaded onto Atlas.ti, the digital records were reviewed repeatedly to identify the activities that each city implemented to develop its own smart city development strategy. During the coding process, every activity was assigned a code, so as the sections of text or other data items describing the following attributes[5]: (1) objectives of the activity; (2) generated or expected outcomes; and (3) entities involved in its development, that is, organizations and citizens. The coding process results in four detailed reports in which the program of activities of each city is assembled and the data necessary to study it is arranged in a structured and well-organized form.

The reports were generated by using Atlas.ti's output function codebook and used to (1) populate the first database and (2) structure the second one, in which the organizations identified during the coding process are individually listed and classified according to their type (see Fig. 5.4). The information necessary to classify the organizations was obtained from their official websites, because all the information which was necessary to complete this task could not be sourced from the digital records. In addition, the data related to each activity was checked to establish whether citizens have been engaged and have taken part in the design and implementation process. These actions were instrumental in assembling the interorganizational collaborative networks of the four smart

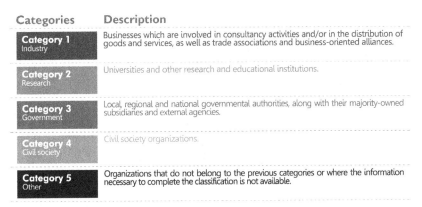

Categories	Description
Category 1 Industry	Businesses which are involved in consultancy activities and/or in the distribution of goods and services, as well as trade associations and business-oriented alliances.
Category 2 Research	Universities and other research and educational institutions.
Category 3 Government	Local, regional and national governmental authorities, along with their majority-owned subsidiaries and external agencies.
Category 4 Civil society	Civil society organizations.
Category 5 Other	Organizations that do not belong to the previous categories or where the information necessary to complete the classification is not available.

FIG. 5.4 Classification system 3.

4. As Gibbs (2007: 38) explains, "coding is how you define what the data you are analyzing is about. It involves identifying and recording one or more passages of text or other data items such as the part of pictures that, in some sense, exemplify the same theoretical or descriptive idea. Usually, several passages are identified, and they are then linked with a name for that idea - the code. Thus, all the text and so on that is about the same thing or exemplifies the same thing is coded with the same name."

5. The data items different from text include pictures, maps, technical drawings, and sections of audio and video files.

city development strategies and establish whether their structure is based on a double- or quadruple-helix collaborative model (Dichotomy 2).

5.3 A multiple case study analysis into European best practices

The coding process made it possible to map 263 activities, whose breakdown by city and category is summarized in Fig. 5.5 and fully exposed in Appendix A to this book (see appendix section). The validity of the hypotheses that each dichotomy proposes in a European context was tested by analyzing these activities, allowing for the case studies' approach to smart city development to be explained.

5.3.1 Dichotomy 1: Technology-led or holistic strategy

Amsterdam, Barcelona, Helsinki, and Vienna have adopted a very similar approach to smart city development and implemented strategies that give equal importance

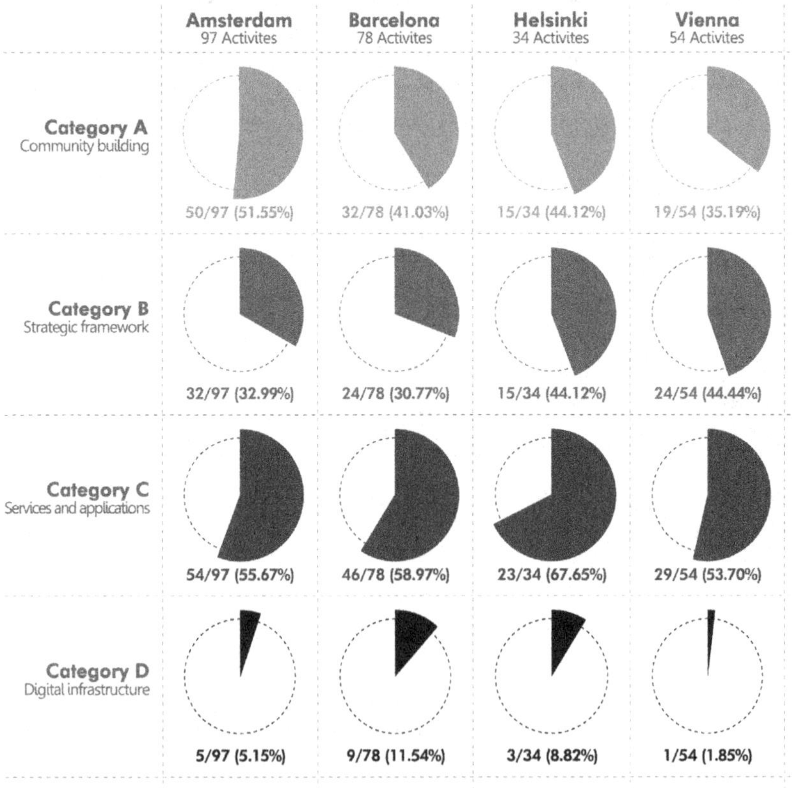

FIG. 5.5 Activities by city and category.

to (1) the deployment of ICT solutions for tackling urban sustainability issues and (2) the development of both a strategic framework and an open and inclusive collaborative environment for enabling the progressive deployment of such technological solutions. This provides evidence of these best practices' decision to embrace a holistic vision of smart cities and consider them not as technology-only focused systems resulting from the massive combination of interconnected ICT devices and applications, but as socio-technical systems in which technological development is aligned with human, social, cultural, economic, and environmental factors.

This assumption can be demonstrated by looking at Fig. 5.6. When comparing the breakdown of activities by group of categories, they appear to be equally divided in each strategy. On the one hand, the first group includes the activities belonging to at least one of the first two categories, that is, "A. Community Building" and "B. Strategic Framework." These activities are completely or partially focused on building the cities' capacity to support smart city development by: (1) establishing a comprehensive strategic framework able to provide long-term sustainability and drive the efforts of individuals and organizations toward the same direction; and (2) creating an open, inclusive, and engaging collaborative environment able to strengthen the abilities of such individuals and organizations to act in concert and actively participate in the co-creation of ICT-related initiatives that bring innovation into the urban environment and support urban sustainability.

For example, with the projects iCity, CitySDK, Commons4EU, Smart Together, and Open Cities, the four cities have developed and deployed new user-driven innovation methodologies to empower local communities and increase their degree of participation in the smart city domain and to foster co-creation processes of digital services of public interest (Van Steenwinkel et al., 2012; Bria et al., 2015). To further stimulate collaboration, Amsterdam has also launched Startupbootcamp, an accelerator program that connects

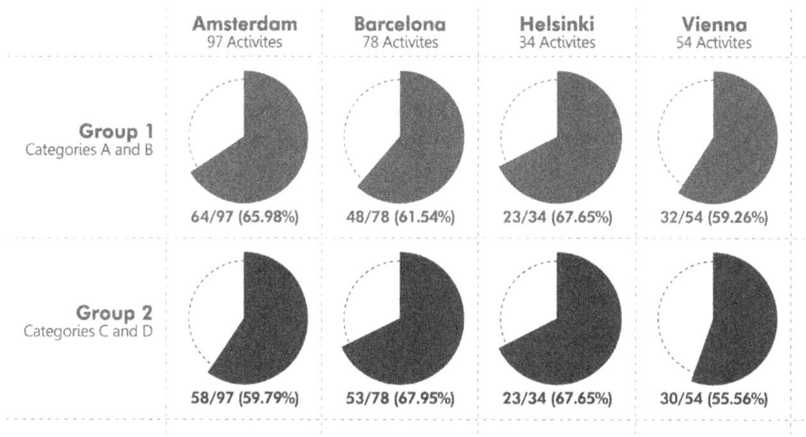

FIG. 5.6 Activities by group of categories.

start-ups working in the field of smart cities with mentors, potential partners, and investors who help improve the quality of their products and services. This activity aims at boosting the city's entrepreneurial culture and accelerating the development of new city-scale digital innovation initiatives.

Additional examples of capacity-building activities are as follows:

- CLUE, TRANSFORM, and Urban Learning, three European projects that allow Vienna, Barcelona, and Amsterdam to improve the capability of their city governments to deliver policies and programs for fighting climate change with ICT solutions (Brandt et al., 2014; CLUE Project Partners, 2014; Hartmann et al., 2015; Hemis et al., 2017);
- EUNOIA, which facilitates citizen and stakeholder involvement in the co-creation of sustainable urban mobility policies that the city of Barcelona can benefit from (Ahrend et al., 2013);
- Helsinki Loves Developers, in which regular meetings are organized in order to open a dialogue among Helsinki's app developers on the benefits of open data and enhance their collaboration (Forum Virium Helsinki, 2014);
- The project FIREBALL, in which Barcelona and Helsinki, along with Lisbon, Manchester, Thessaloniki, and Oulu, engage in a knowledge-sharing process for strengthening their understanding of what drivers and bottlenecks influence smart city development strategies (Schaffers et al., 2012);
- Cibernarium, a training program that aims to increase the knowledge, skills, attitudes, and behaviors in the effective use of digital devices of Barcelona's professionals and citizens.

The second group of activities is instead composed of projects and initiatives in which the deployment of ICT services, applications, and infrastructure components in the built environment is among the objectives. Examples of technological solutions include: mobile apps and open-source platforms for planning customized urban routes in Barcelona and Helsinki; agent-based simulation tools based on 3-D visual analytics for assessing Barcelona's urban mobility; QR codes allowing visitors to obtain free guided tours along some of Helsinki's sights by using their smartphones; new public Wi-Fi hot spots in Barcelona and Amsterdam; a platform for stimulating the use of renewable energy and changing energy consumption behaviors of Amsterdam's city users; and decision-supporting tools for managing the urban energy infrastructure and mobility systems in Vienna and Helsinki (City of Barcelona, 2012c; Rafiq et al., 2013; Sanseverino et al., 2014, 2017; Wiener Modellregion and Climate and Energy Fund, 2014; Bednar et al., 2016; Marguerite et al., 2016; Ahrend et al., 2013).[6]

6. Additional information about the projects discussed in this section can be found in the official websites: http://smarter-together.eu (Smart Together), https://www.startupbootcamp.org (Startupbootcamp), https://dev.hel.fi (Helsinki Loves Developers), https://cibernarium.barcelonactiva.cat (Cibernarium), https://amsterdamsmartcity.com/projects/energy-atlas (Energy Atlas), http://eunoia-project.eu (Eunoia), and https://cordis.europa.eu/project/rcn/95851_en.html (FIREBALL).

5.3.2 Dichotomy 2: Double- or quadruple-helix model of collaboration

The collaborative models that each city adopts to approach smart city development are visually represented by using Gephi. This makes it possible to obtain the visual objects shown in Appendix B, that is, four social-network graphs describing the interactions among the organizations involved in the development of the activities mapped during the coding process, along with their level of participation. In these network graphs, (1) the organizations belonging to each smart city collaborative environment are represented as nodes with a diameter directly proportional to the number of activities that they have contributed to implement, and (2) the edges connect the organizations that have worked together. The stronger the degree of collaboration between two organizations, the higher the weight of the edge that connects them and its thickness in the graph.

The data describing the structures of the networks is summarized in Fig. 5.7. This data makes clear that the design and implementation processes of the four smart city development strategies have required collaborative environments with hundreds of heterogeneous organizations. Barcelona and Vienna, with 407 and 255 nodes, respectively, have the largest and the smallest communities, while the collaborative networks of Amsterdam and Helsinki are instead composed of about 350 nodes each. In addition to being large in size, what these networks also have in common is the distribution of organizations by type. With a level of collaboration between 46 and 56%, businesses are always the most active organizations, and they are followed by institutions for education and

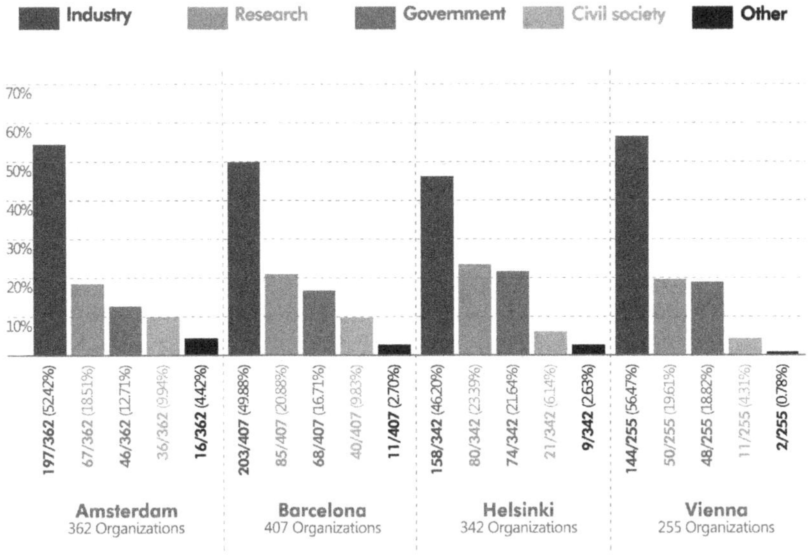

FIG. 5.7 Distribution of organizations by type.

research, which represent approximately 20% of each collaborative network. The remaining share is divided between government and civil society. However, the breakdown of the figures shows that the involvement of the former varies between 13% and 22%, while the latter always remains below 10%.

The collaboration between public and private sector is therefore the core engine behind the four smart city development strategies under investigation and the programs of activities that they have implemented. The results of the analysis show beyond doubt that these programs mainly result from a triple-helix model of collaboration based on the interaction between research, industry, and government. Civil society organizations are the less represented organization type.

The data suggests that civil society organizations are not fully integrated in the collaborative environments. However, when looking at the data in Fig. 5.8, which informs on the number of activates that citizens have been actively involved in the implementation of, it is also clear that the four cities have made an effort to connect smart city development and civil society by stimulating the active involvement of citizens in the development of smart city projects and initiatives. Despite being found only in a limited number of initiatives, such an effort provides evidence of an attempt to move toward a quadruple-helix collaborative model and the open and user-centric innovation approach it stands for (Arnkil et al., 2010; Cavallini et al., 2016). This aim is clearly expressed in the strategic frameworks that the four cities have developed for guiding and regulating smart city development (City of Amsterdam, 2011, 2014a,b, 2015; City of Barcelona and Doxa Consulting, 2012; City of Barcelona, 2012a,b, 2014; City of Vienna, 2014; City of Helsinki, 2015).

The analysis of the activities shows that citizens have been asked to participate as either (1) users who test ICT solutions and provide feedback, (2) developers who are given support for producing new digital services of public interest,

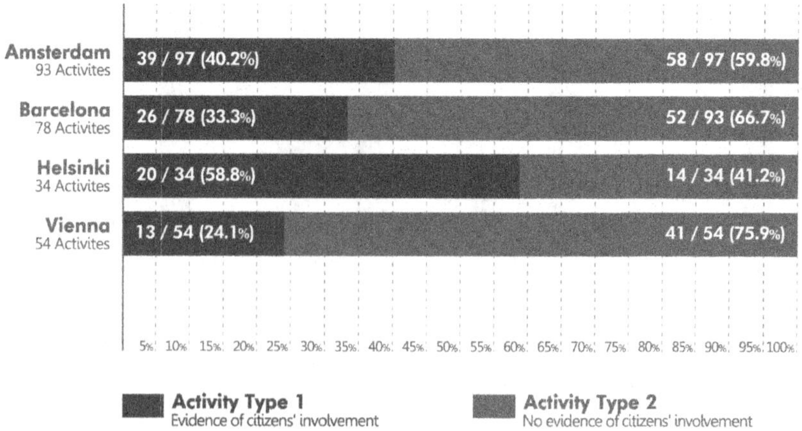

FIG. 5.8 Citizens' involvement in smart city activities.

or (3) residents expressing their ideas and needs during workshops and meetings with other stakeholders. For example, citizens have been invited to attend a series of stakeholders' forums and collaborate in producing Vienna's smart city strategic framework. These forums have been conceived as discussion events for exchanging ideas and ensuring greater transparency, participation, and collaboration in the smart city domain. This approach is also adopted by Amsterdam, where group meetings and workshops have been frequently organized, in which citizens have been provided with the opportunity to collectively discuss both their specific needs and potential ICT-driven projects and initiatives able to meet them (City of Vienna et al., 2011, 2013; City of Vienna, 2012, 2013a,b, 2016; Mora and Bolici, 2017).

In addition, the Living Lab methodology[7] has been used to increase citizens' participation in the testing phases of the ICT solutions and systems to be deployed in the built environment, so as to further develop and network public services. During the delivery of the project Street Smart, for example, Helsinki has piloted a mobile application with a group of citizens who have been asked to provide feedback through an online questionnaire.[8] The same approach has been used in Barcelona during the piloting phase of the decision support system for monitoring buildings' energy consumption that has resulted from the project BESOS.

Additional examples of projects in which the four cities have adopted user-centric innovation methodologies include the following (Amsterdam Innovation Motor and Liander, 2011; Brinkman, 2011; Lievens et al., 2011; Aspern Smart City Research, 2015; Bria et al., 2015; Henriquez, 2015; Panos et al., 2016; Muhlmann, 2017):

- APOLLON: citizen engagement has been instrumental in co-designing a methodology for building cross border Living Labs networks supporting smart city development;
- Sustainable Neighborhood Geuzenveld: more than 500 smart meters and 60 in-home energy feedback displays have been installed in the New West district of Amsterdam, and a user participation program has been launched to allow local residents to interact with one another and compare their consumption patterns and energy saving issues;
- West Orange: five hundred Amsterdam's households have been involved in the testing process of a new wireless energy feedback display and its evaluation for potential scaling-up;
- Smart Citizen Kit: two groups of Barcelona and Amsterdam's local residents have offered to participate in piloting the Smart Citizen Kit, a low-cost

7. In the framework of smart city development, the Living Lab methodology is used to make the deployment of ICT solutions in the built environment more effective by strengthening the collaboration between developers and end users, who are engaged as first adopters during pilot tests (Bergvall-Kåreborn et al., 2009; Schaffers et al., 2011; Baccarne et al., 2014).

8. Additional information on the Street Smart project can be found at https://helsinkistreetlab.fi.

sensing kit that enables the environmental data of a city to be captured by means of crowdsourcing (see Chapter 2 for additional information on this smart technology);

- Climate Street: in order to prepare for a city-scale deployment, a combination of ICT solutions for improving urban sustainability has been tested by a group of approximately 120 entrepreneurs whose commercial activities are located in Utrechtsestraat, a shopping street closed to the City Centre district of Amsterdam;
- Smarter Together: a 25 million Euro project in which six neighborhoods belonging to three European cities (Lyon, Munuch, and Vienna) have experimented innovative co-creation processes for enabling smart city development;
- Smart Challenge: a challenge has been set up for three Amsterdam-based organizations, which have been invited to use Wattcher, an ICT device providing insight into energy consumption patterns, and to compete in saving the largest amount of energy.

The active involvement of civil society in the smart city domain has also been encouraged by means of hackathons and competitions, in which citizens have been invited to apply their knowledge and skills for developing new digital services able to face urban sustainability issues. These events have been organized to nurture citizens' entrepreneurial creativity and digital talent. For example, in 2012, the city government of Barcelona hosted BCN Apps Jam: Recicla!, a ten-hour marathon focusing on the development of applications for encouraging recycling. Three years later, as part of the iCity project, Barcelona also collaborated in organizing the three-day event called Smart Cities Hackathon, which took place simultaneously in 27 cities around the world. During this event, teams of developers were tasked with designing new digital applications for tackling a group of preselected challenges. That very same year, Barcelona also launched Smart City App Hack, an online international competition that resulted in more than 70 smart city apps. Additional examples of hackathons and competitions that were captured during the mapping exercise include the following: Apps4bcn competition, Apps for Amsterdam, Apps4Finland, Open Helsinki - Hack at Home, and Open Finland Challenge (Afman et al., 2011; City of Barcelona, 2012d, 2015a,b; Forum Virium Helsinki, 2014, 2015; Mora and Bolici, 2016, 2017).

5.3.3 Dichotomy 3: Top-down or bottom-up approach

Amsterdam, Barcelona, Helsinki, and Vienna's approach to smart city development combines top-down and bottom-up approaches. The four city governments are among the most active organizations in each collaborative environment and have contributed to carry out between 44 and 91% of the total activities (see Appendix A). This data suggests local governments have played a crucial role, and it also provides evidence of their commitment to supporting smart city development. In addition, by looking at the objectives and outcomes related to the activities they have undertaken, it is possible to note that the city governments have not made use of their position to centralize the implementation process of the smart city development strategies but acted instead as leaders who aim to: (1) encourage the establishment of an open, inclusive, and cohesive collaborative environment by bringing large groups of individuals and organizations together; (2) provide these large communities with a strategic framework able to guide their efforts toward the same direction and make full use of both their collective intelligence and common interest in smart city development; (3) enable this collaborative environment to continuously increase in size; and (4) stimulate bottom-up development processes.

The four city governments meet these objectives by adopting a similar approach. First of all, each city is provided with a strategic framework composed of policy documents that formally state the city government's commitment to support smart city development and (1) provide long-term vision, (2) establish the objectives to be achieved in order for local communities to prosper, (3) suggest the main application domains and urban sustainability issues to focus attention on, and (4) set up the governance systems for enabling and speeding up the transition process toward becoming smart and embrace an ICT-driven approach to urban sustainability (City of Amsterdam, 2011, 2014a,b, 2015; City of Barcelona and Doxa Consulting, 2012; City of Barcelona, 2012a,b, 2014; City of Vienna, 2014; City of Helsinki, 2015).

City governments have also made an effort to increase the know-how of local communities in relation to urban technologies and their capability to manage smart city development. This has been done by supporting the making process and deployment of new planning and operational tools, user-driven innovation methodologies, recommendations, guidelines, standards and technical requirements, and evaluation and assessment methodologies (Brandt et al., 2014; Hartmann et al., 2015; Hemis et al., 2017; CLUE Project Partners, 2014; City of Barcelona, 2014; Bria et al., 2015; Amsterdam Innovation Motor and Liander, 2011).[9] In addition, the local governments collaborate in organizing and hosting forums, conferences, workshops, learning programs, and meetings dealing with smart city development in order to: collect ideas, comments, and feedback about the cities' ICT requirements; generate interest; inform the community; engage new stakeholders and make the collaborative environment larger; raise public awareness of the potential benefits that ICTs can produce in urban environments; increase digital literacy; and stimulate collaboration (City of Vienna, 2012, 2013a,b; Forum Virium Helsinki, 2014; Mora and Bolici, 2016, 2017; Amsterdam Innovation Motor and Liander, 2011; City of Barcelona and Doxa Consulting, 2012).[10]

9. See also the following projects: CityOpt (http://www.cityopt.eu), TRANSFORM (http://urban-transform.eu), PUMAS (www.pumasproject.eu), TRANSFORM+ (http://www.transform-plus.at), EU-GUGLE (http://eu-gugle.eu), and INNOSPIRIT (http://www.innospirit.org).

10. See also Digital City Wien (https://digitalcity.wien).

The work of the local governments is also instrumental in: (1) building platforms for open-data provision and organizing hackathons and competitions for providing IT-skilled individuals and organizations with the knowledge platform that they need to produce new applications and digital services by using public data (Afman et al., 2011; Forum Virium Helsinki, 2014, 2015; Mora and Bolici, 2016, 2017)[11]; and (2) setting up dedicated working groups that are tasked with managing smart city development and the multidisciplinary, heterogeneous, and technologically innovative environment necessary to make it work and grow. These groups mainly cover the areas of coordination, stakeholder management and engagement, citywide monitoring and assessment of smart city projects, communication, and promotion. In addition, they are requested to accelerate the progressive integration of new digital services and technological infrastructures within the city in the short and medium term by: extending participation and strengthening the capacity of citizens and organizations for collaboration in the field of smart cities; forming consortia of cross sectoral partners for designing and implementing innovative ICT-related projects and initiatives; offering access to regional and international networks; and providing interested stakeholders with information on financial instruments which can be deployed to support smart city projects and initiatives.

The best practice analysis shows that the responsibility for managing these functions and establishing a strong collaborative culture is assigned to:

- the Amsterdam Economic Board, which is coordinating Amsterdam Smart City, a collaborative platform resulting from a public-private program launched in 2009[12];
- Forum Virium Helsinki (2015), a nonprofit organization owned by the City of Helsinki;
- TINA Vienna, which is part of Wien Holding GmbH (2012), a holding company of the City of Vienna that carries out community tasks (City of Vienna, 2014);
- the Barcelona City Council's Municipal Institute of Information Technology (City of Barcelona, 2012b, 2016).

5.3.4 Dichotomy 4: Monodimensional or integrated intervention logic

The analysis of the activities belonging to the category "C. Services and Applications" shows that the four cities have adopted an integrated intervention logic, which covers a mix of application domains. However, when comparing

11. Examples of open-data platforms include the following: Amsterdam City Data (https://data.amsterdam.nl), Open Data BCN (http://opendata-ajuntament.barcelona.cat), Helsinki Region Infoshare (http://www.hri.fi), and Open Government Vienna (https://www.data.gv.at).
12. The Amsterdam Smart City program was launched in 2009 by Amsterdam Innovation Motor and Liander (2011), in close cooperation with the City of Amsterdam. In 2013, the Amsterdam Innovation Motor became part of the Amsterdam Economic Board (The Technopolicy Network, 2014; Amsterdam Innovation Motor, 2009). It is important to note that, in the analysis of the Amsterdam's smart city collaborative network, the two entities have been merged.

the cities' level of interest in each application domain, significant dissimilarities can be captured (see Fig. 5.9).

Vienna and Amsterdam's interest in smart city development is mainly oriented toward smart transport, smart building, and smart grid solutions for low-carbon and energy-efficient urban environments. Most of the ICT solutions enabling smart city development are deployed to fight climate change and boost energy efficiency in mobility and transport (C.05), buildings and city districts (C.06), and power infrastructures (C.01). Their approach to smart city development is therefore aligned with the European Commission's interpretation of smart cities. However, the data reveals that both cities have extended such a monodimensional vision by focusing attention on additional policy domains and urban sustainability challenges. For example, technological solutions are deployed to: improve the management of natural resources other than energy; increase the quality of public transport services by providing citizens with real-time information; stimulate collaboration and communication between residents, businesses, governmental authorities, and welfare organizations by means of digital platforms; provide citizens with digital solutions for remote working; and improve people's health and well-being in the context of an aging population.

The interest in transport is also shared by Barcelona and Helsinki, where, respectively, 33 and 43% of the smart city solutions integrated in the urban environment are linked to this application domain. However, most of their initiatives relates to e-government (C.11), where ICT solutions are intended to increase the convenience and accessibility of public data and public services. Also, Barcelona and Helsinki are both particularly active in the field of health and social inclusion (C.07), in which ICTs are mainly deployed to assist elderly people in their everyday activities.[13]

5.4 Strategic principles for smart city development: Lessons from Europe

In May 2016, the European Union's ministers responsible for Urban Matters agreed to establish an Urban Agenda for the European member states. This agenda promotes a new model of urban development and contributes to the implementation of both the United Nations' 2030 Agenda for Sustainable Development and the New Urban Agenda issued by the Habitat III Secretariat. These three international policy documents all stress the important role that sustainable urban development plays in increasing economic prosperity, social

13. See the following projects: CO2 Neutrale, SternE, SeniorTab, Citybike Wien, *E*-Taxis, SMILE, AnachB, Wien.at live-App, Open Government Data, Wien Gestalten (https://smartcity.wien.gv.at), Smart Citizen Kit, Smart Work@Ijburg, Health-Lab, Change by Us in Amsterdam (https://amsterdamsmartcity.com), Smart Urban Spaces (http://www.smarturbanspaces.org), Projecte Radars, Servei de teleassistència municipal, Vincles BCN, and EsclaTIC (http://ajuntament.barcelona.cat/digital).

	Amsterdam 97 Activites	Barcelona 78 Activites	Helsinki 34 Activites	Vienna 54 Activites
Category C Services and applications	54/93 (58.06%)	46/78 (58.97%)	23/34 (67.65%)	29/54 (53.70%)
C.01 Energy networks	15/54 (27.8%)	3/46 (6.5%)	2/23 (8.7%)	8/29 (27.6%)
C.02 Air	20/54 (37.0%)	12/46 (26.1%)	2/23 (8.7%)	3/29 (10.3%)
C.03 Water	1/54 (1.9%)	1/46 (2.2%)	0/23 (0.0%)	1/29 (3.4%)
C.04 Waste	1/54 (1.9%)	1/46 (2.2%)	0/23 (0.0%)	1/29 (3.4%)
C.05 Mobility and transport	16/54 (29.6%)	15/46 (32.6%)	10/23 (43.5%)	12/29 (41.4%)
C.06 Buildings and districts	27/54 (50.0%)	5/46 (10.9%)	2/23 (8.7%)	11/29 (37.9%)
C.07 Health and social inclusion	1/54 (1.9%)	8/46 (17.4%)	3/23 (13.0%)	2/29 (6.9%)
C.08 Culture and recreation	1/54 (1.9%)	2/46 (4.3%)	2/23 (8.7%)	0/29 (0.0%)
C.09 Education	0/54 (0.0%)	0/46 (0.0%)	0/23 (0.0%)	0/29 (0.0%)
C.10 Public security and justice	3/54 (5.6%)	2/46 (4.3%)	0/23 (0.0%)	0/29 (0.0%)
C.11 E-government	11/54 (20.4%)	28/46 (60.9%)	15/23 (65.2%)	6/29 (20.7%)
C.12 Other	2/54 (3.7%)	1/46 (2.2%)	0/23 (0.0%)	0/29 (0.0%)

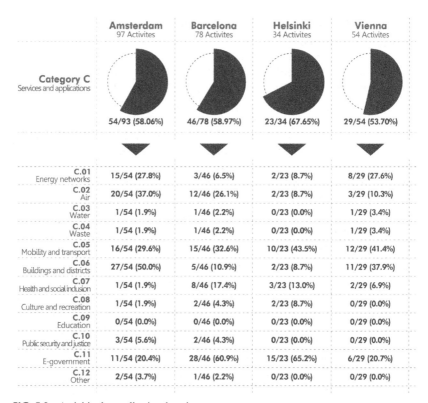

FIG. 5.9 Activities by application domain.

and territorial cohesion, and well-being at a global level. They also recognize smart city development as an integral part of sustainable urban development processes, pointing out that smart technologies provide cities with the opportunity to become more sustainable (European Commission, 2016; United Nations, 2015, 2017).

The United Nations' policy paper on urban services and technology further emphasizes this recommendation by highlighting the potential that smart city development has to support transformative changes in society by helping cities to address the increasingly complex challenges that they are currently facing. However, this policy paper also recognizes the presence of a knowledge gap with regard to how cities can enable such a development and, in response, calls for a better theoretical and practical understanding that current research on smart cities is still unable to offer (United Nations, 2016).

The ambiguity generated by the four dichotomies captured in the previous chapters provides a fundamental challenge that must be addressed before it is possible to clearly articulate what needs to be done in order for urban environments to be successful in enabling smart city development. The deductive multiple case study analysis that this chapter reports on does help meet this challenge.

It focuses attention on Europe, where the validity of the hypotheses that each dichotomy proposes is tested by examining the way in which four best practices have gone about the design and implementation of their smart city development strategies. The results of this analysis are summarized in Fig. 5.10, which shows the choices that have allowed Amsterdam, Barcelona, Helsinki, and Vienna to

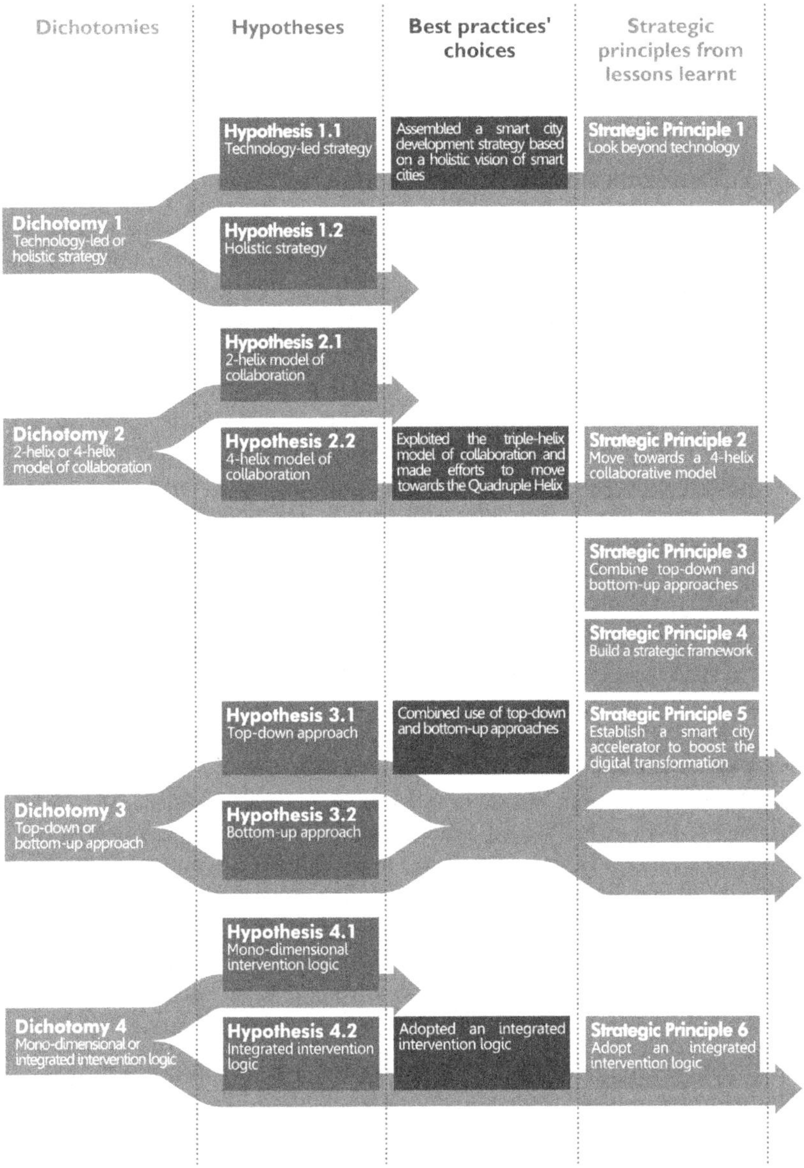

FIG. 5.10 Results of the hypothesis-testing process: best practices' choices and strategic principles from lessons learned.

address the dichotomous nature of smart city research and successfully enable ICT-related development and innovation in urban environments.

The lessons learned and new insights captured by this best practice analysis make it possible to establish a set of strategic principles instructing European cities on the path to follow in designing and implementing smart city development strategies able to produce meaningful results and be successful in meeting urban challenges by means of ICT solutions. These strategic principles are proposed to support decision-making processes in the field of smart city development and speed up the effective deployment of smart technologies in European urban environments.

5.4.1 Strategic principle 1: Look beyond technology

Enabling smart city development is a challenge going far beyond technology. These four leading European smart cities have proved to be complex socio-technical systems in which smart city development results from the integration of new ICT services, applications, and systems for either resolving or mitigating urban challenges. The development process of this technological layer is progressive and recalls the idiomatic expression of urban acupuncture, which refers to the approach of Jaime Lerner to modern urban development, that is, to continuously implement large numbers of small-scale projects that progressively improve the urban context instead of relying upon massive urban renewal projects (Lerner, 2014). This approach suggests dealing with sustainable urban development in an era of constrained budgets and limited resources requires a more dynamic, flexible, and community-based line of action. The European best practices have applied the concept of urban acupuncture in the field of smart city development, which has been enabled by the continuous implementation of short- and medium-term ICT-related interventions that have gradually transformed the cities into smart environments.

However, to let this progressive digital transformation take place, the case studies show that significant efforts must be oriented toward building the capacity of the city to integrate and deploy such technological solutions. This requires cities to: (1) align technological development with the contents of a holistic and comprehensive strategic framework able to provide long-term sustainability and drive individuals and organizations in the same direction; and (2) build an open, inclusive, and engaging collaborative environment that strengthen the capacity of these individuals and organizations to work together and actively participate in the co-creation of ICT-driven initiatives that accelerate urban sustainability.

5.4.2 Strategic principle 2: Move toward a quadruple-helix collaborative model

Collaboration is key to successful implementation of smart city development strategies, and supporting the growth of an open, inclusive, and engaging collaborative environment is pivotal to this. In developing this collaborative environment, it is important to (1) rely on public and private sector collaboration, (2) institute the industry-government-research relationships of the triple-helix collaborative model (Deakin, 2014a,b; Deakin and Leydesdorff, 2014), and (3) make significant efforts to strengthen the participatory qualities of civil society by progressively moving toward a quadruple-helix model of stakeholder engagement and the open and user-centric approach to innovation that such a model promotes (Arnkil et al., 2010; Carayannis and Campbell, 2014; Cavallini et al., 2016).

Strong engagement mechanisms and user-driven innovation methodologies are necessary to bring together large communities composed of heterogeneous organizations representing the triple helix and to increase citizens and civil society organizations' participation in co-creation processes of digital services of public interest. However, working with citizens sets a complex challenge because it requires moving away from "an era of linear, top-down and expert-driven development, production and services (and start) practicing with different forms and levels of co-production" (Arnkil et al., 2010: III). But the results are worth the effort, because a higher level of citizen engagement makes it possible to gain high-value place-based knowledge that can be exploited in the integration and deployment process of ICT-related urban innovations (Mathie and Cunningham, 2003; Curwell et al., 2005; Deakin and Allwinkle, 2007; Torres et al., 2006; Veeckman and van der Graaf, 2014; Bria et al., 2015; Gooch et al., 2015). As suggested by the United Nations' guidelines for sustainable and socially inclusive urban infrastructure, citizen participation can "improve the quality of decision making and facilitate the execution of actions, (…) provide a better way of dealing with cross-cutting issues, (…) and help ensure that actions taken and services provided reflect the needs of people more adequately" (Santucci et al., 2011: 52).

Engagement plans and stakeholder analysis techniques can be useful tools for mapping key actors and understanding both their interests and the potential contribution they may offer (Brandon et al., 2017; Future Cities Catapult and Arup, 2017; Moghadam et al., 2017). Examples of stakeholder engagement for managing smart city development strategies are described in research by Ielite et al. (2015) and Mayangsari and Novani (2015), which respectively report on the experiences of Riga and Bandung.

5.4.3 Strategic principle 3: Combine top-down (government-led) and bottom-up (community-driven)

As suggested in research by Breuer et al. (2014), Lee et al. (2014), Exner (2015), Angelidou (2017), and Mora and Bolici (2016, 2017), smart city development "requires a two-pronged approach: top-down (government-led) to build foundations and bottom-up (community-driven)" (Estevez et al., 2016: VII). "A purely top-down view on the smart city carries a danger of authoritarianism with it, while a bottom-up-only approach leans towards chaos and lack of long-term vision" (Breuer et al., 2014: 162). Therefore, they need to be combined.

Governments have a central role in the design and implementation of strategies for smart city development, but their activity needs to be oriented toward creating the favorable conditions for individuals and organizations to pool their knowledge, skills, and interests and collaborate in delivering smart city initiatives. To achieve this aim, city governments are required to put smart city development among the priorities of their political agenda and assemble a strategic framework and a smart city accelerator, which are both instrumental in: (1) building the open, inclusive, and cohesive collaborative environment needed to activate smart city development and the bottom-up development process required to achieve this; (2) facilitating the creation of partnerships for jointly implementing ICT-related initiatives; and (3) coordinating the efforts of this collaborative environment toward achieving a common set of goals that reflect the vision and priorities of the city.

In addition, the local government's action is needed to improve the capacity of the city to enable smart city development. This can be done through activities that aim to: generate feedback on the cities' ICT requirements and new ideas for ICT-related projects, generate interest and inform the community, stimulate collaboration, engage new stakeholders and help the collaborative environment to grow, raise public awareness of the potential benefits that ICTs can produce in urban environments, and increase the level of digital literacy within the city.

Open-data initiatives like app contests, hackathons, and codefests are an interesting example of actions for building capacity by raising awareness, increasing participation, and stimulating community-driven development in the smart city domain, especially from citizens. By hosting these events, city governments bring together groups of IT-skilled individuals that are invited to conceive new digital applications to address urban concerns by using public data (Johnson and Robinson, 2014; Irani, 2015; Komssi et al., 2015; Lodato and DiSalvo, 2016; Carr and Lassiter, 2017; Concilio et al., 2017).

Forums, conferences, workshops, and training courses are additional activities that cities are using to increase their capacity to sustain smart city development. Barcelona has been organizing the Smart City Expo World Congress since 2011. This event has become a leading global platform for experts working in the field of smart city development, which are brought together to share knowledge and debate.[14] Barcelona has also launched a smart education program for primary and secondary schools in order to bring the concepts of innovation and smartness to kids through practical activities and workshops. Turin, in the north of Italy, has instead offered intensive training courses on the management of smart city development strategies to executives and directors working for the city government (Pisu, 2015).

14. Additional information on the Smart City Expo World Congress and Barcelona's Smart Education program can be found at http://www.smartcityexpo.com and http://cordis.europa.eu/news/rcn/136756_it.html.

5.4.4 Strategic principle 4: Build a strategic framework

The policy documents composing the city's strategic framework for smart city development need to clearly establish a long-term vision highlighting ambitions and motivations driving the smart city transformation process, the expected outcomes and targets to achieve by deploying ICT solutions, the main application domains to focus attention on, and the working group responsible for managing and accelerating the implementation of the strategy.

Along with Amsterdam, Barcelona, Helsinki, and Vienna, further examples of cities that have designed comprehensive strategic frameworks for driving smart city development include New York, Turin, Heraklion, and Birmingham. "New York has created a stand-alone strategy in the early 2010s but has now integrated its digital plans within the overall city vision in order to help think about technology more holistically" (Future Cities Catapult and Arup, 2017: 23). Turin's strategic framework was launched in 2013 and resulted from an elaboration process based on strategic urban planning principles. More than 350 key experts representing governmental authorities, businesses, universities, research centers, and civil society organizations were involved (Carcillo and Macii, 2013; Deambrogio, 2013). The same participatory approach has been applied by Heraklion in Greece and Birmingham in the United Kingdom. Both cities have designed strategic plans for smart city development in order to help the stakeholders to work together instead of operating independently of one another (URBACT Secretariat, 2017; City of Birmingham, 2012, 2014).

Despite being at an early stage of investigation (Komninos, 2014; Angelidou, 2014; Ben Letaifa, 2015; Bolici and Mora, 2015; Mora and Bolici, 2016, 2017; Marsal-Llacuna and Segal, 2016, 2017), strategic planning tools and techniques appear to be particularly useful when adopted to deal with the design process of such strategic frameworks. For example, scenario building, collaborative vision building, stakeholder analyses, and focus groups have been deployed by the city of Vienna to produce a long-term vision, along with a roadmap and an action plan for guiding the city's urban transformation dynamics in the smart city domain (Hofstetter and Vogl, 2011). In addition, potential for smart city development can be tested by means of SWOT (strengths, weaknesses, opportunities, and threats) analyses (Álvarez-García et al., 2017).

5.4.5 Strategic principle 5: Boost the digital transformation by establishing a smart city accelerator

In addition to the strategic framework, local governments are also required to assemble a smart city accelerator, a working group that is dedicated to accelerating the progressive transformation of the city in a smart environment by strengthening the capacity of individuals and organizations to collaborate in delivering innovative ICT-related initiatives. Based on the lessons learned with the best practice analysis, the main activities that these working groups need to carry out are the following: boost the production of new ideas for ICT-related interventions; engage new potential partners and facilitate the creation of new consortia; provide information on financial instruments and funding mechanisms that can be used to support projects and initiatives; offer access to local, regional, and international networks; monitor the ICT-related interventions and assure that they are aligned with the contents of the strategic framework; and facilitate the creation of new partnerships and the acquisition of new resources by promoting the smart city development strategy of the city.

Considering the experiences of Amsterdam, Barcelona, Helsinki, and Vienna, the smart city accelerators can be (1) part of either the city council or other existing organizations that carry out community tasks or (2) set up by establishing new public-private organizations that are autonomous and provided with independent legal identities. Examples of the latter type can also be found in Genoa and Turin, where the smart city development strategies are respectively managed by the Genoa Smart City Association and Torino Smart City Foundation. Both organizations have resulted from the collaboration between the city government and a group of public and private organizations, which belong to the metropolitan area of the city and represent industry, government, and research (Deambrogio, 2013; Sanseverino et al., 2014; Grossi and Pianezzi, 2017). Unfortunately, no research has been conducted yet to investigate how these different types of smart city accelerators work, especially in different urban contexts, and what benefits and disadvantages each option generates.

5.4.6 Strategic principle 6: Adopt an integrated intervention logic

The energy-driven interpretation of smart city development sets boundaries that cities need to overcome. Smart city development pathways need to be shaped according to the socio-economic and cultural background of cities, and the selection of the application domains depends on local context factors (Neirotti et al., 2014). These factors include the urban challenges that the city has to tackle, which are not always energy or environmental-related. Therefore, it is important to adopt an integrated intervention logic that cuts across the multitude of application domains that smart city development represents and extends the benefits that ICT solutions can offer to any policy sectors of the city where there is need for improvement. This requires cities to have a clear understanding of both the urban issues limiting their sustainable growth and the technological advancements to be deployed in order to either mitigate or fully resolve such issues.

Once again, strategic planning tools and techniques can help obtain this knowledge related to urban issue and technological fixes. For example, open consultations through digital platforms and applications can be deployed to actively engage citizens and other relevant stakeholders in the identification of urban issues and local needs (Pentikousis et al., 2011). Issues and possible technological solutions may then be matched by adopting strategic decision processes, such as technology roadmapping. Roadmapping processes for smart city development have been successfully adopted by Birmingham (Fullard, 2016) and analyzed by Lee et al. (2013), whose research shares a methodological approach that can be adopted in any urban contexts.

5.5 Toward a smart-city knowledge platform

This chapter formulates a set of strategic principles that European cities should take into consideration in order to successfully design and implement smart city development strategies. These principles suggest enabling smart city development in Europe requires to:

- look beyond technology;
- move toward a quadruple-helix collaborative model;
- combine top-down (government-led) and bottom-up (community-driven);
- build a smart city strategic framework;
- boost the digital transformation by establishing a smart city accelerator;
- adopt an integrated intervention logic.

The strategic principles that this chapter proposes are sourced from a multiple case study analysis that focuses attention on four European best practices: Amsterdam, Barcelona, Helsinki, and Vienna. Further research is therefore needed to generalize the lessons that have been learned with this analysis to regional contexts beyond Europe and continue to build the know-how necessary to fully overcome the knowledge gap that the dichotomous nature of smart city research has generated. This requires smart city researchers to (1) identify examples of both leading and unsuccessful smart city development strategies belonging to non-European countries and (2) process additional case study analyses to test the validity of the strategic principles that this chapter puts forward.

Extending the generalization of this chapter's findings by conducting additional research into the design and implementation of smart city development strategies is also instrumental in enabling peer-learning and knowledge transfer processes able to support evidence-based decision-making. The scientific literature demonstrates that a large number of cities across Europe and beyond are working on strategies for enabling smart city development. Gathering, codifying, and sharing the practical knowledge produced by these real-life experiences, in the form of good practices and recommendations, is key to succeed in dealing with the ambiguity surrounding smart city development strategies and their design and implementation process. This knowledge can be exploited to create the conditions for continuous learning and innovation, which both serve to accelerate the adoption of strategies that progress smart city development. For example, such a knowledge can be used for: (1) building transnational knowledge-sharing platforms that connect cities together and let them learn from each other, as in the case of the digital market place of the European Innovation Partnership on Smart Cities and Communities (EIP-SCC)[15]; (2) developing and delivering learning events and educational strategies; and (3) supporting the production and deployment of decision-making support tools for underpinning the design and implementation of smart city development strategies.

Future research should also be conducted into the application of strategic planning tools and techniques in the field of smart city development. The research activity that this chapter reports on suggests this area is promising and a number of cities are already experimenting in this innovative domain. Examples of highly valuable research activates aiming at increasing the collective understanding in this knowledge domain include the following: mapping what strategic planning tools and techniques are being used; providing detailed examples able to explain why and how to apply them; and identifying additional instruments that have not been deployed yet but that hold promise for the future.

References

Achaerandio, R., Gallotti, G., Curto, J., Bigliani, R., Maldonado, F., 2011. Smart Cities Analysis in Spain. White paper, IDC. http://www.idc.com/getdoc.jsp?containerId=EIRS56T. (Accessed August 6, 2014).

Afman, S., Boonstra, R., Demeyer, T., Gallyas, K., Jansen-Dings, I., Kresin, F., Reitenbach, M., Schot, M., Slaghuis, L., 2011. Apps for Amsterdam: A City Opening Up. Waag Society. https://waag.org/sites/waag/files/public/Publicaties/A4A_OpenCities_pub.pdf. (Accessed September 5, 2016).

Ahrend, R., Amini, L., Baeza-Yates, R., Ballesteros, P., Barthélemy, M., Batty, M., Dum, R., García-Cantú, O., Haon, S., Harrison, C., Heimgartner, C., Herranz, R., Lobo, J., Loreto, V., Lucio, A., Nijkamp, P., Pumain, D., Ramasco, J., San Miguel, M., Serret, A., Sgard, F., Simmonds, D., Snickars, F., Svanfeldt, C., Tábara, J.D., Willumsen, L., 2013. Global Systems Science and Urban Development. EUNOIA Consortium. http://www.eunoia-project.eu/media/uploads/deliverables/EUNOIA_D1.3_Final_Report_Publishable_Summary.pdf. (Accessed March 4, 2016).

Albino, V., Berardi, U., Dangelico, R.M., 2015. Smart cities: definitions, dimensions, performance, and initiatives. J. Urban Technol. 22 (1), 3–21.

Álvarez-García, J., de la Cruz del Río-Rama, M., Vázquez-Huerta, G., Rueda-Armengot, C., 2017. Smart city and tourism: an analysis of development of Caceres (Spain) as a smart city. In: Peris-Ortiz, M., Bennett, D.R., Pérez-Bustamante Yábar, D. (Eds.), Sustainable Smart Cities: Creating Spaces for Technological, Social and Business Development. Springer, Cham, pp. 199–218.

Amsterdam Innovation Motor, 2009. Amsterdam Capital of Science: ICT in Business. Amsterdam Innovation Motor. http://www.amsterdameconomicboard.com/download.php?itemID=294. (Accessed August 8, 2016).

Amsterdam Innovation Motor, and Liander, 2011. Smart Stories. Amsterdam Smart City. https://issuu.com/amsterdamsmartcity/docs/smart_stories. (Accessed August 5, 2016).

Amsterdam Smart City, 2011. Smart Stories. Amsterdam Smart City. https://issuu.com/amsterdamsmartcity/docs/smart_stories. (Accessed August 5, 2016).

Angelidou, M., 2014. Smart city policies: a spatial approach. Cities: Int. J. Urban Policy Plann. 41 (Suppl 1), S3–S11.

15. See http://eu-smartcities.eu.

Angelidou, M., 2017. The role of smart city characteristics in the plans of fifteen cities. J. Urban Technol. 24 (4), 3–28.

Arnkil, R., Järvensivu, A., Koski, P., Piirainen, T., 2010. Exploring Quadruple Helix: Outlining User-oriented Innovation Models. Working paper, University of Tampere. https://tampub.uta.fi/bitstream/handle/10024/65758/978-951-44-8209-0.pdf?sequence=1. (Accessed July 10, 2016).

Aspern Smart City Research, 2015. Aspern Smart City Research: Energieforschung Gestaltet Energiezukunft. Aspern Smart City Research. http://www.ascr.at/wp-content/uploads/2015/09/ASCR_Folder_dt.pdf. (Accessed May 3, 2017).

Baccarne, B., Schuurman, D., Mechant, P., De Marez, L., 2014. The role of urban living labs in a smart city. In: XXV ISPIM Innovation Conference: Innovation for Sustainable Economy & Society, Dublin. June. International Society for Professional Innovation Management, Manchester, pp. 8–11.

Bednar, T., Bothe, D., Forster, J., Fritz, S., Haufe, N., Kaufmann, T., Eder-Neuhauser, P., Pfaffenbichler, P., Rab, N., Schleicher, J., Weinwurm, G., Winkler, C., Ziegler, M., 2016. URBEN-DK: Results Report. Report, TU Wien. https://urbem.tuwien.ac.at/fileadmin/t/urbem/files/URBEM_Ergebnisbericht_Einzelseiten_EN.pdf. (Accessed August 5, 2017).

Ben Letaifa, S., 2015. How to strategize smart cities: revealing the SMART model. J. Bus. Res. 68 (7), 1414–1419.

Bergvall-Kåreborn, B., Ihlström Eriksson, C., Ståhlbröst, A., Svensson, J., 2009. A milieu for innovation – defining living labs. In: Proceedings of the 2nd ISPIM Innovation Symposium, New York City, NY, 6–9 December 2009. International Society for Professional Innovation Management (ISPIM), Manchester.

Bolici, R., Mora, L., 2015. Urban regeneration in the digital era: how to develop smart city strategies in large European cities. TECHNE: J. Technol. Architect. Environ. 5 (2), 110–119.

Brandon, P.S., Lombardi, P., Shen, G.Q. (Eds.), 2017. Future Challenges in Evaluating and Managing Sustainable Development in the Built Environment. John Wiley & Sons Ltd., Oxford.

Brandt, N., Cambell, F., Deakin, M., Johansson, S., Malmström, M., Mulder, K., Pesch, U., Shahrokni, H., Tatarchenko, O., Årman, L., 2014. European Cities Moving Towards Climate Neutrality. http://www.clue-project.eu/getfile.ashx?cid=69201&cc=5&refid=6. (Accessed July 8, 2017).

Breuer, J., Walravens, N., Ballon, P., 2014. Beyond defining the smart city: meeting top-down and bottom-up approaches in the middle. TeMA: J. Land Use Mobility Environ. 7, 153–164.

Bria, F., Gascó, M., Halpin, H., Baeck, P., Almirall, E., Kresin, F., 2015. Growing a Digital Social Innovation Ecosystem for Europe: DSI Final Report. European Union. https://www.nesta.org.uk/sites/default/files/dsireport.pdf. (Accessed January 3, 2017).

Brinkman, J., 2011. Supporting sustainability through smart infrastructures: the case of Amsterdam. Netw. Industr. Quart. 13 (3), 22–25.

Carayannis, E.G., Campbell, D., 2014. Developed democracies versus emerging autocracies: arts, democracy, and innovation in quadruple Helix innovation systems. J. Innov. Entrepreneurship 3 (12), 1–23.

Carcillo, F., Macii, E., 2013. Torino Smart City: Strategic Planning and Practical Deployment. City of Turin and Polytechnic University of Turin. https://events.hkstp.org/events/Past_AIS/CMS/files/03_Franco_and_Enrico_web_.pdf. (Accessed October 10, 2016).

Carr, S.J., Lassiter, A., 2017. Big data, small apps: premises and products of the civic hackathon. In: Thakuriah, P., Tilahun, N., Zellner, M. (Eds.), Seeing Cities Through Big Data. Springer, Cham, pp. 543–559.

Cavallini, S., Soldi, R., Friedl, J., Volpe, M., 2016. Using the Quadruple Helix Approach to Accelerate the Transfer of Research and Innovation Results to Regional Growth. European Union – Committee of the Regions. http://cor.europa.eu/en/documentation/studies/Documents/quadruple-helix.pdf. (Accessed November 8, 2016).

Cisco Systems, 2016a. Cisco Smart+Connected Digital Platform: At-a-glance. Cisco Systems. http://www.cisco.com/c/dam/en_us/solutions/industries/docs/at-a-glance-c45-736521.pdf. (Accessed June 20, 2017).

Cisco Systems, 2016b. Cisco Smart+Connected Digital Platform: Data Sheet. Cisco Systems. http://www.cisco.com/c/dam/en_us/solutions/industries/docs/datasheet-c78-737127.pdf. (Accessed June 20, 2017).

City of Amsterdam, 2011. Structuurvisie Amsterdam 2040: Economisch Sterk En Duurzaam. City of Amsterdam. http://www.amsterdam.nl/publish/pages/434856/structuurvisie_def_maart2011_web.pdf. (Accessed July 15, 2016).

City of Amsterdam, 2014a. De Circulaire Metropool Amsterdam 2014–2018. City of Amsterdam, http://www.amsterdam.nl/publish/pages/599296/de_circulaire_metropool_amsterdam_2014_2018_printversie_2mb_versie_-_20140618.pdf. (Accessed July 15, 2016).

City of Amsterdam, 2014b. European Strategy for Amsterdam: Progress in Sustainable Urban Development in 2013. City of Amsterdam. http://www.amsterdam.nl/publish/pages/600373/european_strategy_web.pdf. (Accessed July 15, 2016).

City of Amsterdam, 2015. Sustainable Amsterdam: Agenda for Renewable Energy, Clear Air, a Circular Economy and a Climate-resilient City. City of Amsterdam. https://www.amsterdam.nl/publish/pages/675721/sustainable_amsterdam_27-3-2015.pdf. (Accessed August 2, 2016).

City of Barcelona, 2012a. Marc Estratègic I Full De Ruta 2012–2015. City of Barcelona. http://www.bcn.cat/pdf/bases_pam/document_base.pdf. (Accessed August 25, 2016).

City of Barcelona, 2012b. Mesura De Govern MES: L'estratègia TIC De L'Ajuntament De Barcelona Al Servei De La Ciutat I Dels Ciutadans. City of Barcelona. http://governobert.bcn.cat/sites/default/files/MG_Cultura_TIC_300312.pdf. (Accessed August 25, 2016).

City of Barcelona, 2012c. User Manual: Barcelona WiFi. City of Barcelona. http://ajuntament.barcelona.cat/barcelonawifi/docs/en/manual.pdf. (Accessed October 12, 2016).

City of Barcelona, 2012d. Barcelona Impulsa El Reciclatge a Través De La Tecnologia Per a Mòbils En El Dia Internacional De La Prevenció De Residus. Press release, City of Barcelona. http://ajuntament.barcelona.cat/premsa/2012/05/17/barcelona-impulsa-el-reciclatge-a-traves-de-la-tecnologia-per-a-mobils-en-el-dia-internacional-de-la-prevencio-de-residus/. (Accessed September 10, 2016).

City of Barcelona, 2014. Mesura De Govern. Pla Director De Les TIC: Desplegament D'Infraestructures "Smart" a L'Espai Públic (PDTIC). City of Barcelona. http://governobert.bcn.cat/sites/default/files/Pla%20Director%20de%20les%20TIC.pdf. (Accessed August 25, 2016).

City of Barcelona, 2015a. Barcelona Acull Dos Hackathons Sobre Smart Cities Aquest Cap De Setmana. Press release, City of Barcelona. http://ajuntament.barcelona.cat/premsa/2015/02/20/barcelona-acull-dos-hackathons-sobre-smart-cities-aquest-cap-de-setmana/. (Accessed September 10, 2016).

City of Barcelona, 2015b. Barcelona Tendrá Cuatro Aplicaciones En La Final Global De Smart City App Hack. Press release, City of Barcelona. http://barcelona.smartcityapphack.com/2015/11/10/barcelona-tendra-cuatro-aplicaciones-en-la-final-global-de-smart-city-app-hack/. (Accessed September 10, 2016).

City of Barcelona, 2016. IMI - Municipal Institute of Information Technology. City of Barcelona. http://ajuntament.barcelona.cat/imi/en/documents. (Accessed December 5, 2016).

City of Barcelona, and Doxa Consulting, 2012. Barcelona Smart City: The Vision, Focus and Projects of the City of Barcelona in the Context of Smart Cities. City of Barcelona. http://ibarcelona.bcn.cat/sites/default/files/vision_focus_and_projects_of_bcn_in_smart_cities_context.pdf. (Accessed August 25, 2016).

City of Birmingham, 2012. Birmingham's Smart City Commission Vision. City of Birmingham. http://s3-eu-west-1.amazonaws.com/digitalbirmingham/resources/Birminghams-Smart-City-Commission-Vision-FINAL-VERSION.pdf. (Accessed August 7, 2016).

City of Birmingham, 2014. The Roadmap to a Smarter Birmingham. City of Birmingham. https://birminghamsmartcity.files.wordpress.com/2014/03/birmingham_smart_city_roadmap_03_03_20141.pdf. (Accessed August 7, 2016).

City of Helsinki, 2015. Helsingin Kaupungin Tietotekniikkaohjelma 2015–2017. City of Helsinki. http://www.hel.fi/static/helsinki/julkaisut/tietotekniikkaohjelma.pdf. (Accessed September 8, 2016).

City of Vienna, 2012. Smart City Wien Stakeholder Forum: Wo Stehen Wir. City of Vienna. https://www.wien.gv.at/stadtentwicklung/studien/pdf/b008327.pdf. (Accessed September 1, 2016).

City of Vienna, 2013a. Smart City Wien Stakeholder Forum: Auf Dem Weg Zur Smart City Wien Rahmenstrategie. City of Vienna. https://www.wien.gv.at/stadtentwicklung/studien/pdf/b008381.pdf. (Accessed September 1, 2016).

City of Vienna, 2013b. Smart City Wien Stakeholder Forum: Innovation Durch Smarte Projekte. City of Vienna. https://www.wien.gv.at/stadtentwicklung/studien/pdf/b008328.pdf. (Accessed September 1, 2016).

City of Vienna, 2014. Smart City Wien: Framework Strategy. City of Vienna. https://smartcity.wien.gv.at/site/files/2014/09/SmartCityWien_FrameworkStrategy_english_doublepage.pdf. (Accessed August 30, 2016).

City of Vienna, 2016. Stakeholder-Prozesse – Smart City Wien. City of Vienna. https://www.wien.gv.at/stadtentwicklung/projekte/smartcity/stakeholder.html. (Accessed September 1, 2016).

City of Vienna, 3420 Aspern Development AG, Siemens AG Österreich, Österreichisches Forschungs- und Prüfzentrum Arsenal GesmbH, raum & kommunikation GmbH, Vienna University of Technology, Energieinstitut der Wirtschaft GmbH, and Austrian Institute of Technology GmbH, 2011. Smart City Wien: Short Report. Climate and Energy Fund. http://www.smartcities.at/assets/Projektberichte/Endbericht-Kurzfassung/Endbericht-K11NE2F00030-Wien-kurz-dt-engl-v1.0.pdf. (Accessed September 1, 2016).

City of Vienna, 3420 Aspern Development AG, Siemens AG Österreich, Österreichisches Forschungs- und Prüfzentrum Arsenal GesmbH, raum & kommunikation GmbH, Vienna University of Technology, Energieinstitut der Wirtschaft GmbH, and Austrian Institute of Technology GmbH, 2013. Smart City Wien: Vision 2050, Roadmap for 2020 and Beyond, Action Plan for 2012–15. https://www.wien.gv.at/stadtentwicklung/studien/pdf/b008218.pdf. (Accessed September 1, 2016).

CLUE Project Partners, 2014. Practices, Tools and Policies: European Cities Moving Towards Climate Neutrality. Report, http://www.clue-project.eu/getfile.ashx?cid=503736&cc=3&refid=18. (Accessed March 10, 2016).

Cohen, B., 2012a. The 10 Smartest Cities on the Planet. Fast Company. http://www.fastcoexist.com/1679127/the-top-10-smart-cities-on-the-planet. (Accessed October 2, 2014).

Cohen, B., 2012b. The 10 Smartest European Cities. Fast Company. http://www.fastcoexist.com/1680856/the-top-10-smartest-european-cities. (Accessed August 2, 2014).

Cohen, B., 2014. The 10 Smartest Cities in Europe. Fast Company. http://www.fastcoexist.com/3024721/the-10-smartest-cities-in-europe?partner=rss&utm_source=feedburner&utm_medium=feed&utm_campaign=Feed%3A+fastcoexist%2Ffeed+%28Co.Exist%29. (Accessed August 2, 2014).

Concilio, G., Molinari, F., Morelli, N., 2017. Empowering citizens with open data by urban hackathons. In: 2017 Conference for E-Democracy and Open Government (CeDEM), Krems, 17–19 May 2017. Institute of Electrical and Electronics Engineers (IEEE), Piscataway, NJ, pp. 125–134.

Creswell, J.W., 2009. Research Design: Qualitative, Quantitative, and Mixed Methods Approaches, third ed. SAGE Publications, Thousand Oaks, CA.

Curwell, S., Deakin, M., Cooper, I., Paskaleva-Shapira, K., Ravetz, J., Babicki, D., 2005. Citizens' expectations of information cities: implications for urban planning and design. Build. Res. Inf. 33 (1), 55–66.

Deakin, M., 2014a. Smart cities: the state-of-the-art and governance challenge. Triple Helix 1 (7), 1–16.

Deakin, M. (Ed.), 2014b. Smart Cities: Governing, Modelling and Analysing the Transition. Routledge, New York City, NY.

Deakin, M., Allwinkle, S., 2007. Urban regeneration and sustainable communities: the role of networks, innovation, and creativity in building successful partnerships. J. Urban Technol. 14 (1), 77–91.

Deakin, M., Leydesdorff, L., 2014. The triple helix model of smart cities: a neo-evolutionary perspective. In: Deakin, M. (Ed.), Smart Cities: Governing, Modelling and Analyzing the Transition. Routledge, New York, NY, pp. 134–149.

Deambrogio, E., 2013. Towards Torino Smart City. City of Turin. https://www.itu.int/en/ITU-T/climatechange/symposia/201305/Documents/info/Presentations/s7p6-ElenaDeambrogio.pdf. (Accessed March 5, 2016).

Eisenhardt, K.M., 1989. Building theories from case study research. Acad. Manag. Rev. 14 (4), 532–550.

Eisenhardt, K.M., Graebner, M.E., 2007. Theory building from cases: opportunities and challenges. Acad. Manag. J. 50 (1), 25–32.

Estevez, E., Vasco Lopes, N., Janowski, T., 2016. Smart Sustainable Cities – Reconnaissance Study. United Nations University and International Development Research Center (IDRC). http://collections.unu.edu/eserv/UNU:5825/Smart_Sustainable_Cities_v2final.pdf. (Accessed October 8, 2017).

European Commission, 2014. Barcelona Is "iCapital" of Europe. Press release, European Commission. http://europa.eu/rapid/press-release_IP-14-239_en.htm?locale=en. (Accessed March 13, 2014).

European Commission, 2016. Urban Agenda for the EU: Pact of Amsterdam. European Commission. https://ec.europa.eu/futurium/en/system/files/ged/pact-of-amsterdam_en.pdf. (Accessed December 10, 2017).

Exner, J., 2015. smart cities - field of application for planning support systems in the 21st century? In: Proceedings Computers in Urban Planning and Urban Management 2015, Cambridge, MA, 7–10 July 2015. Massachusetts Institute of Technology, Cambridge, MA.

Forum Virium Helsinki, 2014. Forum Virium Helsinki. Presentation. Forum Virium Helsinki. https://forumvirium.fi/en/introduction/materials. (Accessed September 5, 2016).

Forum Virium Helsinki, 2015. Building an Open City. Forum Virium Helsinki. https://forumvirium.fi/en/introduction/materials. (Accessed September 5, 2016).

Fullard, A., 2016. Information Communication Technology and Digital Strategy 2016-2021. City of Birmingham. https://www.birmingham.gov.uk/download/downloads/id/5029/birmingham_city_council_ict_and_digital_strategy_2016-2021.pdf. (Accessed December 20, 2017).

Future Cities Catapult, and Arup, 2017. Smart City Strategies: A Global Review. Future Cities Catapult. http://futurecities.catapult.org.uk/wp-content/uploads/2017/11/GRSCS-Final-Report.pdf. (Accessed December 12, 2017).

George, A.L., Bennett, A., 2005. Case Studies and Theory Development in the Social Sciences. MIT Press, Cambridge, MA.

Gibbs, G.R., 2007. Analysing Qualitative Data. SAGE Publications, Thousand Oaks, CA.

Gibson, J., Robinson, M., Cain, S., 2015. City Initiatives for Technology, Innovation and Entrepreneurship: A Resource for City Leadership. Nesta, Accenture and Future Cities Catapult. http://citie.org/assets/uploads/2015/04/CITIE_Report_2015.pdf. (Accessed August 10, 2016).

Giffinger, R., Ferter, C., Kramar, H., Kalasek, R., Pichler-Milanović, N., Meijers, E., 2007. Smart Cities: Ranking of European Medium-sized Cities. Research report, Vienna University of Technology – Centre of Regional Science (SRF). http://www.smart-cities.eu/download/smart_cities_final_report.pdf. (Accessed May 9, 2012).

Gooch, D., Wolff, A., Kortuem, G., Brown, R., 2015. Reimagining the role of citizens in smart city projects. In: UbiComp/ISWC'15 Adjunct: Adjunct Proceedings of the 2015 ACM International Joint Conference on Pervasive and Ubiquitous Computing and Proceedings of the 2015 ACM International Symposium on Wearable Computers, Osaka, 7–11 September 2015. ACM, New York, NY, pp. 1587–1594.

Grossi, G., Pianezzi, D., 2017. Smart cities: utopia or neoliberal ideology? Cities: Int. J. Urban Policy Plann. 69, 79–85.

Hartmann, S., Hlava, P., Tiede, L., Kintisch, M., Mollay, U., Schremmer, C., Brajovic, T., Breitfuss, A., Leitner, S., Brus, T., Weninger, K., Kalasek, R., 2015. Transformation Agenda Vienna. Report, http://urbantransform.eu/wp-content/uploads/sites/2/2015/07/D2.2_Transformation-Agenda-Vienna.pdf. (Accessed May 12, 2016).

Hemis, H., Schmid, W., Gigler, U., den Boogert, G., Muller, S., Stock, H., Uuong, D., Emery, S., Meskel, E., Weber, P., Jaeger, J., Ljungqvist, L., Geier, S., Olszak, A., Wróblewski, M., Santman, M., Malnar Neralić, S., Mornar, N., Matasović, M., Zidar, M., 2017. Integrating Energy in Urban Planning Processes – Insights From Amsterdam/Zaanstad, Berlin, Paris, Stockholm, Vienna, Warsaw and Zagreb. Report, http://www.urbanlearning.eu/fileadmin/user_upload/documents/D4-2_Synthesis-report_upgraded_processes_final_170807.pdf. (Accessed September 5, 2017).

Henriquez, L., 2015. The Amsterdam Smart Citizens Lab: Towards Community Driven Data Collection. Waag Society and AMS Institute. https://waag.org/sites/waag/files/public/media/publicaties/amsterdam-smart-citizen-lab-publicatie.pdf. (Accessed November 10, 2016).

Hofstetter, K., Vogl, A., 2011. Smart city Wien: Vienna's stepping stone into the European future of technology and climate. In: Schrenk, M., Popovich, V.V., Zeile, P. (Eds.), REAL CORP 2011. Change for Stability: Lifecycles of Cities and Regions. The Role and Possibilities of Foresighted Planning in Transformation Processes. Proceedings of 16th International Conference on Urban Planning, Regional Development and Information Society, Essen, 18–20 May 2011. Competence Center of Urban and Regional Planning (CORP), Schwechat, pp. 1373–1382.

Hollands, R.G., 2008. Will the real smart city please stand up? City: Anal. Urban Trends Culture Theory Policy Action 12 (3), 303–320.

IBM Corporation, 2017. IBM Smarter Planet. Website, http://www-03.ibm.com/ibm/history/ibm100/us/en/icons/smarterplanet/. (Accessed March 20, 2017).

IDC, 2016. IDC Smart Cities Österreich 2016 Studie. IDC. http://idc-austria.at/de/research/local-studies. (Accessed August 10, 2017).

Ielite, I., Olevsky, G., Safiulins, T., 2015. Identification and prioritization of stakeholders in the planning process of sustainable development of the smart city. In: 2015 IEEE Seventh International Conference on Intelligent Computing and Information Systems (ICICIS'15), Cairo, 12–14 December 2015. Institute of Electrical and Electronics Engineers (IEEE), Piscataway, NJ, pp. 251–257.

Irani, L., 2015. Hackathons and the making of entrepreneurial citizenship. Sci. Technol. Hum. Values 40 (5), 799–824.

Johnson, P., Robinson, P., 2014. Civic hackathons: innovation, procurement, or civic engagement? Rev. Policy Res. 31 (4), 349–357.

Komninos, N., 2014. The Age of Intelligent Cities: Smart Environments and Innovation-For-All Strategies. Routledge, New York City, NY.

Komssi, M., Pichlis, D., Raatikainen, M., Kindström, K., Järvinen, J., 2015. What are hackathons for? IEEE Softw. 32 (5), 60–67.

Kotkin, J., 2009. The World's Smartest Cities. Forbes. http://www.forbes.com/2009/12/03/infrastructure-economy-urban-opinions-columnists-smart-cities-09-joel-kotkin.html. (Accessed September 5, 2016).

Lee, J., Hancock, M.G., Hu, M., 2014. Towards an effective framework for building smart cities: lessons from Seoul and San Francisco. Technol. Forecast. Soc. Chang. 89, 80–99.

Lee, J.H., Phaal, R., Lee, S., 2013. An integrated service-device-technology roadmap for smart city development. Technol. Forecast. Soc. Chang. 80 (2), 286–306.

Lerner, J., 2014. Urban Acupuncture: Celebrating Pinpricks of Change that Enrich City Life. Island Press, Washington, DC.

Lievens, B., Schaffers, H., Turkama, P., Stahlbrost, A., Ballon, P., 2011. Cross border living labs networks to support SMEs accessing new markets. In: Cunningham, P., Cunningham, M. (Eds.), EChallenges E-2011 Conference Proceedings, Florence, 26–28 October 2011. International Information Management Corporation (IIMC), Dublin, pp. 1–8.

Lodato, T.J., DiSalvo, C., 2016. Issue-oriented hackathons as material participation. New Media and Society 18 (4), 539–557.

Manville, C., Cochrane, G., Cave, J., Millard, J., Pederson, J.K., Thaarup, R.K., Liebe, A., Wissner, M., Massink, R., Kotterink, B., 2014. Mapping Smart City in the EU. European Parliament – Directorate-General for Internal Policies. http://www.europarl.europa.eu/RegData/etudes/etudes/join/2014/507480/IPOL-ITRE_ET(2014)507480_EN.pdf. (Accessed February 5, 2014).

Marguerite, C., Pardo Garcia, N., Haslinger, E., Monteverdi, I., Santicelli, G., Abdurafikov, R., 2016. CityOpt – Holistic Simulation and Optimization of Energy Systems in Smart Cities: Vienna Demonstrator. Report, http://cityopt.eu/Deliverables/D33.pdf. (Accessed February 1, 2017).

Marsal-Llacuna, M., Segal, M.E., 2016. The intelligenter method (I) for making "smarter" city projects and plans. Cities: Int. J. Urban Policy Plann. 55, 127–138.

Marsal-Llacuna, M., Segal, M.E., 2017. The intelligenter method (II) for "smarter" urban policy-making and regulation drafting. Cities: Int. J. Urban Policy Plann. 61, 83–95.

Mathie, A., Cunningham, G., 2003. From clients to citizens: asset-based community development as a strategy for community-driven development. Dev. Pract. 13 (5), 474–486.

Mayangsari, L., Novani, S., 2015. Multi-stakeholder co-creation analysis in smart city management: An experience from Bandung, Indonesia. Procedia Manuf. 4, 315–321.

Meijer, A., Bolivar, M.P.R., 2016. Governing the smart city: a review of the literature on smart urban governance. Int. Rev. Adm. Sci. 82 (2), 392–408.

Moghadam, S.T., Lombardi, P., Mutani, G., 2017. A mixed methodology for defining a new spatial decision analysis towards low carbon cities. Procedia Eng. 198, 375–385.

Mora, L., Bolici, R., 2016. The development process of smart city strategies: the case of Barcelona. In: Rajaniemi, J. (Ed.), Re-City: Future City – Combining Disciplines. Juvenes print, Tampere, pp. 155–181.

Mora, L., Bolici, R., 2017. How to become a smart city: learning from Amsterdam. In: Bisello, A., Vettorato, D., Stephens, R., Elisei, P. (Eds.), Smart and Sustainable Planning for Cities and Regions: Results of SSPCR 2015. Springer, Cham, pp. 251–266.

Muhlmann, P., 2017. Smart City Wien: The City for Life. TINA Vienna GmbH. https://www.publicconsulting.at/fileadmin/user_upload/media/kpc-consulting/Austrian_CC_Workshop_2017/2._P._Muehlmann_Tina_Vienna_Austrian_CC_WS_2017.pdf. (Accessed August 5, 2017).

Neirotti, P., De Marco, A., Cagliano, A.C., Mangano, G., Scorrano, F., 2014. Current trends in smart city initiatives: some stylised facts. Cities: Int. J. Urban Policy Plann. 38, 25–36.

Panos, A., Rueda, M.L., Gonçalves, F., Águas, M., Cabral Pinto, F., García, D., 2016. D7.2 BESOS Evaluation and Assessment. Report, Hypertech. http://cordis.europa.eu/docs/projects/cnect/3/608723/080/deliverables/001-BesosD72EvaluationandAssessment6.pdf. (Accessed November 10, 2016).

Patton, M.Q., 2002. Qualitative Research and Evaluation Methods, third ed. SAGE Publications, Thousand Oaks, CA.

Pentikousis, K., Zhu, D., Wang, H., 2011. Network infrastructure at the crossroads: the emergence of smart cities. In: 2011 15th International Conference on Intelligence in Next Generation Networks, Berlin, 4-7 October 2011. Institute of Electrical and Electronics Engineers (IEEE), Piscataway, NJ, pp. 109–114.

Pisu, S., 2015. Turin's Smart City Strategy and Projects. Fondazione Torino Wireless. https://www.sas.com/content/dam/SAS/ru_ru/image/events/SAS-Forum-Russia/Presentation/Intelligence_in_the_Public_Sector/02_Torino_Smart_City_practices_current_projects_and_initiatives-(SFR2015).pdf. (Accessed October 10, 2016).

Rafiq, G., Talha, B., Pätzold, M., Gato Luis, J., Ripa, G., Carreras, I., Coviello, C., Marzorati, S., Perez Rodriguez, G., Herrero, G., Desaeger, M., 2013. What's new in intelligent transportation systems? An overview of European projects and initiatives. IEEE Veh. Technol. Mag. 8 (4), 45–69.

Reviglio, E., Camerano, S., Carriero, A., Del Bufalo, G., Alterio, D., Calderini, M., De Marco, A., Michelucci, F.V., Neirotti, P., Scorrano, F., 2013. Smart City: Development Projects and Financial Instruments. Report, Cassa depositi e prestiti. http://www.cassaddpp.it/static/upload/mon/monographic-report_smart-city.pdf. (Accessed February 26, 2014).

Riva Sanseverino, E., Riva Sanseverino, R., Vaccaro, V. (Eds.), 2017. Smart Cities Atlas: Western and Eastern Intelligent Communities. Springer, Cham.

Riva Sanseverino, E., Riva Sanseverino, R., Vaccaro, V., Zizzo, G. (Eds.), 2014. Smart Rules for Smart Cities: Managing Efficient Cities in Euro-Mediterranean Countries. Springer, Cham.

Robson, C., 1993. Real World Research: A Resource for Users of Social Research Methods in Applied Settings. John Wiley & Sons Ltd., Hoboken, NJ.

Santucci, L., Oele, J., Jordán, R., Valenzuela, B., Barth, B., Stipisic, M.M., Andersson, K., Wehmer, N., 2011. Are We Building Competitive and Liveable Cities? Guidelines for Developing Eco-efficient and Socially Inclusive Infrastructure. United Nations. http://www.cepal.org/publicaciones/xml/9/52019/Guidelines.pdf. (Accessed May 10, 2014).

Schaffers, H., Komninos, N., Pallot, M., Aguas, M., Almirall, E., Bakici, T., Barroca, J., Carter, D., Corriou, M., Fernadez, J., Hielkema, H., Kivilehto, A., Nilsson, M., Oliveira, A., Posio, E., Sällström, A., Santoro, R., Senach, B., Torres, I., Tsarchopoulos, P., Trousse, B., Turkama, P., Lopez Ventura, J., 2012. Smart Cities as Innovation Ecosystems Sustained by the Future Internet. White paper, http://hal.archives-ouvertes.fr/docs/00/76/96/35/PDF/FIREBALL-White-Paper-Final2.pdf. (Accessed August 24, 2011).

Schaffers, H., Sällström, A., Pallot, M., Hernández-Muñoz, J.M., Santoro, R., Trousse, B., 2011. Integrating living labs with future internet experimental platforms for co-creating services within smart cities. In: Thoben, K., Stich, V., Imtiaz, A. (Eds.), 2011 17th International Conference on Concurrent Enterprising (ICE), Aachen, 20–22 June 2011. Institute of Electrical and Electronics Engineers (IEEE), Piscataway, NJ, pp. 1–11.

Strauss, A., Corbin, J.M., 1990. Basics of Qualitative Research: Grounded Theory Procedures and Techniques. SAGE Publications, Thousand Oaks, CA.

The Technopolicy Network, 2014. Amsterdam Innovation Motor. The Technopolicy Network. http://technopolicy.net/index.php?option=com_content&view=article&id=41&Itemid=59. (Accessed August 8, 2016).

Torres, L., Vicente, P., Acerete, B., 2006. E-governance developments in European Union cities: reshaping Government's relationship with citizens. Governance: Int. J. Policy Admin. Inst. 19 (2), 277–302.

United Nations, 2015. Transforming Our World: The 2030 Agenda for Sustainable Development. A/RES/70/1, United Nations. https://sustainabledevelopment.un.org/content/documents/21252030%20Agenda%20for%20Sustainable%20Development%20web.pdf. (Accessed December 10, 2017).

United Nations, 2016. Policy Paper 9: Urban Services and Technology. A/CONF.226/PC.3/22, United Nations. http://habitat3.org/wp-content/uploads/Policy-Paper-9-English.pdf. (Accessed December 10, 2017).

United Nations, 2017. New Urban Agenda. A/RES/71/256, United Nations. http://habitat3.org/wp-content/uploads/NUA-English.pdf. (Accessed December 10, 2017).

URBACT Secretariat, 2017. URBACT Good Practice Summary: Summary of Good Practice for Heraklion, Crete, Greece. URBACT Secretariat. http://urbact.eu/file/16763/download?token=SvyHrUQW. (Accessed August 15, 2017).

Van Steenwinkel, F., Potts, M., Glickman, Y., Strick, L., 2012. D3.1 Proposed Methodology for iCities Digital Assessment. CISCO and Fraunhofer. http://www.icityproject.eu/sites/default/files/iCity_D3.1_0.pdf. (Accessed November 10, 2016).

Veeckman, C., van der Graaf, S., 2014. The city as living laboratory: a playground for the innovative development of smart city applications. In: 2014 International ICE Conference on Engineering, Technology and Innovation (ICE), Bergamo, 23–25 June 2014. Institute of Electrical and Electronics Engineers (IEEE), Piscataway, NJ.

Velthausz, D., 2011. Amsterdam Smart City. Amsterdam Smart City. http://www.slideshare.net/llisa/amsterdam-smart-city-eng-presentation-2-32011-7131457. (Accessed August 2, 2016).

Wien Holding GmbH, 2012. Quality of Life for Vienna. Wien Holding GmbH. https://www.wien-holding.at/tools/uploads/folderbroschueren/WienHolding-English.pdf. (Accessed October 20, 2016).

Wiener Modellregion, and Climate and Energy Fund, 2014. Statusbericht Der Wiener Modellregion "E-Mobility nn Demand". Report, Wiener Modellregion and Climate and Energy Fund. https://www.klimafonds.gv.at/assets/Uploads/Themenprojekte/Modellregionen/e-mobility-on-demand-Wien/201504-Statusberichtemobility-on-demand-Wienfinal.pdf. (Accessed October 9, 2015).

Yin, R.K., 2009. Case Study Research: Design and Methods, fourth ed. SAGE Publications, Thousand Oaks, CA.

Zelt, T., Ibel, J., Tuncer, F., 2017. THINK ACT: Smart City. Smart Strategy, Roland Berger GmbH. https://www.rolandberger.com/publications/publication_pdf/ta_17_008_smart_cities_online.pdf. (Accessed August 31, 2017).

Chapter 6

Smart city development in North America

Chapter outline

6.1 The architecture of smart cities

Two critical lessons can be distilled from the multiple case study analysis into European best practices and insight that this offers into smart city development. The previous study demonstrates that enabling smart city development requires cities to cope with the complexity of a socio-technical transformation, which is triggered by the alignment between technological development and human, social, cultural, economic, and environmental factors. In addition, European best practices clearly show that this alignment calls for smart city development strategies capable of assembling four complementary building blocks, basic units that are embedded in the structure of the city and whose connection enables smart city development. These building blocks constitute the core components of a smart city and expose its complex architecture (see Figs. 6.1 and 6.2).

The first building block is a collaborative environment which brings together the industry-government-research relationships of the triple-helix collaborative model and the participatory qualities of civil society organizations and citizens. This environment creates the conditions for individuals and organizations to pool their knowledge, skills, and interests and to collaborate in designing and implementing a citywide smart city development strategy. Evidence

Untangling Smart Cities. https://doi.org/10.1016/B978-0-12-815477-9.00006-2

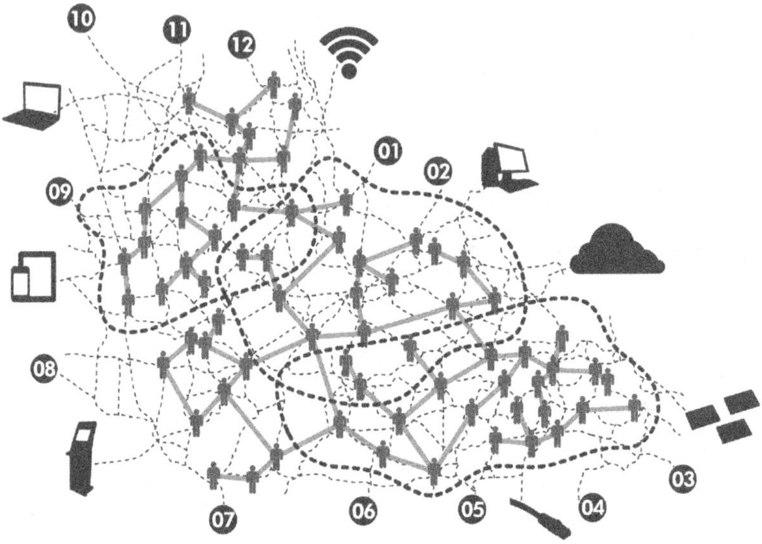

FIG. 6.1 The architecture of smart cities.

from Europe suggests building such an environment requires cities to encourage public-private collaboration and raise the active involvement of civil society in the smart city domain, stimulate bottom-up development processes exploiting ICT-related innovations, increase digital literacy, and improve the level of understanding of city stakeholders on the benefits that smart city development can generate.

The second building block is a comprehensive strategic framework for regulating the smart city transformation process, which is developed to guide the efforts of individuals and organizations belonging to the collaborative environment toward the same direction. The strategic framework is established by the local government and should (1) provide long-term vision, (2) establish the objectives to be achieved through the deployment of ICT solutions, (3) suggest the main application domains and urban sustainability issues to focus attention on, (4) establish standards, technical requirements, and methods for evaluating both results and progress, and (5) set up the governance system necessary to regulate the transition to smart cities and development of an ICT-driven approach to urban sustainability. This governance system includes a smart city accelerator, a working group dedicated to accelerating the progressive transformation of the city in a smart environment. This smart city accelerator can be either a public-private organization with independent legal identity or a working group embedded in the city government's organizational structure.

The third building block is a city-scale network infrastructure composed of hardware and software resources. This technological infrastructure supports data transmission and provides city users with access to ICT services and applications

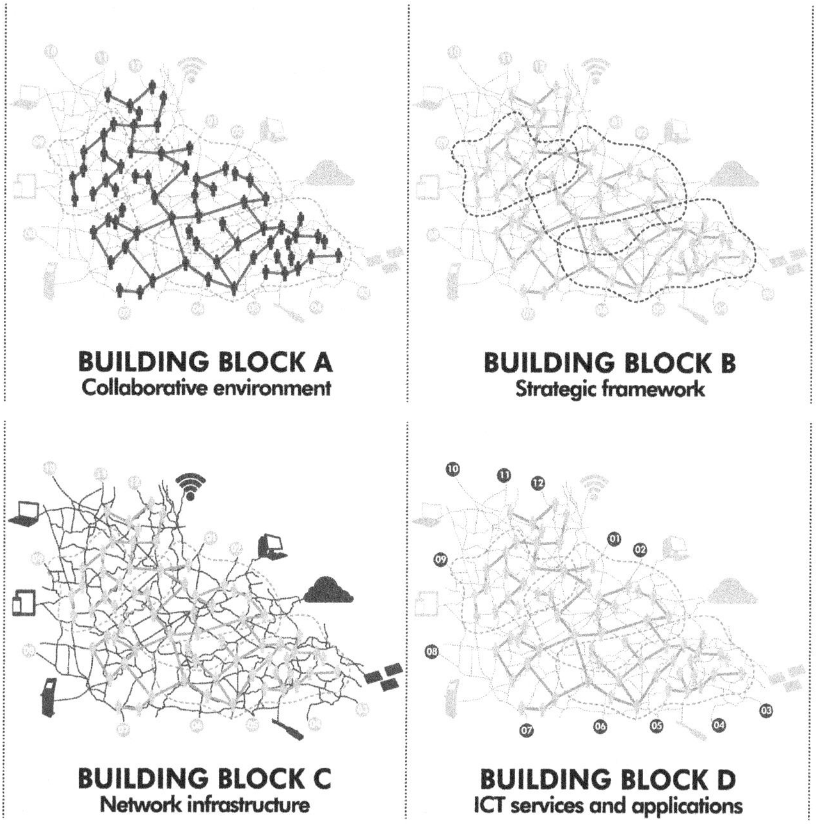

FIG. 6.2 The architecture of smart cities: building blocks. Building Block D—Application domains: Energy networks (01), Air (02), Water (03), Waste (04), Mobility and transport (05), Buildings and districts (06), Health and social inclusion (07), Culture and recreation (08), Education (09), Public security and justice (10), E-government (11), and Others (12).

deployed to address urban sustainability issues. These digital solutions shape the last building block of the smart city, and their uptake is based on an integrated intervention logic that cuts across a multitude of application domains.

Taking into account this insight, it is possible to formulate the following hypothesis: establishing and gathering together these four components is essential for successfully enabling the ICT-driven approach to urban sustainability that smart city development stands for. However, so far, the evidence available to verify such a theoretical premise is limited to the research conducted on European smart cities, and this restricts the possibility of drawing broad inferences of wider significance. Additional research is needed to prove the value of this theory in regional contexts other than Europe, and the acquisition of the empirical evidence necessary to achieve this aim should be considered a priority, because it can further mitigate the negative effects that the dichotomous nature of smart city research is producing.

This chapter reports on the findings of a deductive case study analysis that helps meet this challenge. In the following paragraphs, attention will be shifted from Europe to North America, where the validity of the proposed theory is tested by investigating the ongoing efforts that New York City has made to successfully deploy ICT solutions against sustainability issues. These efforts are captured from a detailed investigation into the extensive program of activities that New York has embarked upon to become a world-leading example of smart city development. Such a program covers 30 years of intensive work, from 1989 to 2018, and is composed of almost 900 activities, which have been mapped by examining more than 800 digital records reporting on New York City's smart city development strategy.

The chapter is organized in three main sections and opens up with Section 6.2, in which the research methodology designed to conduct the analytic process is presented. This methodological approach proposes a single case study analysis in which the examination is conducted by building on the feasibility of the multiple case study analysis presented in Chapter 5. The results of the analysis, which are presented in Section 6.3, suggest success in enabling smart city development in North America depends upon the correct assembling of the four building blocks exposed by the European best practices. Finally, Section 6.4 concludes the chapter by discussing the significance of this finding in relation to the available literature reporting on additional smart city development practices in North American cities: Camden, Kansas City, Mexico City, Philadelphia, Quebec City, and Seattle. This complementary research activity brings together further evidence to prove the validity of the initial hypothesis and broader generalization of the insight captured at the European level.

6.2 Hypothesis testing with case study research: Phase 2

As anticipated in Chapter 2, smart cities are a global phenomenon, which is fast expanding not only in European regions but also in American and Asian land. This is demonstrated by the large number of available studies that investigate smart city development in Asia, Australia, and the Americas. Overall, the literature resulting from these studies captures 240 cities in which documented evidence has been provided of attempts to push urban sustainability forward by means of ICT solutions. These cities are listed in Table 6.1, along with the 21 countries where they are located and the publications which they have been sourced from.

To prove that the validity of the initial theory can be extended to North America, a five-stage hypothesis-testing process is conducted that relies on a best practice analysis. The stages are organized as follows: (1) identification of an initial population of interest for the experiment, (2) selection of a best

TABLE 6.1 Smart city development in Asia, Australia, and the Americas

Continent	Country	Smart city cases		References
		No	Cities	
Asia	China	31	Beijing, Changsha, Chengdu, Chongming District, Chongqing, Dongtan, Foshan, Guiyang, Hong Kong, Huaibei, Kaifeng, Langfang, Nanjing, Ningbo, Rizhao, Shanghai, Shenyang, Shenzhen, Suzhou, Tangshan, Tianjin, Urumqi, Weihai, Wuhan, Wuxi, Xi'an, Xiamen, Yangzhou, Yinggehai, Yishanwan, Zhuhai	Anderson et al. (2012), Anrong et al. (2016), ARUP (2013), Caprotti et al. (2017), Joss (2011), Joss et al. (2011), Ju et al. (2018), Komninos (2011), Lu et al. (2018), Wang and Wang (2017), Zhang et al. (2014)
Asia	India	99	Agartala, Agra, Ahmedabad, Ajmer, Aligarh, Allahabad, Amravati, Amritsar, Aurangabad, Auroville, Bareilly, Belagavi, Belgaum, Bhagalpur, Bhopal, Bhubaneswar, Bidhannagar, Bihar Sharif, Bilaspur, Chandigarh, Changodar, Chennai, Coimbatore, Dahej, Dahod, Davangere, Dharamshala, Dholera, Dindigul, Erode, Faridabad, Gandhinagar, Ghaziabad, Gujarat International Financial Tec-City, Guwahati, Gwalior, Haldia, Hubballi-Dharwad, Imphal, Indore, Jabalpur, Jaipur, Jalandhar, Jhansi, Kakinada, Kalyan-Dombivali, Kanpur, Karnal, Kochi, Kohima, Kota, Kottayam, Lavasa, Lucknow, Ludhiana, Madurai, Manesar Bawal, Mangaluru, Moradabad, Nagpur, Namchi, Nashik, NDMC, New Delhi, New Town Kolkata, Panaji, Port Blair, Pune, Puri, Raipur, Rajkot, Rampur, Ranchi, Rourkela, Sagar, Saharanpur, Salem, Sanand, Shendra, Shillong, Shivamogga, Solapur, Surat, Thane, Thanjavur, Thoothukudi, Tiruchirappalli, Tirupati, Tiruppur, Tumkur, Udaipur, Ujjain, Vadodara, Varanasi, Vellore, Visakhapatnam, Vrindavan, Warangal	Anderson et al. (2012), Datta (2015), Gupta and Hall (2017), Joss (2011), Joss et al. (2011), National League of Cities (2016)

Continued

TABLE 6.1 Smart city development in Asia, Australia, and the Americas—cont'd

Continent	Country	Smart city cases		References
		No	Cities	
Asia	Indonesia	8	Bandung, Bontang, Denpasar, Magelang, Makasar, Palembang, Pontianak, Surabaya	Sandhi Firmanyah et al. (2017)
Asia	Japan	17	Fujisawa, Iida, Kawasaki, Kitakyushu, Kyoto, Minamata Miyakojima, Obihiro, Osaka, Sakai, Shimokawa, Tajimi, Tokyo, Toyama, Toyota, Yokohama, Yusuhara	Fietkiewicz and Stock (2015), Joss (2011), Joss et al. (2011)
Asia	Malaysia	1	Cyberjaya	Angelidou (2017)
Asia	Philippines	1	Puerto Princesa	Joss (2011), Joss et al. (2011)
Asia	Russia	2	Mirny, Skolkovo	Angelidou (2017), Joss (2011), Joss et al. (2011)
Asia	Saudi Arabia	9	Dammam, Jeddah, Jubail, Jubail Industrial City, King Abdullah Economic City, Madinah, Makkah, Riyadh, Yanbu Industrial City	Aina (2017), Anderson et al. (2012), Angelidou (2017)
Asia	Singapore	1	Singapore	Angelidou (2014), Angelidou (2017), Cisco Systems (2012), Kong and Woods (2018), Phumpiu Chang and Rivera Kuri (2014)
Asia	South Korea	7	Busan, Gwanggyo, Incheon, Sejong, Seoul, Songdo, Suwon	Acuto et al. (2018), Anderson et al. (2012), Angelidou (2014), Angelidou (2017), Cisco Systems (2012), Joss (2011), Joss et al. (2011), Kolotouchkina and Seisdedos (2018), Lee et al. (2014), Selinger and Kim (2015), Shwayri (2013)

Asia	Taiwan	2	Kaohsiung, Taoyuan	Anderson et al. (2012), Joss (2011), Joss et al. (2011)
Asia	The United Arab Emirates	1	Masdar	Anderson et al. (2012), Angelidou (2017), Cugurullo (2013), Kolotouchkina and Seisdedos (2018)
North America	Canada	11	Fredericton, Moncton, Montreal, Ottawa, Quebec City, Saint John, Toronto, Vancouver, Victoria, Windsor-Essex, Winnipeg	Alawadhi et al. (2012), Anderson et al. (2012), Arif et al. (2015), Joss (2011), Joss et al. (2011), Leydesdorff and Deakin (2011)
North America	Central America	1	Panama City	Joss (2011), Joss et al. (2011)
North America	Mexico	1	Mexico City; Monterrey	Acuto et al. (2018), Alawadhi et al. (2012), Phumpiu Chang and Rivera Kuri (2014)
North America	The United States	31	Alexandria, VA; Arcosanti, AZ; Austin, TX; Beaufort, SC; Boston, MA; Boulder, CO; Bristol, VA; Camden, NJ; Charlotte, NC; Chattanooga, TN; Chicago, IL; Cleveland, OH; Columbus, OH; Dakota County, MN; Denver, CO; Destiny, FL; Dublin, OH; Fitchburg, WI; Greensburg, KS; Ithaca, NY; Kansas City, MO; Ketchum, ID; Louisville, KY; New York City, NY; Philadelphia, PA; Portland, OR; Providence, RI; Rohnert Park, CA; San Francisco, CA; Scottsdale, AZ; Seattle, WA; South Bend, IN; Washington, DC	Acuto et al. (2018), Alawadhi et al. (2012), Anderson et al. (2012), Angelidou (2014), Angelidou (2017), Arif et al. (2015), ARUP (2013), Cisco Systems (2012), Dierwechter (2013), Joss (2011), Joss et al. (2011), Lee et al. (2014), McLean et al. (2016), McNeill (2016), National League of Cities (2016), Sarma and Sunny (2017), Shelton et al. (2015), The United States Conference of Mayors and IHS Markit (2017), Walters (2011), Wiig (2015), Wiig (2018)

Continued

TABLE 6.1 Smart city development in Asia, Australia, and the Americas—cont'd

		Smart city cases		
Continent	Country	No	Cities	References
South America	Brazil	7	Belo Horizonte, Curitiba, Pedra Branca, Porto Alegre, Recife, Rio de Janeiro, São Carlos	Anderson et al. (2012), Angelidou (2014), Angelidou (2017), ARUP (2013), Cisco Systems (2012), Gaffney and Robertson (2018), Goodspeed (2015), Joss (2011), Joss et al. (2011), Macke et al. (2018), Phumpiu Chang and Rivera Kuri (2014), Ueyama et al. (2017), Viale Pereira et al. (2017)
South America	Colombia	1	Medellin	Acuto et al. (2018)
South America	Ecuador	2	Bahía de Caráquez, Loja	Joss (2011), Joss et al. (2011)
Australia	Australia	4	Ballarat, Ipswich, Melbourne, Sydney	Anderson et al. (2012), Joss (2011), Joss et al. (2011)
Australia	New Zealand	1	Waitakere	Joss (2011), Joss et al. (2011)

practice, (3) data collection, (4) data processing through systematic coding, and (5) analysis of the results.

Firstly, an extreme case of smart city was selected (Yin, 2009), a North American city that has shown success in approaching smart city development. The North American cities listed in Table 6.1 were considered as the initial population and the sampling process, which was conducted by means of a theoretical approach (Eisenhardt, 1989; George and Bennett, 2005; Robson, 1993; Yin, 2009), led to the selection of New York City. With more than 8 million inhabitants, New York City is the most populous city in the United States, and its success in the field of smart city development is demonstrated by the data presented in Table 6.2. This data suggests the American metropolis is an internationally recognized best practice in the field of smart city development, which has received many awards in recognition of its success in using ICT to improve the sustainability of urban operations and infrastructure.

TABLE 6.2 The success of New York City in the field of smart cities: awards and positions in national and international ranking systems

Reference	Evidence of success
Berrone and Ricart (2018)	In the 2018 edition of the IESE Cities in Motion Index (CIMI), whose evaluation system is based on 83 indicators covering 10 key areas, New York City leads the top 10 list of the world smartest cities. One hundred sixty-five cities and 80 countries are included in the analysis
Eden Strategy Institute and ONG&ONG (2018)	Eden Strategy Institute and ONG&ONG design a ranking system to evaluate the performance of the approach to smart city development applied by 140 cities and identify the best-performing cities. New York City leads the group of 12 North American cities included in the top 50 smart cities and is also ranked fourth in the world, after London, Singapore, and Seoul
Woetzel et al. (2018)	The McKinsey Global Institute conducts a survey that compares smart city development practices in 50 cities around the world. The results show that New York has effectively managed smart city development, becoming one of the world's leading smart cities
Berrone and Ricart (2017)	The 2017 edition of the IESE Cities in Motion Index confirms the quality of New York City's performance in the field of smart city development. As in the 2018 edition, New York City reaches the top position and is identified once again as the world leader smart city. This edition of the IESE Cities in Motion Index includes 180 cities representing more than 80 countries

Continued

TABLE 6.2 The success of New York City in the field of smart cities: awards and positions in national and international ranking systems—cont'd

Reference	Evidence of success
City of New York (2016)	New York City is named best smart city at the 2016 edition of the World Smart City Awards. The award recognizes the success of the city government in leveraging smart technologies to support urban sustainability
Gibson et al. (2015)	The collaboration between Nesta, Accenture, and the Future Cities Catapult produces a diagnostic tool for measuring and benchmarking the performance of city governments' policy for supporting urban innovation. This tool is deployed to compare 40 leading cities from around the world. The report presenting the findings of the analysis suggests New York City is the top performer globally for 2015
Rich (2012)	New York City is among the award recipients of the Center for Digital Government's Cybersecurity Leadership and Innovation Awards 2012. The award recognizes the leadership and innovation capacity of New York City in the field of cybersecurity technology services
City of New York (2011)	The New York City Department of Information Technology and Telecommunications (DoITT) is the winner of the ISE North America Project Award 2011 - Government Category. DoITT obtains this prize in recognition of its outstanding leadership in risk management, data asset protection, regulatory compliance, privacy, and network security
Heaton (2011)	The City of New York is among the seven city governments recognized by the Public Technology Institute with the Web 2.0 State and Local Government Awards for Excellence. The award acknowledges New York City's innovative use of Web 2.0 applications and social media tools to engage citizens, improve efficiency, and increase accountability
City of New York (2010b)	New York City is recognized with a Digital Government Achievement Award for the design and implementation of 311Online and its capability to improve the quality of public service delivery. The city government receives the award from the Center for Digital Government, a national research and advisory institute focusing attention on ICT-related policies and practices in state and local government

TABLE 6.2 The success of New York City in the field of smart cities: awards and positions in national and international ranking systems—cont'd

Reference	Evidence of success
City of New York (2010c)	New York City's Reinvent Payphones Challenge and LinkNYC are recognized as 2015 Bright Ideas in government. The Bright Ideas program is managed by the Ash Center for Democratic Governance and Innovation at Harvard University.
City of New York (2010d)	HHS-Connect, NYCStat Stimulus Tracker, and 311 Online, three smart city initiatives implemented by New York City, are awarded at Computerworld's 22nd Annual Laureates Medal Ceremony & Gala Awards. This awards program recognizes projects that have been able to use digital technology to produce positive transformational changes in society
Lay (2010)	The Center for Digital Government conducts an annual Digital Cities Survey, which is open to all US cities with more than 30,000 inhabitants. The survey aims at identifying the cities that are making the most of digital technologies in the fight against unsustainable development patterns. The 10th edition of the survey announces that New York City is among the top-ranked local governments
City of New York (2009)	NYC.gov, the official website of the City of New York, is the recipient of the 2009 Municipal Web Portal Excellence Award. The awarding of this prize, which recognizes North American cities with cutting-edge government websites, is based upon a survey conducted at Rutgers University
City of New York (2007)	ACCESS NYC, a digital service that offers New Yorkers with a single point of access to government-led human service benefit programs, is recognized by the International Data Group with an InfoWorld 100 Award. These annual awards recognize the 100 most innovative ICT solutions which display how technological innovation can help public and private organizations to meet their objectives

To establish whether New York City's smart city development strategy has taken into account the four building blocks under investigation, the activities that the city has implemented to enable smart city development were mapped and analyzed by cross-referencing the qualitative data extracted from multiple sources provided by both internal and external observers. This approach to data collection, which has proved effective in the case study analysis of the previous chapter, strengthened the quality of the analytic process and enabled data triangulation, making it possible to test validity through the convergence of information (Yin, 2009).

The data sources were grouped by using the same classification system proposed in the previous case study analysis. Digital records produced by the city government were considered as primary sources. These records provided first-hand information on the city's smart city development strategy and include the following data items: agendas; minutes of meetings; news and press releases; newsletters; fact sheets; internal correspondence; transcripts of hearing testimonies and formal talks delivered during public events and conferences; conference presentations; the City of New York's official websites; and other government documents, that is, reports, plans, requests for either proposals, information or expressions of interest, programs, agreements, public hearing notices, project proposals, policy and procedure notices, executive orders, directives, memoranda of understanding, codes, standards, and local laws. Additional data was acquired from digital records released by other private and public organizations that have (1) collaborated with the city government in designing and implementing the smart city development strategy of New York City or (2) reported on such a strategy by acting as external observers. These additional sources were used to acquire secondary data and mainly include reports, news and press releases, independent blogs releasing community news, and articles published in online magazines, newspapers, and academic journals.

Overall, 847 digital records in either written, audio, or video form were collected and processed. The search phase leading to the identification of such records was conducted between April and May 2018. After being identified, all the records were catalogued in a single dataset, in which the following information was included: (1) titles, (2) publication dates, (3) names of the organizations authoring the contents, and (4) web address from which the records were accessed (see Appendix C).

Systematic coding was then used to synthesize the large volume of qualitative data that has been gathered and to identify the smart city-related activities embedded in the intricate texture of information that this data has generated. As with Chapter 5, this search activity was managed by deploying the software Atlas.ti as a support tool and following the procedure suggested in the research of Eisenhardt (1989), Robson (1993), Strauss and Corbin (1990), and Gibbs (2007). The digital records were first uploaded onto Atlas.ti, where each was automatically assigned a unique identification number. Subsequently, all records were examined repeatedly to capture the activities that the city implemented to develop its own smart city development strategy. During the coding process, a code was generated for each activity and used to label the data segments describing their features. Attention was focused on the following information: (1) the objectives pursued thoroughly the implementation of each activity, (2) the generated or expected outcomes, (3) the date when the activities were implemented, and (4) the actors involved in their implementation process,

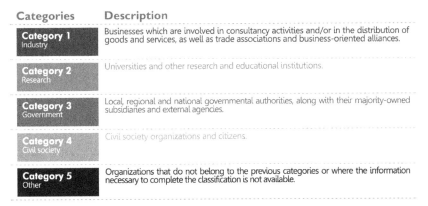

Categories	Description
Category 1 Industry	Businesses which are involved in consultancy activities and/or in the distribution of goods and services, as well as trade associations and business-oriented alliances.
Category 2 Research	Universities and other research and educational institutions.
Category 3 Government	Local, regional and national governmental authorities, along with their majority-owned subsidiaries and external agencies.
Category 4 Civil society	Civil society organizations and citizens.
Category 5 Other	Organizations that do not belong to the previous categories or where the information necessary to complete the classification is not available.

FIG. 6.3 Classification system for collaborative environment.

which were subsequently grouped in the four categories showed in Fig. 6.3.[1] A complete list of the organizations identified during the mapping process is provided in Appendix D.

The coding process supported the progressive assembling of the program of activities that elevate New York City into a world-leading example of smart city development. Such a program covers a 30-year time frame, from 1989 to 2018, and is composed of 865 activities. The mapping exercise was followed by an analysis of the activities, which was conducted through close examination of 3263 coded data segments. The analysis groups the activities according to the contribution they make to the development of the four building blocks: (A) collaborative environment, (B) strategic framework, (C) network infrastructure, and (D) ICT services and applications.

To establish whether the intervention logic applied in New York City cuts across the multitude of application domains that smart city development represents, the activities contributing to the shaping of "Building Block D" were then assigned to one or more application domains. This activity was carried out by using the classification system presented in Fig. 6.4, which is the same system introduced in the previous chapter for supporting the European best practice analysis. Exactly as in that circumstance, the selection of the domains depended upon which policy sectors benefit from the ICT services and applications that each activity enables.

The coding process concludes with the creation of a codebook (Lavrakas, 2008) and a correlation matrix. The correlation matrix outlines the connection between each single activity and the digital records from which coded data

1. The classification system used to group the entities involved in the smart city development strategy of New York City builds on the classification system structured for the European best practice analysis (see Chapter 5). "Civil society" is the only category that was subject to changes. In the framework of this study, this category does not include only civil society organizations but extends to citizens.

Application domain	Description
C.01 Energy networks	To increase the efficiency and sustainability of either street lighting or networks for producing, storing and distributing energy.
C.02 Air	To ensure a better air quality in outdoor environments.
C.03 Water	To improve water resource management.
C.04 Waste	To improve waste management processes.
C.05 Mobility and transport	To provide city users with more sustainable and accessible transport systems and to address mobility issues.
C.06 Buildings and districts	To improve the efficiency, accessibility and management systems of buildings and districts.
C.07 Health and social inclusion	To improve the quality, accessibility and organization of health services and to support social inclusion and wellbeing.
C.08 Culture and recreation	To ensure a better protection of and access to both tangible and intangible cultural heritage and enhance their cultural value, and to help city users access recreational and cultural opportunities.
C.09 Education	To increase the quality of formal and informal teaching and learning processes.
C.10 Public security and justice	To ensure safety and security in urban spaces and to enhance criminal justice systems.
C.11 E-government	To apply ICT solutions to internal government functions and procedures with the purpose of enhancing their efficiency and to increase the accessibility and transparency of city data and information.
C.12 Other	ICT services and applications aiming at producing benefits different than those related to the previous application domains.

FIG. 6.4 Classification system for ICT services and applications.

segments describing its features were extracted. The codebook presents itself as a spreadsheet that serves three main purposes: (1) to gather together the activities as a temporal sequence of events; (2) to provide a short description of all the activities and the list of entities involved in their implementation, that is, organizations or citizens; and (3) to show which building blocks each activity relates to.

6.3 Smart city development in New York City

Figs. 6.5 and 6.6 provide a snapshot of the results obtained through the coding process. The data suggests New York City has invested in a citywide strategy that focuses attention on each one of the four building blocks. Most of the activities offer a contribution to the development of the strategic framework (Building Block B) and the integration of ICT services and applications (Building Block D), which respectively relate to 35.7% and 48.0% of the total activities. The development of the network infrastructure (Building Block C) and collaborative environment

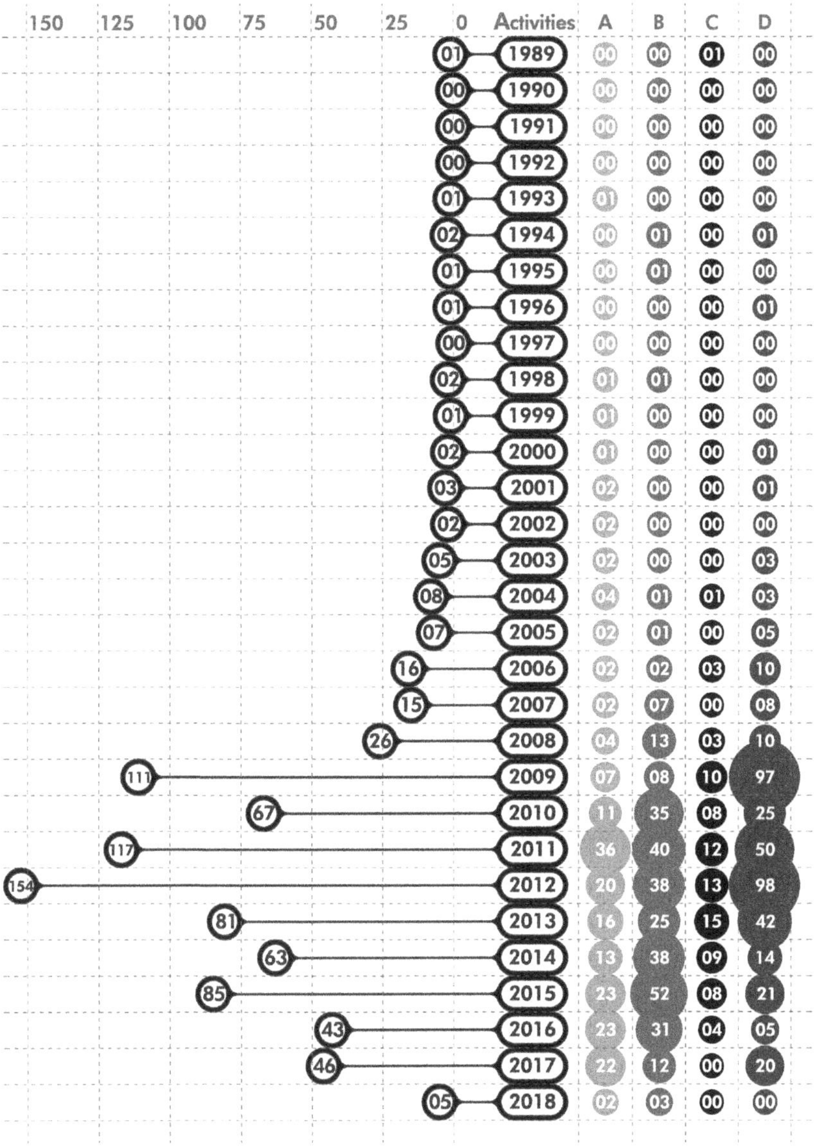

FIG. 6.5 Activities by year.

(Building Block A) is instead linked to a lower number of activities, that is, 197 and 87 out of 865, respectively, which are the equivalent of 22.8% and 10.1%.

Despite the differences, it is important to note that these figures do not reveal the degree of commitment related to each building block. A higher value does not necessary correspond to a more significant investment or a greater level of importance. These figures should rather be considered as an initial proof of the

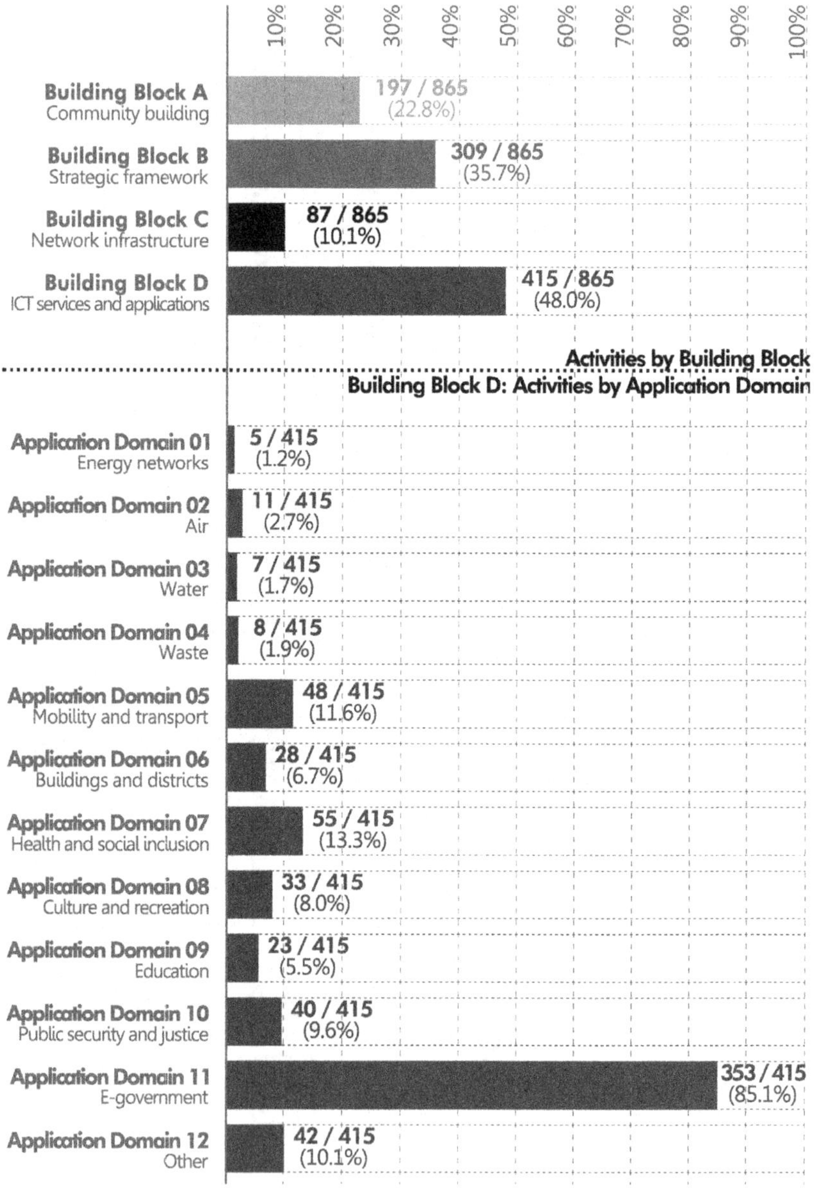

FIG. 6.6 Activities by building block.

alignment between the approach to smart city development of the New York City and the presence of the four building blocks and assembling process observed in European smart city development practices. This alignment is further revealed in the following subsections, which describe how each building block has been developed in the framework of New York City's smart city development strategy.

For each building block, a written account of connected events is provided that explains the strategic approach adopted. The data necessary to elaborate these accounts is sourced from a high number of digital records collected during the search phase. To preserve the quality of the narrative and avoid excessive fragmentation of the text, all the digital records used to support the discussion have been grouped together in Table 6.3, where they have been assigned the same coding system used in Appendix C, the dataset in which all the records are catalogued. Overall the following discussion section draws upon more than 300 data items.

TABLE 6.3 Data sources by publication year

Publication year	Data sources
2006	DR010, DR014
2007	DR020, DR022, DR024, DR025, DR026
2008	DR031, DR032, DR034
2009	DR041, DR042, DR043, DR049, DR050, DR052, DR054, DR055
2010	DR061, DR062, DR063, DR066, DR067, DR071, DR072, DR079, DR080, DR082, DR083, DR089, DR091, DR092, DR094, DR095, DR096, DR097, DR098, DR099, DR100, DR101, DR103, DR105, DR106, DR107, DR108
2011	DR110, DR114, DR115, DR118, DR120, DR121, DR124, DR125, DR127, DR128, DR130, DR132, DR133, DR134, DR135, DR136, DR137, DR138, DR139, DR140, DR142, DR143, DR144, DR145, DR146, DR147, DR150, DR151, DR152, DR153, DR154, DR159, DR160, DR162, DR163, DR164, DR165, DR167, DR168, DR169, DR173, DR174, DR177, DR182
2012	DR184, DR186, DR187, DR188, DR189, DR191, DR194, DR196, DR197, DR198, DR199, DR201, DR202, DR205, DR206, DR209, DR210, DR212, DR214, DR215, DR216, DR218, DR220, DR222, DR223, DR229, DR231, DR233, DR235, DR236, DR237, DR239, DR240, DR241, DR242, DR244, DR245, DR246, DR249, DR250, DR251, DR252, DR253, DR254, DR255, DR256, DR257, DR260, DR261, DR264, DR267
2013	DR271, DR273, DR276, DR278, DR279, DR280, DR283, DR286, DR287, DR288, DR292, DR294, DR295, DR299, DR300, DR301, DR305, DR308, DR312, DR313, DR314, DR315, DR316, DR322, DR323, DR324, DR329, DR330, DR334, DR335, DR336, DR338, DR339, DR340, DR348, DR350, DR351, DR352, DR355, DR356, DR357, DR359, DR367

Continued

TABLE 6.3 Data sources by publication year—cont'd

Publication year	Data sources
2014	DR369, DR370, DR371, DR372, DR373, DR374, DR375, DR378, DR380, DR382, DR387, DR388, DR389, DR390, DR392, DR393, DR394, DR399, DR401, DR402, DR403, DR404, DR405, DR406, DR407, DR409, DR410, DR413, DR414, DR415, DR416, DR417, DR418, DR420, DR421, DR422, DR423, DR424, DR425, DR426, DR428, DR430, DR431, DR432, DR435, DR436, DR437, DR438, DR440, DR443
2015	DR450, DR452, DR453, DR457, DR458, DR459, DR463, DR464, DR465, DR466, DR468, DR469, DR473, DR474, DR475, DR476, DR477, DR479, DR480, DR481, DR483, DR486, DR487, DR488, DR491, DR492, DR493, DR499, DR500
2016	DR503, DR504, DR505, DR506, DR507, DR508, DR509, DR510, DR515, DR518, DR521, DR522, DR523, DR526, DR527, DR528, DR532, DR533, DR534, DR535, DR537, DR540, DR541, DR543, DR544, DR545, DR546, DR547, DR550, DR551, DR552, DR558
2017	DR569, DR570, DR571, DR573, DR577, DR578, DR582, DR583, DR586, DR587, DR588, DR600, DR601
2018	DR608, DR620
N/A	DR622, DR623, DR631, DR635, DR643, DR644, DR645, DR649, DR736, DR817, DR844, DR845, DR846

6.3.1 Building Block A: Collaborative environment

To obtain a visual representation of the collaborative model that the city has adopted to approach smart city development and support the interpretation process, the data previously collected was processed by means of Gephi. This activity resulted in the two-dimensional network graph showed in Fig. 6.7. In the graph the 532 actors collaborating in enabling smart city development in New York City are shown as nodes, and the interactions between them are represented by means of edges. The network is drawn by applying the force-directed layout algorithm designed by Fruchterman and Reingold (1991).

In the graph, the colors of the nodes are assigned upon the category they have been associated with, that is, industry, government, research and education, or civil society, and their diameter is directly proportional to the number of activities they have been involved in. In addition, the position of the nodes reflects their degree of centrality, which is defined as the number of edges incident upon every single node (Butts, 2008). The degree of centrality exposes the

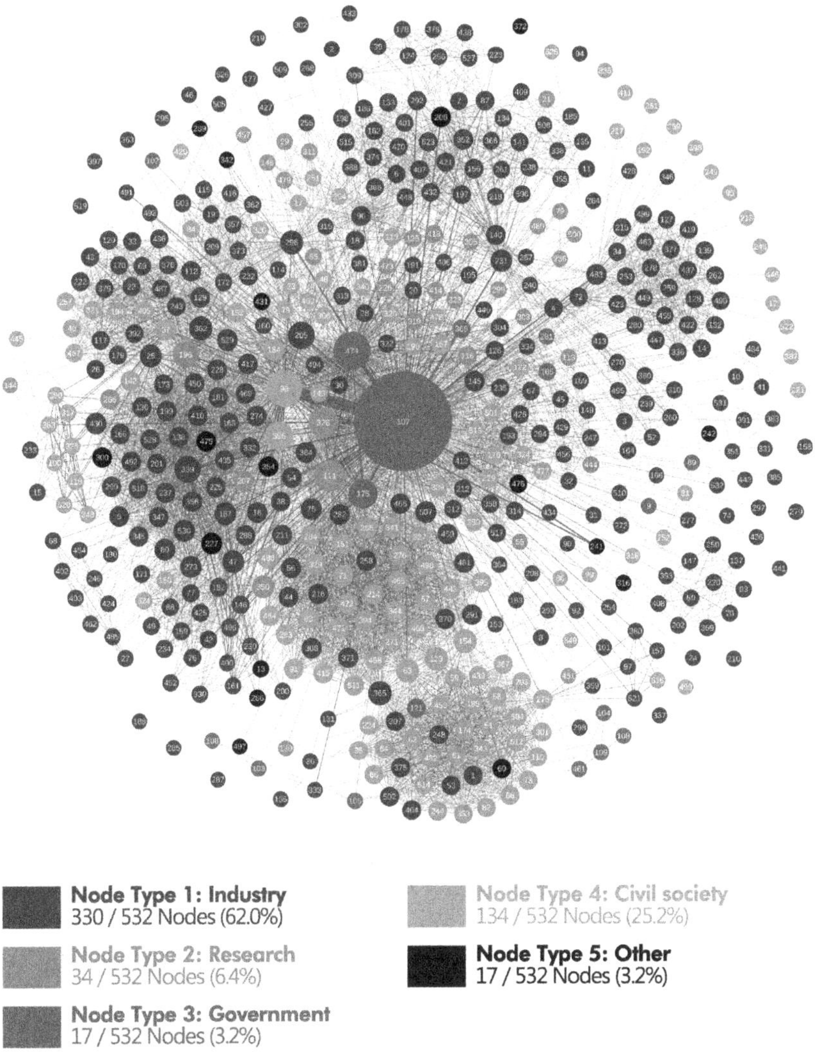

FIG. 6.7 New York City's smart city development strategy: collaborative environment.

level of collaboration between the nodes, hence a higher centrality in the graph corresponds to a stronger level of collaboration with other nodes. Finally, the line segments joining the pairs of nodes are assigned a weight directly proportional to the degree of collaboration. The number of activities in which two actors collaborate is registered by the thickness of the edge that links them. The lack of connection between two nodes expresses the absence of direct collaboration.

The analysis of the network suggests New York City's approach to smart city development lies in the innovation capacity generated by a quadruple-helix collaborative model of stakeholder engagement. The collaborative environment is composed of heterogeneous actors representing different institutional contexts, whose activities create an innovation ecosystem where values, expectations, and knowledge are shared for the benefit of all the participants. When looking at the distribution of entities by category, businesses, trade associations, and business-oriented alliances emerge as the most active organizations, and they are followed by civil society. Sixty-two percent of the total nodes represent industry, while civil society organizations and citizens account for 25.2% of the network. With 6.4% and 3.2%, respectively, research and educational institutions and governmental authorities are the less represented categories. However, a closer look at the data describing the degree of centrality and levels of participation exposes the critical role that the government sector has played in the design and implementation process of New York City's smart city development strategy.

Along with citizens and two New York City-based universities (City University of New York and New York University), the government sector occupies a central position in the multistakeholder governance system driving the smart city development strategy of New York City. The Federal Government of the United States, the New York State, and the City of New York are among the actors with greatest centrality and participation (see Tables 6.4 and 6.5).

TABLE 6.4 Entities with highest degree of centrality

Entity				
ID Code	Name	Category	Number of activities	Degree of centrality
107	City of New York	GOV	627	497
474	New York State	GOV	22	223
98	Citizens	CIV	267	211
111	City University of New York	RES	14	167
328	New York University	RES	14	152
175	Federal Government of the United States	GOV	14	148
396	Robin Hood Foundation	CIV	4	141
205	Google	IND	10	125
339	NY Tech Alliance	IND	11	122
196	General Assembly	RES	6	116

IND, industry; *RES*, research and education; *GOV*, government; *CIV*, civil society.

TABLE 6.5 Entities with highest level of participation

Entity ID Code	Name	Category	Number of activities	Degree of centrality
107	City of New York	GOV	627	497
98	Citizens	CIV	267	211
483	Time Warner Cable	IND	24	57
474	New York State	GOV	22	223
111	City University of New York	RES	14	167
328	New York University	RES	14	152
175	Federal Government of the United States	GOV	14	148
339	NY Tech Alliance	IND	11	122
231	IBM	IND	11	74
205	Google	IND	10	125
296	Microsoft	IND	10	89

IND, industry; *RES*, research and education; *GOV*, government; *CIV*, civil society.

However, the data in Fig. 6.8 clearly demonstrates that the latter has taken a leading position in this system. The city government has the highest degree of centrality, and by supporting the implementation of 627 of the 865 activities that have been mapped, it is also the most active organization.

The city government is deeply involved in the construction of all the building blocks. Most of its effort is oriented toward shaping the citywide strategic framework for smart city development and cultivating a local smart city collaborative environment able to support ICT-related urban development and innovation. The City of New York has taken part in almost all the activities related to both building blocks. However, the data demonstrates that the attention of the local government is also focused on supporting the technological upgrade of the city's ICT infrastructure, an activity that industrial partners and civil society have significantly helped with. The citywide network infrastructure and the ICT solutions and applications it supports the use of are indeed the outcome of the combined effort of civil society organizations, citizens, and city government.

In this collaboration the city government mainly acts as a leader who facilitates community development and nurtures bottom-up smart city development. Its action is very much oriented toward empowering civil society and other city

Level of aggregation 1
Organization categories

	IND	RES	GOV	CIV
Building Block A Community building	48 / 197 24.4%	29 / 197 14.7%	187 / 197 94.9%	74 / 197 37.6%
Building Block B Strategic framework	45 / 309 14.6%	11 / 309 3.6%	308 / 309 99.7%	31 / 309 10.0%
Building Block C Network infrastructure	52 / 87 59.8%	3 / 87 3.4%	68 / 87 78.2%	20 / 87 23.0%
Building Block D ICT services and applications	44 / 415 10.6%	3 / 415 0.7%	206 / 415 49.6%	206 / 415 49.6%

Level of aggregation 2
Organizations

	NYS	NYC	USGOV
Building Block A Community building	8 / 197 4.1%	187 / 197 94.9%	6 / 197 3.0%
Building Block B Strategic framework	8 / 309 2.6%	308 / 309 99.7%	6 / 309 1.9%
Building Block C Network infrastructure	4 / 87 4.6%	68 / 87 78.2%	1 / 87 1.1%
Building Block D ICT services and applications	5 / 415 1.2%	206 / 415 49.6%	4 / 415 1.0%

FIG. 6.8 Levels of participation by building block. *IND*, industry; *RES*, research and education; *GOV*, government; *CIV*, civil society; *NYS*, New York State; *NYC*, New York City; *USGOV*, Federal Government of the United States.

stakeholders in designing and producing ICT solutions of public value for facing New York City's urban challenges. This suggests New York City does not place smart city development entirely in the hands of large corporations and the business sector, but seeks talent, knowledge, and entrepreneurial spirit within the local community. Evidence of this approach can also be found when analyzing the list of activities that the local government has been involved in. These activities are discussed in the following paragraphs, along with some practical examples, which are extracted from the codebook and provided for elucidatory purposes.

The city government engages in a series of activities focused on increasing digital literacy by way of training workshops, thematic courses, training sessions, and through mentoring and personal development programs. The Supported Training and Employment Preparation Services (NYC STEPS) program and the New York City IT Fellows program are two examples of city-led training opportunities committed to the achievement of this aim. The former results from a city-led consortium composed of several city agencies, the educational technology company Skillsoft, the cloud data service company NetApp, and Microsoft. Their collaboration has made it possible to design and launch a program that aims to provide training in workplace and computer skills to New Yorkers and that prepares them to access entry-level jobs in the technology industry. In addition, to recruit new talent and raise awareness as to the importance of technology in urban management, the NYC Department of Information Technology and Telecommunications (DoITT)[2] launched the New York City IT Fellows program. This is a 9-month fellowship designed to bring college graduates into local government and provide them with a strategic perspective on the IT issues and opportunities confronted by technology professionals working for the City of New York.

The action of the city government also denotes its commitment to raising awareness as to the role that ICT plays in improving urban sustainability. This is achieved by way of thematic events that disseminate knowledge through formal presentations and speeches targeting both professional and nonprofessional audiences. These public events are also instrumental in facilitating networking and the formation of new partnerships. For example, in 2006, the International Academy of Digital Arts and Sciences (IADAS) and the NYC Mayor's Office of Media and Entertainment (MOME) organized the first edition of the Internet Week New York, an annual festival which is driven by the ambition to connect the members representing the digital community of New York. Over the years, the Internet Week has grown from a few events to a crowded week, with more than 45,000 people participating in over 250 events around the city.

In the framework for the 2012 edition of the Internet Week, DoITT organized the discussion session entitled "NYC Open Data: Unlock It!" The session aims at introducing the public to the policies and technical standards related to opening up New York City's government data. An additional example is the NYC Data Week, whose first edition took place in 2012. The NYC Data Week results from the partnership between the learning company O'Reilly and DoITT. This event is designed to showcase data-driven innovation projects across different sectors and to increase the local community's awareness of how open data can be used to make urban environments more sustainable.

2. DoITT was established in 1995 and represents the information technology and telecommunications agency of the municipal government.

Stimulating public-private collaboration is an additional objective of the action undertaken by the city government. This objective is met by issuing requests for proposals and information soliciting potential industrial partners to supply IT assets that are valuable for the city, knowledge, or ideas for technological solutions to urban issues. The activities that can be cited are many. For example, in 2009, DoITT issued a request for information directed to technology providers interested in establishing a public Wi-Fi service in New York City's parks and other open spaces. Also, a few months later, the NYC Economic Development Corporation (NYCEDC)[3] issued a request for expressions of interest inviting citizens, software developers, and professionals to advise the city government on what public datasets should be released in an open data format.

In addition, between 2012 and 2016, DoITT released requests for either proposals, information, or expressions of interest in an effort to:

- outline the goals of the comprehensive redesign of NYC.gov,[4] which was intended to enhance the user experience;
- perform market research regarding soon-to-be-available telecommunication service offerings and help the city to obtain them efficiently and effectively;
- foster public feedback on the long-term viability of city-regulated public pay telephones;
- seek qualified vendors interested in providing system integration services for other agencies, offices, boards, and commissions;
- install, operate, and maintain public communications structures in the five boroughs of New York City[5] and transform its network of public pay telephones into Wi-Fi hotspots and information hubs;
- solicit ideas on how to maintain and improve the existing level of service and resiliency of the New York City Wireless Network (NYCWiN)[6] while lowering operating costs;
- identify providers able to offer qualified citywide information technology and telecommunications consulting services;
- identify possible paths to implementation of a Next Generation 911 system in New York City, which should provide for seamless transfer of digital information from the public to emergency responders.

The City of New York also tries to work with industrial partners and research institutions to accelerate the setting up of New York City-based laboratories,

3. NYC Economic Development Corporation (NYCEDC) is part of the city government's organizational structure and performs economic development services. Its activity aims at fostering economic development in New York City. More information can be found at https://www.nycedc.com.

4. NYC.gov is the official website of the City of New York: https://www1.nyc.gov.

5. New York City comprises five county-level administrative divisions that are called boroughs: Manhattan, Brooklyn, Queens, the Bronx, and Staten Island.

6. The New York City Wireless Network (NYCWiN) is a government-dedicated broadband wireless infrastructure that supports the city government's operations by providing its units with access to high-speed voice and video communications and data transfers.

research centers, working groups, and companies interested in improving the city's capability to operate in the field of smart cities and address its most pressing urban challenges by means of ICT solutions. With the Applied Sciences NYC initiative, for example, the city government attempts to find universities willing to set up and operate either new or expanded engineering campuses in the city in exchange for access to city-owned land and financial resources. In October 2011, after issuing a request for proposals, the city government signed three agreements. The first one provided a consortium led by Cornell University and the Israel Institute of Technology (Technion) with land on Roosevelt Island and $100 million in city capital to build the Cornell-Technion Innovation Institute. The second agreement was signed with an NYU-led consortium, which contributed to the development of the Center for Urban Science and Progress in Downtown Brooklyn. This consortium includes the ICT multinational companies IBM and Cisco Systems, along with the following academic institutions: New York University, City University of New York, Carnegie Mellon University, University of Toronto, University of Warwick, and Indian Institute of Technology Bombay. The last agreement relates to the Columbia University's proposal to lead the creation of a new Institute for Data Sciences and Engineering.

In addition to the Applied Sciences NYC initiative, NYCEDC, Columbia University, New York University, and the City University of New York have launched the NYC Urban Technology Innovation Center. This activity aims to promote the development and commercialization of smart building technologies in New York City. The Center connects universities conducting research in this field, the companies creating innovative technologies for smart buildings, and those building owners who are looking to benefit from the latest ICT solutions and are willing to provide real-life test environments. NYCEDC has also launched Urban Tech NYC, an accelerator program providing affordable space and prototyping equipment to entrepreneurs and innovators interested in addressing the city's most pressing urban challenges by developing new ICT solutions.

The city government's commitment to supporting community development and bottom-up smart city development can also be captured by looking at its efforts to engage the public in co-design workshops, public hearings, and open consultations. These activities are conducted in order to capture the needs of the citizens and ensure that they are at the heart of the city's smart city development strategy. For example, during the Open Data Policy Hack Day organized by DoITT, the city government met with the representatives of the New York City's open data community to collectively discuss opportunities and challenges related to the use of open data. Participants included policymakers, technologists, civic hackers, app developers, academics, journalists, and open data enthusiasts. Another similar event took place in 2016, when the City of New York hosted a Broadband Data Dig at the Brooklyn Public Library. During this event, policy experts, civic technologists, and data scientists were asked to

(1) analyze the New York City's broadband strategy, (2) develop recommendations on how to improve it, (3) help develop solutions to address broadband inequities, and (4) design broadband data collection and maintenance policies.

The citywide engagement tour is another example worth mentioning. This initiative, conducted by DoITT and the NYC Mayor's Office of Data Analytics (MODA),[7] allowed the city government to capture the common needs, priorities, gaps, issues, and opportunities across user types and domain areas in relation to open data. The tour was instrumental in interacting with already active users, who were asked to provide feedback on the New York City's open data policy and advise on how to improve it in the light of their expectations. In addition, during the tour, representatives of both city agencies engaged New Yorkers throughout the city to provide potential users unfamiliar with open data with knowledge support.

To look beyond the corporate smart city model, the City of New York has also incorporated creativity, experimentation, and the element of play into its smart city development strategy. This has been done by stimulating citizen engagement and collaboration through the organization of competitions, challenges, and hackathons, which have been backed by a robust open data policy encouraging the informed reuse of the more than 1000 public datasets that the city government shares on its open data portal. The NYC BigApps competition is the best example underscoring the city government's intention to tap into the knowledge, entrepreneurial spirit, and IT-related skills of the public. NYC BigApps is an annual competition which invites software developers and members of the civil society to create web and mobile applications that leverage city-owned data and technology able to address the urban challenges that New Yorkers face. The first edition of the contest was launched in 2009 by DoITT, NYCEDC, and Devpost (former ChallengePost), a private company specialized in the organization of online and in-person hackathons. The most recent edition was conducted in 2017. Hundreds of digital applications have been produced in this 18-year time frame, demonstrating this initiative's capability to make public data and public engagement become meaningful for sustainable urban development.

6.3.2 Building Block B: Strategic framework

The data generated from the analysis of both the collaborative environment and levels of participation suggests the local government is deeply involved in the design and implementation of the smart city development strategy of New York

7. The NYC Mayor's Office of Data Analytics (MODA) is a governmental agency that acts as a civic intelligence center. Its main responsibilities include: (1) designing data-driven solutions to issues affecting the government of New York City's capacity to deliver public services, (2) facilitating data sharing across city government's units, and (3) collaborating with DoITT in making New York City's open data legislation effective. See MODA's official website for additional information: https://www1.nyc.gov/site/analytics/about/about-office-data-analytics.page.

City and its commitment plays a critical role. The analysis also shows that, when it comes to smart city development, the city government seems to value teamwork and group collaboration over individual contributions. As a result, a large collaborative environment has grown, in which large groups of organizations and individuals are brought together to partner in jointly implementing ICT-related initiatives that facilitate smart city development. In addition, to support these actors and help them act in concert, a citywide strategic framework has been created, which combines policy direction with operational action.

This framework is composed of government documents, which together form a set of guidelines governing the city's approach to smart city development. These documents include: city laws and executive orders directing decision-making and operations supporting smart city development; long-term sustainability plans; ICT-related strategic plans, action plans, and roadmaps setting the course of actions and strategic principles to follow; and ICT regulations on requirements, deployment processes, and standards of technology implementation.

The strategic framework for smart city development results from a multilevel governance structure. The top level is represented by the NYC Office of the Mayor, which heads up the executive branch of the government of New York City. This office is responsible for (1) the effectiveness and integrity of the city government's operations, (2) establishing the policies and procedures and governance structure that are necessary to accomplish them, and (3) defining a long-term vision and the direction for the city, devising sustainability goals and objectives.

Vision, objectives, and policy direction are clearly stated in the sustainability plans that the NYC Office of the Mayor has been designing in collaboration with other city agencies, offices, boards and commissions, and external public and private stakeholders, including civil society organizations and citizens. The most recent, "One New York: The Plan for a Strong and Just City" (OneNYC), was released in 2015. This plan offers a blueprint for tackling New York City's most significant challenges. According to the trend analysis and data that the plan reports on, these challenges are four: urban environmental conditions and climate change, population growth, aging infrastructure, and increasing inequality. For each challenge, OneNYC identifies a set of goals and targets to achieve, along with a list of supporting initiatives to be implemented in order to meet the expected targets. Overall, the plan details more than 25 goals, and to track the progress that has been made in meeting them, a set of key indicators has been developed, which the city government reports on each year.

OneNYC recognizes that digital technology and the exponential growth of available data are transforming every sector of society, including government, and exposes a commitment to take advantage of the potential these global trends have to enhance urban sustainability in New York City. This commitment is in line with and builds on the long-term sustainability plans that the city government released before 2015.[8] In acknowledging that new technologies and regulatory frameworks are key to achieving the ambition of a sustainable New York City, OneNYC identifies a series of ICT-related initiatives, which in turn tackle each one of the four challenges.

To make sure that smart city solutions are correctly introduced within the city and become a tool for delivering urban sustainability, the NYC Office of the Mayor has established a technology governance structure, whose action is instructed by means of city laws and executive orders. This governance structure has been operating since 1998, the year in which the Technology Steering Committee was formed and tasked with working across city government's agencies and offices to coordinate and oversight technology plans and initiatives, along with monitoring policies, standards, and procedures. The steering committee is led by the chief technology officer and consists also of the commissioner that heads DoITT and the director of the NYC Office of Management and Budget.[9] Under this arrangement, the NYC Office of the Chief Technology Officer and DoITT have also been requested to work in close conjunction with all the other units of the city government and provide the committee with the operational assistance necessary to its functioning.

A detailed examination of the contribution offered by city agencies, offices, boards, and commissions to the activities implemented for enabling smart city development suggests this internal collaboration has been successfully activated and DoITT has taken a leadership position, becoming a smart city accelerator for New York City. The chart in Fig. 6.9 shows the organizational structure of the government of New York City and reports on the results of an attempt to spotlight the agencies, offices, boards, and commissions that have been active in advancing the city's ambition to become smart. The results of this matching exercise demonstrate that smart city development has been approached collectively and cuts across different sectors and divisions. In addition, by capturing the level of participation of each unit, Fig. 6.10 contributes additional data that makes it possible to point out the centrality of DoITT in the operational actions.

DoITT acts as the technology leader of New York City, and its overall contribution accounts for about 70% of the city government's effort to make

8. This commitment clearly emerges in PlaNYC, a comprehensive plan that the city government designed to expose the journey toward achieving the sustainability goals for New York City. PlaNYC was released in 2007 by the Bloomberg administration, which served from 2002 to 2013.

9. This approach to overseeing ICT-related projects and policies was subject to progressive adjustments over the years and was temporarily suspended under the Bloomberg administration, between 2010 and 2014, when DoITT was given primary responsibility for the technology sector and the Technology Steering Committee was terminated. However, this revised structure suffered from some unsuccessful citywide ICT initiatives that have convinced the De Blasio administration to bring back the Technology Steering Committee in 2015.

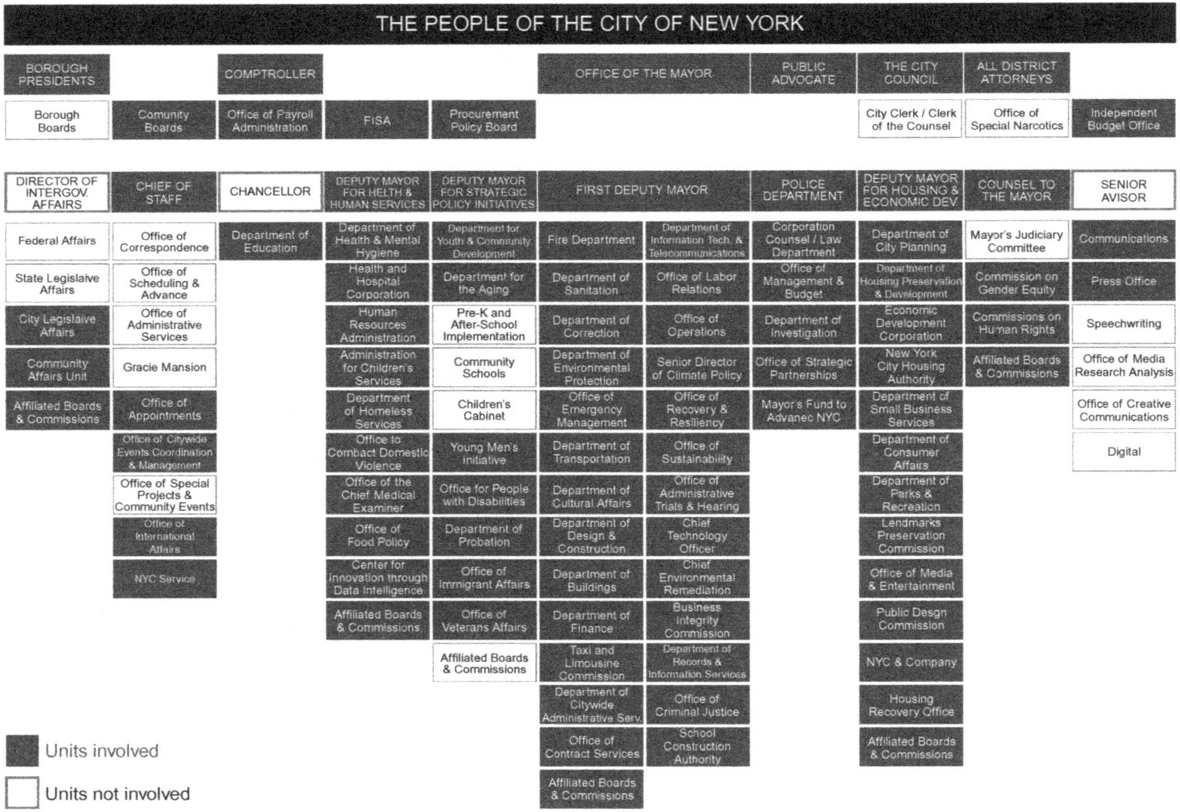
THE PEOPLE OF THE CITY OF NEW YORK
BOROUGH PRESIDENTS
COMPTROLLER
OFFICE OF THE MAYOR
PUBLIC ADVOCATE
THE CITY COUNCIL
ALL DISTRICT ATTORNEYS
Borough Boards
Comunity Boards
Office of Payroll Administration
FISA
Procurement Policy Board
City Clerk / Clerk of the Counsel
Office of Special Narcotics
Independent Budget Office
DIRECTOR OF INTERGOV. AFFAIRS
CHIEF OF STAFF
CHANCELLOR
DEPUTY MAYOR FOR HELTH & HUMAN SERVICES
DEPUTY MAYOR FOR STRATEGIC POLICY INITIATIVES
FIRST DEPUTY MAYOR
POLICE DEPARTMENT
DEPUTY MAYOR FOR HOUSING & ECONOMIC DEV.
COUNSEL TO THE MAYOR
SENIOR AVISOR
Federal Affairs
State Legislaive Affairs
City Legislaive Affairs
Community Affairs Unit
Affiliated Boards & Commissions
Office of Correspondence
Office of Scheduling & Advance
Office of Administrative Services
Gracie Mansion
Office of Appointments
Office of Citywide Events Coordination & Management
Office of Special Projects & Community Events
Office of International Affairs
NYC Service
Department of Education
Department of Health & Mental Hygiene
Health and Hospital Corporation
Human Resources Administration
Administration for Children's Services
Department of Homeless Services
Office to Combact Domestic Violence
Office of the Chief Medical Examiner
Office of Food Policy
Center for Innovation through Data Intelligence
Affiliated Boards & Commissions
Department for Youth & Community Development
Department for the Aging
Pre-K and After-School Implementation
Community Schools
Children's Cabinet
Young Men's Initiative
Office for People with Disabilities
Department of Probation
Office of Immigrant Affairs
Office of Veterans Affairs
Affiliated Boards & Commissions
Fire Department
Department of Sanitation
Department of Correction
Department of Environmental Protection
Office of Emergency Management
Department of Transportation
Department of Cultural Affairs
Department of Design & Construction
Department of Buildings
Department of Finance
Taxi and Limousine Commission
Department of Citywide Administrative Serv.
Office of Contract Services
Affiliated Boards & Commissions
Department of Information Tech. & Telecommunications
Office of Labor Relations
Office of Operations
Senior Director of Climate Policy
Office of Recovery & Resiliency
Office of Sustainability
Office of Administrative Trials & Hearing
Chief Technology Officer
Chief Environmental Remediation
Business Integrity Commission
Department of Records & Information Services
Office of Criminal Justice
School Construction Authority
Corporation Counsel / Law Department
Office of Management & Budget
Department of Investigation
Office of Strategic Partnerships
Mayor's Fund to Advanec NYC
Department of City Planning
Department of Housing Preservation & Development
Economic Development Corporation
New York City Housing Authority
Department of Small Business Services
Department of Consumer Affairs
Department of Parks & Recreation
Lendmarks Preservation Commission
Office of Media & Entertainment
Public Desgn Commission
NYC & Company
Housing Recovery Office
Affiliated Boards & Commissions
Mayor's Judiciary Committee
Commission on Gender Equity
Commissions on Human Rights
Affiliated Boards & Commissions
Communications
Press Office
Speechwriting
Office of Media Research Analysis
Office of Creative Communications
Digital
Units involved
Units not involved

FIG. 6.9 Government of New York City: units actively involved in enabling smart city development. (The figure pictures how the organization of the city government was structured in October 2018. The data necessary to develop this figure was extracted from the official organizational chart, which can be downloaded from NYC.gov.)

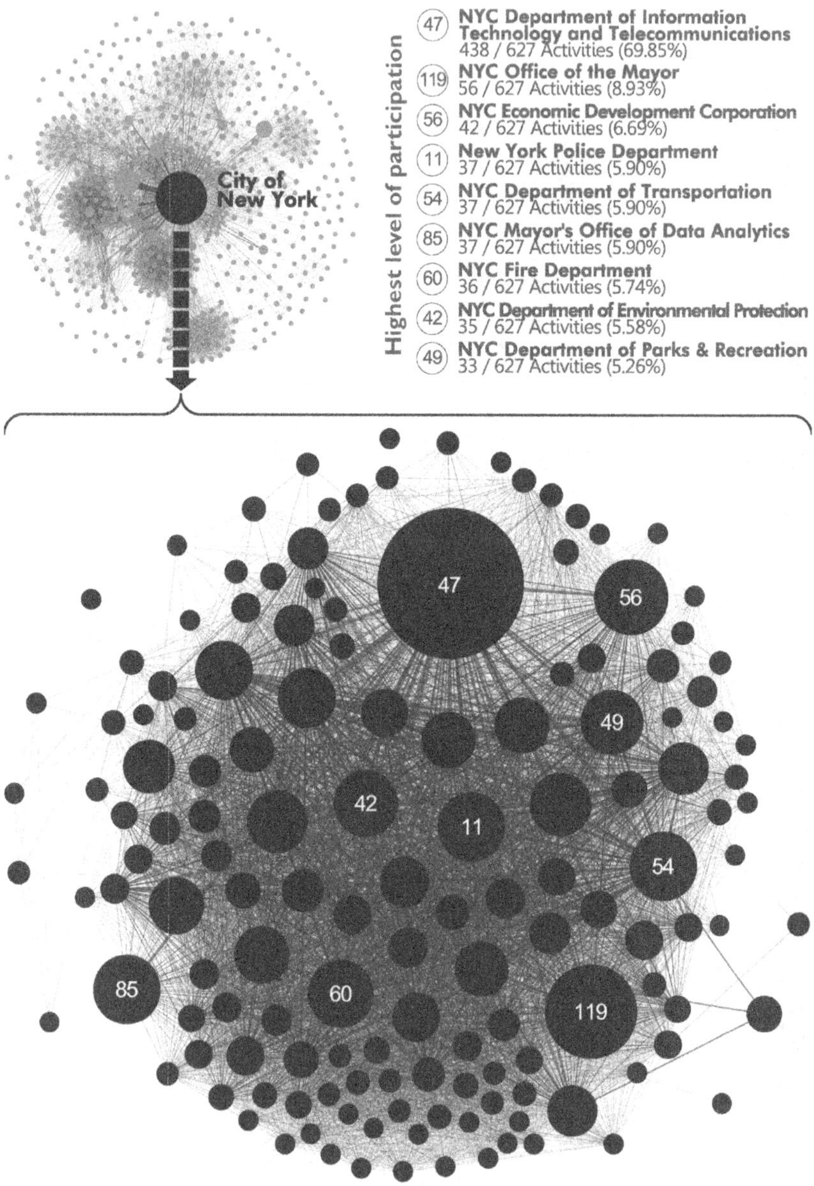

FIG. 6.10 Government of New York City: internal collaboration and levels of participation.

smart city development possible. The analysis of such a contribution suggests DoITT's main tasks and objectives are the followings:

- Designing and operationalizing a comprehensive technology strategy for coordinated, effective, and efficient citywide IT implementation and ensuring its alignment with the city's sustainability priorities and technology-related policy;

- Establishing IT regulations on requirements, deployment processes, and standards on technology implementation that internal and external stakeholders are required to take into account when interacting with the city's information and technology assets;
- Ensuring the availability and functioning of a citywide broadband infrastructure for high-speed Internet access that all stakeholders can benefit from, in particular, by coordinating the efforts to increase free and low-cost broadband service across the five boroughs;
- Supporting external stakeholders in developing and deploying new digital services and infrastructure solutions, which aim to improve the quality of public service delivery;
- Providing city agencies, offices, boards, and commissions with continuous support and assistance in order to solve their issues by means of either tailored technology-driven solutions or common solutions to share in a standardized infrastructure environment;
- Ensuring transparency and fostering civic innovation by carrying out the open data legislation of New York City.

This list of tasks demonstrates that, depending on the situations, DoITT acts as either a service provider, an advisor, or a broker, and it offers structured oversight for the diverse portfolio of technology projects serving the city. In addition, the analysis exposes two factors that appear critical in allowing DoITT to accomplish its mission effectively. The first one is an intensive collaboration with both internal stakeholders (city governments' units) and external stakeholders, including the public, which is frequently asked to collaborate in addressing urgent needs and helping to develop solutions by means of competitions, community workshops, surveys, and polls. DoITT is very much involved in organizing initiatives focused on citizen engagement, like the NYC BigApps competion, but it also collaborates in organizing outreach and networking events. These events aim to showcase smart city projects and initiatives taking place in New York City and attempt to expand the smart city collaborative environment by attracting the attention of potential new stakeholders interested in supporting New York City's transformation in a smart environment.

The second critical factor is a continuous process of internal improvement, which optimizes DoITT's organizational structure and expands its working capacity. This includes a significant effort in: (1) improving procedures related to IT contracting and vendor accountability, by identifying best practices for vendor selection and compensation, increasing transparency in vendor engagements and tracking and monitoring their activity; and (2) developing targeted initiatives focused on providing its staff with training opportunities for their jobs and new skill sets for professional growth. These professional development initiatives aim to improve the agency's in-house capacity to insource IT work and reduce the need to rely on external consultants.

6.3.3 Building Block C: Network infrastructure

The network infrastructure serving New York City is built upon a robust collaboration between public and private sectors. DoITT devises the telecommunications strategies for extending broadband adoption across the five boroughs. In addition, it coordinates the city's efforts to overcome disparities in access by combining affordable broadband subscriptions, public computer centers, school programs, and the integration of wireless technologies for free Internet access in public spaces. DoITT ensures that these strategies are implemented by means of coalitions with industrial partners and civil society organizations, which are regulated by formal agreements. These public-private partnerships are activated due to their potential to "foster innovative approaches (to broadband adoption) and help avoid duplication and waste" of resources (City of New York, 2010a: 3).

DoITT's strategies are instrumental in achieving the ambition of New York City "to ensure high-quality Internet everywhere, [...] eliminate cost as a barrier to access, and [...] make the Internet a just and equitable platform" (City of New York, 2018b: 38). This ambition is clearly stated in OneNYC, which recognizes Internet access "as a prerequisite for full participation in the city's economic and civic life" and establishes the following goal: "making sure every New Yorker has affordable, high-speed internet access by 2025" (City of New York, 2018b: 38). Achieving this objective would close the divide in broadband adoption first reported on by DoITT in 2008, after conducting an assessment of the broadband deployment and adoption across the five boroughs. This assessment study gathered input from residents and hundreds of institutional stakeholders representing the public, private, and nonprofit sectors. The findings exposed the existence of a digital divide in broadband adoption, in particular in lower-income communities. The gap in broadband adoption that this divide registers is also acknowledged by OneNYC, which states "more than one-third of the lowest-income New Yorkers [...] lack broadband Internet access, which hinders their communications and access to City services" (City of New York, 2018a: 35).

To move toward citywide and affordable Internet access, the government of New York City has launched a suite of complementary initiatives driven by a concerted and coordinated public-private effort. Some of the most relevant initiatives include: (1) NYC Connected Communities, (2) NYC Connected Foundations, (3) NYC Connected Learning, (4) ConnectNYC, (5) Connect IBZ, (6) the renewal of the cable television franchise, and (7) LinkNYC.

In 2010 the government of New York City was awarded 42 million dollars in the form of three competitive grants from the Federal Government. Fourteen million dollars were used to support the NYC Connected Communities initiative, which made it possible to significantly expand the availability and capacity of public computer centers in the highest poverty areas of the city. According to the statistics provided by the City of New York, with this action, more than 1000 new workstations were brought to 40,000 users across approximately

100 libraries, public housing facilities, senior centers, and community centers throughout the five boroughs.

The remaining 28 million dollars represent the investment for NYC Connected Foundations and NYC Connected Learning, which were awarded 6 and 22 million dollars, respectively. NYC Connected Foundations targets New York City's transfer school students, namely, those students between the ages of 16 and 21 who have disengaged from high school and are not on track to graduate. As part of an effort to help them develop the skills necessary for graduation and a successful transition to either college or work, students and their families at 43 transfer high schools have received computer training, computer equipment, and Internet access subsidies after completing a 57-hour broadband training course. NYC Connected Learning builds on NYC Connected Foundations and continues providing students with IT support. This second initiative is instrumental in providing more than 18,000 low-income sixth grade students and 40,000 public school household members with free home computers, discounted broadband service, high-quality digital educational resources, and digital literacy training to boost educational outcomes over 3 academic years.

Reducing the existing gap in broadband Internet access across New York City is also the main objective of ConnectNYC and Connect IBZ, two city-sponsored programs that were launched by NYCEDC. Both programs provide unwired and underwired zones of the city with an opportunity to connect to fiber infrastructure. This initiative addresses challenges facing fiber optic expansion by expediting build-out and efficiently bringing together commercial and industrial business demand for an improved broadband connectivity.

Additional public broadband adoption and broadband-related economic development benefits also result from the renewal of the cable television franchise contracts that DoITT have awarded to Time Warner Cable and Cablevision Systems.[10] As part of the franchise renewal agreement: (1) both companies bring communication infrastructure to underserved commercial, industrial, and manufacturing locations in support of the city's economic development initiatives; (2) Cablevision Systems agree to provide free commercial-grade Internet service to all public libraries in its service area; and (3) Time Warner Cable agrees to create 40 public computer centers, in partnership with local not-for-profit organizations, to provide free broadband access to low-income communities across the city. In addition, Time Warner Cable and Cablevision Systems accept to equip 32 New York City's parks across the five boroughs with Wi-Fi service and maintain the systems for 10 years.

The availability of mobile Internet connection in open spaces is further expanded by AT&T, which partners with the NYC Department of Parks and Recreation and starts offering Wi-Fi connection free of charge in 20 parks across

10. Time Warner Cable and Cablevision Systems are two former American cable television providers with headquarters in New York City.

the five boroughs. However, the limited extension of the service convinces the city government to seek for alternative solutions able to provide a citywide extension of the Wi-Fi service. The solution surfaces in the form of an request for proposals issued by DoITT in 2014, which results in the government of New York City authorizing CityBridge[11] to install, operate, and maintain LinkNYC.

LinkNYC is the citywide wireless network that is intended to replace the aging network of public pay telephones with state-of-the-art kiosks bringing free Wi-Fi at the street level. The kiosks composing the network are called Links and, according to the agreement, are built at no cost to New Yorkers because they are entirely funded from the advertising revenue they generate. Links are designed to offer high-speed and free Wi-Fi connection, as well as a range of other services, including free phone calls to anywhere in the United States, a touchscreen tablet interface to access city services, wayfinding, easy access to 911 and 311 calls, free cell phone charging, and digital displays for advertising and public service announcements. The implementation of LinkNYC was officially launched in February 2016, with a plan calling for a total of 7500 LinkNYC kiosks across all five boroughs.

In addition to improving the access to broadband services for residents and businesses, DoITT's effort is also oriented toward designing, building, and maintaining an enterprise-level infrastructure environment able to support city operations. This consolidated environment makes it possible for New York to avoid the higher maintenance costs that multiple city-agency-owned networks would otherwise generate. It is made up of four core infrastructure components, which surface from DoITT-led initiatives: (1) CityNet, the city's institutional fiber network for voice and data communications; (2) the New York City Wireless Network (NYCWiN); (3) the CITIServ shared services environment; and (3) the Citywide Radio Network (CRN).

NYCWiN and the CRN provide wireless services to all city governments' units, eliminating the need to build agency-owned and agency-maintained systems. The CRN was built in 2009 and made it possible to migrate first responders and public safety agencies onto a common frequency. This network supports analog and digital communications and has enhanced both citywide interoperability and radio coverage within the five boroughs, including the waterways surrounding New York City. NYCWiN is instead a broadband wireless infrastructure created to support public safety and other city operations. Its construction started in 2006, with a pilot project in which DoITT collaborated with Northrop Grumman Corporation and Motorola to test two competing wireless technologies for potential citywide implementation. Testing these technological solutions was critical and the 12-week head-to-head demonstration that took place made it possible to select the most suitable technical solutions for building NYCWiN, the citywide

11. CityBridge is a consortium consisting of six New York City-based private companies operating in the ICT sector. These companies are Titan, Control Group, Qualcomm, Comark, Transit Wireless, and Antenna Design.

mobile wireless network. The cost of the pilot program is estimated to be 2.7 million dollars, which is a relatively small layout of expenditure when compared with the overall cost of building a citywide Wi-Fi network and maintaining it for a 5-year period. A cost that was expected to be $500 million. The pilot provided the city with the proof of concept necessary to guide a selection process leading to this huge scale-up investment.

However, in 2015, the city government estimated that NYCWiN was costing over 40 million dollars a year in operations and maintenance, and an investment of hundreds of millions in upgrades would have been necessary in the near future to maintain the functionality of the network. To gather ideas on how to improve its efficiency while reducing operation and maintenance costs, DoITT released a request for interest and information, soliciting the intervention of private companies, but none of the responses offered cost-effective solutions. Considering the lack of alternative solutions, in 2017, DoITT decided to transition city governments' units from NYCWiN to commercial carriers. The formal statement on this transfer, which was released by the commissioner heading DoITT, describes this change as a measure of financial prudence.

The consolidated and coordinated approach to network infrastructure has also led to the launching of the NYC Citywide IT Infrastructure Services (CITIServ) program and completion of CityNet, a network solution unifying the city's data communications and sharing of data among city agencies. CITIServ focused primarily on data center consolidation and made it possible to optimize and modernize the city's IT infrastructure by unifying more than 50 data centers that the government of New York City was operating. The main benefits that the CITIServ environment has produced include the followings: (1) lower operational costs, in particular by reducing the need to purchase, support, and maintain new hardware at the individual agency level; (2) reduced infrastructure footprint; (3) improved level of data security; and (4) improved service for a broad range of city entities, which are provided with a unified set of IT-related shared services and applications.

6.3.4 Building Block D: ICT services and applications

Fig. 6.6 shows that New York City has approached smart city development by adopting an integrated intervention logic. Its strategy cuts across all the application domains that smart city development represents and extends the benefits that ICT solutions can produce to multiple policy sectors. In addition, the data in Figs. 6.8 and 6.9 demonstrates that such an intervention logic is underpinned by a high-level of cross departmental and interorganizational collaboration. This intensive process of collaboration among stakeholders, either internal or external, is pivotal in governing the city's uptake of new ICT services and applications. Such a collaboration takes the form of small working groups, which organize their action around deploying ICT services and applications that are able to hit the sustainability issues affecting the core policy sectors of the city.

The city government has a central role in enabling and maintaining the stability of this collaborative model, which is driven by alliances connecting representatives of DoITT and other agencies and offices of the local government, industrial partners, and civil society (see Fig. 6.8). This collaboration has powered an innovation process that makes it possible for the city to enhance the efficiency of internal government functions and procedures by means of new ICT solutions. DoITT has developed a sustained track record of successfully completing ICT-related projects that provide city governments' units with technology-driven solutions for making public service delivery more efficient and enhancing business-to-government and resident-to-government interactions. These projects mainly rely on the know-how of DoITT's staff members. However, when additional knowledge is necessary, the expertise of IT companies acting as service providers or IT consultants is requested.

New York City government's agencies and offices have also made significant efforts to improve the accessibility of city-owned data and facilitate civic hacking. This bottom-up development process is based on the organizations of public contests in which citizens are invited to exploit such a data in the delivery of new software applications able to address the issues that trouble city users. The success of this bottom-up development process is demonstrated by the many technological solutions that independent groups of citizens have produced over the years and their central role in the smart city collaborative environment of New York City: 46.7% of the total activities contributing to the development of "Building Block D" have been implemented by independent developers in the framework of app competitions (see Fig. 6.7 and Appendix D).

6.4 Extending the generalization

This best practice analysis demonstrates that the validity of the building blocks and strategic principles identified in Chapter 5 goes beyond the European context and extends into North America. New York City further confirms that smart city development requires much more than technology in order to be successful in nurturing urban sustainability and is enabled by a socio-technical transformation in which technological development is aligned with human, social, cultural, economic, and environmental factors. New York City also demonstrates that such an alignment calls for strategies capable of assembling the four complementary building blocks exposed by European best practices and embed them into the structure of the city. The investigation clearly suggests that these building blocks constitute the core components of a smart city.

Further evidence proving the validity of the initial hypothesis and broader generalization of the findings captured at the European level can also be drawn from the available literature that reports on additional North American smart city development practices. Such a literature offers additional insight into how smart city development takes place in North America, which further substantiates the findings of this study and is instrumental in overcoming what might otherwise be seen as the limitations of a single case study. The value of these additional case studies lies in the opportunity that they offer to triangulate the process of smart city development in New York City with other North American experiences, thereby improving the robustness and reliability of this study's findings through cross verification from multiple sources. This additional evidence is offered in the following paragraphs, which introduce the lessons learned from the analysis of how smart city development has been approached by the cities of: Camden, New Jersey; Kansas City, Missouri; Mexico City, Mexico; Philadelphia, Pennsylvania; Quebec City, Canada; and Seattle, Washington.

6.4.1 Philadelphia, Quebec City, Mexico City and Seattle

Alawadhi et al. (2012) conduct a set of interviews with city government representatives responsible for implementing smart city initiatives in four North American cities: Philadelphia, Seattle, Quebec City, and Mexico City. Philadelphia and its approach to smart city development are also examined in research by Wiig (2015, 2016) and Shelton et al. (2015), who focuses attention on the Digital On-Ramps initiative, a smart city project born in the framework of the IBM's Smarter Cities Challenge. Overall, the lessons learned from these four cities on how to approach smart city development align with the experience of New York City, in particular in confirming the importance of setting up a (1) quadruple-helix collaborative environment, (2) strategic framework, (3) smart city accelerator, (4) multilevel governance structure, and (5) technological infrastructure for supporting the provision of digital services and applications.

The multiple case study analysis presented by Alawadhi et al. (2012) confirms that the main challenges imposed by smart city development are mainly organizational than technology-related. Among the characteristics that these four cities share, the authors report on the change in the organizational culture, which they had to face in order to approach smart city development. A more open and collaborative environment is identified as a critical element for smart city development practices, as well as collaboration, communication and the sharing of resources, commitment, and information among internal and external stakeholders. The data provided by the interviewees suggests the smart city development strategies of these four cities are based on the collaboration between industry, governmental authorities, universities, and civil society, and particular attention has been focused on enhancing the participation of citizens and capturing their knowledge of the urban environment.

In addition to this quadruple-helix collaborative environment, the presence of two additional elements was found essential. The first one is a leading agency or department within the city government's structure, which is tasked with coordinating the smart development strategy and linking together internal and external stakeholders. The second element is a strategic framework setting up the policy context for smart city development. This framework is described as a combination of policy direction from the highest-ranking officials in the city government and a political position that clearly states the importance of embracing an ICT-driven approach to urban sustainability.

Finally, the study captures the respondents' views regarding the network infrastructure composing "Building Block C." According to the findings, the interviewees agree in expressing the fundamental role that such an infrastructure and its components have in enabling smart city development, in particular in relation to creating the capacity for delivering digital services and applications. In addition, the interviews have also highlighted the collaborative efforts necessary to build the network infrastructure and the need to bridge digital divide to guarantee equal access to the Internet.

In exposing the development process of Digital On-Ramps, Wiig (2015, 2016) and Shelton et al. (2015) continue the investigation of Philadelphia's approach to smart city development and serve to highlight the incapacity of this digital application to deliver the expected outcome: "solving unemployment for 500,000 marginalized city residents" (Wiig, 2016: 353). This initiative is developed in the context of the IBM's Smart Cities Challenge, and the case study analysis shows that the lack of meaningful benefits was mainly caused by (1) a technocratic vision of smart city development, (2) a double-helix collaborative model in which citizens where included only in the project's narrative instead of being part of the implementation process, and (3) a weak strategic framework built on an unreliable policy direction and bombastic expectations. These results expose the "a-spatiality of techno-utopian smart city policies" raising from the belief of the city government in the corporate smart city model, which proposes one-size-fits-all technological fixes instead of taking "into consideration the material geography of [...] urban problems" (Wiig, 2016: 548).

6.4.2 Camden

"Achieving a safe city takes more than a surveillance-based technological fix" (Wiig, 2018: 417) is the statement that perhaps best summarizes the failure of Camdem's citywide surveillance system for reducing crime rates. Camden is one of the most dangerous cities in North America and ensuring public safety is therefore one of the main priorities in the urban regeneration agenda designed by the local government. However, the technology-driven approach that the city has decided to adopt in order to tackle this pressing issue has proved to be unsuccessful. As in the case of Philadelphia's Digital On-Ramps initiative, the experience of Camden further exposes the limitations of the corporate smart city model and the need for cities to embrace a much more progressive and holistic view of smart city development practices.

As Wiig (2018) reports, the city government pictured the installation of a high-technology system for automated surveillance as the main pillar of a regeneration process unable to produce the expected results. The analysis suggests Camden's approach to smart city development was driven by the misperception of the market-driven rationality cultivated by the corporate smart city model, which has prevented the local government from looking beyond technology. This attempt to embrace smart city development fell short of the city's expectations due to the deployment of a strategic framework that underestimated the complex socio-economic and cultural implications of a public safety crisis, which it sought to address. This is because the one-size-fits-all technology-driven solution adopted has proved to lack the strategic means needed for this smart city development to meet the intended sustainability goal.

6.4.3 Kansas City

Enabling smart city development requires cities to set in motion quadruple-helix-based collaborative environments able to combine open innovation, bottom-up development activities, and local entrepreneurship in a civic context. This key lesson clearly emerges in the analysis of New York City and is also echoed in research by Sarma and Sunny (2017), who focus their attention on the approach to smart city development of Kansas City. In these collaborative environments, local communities are provided with the possibility to leverage creativity, IT skills, and entrepreneurial spirit for producing smart city solutions that the city can benefit from.

The case study analysis of Kansas City provides additional evidence suggesting that technology-driven civic entrepreneurship is triggered by the combination of open data, network infrastructure, citizen engagement mechanisms, and a strategic framework that provides policy direction and clearly exposes the sustainability issues that the city is required to deal with. Kansas City has combined living lab methodology and partnership programs to mix these key elements together and attract aspiring civic entrepreneurs interested in co-creating new ICT solutions in collaboration with public and private stakeholders. This approach has become the means by which to enhance urban development under the smart city paradigm and progress this by "creating an urban ecosystem geared toward civic value through entrepreneurship" (Sarma and Sunny, 2017: 848).

References

Acuto, M., Steenmans, K., Iwaszuk, E., Ortega-Garza, L., 2018. Informing urban governance? Boundary-spanning organisations and the ecosystem of urban data. Area, 1–10. https://doi.org/10.1111/area.12430.

Aina, Y.A., 2017. Achieving smart sustainable cities with GeoICT support: the Saudi evolving smart cities. Cities: Int. J. Urban Policy Plann. 71, 49–58.

Alawadhi, S., Aldama-Nalda, A., Chourabi, H., Gil-Garcia, R.J., Leung, S., Mellouli, S., Nam, T., Pardo, T.A., Scholl, H.J., Walker, S., 2012. Building understanding of smart city initiatives. In: Scholl, H.J., Janssen, M., Wimmer, M.A., Moe, C.E., Flak, L.S. (Eds.), Electronic Government: 11th IFIP WG 8.5 International Conference, EGOV 2012, Kristiansand, Norway, September 3–6, 2012. Proceedings. Springer, Berlin, pp. 40–53.

Anderson, J., Fisher, D., Witters, L., 2012. Getting Smart About Smart Cities: Understanding the Market Opportunity in the Cities of Tomorrow. Alcatel-Lucent. http://www2.alcatel-lucent.com/knowledge-center/admin/mci-files-1a2c3f/ma/Smart_Cities_Market_opportunity_MarketAnalysis.pdf. (Accessed January 1, 2013).

Angelidou, M., 2014. Smart city policies: a spatial approach. Cities: Int. J. Urban Policy Plann. 41 (Suppl 1), S3–S11.

Angelidou, M., 2017. Smart city planning and development shortcomings. TeMA. J. Land Use Mobil. Environ. 10, 77–94.

Anrong, D., Gongli, L., Juan, L., Xianjuan, K., 2016. Research on smart community planning of Yishanwan, China towards new urbanization. Int. Rev. Spatial Plann. Sustain. Dev. 4 (1), 78–90.

Arif, H., Cole, R.J., Cole, I.A., 2015. Experiments with smart zoning for smart cities. In: Araya, D. (Ed.), Smart Cities as Democratic Ecologies. Palgrave Macmillan, London, pp. 173–199.

ARUP, 2013. Global Innovators: International Case Studies on Smart Cities. BIS Research Paper n°135, Government of the United Kingdom – Department for Business, Innovation and Skills. https://www.gov.uk/government/uploads/system/uploads/attachment_data/file/249397/bis-13-1216-global-innovators-international-smart-cities.pdf. (Accessed September 8, 2016).

Berrone, P., Ricart, J.E., 2017. IESE Cities in Motion Index 2017. University of Navarra. https://www.mos.ru/upload/documents/files/9743/IESECitiesinMotionIndexIESECitiesinMotionIndex.pdf. (Accessed January 30, 2019).

Berrone, P., Ricart, J.E., 2018. IESE Cities in Motion Index 2018. University of Navarra. https://media.iese.edu/research/pdfs/ST-0471-E.pdf. (Accessed January 30, 2019).

Butts, C.T., 2008. Social network analysis: a methodological introduction. Asian J. Soc. Psychol. 11 (1), 13–41.

Caprotti, F., Cowley, R., Bailey, I., Joss, S., Sengers, F., Raven, R., Spaeth, P., Jolivet, E., Tan-Mullins, M., Cheshmehzangi, A., Xie, L., 2017. Smart Eco-City Development in Europe and China: Opportunities, Drivers and Challenges. University of Exeter. https://ore.exeter.ac.uk/repository/handle/10871/29876. (Accessed January 3, 2019).

Cisco Systems, 2012. Smart Cities Exposé: 10 Cities in Transition. Cisco Systems. http://www.pageturnpro.com/Cisco/41742-Smart-Cities-Expose-10-Cities-in-Transition/index.html#44. (Accessed January 5, 2013).

City of New York, 2007. ACCESS NYC Awarded as One of Infoworld's 100 Most Innovative IT Solutions for 2007. Press Release, City of New York – Department of Information Technology & Telecommunications. https://www1.nyc.gov/site/doitt/about/pr-071113.page. (Accessed January 2, 2019).

City of New York, 2009. New York City Recognized with 2009 Municipal Web Portal Excellence Award. Press Release, City of New York – Department of Information Technology & Telecommunications. https://www1.nyc.gov/site/doitt/about/pr-090513.page. (Accessed January 2, 2019).

City of New York, 2010a. Department of Information Technology and Telecommunications Testimony Before the City Council Committee on Technology. Oversight on Broadband Adoption: Closing the Digital Divide. City of New York. https://www1.nyc.gov/assets/doitt/downloads/pdf/broadband_adoption_092710.pdf. (Accessed January 2, 2019).

City of New York, 2010b. Mayor Bloomberg Announces 311online Wins Digital Government Achievement Award. Press Release, City of New York. https://www1.nyc.gov/office-of-the-mayor/news/396-10/mayor-bloomberg-311online-wins-digital-government-achievement-award. (Accessed January 2, 2019).

City of New York, 2010c. Reinvent Payphones Challenge/LinkNYC Recognized As 2015 Harvard Ash Center Bright Idea in Government. Press Release, City of New York. https://www1.nyc.gov/assets/doitt/downloads/pdf/Bright_Ideas_Press_Release_FINAL.pdf. (Accessed January 2, 2019).

City of New York, 2010d. Statement of Mayor Michael R. Bloomberg on Honors for Three City Technology Initiatives. Press Release, City of New York. https://www1.nyc.gov/office-of-the-mayor/news/263-10/statement-mayor-michael-bloomberg-honors-three-city-technology-initiatives. (Accessed January 2, 2019).

City of New York, 2011. Annual Report 2011. Enabling the Connected City: Year in Review. City of New York – Department of Information Technology & Telecommunications. https://www1.nyc.gov/assets/doitt/downloads/pdf/doitt_2011_annual_report.pdf. (Accessed January 2, 2019).

City of New York, 2016. New York Named "2016 Best Smart City," NYC to Host 2017 International Conference on Urban Technology at Brooklyn Navy Yard. Press Release, City of New York. https://www1.nyc.gov/office-of-the-mayor/news/909-16/new-york-named-2016-best-smart-city-nyc-host-2017-international-conference-urban. (Accessed January 2, 2019).

City of New York, 2018a. One New York: The Plan for a Strong and Just City. City of New York. https://onenyc.cityofnewyork.us/wp-content/uploads/2018/04/OneNYC-1.pdf. (Accessed January 2, 2019).

City of New York, 2018b. OneNYC 2018: Progress Report. City of New York. https://onenyc.cityofnewyork.us/wp-content/uploads/2018/05/OneNYC_Progress_2018.pdf. (Accessed January 2, 2019).

Cugurullo, F., 2013. How to build a sandcastle: an analysis of the genesis and development of Masdar City. J. Urban Technol. 20 (1), 23–37.

Datta, A., 2015. New urban utopias of postcolonial India: entrepreneurial urbanization in Dholera Smart City, Gujarat. Dialogues Hum. Geogr. 5 (1), 3–22.

Dierwechter, Y., 2013. Smart city-regionalism across Seattle: progressing transit nodes in labor space? Geoforum 49, 139–149.

Eden Strategy Institute, & ONG&ONG, 2018. Top 50 Smart City Governments. Eden Strategy Institute. https://static1.squarespace.com/static/5b3c517fec4eb767a04e73ff/t/5b513c57aa4a99f62d168e60/1532050650562/Eden-OXD_Top+50+Smart+City+Governments.pdf. (Accessed January 20, 2019).

Eisenhardt, K.M., 1989. Building theories from case study research. Acad. Manag. Rev. 14 (4), 532–550.

Fietkiewicz, K.J., Stock, W.G., 2015. How smart are Japanese cities? An empirical investigation of infrastructures and governmental programs in Tokyo, Yokohama, Osaka and Kyoto. In: Bui, T.X., Sprague, R.H. (Eds.), Proceedings of the 48th Hawaii International Conference on System Sciences (HICSS), Kauai, HI, 5–8 January 2015. Institute of Electrical and Electronics Engineers (IEEE), Piscataway, NJ, pp. 2345–2354.

Fruchterman, T.M.J., Reingold, E.M., 1991. Graph drawing by force-directed placement. Softw. Pract. Exp. 21 (11), 1129–1164.

Gaffney, C., Robertson, C., 2018. Smarter than smart: Rio De Janeiro's flawed emergence as a smart city. J. Urban Technol. 25 (3), 47–64.

George, A.L., Bennett, A., 2005. Case Studies and Theory Development in the Social Sciences. MIT Press, Cambridge, MA.

Gibbs, G.R., 2007. Analysing Qualitative Data. SAGE Publications, Thousand Oaks, CA.

Gibson, J., Robinson, M., Cain, S., 2015. City Initiatives for Technology, Innovation and Entrepreneurship: A Resource for City Leadership. Nesta, Accenture and Future Cities Catapult. https://media.nesta.org.uk/documents/citie_report_2015.pdf. (Accessed January 2, 2019).

Goodspeed, R., 2015. Smart cities: moving beyond urban cybernetics to tackle wicked problems. Camb. J. Reg. Econ. Soc. 8 (1), 79–92.

Gupta, K., Hall, R.P., 2017. The Indian Perspective of Smart Cities. In: Proceedings of the 2017 Smart City Symposium Prague (SCSP), Prague, 25–26 May 2017. Institute of Electrical and Electronics Engineers, Piscataway, NJ.

Heaton, B., 2011. 17 State and Local Governments Honored for Web 2.0 and Social Media. Press Release, e.Republic. http://www.govtech.com/e-government/Governments-Honored-Web-20-and-Social-Media-.html. (Accessed January 30, 2019).

Joss, S., 2011. Eco-cities: the mainstreaming of urban sustainability – key characteristics and driving factors. Int. J. Sustain. Dev. Plan. 6 (3), 268–285.

Joss, S., Tomozeiu, D., Cowley, R., 2011. Eco-Cities – A Global Survey 2011: Eco-City Profiles. University of Westminster. https://www.westminster.ac.uk/file/12651/download. (Accessed February 2, 2012).

Ju, J., Liu, L., Feng, Y., 2018. Citizen-centered big data analysis-driven governance intelligence framework for smart cities. Telecommun. Policy 42, 881–896. https://doi.org/10.1016/j.telpol.2018.01.003.

Kolotouchkina, O., Seisdedos, G., 2018. Place branding strategies in the context of new smart cities: Songdo IBD, Masdar and Skolkovo. Place Brand. Public Diplomacy 14 (2), 115–124.

Komninos, N., 2011. Intelligent cities: variable geometries of spatial intelligence. Intell. Build. Int. 3 (3), 172–188.

Kong, L., Woods, O., 2018. The ideological alignment of smart urbanism in Singapore: critical reflections on a political paradox. Urban Stud. 55 (4), 679–701.

Lavrakas, P.J. (Ed.), 2008. Encyclopedia of Survey Research Methods. SAGE Publications, Thousand Oaks, CA.

Lay, C., 2010. 10th Annual Digital Cities Survey: 2010 Results. Press Release, e.Republic. http://www.govtech.com/dc/digital-cities/102472074.html. (Accessed January 30, 2019).

Lee, J., Hancock, M.G., Hu, M., 2014. Towards an effective framework for building smart cities: lessons from Seoul and San Francisco. Technol. Forecast. Soc. Chang. 89, 80–99.

Leydesdorff, L., Deakin, M., 2011. The triple-helix model of smart cities: a neo-evolutionary perspective. J. Urban Technol. 18 (2), 53–63.

Lu, H., de Jong, M., ten Heuvelhof, E., 2018. Explaining the variety in smart Eco City development in China-what policy network theory can teach us about overcoming barriers in implementation? J. Clean. Prod. 196, 1–15.

Macke, J., Casagrande, R.M., Sarate, R., J. A., & Silva, K. A., 2018. Smart City and quality of life: Citizens' perception in a Brazilian case study. J. Clean. Prod. 182, 717–726.

McLean, A., Bulkeley, H., Crang, M., 2016. Negotiating the urban smart grid: socio-technical experimentation in the City of Austin. Urban Stud. 53 (15), 3246–3263.

McNeill, D., 2016. Governing a City of unicorns: technology capital and the urban politics of San Francisco. Urban Geogr. 37 (4), 494–513.

National League of Cities, 2016. Trends in Smart City Development: Case Studies and Recommendations. Research Report, National League of Cities. https://www.nlc.org/sites/default/files/2017-01/Trends%20in%20Smart%20City%20Development.pdf. (Accessed August 2, 2018).

Phumpiu Chang, P., Rivera Kuri, J., 2014. Monterrey envisioned as a smart city developed through international model examples. In: Marchettini, N., Brebbia, C., Pulselli, R., Bastianoni, S. (Eds.), The Sustainable City IX. WIT Press, Southampton, pp. 51–64.

Rich, S., 2012. New York City and Texas Honored for Cybersecurity Leadership. Press Release, e.Republic. http://www.govtech.com/pcio/CDG-Cyber-Security-Awards-2012.html. (Accessed January 15, 2019).

Robson, C., 1993. Real World Research: A Resource for Users of Social Research Methods in Applied Settings. John Wiley & Sons Ltd., Hoboken, NJ.

Sandhi Firmanyah, H., Supangkat, S.H., Arman, A.A., Adhitya, R., 2017. Searching Smart City in Indonesia through maturity model analysis: case study in 10 cities. In: Proceedings of the 2017 International Conference on ICT for Smart Society (ICISS), Tangerang, 20-21 September 2017. Institute of Electrical and Electronics Engineers (IEEE), Piscataway, NJ.

Sarma, S., Sunny, S.A., 2017. Civic entrepreneurial ecosystems: smart city emergence in Kansas City. Bus. Horiz. 60 (6), 843–853.

Selinger, M., Kim, T., 2015. Smart city needs smart people: Songdo and smart + connected learning. In: Araya, D. (Ed.), Smart Cities as Democratic Ecologies. Palgrave Macmillan, London, pp. 159–172.

Shelton, T., Zook, M., Wiig, A., 2015. The 'actually existing smart city'. Camb. J. Reg. Econ. Soc. 8 (1), 13–25.

Shwayri, S.T., 2013. A model Korean ubiquitous eco-city? The politics of making Songdo. J. Urban Technol. 20 (1), 39–55.

Strauss, A., Corbin, J.M., 1990. Basics of Qualitative Research: Grounded Theory Procedures and Techniques. SAGE Publications, Thousand Oaks, CA.

The United States Conference of Mayors, & IHS Markit, 2017. Cities of the 21st Century: 2016 Smart Cities Survey. The United States Conference of Mayors. https://www.usmayors.org/wp-content/uploads/2017/02/2016SmartCitiesSurvey.pdf. (Accessed October 4, 2018).

Ueyama, J., Faiçal, B.S., Mano, L.Y., Bayer, G., Pessin, G., Gomes, P.H., 2017. Enhancing reliability in wireless sensor networks for adaptive river monitoring systems: reflections on their long-term deployment in Brazil. Comput. Environ. Urban. Syst. 65, 41–52.

Viale Pereira, G., Cunha, M.A., Lampoltshammer, T.J., Parycek, P., Gregianin Testa, M., 2017. Increasing collaboration and participation in smart city governance: a cross-case analysis of smart city initiatives. Inf. Technol. Dev. 23 (3), 526–553.

Walters, D., 2011. Smart cities, smart places, smart democracy: form-based codes, electronic governance and the role of place in making smart cities. Intell. Build. Int. 3 (3), 198–218.

Wang, F., Wang, K., 2017. Assessing the effect of eco-city practices on urban sustainability using an extended ecological footprint model: a case study in Xi'an, China. Sustainability 9 (9), 1591–1606.

Wiig, A., 2015. IBM's smart city as techno-utopian policy mobility. City: Anal. Urban Trends Culture Theory Policy Action 19 (2–3), 258–273.

Wiig, A., 2016. The empty rhetoric of the smart city: from digital inclusion to economic promotion in Philadelphia. Urban Geogr. 37 (4), 535–553.

Wiig, A., 2018. Secure the city, revitalize the zone: smart urbanization in Camden, New Jersey. Environ. Plann. C: Polit. Space 36 (3), 403–422.

Woetzel, J., Remes, J., Boland, B., Lv, K., Sinha, S., Strube, G., Means, J., Law, J., Cadena, A., von der Tann, V., 2018. Smart Cities: Digital Solutions for a More Livable Future. McKinsey & Company. https://www.mckinsey.com/~/media/McKinsey/Industries/Capital%20Projects%20and%20Infrastructure/Our%20Insights/Smart%20cities%20Digital%20solutions%20for%20a%20more%20livable%20future/MGI-Smart-Cities-Full-Report.ashx. (Accessed January 15, 2019).

Yin, R.K., 2009. Case Study Research: Design and Methods, 4 ed. SAGE Publications, Thousand Oaks, CA.

Zhang, Y., Zhou, K., Li, X., 2014. Study on the construction of smart agricultural demonstration park. Int. J. Smart Home 8 (5), 261–268.

Chapter 7

The social shaping of smart cities

Chapter outline

7.1 Smart cities and the dynamics of expectations

Seeking for innovations capable of contributing to the creation of more sustainable urban development paths is a future-oriented activity, whose aim is to reframe existing urban sustainability dynamics and improve their functioning (Adams et al., 2016). These improvements, which can be either incremental or radical, take different forms, and a very large number of representative cases can be provided. For example, innovations leading to more sustainable urban environments can surface as new collaborative models for designing urban development projects and strategies (Boyer, 2015; Moulaert et al., 2007), new business models for fostering the collaborative consumption of public services (Ma et al., 2018), cultural and political changes (Kagan et al., 2018), or new technological solutions (Batty et al., 2012; Kim et al., 2017; McCormick and Kiss, 2015).

Forecasting the future is a key component of innovation processes, and the potential changes emerging from the search for alternative states generate expectations, especially when technology-related advancements are brought forward. In this context, expectations can be defined as "real-time representations of future technological situations and capabilities," which link the prospect of new solutions to existing social issues (Borup et al., 2006: 286). The critical role that expectations play in shaping technological progress is widely recognized, and analyzing how they both evolve and influence technology-related innovation processes in different sectors has become a key priority for researchers interested in better understanding how innovation works (Borup et al., 2006;

Untangling Smart Cities. https://doi.org/10.1016/B978-0-12-815477-9.00007-4

Brown and Michael, 2003; Khodayaria and Aslani, 2018; Kriechbaum et al., 2018; Ruef and Markard, 2010; van Lente and Bakker, 2010; van Lente et al., 2013).

Research in this knowledge domain has demonstrated that anticipatory expectations do not evolve along linear patterns (Geels and Raven, 2006), but "change over time in response and adaptation to new conditions or emergent problems" (Borup et al., 2006: 286). In addition, when comparing these patterns across different technological advancements, no single pattern surfaces due to the presence of variations and a high level of unpredictability. Of particular relevance in exposing this condition is the contribution offered by van Lente et al. (2013), who compared how expectations changed over time in the innovation processes leading to three new technological advancements: the voice over internet protocol (VoIP), gene therapy, and high-temperature superconductivity.

But the complexity of this phenomenon has not stopped researchers from attempting to distill a sequence of stages able to describe how expectations and the degree of maturity of technological innovations evolve together. One of the most popular results of this search is the hype cycle model designed by Gartner[1] (Fenn and Raskino, 2008; Sumic et al., 2009), which has obtained substantial attention from both practitioners and academics (Aslani et al., 2018; Campani and Vaglio, 2015; Dedehayir and Steinert, 2016; Ghubril and Prentice, 2014; Järvenpää and Mäkinen, 2008; Khodayaria and Aslani, 2018; O'Leary, 2008). This model has been strongly criticized for its tendency to picture a very unpredictable process in a too generalized, rigid, and linear form (Borup et al., 2006), while ignoring the methodological incongruencies and theoretical limitations that Järvenpää and Mäkinen (2008) and Dedehayir and Steinert (2016) have exposed with clarity. However, despite these deficiencies, the contribution that the hype cycle offers to the study of how expectations affect innovation processes lies in the capacity it has to further highlight the importance of peak-disappointment-recovery sequences generated by hyped behaviors. This is a critical component of technological innovation processes that many investigations have focused attention on, making significant efforts to describe it through coherent mathematical conceptualizations (Campani and Vaglio, 2015; Dedehayir and Steinert, 2016; Goldenberg et al., 2002; Jun, 2012; Mahajan and Muller, 1996; Phillips, 2007; Rogers, 2003; Silvestrini et al., 2017; van Lente et al., 2013).

Hyped behaviors frequently emerge in innovation processes, regardless of the sector, and they result in hype-type evolution curves that are composed of the three sequential stages outlining peak-disappointment-recovery patterns. Significant efforts have been made to investigate such a pattern, which has been documented, for example, in the cases of stationary fuel cells (Ruef and Markard, 2010), photovoltaic technology (Kriechbaum et al., 2018), digital

1. Gartner is a North America-based advisory company which operates worldwide, and a significant part of its research activity focuses on capturing and analyzing emerging developments in the information technology sector.

versatile disc (DVD) technology (Järvenpää and Mäkinen, 2008), organic light-emitting diode (OLED) technology (Campani and Vaglio, 2015), energy storage systems (Khodayaria and Aslani, 2018), and biogas development (Geels and Raven, 2006).

The peak-disappointment-recovery pattern that these studies put forward is shown in Fig. 7.1. After a potential technological breakthrough is triggered, a mix of positive and negative expectations begins to emerge. When the positive expectations exceed the concerns, the faith in the benefits that the technological breakthrough may produce starts rising and powers the innovation process. However, these expectations are not always realistic; they can be exaggerated and produce hypes. In the short term, the enthusiastic expectations that hypes generate can become instrumental in attracting interest, fostering commitment, and boosting the development of the new vision. But when it becomes clear that the excessively optimistic ambitions cannot be realized, the hype stops, and a feeling of disappointment surfaces, which results from the discovery that the expected scenario is not as good as the hype suggests. This disillusionment triggers a recovery stage during which adjusting the exaggerated expectations to longer time horizons becomes essential to discern the hype from the reality and to demonstrate whether the proposed technological development can become meaningful.

As history demonstrates, urban utopias have a tendency to generate hypes in relation to the benefits that technological progress can grant access to, and smart cities exemplify this tendency. When looking at the results of the investigation that this book reports on, a hype can be identified in the first two decades of research, whereby the technocentric urban utopia imagined by the corporate

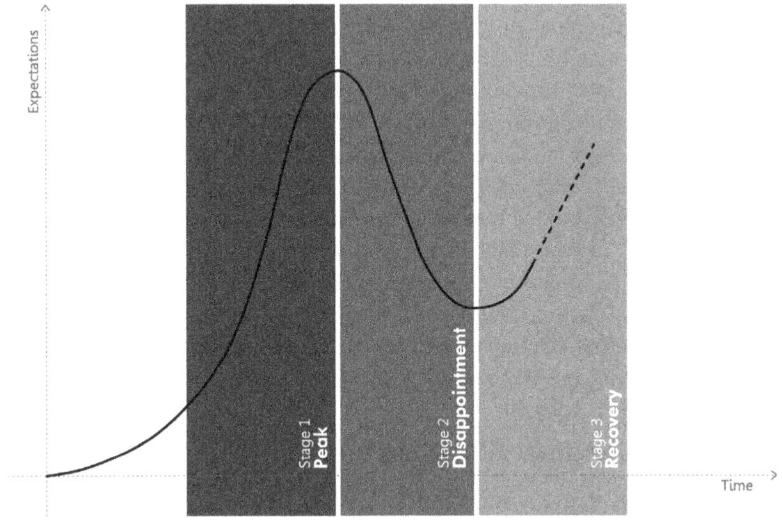

FIG. 7.1 The hype-type evolution curves of innovation processes.

sector took root and started to grow. This hype was then followed by a clear downscaling of expectations, which was caused by disappointment in the outcomes of the first experiments embracing the utopian vision and its driving principles: technological determinism, strong market orientation, top-down and industry-driven development process, double-helix collaborative model, and the a-spatiality of one-size-fits-all solutions to urban problems (Cardullo and Kitchin, 2019; Datta, 2015a, 2015b; Grossi and Pianezzi, 2017; Marvin et al., 2016; McNeill, 2015, 2016; Pollio, 2016; Shelton et al., 2015; Soderstrom et al., 2014; Valdez et al., 2018; Wiig, 2015, 2016)

Surrounded by highly optimistic expectations and an unconditional faith in technological progress, smart city development was immediately championed by the corporate sector as an innovative approach to urban sustainability. However, this happened long before it was possible to obtain the evidence needed to (1) showcase the benefits that smart city development can produce and (2) structure an operating model able to explain how such a development should be managed to support sustainable urban development. As soon as the technocentric urban utopia pictured by the corporate sector was found to be incapable of delivering the expected benefits, skepticism started to emerge, and the scientific community has immediately pushed for a more progressive understanding of smart cities (Ahvenniemi et al., 2017; Colding and Barthel, 2017; Deakin and Al Wear, 2011; Hollands, 2008, 2015; Kitchin, 2015; Yigitcanlar and Kamruzzaman, 2018; Yigitcanlar et al., 2019).

7.2 Separating the hype from reality: Key lessons and recommendations

When untangled from the technocentric urban utopia that the corporate sector has imagined, smart cities do have the potential to develop into innovation systems that set the stage for a technology-enabled approach to urban sustainability. However, this requires separating the hype that the utopian thinking has generated about smart city development from the reality. The following paragraphs sum up the key lessons and recommendations that this book can offer to help the community of stakeholders that are involved in smart city research, policy, and practice, to "see beyond the hype" (Lavine, 2010: 1470). This contribution will help develop the "critical understanding of smart urbanism" (Luque-Ayala and Marvin, 2015: 2113) that is necessary to replace the conceptualizations that have generated the hype, with a progressive, constructivist, and human vision of smart city development that can meet the expectations that society has of it (Caragliu et al., 2011; Deakin and Al Wear, 2011; Hollands, 2008, 2015; Kitchin, 2015).

7.2.1 Reframing smart city research

The results of the analyses suggest that, despite the differences in interpreting the smart city concept that has developed over the last three decades, an initial common understanding emerges. In this respect, representatives of academia, industry, government, and civil society organizations all expect smart city development to become a technology-enabled approach to urban sustainability. In addition, the investigation demonstrates that successfully embracing smart city development requires a collective effort triggered by two complementary forces. On the one hand, there is the faith in the progress of technological advancement exposed by the utopian thinking of the corporate sector. On the other, the knowledge, skills, and interests of a quadruple-helix collaborative environment that offers civil society a safeguard against the technological determinism that the utopia imposes and that serves to shape the need for technological innovation in response to the requirements of urban sustainability. This emerging theory is grounded on the evidence that the best practice analyses have offered, which suggests smart cities can become meaningful only when the technocentric and market-oriented development logic they are currently founded on is replaced with the collaborative efforts of an open community whose actions are based on a holistic interpretation of smart city development.

Unfortunately, rather than promoting such a holistic interpretation, smart city research currently exhibits division, a lack of cohesion, and the presence of a limited intellectual exchange. As a result, it falls short of providing the comprehensive and interdisciplinary understanding of the subject that is necessary to inform smart city development policy and practice. Research around smart cities appears to be mainly driven by technology-related considerations, which have taken center stage in the smart city discourse. As a result, any consideration as to the social shaping (Williams and Edge, 1996) of smart cities has tended to be overshadowed, and the research investigating how to successfully manage socio, cultural, political, economic, and environmental factors when designing and implementing smart city development strategies has remained at a preliminary stage (Birbi and Krogstie, 2017; Martin et al., 2018).

The technological component of smart cities cannot emerge as a response to market forces and does not develop according to "an inner technical logic, but is instead a social product, patterned by the conditions of its creation and use" (Williams and Edge, 1996: 866). Years of research efforts in the field of science, technology, and society studies have clearly demonstrated that technological artifacts and systems are the outcome of strategic choices and social forces, and this negotiability exposes the social shaping of technological transformations (Aibar and Bijker, 1997; Bijker, 2008, 2010; Bijker and Law, 1992; Hommels, 2005; Orlikowski, 1992; Pinch and Bijker, 1984). This indicates that attempting to grasp the complexity of smart cities without considering their social shaping will leave the expectations that society has of smart city development as an innovative approach to urban sustainability unrealized.

A novel approach to scientific research that works across traditional discipline boundaries and promotes a constructivist view of smart city development is required to generate this missing insight, which lies in the intersection between engineering and technology disciplines and social sciences. Exactly as

Acuto et al. (2018: 2) point out in relation to the current state of urban science, the study of smart city development "needs to become more than the sum of its parts" and orient towards a more holistic line of enquiry that prioritize the generation of "actionable knowledge" (Bai et al., 2016: 71) able to foster "scientifically driven" smart city development policy and practice (Acuto, 2018: 166). Otherwise the dichotomous nature of smart city research and the technocentric imaginary of smart cities that feeds the utopia of the corporate sector will continue to last, so do their negative effects.

With the emergence of complex interactions between urban development dynamics and digital components, a stronger connection among disciplinary patterns is key to obtain a comprehensive understanding of the sociotechnical challenges that smart city development poses. An interdisciplinarity approach can overcome some of the most relevant existing knowledge gaps, which are mainly related to the strategic and organizational components of smart cities. The followings are some of the questions that these gaps pose for smart city researchers, and despite their high relevance an insufficient research effort has been identified:

- What key performance indicators and metrics best measure the effectiveness of the ICT-driven approach to urban sustainability that smart city development promotes? (Ahvenniemi et al., 2017; Hara et al., 2016; Klopp and Petretta, 2017; Marsal-Llacuna et al., 2015)
- What are the cultural, technological, financial, and organizational barriers to smart city development as an ICT-driven approach to urban sustainability, and what measures should be used to overcome the limitations that these barriers generate? (Angelidou, 2014; Ann Keller et al., 2012; Mosannenzadeh et al., 2017)
- What business models should be adopted to build a platform of ICT solutions for urban sustainability that is inclusive, safe, and resilient? (Díaz-Díaz et al., 2017; Walravens, 2015b)
- What are the activities, phases, and standards to be considered when designing and implementing strategies for enabling smart city development? (Ben Letaifa, 2015; Bolici and Mora, 2015; Komninos, 2014; Mora and Bolici, 2016, 2017; Mora et al., 2019; van Winden and van den Buuse, 2017; Wu et al., 2018)
- How can privacy concerns and controversy arising from the technological solutions embedded in smart environments be detected and managed? (Kitchin, 2014; van Zoonen, 2016)
- What tools and techniques can be deployed to boost the active participation of citizens in smart city development practice? (Cardullo and Kitchin, 2019; Castelnovo et al., 2016; Hollands, 2015; Johnson and Robinson, 2014; Joss et al., 2017; Snow et al., 2016)
- What are the dynamics of the governance systems regulating the development of smart cities as ecosystems of ICT-driven innovations for urban

sustainability and wealth creation? (Leydesdorff and Deakin, 2011; Macke et al., 2018; Sauer, 2012; Voytenko et al., 2016)

- What frameworks can be deployed to design and evaluate policy measures in the field of smart city development and ICT-enabled urban innovation? (Woolthuis et al., 2005)
- How can cities cope with the negative externalities that the failure of technology-driven public sector projects can generate? (Nam and Pardo, 2011b)

7.2.2 Smart cities as complex adaptive systems for urban innovation

Smart cities should be considered as socially shaped innovation systems for supporting a technology-enabled approach to urban sustainability (Bijker, 2010; Williams and Edge, 1996), and this book is instrumental in exposing the complex nature of their architecture. The findings of the investigation suggest enabling smart city development requires a local platform of ICT solutions to urban challenges within the built environment. The design and construction of this platform is progressive and depends upon a dynamic, flexible, and community-based line of action, whereby groups of actors belonging to a large collaborative environment engage in joint initiatives leading to the continuous implementation of ICT-related interventions that constantly improve urban sustainability.

However, the organizational dynamics governing smart city collaborative environments have not yet been sufficiently examined. Filling such a knowledge gap by adopting an interdisciplinary approach driven by the use of "organizational theory lenses" (Arellano-Gault et al., 2013: 145) is a relevant objective for future research. This book helps fill such a knowledge gap by demonstrating that (1) smart city development is a knowledge-intensive activity in which collaboration and collective action have a central role and (2) smart city collaborative environments are effective when the industry-government-research relationships of the triple-helix collaborative model and the participatory qualities of civil society organizations and citizens are brought together (Deakin and Leydesdorff, 2014; Dixon et al., 2018; van Waart et al., 2016). As Walravens (2015a) points out, this combination activates a form of "collective intelligence" (Woolley et al., 2010: 686) that triggers the ICT-related urban innovation process and provides smart city development strategies with long-term effectiveness.

How actors connect and relate to one another is critical to the survival of smart cities, and understanding the complex dynamics governing such a collaborative space represents a fundamental issue of contemporary organization studies. This issue relates to the "changing nature of Weberian bureaucracy" (Kornberger et al., 2017a, b: 181) and is well captured by Arellano-Gault et al. (2013) and Kornberger et al. (2017a, b), who both explore how bureaucratic organizations, such as local governments, are adapting their organizational dynamics to operate under the circumstances of an increased openness, transparency, and interaction with the external environment.

This book's investigation demonstrates that the rigidity of public sector bureaucracies does not offer the appropriate organizational arrangement for supporting smart city development. The traditional image of the public sector as the provider of welfare cannot cope with the complexity of an ICT-driven approach to urban sustainability, which requires the paradigm shift introduced by the era of open innovation (Chesbrough, 2003a, b; Chesbrough et al., 2006) and the idea that "a single organization cannot innovate in isolation" (Dahlander and Gann, 2010: 699). A "new urban governance" (Mason, 2007: 2366) is required to enable smart city development in which the public sector "has a new role of acting as a broker in the creation of value" (Jackson, 2001: 5) and becomes "an enabler, a catalytic agent facilitating provision and action by and through" (Stoker, 1998: 34) intersectoral collaborative partnerships (Deakin, 2014b; Schaffers et al., 2011; Walravens, 2015a). However, additional research is necessary to establish whether the number of strategic alliances affects the performance of the collaborative environment and if there is an optimal level of variety to reach (Dong and McCarthy, 2019).

When analyzing the evidence collected during the best practice analyses, it is also clear that smart city collaborative environments display many properties that resemble complex adaptive systems (Batty, 2008, 2013b; Martin and Sunley, 2007; McKelvey, 2004; Plsek and Greenhalgh, 2001), where innovation is "co-created interactively by participants of collaborative networks" (Russell and Smorodinskaya, 2018: 115). These properties include the following:

- Requisite variety and dispersed interaction: the system is composed of heterogeneous agents that are active in parallel.
- Continual adaptation and perpetual novelty: the system and the broader environment in which it is embedded co-evolve.
- Nested systems: multiple levels of organizations overlap.
- Iteration: small changes lead to larger effects.
- Openness: the boundary separating the system from the broader environment is indefinable.
- Inherent unpredictability and nonlinearity: the behavior of all actors is unpredictable over time, sensitive to small changes, and often nonlinear.

Smart city collaborative environments are not fixed, but continually adapt in and evolve with the broader urban environment that they are part of. This mutual influence is evident when looking at the alignment between ICT solutions and urban challenges that adapt to ever-shifting sustainability priorities. Therefore, collaborative environments for enabling smart city development and the broader urban environment strongly influence each other, but the boundary dividing these two entities is not easily definable. This is because smart city collaborative environments are open, inclusive, and composed of a large number of heterogeneous actors that can be located everywhere, either internally or externally to the outer limits of the urban environment. These actors represent different institutional contexts (government, research and education, industry, and civil society), and they work in parallel, usually in subgroups, and the order of the collaborative environment depends upon their mutually self-reinforcing interactions. These interactions create an innovation system where (1) values, expectations, and resources belonging to different actors are brought together and aligned to create value for all the participants and (2) bottom-up and top-down forces are complementary in nature and instigate evolutionary processes that sustain urban development.

The multiple-case study analyses demonstrate that adopting an open and inclusive quadruple-helix approach to the design and implementation process of smart city development strategies allows cities to simultaneously engage with top-down and bottom-up development, whose combination is key to looking beyond the corporate smart city model. In this process, the active involvement of citizens and their knowledge resources, entrepreneurial spirit, and problem-solving skills have emerged as critical assets and a valuable layer of intelligence (Gooch et al., 2015). But the analysis also demonstrates that, to be effective, this involvement needs to go beyond "citizens participating in computational sensing and monitoring practices" (Gabrys, 2014: 32) and rhetoric-based discourses (Cardullo and Kitchin, 2018; Cardullo et al., 2019; Shelton and Lodato, 2019).

This book's investigation shows that citizens can have different roles (Berntzen and Johannessen, 2016) and tend to participate in shaping smart city development strategies by acting as (1) users who test ICT solutions and provide feedback; (2) developers of new digital services of public interest for assembling the platform of ICT solutions to urban issues; and (3) residents who help frame their city's smart city development strategy by reporting on their ideas, needs, and knowledge of urban challenges. In addition, the investigation makes clear that drawing from and collaborating with civil society requires cities to confront the exclusion that the digital divide and lack of digital literacy can generate (Vanolo, 2014) and to help citizens understand and benefit from the possibilities that smart city development introduces (Capdevila and Zarlenga, 2015; Hemment and Townsend, 2013; IET, 2016; Thomas et al., 2016).

Overall, despite some differences in the degree of involvement that surface when comparing the case studies, the contribution offered by citizens has always proven tangible and critical in supporting smart city development in every city. However, the results also provide additional evidence suggesting that citizen participation in the smart city domain is circumscribed (Cardullo and Kitchin, 2019; IET, 2016; Shelton and Lodato, 2019). When looking at the programs of activities composing the four smart city development strategies, groups of citizens are found engaged in the development of the technological infrastructure (Building block C) and the production of ICT services and applications that are deployed to address urban sustainability challenges (Building block D), but their input becomes very limited when related to the decision-making process for setting up the collaborative environment (Building block A) and citywide strategic framework (Building block B). The latter components result mainly from the action of representatives of the triple helix, in particular the city government.

This shortcoming has led many commenters to question the democratic value of smart city development strategies (Cardullo and Kitchin, 2018; Cardullo et al., 2019; Cowley et al., 2018; Gardner and Hespanhol, 2018; Joss et al., 2017; Shelton and Lodato, 2019) and carries the risk of assembling strategic approaches that grow "without sufficient insight into what people actually want them to deliver" (IET, 2016: 2). Therefore, much more should be done to involve the public and improve the synergy between the four helixes, but this requires an improved understanding of what organizational challenges affect this synergy (Mendoza Moheno et al., 2017) and what public engagement mechanisms are most suitable to support effective participation practices and foster deliberative democracy in the smart city domain (Valdez et al., 2018).

"A theory or model that predicts or describes how to enable effective involvement" (Rowe and Frewer, 2005: 252) in smart city development practice is still missing, as well as tailored tools and techniques for assessing the degree to which smart city development strategies reflect the expectations of all the institutional actors involved, including the public. Only a few experiments can be cited that have tried to overcome this gap by testing the use of stakeholder analysis techniques (Mayangsari and Novani, 2015) and multicriteria analysis methodologies in the smart city domain (Kourtit et al., 2014; Lombardi et al., 2012; Brorström et al., 2018). However, despite proving beneficial in supporting decision-making processes in different sectors (Bryson, 1988, 1995; Bryson and Anderson, 2000; Caniato et al., 2014; Tzeng et al., 2005), the use of these strategic planning tools has not yet found large application in the field of smart cities. This shortfall points out the lack of strategy affecting smart city development theory and practice, a key limitation that is discussed in the following section of the chapter.

7.2.3 Strategizing and operationalizing the smart city

While analyzing the conceptualization and design phases of mobile collaborative systems, Herskovic et al. (2011) explain that developers tend to consider only some requirements, which they consider critical, without realizing either the presence or the importance of many others. The existence of this shortcoming is also highlighted by Rey et al. (2012) and Sahai et al. (2005), whose attention shifts from computer science to public health. Their research demonstrates that the statistics on gastroparesis and injuries can be affected by unrecognized or hidden cases that are not documented, and the wrong statistical representation resulting from this lack of insight can be critical enough to mislead decision-making processes. In these studies, this phenomenon is called the "Iceberg effect": only a few factors affecting an event or situation are visible to those observing and analyzing it, while most factors remain hidden, and these might include some of the most critical (see Fig. 7.2).

The iceberg effect represents one of the main limitations of smart city theory and practice. This is because the utopian thinking of the corporate sector that

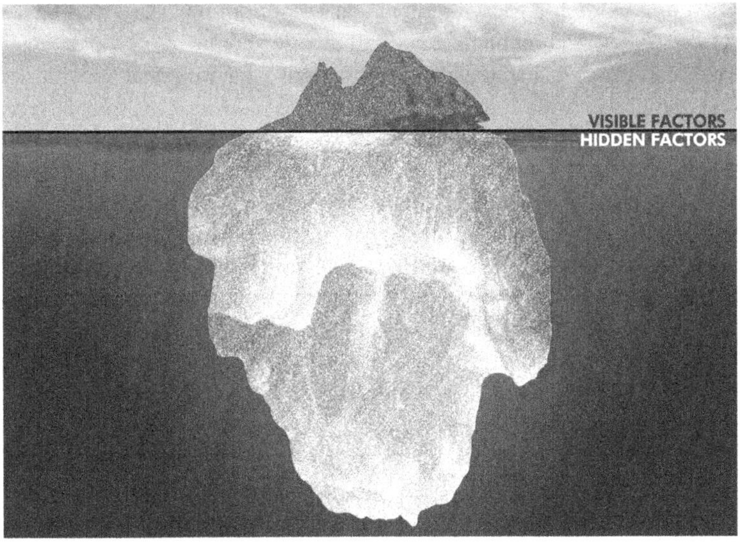

FIG. 7.2 The iceberg effect.

fuels the technocentric image has inhibited any serious investigation into the social shaping of smart cities. Over the past 30 years, the social has been kept out of sight, as a factor that remains below the waterline and does not influence the effectiveness of smart city development. As a result, a number of smart city development paths have grown, which have proved incapable of enabling an ICT-driven approach to urban sustainability due to the tendency they have exposed to underestimate the nontechnical components of smart cities (Angelidou, 2014; Ben Letaifa, 2015; Bolici and Mora, 2015; Mora and Bolici, 2016, 2017; Nam and Pardo, 2011a; Schaffers et al., 2011; Yigitcanlar et al., 2019).

The case study analyses reported on in this book demonstrate that strategizing smart city development practice is essential to cope with the complexity of a sociotechnical transformation that is triggered by the alignment between technological development and human, social, cultural, economic, and environmental factors. In addition, the findings clearly show that this alignment can be achieved only when the following strategic principles are embraced:

- looking beyond technology
- moving towards a quadruple-helix collaborative model
- combining top-down (government-led) and bottom-up (community-driven) development
- building a smart city strategic framework
- establishing a smart city accelerator
- adopting an integrated intervention logic

The results of the analyses demonstrate that the adoption of this initial set of strategic principles, which future research requires to expand, is effective in helping cities assemble four complementary building blocks, which have now surfaced as the core components of smart city developments.

The first building block is the collaborative environment previously described, which is required to bring together the industry-government-research relationships of the triple-helix and civil society (Deakin, 2014a; Deakin and Leydesdorff, 2014; Komninos, 2014; Schaffers et al., 2011). Evidence from the analyses suggests building such an environment requires to encourage public-private collaboration and raise the active involvement of civil society in the smart city domain, stimulate bottom-up development processes exploiting ICT-related innovations, increase digital literacy, and improve the level of understanding of city stakeholders on the benefits that smart city development can generate.

The second building block is a comprehensive strategic framework for regulating the adoption of the smart city approach to urban sustainability, which is developed to link "longer term strategic planning to short-term thinking" (Batty, 2013a: 274) and guide the efforts of individuals and organizations involved in this "community-led transition" (Deakin and Al Wear, 2011: 144) in the same direction. The strategic framework should be developed through a consensus-building process led by the local government and (1) provide long-term vision; (2) establish the objectives to be achieved through the deployment of ICT solutions; (3) suggest the main application domains and urban sustainability issues to focus attention on; (4) establish standards, technical requirements, and methods for evaluating both results and progress; and (5) set up the governance system necessary to regulate the transition to a smart city approach to urban sustainability. This governance system includes a working group dedicated to accelerating the progressive transformation of the city in a smart environment. This working group, which has been called smart city accelerator, can be embedded in the city government's organizational structure or take the form of a public-private organization with independent legal identity.

The third building block is a city-scale network infrastructure composed of hardware and software resources. This technological infrastructure is required to support data transmission and provide city users with access to ICT services and applications deployed to address urban sustainability issues. These digital solutions shape the last building block of smart cities, and their uptake should be based on an integrated intervention logic that cuts across a multitude of application domains, whose selection depends on the sustainability issues of local communities.

The contribution that this investigation offers in extending the theory underpinning smart city development practice is significant. However, additional research is needed to understand whether the validity of the strategic principles and insight into the architecture of smart cities that this book captures can be extended beyond Europe and North America. Conducting additional research into the design and implementation of smart city development strategies is needed urgently and will be instrumental in enabling peer-learning and knowledge transfer processes able to support evidence-based decision-making. A large number of cities across the world are working on strategies for enabling smart city development. Gathering, codifying, and sharing the know-how produced by these real-life experiences, in the form of good practices and recommendations, is key to successfully dealing with the ambiguity surrounding smart city development practice. This knowledge can be exploited to create the conditions for continuous learning and accelerate the adoption of smart city development, in which strategic planning can provide a significant contribution.

As already pointed out in the previous chapters, strategic planning for smart cities continues to remain a largely unexplored knowledge domain (Angelidou, 2014), and the research that attempts to model and operationalize smart city development strategies is still in progress. Expanding these two research areas is key to develop decision-making support tools, which practitioners can effectively deploy, and to succeed in dealing with the existing knowledge gap dividing theory and practice that the dichotomous nature of smart city research has contributed to engender. Significant efforts will be necessary to meet this target, but the results obtained so far suggest research is lagging behind and does not meet the expectations of the stakeholders actively engaged in smart city development practice.

The work conducted by the British Standards Institution (BSI) is one of the most discussed attempts to operationalize the smart city approach to urban sustainability (Caird, 2018; Caird and Hallett, 2019; Joss et al., 2017) and build the missing "interface between research, policy, and practice" (Joss et al., 2017: 30). After a 5-year open consultation process with city leaders and key experts, BSI has released a suite of ISO standards that offer a common conceptual and practical interpretation of smart city development that intend to improve decision-making. However, despite being an extremely advanced example of a decision support system for smart city development strategies, these standards display "unresolved issues and some persistent contradictions" (Joss et al., 2017: 29) and do not possess the level of detail that is necessary to provide a comprehensive and in-depth understanding of how the strategic process leading to successful smart city developments should be assembled as a step-wise logic.

Further studies have been conducted to overcome this knowledge gap (see Ben Letaifa, 2015; Bolici and Mora, 2015; Komninos, 2014; Mora and Bolici, 2016, 2017; Zygiaris, 2013). But notwithstanding the significance of the output produced by these studies, which have provided some of the first roadmaps and planning frameworks for smart city development strategies, their preliminary nature is still evident (Lee et al., 2014), especially in relation to evaluation and reporting methodologies (Caird and Hallett, 2019; Kourtit et al., 2014; Lombardi et al., 2012). This opens up new possibilities for future collaborative and interdisciplinary research aimed at tracing pathways able to transform the utopian smart cities of the corporate sector into innovation systems capable of nurturing a technology-enabled urban sustainability.

References

Acuto, M., 2018. Global science for city policy. Science 359 (6372), 165–166.

Acuto, M., Parnell, S., Seto, K.C., 2018. Building a global urban science. Nat. Sustain. 1, 2–4.

Adams, R., Jeanrenaud, S., Bessant, J., Denyer, D., Overy, P., 2016. Sustainability-oriented innovation: a systematic review. Int. J. Manag. Rev. 18, 180–205.

Ahvenniemi, H., Huovila, A., Pinto-Seppä, I., Airaksinen, M., 2017. What are the differences between sustainable and smart cities? Cities: Int. J. Urban Policy Plan. 60, 234–245.

Aibar, E., Bijker, W.E., 1997. Constructing a city: the Cerdà plan for the extension of Barcelona. Sci. Technol. Hum. Values 22 (1), 3–30.

Angelidou, M., 2014. Smart city policies: a spatial approach. Cities: Int. J. Urban Policy Plan. 41 (Supplement 1), S3–S11.

Ann Keller, S., Koonin, S.E., Shipp, S., 2012. Big data and city living—what can it do for us? Significance 9 (4), 4–7.

Arellano-Gault, D., Demortain, D., Rouillard, C., Thoenig, J., 2013. Bringing public organization and organizing back in. Organ. Stud. 34 (2), 145–167.

Aslani, A., Mazzuca-Sobczuk, T., Eivazi, S., Bekhrad, K., 2018. Analysis of bioenergy technologies development based on life cycle and adaptation trends. Renew. Energy 127, 1076–1086.

Bai, X., Surveyer, A., Elmqvist, T., Gatzweiler, F.W., Guneralp, B., Parnell, S., Prieur-Richard, A., Shrivastava, P., Siri, J.G., Stafford-Smith, M., Toussaint, J., Webb, R., 2016. Defining and advancing a systems approach for sustainable cities. Curr. Opin. Environ. Sustain. 23, 69–78.

Batty, M., 2008. The size, scale, and shape of cities. Science 319 (5864), 769–771.

Batty, M., 2013a. Big data, smart cities and city planning. Dialog. Hum. Geogr. 3 (3), 274–279.

Batty, M., 2013b. The New Science of Cities. The MIT Press, Cambridge, MA.

Batty, M., Axhausen, K.W., Giannotti, F., Pozdnoukhov, A., Bazzani, A., Wachowicz, M., Ouzounis, G., Portugali, Y., 2012. Smart cities of the future. Eur. Phys. J. Special Top. 214 (1), 481–518.

Ben Letaifa, S., 2015. How to strategize smart cities: revealing the SMART model. J. Bus. Res. 68 (7), 1414–1419.

Berntzen, L., Johannessen, M.R., 2016. The role of citizen participation in municipal smart city projects: lessons learned from Norway. In: Gil-Garcia, J.R., Pardo, T.A., Nam, T. (Eds.), Smarter as the New Urban Agenda: A Comprehensive View of the 21st Century City. Springer, Cham, pp. 299–314.

Bijker, W.E., 2008. Social construction of technology. In: Donsbach, W. (Ed.), The International Encyclopedia of Communication. John Wiley & Sons, Chichester, pp. 1–5.

Bijker, W.E., 2010. How is technology made?—That is the question! Camb. J. Econ. 34 (1), 63–76.

Bijker, W.E., Law, J. (Eds.), 1992. Shaping Technology/Building Society: Studies in Sociotechnical Change. MIT Press, Cambridge, MA.

Birbi, S.E., Krogstie, J., 2017. On the social shaping dimensions of smart sustainable cities: a study in science, technology, and society. Sustain. Cities Soc. 29, 219–246.

Bolici, R., Mora, L., 2015. Urban regeneration in the digital era: how to develop smart city strategies in large European cities. TECHNE: J. Technol. Architect. Environ. 5 (2), 110–119.

Borup, M., Brown, N., Konrad, K., Van Lente, H., 2006. The sociology of expectations in science and technology. Tech. Anal. Strat. Manag. 18 (3-4), 285–298.

Boyer, R.H.W., 2015. Grassroots innovation for urban sustainability: comparing the diffusion pathways of three Ecovillage projects. Environ. Plan. A: Econ. Space 45, 320–337.

Brorström, S., Argento, D., Grossi, G., Thomasson, A., Almqvist, R., 2018. Translating sustainable and smart city strategies into performance measurement systems. Publ. Money Manage. 38 (3), 193–202.

Brown, N., Michael, M., 2003. A sociology of expectations: retrospecting prospects and prospecting retrospects. Tech. Anal. Strat. Manag. 15 (1), 3–18.

Bryson, J.M., 1988. A strategic planning process for public and non-profit organizations. Long Range Plan. 21 (1), 73–81.

Bryson, J.M., 1995. Strategic Planning for Public and Non-profit Organizations: A Guide to Strengthening and Sustaining Organizational Achievement. Jossey-Bass, San Francisco, CA.

Bryson, J.M., Anderson, S.R., 2000. Applying large-group interaction methods in the planning and implementation of major change efforts. Public Adm. Rev. 60 (2), 143–162.

Caird, S., 2018. City approaches to smart city evaluation and reporting: case studies in the United Kingdom. Urban Res. Pract. 11 (2), 159–179.

Caird, S., Hallett, S.H., 2019. Towards evaluation design for smart city development. J. Urban Des. 24 (2), 188–209.

Campani, M., Vaglio, R., 2015. A simple interpretation of the growth of scientific/technological research impact leading to hype-type evolution curves. Scientometrics 103 (1), 75–83.

Caniato, M., Vaccari, M., Visvanathan, C., Zurbrügg, C., 2014. Using social network and stakeholder analysis to help evaluate infectious waste management: a step towards a holistic assessment. Waste Manag. 34 (5), 938–951.

Capdevila, I., Zarlenga, M.I., 2015. Smart city or smart citizens? The Barcelona case. J. Strateg. Manag. 8 (3), 266–282.

Caragliu, A., Del Bo, C., Nijkamp, P., 2011. Smart cities in Europe. J. Urban Technol. 18 (2), 65–82.

Cardullo, P., Kitchin, R., 2018. Smart urbanism and smart citizenship: the neoliberal logic of 'citizen-focused' smart cities in Europe. Environ. Plan. C: Polit. Space https://doi.org/10.1177/0263774X18806508.

Cardullo, P., Kitchin, R., 2019. Being a 'citizen' in the smart city: up and down the scaffold of smart citizen participation in Dublin, Ireland. GeoJournal 84 (1), 1–13.

Cardullo, P., Kitchin, R., Di Feliciantonio, C., 2019. Living labs and vacancy in the neoliberal city. Cities: Int. J. Urban Policy Plan. 73, 44–50.

Castelnovo, W., Misuraca, G., Savoldelli, A., 2016. Smart cities governance: the need for a holistic approach to assessing urban participatory policy making. Soc. Sci. Comput. Rev. 34 (6), 724–739.

Chesbrough, H., 2003a. Open Innovation: The New Imperative for Creating and Profiting From Technology. Harvard Business Press, Boston, MA.

Chesbrough, H., 2003b. The logic of open innovation: managing intellectual property. Calif. Manag. Rev. 45 (3), 33–58.

Chesbrough, H., Vanhaverbeke, W., West, J. (Eds.), 2006. Open Innovation: Researching a New Paradigm. Oxford University Press, Oxford.

Colding, J., Barthel, S., 2017. An urban ecology critique on the "smart city" model. J. Clean. Prod. 164, 95–101.

Cowley, R., Joss, S., Dayot, Y., 2018. The smart city and its publics: insights from across six UK cities. Urban Res. Pract. 11 (1), 53–77.

Dahlander, L., Gann, D.M., 2010. How open is innovation? Res. Policy 39, 699–709.

Datta, A., 2015a. A 100 smart cities, a 100 utopias. Dialog. Hum. Geogr. 5 (1), 49–53.

Datta, A., 2015b. New urban utopias of postcolonial India: entrepreneurial urbanization in Dholera smart city, Gujarat. Dialog. Hum. Geogr. 5 (1), 3–22.

Deakin, M., 2014a. Smart cities: the state-of-the-art and governance challenge. Triple Helix 1 (7), 1–16.

Deakin, M. (Ed.), 2014b. Smart Cities: Governing, Modelling and Analysing the Transition. Routledge, New York City, NY.

Deakin, M., Al Wear, H., 2011. From intelligent to smart cities. Intell. Build. Int. 3 (3), 140–152.

Deakin, M., Leydesdorff, L., 2014. The Triple Helix model of smart cities: a neo-evolutionary perspective. In: Deakin, M. (Ed.), Smart Cities: Governing, Modelling and Analyzing the Transition. Routledge, New York, NY, pp. 134–149.

Dedehayir, O., Steinert, M., 2016. The hype cycle model: a review and future directions. Technol. Forecast. Social Change 108, 28–41.

Díaz-Díaz, R., Muñoz, L., Pérez-González, D., 2017. The business model evaluation tool for smart cities: application to SmartSantander use cases. Energies 10, 262–292.

Dixon, T., Montgomery, J., Horton-Baker, N., Farrelly, L., 2018. Using urban foresight techniques in city visioning: lessons from the reading 2050 vision. Local Econ.: J. Local Econ. Policy Unit 33 (9), 777–799.

Dong, J.Q., McCarthy, K.J., 2019. When more isn't Merrier: pharmaceutical alliance networks and breakthrough innovation. Drug Discov. Today 24 (3), 673–677.

Fenn, J., Raskino, M., 2008. Mastering the Hype Cycle: How to Choose the Right Innovation at the Right Time. Harvard Business Press, Boston, MA.

Gabrys, J., 2014. Programming environments: environmentality and citizen sensing in the smart city. Environ. Plan. D: Soc. Space 32 (1), 30–48.

Gardner, N., Hespanhol, L., 2018. SMLXL: scaling the smart city, from metropolis to individual. City Cult. Soc. 12, 54–61.

Geels, F., Raven, R., 2006. Non-linearity and expectations in niche-development trajectories: ups and downs in dutch biogas development (1973–2003). Tech. Anal. Strat. Manag. 18 (3-4), 375–392.

Ghubril, A. C., & Prentice, S. (2014). Hype Cycle for Human-Computer Interaction, 2014. Gartner. https://www.gartner.com/doc/2822817/hype-cycle-humancomputer-interaction (Accessed 10.09.2017).

Goldenberg, J., Libai, B., Muller, E., 2002. Riding the saddle: how cross-market communications can create a major slump in sales. J. Mark. 66 (2), 1–16.

Gooch, D., Wolff, A., Kortuem, G., Brown, R., 2015. Reimagining the role of citizens in smart city projects. In: UbiComp/ISWC'15 Adjunct: Adjunct Proceedings of the 2015 ACM International Joint Conference on Pervasive and Ubiquitous Computing and Proceedings of the 2015 ACM International Symposium on Wearable Computers, Osaka, 7–11 September 2015. ACM Press, New York, NY, pp. 1587–1594.

Grossi, G., Pianezzi, D., 2017. Smart cities: utopia or neoliberal ideology? Cities: Int. J. Urban Policy Plan. 69, 79–85.

Hara, M., Nagao, T., Hannoe, S., Nakamura, J., 2016. New key performance indicators for a smart sustainable city. Sustainability 8 (3), 1–19.

Hemment, D., Townsend, A. (Eds.), 2013. Smart Citizens. FutureEverything, Manchester.

Herskovic, V., Ochoa, S.F., Pino, J.A., Neyem, A., 2011. The Iceberg effect: behind the user interface of mobile collaborative systems. J. Univ. Comput. Sci. 17 (2), 183–202.

Hollands, R.G., 2008. Will the real smart city please stand up? City: Anal. Urban Trends Cult. Theory Policy Action 12 (3), 303–320.

Hollands, R.G., 2015. Critical interventions into the corporate smart city. Camb. J. Reg. Econ. Soc. 8 (1), 61–77.

Hommels, A., 2005. Unbuilding Cities: Obduracy in Urban Sociotechnical Change. MIT Press, Cambridge, MA.

IET (2016). Smart Cities: Time to Involve the People?. The Institution of Engineering and Technology (IET). https://www.theiet.org/impact-society/factfiles/built-environment/smart-cities/. (Accessed 10.12.2018).

Jackson, P.M., 2001. Public sector added value: can bureaucracy deliver? Publ. Adm. 79 (1), 5–28.

Järvenpää, H.M., Mäkinen, S.J., 2008. An empirical study of the existence of the hype cycle: a case of DVD technology. In: 2008 IEEE International Engineering Management Conference, Europe: Managing Engineering, Technology and Innovation for Growth, Estoril, 28–30 June 2008. Institute of Electrical and Electronics Engineers (IEEE), Piscataway, NJ, pp. 1–5.

Johnson, P., Robinson, P., 2014. Civic Hackathons: innovation, procurement, or civic engagement? Rev. Policy Res. 31 (4), 349–357.

Joss, S., Cook, M., Dayot, Y., 2017. Smart cities: towards a new citizenship regime? A discourse analysis of the British smart city standard. J. Urban Technol. 24 (4), 29–49.

Jun, S., 2012. A comparative study of hype cycles among actors within the socio-technical system: with a focus on the case study of hybrid cars. Technol. Forecast. Social Change 79, 1413–1430.

Kagan, S., Hauerwaas, A., Holz, V., Wedler, P., 2018. Culture in sustainable urban development: practices and policies for spaces of possibility and institutional innovations. City Cult. Soc. 13, 32–45.

Khodayaria, M., Aslani, A., 2018. Analysis of the energy storage technology using hype cycle approach. Sustain. Energy Technol. Assess. 25, 60–74.

Kim, T., Ramos, C., Mohammed, S., 2017. Smart city and IoT. Futur. Gener. Comput. Syst. 76, 159–162.

Kitchin, R., 2014. The real-time city? Big data and smart urbanism. GeoJournal 79 (1), 1–14.

Kitchin, R., 2015. Making sense of smart cities: addressing present shortcomings. Camb. J. Reg. Econ. Soc. 8 (1), 131–136.

Klopp, J.M., Petretta, D.L., 2017. The urban sustainable development goal: indicators, complexity and the politics of measuring cities. Cities: Int. J. Urban Policy Plan. 63, 92–97.

Komninos, N., 2014. The Age of Intelligent Cities: Smart Environments and Innovation-For-All Strategies. Routledge, New York City, NY.

Kornberger, M., Meyer, R.E., Brandtner, C., Höllerer, M.A., 2017a. When Bureaucracy Meets the Crowd: Studying "Open Government" in the Vienna City Administration. Organ. Stud. 38 (2), 179–200.

Kornberger, M., Meyer, R.E., Brandtner, C., Höllerer, M.A., 2017b. When bureaucracy meets the crowd: studying "open government" in the Vienna city administration. Organ. Stud. 38 (2), 179–200.

Kourtit, K., Deakin, M., Caragliu, A., Del Bo, C., Nijkamp, P., Lombardi, P., Giordano, S., 2014. An advanced triple helix network framework for smart cities performance. In: Deakin, M. (Ed.), Smart Cities: Governing, Modelling and Analyzing the Transition. Routledge, New York, NY, pp. 196–216.

Kriechbaum, M., López Prol, J., Posch, A., 2018. Looking back at the future: dynamics of collective expectations about photovoltaic technology in Germany & Spain. Technol. Forecast. Social Change 129, 76–87.

Lavine, M., 2010. What would A. G. Bell say now? Science 329 (5998), 1470.

Lee, J., Hancock, M.G., Hu, M., 2014. Towards an effective framework for building smart cities: lessons from Seoul and San Francisco. Technol. Forecast. Soc. Change 89, 80–99.

Leydesdorff, L., Deakin, M., 2011. The triple-helix model of smart cities: a neo-evolutionary perspective. J. Urban Technol. 18 (2), 53–63.

Lombardi, P., Giordano, S., Farouh, H., Yousef, W., 2012. Modelling the smart city performance. Innovation: Eur. J. Soc. Sci. Res. 25 (2), 137–149.

Luque-Ayala, A., Marvin, S., 2015. Developing a critical understanding of smart urbanism? Urban Stud. 52 (12), 2105–2116.

Ma, Y., Rong, K., Mangalagiu, D., Thornton, T.F., Zhu, D., 2018. Co-evolution between urban sustainability and business ecosystem innovation: evidence from the sharing mobility sector in Shanghai. J. Clean. Prod. 188, 942–953.

Macke, J., Casagrande, R.M., Sarate, J.A.R., Silva, K.A., 2018. Smart city and quality of life: citizens' perception in a Brazilian case study. J. Clean. Prod. 182, 717–726.

Mahajan, V., Muller, E., 1996. Timing, diffusion, and substitution of successive generations of technological innovations: the IBM mainframe case. Technol. Forecast. Soc. Change 51 (2), 109–132.

Marsal-Llacuna, M., Colomer-Llinàs, J., Meléndez-Frigola, J., 2015. Lessons in urban monitoring taken from sustainable and livable cities to better address the smart cities initiative. Technol. Forecast. Soc. Change 90, 611–622.

Martin, C.J., Evans, J., Karvonen, A., 2018. Smart and sustainable? Five tensions in the visions and practices of the smart-sustainable city in Europe and North America. Technol. Forecast. Social Change 133, 269–278.

Martin, R., Sunley, P., 2007. Complexity thinking and evolutionary economic geography. J. Econ. Geogr. 7 (5), 573–601.

Marvin, S., Luque-Ayala, A., McFarlane, C. (Eds.), 2016. Smart Urbanism: Utopian Vision or False Dawn? Routledge, New York City, NY.

Mason, M., 2007. Collaborative partnerships for urban development: a study of the vancouver agreement. Environ. Plan. A: Econ. Space 39 (10), 2366–2382.

Mayangsari, L., Novani, S., 2015. Multi-stakeholder co-creation analysis in smart city management: an experience from Bandung, Indonesia. Procedia Manuf. 4, 315–321.

McCormick, K., Kiss, B., 2015. Learning through renovations for urban sustainability: the case of the Malmö innovation platform. Curr. Opin. Environ. Sustain. 16, 44–50.

McKelvey, B., 2004. Toward a complexity science of entrepreneurship. J. Bus. Ventur. 19 (3), 313–341.

McNeill, D., 2015. Global firms and smart technologies: IBM and the reduction of cities. Trans. Inst. Br. Geogr. 40 (4), 562–574.

McNeill, D., 2016. Governing a city of unicorns: technology capital and the urban politics of San Francisco. Urban Geogr. 37 (4), 494–513.

Mendoza Moheno, J., Hernández Calzada, M.A., Salazar Hernández, B.C., 2017. Organizational challenges for building smart cities. In: Peris-Ortiz, M., Bennett, D.R., Pérez-Bustamante Yábar, D. (Eds.), Sustainable Smart Cities: Creating Spaces for Technological, Social and Business Development. Springer, Cham, pp. 89–99.

Mora, L., Bolici, R., 2016. The development process of smart city strategies: the case of Barcelona. In: Rajaniemi, J. (Ed.), Re-City: Future City—Combining Disciplines. Juvenes Print, Tampere, pp. 155–181.

Mora, L., Bolici, R., 2017. How to become a smart city: learning from Amsterdam. In: Bisello, A., Vettorato, D., Stephens, R., Elisei, P. (Eds.), Smart and Sustainable Planning for Cities and Regions: Results of SSPCR 2015. Springer, Cham, pp. 251–266.

Mora, L., Deakin, M., Reid, A., Angelidou, M., 2019. How to overcome the dichotomous nature of smart city research: proposed methodology and results of a pilot study. J. Urban Technol. 26 (2), 89–128.

Mosannenzadeh, F., Bisello, A., Vaccaro, R., D'Alonzo, V., Hunter, G.W., Vettorato, D., 2017. Smart energy city development: a story told by urban planners. Cities: Int. J. Urban Policy Plan. 64, 54–65.

Moulaert, F., Martinelli, F., González, S., Swyngedouw, E., 2007. Introduction. Social innovation and governance in European cities: urban development between path dependency and radical innovation. Eur. Urban. Region. Stud. 14 (3), 195–209.

Nam, T., Pardo, T.A., 2011a. Conceptualizing smart city with dimensions of technology, people and institutions. In: Bertot, J., Nahon, K., Chun, S.A., Luna-Reyes, L., Atluri, V. (Eds.), Proceedings of the 12th Annual International Conference on Digital Government Research: Digital Government Innovation in Challenging Times, College Park, MD, 12–15 June 2011. ACM Press, New York City, NY, pp. 282–291.

Nam, T., Pardo, T.A., 2011b. Smart city as urban innovation: focusing on management, policy, and context. In: Estevez, E., Janssen, M. (Eds.), Proceedings of the 5th International Conference on Theory and Practice of Electronic Governance (ICEGOV2011), Tallinn, 26–28 September 2011. ACM Press, New York City, NY, pp. 185–194.

O'Leary, D.E., 2008. Gartner's hype cycle and information system research issues. Int. J. Account. Inf. Syst. 9, 240–252.

Orlikowski, W.J., 1992. The duality of technology: rethinking the concept of technology in organizations. Organ. Sci. 3 (3), 398–427.

Phillips, F., 2007. On S-curves and tipping points. Technol. Forecast. Soc. Change 74 (6), 715–730.

Pinch, T.J., Bijker, W.E., 1984. The social construction of facts and artefacts: or how the sociology of science and the sociology of technology might benefit each other. Soc. Stud. Sci. 14 (3), 399–441.

Plsek, P.E., Greenhalgh, T., 2001. The challenge of complexity in health care. Br. Med. J. 323, 625–628.

Pollio, A., 2016. Technologies of austerity urbanism: the "smart city" agenda in Italy (2011–2013). Urban Geogr. 37 (4), 514–534.

Rey, E., Choung, R.S., Schleck, C.D., Zinsmeister, A.R., Talley, N.J., Locke, G.R., 2012. Prevalence of hidden gastroparesis in the community: the gastroparesis "Iceberg". J. Neurogastroenterol. Motil. 18 (1), 34–42.

Rogers, E.M., 2003. Diffusion of Innovations, fifth ed. Free Press, New York City, NY.

Rowe, G., Frewer, L.J., 2005. A typology of public engagement mechanisms. Sci. Technol. Hum. Values 30 (2), 251–290.

Ruef, A., Markard, J., 2010. What happens after a hype? How changing expectations affected innovation activities in the case of stationary fuel cells. Tech. Anal. Strat. Manag. 22 (3), 317–338.

Russell, M.G., Smorodinskaya, N.V., 2018. Leveraging complexity for ecosystemic innovation. Technol. Forecast. Social Change 136, 114–131.

Sahai, V.S., Ward, M.S., Zmijowskyj, T., Rowe, B.H., 2005. Quantifying the Iceberg effect for injury: using comprehensive community health data. Can. J. Publ. Health 96 (5), 328–332.

Sauer, S., 2012. Do smart cities produce smart entrepreneurs? J. Theor. Appl. Electron. Commer. Res. 7 (3), 63–73.

Schaffers, H., Komninos, N., Pallot, M., Trousse, B., Nilsson, M., Oliveira, A., 2011. Smart cities and the future internet: towards cooperation frameworks for open innovation. In: Domingue, J., Galis, A., Gavras, A., Zahariadis, T., Lambert, D., Cleary, F., Daras, P., Krco, S., Muller, H., Li, M., Schaffers, H., Lotz, V., Alvarez, F., Stiller, B., Karnouskos, S., Avessta, S., Nillson, M. (Eds.), The Future Internet. Future Internet Assembly 2011: Achievements and Technological Promises. Springer, Berlin, pp. 431–446.

Shelton, T., Lodato, T., 2019. Actually existing smart citizens: expertise and (non)participation in the making of the smart city. City: Anal. Urban Trends Cult. Theory Policy Action 23 (1), 35–52.

Shelton, T., Zook, M., Wiig, A., 2015. The 'actually existing smart city'. Camb. J. Reg. Econ. Soc. 8 (1), 13–25.

Silvestrini, P., Amato, U., Vettoliere, A., Silvestrini, S., Ruggiero, B., 2017. Rate equation leading to hype-type evolution curves: a mathematical approach in view of analysing technology development. Technol. Forecast. Social Change 116, 1–12.

Snow, C.C., Håkonsson, D.D., Obel, B., 2016. A smart city is a collaborative community: lessons from smart Aarhus. Calif. Manag. Rev. 59 (1), 92–108.

Soderstrom, O., Paasche, T., Klauser, F., 2014. Smart cities as corporate storytelling. City: Anal. Urban Trends Cult. Theory Policy Action 18 (3), 307–320.

Stoker, G., 1998. Public-private partnerships and urban governance. In: Pierre, J. (Ed.), Partnerships in Urban Governance: European and American Experiences. Palgrave, New York City, NY, pp. 34–51.

Sumic, Z., Harrison, K., Moore, C., Steenstrup, K., Koslowski, T., & Pescatore, J. (2009). Hype Cycle for Utility Industry Operational and Energy Technologies, 2009. Gartner. https://www.gartner.com/doc/1077912/hype-cycle-utility-industry-operational. (Accessed 10.09.2017).

Thomas, V., Wang, D., Mullagh, L., Dunn, N., 2016. Where's Wally? In search of citizen perspectives on the smart city. Sustainability 8 (3), 207–220.

Tzeng, G., Lin, C., Opricovic, S., 2005. Multi-criteria analysis of alternative-fuel buses for public transportation. Energy Policy 33 (11), 1373–1383.

Valdez, A., Cook, M., Potter, S., 2018. Roadmaps to utopia: tales of the smart city. Urban Stud. 55 (15), 3385–3403.

van Lente, H., Bakker, S., 2010. Competing expectations: the case of hydrogen storage technologies. Tech. Anal. Strat. Manag. 22 (6), 693–709.

van Lente, H., Spitters, C., Peine, A., 2013. Comparing technological hype cycles: towards a theory. Technol. Forecast. Soc. Change 80, 1615–1628.

van Waart, P., Mulder, I., de Bont, C., 2016. A participatory approach for envisioning a smart city. Soc. Sci. Comput. Rev. 34 (6), 708–723.

van Winden, W., van den Buuse, D., 2017. Smart city pilot projects: exploring the dimensions and conditions of scaling up. J. Urban Technol. 24 (4), 51–72.

van Zoonen, L., 2016. Privacy concerns in smart cities. Gov. Inf. Q. 33 (3), 472–480.

Vanolo, A., 2014. Smartmentality: the smart city as disciplinary strategy. Urban Stud. 51 (5), 883–898.

Voytenko, Y., McCormick, K., Evans, J., Schliwa, G., 2016. Urban living labs for sustainability and low carbon cities in Europe: towards a research Agenda. J. Clean. Prod. 123, 45–54.

Walravens, N., 2015a. Mobile city applications for Brussels citizens: smart city trends, challenges and a reality check. Telematics Inform. 32 (2), 282–299.

Walravens, N., 2015b. Qualitative indicators for smart city business models: the case of mobile services and applications. Telecommun. Policy 39 (3-4), 218–240.

Wiig, A., 2015. IBM's smart city as techno-utopian policy mobility. City: Anal. Urban Trends Cult. Theory Policy Action 19 (2-3), 258–273.

Wiig, A., 2016. The empty rhetoric of the smart city: from digital inclusion to economic promotion in Philadelphia. Urban Geogr. 37 (4), 535–553.

Williams, R., Edge, D., 1996. The social shaping of technology. Res. Policy 25, 865–899.

Woolley, A.W., Chabris, C.F., Pentland, A., Hashmi, N., Malone, T.W., 2010. Evidence for a collective intelligence factor in the performance of human groups. Science 330 (6004), 686–688.

Woolthuis, R.K., Lankhuizen, M., Gilsing, V., 2005. A system failure framework for innovation policy design. Technovation 25, 609–619.

Wu, Y., Zhang, W., Shen, J., Mo, Z., Peng, Y., 2018. Smart city with chinese characteristics against the background of big data: idea, action and risk. J. Clean. Prod. 173, 60–66.

Yigitcanlar, T., Kamruzzaman, M., 2018. Does smart city policy lead to sustainability of cities? Land Use Policy 73, 49–58.

Yigitcanlar, T., Kamruzzaman, M., Foth, M., Sabatini-Marques, J., da Costa, E., Ioppolo, G., 2019. Can cities become smart without being sustainable? A systematic review of the literature. Sustain. Cities Soc. 45, 348–365.

Zygiaris, S., 2013. Smart city reference model: assisting planners to conceptualize the building of smart city innovation ecosystems. J. Knowl. Econ. 4 (2), 217–231.

Appendix A

See Tables A.1–A.4.

TABLE A.1 Amsterdam's smart city development strategy: activities by category and application domain

Activity		Category				Application domain											
ID code	Name	A	B	C	D	C.01	C.02	C.03	C.04	C.05	C.06	C.07	C.08	C.09	C.10	C.11	C.12
AMS.ACT.0001	3D Print Canal House			X							X						
AMS.ACT.0002	Amstel 3D Pilot			X												X	
AMS.ACT.0003	Amsterdam ArenA			X			X				X						
AMS.ACT.0004	Amsterdam ArenA Innovation Center	X															
AMS.ACT.0005	Amsterdam free Wi-fi				X												
AMS.ACT.0006	Amsterdam Rainproof	X															
AMS.ACT.0007	**Amsterdam Smart Citizens Lab**	X	X														
AMS.ACT.0008	Amsterdam Smart City		X														
AMS.ACT.0009	AmsterdamOpent.nl	X		X												X	
AMS.ACT.0010	Amsterdamse Zoncoalitie	X															
AMS.ACT.0011	**Apollon**	X	X														

AMS.ACT.0012	**Apps for Amsterdam**	X															
AMS.ACT.0013	**Apps4EU**	X	X														
AMS.ACT.0014	**Arrowhead**			X		X					X						
AMS.ACT.0015	**Besmettelijke Buurtkracht 2.0**	X															
AMS.ACT.0016	Fuel cell technology		X	X							X						
AMS.ACT.0017	**Buiksloterham**	X	X														
AMS.ACT.0018	**Sustainable Neighborhood Geuzenveld**	X		X		X	X				X						
AMS.ACT.0019	**CITY-ZEN**	X	X	X		X	X				X						
AMS.ACT.0020	**CitySDK**	X		X	X					X							
AMS.ACT.0021	Civocracy			X												X	
AMS.ACT.0022	**Commons4EU**	X	X														
AMS.ACT.0023	Concept ICT-visie Amsterdam 2020		X														
AMS.ACT.0024	**D-CENT**			X													
AMS.ACT.0025	De Circulaire Metropool Amsterdam 2014–18		X														

Continued

TABLE A.1 Amsterdam's smart city development strategy: activities by category and application domain—cont'd

Activity		Category				Application domain											
ID code	Name	A	B	C	D	C.01	C.02	C.03	C.04	C.05	C.06	C.07	C.08	C.09	C.10	C.11	C.12
AMS.ACT.0026	The Digital Road Authority—Incident Management			X						X					X		
AMS.ACT.0027	The Green Canals of Amsterdam		X	X							X		X				
AMS.ACT.0028	**IJburg YOU decide**	X	X														
AMS.ACT.0029	**Digilab HvA**	X															
AMS.ACT.0030	**Digital city card**			X												X	
AMS.ACT.0031	Energy Atlas	X		X												X	
AMS.ACT.0032	Energetic Zuidoost	X	X														
AMS.ACT.0033	**Energy Management Haarlem**	X	X	X							X						
AMS.ACT.0034	Energy storage for households			X		X					X						
AMS.ACT.0035	European Strategy for Amsterdam		X														
AMS.ACT.0036	FIREBALL		X														
AMS.ACT.0037	Flexible street lighting			X		X											

AMS.ACT.0038	Self-sufficient Pampus		X	X							X						
AMS.ACT.0039	Municipal buildings			X		X	X				X						
AMS.ACT.0040	geWoonboot	X															
AMS.ACT.0041	Fiber to the Home for IJburg				X												
AMS.ACT.0042	**Health Lab**	X		X								X					
AMS.ACT.0043	The smart home			X				X			X						
AMS.ACT.0044	**iBeacon Living Lab**	X			X												
AMS.ACT.0045	**Icing Project**	X	X	X												X	
AMS.ACT.0046	**iCity**	X	X		X												
AMS.ACT.0047	**Idee voor je buurt (Change by Us in Amsterdam)**			X												X	
AMS.ACT.0048	IREEN	X	X														
AMS.ACT.0049	Ito Tower			X							X						
AMS.ACT.0050	**Climate street**	X	X	X		X	X		X	X	X						
AMS.ACT.0051	**Knowledge mile—Kennis straat**	X															
AMS.ACT.0052	Koplopers D-020	X															

Continued

TABLE A.1 Amsterdam's smart city development strategy: activities by category and application domain—cont'd

Activity		Category				Application domain											
ID code	Name	A	B	C	D	C.01	C.02	C.03	C.04	C.05	C.06	C.07	C.08	C.09	C.10	C.11	C.12
AMS.ACT.0053	Last mile logistics: Foodlogica			X			X			X							
AMS.ACT.0054	**MOBI.Europe**			X			X			X							
AMS.ACT.0055	Moet je Watt—Charging system			X		X				X							
AMS.ACT.0056	Molen van Sloten	X															
AMS.ACT.0057	Monumental buildings	X	X														
AMS.ACT.0058	**Beautiful, Smart, Sustainable Wildeman**	X	X														
AMS.ACT.0059	MX3D Bridge project			X							X						
AMS.ACT.0060	NxtCity Amsterdam	X															
AMS.ACT.0061	Oosterlicht, project of Zuiderlicht	X		X			X				X						
AMS.ACT.0062	**Open Cities**	X	X	X												X	
AMS.ACT.0063	OrangeGas		X														

AMS.ACT.0064	PICO—Tool Project for Innovative Communication and Design			X												X	
AMS.ACT.0065	**PLAYDECIDE Game at NEMO**	X															
AMS.ACT.0066	Ring-Ring	X															
AMS.ACT.0067	Smart Parking			X			X			X					X		
AMS.ACT.0068	Smart Work@ IJburg			X						X							X
AMS.ACT.0069	**Smart Schools Contest**	X		X												X	
AMS.ACT.0070	**Smart sports parks**	X		X							X						
AMS.ACT.0071	**Smart Students**	X															
AMS.ACT.0072	**Smart Challenge**	X		X			X				X						
AMS.ACT.0073	**Smart Citizen Kit**	X		X			X				X					X	
AMS.ACT.0074	**Smart Electric Energy Boat**		X	X		X				X	X						
AMS.ACT.0075	**Smart Entrepreneurial Lab**	X															
AMS.ACT.0076	Smart Lights in Metropolitan Areas			X		X											

Continued

TABLE A.1 Amsterdam's smart city development strategy: activities by category and application domain—cont'd

Activity		Category				Application domain											
ID code	Name	A	B	C	D	C.01	C.02	C.03	C.04	C.05	C.06	C.07	C.08	C.09	C.10	C.11	C.12
AMS.ACT.0077	Smart Living showroom	X															
AMS.ACT.0078	**Solar Gambling**	X															
AMS.ACT.0079	City distribution: Cargohopper			X			X			X					X		
AMS.ACT.0080	District heating and comfort cooling for Houthaven quarter			X		X	X				X						
AMS.ACT.0081	StartUpBootcamp Smart City and Living	X															
AMS.ACT.0082	Structuurvisie Amsterdam 2040: Economisch Sterk En Duurzaam		X														
AMS.ACT.0083	**SUPERHUB**		X	X			X			X							
AMS.ACT.0084	TPEX—Smart Airmiles			X			X			X							X
AMS.ACT.0085	Transformation Agenda for Low Carbon Cities	X	X														
AMS.ACT.0086	Urban Learning	X	X														
AMS.ACT.0087	**Vehicle2Grid**		X	X		X				X	X						

AMS.ACT.0088	Ship to grid			X		X	X			X							
AMS.ACT.0089	**Watt for Watt**	X															
AMS.ACT.0090	WEGO Car sharing			X						X							
AMS.ACT.0091	**West Orange**	X		X			X				X						
AMS.ACT.0092	Laws and regulations in Zuidoost		X														
AMS.ACT.0093	Yeller: share your taxi			X						X							
AMS.ACT.0094	Zaans warmtenet			X			X				X						
AMS.ACT.0095	ZO flexibel			X		X	X				X						
AMS.ACT.0096	Sunny Soccer Southern Light			X		X					X						
AMS.ACT.0097	Swimming pools	X		X			X				X						

A, community building; B, strategic framework; C, services and applications; D, digital infrastructure; C.01, energy networks; C.02, air; C.03, water; C.04, waste; C.05, mobility and transport; C.06, buildings and districts; C.07, health and social inclusion; C.08, cultural and recreation; C.09, education; C.10, public security and justice; C.11, e-government; C.12, others. Activities in bold: evidence of citizens' involvement.

TABLE A.2 Barcelona's smart city development strategy: activities by category and application domain

Activity		Category				Application domain											
ID code	Name	A	B	C	D	C.01	C.02	C.03	C.04	C.05	C.06	C.07	C.08	C.09	C.10	C.11	C.12
BAR. ACT.0001	apparkB			X			X			X						X	
BAR. ACT.0002	**Apps4bcn competition**	X															
BAR. ACT.0003	**Apps4bcn platform**	X		X												X	
BAR. ACT.0004	**Apps4EU**	X	X														
BAR. ACT.0005	Area DUM			X			X			X						X	
BAR. ACT.0006	**Arrowhead**			X		X					X						
BAR. ACT.0007	Barcelona's Smart City Strategy		X														
BAR. ACT.0008	Barcelona Wi-Fi				X												
BAR. ACT.0009	**BCN Apps Jam: Recicla**	X															

BAR. ACT.0010	BCN Contactless			X													X
BAR. ACT.0011	BCN Inclou			X								X				X	
BAR. ACT.0012	**Besos**	X	X	X		X	X			X	X					X	
BAR. ACT.0013	bigov Better City Indicators			X												X	
BAR. ACT.0014	Bústia Ciutadana	X		X												X	
BAR. ACT.0015	Cibernarium	X															
BAR. ACT.0016	City OS				X												
BAR. ACT.0017	**CitySDK**	X		X	X					X							
BAR. ACT.0018	CloudBCN	X		X												X	
BAR. ACT.0019	CloudOpting	X		X												X	
BAR. ACT.0020	Clue		X														

Continued

TABLE A.2 Barcelona's smart city development strategy: activities by category and application domain—cont'd

Activity		Category				Application domain											
ID code	Name	A	B	C	D	C.01	C.02	C.03	C.04	C.05	C.06	C.07	C.08	C.09	C.10	C.11	C.12
BAR. ACT.0021	**Commons4EU**	X	X														
BAR. ACT.0022	**D-CENT**			X												X	
BAR. ACT.0023	Dark fiber network				X												
BAR. ACT.0024	DC4Cities		X	X			X				X						
BAR. ACT.0025	EsclaTIC			X								X					
BAR. ACT.0026	eServices Platform (eTramits)			X												X	
BAR. ACT.0027	**Eunoia**	X	X	X			X			X							
BAR. ACT.0028	FIREBALL		X														
BAR. ACT.0029	Geoportal	X		X												X	
BAR. ACT.0030	Google Maps Transit			X						X						X	
BAR. ACT.0031	Govern Obert (GO!) portal	X		X												X	

BAR. ACT.0032	GrowSmarter			X		X	X		X	X	X						
BAR. ACT.0033	iBicing			X			X			X							
BAR. ACT.0034	**ICING Project**	X	X	X												X	
BAR. ACT.0035	**iCity**	X	X		X												
BAR. ACT.0036	idBCN			X												X	
BAR. ACT.0037	Insight		X	X												X	
BAR. ACT.0038	Live	X															
BAR. ACT.0039	Mapa Barcelona + Sostenible	X		X											X		
BAR. ACT.0040	Programa d'Actuació Municipal 2012–15		X														
BAR. ACT.0041	Mesura de Govern MES		X														
BAR. ACT.0042	Mesura de govern MITIC		X														

Continued

TABLE A.2 Barcelona's smart city development strategy: activities by category and application domain—cont'd

Activity		Category				Application domain											
ID code	Name	A	B	C	D	C.01	C.02	C.03	C.04	C.05	C.06	C.07	C.08	C.09	C.10	C.11	C.12
BAR. ACT.0043	Pla Director de les TIC		X														
BAR. ACT.0044	**MOLECULES**		X	X			X			X							
BAR. ACT.0045	**mSchool**	X															
BAR. ACT.0046	Oficina Virtual d'Atenció Ciutadana			X												X	
BAR. ACT.0047	**Open Cities**	X	X	X												X	
BAR. ACT.0048	Open-DAI			X												X	
BAR. ACT.0049	OpenData BCN	X		X												X	
BAR. ACT.0050	Pla Barcelona 2.0		X														
BAR. ACT.0051	Project Management Office (PMO)		X														
BAR. ACT.0052	**Projecte Radars**	X		X								X					

BAR. ACT.0053	Prometteo			X								X					
BAR. ACT.0054	Semàfors intel·ligents			X						X		X			X		
BAR. ACT.0055	Sensors' management platform		X		X												
BAR. ACT.0056	Sentilo: Plataforma de Sensors i Actuadors de Barcelona (PSAB)			X												X	
BAR. ACT.0057	Servei de teleassistència municipal			X								X				X	
BAR. ACT.0058	Sistema de aparcamiento inteligente			X			X			X						X	
BAR. ACT.0059	Situation room		X	X												X	
BAR. ACT.0060	**Smart Cities Hackathon**	X															
BAR. ACT.0061	**Smart Citizen Kit**	X		X			X				X					X	
BAR. ACT.0062	**Smart City App Hack**	X															

Continued

TABLE A.2 Barcelona's smart city development strategy: activities by category and application domain—cont'd

Activity		Category				Application domain											
ID code	Name	A	B	C	D	C.01	C.02	C.03	C.04	C.05	C.06	C.07	C.08	C.09	C.10	C.11	C.12
BAR. ACT.0063	Smart City Campus	X															
BAR. ACT.0064	Smart City Expo World Congress	X															
BAR. ACT.0065	**Smart education**	X															
BAR. ACT.0066	**Smart hort**	X															
BAR. ACT.0067	SmartBarcino			X									X				
BAR. ACT.0068	**smartCEM**		X				X			X							
BAR. ACT.0069	Smartquesina			X	X					X							
BAR. ACT.0070	**SUPERHUB**		X	X			X			X							
BAR. ACT.0071	Telegestió del reg			X				X									
BAR. ACT.0072	TMB Virtual			X						X						X	

BAR. ACT.0073	Transformation Agenda for Low Carbon Cities	X	X														
BAR. ACT.0074	**Urban Lab Challenge**	X															
BAR. ACT.0075	Urban Platform				X												
BAR. ACT.0076	**Vincles BCN**			X								X				X	
BAR. ACT.0077	**Virtual memory of the elder**	X		X								X	X				
BAR. ACT.0078	Wi-Fi vía pública				X												

A, community building; B, strategic framework; C, services and applications; D, digital infrastructure; C.01, energy networks; C.02, air; C.03, water; C.04, waste; C.05, mobility and transport; C.06, buildings and districts; C.07, health and social inclusion; C.08, cultural and recreation; C.09, education; C.10, public security and justice; C.11, e-government; C.12, others. Activities in bold: evidence of citizens' involvement.

TABLE A.3 Helsinki's smart city development strategy: activities by category and application domain

Activity		Category				Application domain											
ID code	Name	A	B	C	D	C.01	C.02	C.03	C.04	C.05	C.06	C.07	C.08	C.09	C.10	C.11	C.12
HEL. ACT.0001	**Apollon**	X	X														
HEL. ACT.0002	**Apps4EU**	X	X														
HEL. ACT.0003	**Arrowhead**			X		X					X						
HEL. ACT.0004	**CITYOPT**	X	X	X		X					X						
HEL. ACT.0005	**CitySDK**	X		X	X					X							
HEL. ACT.0006	**Commons4EU**	X	X														
HEL. ACT.0007	**D-CENT**			X													
HEL. ACT.0008	**Digital City Card**			X												X	
HEL. ACT.0009	EMPOWER		X	X			X			X						X	
HEL. ACT.0010	FIREBALL		X														

HEL. ACT.0011	Forum Virium Helsinki		X														
HEL. ACT.0012	Helsinki App Store			X												X	
HEL. ACT.0013	Helsinki ICT program 2015–17		X														
HEL. ACT.0014	**Helsinki Loves Developers**	X															
HEL. ACT.0015	Helsinki Region Infoshare	X		X												X	
HEL. ACT.0016	Helsinki region intelligent traffic services			X						X						X	
HEL. ACT.0017	**ICING Project**	X	X	X												X	
HEL. ACT.0018	m.hubi Platform			X						X						X	
HEL. ACT.0019	**Nappula**	X		X								X					
HEL. ACT.0020	**Open Cities**	X	X	X												X	
HEL. ACT.0021	**Open Finland Challenge**	X															

Continued

TABLE A.3 Helsinki's smart city development strategy: activities by category and application domain—cont'd

Activity		Category				Application domain											
ID code	Name	A	B	C	D	C.01	C.02	C.03	C.04	C.05	C.06	C.07	C.08	C.09	C.10	C.11	C.12
HEL. ACT.0022	**Open Helsinki—Hack at Home**	X															
HEL. ACT.0023	Raksa.info			X												X	
HEL. ACT.0024	**Save energy**	X	X	X						X						X	
HEL. ACT.0025	SAWE		X														
HEL. ACT.0026	Silver		X	X								X					
HEL. ACT.0027	**Smart City App Hack**	X															
HEL. ACT.0028	**Smart Urban Spaces**		X	X	X					X		X					
HEL. ACT.0029	**Street smart**	X		X									X			X	
HEL. ACT.0030	**SUPERHUB**		X	X			X			X							
HEL. ACT.0031	Traffic information platform			X						X						X	

HEL. ACT.0032	Ubiquitous Helsinki (Desktop HUBI.portal)			X						X						X	
HEL. ACT.0033	Urbanflow Helsinki			X	X											X	
HEL. ACT.0034	**Walk and Feel Helsinki**			X						X			X			X	

A, community building; B, strategic framework; C, services and applications; D, digital infrastructure; C.01, energy networks; C.02, air; C.03, water; C.04, waste; C.05, mobility and transport; C.06, buildings and districts; C.07, health and social inclusion; C.08, cultural and recreation; C.09, education; C.10, public security and justice; C.11, e-government; C.12, others. Activities in bold: evidence of citizens' involvement.

TABLE A.4 Vienna's smart city development strategy: activities by category and application domain

Activity		Category				Application domain											
ID code	Name	A	B	C	D	C.01	C.02	C.03	C.04	C.05	C.06	C.07	C.08	C.09	C.10	C.11	C.12
VIE. ACT.0001	AnachB—smart von A nach B			X						X						X	
VIE. ACT.0002	**Arrowhead**			X		X					X						
VIE. ACT.0003	Aspern.mobil	X	X														
VIE. ACT.0004	Boutiquehotel Stadthalle: Stadthotel mit Null-Energie-Bilanz			X							X						
VIE. ACT.0005	Competencies for a Sustainable Socio-Economic Development	X															
VIE. ACT.0006	Citybike Wien			X			X			X							
VIE. ACT.0007	**CITYOPT**	X	X	X		X					X						
VIE. ACT.0008	CLUE		X														

VIE. ACT.0009	CO2 neutrale post			X		X	X			X	X						
VIE. ACT.0010	Die MA 48 Mist App			X					X								
VIE. ACT.0011	**Digital Agenda Wien**	X	X														
VIE. ACT.0012	Digital Salon	X															
VIE. ACT.0013	DigitalCity.Wien	X															
VIE. ACT.0014	**DigitalCity.Wien Action Day**	X															
VIE. ACT.0015	E-mobility on demand			X						X							
VIE. ACT.0016	E-taxis			X			X			X							
VIE. ACT.0017	Energiespar-Bim			X						X							
VIE. ACT.0018	EOS—Energie aus Klärschlamm			X		X											
VIE. ACT.0019	EU-GUGLE: Sustainable renovation models for smarter cities			X							X						

Continued

TABLE A.4 Vienna's smart city development strategy: activities by category and application domain—cont'd

Activity		Category				Application domain											
ID code	Name	A	B	C	D	C.01	C.02	C.03	C.04	C.05	C.06	C.07	C.08	C.09	C.10	C.11	C.12
VIE. ACT.0020	Forschungsprojekt Smart.Monitor		X														
VIE. ACT.0021	INNOSPIRIT		X														
VIE. ACT.0022	INWAPO		X														
VIE. ACT.0023	IREEN		X														
VIE. ACT.0024	LED-Technik in der öffentlichen Beleuchtung			X		X											
VIE. ACT.0025	**Open Government Data**	X		X												X	
VIE. ACT.0026	Optihubs		X														
VIE. ACT.0027	**Photovoltaik-Dachgarten**			X							X						
VIE. ACT.0028	Programm Klimaaktiv Erneuerbare Wärme	X	X														
VIE. ACT.0029	PUMAS	X	X	X						X							

VIE. ACT.0030	**Smart Cities Demo Aspern**			X		X					X						
VIE. ACT.0031	**Seniortab**			X								X					
VIE. ACT.0032	Skopje Urban Transport		X														
VIE. ACT.0033	**Smart City Wien Framework Strategy**		X														
VIE. ACT.0034	**Smart City Wien project**	X	X														
VIE. ACT.0035	Smart Hubs 2.0		X														
VIE. ACT.0036	**Smart services**		X														
VIE. ACT.0037	Smart Verteilerkreis	X	X	X						X							
VIE. ACT.0038	**Smarter Together**	X	X	X						X	X						
VIE. ACT.0039	**SMILE (Die Mobilitätsplattform der Zukunft)**			X						X						X	
VIE. ACT.0040	Social City Wien—Plattform für gesellschaftliche Innovation	X															

Continued

TABLE A.4 Vienna's smart city development strategy: activities by category and application domain—cont'd

Activity		Category				Application domain											
ID code	Name	A	B	C	D	C.01	C.02	C.03	C.04	C.05	C.06	C.07	C.08	C.09	C.10	C.11	C.12
VIE. ACT.0041	SternE—Erneuerbare Energie in der Hauptkläranlage			X				X									
VIE. ACT.0042	Technologiezentrum aspern IQ	X		X							X						
VIE. ACT.0043	TINA Vienna GmbH		X														
VIE. ACT.0044	TRANSFORM+	X	X														
VIE. ACT.0045	Transformation Agenda for Low Carbon Cities	X	X														
VIE. ACT.0046	Trinkwasserkraftwerke			X		X											
VIE. ACT.0047	Urban Learning	X	X														
VIE. ACT.0048	URBEM-DK		X	X		X				X	X						
VIE. ACT.0049	Virtual Office			X												X	
VIE. ACT.0050	Weatherpark			X							X						

VIE. ACT.0051	Wien Gestalten	X		X								X				X	
VIE. ACT.0052	wien.at live-App			X						X						X	
VIE. ACT.0053	wien.at Public WLAN				X												
VIE. ACT.0054	ZENEM (Zukünftige Energienetze mit Elektromobilität)		X														

A, community building; B, strategic framework; C, services and applications; D, digital infrastructure; C.01, energy networks; C.02, air; C.03, water; C.04, waste; C.05, mobility and transport; C.06, buildings and districts; C.07, health and social inclusion; C.08, cultural and recreation; C.09, education; C.10, public security and justice; C.11, e-government; C.12, others. Activities in bold: evidence of citizens' involvement.

Appendix B

See Figs. B.1–B.4.

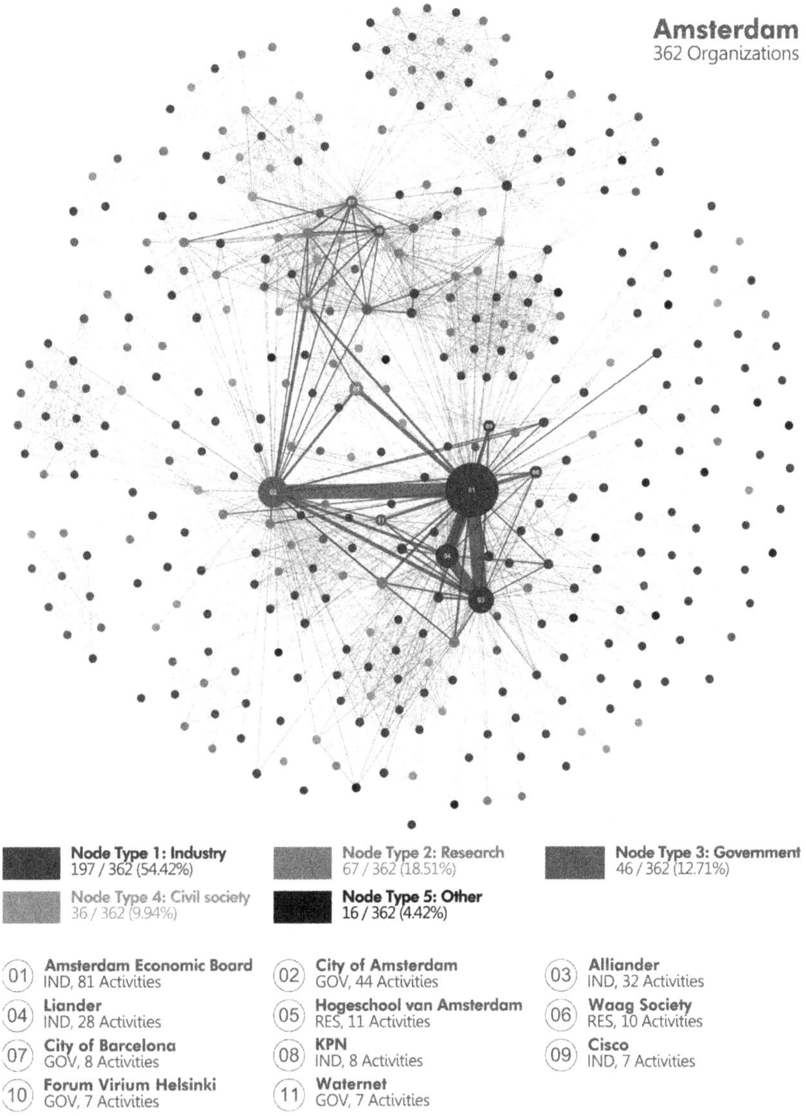

FIG. B.1 Amsterdam's smart city development strategy: collaborative environment.

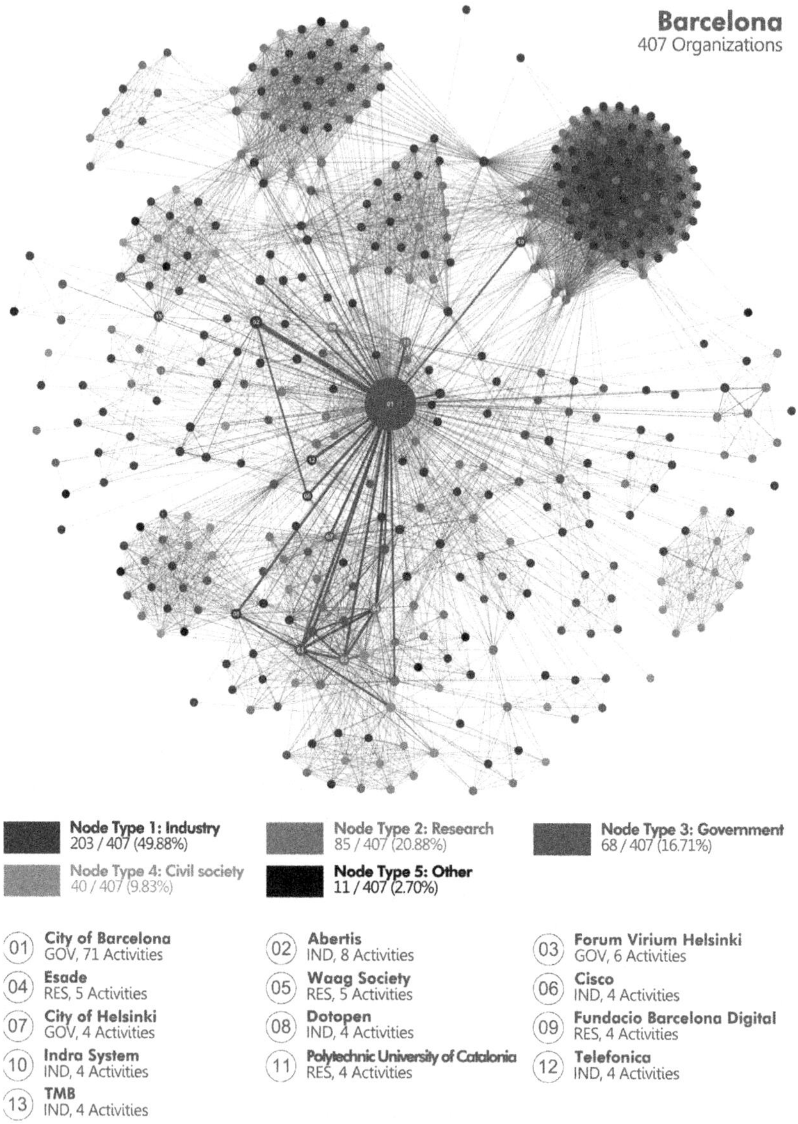

FIG. B.2 Barcelona's smart city development strategy: collaborative environment.

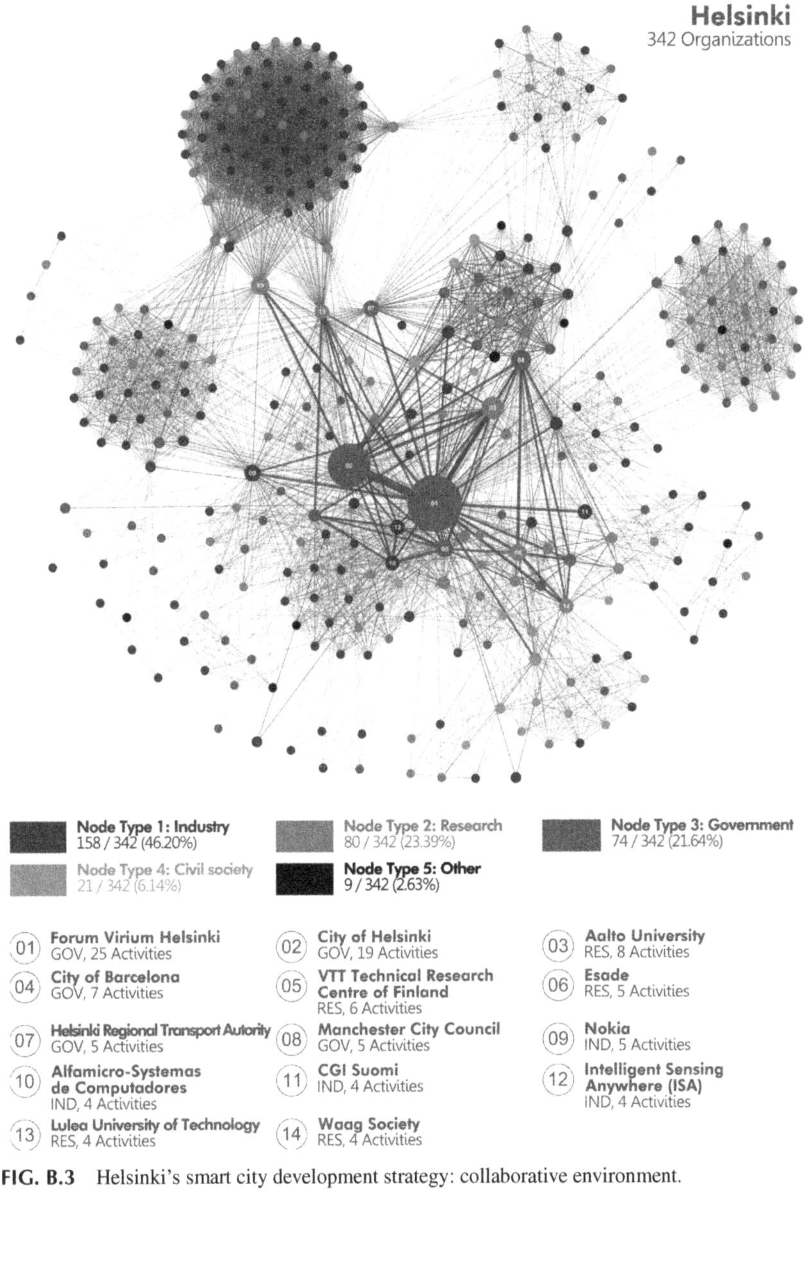
Helsinki
342 Organizations
Node Type 1: Industry
158 / 342 (46.20%)
Node Type 2: Research
80 / 342 (23.39%)
Node Type 3: Government
74 / 342 (21.64%)
Node Type 4: Civil society
21 / 342 (6.14%)
Node Type 5: Other
9 / 342 (2.63%)
01 Forum Virium Helsinki
GOV, 25 Activities
02 City of Helsinki
GOV, 19 Activities
03 Aalto University
RES, 8 Activities
04 City of Barcelona
GOV, 7 Activities
05 VTT Technical Research Centre of Finland
RES, 6 Activities
06 Esade
RES, 5 Activities
07 Helsinki Regional Transport Autority
GOV, 5 Activities
08 Manchester City Council
GOV, 5 Activities
09 Nokia
IND, 5 Activities
10 Alfamicro-Systemas de Computadores
IND, 4 Activities
11 CGI Suomi
IND, 4 Activities
12 Intelligent Sensing Anywhere (ISA)
IND, 4 Activities
13 Lulea University of Technology
RES, 4 Activities
14 Waag Society
RES, 4 Activities

FIG. B.3 Helsinki's smart city development strategy: collaborative environment.

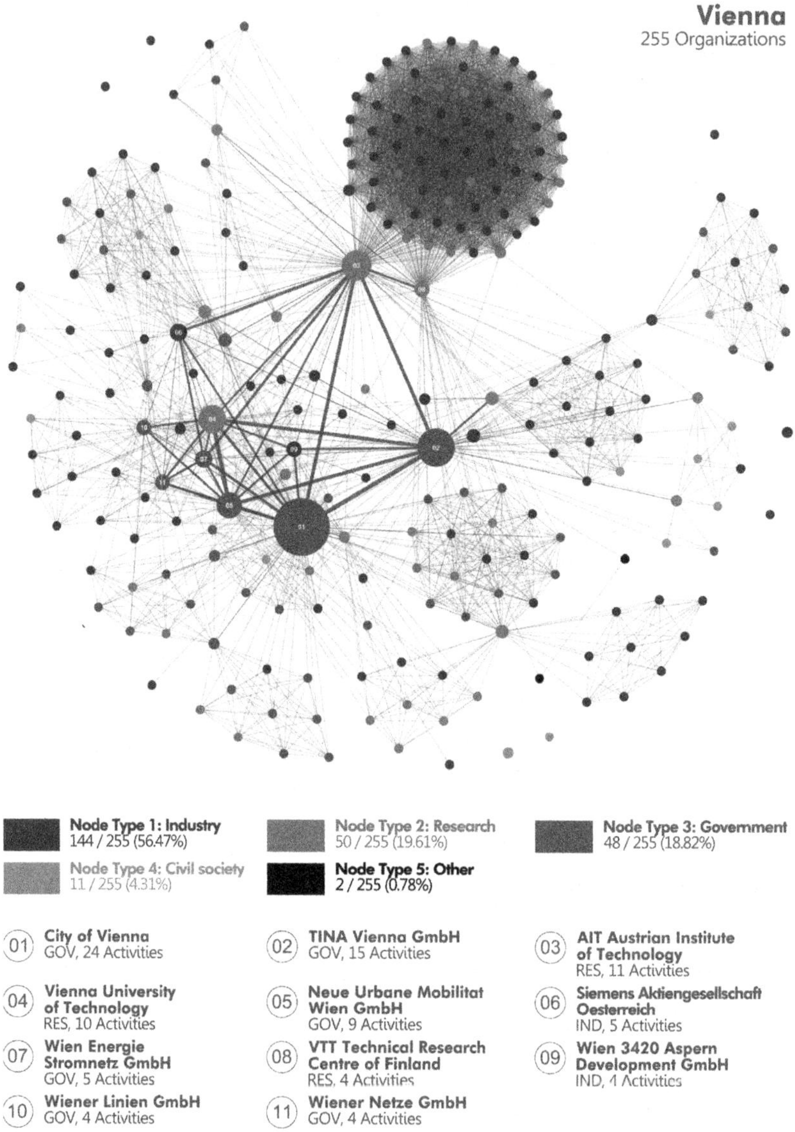
Vienna
255 Organizations
Node Type 1: Industry
144 / 255 (56.47%)
Node Type 2: Research
50 / 255 (19.61%)
Node Type 3: Government
48 / 255 (18.82%)
Node Type 4: Civil society
11 / 255 (4.31%)
Node Type 5: Other
2 / 255 (0.78%)
01 City of Vienna
GOV, 24 Activities
02 TINA Vienna GmbH
GOV, 15 Activities
03 AIT Austrian Institute of Technology
RES, 11 Activities
04 Vienna University of Technology
RES, 10 Activities
05 Neue Urbane Mobilitat Wien GmbH
GOV, 9 Activities
06 Siemens Aktiengesellschaft Oesterreich
IND, 5 Activities
07 Wien Energie Stromnetz GmbH
GOV, 5 Activities
08 VTT Technical Research Centre of Finland
RES, 4 Activities
09 Wien 3420 Aspern Development GmbH
IND, 4 Activities
10 Wiener Linien GmbH
GOV, 4 Activities
11 Wiener Netze GmbH
GOV, 4 Activities

FIG. B.4 Vienna's smart city development strategy: collaborative environment.

Appendix C

See Table C.1.

TABLE C.1 Digital records collected during the search phase

ID	Date	Producer	Title	Source
DR001	2004	City of New York	Mayor Michael R. Bloomberg and Governor George E. Pataki Announce Historic Plan to Create Convention Corridor on Manhattan's West Side, Including Expanded Javits Center and New 75,000 Seat Sports and Convention Center	http://www1.nyc.gov/office-of-the-mayor/news/067-04/mayor-michael-bloomberg-governor-george-e-pataki-historic-plan-create
DR002	2004	City of New York	Franchise Agreement Between the City of New York and Clearlinx Network Corporation	https://www1.nyc.gov/assets/doitt/downloads/pdf/2004_ClearLinx_Poletop_Agreement_FINAL.pdf
DR003	2004	City of New York	Franchise Agreement Between the City of New York and Crown Castle Solutions Corporation	https://www1.nyc.gov/assets/doitt/downloads/pdf/2004_Crown_Castle_Poletop_Agreement_FINALsigned.pdf
DR004	2004	City of New York	Franchise Agreement Between the City of New York and Nextel of New York, Inc.	https://www1.nyc.gov/assets/doitt/downloads/pdf/2004_Nextel_Poletop_Agreement_FINALsigned.pdf
DR005	2005	The New York Times	City's 311 Help Line Plans to Add Data on Social Services	http://www.nytimes.com/2005/11/11/nyregion/citys-311-help-line-plans-to-add-data-on-social-services.html
DR006	2005	City of New York	Mayor Michael R. Bloomberg Announces Merger of WNYE-TV and WNYE-FM with NYC TV	http://www1.nyc.gov/office-of-the-mayor/news/038-05/mayor-michael-bloomberg-merger-wnye-tv-wnye-fm-nyc-tv

DR007	2005	City of New York	Mayor Michael R. Bloomberg Congratulates NYC TV on Winning Eight New York Emmy Awards	http://www1.nyc.gov/office-of-the-mayor/news/123-05/mayor-michael-bloomberg-congratulates-nyc-tv-winning-eight-new-york-emmy-awards
DR008	2005	City of New York	Mayor Bloomberg Announces Major Expansion of the 3-1-1 Citizen Service Center to Include Information on Social and Nonprofit Services	http://www1.nyc.gov/office-of-the-mayor/news/419-05/mayor-bloomberg-major-expansion-the-3-1-1-citizen-service-center-include
DR009	2005	City of New York	Department of Information Technology and Telecommunications Commissioner Gino Menchini and NYPD Commissioner Raymond W. Kelly Announce that all Nomadic Voip Telephone Companies are Now Properly Sending Calls to the City's 911 Call Center	https://www1.nyc.gov/site/doitt/about/pr-050831.page
DR010	2006	City of New York	Mayor Bloomberg Announces Pilot Program to Test Wireless Technologies to Create High Speed Wireless Data Network for New York City Police and Fire Departments	http://www1.nyc.gov/office-of-the-mayor/news/145-06/mayor-bloomberg-pilot-program-test-wireless-technologies-create-high-speed-wireless
DR011	2006	City of New York	Mayor Bloomberg Appoints Paul J. Cosgrave as Commissioner of the Department of Information Technology and Telecommunications	http://www1.nyc.gov/office-of-the-mayor/news/204-06/mayor-bloomberg-appoints-paul-j-cosgrave-commissioner-the-department-information

Continued

TABLE C.1 Digital records collected during the search phase—cont'd

ID	Date	Producer	Title	Source
DR012	2006	City of New York	Mayor Bloomberg and WBNC General Manager Frank Comerford Announce WNBC will Broadcast NYC TV Programming	http://www1.nyc.gov/office-of-the-mayor/news/291-06/mayor-bloomberg-wnbc-general-manager-frank-comerford-wnbc-will-broadcast-nyc-tv
DR013	2006	City of New York	Mayor Bloomberg Announces NYC TV Series "Secrets of New York" Will Be Aired Nationwide on PBS Stations	http://www1.nyc.gov/office-of-the-mayor/news/315-06/mayor-bloomberg-nyc-tv-series-secrets-new-york-will-be-aired-nationwide-pbs
DR014	2006	City of New York	Mayor Bloomberg Announces Selection Of Northrop Grumman To Build High Speed Wireless Data Network For Police Officers, Firefighters And Other City Workers	http://www1.nyc.gov/office-of-the-mayor/news/326-06/mayor-bloomberg-selection-northrop-grumman-build-high-speed-wireless-data-network
DR015	2006	City of New York	Department of Information Technology and Telecommunications Commissioner Cosgrave Announces Annual Excellence in Technology Awards	https://www1.nyc.gov/site/doitt/about/pr-061102.page
DR016	2006	City of New York	Department of Information Technology and Telecommunications Commissioner Cosgrave Announces Launch of NYCityMap on nyc.gov	https://www1.nyc.gov/site/doitt/about/pr-061130.page
DR017	2006	City of New York	Mayor Bloomberg Announces Creation of Office of Long-term Planning and Sustainability	https://www1.nyc.gov/office-of-the-mayor/news/335-06/mayor-bloomberg-creation-office-long-term-planning-sustainability#/3

DR018	2007	International Downtown Association	IDA 53rd Annual Conference and World Congress	http://www.nyc.gov/html/sbs/downloads/pdf/Conference%20brochure.pdf
DR019	2007	City of New York	Mayor Bloomberg Announces Record New York Emmy Nominations for NYC TV	http://www1.nyc.gov/office-of-the-mayor/news/046-07/mayor-bloomberg-record-new-york-emmy-nominations-nyc-tv
DR020	2007	City of New York	Mayor Bloomberg Announces Release of Planit, New York City's First-Ever Comprehensive Technology Strategy	http://www1.nyc.gov/office-of-the-mayor/news/396-07/mayor-bloomberg-release-i-planit-i-new-york-city-s-first-ever-comprehensive
DR021	2007	City of New York	Department of Information Technology and Telecommunications and the Office of Deputy Mayor for Health & Human Services Awarded for Development of Access NYC	https://www1.nyc.gov/site/doitt/about/pr-070524.page
DR022	2007	City of New York	Department of Information Technology and Telecommunications Commissioner Cosgrave Announces Annual Excellence in Technology Awards	https://www1.nyc.gov/site/doitt/about/pr-071101.page
DR023	2007	City of New York	Access NYC Awarded as One of Infoworld's 100 Most Innovative IT Solutions for 2007	https://www1.nyc.gov/site/doitt/about/pr-071113.page
DR024	2007	City of New York	Mayor Bloomberg Presents PlaNYC: A Greener, Greater New York	https://www1.nyc.gov/office-of-the-mayor/news/119-07/mayor-bloomberg-presents-planyc-a-greener-greater-new-york#/2
DR025	2007	City of New York	PlaNYC: A Greener, Greater New York	http://www.nyc.gov/html/planyc/downloads/pdf/publications/full_report_2007.pdf

Continued

TABLE C.1 Digital records collected during the search phase—cont'd

ID	Date	Producer	Title	Source
DR026	2007	Taylor & Francis	Citynet^{SM} New York City's Data Communications Network	https://www.tandfonline.com/doi/abs/10.1080/10630739308724471?journalCode=cjut20
DR027	2008	SILive.com	Staten Island's CB1 Gets New Home on the Web	http://www.silive.com/news/index.ssf/2008/04/staten_islands_cb1_gets_new_ho.html
DR028	2008	City of New York	Mayor Bloomberg and Commissioner Cosgrave Congratulate 311 on Five Years of Service	http://www1.nyc.gov/office-of-the-mayor/news/082-08/mayor-bloomberg-commissioner-cosgrave-congratulate-311-five-years-service
DR029	2008	City of New York	Deputy Mayor Lieber and Commissioner Cosgrave Announce Agreement With Verizon to Offer Competitive Cable Television Service to Every New York City Household	http://www1.nyc.gov/office-of-the-mayor/news/156-08/deputy-mayor-lieber-commissioner-cosgrave-agreement-verizon-offer-competitive
DR030	2008	City of New York	Mayor Bloomberg and Commissioner Cosgrave Congratulate 311 Customer Service Center on Municipal Art Society Annual Award	http://www1.nyc.gov/office-of-the-mayor/news/269-08/mayor-bloomberg-commissioner-cosgrave-congratulate-311-customer-service-center-municipal-art
DR031	2008	City of New York	Franchise Agreement Between The City of New York and Lexent Metro Connect, LLC	https://www1.nyc.gov/assets/doitt/downloads/pdf/2008_Franchise_Agreement_Lexent.pdf
DR032	2008	City of New York	Franchise Agreement Between The City of New York and NextG Networks of NY, Inc.	https://www1.nyc.gov/assets/doitt/downloads/pdf/2008_Franchise_Agreement_NextG.pdf
DR033	2008	City of New York	New York State and New York City Bring Together World Leading Technology Companies and State MWBE Firms for Jumpstart Event	https://www1.nyc.gov/assets/doitt/downloads/pdf/tech_sector_mwbe_20081106.pdf

DR034	2008	City of New York	DoITT Honored for IT Innovation and Excellence at Annual "Best of New York" Awards Ceremony	https://www1.nyc.gov/site/doitt/about/pr-080319.page
DR035	2008	City of New York	DoITT Issues Open Solicitation for New Cable Television Providers	https://www1.nyc.gov/site/doitt/about/pr-080411.page
DR036	2008	City of New York	DoITT Commissioner Cosgrave and CAU Commissioner Parvizi Join Staten Island Officials at Launch of New Community Board 1 Website	https://www1.nyc.gov/site/doitt/about/pr-080414.page
DR037	2008	City of New York	Department of Information Technology and Telecommunications Commissioner Cosgrave Announces Annual Excellence in Technology Award Winners	https://www1.nyc.gov/site/doitt/about/pr-081106.page
DR038	2008	City of New York	Audit Report on the Development and Implementation of the Notice of Violation Administration System by the Department of Sanitation	https://comptroller.nyc.gov/wp-content/uploads/documents/7A08_056.pdf
DR039	2009	The New York Times	To Do More With Less, Governments Go Digital	http://www.nyc.gov/html/sbs/downloads/pdf/press_clips/pressclip_2009_10_11_NYT.pdf
DR040	2009	City of New York	Mayor Bloomberg, Doitt Commissioner Cosgrave, and NYC Media Group President Arick Wierson Launch New Transmitter Site for WNYE 91.5 FM Radio New York at 4 Times Square	http://www1.nyc.gov/office-of-the-mayor/news/109-09/mayor-bloomberg-doitt-commissioner-cosgrave-nyc-media-group-president-arick-wierson-launch
DR041	2009	City of New York	Mayor Bloomberg Announces Five Technology Initiatives to Improve Accessibility, Transparency and Accountability Across City Government	http://www1.nyc.gov/office-of-the-mayor/news/294-09/mayor-bloomberg-five-technology-initiatives-improve-accessibility-transparency

Continued

TABLE C.1 Digital records collected during the search phase—cont'd

ID	Date	Producer	Title	Source
DR042	2009	City of New York	Mayor Bloomberg Unveils Connected City Initiative	http://www1.nyc.gov/office-of-the-mayor/news/432-09/mayor-bloomberg-connected-city-initiative
DR043	2009	ASIS International	Rough Waters, Smooth Response	https://www1.nyc.gov/assets/doitt/downloads/pdf/1010_case_study.pdf
DR044	2009	City of New York	Department of Information Technology & Telecommunications: Language Access Plan	https://www1.nyc.gov/assets/doitt/downloads/pdf/lap_doitt.pdf
DR045	2009	City of New York	Department of Information Technology and Telecommunications Commissioner Cosgrave Congratulates 311 on Record Level of Calls and New Services in 2008	https://www1.nyc.gov/site/doitt/about/pr-090105.page
DR046	2009	City of New York	BBC World News Marks Return to New York City With Mayor Michael Bloomberg Interview on NYCTV	https://www1.nyc.gov/site/doitt/about/pr-090320.page
DR047	2009	City of New York	Department of Information Technology and Telecommunications Commissioner Paul J. Cosgrave Announces Launch of NYCityMap 2.0	https://www1.nyc.gov/site/doitt/about/pr-090414.page
DR048	2009	City of New York	New York City Recognized With 2009 Municipal Web Portal Excellence Award	https://www1.nyc.gov/site/doitt/about/pr-090513.page
DR049	2009	City of New York	Department of Information Technology and Telecommunications and Northrop Grumman Corporation Announce the New York City Wireless Network is Operational Citywide	https://www1.nyc.gov/site/doitt/about/pr-090519.page

DR050	2009	City of New York	Department of Information Technology and Telecommunications and BMC Software Announce Significant Improvements in Customer Service Delivery	https://www1.nyc.gov/site/doitt/about/pr-090624.page
DR051	2009	City of New York	Department of Information Technology and Telecommunications Seeks Partner to Administer and Promote ".nyc"	https://www1.nyc.gov/site/doitt/about/pr-091005.page
DR052	2009	City of New York	Department of Information Technology and Telecommunications Presents 2009 Excellence in Technology Award Program Winners	https://www1.nyc.gov/site/doitt/about/pr-091016.page
DR053	2009	Manhattan Institute for Policy Research	How New York Became Safe: The Full Story	https://www.city-journal.org/html/how-new-york-became-safe-full-story-13197.html
DR054	2009	City of New York	American Recovery and Reinvestment Act of 2009 Broadband Initiatives: Comments of the City of New York. April 13, 2009	https://www1.nyc.gov/assets/doitt/downloads/pdf/ntia_arra_city_of_new_york.pdf
DR055	2009	City of New York	Internet Week Returns June 2009	http://www.nyc.gov/html/film/html/news_2008/120108_internet_week_2009.shtml
DR056	2009	Narrative Content Group	Con Ed Launches Smart Grid Pilot Project in New York City	https://www.treehugger.com/clean-technology/con-ed-launches-smart-grid-pilot-project-in-new-york-city.html
DR057	2009	Globe Business Media Group	New asbestos rules for the City of New York	https://www.lexology.com/library/detail.aspx?g=be41af9d-48c3-4012-a7e5-70740c3b8094

Continued

TABLE C.1 Digital records collected during the search phase—cont'd

ID	Date	Producer	Title	Source
DR058	2009	StreetInsider.com	New York Fire Department Selects IBM (IBM) to build State-of-the-Art System for Collecting and Sharing Data	https://www.streetinsider.com/Corporate+News/New+York+Fire+Department+Selects+IBM+%28IBM%29+to+build+State-of-the-Art+System+for+Collecting+and+Sharing+Data/4294270.html
DR059	2010	Curbed	Aerial NYC Map Adds More Historic Photos, Remains Awesome	http://ny.curbed.com/archives/2010/07/21/aerial_nyc_map_adds_more_historic_photos_remains_awesome.php
DR060	2010	New York Post	Microsoft deal saves city macro-hard cash	http://nypost.com/2010/10/21/microsoft-deal-saves-city-macro-hard-cash/
DR061	2010	Observer	Steve Ballmer and Mayor Bloomberg Put NYC on Microsoft's Cloud	http://observer.com/2010/10/steve-ballmer-and-mayor-bloomberg-put-nyc-on-microsofts-cloud/
DR062	2010	TechCrunch	NYC To Get Wi-Fi In Parks, But It's Free For Only 30 Minutes Per Month	http://techcrunch.com/2010/09/15/nyc-to-get-wi-fi-in-parks-but-its-free-for-only-30-minutes-per-month/
DR063	2010	ADVFN	Microsoft Agrees To Combine NYC License Pacts, Saving City $50 Million	http://www.advfn.com/news_Microsoft-Agrees-To-Combine-NYC-License-Pacts-Sav_44870609.html
DR064	2010	CIO Insight	New York City's IT Roadmap	http://www.cioinsight.com/c/a/Case-Studies/New-York-Citys-IT-Roadmap-636940
DR065	2010	Computerworld	Microsoft takes cloud fight to Google	http://www.computerworld.com/article/2513565/cloud-computing/microsoft-takes-cloud-fight-to-google.html

DR066	2010	DSLReports	Time Warner, Cablevision Offering "Free" NYC Park Wi-Fi	http://www.dslreports.com/shownews/Time-Warner-Cablevision-Offering-Free-NYC-Park-WiFi-110366
DR067	2010	Gotham Gazette	High Speed Internet Access Opens Another Digital Divide	http://www.gothamgazette.com/index.php/development/546-high-speed-internet-access-opens-another-digital-divide
DR068	2010	e.Republic	10th Annual Digital Cities Survey—2010 Results	http://www.govtech.com/dc/digital-cities/102472074.html
DR069	2010	e.Republic	G7: CIOs From Seven Big-Cities Work Together to Develop Open-Source IT Solutions	http://www.govtech.com/e-government/G7-Big-City-CIOs-Work-to-Develop-Open-Source-IT-Solutions.html
DR070	2010	e.Republic	New York City's Digital Map Puts In-Depth GIS Data a Few Clicks Away	http://www.govtech.com/e-government/New-York-City-Digital-Map.html
DR071	2010	InformationWeek	Microsoft Signs NYC To Cloud Computing Deal	http://www.informationweek.com/government/open-government/microsoft-signs-nyc-to-cloud-computing-deal/d/d-id/1093490?cid=rssfeed_iwk_all
DR072	2010	InformationWeek	New York As IT Center Of The World	http://www.informationweek.com/government/open-government/new-york-as-it-center-of-the-world/d/d-id/1093629?cid=rssfeed_iwk_all
DR073	2010	MediaPost	NYC Includes "Cord-Cutter" Provision For TWC, Cablevision	http://www.mediapost.com/publications/article/135857/nyc-includes-cord-cutter-provision-for-twc-cabl.html

Continued

TABLE C.1 Digital records collected during the search phase—cont'd

ID	Date	Producer	Title	Source
DR074	2010	City of New York	Maximizing Efficiency in NYC Government: A Plan to Consolidate and Modernize Back-Office Operations	http://www.nyc.gov/html/om/pdf/2010/pr316-10_report.pdf
DR075	2010	The New York Times	Insights From a Week as a 311 Operator in N.Y.	http://www.nytimes.com/2010/05/16/nyregion/16three11.html
DR076	2010	The New York Times	Cable Contract Has Fines for Late Service Calls	http://www.nytimes.com/2010/09/15/nyregion/15cable.html
DR077	2010	The New York Times	An Appointment with the Cable Guy?	http://www.nytimes.com/2010/09/19/opinion/19sun4.html
DR078	2010	The New York Times	Microsoft and New York in Software Deal	http://www.nytimes.com/2010/10/21/technology/21soft.html?_r=2&ref=microsoft_corporation
DR079	2010	PCWorld	Microsoft Signs Cloud Deals With California, New York City	http://www.pcworld.com/article/208332/microsoft_signs_cloud_deals_with_california_new_york_city.html
DR080	2010	Transportation Alternatives	This is How They Do-ITT	http://www.transalt.org/news/magazine/2010/Spring/10
DR081	2010	New York Public Radio	No More Wait for the Cable Man?	http://www1.wnyc.org/story/94413-no-more-wait-cable-man/
DR082	2010	City of New York	Mayor Bloomberg Announces Winners Of Inaugural Nyc Bigapps Competition	http://www1.nyc.gov/office-of-the-mayor/news/062-10/mayor-bloomberg-winners-inaugural-nyc-bigapps-competition

DR083	2010	City of New York	Mayor Bloomberg And Information Technology And Telecommunications Commissioner Post Start Overhaul Of Data Infrastructure At More Than 40 City Agencies	http://www1.nyc.gov/office-of-the-mayor/news/089-10/mayor-bloomberg-information-technology-telecommunications-commissioner-post-start#/0
DR084	2010	City of New York	Mayor Bloomberg And Domestic Violence Commissioner Jimenez Open New York City's Third Family Justice Center	http://www1.nyc.gov/office-of-the-mayor/news/164-10/mayor-bloomberg-domestic-violence-commissioner-jimenez-open-new-york-city-s-third-family
DR085	2010	City of New York	Mayor Bloomberg Answers "100 Millionth" Call To 311	http://www1.nyc.gov/office-of-the-mayor/news/203-10/mayor-bloomberg-answers-100-millionth-call-311
DR086	2010	City of New York	Mayor Bloomberg Launches Language Gateway	http://www1.nyc.gov/office-of-the-mayor/news/233-10/mayor-bloomberg-launches-language-gateway
DR087	2010	City of New York	Statement Of Mayor Michael R. Bloomberg On Honors For Three City Technology Initiatives	http://www1.nyc.gov/office-of-the-mayor/news/263-10/statement-mayor-michael-bloomberg-honors-three-city-technology-initiatives
DR088	2010	City of New York	Mayor Bloomberg Announces Board Members Of The New Brooklyn Bridge Park Corporation	http://www1.nyc.gov/office-of-the-mayor/news/319-10/mayor-bloomberg-board-members-the-new-brooklyn-bridge-park-corporation
DR089	2010	City of New York	Statement Of Mayor Michael R. Bloomberg On $20 Million In Federal Stimulus Awards For Broadband Adoption And Expansion	http://www1.nyc.gov/office-of-the-mayor/news/388-10/statement-mayor-michael-bloomberg-20-million-federal-stimulus-awards-broadband

Continued

TABLE C.1 Digital records collected during the search phase—cont'd

ID	Date	Producer	Title	Source
DR090	2010	City of New York	Mayor Bloomberg Announces 311online Wins Digital Government Achievement Award	http://www1.nyc.gov/office-of-the-mayor/news/396-10/mayor-bloomberg-311online-wins-digital-government-achievement-award
DR091	2010	City of New York	Mayor Bloomberg Launches Nyc Bigapps 2.0 Competition	http://www1.nyc.gov/office-of-the-mayor/news/430-10/mayor-bloomberg-launches-nyc-bigapps-2-0-competition
DR092	2010	City of New York	Mayor Bloomberg And Microsoft Ceo Steve Ballmer Announce First Of Its Kind Partnership To Keep New York City At The Cutting Edge Of Technological Innovation While Saving Taxpayer Dollars	http://www1.nyc.gov/office-of-the-mayor/news/439-10/mayor-bloomberg-microsoft-ceo-steve-ballmer-first-its-kind-partnership-keep-new#/2
DR093	2010	Personal Democracy Forum	Personal Democracy Forum—Public Event (5/19), New York: Part 4	https://www.youtube.com/watch?v=0bLbtIuwdOQ
DR094	2010	City of New York	DoITT News: Microsoft Agreement	https://www.youtube.com/watch?v=bZQPjlcA5CI
DR095	2010	City of New York	30 Day Report: Enabling the Connected City	https://www1.nyc.gov/assets/doitt/downloads/pdf/30_day_report.pdf
DR096	2010	City of New York	Department of Information Technology and Telecommunications Testimony Before the City Council Committee on Technology Oversight on Broadband Adoption: Closing the Digital Divide. Monday, September 27, 2010	https://www1.nyc.gov/assets/doitt/downloads/pdf/broadband_adoption_092710.pdf

DR097	2010	City of New York	NYC Dept. of Information Technology & Telecommunications (DoITT)	https://www1.nyc.gov/assets/doitt/downloads/pdf/cm_cabrera_120810.pdf
DR098	2010	City of New York	Department of Information Technology and Telecommunications Testimony Before the City Council Committees on Finance, Land Use and Technology: Fiscal Year 2011 Executive Budget. Tuesday, May 25, 2010	https://www1.nyc.gov/assets/doitt/downloads/pdf/doitt_exec_budget_testimony_fy2011.pdf
DR099	2010	City of New York	Department of Information Technology and Telecommunications Testimony Before the City Council Committees on Land Use and Technology: Fiscal Year 2011 Preliminary Budget. Thursday, March 11, 2010	https://www1.nyc.gov/assets/doitt/downloads/pdf/doitt_prelim_budget_testimony_fy2011.pdf
DR100	2010	City of New York	Executive Order No. 140: Authorizing the Department of Information Technology and Telecommunications to Consolidate the Infrastructure of and Establish Coordinated Citywide Policies for Information Technology and Telecommunications for the City of New York	https://www1.nyc.gov/assets/doitt/downloads/pdf/eo_140.pdf
DR101	2010	City of New York	NYC Connected Communities: Fact Sheet	https://www1.nyc.gov/assets/doitt/downloads/pdf/fact_sheet_pcc.pdf
DR102	2010	City of New York	NYC Connected Foundations: Fact Sheet	https://www1.nyc.gov/assets/doitt/downloads/pdf/fact_sheet_sba.pdf
DR103	2010	City of New York	Department of Information Technology and Telecommunications Testimony Before the City Council Committee on Technology: Oversight on New York City's Mobile Workforce. Tuesday, October 19, 2010	https://www1.nyc.gov/assets/doitt/downloads/pdf/mobile_workforce_101910.pdf

Continued

TABLE C.1 Digital records collected during the search phase—cont'd

ID	Date	Producer	Title	Source
DR104	2010	City of New York	Department of Information Technology and Telecommunications Testimony Before the City Council Subcommittee on Zoning and Franchises Public Pay Telephone Authorizing Resolution Monday, May 17, 2010	https://www1.nyc.gov/assets/doitt/downloads/pdf/mtf_authorizing_resolution_051710.pdf
DR105	2010	City of New York	Department of Information Technology and Telecommunications Testimony Before the New York City Council Committee on Technology. Re: Intro. 029-10—Open Data Standards for City Agencies. Monday, June 21, 2010	https://www1.nyc.gov/assets/doitt/downloads/pdf/testimony_open_data_6_21_10.pdf
DR106	2010	City of New York	Mayor Bloomberg And New York City Housing Authority Chairman Rhea Rename Bronx Development In Honor Of U.S. Supreme Court Justice Sonia Sotomayor	https://www1.nyc.gov/office-of-the-mayor/news/253-10/mayor-bloomberg-re-invent-nyc-gov-hackathon-encourage-developers-designers-to
DR107	2010	City of New York	Deputy Mayor Goldsmith and Department of Information Technology and Telecommunications Commissioner Post Recognize 2010 Excellence in Technology Award Program Winners	https://www1.nyc.gov/site/doitt/about/pr-101104.page
DR108	2010	NBC	Internet Week to Be Bigger and Better This Year	https://www.nbcnewyork.com/news/local/Internet-Week-To-Be-Bigger-and-Better--95430474.html
DR109	2010	City of New York	Energy Efficiency Operations & Maintenance Plan	http://www.nyc.gov/html/dem/downloads/pdf/EEOM_Plan.pdf

DR110	2011	American City and County	Cities work together on new web apps	http://americancityandcounty.com/technology/social-media-apps-20111114
DR111	2011	Computerworld	21st Century Achievement Award Winners & Finalists	http://events.computerworld.com/ehome/index.php?eventid=11545&tabid=12624&)
DR112	2011	GovFresh	2011 GovFresh Awards winners	http://govfresh.com/2011/12/2011-govfresh-awards-winners/
DR113	2011	New York Post	Live-vid scouting units roll between li'l flakes	http://nypost.com/2011/01/08/live-vid-scouting-units-roll-between-lil-flakes/
DR114	2011	Urgent Communications	NYC operates government-only mobile broadband network	http://urgentcomm.com/networks_and_systems/news/nyc-mobile-broadband-network-20110215
DR115	2011	DNAinfo	City Solicits Big Ideas in New BigApps Challenge	http://www.dnainfo.com/new-york/20110621/manhattan/city-solicits-big-ideas-new-bigapps-challenge
DR116	2011	e.Republic	Best of New York Awards 2011	http://www.govtech.com/cdg/best-of-new-york/Best-of-New-York-Awards-2011.html
DR117	2011	e.Republic	17 State and Local Governments Honored for Web 2.0 and Social Media	http://www.govtech.com/e-government/Governments-Honored-Web-20-and-Social-Media-.html
DR118	2011	e.Republic	5 Government Procurement Practices That Stifle Innovation	http://www.govtech.com/pcio/articles/5-Government-Procurement-Practices-That-Stifle-Innovation.html
DR119	2011	e.Republic	2011 Best of New York Winners Honored	http://www.govtech.com/policy-management/2011-Best-of-New-York-Winners-Honored.html

Continued

TABLE C.1 Digital records collected during the search phase—cont'd

ID	Date	Producer	Title	Source
DR120	2011	e.Republic	New York City CIO Carole Post Named State's IT Official of the Year	http://www.govtech.com/policy-management/New-York-City-CIO-Carole-Post-040611.html?elq=0a892defb04840868910d0fb36922910
DR121	2011	InformationWeek	New York Touts "Open Gov" Progress	http://www.informationweek.com/government/leadership/new-york-touts-open-gov-progress/d/d-id/1098229?
DR122	2011	InformationWeek	The Government CIO 50: Vision, Influence, And Results	http://www.informationweek.com/government/leadership/the-government-cio-50-vision-influence-and-results/d/d-id/1096425?
DR123	2011	NextGov	Kundra seeks IT cooperation with state and local governments	http://www.nextgov.com/mobile/2011/05/kundra-seeks-it-cooperation-with-state-and-local-governments/49019/
DR124	2011	City of New York	Road Map for the Digital City: Achieving New York City's Digital Future	http://www.nyc.gov/html/media/media/PDF/90dayreport.pdf
DR125	2011	City of New York	NYC Citywide IT Infrastructure Services (CITIServ) Program	http://www.nyc.gov/html/om/pdf/2011/pr064-11_fact_sheet.pdf
DR126	2011	City of New York	New TLC Service Allows Renewing Driver Licensees to Pay Fees Online with Credit Cards	http://www.nyc.gov/html/tlc/downloads/pdf/press_release_04_27_2011.pdf
DR127	2011	City of New York	NYC BigApps Past Competitions	http://www.nycedc.com/services/nyc-bigapps/past-competitions
DR128	2011	City of New York	Wi-Fi in Parks	http://www.nycgovparks.org/facilities/wifi

DR129	2011	The New York Times	Snowstorm That Wasn't Finds City Well Prepared	http://www.nytimes.com/2011/01/08/nyregion/08snow.html?_r=1&adxnnl=1&partner=rss&emc=rss&adxnnlx=1294502484-OKXy9HsV+AWne6HqUmP8hQ
DR130	2011	RCR Wireless News	New York City delivers mobility in a carrier-free world	http://www.rcrwireless.com/20110419/carriers/new-york-city-delivers-mobility-in-a-carrier-free-world
DR131	2011	New York Public Radio	NYC Releases More Data Sets, Updates Portal	http://www.wnyc.org/story/106441-show-and-tell-nyc-officials-demonstrate-new-snow-response-tools/
DR132	2011	New York Public Radio	Stung by IT Capers, City "Insources" Union Talent	http://www.wnyc.org/story/120048-stung-it-capers-city-insources-union-talent/
DR133	2011	City of New York	Mayor Bloomberg Launches Nyc Urban Technology Innovation Center	http://www1.nyc.gov/office-of-the-mayor/news/022-11/mayor-bloomberg-launches-nyc-urban-technology-innovation-center
DR134	2011	City of New York	Mayor Bloomberg Opens New Consolidated Data Center To House Technology Infrastructure Of More Than 40 City Agencies	http://www1.nyc.gov/office-of-the-mayor/news/064-11/mayor-bloomberg-opens-new-consolidated-data-center-house-technology-infrastructure-more-than#/0
DR135	2011	City of New York	Mayor Bloomberg Announces Winners Of Nyc Bigapps 2.0 Competition	http://www1.nyc.gov/office-of-the-mayor/news/104-11/mayor-bloomberg-winners-nyc-bigapps-2-0-competition
DR136	2011	City of New York	Mayor Bloomberg And Chief Digital Officer Rachel Sterne Unveil Road Map For The Digital City—A Plan To Make New York The Nation's Leading Digital City	http://www1.nyc.gov/office-of-the-mayor/news/158-11/mayor-bloomberg-chief-digital-officer-rachel-sterne-em-road-map-the-digital#/3

Continued

TABLE C.1 Digital records collected during the search phase—cont'd

ID	Date	Producer	Title	Source
DR137	2011	City of New York	Mayor Bloomberg And At&t Chairman And Ceo Randall Stephenson Launch Free Wi-fi Service In 20 New York City Parks	http://www1.nyc.gov/office-of-the-mayor/news/202-11/mayor-bloomberg-at-t-chairman-ceo-randall-stephenson-launch-free-wi-fi-service-20-new#/0
DR138	2011	City of New York	Mayor Bloomberg And New York City Housing Authority Chairman Rhea Rename Bronx Development In Honor Of U.S. Supreme Court Justice Sonia Sotomayor	http://www1.nyc.gov/office-of-the-mayor/news/253-10/mayor-bloomberg-re-invent-nyc-gov-hackathon-encourage-developers-designers-to
DR139	2011	City of New York	Mayor Bloomberg Announces New, Real-time Traffic Management System To Reduce Congestion In Midtown Manhattan	http://www1.nyc.gov/office-of-the-mayor/news/257-11/mayor-bloomberg-new-real-time-traffic-management-system-reduce-congestion-midtown
DR140	2011	City of New York	Mayor Bloomberg Launches Nyc Bigapps 3.0 Competition, Announces New Technology Council And Immigration Seminars For Start-ups	http://www1.nyc.gov/office-of-the-mayor/news/359-11/mayor-bloomberg-launches-nyc-bigapps-3-0-competition-new-technology-council-and#/4
DR141	2011	TENANDISE	2011 ISE North America Government Project Award Winner DoITT	https://www.youtube.com/watch?v=xmeVBv72TcA
DR142	2011	City of New York	Franchise Agreement Between The City of New York and Mobilitie Investments II, LLC	https://www1.nyc.gov/assets/doitt/downloads/pdf/2011_Poletop_Franchise_Agreement_FINAL_Mobilitie_Investments_II_LLC.pdf

DR143	2011	City of New York	Franchise Agreement Between The City of New York and Xchange Telecom Corp.	https://www1.nyc.gov/assets/doitt/downloads/pdf/2011_Poletop_Franchise_Agreement_FINAL_Xchange_Telecom_Corp.pdf
DR144	2011	City of New York	NYC Department of Information Technology & Telecommunications (DoITT)	https://www1.nyc.gov/assets/doitt/downloads/pdf/beyond_beltway.pdf
DR145	2011	City of New York	Driving Innovation in Government	https://www1.nyc.gov/assets/doitt/downloads/pdf/big_cities_cio_042811.pdf
DR146	2011	City of New York	Testimony of Caswell F. Holloway Deputy Mayor for Operations, City of New York Before the New York City Council Committees on Contracts and Technology	https://www1.nyc.gov/assets/doitt/downloads/pdf/cfh_testimony_10_31_2011.pdf
DR147	2011	City of New York	Department of Information Technology & Telecommunications—2010 Annual Report. Enabling the Connected City: Year in Review	https://www1.nyc.gov/assets/doitt/downloads/pdf/doitt_2010_annual_report.pdf
DR148	2011	City of New York	2011 Excellence in Technology Awards Program: 10th Anniversary. Award Winner Descriptions. November 15, 2011	https://www1.nyc.gov/assets/doitt/downloads/pdf/etap_111611_v7_2011.pdf
DR149	2011	City of New York	Evolution of the Data Center	https://www1.nyc.gov/assets/doitt/downloads/pdf/evolution_data_center_060711.pdf
DR150	2011	City of New York	Department of Information Technology and Telecommunications Testimony Before the City Council Committees on Finance, Land Use and Technology: Fiscal Year 2012 Executive Budget. Wednesday, May 25, 2011	https://www1.nyc.gov/assets/doitt/downloads/pdf/fiscal_2012_exec_budget.pdf

Continued

TABLE C.1 Digital records collected during the search phase—cont'd

ID	Date	Producer	Title	Source
DR151	2011	City of New York	Department of Information Technology and Telecommunications Testimony Before the City Council Committees on Finance, Land Use and Technology: Fiscal Year 2011 Preliminary Budget. Wednesday, March 16, 2011	https://www1.nyc.gov/assets/doitt/downloads/pdf/fy_2012_prelim_budget_testimony.pdf
DR152	2011	City of New York	Driving Innovation in Government	https://www1.nyc.gov/assets/doitt/downloads/pdf/infoweek_leadership_forum_050311.pdf
DR153	2011	City of New York	Department of Information Technology and Telecommunications Testimony Before the City Council Committees on Technology and Parks & Recreation: Oversight on Internet Access in Public Parks. Wednesday, January 26, 2011	https://www1.nyc.gov/assets/doitt/downloads/pdf/internet_access_in_public_parks_1_26_11.pdf
DR154	2011	City of New York	IT Shared Services in a Federated Enterprise	https://www1.nyc.gov/assets/doitt/downloads/pdf/it_shared_services_052511.pdf
DR155	2011	City of New York	Before the Federal Communications Commission in the Matter of Acceleration of Broadband Deployment: Expanding the Reach and Reducing the Cost of Broadband Deployment by Improving Policies Regarding Public Rights of Way and Wireless Facilities Siting. Comments of the City of New York	https://www1.nyc.gov/assets/doitt/downloads/pdf/nyc_comments_acceleration_broadband.pdf
DR156	2011	City of New York	Before the Federal Communications Commission in the Matter of Basic Service Tier Encryption Compatibility Between Cable Systems and Consumer Electronics Equipment: Comments of the City of New York	https://www1.nyc.gov/assets/doitt/downloads/pdf/nyc_comments_cable_systems.pdf

DR157	2011	City of New York	Before the Federal Communications Commission in the Matter of Lifeline and Link Up Reform and Modernization Federal-State Joint Board on Universal Service Lifeline and Link Up: Comments of the City of New York	https://www1.nyc.gov/assets/doitt/downloads/pdf/nyc_comments_lifeline_linkup.pdf
DR158	2011	City of New York	Before the Federal Communications Commission in the Matter of Acceleration of Broadband Deployment: Expanding the Reach and Reducing the Cost of Broadband Deployment by Improving Policies Regarding Public Rights of Way and Wireless Facilities Siting. Reply Comments of the City of New York	https://www1.nyc.gov/assets/doitt/downloads/pdf/nyc_reply_comments_acceleration_broadband.pdf
DR159	2011	City of New York	NYC Steps	https://www1.nyc.gov/assets/doitt/downloads/pdf/nyc_steps.pdf
DR160	2011	City of New York	OpenGov Camp	https://www1.nyc.gov/assets/doitt/downloads/pdf/opengov_camp_060211.pdf
DR161	2011	City of New York	Standards for On-Street Communications Pedestal Structures	https://www1.nyc.gov/assets/doitt/downloads/pdf/Ped_STANDARDS_Revised_2011.pdf
DR162	2011	City of New York	Department of Information Technology and Telecommunications Testimony Before the City Council Committee on Technology in Government: Oversight Hearing on Establishing Citywide IT Strategy. Friday, April 15, 2011	https://www1.nyc.gov/assets/doitt/downloads/pdf/testimony_establishing_citywide_it_strategy.pdf
DR163	2011	InformationWeek	Government CIO 50	https://www1.nyc.gov/assets/doitt/downloads/pdf/week_top_50.pdf

Continued

TABLE C.1 Digital records collected during the search phase—cont'd

ID	Date	Producer	Title	Source
DR164	2011	City of New York	Mayor Bloomberg Launches Nyc Urban Technology Innovation Center	https://www1.nyc.gov/office-of-the-mayor/news/022-11/mayor-bloomberg-launches-nyc-urban-technology-innovation-center
DR165	2011	City of New York	Mayor Bloomberg And Chief Digital Officer Rachel Sterne Unveil "Road Map For The Digital City"—A Plan To Make New York The Nation's Leading Digital City	https://www1.nyc.gov/office-of-the-mayor/news/158-11/mayor-bloomberg-chief-digital-officer-rachel-sterne-em-road-map-the-digital
DR166	2011	City of New York	Mayor Bloomberg And Media & Entertainment Commissioner Oliver Present 6th Annual "Made In Ny" Awards	https://www1.nyc.gov/office-of-the-mayor/news/192-11/mayor-bloomberg-media-entertainment-commissioner-oliver-present-6th-annual-made-ny-awards
DR167	2011	City of New York	Mayor Bloomberg And At&t Chairman And Ceo Randall Stephenson Launch Free Wi-fi Service In 20 New York City Parks	https://www1.nyc.gov/office-of-the-mayor/news/202-11/mayor-bloomberg-at-t-chairman-ceo-randall-stephenson-launch-free-wi-fi-service-20-new
DR168	2011	City of New York	Mayor Bloomberg Discusses New Additions To City's Parks In Weekly Radio Address	https://www1.nyc.gov/office-of-the-mayor/news/203-11/mayor-bloomberg-new-additions-city-s-parks-weekly-radio-address
DR169	2011	City of New York	Mayor Bloomberg Launches Nyc Bigapps 3.0 Competition, Announces New Technology Council And Immigration Seminars For Start-ups	https://www1.nyc.gov/office-of-the-mayor/news/359-11/mayor-bloomberg-launches-nyc-bigapps-3-0-competition-new-technology-council-and

DR170	2011	City of New York	Mayor Bloomberg And Speaker Quinn Open East Coast Headquarters Of Yelp, Online Service That Connects Users To Local Businesses	https://www1.nyc.gov/office-of-the-mayor/news/381-11/mayor-bloomberg-speaker-quinn-open-east-coast-headquarters-yelp-online-service-that
DR171	2011	City of New York	Mayor Bloomberg Announces "re-invent Nyc.gov" Hackathon To Encourage Developers And Designers To Help Transform New York City's Website	https://www1.nyc.gov/office-of-the-mayor/news/253-11/mayor-bloomberg-re-invent-nyc-gov-hackathon-encourage-developers-designers-to
DR172	2011	City of New York	Deputy Mayor Goldsmith, Operations Director Weinstein and Information Technology Commissioner Post Launch 311 Service Request Map as Part of NYC Simplicity	https://www1.nyc.gov/site/doitt/about/pr-110216.page
DR173	2011	City of New York	Deputy Mayor Goldsmith Launches Change By Us Nyc, a New Social Media Platform that Will Enable New Yorkers to Submit Ideas for Improving the City, then Take Action and Connect to City Resources	https://www1.nyc.gov/site/doitt/about/pr-110707.page
DR174	2011	City of New York	New York City Announces Increased Access to Free Public Broadband, Expansion of Wi-Fi in Public Spaces, and Enhanced Television Services in All Five Boroughs Over Next Nine Years	https://www1.nyc.gov/site/doitt/about/pr-110810.page
DR175	2011	City of New York	Statement of Department Of Information Technology and Telecommunications Commissioner Carole Post on DOI Substantiation of Forgery by City-Contracted Software Company Employee	https://www1.nyc.gov/site/doitt/about/pr-110901.page

Continued

TABLE C.1 Digital records collected during the search phase—cont'd

ID	Date	Producer	Title	Source
DR176	2011	City of New York	City Planning's New Web Application—ZoLa—is One Stop Shop for Zoning Information	https://www1.nyc.gov/site/doitt/about/pr-110907.page
DR177	2011	City of New York	Mayor's Office to Combat Domestic Violence Commissioner Jimenez, Technology Commissioner Post, and Private Sector Partners Host Graduation Ceremony for First "NYC Steps" Class at The NYC Family Justice Center in Queens	https://www1.nyc.gov/site/doitt/about/pr-111028.page
DR178	2011	e.Republic	Beyond Performance Measurement	http://www.governing.com/blogs/bfc/new-york-city-performance-data-analytics.html
DR179	2011	The Wall Street Journal	Mayor Moves Against Drugs	http://online.wsj.com/article/SB10001424052970203430404577095033137451916.html?mod=WSJ_NY_LEFTSecondStories
DR180	2011	The New York Times	City to Crack Down on Illegally Divided Apartments	http://cityroom.blogs.nytimes.com/2011/06/07/city-to-crack-down-on-illegally-divided-apartments/?scp=1&sq=bloomberg%20foreclosure%20illegally%20converted%20apartments&st=cse
DR181	2011	The Wall Street Journal	Mayor Moves Against Drugs	http://online.wsj.com/article/SB10001424052970203430404577095033137451916.html?mod=WSJ_NY_LEFTSecondStories
DR182	2011	City of New York	PlaNYC: A Greener, Greater New York. Update April 2011	http://www.nyc.gov/html/planyc/downloads/pdf/publications/planyc_2011_planyc_full_report.pdf

DR183	2011	City of New York	Mayor Bloomberg And District Attorneys Announce New Effort To Use Data To Fight Financial Crime	https://www1.nyc.gov/office-of-the-mayor/news/040-11/mayor-bloomberg-district-attorneys-new-effort-use-data-fight-financial-crime#/4
DR184	2012	Los Angeles Times	New York City pay phone kiosks become Wi-Fi hot spots	http://articles.latimes.com/2012/jul/12/business/la-fi-tn-nyc-pay-phone-wifi-20120711
DR185	2012	The New York Times	City Seeks to Become a New Internet Address	http://cityroom.blogs.nytimes.com/2012/03/20/city-seeks-to-become-a-new-internet-address/
DR186	2012	The New York Times	City Begins Wi-Fi Pilot Program in 10 Phone Booths	http://cityroom.blogs.nytimes.com/2012/07/11/city-has-begun-converting-pay-phones-into-wi-fi-hot-spots/
DR187	2012	Gothamist	NYC Starts Offering Free, Unlimited WiFi Via Payphone Kiosks	http://gothamist.com/2012/07/11/nyc_starts_offering_free_unlimited.php
DR188	2012	City of New York	City's First Sustainability Hackathon Brings Local Tech Community Together To Help Create A Greener, Greater NYC With Apps For Bicycle Sharing, Recycling, Finding Markets With Fresh Food And More	http://home.nyc.gov/html/planyc2030/downloads/pdf/first_sustainability_hackathon_produces_apps.pdf
DR189	2012	Mashable	NYC Is Turning Payphones Into Wi-Fi Hotspots	http://mashable.com/2012/07/11/new-york-payphone-hotspot/
DR190	2012	CBS New York	NYC Officials Offer Tips For National "Protect Your Identity" Week	http://newyork.cbslocal.com/2012/10/23/nyc-officials-offer-tips-for-national-protect-your-identity-week/
DR191	2012	New York Post	City 'i's new phone booths	http://nypost.com/2012/04/08/city-is-new-phone-booths/

Continued

TABLE C.1 Digital records collected during the search phase—cont'd

ID	Date	Producer	Title	Source
DR192	2012	Observer	Mayor Bloomberg's Big Plan to Improve Broadband	http://observer.com/2012/06/mayor-bloombergs-big-plan-to-improve-broadband-for-the-citys-booming-tech-sector/
DR193	2012	Search Engine Watch	Making the Most of the Open Data Movement	http://searchenginewatch.com/sew/how-to/2227494/making-the-most-of-the-open-data-movement#
DR194	2012	TechPresident	Five Ways New York City is Changing its Broadband Policy	http://techpresident.com/news/22442/five-ways-new-york-city-changing-its-broadband-policy
DR195	2012	TechPresident	City CIOs See Inspiration for Civic Hackers in New Federal Portal for City Data	http://techpresident.com/news/22673/city-cios-hope-new-portal-city-and-federal-data-will-spark-new-ideas-insights
DR196	2012	TechPresident	Michael Bloomberg Wants You to Design New York City's Payphone of the Future	http://techpresident.com/news/23237/new-york-city-seeks-invent-payphone-future
DR197	2012	POLITICO	Now that open data is law in New York, meet Carole Post, the enforcer	http://www.capitalnewyork.com/article/media/2012/03/5524037/now-open-data-law-new-york-meet-carole-post-enforcer
DR198	2012	Dataversity	New York City: Taking Smart—And Semantic—Steps To Its Digital Future	http://www.dataversity.net/new-york-city-taking-smart-and-semantic-steps-to-its-digital-future/
DR199	2012	e.Republic	At Issue: Will NYC's Open Data Catch Fire?	http://www.digitalcommunities.com/articles/NYC-Open-Data-Catch-Fire.html?elq=6565685e573d4b3f9338b11efa06ed8c&elqCampaignId=93

DR200	2012	DNAinfo	Mobile Computer Labs Deliver High-Speed Internet to Public Housing	http://www.dnainfo.com/new-york/20120808/claremont/mobile-computer-labs-deliver-high-speed-internet-public-housing
DR201	2012	DNAinfo	Park Slope Community Center Gets New Computer Lab	http://www.dnainfo.com/new-york/20120814/park-slope/park-slope-community-center-gets-new-computer-lab
DR202	2012	AOL	Bloomberg signs NYC 'Open Data Policy' into law, plans web portal for 2018	http://www.engadget.com/2012/03/12/bloomberg-signs-nyc-open-data-policy-into-law-plans-web-porta/
DR203	2012	e.Republic	Cities Aim to Slash 311 Costs Without Affecting Services	http://www.govtech.com/budget-finance/Cities-Aim-to-Slash-311-Phone-Bills-Without-Affecting-311-Services.html
DR204	2012	e.Republic	Cloud Technology Wins in NYC Super Bowl Parade	http://www.govtech.com/e-government/Cloud-Technology-Wins-in-NYC-Super-Bowl-Parade.html
DR205	2012	e.Republic	New York City Readies for a Website Overhaul	http://www.govtech.com/e-government/New-York-City-Readies-for-a-Website-Overhaul.html
DR206	2012	e.Republic	New York City and Texas Honored for Cybersecurity Leadership	http://www.govtech.com/pcio/CDG-Cyber-Security-Awards-2012.html
DR207	2012	e.Republic	Gang of 7 Big-City CIOs Forges Ahead Despite Turnover	http://www.govtech.com/pcio/Gang-of-7-Big-City-CIOs-Forges-Ahead-Despite-Turnover.html
DR208	2012	e.Republic	New York City Shows New Law Enforcement Technology	http://www.govtech.com/public-safety/New-York-City-Shows-New-Law-Enforcement-Technology.html

Continued

TABLE C.1 Digital records collected during the search phase—cont'd

ID	Date	Producer	Title	Source
DR209	2012	InformationWeek	NYC Passes Data Transparency Law	http://www.informationweek.com/regulations/nyc-passes-data-transparency-law/d/d-id/1103263?
DR210	2012	City of New York	NYC DOT Announces Expansion of Midtown Congestion Management System, Receives National Transportation Award	http://www.nyc.gov/html/dot/html/pr2012/pr12_25.shtml
DR211	2012	City of New York	Fire Department: Annual Report 2012/2013	http://www.nyc.gov/html/fdny/pdf/publications/annual_reports/2012_annual_report.pdf
DR212	2012	City of New York	NYCEDC and DoITT Announce the Opening of Public Voting For NYC BigApps 3.0 Competition	http://www.nycedc.com/press-release/nycedc-and-doitt-announce-opening-public-voting-nyc-bigapps-30-competition
DR213	2012	The New York Times	City to Install 'Smart Screens' in Some Public Phone Booths	http://www.nytimes.com/2012/04/09/nyregion/city-to-install-touch-screens-in-public-phone-booths.html?_r=1
DR214	2012	The Slate Group	Michael Bloomberg Wants To Do Something Cool With New York's Phone Booths	http://www.slate.com/blogs/future_tense/2012/12/05/reinvent_payphones_new_york_challenges_techies_to_design_a_better_phone.html
DR215	2012	StateTech	StateTech Interview With New York City CIO Carole Post	http://www.statetechmagazine.com/article/2012/01/nyc-cio-qa
DR216	2012	StateTech	New York City's CIO Discusses Successes and Challenges Towards Consolidation	http://www.statetechmagazine.com/article/2012/01/nycs-it-outlook

DR217	2012	StateTech	Governments Take Different Paths to Cloud Security	http://www.statetechmagazine.com/article/2012/03/governments-take-different-paths-cloud-security
DR218	2012	StateTech	New York City Phone Booths Reborn as Wi-Fi Hotspots	http://www.statetechmagazine.com/article/2012/07/new-york-city-phone-booths-reborn-wi-fi-hotspots
DR219	2012	MetroFocus	Paving a Path for Girls on NYC's Digital Frontier	http://www.thirteen.org/metrofocus/2012/04/paving-a-path-for-girls-in-nycs-digital-frontier/
DR220	2012	MetroFocus	May is Internet Month in New York City	http://www.thirteen.org/metrofocus/2012/05/may-is-internet-month-in-new-york-city/
DR221	2012	MetroFocus	The New Tech Economy: Supporting Every Sector	http://www.thirteen.org/metrofocus/2012/05/the-new-tech-economy-supporting-every-sector/
DR222	2012	MetroFocus	City Announces Plan to Increase Broadband Access	http://www.thirteen.org/metrofocus/2012/06/city-announces-plan-to-increase-broadband-access/
DR223	2012	MetroFocus	Digital Literacy Programs for the Facebook Generation	http://www.thirteen.org/metrofocus/2012/06/digital-literacy-programs-for-the-facebook-generation/
DR224	2012	Time Warner Cable	Time Warner Cable Opens State-of-the-Art Learning Lab at Good Shepherd Services	http://www.timewarnercable.com/content/twc/en/about-us/press/time_warner_cableopensstate-of-the-artlearninglabatgoodshepherds.html
DR225	2012	United Nations	UN awards 44 organizations for public service excellence	http://www.un.org/en/development/desa/news/administration/un-public-service-awards.html

Continued

TABLE C.1 Digital records collected during the search phase—cont'd

ID	Date	Producer	Title	Source
DR226	2012	City of New York	Building Ideas Vol.4	http://www1.nyc.gov/assets/ddc/downloads/town-and-gown/building-ideas-4.pdf
DR227	2012	City of New York	Mayor Bloomberg Announces Completion Of Major Milestones In 911 System Overhaul Sought By The City For Decades	http://www1.nyc.gov/office-of-the-mayor/news/004-12/mayor-bloomberg-completion-major-milestones-911-system-overhaul-sought-the-city#/0
DR228	2012	City of New York	Mayor Bloomberg And Speaker Quinn Launch Online "nyc Street Closures" Map	http://www1.nyc.gov/office-of-the-mayor/news/010-12/mayor-bloomberg-speaker-quinn-launch-online-nyc-street-closures-map
DR229	2012	City of New York	Mayor Bloomberg Signs Legislation Creating A Citywide Comprehensive Open Data Policy	http://www1.nyc.gov/office-of-the-mayor/news/081-12/mayor-bloomberg-signs-legislation-creating-a-citywide-comprehensive-open-data-policy
DR230	2012	City of New York	Mayor Bloomberg Announces Department Of Information Technology & Telecommunications Commissioner Carole Post To Join New York Law School After Leaving City Government	http://www1.nyc.gov/office-of-the-mayor/news/127-12/mayor-bloomberg-department-information-technology-telecommunications-commissioner
DR231	2012	City of New York	Mayor Bloomberg Announces Winners Of Nyc Bigapps 3.0, Third Annual Competition To Create Apps Using Official City Data	http://www1.nyc.gov/office-of-the-mayor/news/138-12/mayor-bloomberg-winners-nyc-bigapps-3-0-third-annual-competition-create-apps-using

DR232	2012	City of New York	Mayor Bloomberg Appoints Rahul N. Merchant As The City's First Chief Information And Innovation Officer	http://www1.nyc.gov/office-of-the-mayor/news/148-12/mayor-bloomberg-appoints-rahul-n-merchant-the-city-s-first-chief-information-innovation
DR233	2012	City of New York	Mayor Bloomberg And Speaker Quinn Announce New Initiatives To Expand New York City's Broadband Connectivity, Bolstering The Growing Tech Sector And Allowing Businesses And Residents To Access High-speed Internet	http://www1.nyc.gov/office-of-the-mayor/news/236-12/mayor-bloomberg-speaker-quinn-new-initiatives-expand-new-york-city-s-broadband
DR234	2012	City of New York	Mayor Bloomberg, Police Commissioner Kelly And Microsoft Unveil New, State-of-the-art Law Enforcement Technology That Aggregates And Analyzes Existing Public Safety Data In Real Time To Provide A Comprehensive View Of Potential Threats And Criminal Activity	http://www1.nyc.gov/office-of-the-mayor/news/291-12/mayor-bloomberg-police-commissioner-kelly-microsoft-new-state-of-the-art-law
DR235	2012	City of New York	Mayor Bloomberg, Department Of Small Business Services And Nyc Digital Along With Google, Mashable And Tumblr Introduce New Technology Toolkit To Help Small Local Businesses Launch And Grow Online	http://www1.nyc.gov/office-of-the-mayor/news/306-12/mayor-bloomberg-department-small-business-services-nyc-digital-with-google-mashable#/0
DR236	2012	City of New York	Mayor Bloomberg Launches Competition To Install Free Fiber Cable Wiring In Growing Businesses Across The Five Boroughs	http://www1.nyc.gov/office-of-the-mayor/news/364-12/mayor-bloomberg-launches-competition-install-free-fiber-cable-wiring-growing-businesses#/0

Continued

TABLE C.1 Digital records collected during the search phase—cont'd

ID	Date	Producer	Title	Source
DR237	2012	City of New York	Mayor Bloomberg, Chief Information & Innovation Officer Merchant and Chief Digital Officer Haot Launch Reinvent Payphones Design Challenge	http://www1.nyc.gov/office-of-the-mayor/news/457-12/mayor-bloomberg-chief-information-innovation-officer-merchant-chief-digital-officer-haot
DR238	2012	City of New York	NYC311	https://www.youtube.com/watch?v=_BTq-Ar7uak
DR239	2012	City of New York	What Can Public Built Environment Data Tell Us?	https://www1.nyc.gov/assets/ddc/downloads/town-and-gown/04-25-12%20Precis.Final.pdf
DR240	2012	City of New York	New York City's Bronx Family Justice Center Hosts Ceremony for First Class of "Nyc Steps" Program Graduates	https://www1.nyc.gov/assets/doitt/downloads/pdf/bx_fjc_graduation_062012.pdf
DR241	2012	Crain Communications	Calling back the pay phone	https://www1.nyc.gov/assets/doitt/downloads/pdf/calling_back_the_pay_phone_11-18-2012.pdf
DR242	2012	City of New York	Change Management Policy	https://www1.nyc.gov/assets/doitt/downloads/pdf/Change_Management.pdf
DR243	2012	City of New York	Commissioner Carole Post's Remarks: Intro 29-A/ Open Data Bill Signing Ceremony	https://www1.nyc.gov/assets/doitt/downloads/pdf/cp_remarks_030712.pdf
DR244	2012	City of New York	James Weldon Johnson Community Center's Learning Lab "Ribbon-Cutting" Remarks of Commissioner Carole Post (as prepared)	https://www1.nyc.gov/assets/doitt/downloads/pdf/cwp_remarks.pdf

DR245	2012	City of New York	Department of Information Technology & Telecommunications—2011 Annual Report. Enabling the Connected City: Year in Review	https://www1.nyc.gov/assets/doitt/downloads/pdf/doitt_2011_annual_report.pdf
DR246	2012	City of New York	Department of Information Technology and Telecommunications Testimony Before the City Council Committees on Finance, Land Use and Technology: Fiscal Year 2013 Executive Budget. Tuesday, May 29, 2012	https://www1.nyc.gov/assets/doitt/downloads/pdf/fy_2013_exec_budget_052912.pdf
DR247	2012	City of New York	Time Warner Cable Learning Lab Opens at the James Weldon Johnson Community Center in Harlem	https://www1.nyc.gov/assets/doitt/downloads/pdf/johnson_center_learning.pdf
DR248	2012	City of New York	Time Warner Cable Learning Lab Opens at the James Weldon Johnson Community Center in Harlem: Pictures	https://www1.nyc.gov/assets/doitt/downloads/pdf/johnson_center_pics.pdf
DR249	2012	City of New York	Department of Information Technology and Telecommunications Testimony Before the City Council Committee on Technology. Oversight on Broadband Adoption: Closing the Digital Divide. Monday, April 23, 2012	https://www1.nyc.gov/assets/doitt/downloads/pdf/oversight_on_broadband_adoption_4_23_12.pdf
DR250	2012	City of New York	Request for Information Regarding the Future of Public Pay Telephones on New York City Sidewalks and Potential Alternative or Additional Forms of Telecommunications Facilities on New York City Sidewalks	https://www1.nyc.gov/assets/doitt/downloads/pdf/payphone_rfi.pdf

Continued

TABLE C.1 Digital records collected during the search phase—cont'd

ID	Date	Producer	Title	Source
DR251	2012	City of New York	New York City's Queens Family Justice Center Hosts Ceremony for Second Class Of NYC Steps Program Graduates	https://www1.nyc.gov/assets/doitt/downloads/pdf/qns_fjc_graduation062012.pdf
DR252	2012	City of New York	Security Architecture Standard	https://www1.nyc.gov/assets/doitt/downloads/pdf/security_architecture_standard.pdf
DR253	2012	City of New York	Request for Information Regarding Provision of Telecommunication Services to the City of New York	https://www1.nyc.gov/assets/doitt/downloads/pdf/telecom_services_rfi.pdf
DR254	2012	City of New York	Department of Information Technology and Telecommunications Testimony Before the City Council Committees on Finance, Land Use and Technology: Fiscal Year 2013 Preliminary Budget. Thursday, March 8, 2012	https://www1.nyc.gov/assets/doitt/downloads/pdf/testimony_fiscal_2013_prelim_budget_3_8_12.pdf
DR255	2012	City of New York	Department of Information Technology and Telecommunications Testimony Before the New York City Council Committee on Technology. Re: Intro. 664-11—Personal Information Security. Thursday, January 19, 2012	https://www1.nyc.gov/assets/doitt/downloads/pdf/testimony_intro_664_personal_infosec_1_19_12.pdf
DR256	2012	City of New York	Mayor Bloomberg Launches Four New City Social Media Channels During Social Media Week	https://www1.nyc.gov/office-of-the-mayor/news/060-12/mayor-bloomberg-launches-four-new-city-social-media-channels-during-social-media-week

DR257	2012	City of New York	Mayor Bloomberg And Columbia University President Bollinger Announce Agreement To Create New Institute For Data Sciences And Engineering	https://www1.nyc.gov/office-of-the-mayor/news/280-12/mayor-bloomberg-columbia-university-president-bollinger-agreement-create-new
DR258	2012	City of New York	Mayor Bloomberg, Department Of Small Business Services And NYC Digital Along With Google, Mashable And Tumblr Introduce New Technology Toolkit To Help Small Local Businesses Launch And Grow Online	https://www1.nyc.gov/office-of-the-mayor/news/306-12/mayor-bloomberg-department-small-business-services-nyc-digital-with-google-mashable
DR259	2012	City of New York	Statements of Chief Policy Advisor Feinblatt and Chief Information and Innovation Officer Merchant on New York City's Participation in Code for America's 2013 Fellowship Program	https://www1.nyc.gov/site/doitt/about/pr-101001.page
DR260	2012	City of New York	Citywide Chief Information & Innovation Officer Merchant, Chief Digital Officer Sterne, Council Member Brewer, Van Wagner Communications, and Titan Announce Free Wi-Fi Service Provided Through Payphone Kiosks	https://www1.nyc.gov/site/doitt/about/pr-120711.page
DR261	2012	City of New York	Department of Information Technology and Telecommunications and Time Warner Cable Business Class Announce $25 Million Investment to Expand Fiber Optic Network to Brooklyn Navy Yard and Key Business Locations Across City	https://www1.nyc.gov/site/doitt/about/pr-120828.page
DR262	2012	City of New York	Statements of Chief Policy Advisor Feinblatt and Chief Information and Innovation Officer Merchant on New York City's Participation in Code for America's 2013 Fellowship Program	https://www1.nyc.gov/site/doitt/about/pr-121001.page

Continued

TABLE C.1 Digital records collected during the search phase—cont'd

ID	Date	Producer	Title	Source
DR263	2012	City of New York	Statement of Citywide Chief Information & Innovation Officer Rahul N. Merchant on Meeting with Japanese Government CIO	https://www1.nyc.gov/site/doitt/about/pr-121016.page
DR264	2012	City of New York	Department of Information Technology & Telecommunications Announces First-Ever	https://www1.nyc.gov/site/doitt/about/pr-121022.page
DR265	2012	International Data Group	How Big Data Save Lives in New York City	http://www.cio.com/article/719926/How_Big_Data_Save_Lives_in_New_York_City
DR266	2012	The Economist	Governing data: Stats and the state	http://www.economist.com/blogs/graphicdetail/2012/07/governing-data
DR267	2012	City of New York	Internet Week NY: May 14-21	https://www.nycedc.com/blog-entry/internet-week-ny-may-14-21
DR268	2012	City of New York	City of New York Office of the Comptroller: Financial Audit	https://comptroller.nyc.gov/wp-content/uploads/documents/7I11_118A.pdf
DR269	2012	Warshaw Group	Warshaw Group Celebrates Eleventh Year as Sponsor of New York City Technology Forum	http://warshawgroup.com/news/warshaw-group-celebrates-eleventh-year-sponsor-new-york-city-technology-forum/
DR270	2013	The New York Times	F.C.C. Seeks Ways to Keep Phones Alive in a Storm	http://bits.blogs.nytimes.com/2013/02/05/f-c-c-revisits-communications-failures-after-hurricane-sandy/
DR271	2013	Mashable	New York City Launches Nation's Largest Free Public Wi-Fi Network	http://mashable.com/2013/12/10/new-york-city-harlem-wi-fi-network/

DR272	2013	Commonwealth of Kentucky	Governor Steve Beshear's Communications Office	http://migration.kentucky.gov/Newsroom/governor/20130430cio.htm
DR273	2013	CBS New York	Verizon Using Microtrenching To Install Fiber-Optic System In NYC	http://newyork.cbslocal.com/2013/04/08/verizon-using-microtrenching-to-install-fiber-optic-system-in-nyc/
DR274	2013	Time	Harlem Gets Wired: Free Public Wi-Fi to Launch Early Next Year	http://techland.time.com/2013/12/11/harlem-gets-wired-free-public-wi-fi-to-launch-early-next-year/
DR275	2013	TechPresident	Under Open Data Law, New York City Begins Herding Its Data	http://techpresident.com/news/23595/nyc-marks-one-year-open-data-law-and-looks-ahead
DR276	2013	TechPresident	Will "Microtrenching" Realize New York City's Gigabit Dreams?	http://techpresident.com/news/23719/microtrenching-puts-fiber-nyc-sidewalks
DR277	2013	TechPresident	Fighting Fires With Data, New York City Launches New Safety Inspection System	http://techpresident.com/news/23884/new-york-city-taps-its-brain-reduce-deaths-fire
DR278	2013	TechPresident	New York City's Latest Open Data Release	http://techpresident.com/news/24367/property-records-and-building-permits-part-new-nyc-open-data-release
DR279	2013	TechPresident	Hearing Highlights Successes and Challenges of NYC's Open Data Law	http://techpresident.com/news/24552/hearing-highlights-successes-and-challenges-nycs-open-data-law
DR280	2013	The New York Times	Could Outmoded Phone Booths Become E.V. Charging Stations?	http://wheels.blogs.nytimes.com/2013/08/14/could-outmoded-phone-booths-become-e-v-charging-stations/?_r=0

Continued

TABLE C.1 Digital records collected during the search phase—cont'd

ID	Date	Producer	Title	Source
DR281	2013	BBC	How New York is releasing its "big data" to the public	http://www.bbc.com/news/technology-24505860
DR282	2013	BBC	New Yorkers are learning to love big data	http://www.bbc.com/news/world-us-canada-24813181
DR283	2013	The Atlantic	Let's Make Old Payphones Into Electric Car Chargers	http://www.citylab.com/cityfixer/2013/09/lets-make-old-payphones-ev-chargers/6760/
DR284	2013	The Atlantic	New York's Real-Time Snow Plow Map to Get its First Major Test This Weekend	http://www.citylab.com/tech/2013/02/new-yorks-real-time-snow-plow-map-get-its-first-real-test-weekend/4639/
DR285	2013	The Atlantic	Why New York City's Open Data Law Is Worth Caring About	http://www.citylab.com/tech/2013/03/why-new-york-citys-open-data-law-worth-caring-about/4904/
DR286	2013	Computerworld	Data centers under water: What, me worry?	http://www.computerworld.com/article/2496633/data-center/data-centers-under-water--what--me-worry-.html
DR287	2013	AOL	NYC awards six Reinvent Payphones finalists, asks public to select favorite via Facebook	http://www.engadget.com/2013/03/06/nyc-reinvent-payphones-finalists/
DR288	2013	AOL	NYC partners with Cablevision, Time Warner Cable to bring WiFi hotspots to city parks	http://www.engadget.com/2013/07/16/nyc-cablevision-time-warner-cable-wifi-hotspots/
DR289	2013	e.Republic	New Kentucky CIO Brings Big Experience	http://www.govtech.com/e-government/New-Kentucky-CIO-Brings-Big-Experience.html?elq=8045a30523064192a20883609e48204d&elqCampaignId=3988

DR290	2013	Inc	NYC Data Tool Gives Small Business an Edge	http://www.inc.com/welcome.html?destination=http://www.inc.com/jill-krasny/nyc-business-atlas-helps-small-businesses.html
DR291	2013	NJ.com	FCC holds Hurricane Sandy hearings into telecom failures, fixes	http://www.nj.com/business/index.ssf/2013/02/fcc_holds_hurricane_sandy_hear.html
DR292	2013	City of New York	Verizon Wireless Continues to Support the Mayor's Office in its Efforts to Combat Domestic Violence in New York City	http://www.nyc.gov/html/ocdv/downloads/pdf/Press_Release_BKFJC_STEPS_graduation_071713.pdf
DR293	2013	City of New York	Read the Report	http://www.nyc.gov/html/sirr/html/report/report.shtml
DR294	2013	City of New York	NYCEDC Announces Launch of NYC Broadband Map to Provide View of Commercial Broadband Infrastructure	http://www.nycedc.com/press-release/nycedc-announces-launch-nyc-broadband-map-provide-view-commercial-broadband
DR295	2013	City of New York	NYCEDC Launches Second Round of ConnectNYC to Construct Free Fiber Cable Wiring For Businesses Across New York City	http://www.nycedc.com/press-release/nycedc-launches-second-round-connectnyc-construct-free-fiber-cable-wiring-businesses
DR296	2013	The New York Times	City's Web Site is Redesigned for First Time in a Decade	http://www.nytimes.com/2013/09/30/nyregion/new-york-citys-internet-site-gets-a-user-friendly-update.html?_r=1
DR297	2013	POLITICO	Wireless carriers MIA during Sandy?	http://www.politico.com/story/2013/02/communication-companies-slammed-at-hearing-87223.html
DR298	2013	StateTech	Proper Planning Kept IT Agencies Afloat During Hurricane Sandy	http://www.statetechmagazine.com/article/2013/04/proper-planning-kept-it-agencies-afloat-during-hurricane-sandy

Continued

TABLE C.1 Digital records collected during the search phase—cont'd

ID	Date	Producer	Title	Source
DR299	2013	The Atlantic	How New York Is Reinventing the Phone Booth	http://www.theatlantic.com/magazine/archive/2013/05/immobile-phones/309291/
DR300	2013	Wired	10-Foot-Tall Double-Sided Touchscreen Wins NYC's Pay Phone Redesign Challenge	http://www.wired.com/2013/03/nyc-pay-phones-redesign-challenge/
DR301	2013	New York Public Radio	Redesigning NYC's 11,412 Payphones for the Digital Age	http://www.wnyc.org/story/273873-redesigning-nycs-11412-payphones-digital-age/
DR302	2013	New York Public Radio	NYC Releases More Data Sets, Updates Portal	http://www.wnyc.org/story/nyc-releases-more-data-sets-updates-website/
DR303	2013	New York Public Radio	WiFi on Wheels Rolls Into Public Housing	http://www.wnyc.org/story/wifi-wheels-rolls-public-housing/
DR304	2013	City of New York	Appendix 11—Written Comments Received on the DEIS	http://www1.nyc.gov/assets/planning/download/pdf/applicants/env-review/east_midtown/append11_feis.pdf
DR305	2013	City of New York	Mayor Bloomberg, Chief Information & Innovation Officer Merchant And Chief Digital Officer Haot Announce Winning Prototypes From "Reinvent Payphones Design Challenge"	http://www1.nyc.gov/office-of-the-mayor/news/086-13/mayor-bloomberg-chief-information-innovation-officer-merchant-chief-digital-officer-haot
DR306	2013	City of New York	Mayor Bloomberg Commemorates Ten Years Of Nyc311, The Nation's Largest And Most Comprehensive 311 Service	http://www1.nyc.gov/office-of-the-mayor/news/089-13/mayor-bloomberg-commemorates-ten-years-nyc311-nation-s-largest-most-comprehensive-311

DR307	2013	City of New York	Mayor Bloomberg Launches Times Square Public Space Recycling Pilot To Make Managing Waste More Efficient	http://www1.nyc.gov/office-of-the-mayor/news/097-13/mayor-bloomberg-launches-times-square-public-space-recycling-pilot-make-managing-waste-more
DR308	2013	City of New York	Mayor Bloomberg Launches Fourth Annual Nyc Bigapps Competition	http://www1.nyc.gov/office-of-the-mayor/news/105-13/mayor-bloomberg-launches-fourth-annual-nyc-bigapps-competition
DR309	2013	City of New York	Mayor Bloomberg And Transportation Commissioner Sadik-khan Announce New Pilot Program To Pay Parking Meters Remotely And Launch Real-time Parking Availability Map	http://www1.nyc.gov/office-of-the-mayor/news/129-13/mayor-bloomberg-transportation-commissioner-sadik-khan-new-pilot-program-pay
DR310	2013	City of New York	Mayor Bloomberg And Fire Commissioner Cassano Announce New Risk-based Fire Inspections Citywide Based On Data Mined From City Records	http://www1.nyc.gov/office-of-the-mayor/news/163-13/mayor-bloomberg-fire-commissioner-cassano-new-risk-based-fire-inspections-citywide#/0
DR311	2013	City of New York	Mayor Bloomberg Signs Legislation Requiring The Creation Of An Interactive Crime-mapping Website	http://www1.nyc.gov/office-of-the-mayor/news/164-13/mayor-bloomberg-signs-legislation-requiring-creation-an-interactive-crime-mapping-website
DR312	2013	City of New York	Mayor Bloomberg Announces Winners Of Nyc Bigapps, Fourth Annual Competition To Create Apps Using City Data	http://www1.nyc.gov/office-of-the-mayor/news/215-13/mayor-bloomberg-winners-nyc-bigapps-fourth-annual-competition-create-apps-using
DR313	2013	City of New York	Mayor Bloomberg And Speaker Quinn Announce New Unique .nyc Web Address For New Yorkers And Businesses	http://www1.nyc.gov/office-of-the-mayor/news/236-13/mayor-bloomberg-speaker-quinn-new-unique-nyc-web-address-new-yorkers-and

Continued

TABLE C.1 Digital records collected during the search phase—cont'd

ID	Date	Producer	Title	Source
DR314	2013	City of New York	Mayor Bloomberg Launches New Redesigned and Redeveloped NYC.gov	http://www1.nyc.gov/office-of-the-mayor/news/314-13/mayor-bloomberg-launches-new-redesigned-redeveloped-nyc-gov#/0
DR315	2013	City of New York	Mayor Bloomberg Announces New Initiatives to Expand Wireless and Broadband Connectivity	http://www1.nyc.gov/office-of-the-mayor/news/315-13/mayor-bloomberg-new-initiatives-expand-wireless-broadband-connectivity
DR316	2013	City of New York	Mayor Bloomberg Announces Country's Largest Continuous Free Public WiFi Network	http://www1.nyc.gov/office-of-the-mayor/news/394-13/mayor-bloomberg-country-s-largest-continuous-free-public-wifi-network
DR317	2013	City of New York	Mayor Bloomberg Launches Times Square Public Space Recycling Pilot To Make Managing Waste More Efficient	https://www1.nyc.gov/office-of-the-mayor/news/097-13/mayor-bloomberg-launches-times-square-public-space-recycling-pilot-make-managing-waste-more
DR318	2013	City of New York	Liu Open-Sources Checkbook NYC	https://comptroller.nyc.gov/wp-content/uploads/2013/07/PR13-06-083.pdf
DR319	2013	City of New York	Using NYC Open Data	https://www.youtube.com/watch?v=xyIRu7uGMIA
DR320	2013	City of New York	Building Ideas Vol.3	https://www1.nyc.gov/assets/ddc/downloads/town-and-gown/building-ideas-3.pdf
DR321	2013	City of New York	Notice of Adoption of Rules	https://www1.nyc.gov/assets/doitt/downloads/pdf/a_doitt_08_15_13_a.pdf

DR322	2013	City of New York	Chief Information & Innovation Officer Progress Report: December 2013	https://www1.nyc.gov/assets/doitt/downloads/pdf/CIIO_Report_12_16_13_FINAL.pdf
DR323	2013	City of New York	Department of Information Technology and Telecommunications Testimony Before the City Council Committees on Land Use and Technology: Fiscal Year 2014 Executive Budget. Wednesday, May 29, 2013	https://www1.nyc.gov/assets/doitt/downloads/pdf/fiscal_2014_exec_budget_testimony.pdf
DR324	2013	City of New York	Department of Information Technology and Telecommunications Testimony Before the City Council Committees on Land Use and Technology: Fiscal Year 2014 Preliminary Budget. Monday, March 18, 2013	https://www1.nyc.gov/assets/doitt/downloads/pdf/fiscal_2014_prelim_budget_3_18_13.pdf
DR325	2013	City of New York	Memorandum of Understanding Pursuant to Health Insurance Portability and Accountability Act	https://www1.nyc.gov/assets/doitt/downloads/pdf/hipaa_multi_agency.pdf
DR326	2013	City of New York	Department of Information Technology and Telecommunications Testimony Before the City Council Committee on Technology: Re: Intro. 0984-2012/Creation & Maintenance of an Interactive Crime Mapping Website. Friday, March 1, 2013	https://www1.nyc.gov/assets/doitt/downloads/pdf/intro_984_crime_mapping_website.pdf
DR327	2013	City of New York	Department of Information Technology and Telecommunications Testimony Before the City Council Committees on Land Use and Technology. Oversight: DoITT's Contract Hiring of Minority and Women Owned Business Enterprises. Date: Monday, October 28, 2013	https://www1.nyc.gov/assets/doitt/downloads/pdf/mwbe_testimony_10_28_13.pdf

Continued

TABLE C.1 Digital records collected during the search phase—cont'd

ID	Date	Producer	Title	Source
DR328	2013	City of New York	Statement of NYC Chief Information & Innovation Officer Rahul N. Merchant to the Federal Communications Commission. PS Docket No. 11-60 Regarding Communications & Hurricane Sandy. Thursday, February 7, 2013	https://www1.nyc.gov/assets/doitt/downloads/pdf/nyc_ciio_statement_to_fcc_ps_docket_no-11-60.pdf
DR329	2013	City of New York	NYC Open Data Plan 2013	https://www1.nyc.gov/assets/doitt/downloads/pdf/nyc_open_data_plan_2013.pdf
DR330	2013	City of New York	Testimony of Michael Flowers—Chief Analytics and Open Platform Officer—before the New York City Council—Committee on Technology. November 20, 2013	https://www1.nyc.gov/assets/doitt/downloads/pdf/Open-Data-Testimony_11_20_13.pdf
DR331	2013	City of New York	Notice of Public Hearing: Opportunity to Comment on Deletion of Obsolete Rules	https://www1.nyc.gov/assets/doitt/downloads/pdf/P_DoITT_06_27_13_a.pdf
DR332	2013	City of New York	Amended Notice of Public Hearing: Opportunity to Comment on Proposed Rules Authorizing and Regulating "Microtrenching" by the City's Telecommunications Franchisees	https://www1.nyc.gov/assets/doitt/downloads/pdf/p_doitt_08_05_13_a.pdf
DR333	2013	City of New York	Before the Federal Communications Commission in the Matter of Implementation of Sections 309(j) and 337 of The Communications Act of 1934 as Amended: Promotion of Spectrum Efficient Technologies on Certain Part 90 Frequencies	https://www1.nyc.gov/assets/doitt/downloads/pdf/signed_waiver_request.pdf

DR334	2013	City of New York	Franchise Agreement Between The City of New York and Stealth Communication Services, LLC	https://www1.nyc.gov/assets/doitt/downloads/pdf/Stealth_Info_Services_Franchise_executed.pdf
DR335	2013	City of New York	Request for Proposals (RFP) for Systems Integration Services for Technology Projects Citywide	https://www1.nyc.gov/assets/doitt/downloads/pdf/sysintegration_citywide_si_services_rfp.pdf
DR336	2013	City and State NY LLC	911 in the Digital Age	https://www1.nyc.gov/assets/doitt/downloads/pdf/the_digital_age.pdf
DR337	2013	City of New York	Statement of Department of Information Technology & Telecommunications Commissioner Rahul N. Merchant Submitted to the Committee on Consumer Affairs & Subcommittee on Zoning & Franchises. Oversight on Time Warner Cable, CBS, and the Consumers Stuck in the Middle Thursday, August 8, 2013	https://www1.nyc.gov/assets/doitt/downloads/pdf/twc_cbs_counci_doitt_statement_080813.pdf
DR338	2013	City of New York	Franchise Agreement Between The City of New York and United Federal Data of New York, LLC	https://www1.nyc.gov/assets/doitt/downloads/pdf/United_Federal_Data_Info_Services_Franchise_executed.pdf
DR339	2013	City of New York	Department of Information Technology and Telecommunications. CIIO Rahul N. Merchant's Remarks: Innovating for the Connected Home, Living Room & TV—NYC MIT Enterprise Forum of NY, Verizon FiOS & Mashable Meetup. Tuesday, May 7,2013	https://www1.nyc.gov/assets/doitt/downloads/pdf/verizon_mit_meetup_rnm_remarks.pdf
DR340	2013	City of New York	NYC Mayor's Office of Media and Entertainment: The 2013 Report	https://www1.nyc.gov/assets/mome/pdf/2013report.pdf

Continued

TABLE C.1 Digital records collected during the search phase—cont'd

ID	Date	Producer	Title	Source
DR341	2013	City of New York	East Midtown Rezoning and Related Actions FEIS: Appendix 11 – Written Comments Received on the DEIS	https://www1.nyc.gov/assets/planning/download/pdf/applicants/env-review/east_midtown/append11_feis.pdf
DR342	2013	City of New York	Mayor Bloomberg And Chancellor Walcott Launch The Gap App Challenge, A New Software Development Contest For Programs To Help Middle School Students Excel In Math	https://www1.nyc.gov/office-of-the-mayor/news/006-13/mayor-bloomberg-chancellor-walcott-launch-gap-app-challenge-a-new-software-development
DR343	2013	City of New York	Mayor Bloomberg Launches Times Square Public Space Recycling Pilot To Make Managing Waste More Efficient	https://www1.nyc.gov/office-of-the-mayor/news/097-13/mayor-bloomberg-launches-times-square-public-space-recycling-pilot-make-managing-waste-more
DR344	2013	City of New York	Mayor Bloomberg And Transportation Commissioner Sadik-khan Announce New Pilot Program To Pay Parking Meters Remotely And Launch Real-time Parking Availability Map	https://www1.nyc.gov/office-of-the-mayor/news/129-13/mayor-bloomberg-transportation-commissioner-sadik-khan-new-pilot-program-pay
DR345	2013	City of New York	Mayor Bloomberg And Media & Entertainment Commissioner Oliver Present Eighth Annual Made In NY" Awards	https://www1.nyc.gov/office-of-the-mayor/news/198-13/mayor-bloomberg-media-entertainment-commissioner-oliver-present-eighth-annual-made-ny-
DR346	2013	City of New York	Mayor Bloomberg And Speaker Quinn Announce New Unique .nyc Web Address For New Yorkers And Businesses	https://www1.nyc.gov/office-of-the-mayor/news/236-13/mayor-bloomberg-speaker-quinn-new-unique-nyc-web-address-new-yorkers-and

DR347	2013	City of New York	Mayor Bloomberg Launches New Redesigned and Redeveloped NYC.gov	https://www1.nyc.gov/office-of-the-mayor/news/314-13/mayor-bloomberg-launches-new-redesigned-redeveloped-nyc-gov
DR348	2013	City of New York	Mayor Bloomberg Releases Update to Digital Roadmap, Plan to Ensure New York City Remains a Leading Global Digital City	https://www1.nyc.gov/office-of-the-mayor/news/338-13/mayor-bloomberg-releases-to-digital-roadmap-plan-ensure-new-york-city-remains-leading
DR349	2013	City of New York	Mayor Bloomberg and Chancellor Walcott Announce AT&T to Donate $1.6 Million to the Fund for Public Schools to Expand Software Engineering Curriculum in High Schools	https://www1.nyc.gov/office-of-the-mayor/news/364-13/mayor-bloomberg-chancellor-walcott-at-t-donate-1-6-million-the-fund-public
DR350	2013	City of New York	New York City's Brooklyn Family Justice Center Hosts Ceremony for First Class of "NYC Steps" Program Graduates	https://www1.nyc.gov/site/doitt/about/pr-130109.page
DR351	2013	City of New York	Department of Information Technology and Telecommunications Marks Major Milestone on Implementation of City's Landmark Open Data Law	https://www1.nyc.gov/site/doitt/about/pr-130307.page
DR352	2013	City of New York	New York City Launches Micro-Trenching Pilot to Enable Rapid Deployment of Fiber Optic Cabling Across the Five Boroughs	https://www1.nyc.gov/site/doitt/about/pr-130402.page
DR353	2013	City of New York	Statement of Chief Information and Innovation Officer Merchant on the Appointment of Deputy Commissioner James Fowler as Kentucky State CIO	https://www1.nyc.gov/site/doitt/about/pr-130430.page

Continued

TABLE C.1 Digital records collected during the search phase—cont'd

ID	Date	Producer	Title	Source
DR354	2013	City of New York	Deputy Mayor Holloway and Office of Emergency Management Commissioner Bruno Announce Final Updated Hurricane Evacuation Zones	https://www1.nyc.gov/site/doitt/about/pr-130618.page
DR355	2013	City of New York	New York City, Cablevision, and Time Warner Cable Launch Public WiFi in 32 Parks Across the Five Boroughs	https://www1.nyc.gov/site/doitt/about/pr-130716.page
DR356	2013	City of New York	Reams of City Data Available for First Time Through New User-Friendly Website	https://www1.nyc.gov/site/doitt/about/pr-130923.page
DR357	2013	City of New York	NYC DataWeek Returns: Second Annual Celebration of Data Innovation	https://www1.nyc.gov/site/doitt/about/pr-131027.page
DR358	2013	City of New York	New York City Felony Crime Data Depicted for First Time on Interactive Map	https://www1.nyc.gov/site/doitt/about/pr-131208.page
DR359	2013	City of New York	PlaNYC: A Stronger, More Resilient New York	http://s-media.nyc.gov/agencies/sirr/SIRR_singles_Hi_res.pdf
DR360	2013	Wired	Alpha Geek: Data Cruncher Uses Code to Solve NYC's Problems	http://www.wired.com/2013/12/lauren-talbot/
DR361	2013	BBC	How New York is releasing its 'big data' to the public	http://www.bbc.co.uk/news/technology-24505860
DR362	2013	TechPresident	Fighting Fires With Data, New York City Launches New Safety Inspection System	http://techpresident.com/news/23884/new-york-city-taps-its-brain-reduce-deaths-fire

DR363	2013	Intelligencer	The City's Big Data Office Knows New York	http://nymag.com/daily/intelligencer/2013/03/meet-numbers-guys-who-run-new-york-city.html
DR364	2013	The New York Times	The Mayor's Geek Squad	http://www.nytimes.com/2013/03/24/nyregion/mayor-bloombergs-geek-squad.html?pagewanted=all
DR365	2013	The Slate Group	Big Data in the Big Apple	http://www.slate.com/articles/technology/future_tense/2013/03/big_data_excerpt_how_mike_flowers_revolutionized_new_york_s_building_inspections.html
DR366	2013	City of New York	Mayor Bloomberg Launches "We Are Made in NY" Initiative to Support Local Tech Industry	https://www.youtube.com/watch?time_continue=18&v=Sv7PH3g69AI
DR367	2013	Laughing Squid	Internet Week New York 2013, A Festival That Celebrates Internet Business & Culture in New York City	https://laughingsquid.com/internet-week-new-york-2013-a-festival-that-celebrates-internet-business-culture-in-new-york-city/
DR368	2013	QED National	QED National Sponsors 2013 New York City Technology Forum	http://www.qednational.com/qed-national-sponsors-2013-new-york-city-technology-forum/
DR369	2014	Mashable	NYC announces free city-wide Wi-Fi with next-gen pay phones	http://mashable.com/2014/11/17/free-nyc-wi-fi-pay-phones/
DR370	2014	New York Post	Plan calls for free Wi-Fi kiosks on city street corners	http://nypost.com/2014/11/18/plan-calls-for-free-wi-fi-kiosks-on-city-street-corners/
DR371	2014	Time	New York Is Transforming Its Old Payphones into Wi-Fi Hotspots	http://time.com/3591964/nyc-payphones-wifi/

Continued

TABLE C.1 Digital records collected during the search phase—cont'd

ID	Date	Producer	Title	Source
DR372	2014	Fast Company	Inside NYC's Bold Plan To Turn Payphones Into Wi-Fi Hotspots	http://www.fastcolabs.com/3033911/inside-nycs-bold-plan-to-turn-payphones-into-wi-fi-hotspots?utm_content=bufferaf696&utm_medium=social&utm_source=twitter.com&utm_campaign=buffer
DR373	2014	Fast Company	New York City's Pay Phones Will Be Replaced By Free Wi-Fi Mobile Charging Stations	http://www.fastcolabs.com/3038678/new-york-citys-pay-phones-will-be-replaced-by-free-wi-fi-mobile-charging-stations
DR374	2014	Kiosk Marketplace	NYC replacing payphones with kiosks	http://www.kioskmarketplace.com/articles/nyc-replacing-payphones-with-kiosks/
DR375	2014	City of New York	NYCEDC Launches Annual NYC BigApps Competition, Which Leverages Strength Of New York City Tech Ecosystem To Make The City a Better Place to Live, Work, Learn And Play	http://www.nycedc.com/press-release/nycedc-launches-annual-nyc-bigapps-competition-which-leverages-strength-new-york-city
DR376	2014	The New York Times	The 21st Century Is Calling, With Wi-Fi Hot Spots	http://www.nytimes.com/2014/05/01/nyregion/the-21st-century-is-calling-with-wi-fi-hot-spots.html?_r=0
DR377	2014	The New York Times	Pay Phones in New York City Will Become Free Wi-Fi Hot Spots	http://www.nytimes.com/2014/11/18/nyregion/pay-phones-in-new-york-city-will-become-free-wi-fi-hot-spots.html
DR378	2014	MetroFocus	New York City's Plan to Bridge the Digital Divide with WiFi	http://www.thirteen.org/metrofocus/2014/06/new-york-citys-plan-to-bridge-the-digital-divide-with-wifi/

DR379	2014	The Washington Post	New York City Unveils the Payphone of the Future and it Does a Whole Lot More Than Make Phone Calls	http://www.washingtonpost.com/blogs/wonkblog/wp/2014/11/17/new-york-city-unveils-the-payphone-of-the-future-and-it-does-a-whole-lot-more-than-make-phone-calls/
DR380	2014	City of New York	Executive Order No. 08: Re-Establishment of the City of New York Technology Steering Committee	http://www1.nyc.gov/assets/home/downloads/pdf/executive-orders/2014/eo_8.pdf
DR381	2014	City of New York	Mayor de Blasio Appoints Anne Roest as Commissioner of Department of Information Technology and Telecommunications	http://www1.nyc.gov/office-of-the-mayor/news/203-14/mayor-de-blasio-appoints-anne-roest-commissioner-department-information-technology-and#/0
DR382	2014	City of New York	Mayor de Blasio Delivers Keynote Address at Internet Week New York 2014	http://www1.nyc.gov/office-of-the-mayor/news/227-14/mayor-de-blasio-delivers-keynote-address-internet-week-new-york-2014#/0
DR383	2014	City of New York	De Blasio Administration Announces Halt To Emergency Communications Technology Project And Orders Immediate Comprehensive Review	http://www1.nyc.gov/office-of-the-mayor/news/228-14/de-blasio-administration-halt-emergency-communications-technology-project-orders
DR384	2014	City of New York	De Blasio Administration Announces Most Comprehensive Review in Years of Existing 911 Emergency Response System	http://www1.nyc.gov/office-of-the-mayor/news/256-14/de-blasio-administration-most-comprehensive-review-years-existing-911-emergency
DR385	2014	City of New York	De Blasio Administration Announces City's 911 Technical Review Recommendations	http://www1.nyc.gov/office-of-the-mayor/news/388-14/de-blasio-administration-city-s-911-technical-review-recommendations

Continued

TABLE C.1 Digital records collected during the search phase—cont'd

ID	Date	Producer	Title	Source
DR386	2014	City of New York	Mayor Bill de Blasio Signs Two Transparency Bills into Law, Announces Public-Private Partnership to Release City Record Data	http://www1.nyc.gov/office-of-the-mayor/news/393-14/mayor-bill-de-blasio-signs-two-transparency-bills-law-public-private-partnership-to#/0
DR387	2014	City of New York	De Blasio Administration Announces Winner of Competition to Replace Payphones with Five-Borough Wi-Fi Network	http://www1.nyc.gov/office-of-the-mayor/news/923-14/de-blasio-administration-winner-competition-replace-payphones-five-borough
DR388	2014	City of New York	Support Pours in For LinkNYC	http://www1.nyc.gov/office-of-the-mayor/news/944-14/support-pours-for-linknyc
DR389	2014	City of New York	Statement From Mayor Bill de Blasio On Today's Approval Of City's LinkNYC Proposal	http://www1.nyc.gov/office-of-the-mayor/news/952-14/statement-mayor-bill-de-blasio-today-s-approval-city-s-linknyc-proposal
DR390	2014	City of New York	Microtrenching Rules	https://rules.cityofnewyork.us/content/microtrenching-rules-1
DR391	2014	New York State	Governor Cuomo Announces First-Ever New York State Broadband Champion Award Winners	https://www.governor.ny.gov/news/governor-cuomo-announces-first-ever-new-york-state-broadband-champion-award-winners
DR392	2014	City of New York	Anti-Virus Security Policy	https://www1.nyc.gov/assets/doitt/downloads/pdf/anti_virus.pdf
DR393	2014	City of New York	Anti-Piracy Policy	https://www1.nyc.gov/assets/doitt/downloads/pdf/anti-piracy.pdf

DR394	2014	City of New York	Applicability Table	https://www1.nyc.gov/assets/doitt/downloads/pdf/applicability_table.pdf
DR395	2014	City of New York	Public Communications Structure Franchise Agreement: Attachment RDR (Resiliency and Disaster Recovery)	https://www1.nyc.gov/assets/doitt/downloads/pdf/Attachment-RDR-Resiliency-and-Disaster-Recovery-(REVISED-FINAL-12-10-2014).pdf
DR396	2014	City of New York	Public Communications Structure Franchise Agreement: Attachment SRV (Services)	https://www1.nyc.gov/assets/doitt/downloads/pdf/Attachment-SRV-Services-(REVISED-FINAL-12-10-2014).pdf
DR397	2014	City of New York	CISO Role	https://www1.nyc.gov/assets/doitt/downloads/pdf/CISO_role.pdf
DR398	2014	City of New York	Comments of the City of New York in Response to Notice of Proposed Rulemaking	https://www1.nyc.gov/assets/doitt/downloads/pdf/City-of-New-York-Wireless-Siting-NPRM-Comments-2-3-2014.pdf
DR399	2014	City of New York	Data Classification Policy	https://www1.nyc.gov/assets/doitt/downloads/pdf/data_classification.pdf
DR400	2014	City of New York	DataShare Overview	https://www1.nyc.gov/assets/doitt/downloads/pdf/datashare_overview_public.pdf
DR401	2014	City of New York	Digital Media Re-use and Disposal Policy	https://www1.nyc.gov/assets/doitt/downloads/pdf/digital_media_reuse.pdf
DR402	2014	City of New York	Statement of Department of Information Technology & Telecommunications Assistant Commissioner Stanley Shor for the Committee on Technology and Subcommittee on Zoning & Franchises Oversight on DoITT's Request for Proposals for NYC Wifi and Communication Hubs. Wednesday, June 18, 2014	https://www1.nyc.gov/assets/doitt/downloads/pdf/doitt_statement_oversight_rfp_commhubs_nyc_wifi.pdf

Continued

TABLE C.1 Digital records collected during the search phase—cont'd

ID	Date	Producer	Title	Source
DR403	2014	City of New York	Request for Proposals for a Franchise to Install, Operate and Maintain Public Communications Structures in the Boroughs of the Bronx, Brooklyn, Manhattan, Queens and Staten Island	https://www1.nyc.gov/assets/doitt/downloads/pdf/DoITT-Public-Communication-Structure-RFP-4-30-14.pdf
DR404	2014	City of New York	Assessment of Key Requirements and Components of the Emergency Communications Transformation Program (ECTP)	https://www1.nyc.gov/assets/doitt/downloads/pdf/ECTP-60-Day-Assessment-140806.pdf
DR405	2014	City of New York	Encryption Policy	https://www1.nyc.gov/assets/doitt/downloads/pdf/encryption.pdf
DR406	2014	City of New York	External Identity Management and Password Policy	https://www1.nyc.gov/assets/doitt/downloads/pdf/external_id_mgmt_and_password_policy.pdf
DR407	2014	City of New York	Department of Information Technology and Telecommunications Testimony Before the City Council Committees on Finance, Land Use and Technology: Fiscal Year 2015 Executive Budget. Thursday, May 22, 2014	https://www1.nyc.gov/assets/doitt/downloads/pdf/Fiscal_2015_Exec_Budget_Testimony.pdf
DR408	2014	City of New York	Department of Information Technology and Telecommunications Testimony Before the City Council Committees on Finance, Land Use and Technology: Fiscal Year 2015 Preliminary Budget. Thursday, March 6, 2014	https://www1.nyc.gov/assets/doitt/downloads/pdf/fiscal-2015-prelim-budget-testimony.pdf

DR409	2014	City of New York	Franchise Agreement for the Installation, Operation, and Maintenance of Public Communications Structures in the Boroughs of the Bronx, Brooklyn, Manhattan, Queens and Staten Island	https://www1.nyc.gov/assets/doitt/downloads/pdf/Franchise-Agreement-for-Public-Communications-Structures-(REVISED-FINAL-12-10-2014).pdf
DR410	2014	City of New York	Identity Management Security Policy	https://www1.nyc.gov/assets/doitt/downloads/pdf/identity_management.pdf
DR411	2014	City of New York	Department of Information Technology and Telecommunications Testimony Before the City Council Committees on Recovery and Resiliency & Fire and Criminal Justice Services. Re: Intro. 0425-2014/Communications Access Planning. Thursday, November 20, 2014	https://www1.nyc.gov/assets/doitt/downloads/pdf/intro-425-Communications-Access-Plan-11-20%2014-final-testimony.pdf
DR412	2014	City of New York	Department of Information Technology and Telecommunications Testimony Before the City Council Committees on Contracts, Technology, and Oversight & Investigations. Re: Intro. 0498-2014/Conflicts of Interest in City Contracts. Monday, December 15, 2014	https://www1.nyc.gov/assets/doitt/downloads/pdf/Intro-498-(CoI-City-Contracts)-FINAL-12-15-14.pdf
DR413	2014	City of New York	Logon Banner Policy	https://www1.nyc.gov/assets/doitt/downloads/pdf/logon_banner_policy.pdf
DR414	2014	City of New York	Franchise Agreement Between The City of New York and Metro Fiber Co., LLC	https://www1.nyc.gov/assets/doitt/downloads/pdf/Metro_Fiber_Co_Info_Srvcs_Franchise.pdf

Continued

TABLE C.1 Digital records collected during the search phase—cont'd

ID	Date	Producer	Title	Source
DR415	2014	City of New York	NYC Open Data Plan 2014	https://www1.nyc.gov/assets/doitt/downloads/pdf/nyc_open_data_plan.pdf
DR416	2014	City of New York	NYC Open Data Plan 2014: Update	https://www1.nyc.gov/assets/doitt/downloads/pdf/nyc-open-data-plan-july-2014-update.pdf
DR417	2014	City of New York	Department of Information Technology and Telecommunications Testimony Before the City Council Committee on Technology: Oversight on Implementation New York City's Open Data Law. Monday, October 27, 2014	https://www1.nyc.gov/assets/doitt/downloads/pdf/Open_Data_Testimony_DoITT.pdf
DR418	2014	City of New York	Testimony of Nicholas O'Brien—Director of Public Affairs for the Mayor's Office of Data Analytics and Acting Open Platform Officer—before the New York City Council—Committee on Technology. October 27, 2014	https://www1.nyc.gov/assets/doitt/downloads/pdf/Open_Data_Testimony_MoDA.pdf
DR419	2014	City of New York	Department of Information Technology and Telecommunications Testimony Before the City Council Committees on Fire & Criminal Justice Services, Public Safety, and Technology. Oversight on Unified Call Taking and FDNY/EMS Emergency Response Protocols. Friday, May 30, 2014	https://www1.nyc.gov/assets/doitt/downloads/pdf/Oversight_UCT_Emergency_Response.pdf
DR420	2014	City of New York	Password Policy	https://www1.nyc.gov/assets/doitt/downloads/pdf/password.pdf

DR421	2014	City of New York	Personnel Security Policy	https://www1.nyc.gov/assets/doitt/downloads/pdf/Personnel_Policy.pdf
DR422	2014	City of New York	Portable Data Security Policy	https://www1.nyc.gov/assets/doitt/downloads/pdf/Portable_Data.pdf
DR423	2014	City of New York	Fact Sheet. Request for Proposals: NYC WiFi & Communication Hubs	https://www1.nyc.gov/assets/doitt/downloads/pdf/Public-Comm-Structures-RFP-Fact-Sheet-04-30-14.pdf
DR424	2014	City of New York	Remote Access Policy	https://www1.nyc.gov/assets/doitt/downloads/pdf/remote_access.pdf
DR425	2014	City of New York	Information Security Policy for Service Providers	https://www1.nyc.gov/assets/doitt/downloads/pdf/service_provider_policy.pdf
DR426	2014	City of New York	Site B Services for Open Systems: V4.1 - Public	https://www1.nyc.gov/assets/doitt/downloads/pdf/site_b_overview_public.pdf
DR427	2014	City of New York	Standard Requirements	https://www1.nyc.gov/assets/doitt/downloads/pdf/standard_requirements_public.pdf
DR428	2014	City of New York	User Responsibilities Policy	https://www1.nyc.gov/assets/doitt/downloads/pdf/user_responsibilities.pdf
DR429	2014	City of New York	Testimony of Jessica Singleton, Office of the Mayor. New York City Council Committee on Technology Hearing on Introduction 471 (We the People Online Petition Bill)	https://www1.nyc.gov/assets/doitt/downloads/pdf/Vacca-WeThePeople-Legislation-10.1.14.pdf
DR430	2014	City of New York	Vulnerability Management Policy	https://www1.nyc.gov/assets/doitt/downloads/pdf/vulnerability_management.pdf

Continued

TABLE C.1 Digital records collected during the search phase—cont'd

ID	Date	Producer	Title	Source
DR431	2014	City of New York	Wireless Security Policy	https://www1.nyc.gov/assets/doitt/downloads/pdf/wireless_security.pdf
DR432	2014	City of New York	Franchise Agreement Between The City of New York and Zenfi Networks, Inc.	https://www1.nyc.gov/assets/doitt/downloads/pdf/Zenfi_Networks_Information_Srvcs_franchise.pdf
DR433	2014	New York City Global Partnership	Best Practice: Affordable Workspace for the Creative and Digital Sector	https://www1.nyc.gov/assets/globalpartners/downloads/pdf/Manchester_EconomicDevelopment_Technology.pdf
DR434	2014	City of New York	Manhattan Community Board 1: Chairperson's Report for August and September 2014	https://www1.nyc.gov/assets/manhattancb1/downloads/pdf/chairperson-reports/sep-2014.pdf
DR435	2014	City of New York	De Blasio Administration Announces Winner of Competition to Replace Payphones with Five-Borough Wi-Fi Network	https://www1.nyc.gov/office-of-the-mayor/news/923-14/de-blasio-administration-winner-competition-replace-payphones-five-borough
DR436	2014	City of New York	Support Pours in For LinkNYC	https://www1.nyc.gov/office-of-the-mayor/news/944-14/support-pours-for-linknyc
DR437	2014	City of New York	New York City Continues Building Upon Open Data Efforts	https://www1.nyc.gov/site/doitt/about/pr-140717.page
DR438	2014	Gotham Gazette	De Blasio Administration, City's Tech Community Prepare for Big Year Two	http://www.gothamgazette.com/index.php/government/5491-de-blasio-administration-citys-tech-community-prepare-for-big-year-two

DR439	2014	Gotham Gazette	City Council Course Offering: Open Data 101	http://www.gothamgazette.com/index.php/government/5444-city-council-course-offering-open-data-101-vacca
DR440	2014	Fortune	Bright lights, big cities, bigger data	http://fortune.com/2014/10/30/bright-lights-big-cities-bigger-data/
DR441	2014	Crain's New York Business	De Blasio names new chief analytics officer	http://www.crainsnewyork.com/article/20141022/TECHNOLOGY/141029947/de-blasio-names-new-chief-analytics-officer
DR442	2014	StateTech	Applying Analytics Can Improve Outcomes	http://www.statetechmagazine.com/article/2014/07/governments-apply-analytics-improve-outcomes
DR443	2014	New York University	Talking Open Data with NYC Stakeholders: A Wrap-Up	http://thegovlab.org/talking-open-data-with-nyc-stakeholders-a-wrap-up/
DR444	2014	TechPresident	With Business Atlas, NYC Analytics Office Looks to 2014	http://techpresident.com/news/24635/business-atlas-nyc-analytics-office-looks-2014
DR445	2014	e.Republic	NYC BigApps Winners Poised to Improve New York	http://www.govtech.com/applications/NYC-BigApps-Winners-Poised-to-Improve-New-York.html
DR446	2014	City of New York	Mayor de Blasio Unveils Digital.NYC, First Ever All-Inclusive Online Hub for City's Tech Ecosystem	https://www.youtube.com/watch?v=0AvZ6tO9_lo&feature=youtu.be
DR447	2014	GovEvents	New York City Technology Forum 2014	https://www.govevents.com/details/12154/new-york-city-technology-forum-2014/
DR448	2014	City of New York	Executive Order No. 08: Re-Establishment of the City of New York Technology Steering Committee	https://www1.nyc.gov/assets/home/downloads/pdf/executive-orders/2014/eo_8.pdf

Continued

TABLE C.1 Digital records collected during the search phase—cont'd

ID	Date	Producer	Title	Source
DR449	2015	Crain Communications	City's 311 hotline is getting some help of its own	http://bit.ly/1QP9Fnp
DR450	2015	Intelligencer	New York City Is Getting Some Technology Upgrades	http://nymag.com/daily/intelligencer/2015/12/new-york-city-is-getting-some-tech-upgrades.html
DR451	2015	State Scoop	New York City refines open data policy with new laws	http://statescoop.com/new-york-city-refines-open-data-policy-new-laws/
DR452	2015	BuzzFeed	NYC Mayor's Office Pushes For Universal Broadband With Three New Initiatives	http://www.buzzfeed.com/johanabhuiyan/internets-for-everyone#.af35d5Ry6
DR453	2015	DailyDooh	LinkNYC Will Help Make New York A Smart City	http://www.dailydooh.com/archives/111250
DR454	2015	Gotham Gazette	Defying National Trends, Women Lead City's Tech Team	http://www.gothamgazette.com/index.php/government/5566-defying-national-trends-women-lead-citys-tech-team
DR455	2015	City of New York	Big Step for Big Data: Yellow/Green Taxi Trip Records Now Available Online	http://www.nyc.gov/html/tlc/downloads/pdf/press_release_08_03_15.pdf
DR456	2015	StateTech	NYC Addresses Challenges in Luring Younger Government Workers	http://www.statetechmagazine.com/article/2015/11/nyc-addresses-challenges-luring-younger-government-workers
DR457	2015	City of New York	Request for Proposals (RFP) Citywide Standby Information Technology and Telecommunications Consulting Services	http://www1.nyc.gov/assets/doitt/downloads/pdf/RFP_Citywide%20ITCS_PIN%2085816P0002.pdf
DR458	2015	City of New York	Building a Smart + Equitable City	http://www1.nyc.gov/assets/forward/documents/NYC-Smart-Equitable-City-Final.pdf

DR459	2015	City of New York	NYC Open Data Plan 2015	http://www1.nyc.gov/assets/home/downloads/pdf/reports/2015/NYC-Open-Data-Plan-2015.pdf
DR460	2015	City of New York	The City Record 04.06.2015	http://www1.nyc.gov/html/dcas/downloads/pdf/cityrecord/cityrecord-04-06-15.pdf
DR461	2015	City of New York	De Blasio Administration Bans Single-Use Styrofoam Products in New York City Beginning July 1, 2015	http://www1.nyc.gov/office-of-the-mayor/news/016-15/de-blasio-administration-bans-single-use-styrofoam-products-new-york-city-beginning-july-1-2015
DR462	2015	City of New York	First Lady Chirlane McCray Highlights New York City's Leadership in Reducing Gender Inequality	http://www1.nyc.gov/office-of-the-mayor/news/158-15/first-lady-chirlane-mccray-highlights-new-york-city-s-leadership-reducing-gender-inequality
DR463	2015	City of New York	Reactions: Mayor de Blasio Releases One New York: The Plan For a Strong and Just City	http://www1.nyc.gov/office-of-the-mayor/news/258-15/reactions-mayor-de-blasio-releases-one-new-york-plan-strong-just-city
DR464	2015	City of New York	De Blasio Administration Releases Audit Report of Verizon's Citywide FiOS Implementation	http://www1.nyc.gov/office-of-the-mayor/news/415-15/de-blasio-administration-releases-audit-report-verizon-s-citywide-fios-implementation
DR465	2015	City of New York	De Blasio Administration Releases Open Data for all, The City's New Open Data Plan	http://www1.nyc.gov/office-of-the-mayor/news/487-15/de-blasio-administration-releases-open-data-all-city-s-new-open-data-plan

Continued

TABLE C.1 Digital records collected during the search phase—cont'd

ID	Date	Producer	Title	Source
DR466	2015	City of New York	Mayor de Blasio and NYCEDC Launch Sixth Annual NYC Bigapps Competition—Challenging NYC's Tech Innovators to Find Lasting Solutions to Four of The City's Most Pressing Issues	http://www1.nyc.gov/office-of-the-mayor/news/494-15/mayor-de-blasio-nycedc-launch-sixth-annual-nyc-bigapps-competition---challenging-nyc-s-tech
DR467	2015	City of New York	Mayor de Blasio, First Lady Mccray, Commissioner Pierre-Louis and Acting Staten Island District Attorney Master Announce Groundbreaking of Fifth NYC Family Justice Center on Staten Island	http://www1.nyc.gov/office-of-the-mayor/news/685-15/mayor-de-blasio-first-lady-mccray-commissioner-pierre-louis-acting-staten-island-district#/0
DR468	2015	City of New York	Transcript: Mayor de Blasio Holds Public Hearing and Signs Intros. 898-A, 890-A, 900-A, 914-A, 915-A, 743-A, 783-A, 956-A, 982-A, and Holds Public Hearing for Intro. 314-A	http://www1.nyc.gov/office-of-the-mayor/news/891-15/transcript-mayor-de-blasio-holds-public-hearing-signs-intros-898-a-890-a-900-a-914-a-
DR469	2015	GigaOm	A guide to New York's plan to cover the city in Wi-Fi hotspots	https://gigaom.com/2015/02/01/link-nyc-explained/
DR470	2015	Next City	The Lamppost That Could Improve Cell Service and Make Money for Cities	https://nextcity.org/daily/entry/zero-site-better-cell-service-cities-lamppost-new-york-city
DR471	2015	NATOA	NATOA Announces Recipients of 2015 Community Broadband Awards for Outstanding Broadband Endeavors	https://www.natoa.org/web/site_news/news_detail/27
DR472	2015	City of New York	Request for Systems Integration Services For 311 Customer Service Management System Replacement and Re-Architecture Project (4/28/2015)	https://www1.nyc.gov/assets/doitt/downloads/pdf/311-rfs.pdf

DR473	2015	City of New York	Reinvent Payphones Challenge/LinkNYC Recognized as 2015 Harvard Ash Center Bright Idea in Government	https://www1.nyc.gov/assets/doitt/downloads/pdf/Bright_Ideas_Press_Release_FINAL.pdf
DR474	2015	City of New York	Preliminary Fiscal 2016 Budget Testimony—Addendum: DoITT Free WiFi Locations, By Borough	https://www1.nyc.gov/assets/doitt/downloads/pdf/budget-testimony-addendum.pdf
DR475	2015	City of New York	Citywide Guidelines for Geographic Information Systems (GIS): Final 1.3—Public	https://www1.nyc.gov/assets/doitt/downloads/pdf/citywide_gis_guidelines_public.pdf
DR476	2015	City of New York	Department of Information Technology and Telecommunications Testimony Before the City Council Committee on Technology Oversight on Open Data and Proposed Legislative Package: Thursday, October 1, 2015	https://www1.nyc.gov/assets/doitt/downloads/pdf/doitt_open_data_testimony_october_2015.pdf
DR477	2015	City of New York	Department of Information Technology and Telecommunications Testimony Before the City Council Committees on Fire and Criminal Justice, Public Safety, Contracts, Oversight and Investigation, and Technology. Re: Examining the New York City Department of Investigation Report on the City's Program to Overhaul the 911 System. Wednesday, February 25, 2015	https://www1.nyc.gov/assets/doitt/downloads/pdf/DOITT-ECTP-Hearing-Testimony.pdf
DR478	2015	City of New York	Rules of the New York City Department of Information Technology and Telecommunications	https://www1.nyc.gov/assets/doitt/downloads/pdf/DoITT-Rules-8-8-2015.pdf
DR479	2015	City of New York	The Excellence in Technology Awards Program (ETAP) 2015	https://www1.nyc.gov/assets/doitt/downloads/pdf/etap_2015.pdf

Continued

TABLE C.1 Digital records collected during the search phase—cont'd

ID	Date	Producer	Title	Source
DR480	2015	City of New York	Department of Information Technology and Telecommunications Testimony Before the City Council Committees on Finance, Land Use and Technology: Fiscal Year 2016 Executive Budget. Thursday, June 4, 2015	https://www1.nyc.gov/assets/doitt/downloads/pdf/fiscal_2016_exec._budget_testimony_final6.4.15.pdf
DR481	2015	City of New York	Department of Information Technology and Telecommunications Testimony Before the City Council Committees on Finance, Land Use and Technology: Fiscal Year 2016 Preliminary Budget. Tuesday, March 10, 2015	https://www1.nyc.gov/assets/doitt/downloads/pdf/fiscal_2016_prelim_budget_testimony.pdf
DR482	2015	City of New York	Request for Proposals for Franchises for the Installation and Use of Telecommunications Equipment and Facilities, Including Base Stations and Access Point Facilities, on City-Owned Street Light Poles, Traffic Light Poles, Highway Sign Support Poles and Certain Utility Poles Located on City Streets, in Connection with the Provision of Mobile Telecommunications Services	https://www1.nyc.gov/assets/doitt/downloads/pdf/mobile-telecom-franchise-rfp.pdf
DR483	2015	City of New York	Department of Information Technology & Telecommunications Testimony Before the City Council Subcommittee on Zoning and Franchises. Re: Intro. 935-2015/Mobile Telecommunications Authorizing Resolution Renewal. Tuesday, January 12, 2016	https://www1.nyc.gov/assets/doitt/downloads/pdf/moda_open_data_testimony_2015.pdf

DR484	2015	City of New York	Department of Information Technology and Telecommunications Testimony Before the New York State Civil Service Commission: IT Non-Competitive Class Titles Proposal. Thursday, December 3, 2015	https://www1.nyc.gov/assets/doitt/downloads/pdf/nyc_it_titles_doitt_final_12_2_15.pdf
DR485	2015	City of New York	Franchise Agreement Between The City of New York and Phoenix Fiber Network, LLC	https://www1.nyc.gov/assets/doitt/downloads/pdf/phoenix_fiber_network_info_srvcs_franchise.pdf
DR486	2015	City of New York	Request for Expressions of Interest and Information (RFEI) on New York City Wireless Network (NYCWiN) Operations and Maintenance Services	https://www1.nyc.gov/assets/doitt/downloads/pdf/rfei/nycwin-ops-maint.pdf
DR487	2015	City of New York	Department of Information Technology and Telecommunications: Strategic Plan 2015-2017	https://www1.nyc.gov/assets/doitt/downloads/pdf/strategic_plan_2015-2017.pdf
DR488	2015	City of New York	Department of Information Technology and Telecommunications: Strategic Plan 2015-2017. 2015 Progress Report	https://www1.nyc.gov/assets/doitt/downloads/pdf/strategic-plan-2015-progress-report.pdf
DR489	2015	City of New York	Testimony of Chris Long Before the City Council Committee on Technology. Re: Intro. 673-2015/ City Website Translation. Re: Intro. 683-2015/ Accessible City Websites. Monday, April 20, 2015	https://www1.nyc.gov/assets/doitt/downloads/pdf/Testimony-for-4-20-Technology-Hearing.pdf
DR490	2015	City of New York	Citywide User Experience Design Guidelines: NYC.gov Style Guide. Final 1.2—Public	https://www1.nyc.gov/assets/doitt/downloads/pdf/user_experience_design_public.pdf

Continued

TABLE C.1 Digital records collected during the search phase—cont'd

ID	Date	Producer	Title	Source
DR491	2015	City of New York	Department of Information Technology and Telecommunications Testimony Before the City Council Committees on Technology and Oversight & Investigations and Subcommittee on Zoning & Franchises. Oversight on The Verizon FiOS Franchise. Wednesday, October 14, 2015	https://www1.nyc.gov/assets/doitt/downloads/pdf/verizon_fios_franchise_oversight_10_14_15final.pdf
DR492	2015	City of New York	Verizon FiOS Implementation Final Audit Report	https://www1.nyc.gov/assets/doitt/downloads/pdf/verizon-audit.pdf
DR493	2015	City of New York	Franchise Agreement Between The City of New York and Zenfi Networks, Inc.	https://www1.nyc.gov/assets/doitt/downloads/pdf/zenfi_executed_franchise_agreement_redacted.pdf
DR494	2015	City of New York	Re: Case 08-V-0624—Petition of Verizon New York, Inc. for a Certificate of Confirmation for its Franchise with the City of New York (New York, Bronx, Queens, Kings and Richmond Counties)	https://www1.nyc.gov/assets/doitt/downloads/pdf/zibelman-aug3.pdf
DR495	2015	City of New York	Building a Smart + Equitable City	https://www1.nyc.gov/assets/forward/documents/NYC-Smart-Equitable-City-Final.pdf
DR496	2015	City of New York	Community Board #1—Manhattan Resolution. Date: July 28, 2015	https://www1.nyc.gov/assets/manhattancb1/downloads/pdf/resolutions/15-07-28.pdf
DR497	2015	City of New York	De Blasio Administration Bans Single-Use Styrofoam Products in New York City Beginning July 1, 2015	https://www1.nyc.gov/office-of-the-mayor/news/016-15/de-blasio-administration-bans-single-use-styrofoam-products-new-york-city-beginning-july-1-2015

DR498	2015	City of New York	First Lady Chirlane McCray Highlights New York City's Leadership in Reducing Gender Inequality	https://www1.nyc.gov/office-of-the-mayor/news/158-15/first-lady-chirlane-mccray-highlights-new-york-city-s-leadership-reducing-gender-inequality
DR499	2015	City of New York	Reactions: Mayor de Blasio Releases One New York: The Plan For a Strong and Just City	https://www1.nyc.gov/office-of-the-mayor/news/258-15/reactions-mayor-de-blasio-releases-one-new-york-plan-strong-just-city
DR500	2015	City of New York	Mayor de Blasio and NYCEDC Launch Sixth Annual NYC Bigapps Competition—Challenging NYC's Tech Innovators to Find Lasting Solutions to Four of The City's Most Pressing Issues	https://www1.nyc.gov/office-of-the-mayor/news/494-15/mayor-de-blasio-nycedc-launch-sixth-annual-nyc-bigapps-competition---challenging-nyc-s-tech
DR501	2015	TrustArc	Internet Week New York	https://www.trustarc.com/calendar-event/internet-week-new-york/
DR502	2015	e.Republic	New York City Technology Forum 2015	http://events.govtech.com/New-York-City-Technology-Forum-2015.html#/speakers
DR503	2016	Fortune	New York Launches Free Wi-Fi Hotspots	http://fortune.com/2016/02/21/nyc-wifi-hotspots/
DR504	2016	Gothamist	Brace For The "Fastest Internet You've Ever Used" At These Free Sidewalk Kiosks	http://gothamist.com/2016/01/05/linknyc_wifi_2_fast_2_furious.php
DR505	2016	Kutv	Can you download me now? NY payphones become Wi-Fi hot spots	http://kutv.com/news/offbeat/can-you-download-me-now-ny-payphones-become-wi-fi-hot-spots
DR506	2016	New York Post	New Yorkers are about to get free Wi-Fi	http://nypost.com/2016/01/10/new-yorkers-are-about-to-get-free-wi-fi/

Continued

TABLE C.1 Digital records collected during the search phase—cont'd

ID	Date	Producer	Title	Source
DR507	2016	Complex Media	New York City's Getting Wi-Fi Hotspots to Replace Pay Phone Boots	http://www.complex.com/pop-culture/2016/01/new-york-city-replacing-pay-phone-booths-with-wifi-hot-spots
DR508	2016	The Daily Dot	Turning old payphones into new opportunities	http://www.dailydot.com/opinion/turning-payphones-into-opportunities-de-blasio-new-york/
DR509	2016	Fast Company	You'll Find The Safest Free Internet Connection With These City Wi-Fi Networks	http://www.fastcompany.com/3055195/elasticity/youll-find-the-safest-free-internet-connection-with-these-city-wi-fi-networks
DR510	2016	MarketWatch	The "mind-boggling" risks your city faces from cyber attackers	http://www.marketwatch.com/story/the-mind-boggling-risks-your-city-faces-from-cyber-attackers-2016-01-04
DR511	2016	City of New York	NYC DOT Advances to Phases Two and Three of Federal Connected Vehicle Pilot Program	http://www.nyc.gov/html/dot/html/pr2016/pr16-094.shtml
DR512	2016	City of New York	The Nature of New York City	http://www.nycgovparks.org/download/summit-2016-DEPTNC-maxwell-emily.pdf
DR513	2016	City of New York	NYC Parks Launches Smart Bench Pilot Program	http://www.nycgovparks.org/news/press-releases?id=21372
DR514	2016	City of New York	NYC Parks Launches Smart Bench Pilot Program: Parks Advances Use of Technology to Improve Green Spaces	http://www.nycgovparks.org/parks/highbridge-park_bronx/pressrelease/21372

DR515	2016	New York Public Radio	Goodbye Pay Phones, Hello LinkNYC	http://www.wnyc.org/story/goodbye-pay-phones-hello-linknyc/
DR516	2016	New York University	Reducing Data Poverty in NYC: Achieving Open Data for All. A Capstone Report	http://www1.nyc.gov/assets/analytics/downloads/pdf/cusp_open_data_poverty_capstone.pdf
DR517	2016	City of New York	Building Ideas Catalogue 02/2016	http://www1.nyc.gov/assets/ddc/downloads/town-and-gown/catalogue/building-ideas-catalogue-feb2016.pdf
DR518	2016	City of New York	New York City's Roadmap to 80x50	http://www1.nyc.gov/assets/sustainability/downloads/pdf/publications/New%20York%20City's%20Roadmap%20to%2080%20x%2050_Final.pdf
DR519	2016	City of New York	2016 NYC Summer Internship Program	http://www1.nyc.gov/html/dcas/downloads/pdf/postings/DOITT-021.pdf
DR520	2016	City of New York	NYC DOT Advances to Phases Two and Three of Federal Connected Vehicle Pilot Program	http://www1.nyc.gov/html/dot/html/pr2016/pr16-094.shtml
DR521	2016	City of New York	OneNYC 2016 Progress Report	http://www1.nyc.gov/html/onenyc/downloads/pdf/publications/OneNYC-2016-Progress-Report.pdf
DR522	2016	City of New York	Mayor de Blasio Announces Public Launch of LinkNYC Program, Largest and Fastest Free Municipal Wi-Fi Network in the World	http://www1.nyc.gov/office-of-the-mayor/news/184-16/mayor-de-blasio-public-launch-linknyc-program-largest-fastest-free-municipal
DR523	2016	City of New York	De Blasio Administration Releases Annual Update to Open Data Plan	http://www1.nyc.gov/office-of-the-mayor/news/618-16/de-blasio-administration-releases-annual-to-open-data-plan

Continued

TABLE C.1 Digital records collected during the search phase—cont'd

ID	Date	Producer	Title	Source
DR524	2016	City of New York	Mayor de Blasio, Formula E Announce Inaugural NYC ePrix Coming To Brooklyn	http://www1.nyc.gov/office-of-the-mayor/news/761-16/mayor-de-blasio-formula-e-inaugural-nyc-eprix-coming-brooklyn
DR525	2016	City of New York	Mayor de Blasio Appoints Miguel A. Gamino Jr. As NYC Chief Technology Officer	http://www1.nyc.gov/office-of-the-mayor/news/843-16/mayor-de-blasio-appoints-miguel-a-gamino-jr-nyc-chief-technology-officer
DR526	2016	City of New York	New York Named "2016 Best Smart City," NYC To Host 2017 International Conference On Urban Technology At Brooklyn Navy Yard	http://www1.nyc.gov/office-of-the-mayor/news/909-16/new-york-named-2016-best-smart-city-nyc-host-2017-international-conference-urban
DR527	2016	City of New York	Open Data For All: 2016 Progress Report	https://opendata.cityofnewyork.us/wp-content/uploads/2017/12/2016_opendataforall.pdf
DR528	2016	Columbia University	Empowering NYC Communities through the Use of NYC Open Data: Capstone Final Report	https://sipa.columbia.edu/file/3355/download?token=B9KidkkT
DR529	2016	City of New York	Disclosure of Donations - November 15, 2016	https://www1.nyc.gov/assets/coib/downloads/pdf2/fundraising_reports/apr_1_16_to_sep_31_16.pdf
DR530	2016	City of New York	Building Ideas Catalogue 03/2016	https://www1.nyc.gov/assets/ddc/downloads/town-and-gown/catalogue/building-ideas-catalogue-mar2016.pdf
DR531	2016	City of New York	Testimony of Anne Roest concerning the FY 2017 Executive Budget: Thursday, May 19, 2016	https://www1.nyc.gov/assets/doitt/downloads/pdf/2016.05.19%20FY17%20Executive%20Budget.pdf

DR532	2016	City of New York	Department of Information Technology & Telecommunications Testimony before the City Council Committee on Technology. RE: Intro. 1158/Reporting on the Routing of Calls Near the Boundaries of NYC	https://www1.nyc.gov/assets/doitt/downloads/pdf/2016.06.17%20DoITT%20Testimony%20Int.%201158.pdf
DR533	2016	City of New York	2016 Annual Report on Implementation of Next Generation 9-1-1 in NYC	https://www1.nyc.gov/assets/doitt/downloads/pdf/DOITT-NG911-LL78-Annual-Report-2016.pdf
DR534	2016	City of New York	Department of Information Technology and Telecommunications Testimony Before the City Council Committee on Technology: Oversight on The Open Data Law and its 2015/2016 Amendments. Wednesday, September 21, 2016	https://www1.nyc.gov/assets/doitt/downloads/pdf/FINAL%209.21.16%20Open%20Data%20Testimony.pdf
DR535	2016	City of New York	Department of Information Technology and Telecommunications Testimony Before the City Council Committees on Finance, Land Use and Technology: Fiscal Year 2017 Preliminary Budget. Tuesday, March 29, 2016	https://www1.nyc.gov/assets/doitt/downloads/pdf/Fiscal-2017-Prelim-Budget-Testimony-FINAL-3.29.16.pdf
DR536	2016	City of New York	Department of Information Technology and Telecommunications Releases Geoclient under an Open Source License	https://www1.nyc.gov/assets/doitt/downloads/pdf/geoclient_release_2016.pdf
DR537	2016	City of New York	Department of Information Technology and Telecommunications Testimony Before the City Council Committees on Technology. Re: Intro. 564-2014/Online Submission of City Business Permits, Licenses and Applications. Tuesday, May 3, 2016	https://www1.nyc.gov/assets/doitt/downloads/pdf/Hearing%20Testimony%20564%202016.05.03.pdf

Continued

TABLE C.1 Digital records collected during the search phase—cont'd

ID	Date	Producer	Title	Source
DR538	2016	City of New York	Department of Information Technology & Telecommunications Testimony Before the New York City Council Committee on Technology. Re: Intro. 626-2015/Personal Information Security & Intro. 1052-2016/City Agency Electronics Disposal. Monday, February 1, 2016	https://www1.nyc.gov/assets/doitt/downloads/pdf/intro_626_1052_2116final.pdf
DR539	2016	City of New York	Department of Information Technology and Telecommunications Testimony Before the City Council Committee on Contracts. Re: Intro. 365-2014/Collaborative Software Purchasing & Intro. 366-2014/Free and Open Source Software. Tuesday, February 23, 2016	https://www1.nyc.gov/assets/doitt/downloads/pdf/intro-365-366-civic-commons-fossa.pdf
DR540	2016	City of New York	Department of Information Technology & Telecommunications Before the City Council Committees on Technology and Public Safety. Re: Intro. 0868-2014 / Creating an Emergency Mobile Text System. Thursday, January 14, 2016	https://www1.nyc.gov/assets/doitt/downloads/pdf/Intro-868-NextGen-911.pdf
DR541	2016	City of New York	Mobile Computing Device Security Policy	https://www1.nyc.gov/assets/doitt/downloads/pdf/mobile_security_policy.pdf
DR542	2016	City of New York	Department of Information Technology & Telecommunications Testimony Before the City Council Subcommittee on Zoning and Franchises. Re: Intro. 935-2015 / Mobile Telecommunications Authorizing Resolution Renewal. Tuesday, January 12, 2016	https://www1.nyc.gov/assets/doitt/downloads/pdf/Mobile-Telecom-Testimony-Jan-2016.pdf

DR543	2016	City of New York	Department of Information Technology and Telecommunications Issues Request for Information for Next Generation 911 System	https://www1.nyc.gov/assets/doitt/downloads/pdf/ng911_rfi_release_final.pdf
DR544	2016	City of New York	Open Data Policy and Technical Standards Manual	https://www1.nyc.gov/assets/doitt/downloads/pdf/nyc_open_data_tsm.pdf
DR545	2016	City of New York	NYC Open Data Plan 2016	https://www1.nyc.gov/assets/doitt/downloads/pdf/open-data-update-2016-final.pdf
DR546	2016	City of New York	Citywide Policy for Performance Testing of Public-Facing Applications: Final 2.0 - Public	https://www1.nyc.gov/assets/doitt/downloads/pdf/performance_testing_public.pdf
DR547	2016	City of New York	Testimony of Stanley Shor, Assistant Commissioner of Franchise Administration Committee on Technology: Oversight—LinkNYC. November 15, 2016	https://www1.nyc.gov/assets/doitt/downloads/pdf/SS%20LinkNYC%20testimony%20FINAL%2011.15.pdf
DR548	2016	City of New York	Streetscape Study of Lower Manhattan: An Analysis of the Sidewalk Features and Public Space of Manhattan Community District 1	https://www1.nyc.gov/assets/manhattancb1/downloads/pdf/studies-and-reports/streetscape-study-final-report-6-21.pdf
DR549	2016	City of New York	NYC DOT Advances to Phases Two and Three of Federal Connected Vehicle Pilot Program	https://www1.nyc.gov/html/dot/html/pr2016/pr16-094.shtml
DR550	2016	City of New York	OneNYC: 2016 Progress Report	https://www1.nyc.gov/html/onenyc/downloads/pdf/publications/OneNYC-2016-Progress-Report.pdf
DR551	2016	City of New York	Mayor de Blasio Announces Public Launch of LinkNYC Program, Largest and Fastest Free Municipal Wi-Fi Network in the World	https://www1.nyc.gov/office-of-the-mayor/news/184-16/mayor-de-blasio-public-launch-linknyc-program-largest-fastest-free-municipal

Continued

TABLE C.1 Digital records collected during the search phase—cont'd

ID	Date	Producer	Title	Source
DR552	2016	City of New York	De Blasio Administration Releases Annual Update to Open Data Plan	https://www1.nyc.gov/office-of-the-mayor/news/618-16/de-blasio-administration-releases-annual-to-open-data-plan
DR553	2016	City of New York	Mayor de Blasio, Formula E Announce Inaugural NYC ePrix Coming To Brooklyn	https://www1.nyc.gov/office-of-the-mayor/news/761-16/mayor-de-blasio-formula-e-inaugural-nyc-eprix-coming-brooklyn
DR554	2016	City of New York	Mayor de Blasio Appoints Miguel A. Gamino Jr. As NYC Chief Technology Officer	https://www1.nyc.gov/office-of-the-mayor/news/843-16/mayor-de-blasio-appoints-miguel-a-gamino-jr-nyc-chief-technology-officer
DR555	2016	City of New York	New York Named "2016 Best Smart City," NYC To Host 2017 International Conference On Urban Technology At Brooklyn Navy Yard	https://www1.nyc.gov/office-of-the-mayor/news/909-16/new-york-named-2016-best-smart-city-nyc-host-2017-international-conference-urban
DR556	2016	City of New York	PPB Rules	https://www1.nyc.gov/assets/mocs/downloads/pdf/PPBRULESFINALEffectiveJuly2016.pdf
DR557	2016	NBC	An Inside Look at the System That Cut Crime in New York By 75 Percent	https://www.nbcnews.com/news/us-news/inside-look-system-cut-crime-new-york-75-percent-n557031
DR558	2016	Adage	Internet Week	https://twitter.com/internetweek?lang=en
DR559	2016	e.Republic	New York City Technology Forum 2016	http://events.govtech.com/New-York-City-Technology-Forum-2016.html

DR560	2017	City of New York	FY 2017 Manhattan Borough Budget Consultations	http://www.nyc.gov/html/mancb3/downloads/budget/2017/FY%2017%20EDC%20MANHATTAN%20NOTES.xlsx
DR561	2017	City of New York	The Brownsville Plan: Our Home, Our Future	http://www1.nyc.gov/assets/hpd/downloads/pdf/community/the-brownsville-plan.pdf
DR562	2017	City of New York	New York City Identity Card Program Quarterly Report	http://www1.nyc.gov/assets/idnyc/downloads/pdf/IDNYC_Q2_6_30_17.pdf
DR563	2017	City of New York	Vision Zero: Year Three Report	http://www1.nyc.gov/html/dcas/downloads/pdf/fleet/Vision_Zero_Year_3_Report.pdf
DR564	2017	City of New York	2017 NYC Summer Internship Program	http://www1.nyc.gov/html/dcas/downloads/pdf/postings/DoITT-030.pdf
DR565	2017	City of New York	Mayor de Blasio Brings NYC's First Neighborhood Innovation Lab for Smart City Technologies to Brownsville	http://www1.nyc.gov/office-of-the-mayor/news/159-17/mayor-de-blasio-brings-nyc-s-first-neighborhood-innovation-lab-smart-city-technologies-to
DR566	2017	City of New York	Transcript: Mayor de Blasio Mayor de Blasio Announces a Comprehensive Set of Strategies to Spur the Creation of 100,000 Jobs	http://www1.nyc.gov/office-of-the-mayor/news/417-17/transcript-mayor-de-blasio-mayor-de-blasio-comprehensive-set-strategies-spur-the
DR567	2017	City of New York	De Blasio Administration Announces Launch of New Smart City Technologies and Young Innovators Program in Brownsville	http://www1.nyc.gov/office-of-the-mayor/news/463-17/de-blasio-administration-launch-new-smart-city-technologies-young-innovators
DR568	2017	City of New York	City Awards Community-Based Organizations $500,000 to Implement Tech Solutions to Enhance Commercial Districts Across NYC	http://www1.nyc.gov/site/sbs/about/pr20170619-NeighborhoodChallenge.page

Continued

TABLE C.1 Digital records collected during the search phase—cont'd

ID	Date	Producer	Title	Source
DR569	2017	City of New York	Open Data for All: 2017 Progress Report	https://moda-nyc.github.io/2017-Open-Data-Report/
DR570	2017	City of New York	Open Data for All: 2017 Progress Report	https://opendata.cityofnewyork.us/wp-content/uploads/2017/07/OD4A-report_2017-1.pdf
DR571	2017	Reboot	Understanding the Users of Open Data: Research Findings	https://opendata.cityofnewyork.us/wp-content/uploads/2017/07/Understanding-the-Users-of-Open-Data_Reboot.pdf
DR572	2017	City of New York	Minutes of Community Board #16—April 25, 2017	https://www1.nyc.gov/assets/brooklyncb16/downloads/pdf/minutes/2017/04-25-2017.pdf
DR573	2017	City of New York	Minutes of Economic Development and Employment Committee—April 04, 2017	https://www1.nyc.gov/assets/brooklyncb2/downloads/pdf/min_ed%26e_1704.pdf
DR574	2017	City of New York	NYC.gov Agency Content Accessibility Issues to Fix	https://www1.nyc.gov/assets/doitt/downloads/excel/nyc-war-appendix-3-content-changes.xls
DR575	2017	City of New York	Testimony of Michael Pastor General Counsel, New York City Department of Information Technology & Telecommunications before the New York City Council Subcommittee on Zoning and Franchises and the Committee on Technology concerning the Charter Communications Franchise Agreement: Tuesday, May 30, 2017	https://www1.nyc.gov/assets/doitt/downloads/pdf/05.30.17%20FINAL%20Spectrum%20Testimony.pdf

DR576	2017	City of New York	Department of Information Technology and Telecommunications Amendment No. 1 to the Franchise Agreement Between the City of New York and CityBridge, LLC for the Installation, Operation, and Maintenance of Public Communications Structures in the Boroughs of the Bronx, Brooklyn, Manhattan, Queens and Staten Island Contract No. RCTI-858-20158202566	https://www1.nyc.gov/assets/doitt/downloads/pdf/amendment_no_1_to_the_public_communications_structure_franchise_agreeme.pdf
DR577	2017	City of New York	Citywide Linking Policy: Final 1.4—Public	https://www1.nyc.gov/assets/doitt/downloads/pdf/citywide_linking_policy_public.pdf
DR578	2017	City of New York	2017 Annual Report on Implementation of Next Generation 9-1-1 in NYC	https://www1.nyc.gov/assets/doitt/downloads/pdf/doitt-ng911-ll78-annual-report-2017.pdf
DR579	2017	City of New York	Department of Information Technology and Telecommunications Testimony Before the New York City Council Committee on Technology. Oversight: Privacy of City Data. Monday, April 24, 2017	https://www1.nyc.gov/assets/doitt/downloads/pdf/DoITT%20Data%20Privacy%20Hearing%20Testimony%20FINAL.pdf
DR580	2017	City of New York	Testimony of the Department of Information Technology and Telecommunications Before the City Council Committee on Technology. September 20, 2017	https://www1.nyc.gov/assets/doitt/downloads/pdf/DoITT%20Open%20Data%20testimony%2009.20.17.pdf
DR581	2017	City of New York	Testimony of the Department of Information Technology and Telecommunications on Int. 1696, A Local Law to Amend the Administrative Code of the City of New York, In Relation to Automated Processing of Data for the Purposes of Targeting Services, Penalties, or Policing to Persons. October 16, 2017	https://www1.nyc.gov/assets/doitt/downloads/pdf/DoITT%20Testimony%20Int%201696%20FINAL.pdf

Continued

TABLE C.1 Digital records collected during the search phase—cont'd

ID	Date	Producer	Title	Source
DR582	2017	City of New York	Department of Information Technology and Telecommunications Testimony Before the City Council Committees on Land Use and Technology: Fiscal Year 2018 Preliminary Budget. Wednesday, March 29, 2017	https://www1.nyc.gov/assets/doitt/downloads/pdf/FINAL%202018%20Prelim%20Budget%20Testimony%20DoITT.pdf
DR583	2017	City of New York	Testimony of Anne Roest Commissioner, New York City Department of Information Technology & Telecommunications before the New York City Council Committees on Finance, Technology and Land Use concerning the FY 2018 Executive Budget. Thursday, May 18, 2017	https://www1.nyc.gov/assets/doitt/downloads/pdf/FINAL%20DoITT%20FY18%20Exec%20Budget%20Testimony.pdf
DR584	2017	City of New York	Dr. Amen Ra Mashriki, Chief Analytics Officer Testimony Before the City Council Committees on Technology. Oversight on MODA's 2016 Open Data Examination and Verification Report. Tuesday, January 24, 2017	https://www1.nyc.gov/assets/doitt/downloads/pdf/Hearing%20Testimony%20MODA%20EV%202017.01.24.pdf
DR585	2017	City of New York	Testimony of The Department of Information Technology and Telecommunications Before the New York City Council Committee on Contracts. October 23, 2017	https://www1.nyc.gov/assets/doitt/downloads/pdf/IT%20contracts%20testimony%20 10-23%20FINAL.pdf
DR586	2017	City of New York	The City of New York Web Accessibility Report	https://www1.nyc.gov/assets/doitt/downloads/pdf/nyc-web-accessibility-report.pdf

DR587	2017	City of New York	Is NYC.ID for You?	https://www1.nyc.gov/assets/doitt/downloads/pdf/NYC.ID-Integration-Guide.pdf
DR588	2017	City of New York	Open Data for All: 2017 Progress Report	https://www1.nyc.gov/assets/doitt/downloads/pdf/OD4A-report_2017.pdf
DR589	2017	City of New York	The Brownsville Request for Proposals	https://www1.nyc.gov/assets/hpd/downloads/pdf/developers/brownsville-rfp-w-appendix.pdf
DR590	2017	City of New York	New York City Identity Card Program Quarterly Report. March 30, 2017–June 29, 2017	https://www1.nyc.gov/assets/idnyc/downloads/pdf/IDNYC_Q2_6_30_17.pdf
DR591	2017	City of New York	Vision Zero: Year Three Report	https://www1.nyc.gov/assets/visionzero/downloads/pdf/vision-zero-year-3-report.pdf
DR592	2017	City of New York	Mayor de Blasio Brings NYC's First Neighborhood Innovation Lab for Smart City Technologies to Brownsville	https://www1.nyc.gov/office-of-the-mayor/news/159-17/mayor-de-blasio-brings-nyc-s-first-neighborhood-innovation-lab-smart-city-technologies-to
DR593	2017	City of New York	Transcript: Mayor de Blasio Mayor de Blasio Announces a Comprehensive Set of Strategies to Spur the Creation of 100,000 Jobs	https://www1.nyc.gov/office-of-the-mayor/news/417-17/transcript-mayor-de-blasio-mayor-de-blasio-comprehensive-set-strategies-spur-the
DR594	2017	City of New York	De Blasio Administration Announces Launch of New Smart City Technologies and Young Innovators Program in Brownsville	https://www1.nyc.gov/office-of-the-mayor/news/463-17/de-blasio-administration-launch-new-smart-city-technologies-young-innovators
DR595	2017	City of New York	Mayor de Blasio and Barcelona Mayor Colau Announce Joint Competition to Make Streets Safer and More Accessible for Pedestrians Who are Blind or Have Low Vision	https://www1.nyc.gov/office-of-the-mayor/news/641-17/mayor-de-blasio-barcelona-mayor-colau-joint-competition-make-streets-safer-more

Continued

TABLE C.1 Digital records collected during the search phase—cont'd

ID	Date	Producer	Title	Source
DR596	2017	City of New York	De Blasio Administration and Brownsville Community Leaders Announce NYCx Co-Lab Challenges in Brownsville	https://www1.nyc.gov/office-of-the-mayor/news/679-17/de-blasio-administration-brownsville-community-leaders-nycx-co-lab-challenges-in
DR597	2017	City of New York	City Awards Community-Based Organizations $500,000 to Implement Tech Solutions to Enhance Commercial Districts Across NYC	https://www1.nyc.gov/site/sbs/about/pr20170619-NeighborhoodChallenge.page
DR598	2017	Crain Communications	IBM's Watson will soon answer your 311 calls	https://www.crainsnewyork.com/article/20170112/TECHNOLOGY/170119941/ibm-s-watson-will-soon-answer-your-311-calls-as-part-of-a-24-million-upgrade-to-the-system
DR599	2017	PostJobFree	Project Manager System	https://www.postjobfree.com/resume/ac137v/azure-tfs-system-search-led-new-york-ny
DR600	2017	Medium	NYC BigApps: Winners	http://www.bigapps.nyc/winners/
DR601	2017	ABC	New York City to launch new emergency notification app, "Notify NYC"	https://abc7ny.com/community-events/nyc-to-launch-new-emergency-notification-app/2442175/
DR602	2017	e.Republic	New York City Technology Forum 2017	http://events.govtech.com/New-York-City-Technology-Forum-2017.html
DR603	2018	City of New York	Learning about NYC: Buildings	https://opendata.cityofnewyork.us/wp-content/uploads/2018/04/Civic-Hall-01.25.18-event_-Buildings.pdf

DR604	2018	City of New York	Learning about NYC: Environment & Sustainability	https://opendata.cityofnewyork.us/wp-content/uploads/2018/08/Civic-Hall-05.01.18-event EnvironmentaAndSustainability.pdf
DR605	2018	City of New York	Open Data User Journey Analysis	https://opendata.cityofnewyork.us/wp-content/uploads/2018/08/Web-Traffic-Research_User-Journey-Presentation_Spring-2018.pdf
DR606	2018	City of New York	Monthly Board Meeting—Minutes: April 24, 2018	https://www1.nyc.gov/assets/brooklyncb15/downloads/pdf/minutes/minutesapr2018.pdf
DR607	2018	City of New York	Minutes of Community Board #16—May 22, 2018	https://www1.nyc.gov/assets/brooklyncb16/downloads/pdf/minutes/2018/05-%2022-2018.pdf
DR608	2018	City of New York	Citywide Application Security Policy	https://www1.nyc.gov/assets/doitt/downloads/pdf/application_development.pdf
DR609	2018	City of New York	Re: Draft letter Report Regarding Charter's Compliance with Article 71 of Franchise Agreement	https://www1.nyc.gov/assets/doitt/downloads/pdf/doitt-final-charter-audit-report-redacted.pdf
DR610	2018	US Court of Appeals for the District of Columbia Circuit	Mozilla Corporation, et al., Against Federal Communications Commission and United States of America: Brief for Amici the City of New York and 27 Other Local Governments, Mayors, and Municipal Organizations in Support of Petitioners	https://www1.nyc.gov/assets/home/downloads/pdf/press-releases/2018/final-nyc-net-neutrality-amicus-brief.pdf
DR611	2018	City of New York	Monthly Meeting. Tuesday, March 27, 2018. Museum of Jewish Heritage, 36 Battery Place	https://www1.nyc.gov/assets/manhattancb1/downloads/pdf/full-board-meeting-minutes/18-03-27.pdf

Continued

TABLE C.1 Digital records collected during the search phase—cont'd

ID	Date	Producer	Title	Source
DR612	2018	City of New York	Business & Consumer Issues Committee Meeting Minutes. April 11, 2018	https://www1.nyc.gov/assets/manhattancb7/downloads/pdf/minutes/2018/min04_18.pdf
DR613	2018	City of New York	AccessibleNYC: An Annual Report on the State of People with Disabilities Living in New York City. 2018 Edition	https://www1.nyc.gov/assets/mopd/downloads/pdf/accessiblenyc-2018.pdf
DR614	2018	City of New York	City Planning Commission. June 27, 2018/ Calendar No. 14. C180203ZSM	https://www1.nyc.gov/assets/planning/download/pdf/about/cpc/180203.pdf
DR615	2018	City of New York	Vision Zero: Year Four Report	https://www1.nyc.gov/assets/visionzero/downloads/pdf/vision-zero-year-4-report.pdf
DR616	2018	City of New York	Transcript: Mayor de Blasio Delivers Remarks at the Center for American Progress' 2018 Ideas Conference	https://www1.nyc.gov/office-of-the-mayor/news/248-18/transcript-mayor-de-blasio-delivers-remarks-the-center-american-progress-2018-ideas
DR617	2018	City of New York	De Blasio Administration Announces Finalists from Tech Companies on Local Climate Action	https://www1.nyc.gov/office-of-the-mayor/news/300-18/de-blasio-administration-finalists-tech-companies-local-climate-action
DR618	2018	City of New York	NYC Emergency Management's Latest 'Prep Talk' Podcast Focuses on Disability Awareness	https://www1.nyc.gov/site/em/about/press-releases/20180716_pr_nycem-latest-prep-talk-podcast-focuses-on-disability-awareness.page
DR619	2018	City of New York	NYCHA, DSNY, MOCTO & NYCEDC Announce Winners of the NYCx Co-Lab Challenge to Reduce Waste and Increase Recycling in Brownsville Houses	https://www1.nyc.gov/site/nycha/about/press/pr-2018/pr-20180423.page

DR620	2018	City of New York	OneNYC 2018: Progress Report	https://onenyc.cityofnewyork.us/wp-content/uploads/2018/05/OneNYC_Progress_2018.pdf
DR621	2018	e.Republic	New York City Technology Forum 2019	http://events.govtech.com/New-York-City-Technology-Forum.html
DR622	N/A	Medium	NYC BigApps: About	http://www.bigapps.nyc/about/
DR623	N/A	City of New York	NYC OpenData Technical Standards Manual (TSM)	http://cityofnewyork.github.io/opendatatsm/
DR624	N/A	City of New York	NYC Developer Portal	http://developer.cityofnewyork.us/
DR625	N/A	City of New York	NYC Developer Portal: Open311 Inquiry	http://developer.cityofnewyork.us/api/open311-inquiry
DR626	N/A	City of New York	NYC Developer Portal: App Showcase	http://developer.cityofnewyork.us/app
DR627	N/A	City of New York	About Population FactFinder	https://popfactfinder.planning.nyc.gov/about#12.25/40.724/-73.9868
DR628	N/A	City of New York	NYC Crime Map	http://maps.nyc.gov/crime/
DR629	N/A	City of New York	NYCityMap	http://maps.nyc.gov/doitt/nycitymap/
DR630	N/A	City of New York	NYC OpenData: About	https://nycopendata.tumblr.com/about
DR631	N/A	City of New York	NYC Open Data	http://nycopendata.tumblr.com/
DR632	N/A	Senior Planet	Senior Planet: Welcome	http://seniorplanet.org/the-center/welcome/
DR633	N/A	Code for America	Government partners	http://www.codeforamerica.org/governments/newyork/
DR634	N/A	LearningTimes	Case Study: DIG/IT and the NYC Department of Education	http://www.learningtimes.com/what-we-do/badges/digit-badges-nycdoe/

Continued

TABLE C.1 Digital records collected during the search phase—cont'd

ID	Date	Producer	Title	Source
DR635	N/A	CityBridge	LinkNYC	http://www.link.nyc/
DR636	N/A	City of New York	About Automated Meter Reading (AMR)	http://www.nyc.gov/html/dep/html/customer_services/amr_about.shtml
DR637	N/A	City of New York	A 21st Century Transportation Department	http://www.nyc.gov/html/dot/downloads/pdf/stratplan_leadership.pdf
DR638	N/A	City of New York	EE 1: Improve Energy Modelling for Building Design	http://www.nyc.gov/html/gbee/downloads/pdf/e&ce_energy_efficiency.pdf
DR639	N/A	City of New York	OC 1: Add Environmental Protection as Fundamental Principal of the Construction Codes	http://www.nyc.gov/html/gbee/downloads/pdf/gctf_all_proposals.pdf
DR640	N/A	City of New York	About Language Gateway	http://www.nyc.gov/html/lg/html/about/about.shtml
DR641	N/A	City of New York	NYC Project—Welcome to the NYC Project site	http://www.nyc.gov/html/nycproject/html/home/home.shtml
DR642	N/A	City of New York	NYC Project—Hybrid Workflow	http://www.nyc.gov/html/nycproject/html/hybrid/hybrid.shtml
DR643	N/A	City of New York	NYC Project—Agile Workflow	http://www.nyc.gov/html/nycproject/html/agile/agile.shtml
DR644	N/A	City of New York	NYC Project—Deliverables	http://www.nyc.gov/html/nycproject/html/deliverables/deliverables.shtml
DR645	N/A	City of New York	NYC Project—Collaboration	http://www.nyc.gov/html/nycproject/html/collaboration/collaboration.shtml

DR646	N/A	City of New York	NYC Project—Practices	http://www.nyc.gov/html/nycproject/html/practices/practices.shtml
DR647	N/A	City of New York	Media Education Programs	http://www.nycgovparks.org/crc
DR648	N/A	Neustar	.nyc	http://www.ownit.nyc/register.php?domain=
DR649	N/A	City of New York	UrbanTech NYC	http://www.urbantechnyc.com
DR650	N/A	City of New York	Applications	http://www1.nyc.gov/connect/applications.page
DR651	N/A	City of New York	Social Media	http://www1.nyc.gov/connect/social-media.page
DR652	N/A	City of New York	Neighborhood Challenge Innovation Competition	http://www1.nyc.gov/nyc-resources/service/2061/neighborhood-challenge-innovation-competition
DR653	N/A	City of New York	Welcome to the Mayor's Office of Data Analytics	http://www1.nyc.gov/site/analytics/index.page
DR654	N/A	City of New York	Invitation for Bids for Closed Captioning Services for Prerecorded, Live and Near-Live Programming—EPIN: 85816B0002	http://www1.nyc.gov/site/doitt/business/closed-captioning-services-download.page
DR655	N/A	City of New York	Contact Center Services RFP—PIN: 85815P0003	http://www1.nyc.gov/site/doitt/business/contact-center-services-download.page
DR656	N/A	City of New York	Media Campaign and Purchasing Services—MOME—PIN: 85816P0003	http://www1.nyc.gov/site/doitt/business/media-campaign-and-purchasing-services-download.page
DR657	N/A	City of New York	NYC Next Generation 9-1-1 Emergency Services—PIN 85817P0002	http://www1.nyc.gov/site/doitt/business/next-gen-911-emergency-services-download.page

Continued

TABLE C.1 Digital records collected during the search phase—cont'd

ID	Date	Producer	Title	Source
DR658	N/A	City of New York	New York City Next Generation 9-1-1 Program Request for Information	http://www1.nyc.gov/site/doitt/business/nyc-next-gen-911-program-download.page
DR659	N/A	City of New York	Open Business Opportunities	http://www1.nyc.gov/site/doitt/business/open-business-opportunities.page
DR660	N/A	City of New York	NYC 3-D Building Model	http://www1.nyc.gov/site/doitt/initiatives/3d-building.page
DR661	N/A	City of New York	LinkNYC	http://www1.nyc.gov/site/doitt/initiatives/linknyc.page
DR662	N/A	City of New York	Guides & App	http://www1.nyc.gov/site/em/ready/guides-resources.page
DR663	N/A	City of New York	Domain Requests	http://www1.nyc.gov/site/forward/initiatives/dotnyc/domain-requests.page
DR664	N/A	City of New York	.nyc Documentation	http://www1.nyc.gov/site/forward/initiatives/dotnyc/dotnycdocs.page
DR665	N/A	City of New York	Neighborhood Domains	http://www1.nyc.gov/site/forward/initiatives/dotnyc/neighborhoods.page
DR666	N/A	City of New York	Introducing .nyc	http://www1.nyc.gov/site/forward/initiatives/dotnyc/nyc.page
DR667	N/A	City of New York	Public Interest Proposals for .nyc Domains	http://www1.nyc.gov/site/forward/initiatives/dotnyc/public-interest-proposals.page

DR668	N/A	City of New York	International Businesses: Welcome to NYC	http://www1.nyc.gov/site/internationalbusiness/index.page
DR669	N/A	City of New York	International Businesses: Additional Industries	http://www1.nyc.gov/site/internationalbusiness/industries/additional-industries.page
DR670	N/A	City of New York	Fashion Industry	http://www1.nyc.gov/site/internationalbusiness/industries/fashion-industry.page
DR671	N/A	City of New York	Industries	http://www1.nyc.gov/site/internationalbusiness/industries/industries.page
DR672	N/A	City of New York	Life Sciences Industry	http://www1.nyc.gov/site/internationalbusiness/industries/life-sciences-industry.page
DR673	N/A	City of New York	Smart Cities and Clean Tech Industry	http://www1.nyc.gov/site/internationalbusiness/industries/smart-cities-and-clean-tech-industry.page
DR674	N/A	City of New York	Technology and Media Industry	http://www1.nyc.gov/site/internationalbusiness/industries/technology-and-media-industry.page
DR675	N/A	City of New York	Fashion Programs	http://www1.nyc.gov/site/internationalbusiness/programs/fashion-programs.page
DR676	N/A	City of New York	Food, Beverage & Retail Programs	http://www1.nyc.gov/site/internationalbusiness/programs/food-beverage-and-retail-programs.page
DR677	N/A	City of New York	Industrial & Manufacturing Programs	http://www1.nyc.gov/site/internationalbusiness/programs/industrial-manufacturing-programs.page

Continued

TABLE C.1 Digital records collected during the search phase—cont'd

ID	Date	Producer	Title	Source
DR678	N/A	City of New York	Life Sciences and Healthcare Programs	http://www1.nyc.gov/site/internationalbusiness/programs/life-sciences-programs.page
DR679	N/A	City of New York	Programs for Any Industry	http://www1.nyc.gov/site/internationalbusiness/programs/programs-for-any-industry.page
DR680	N/A	City of New York	Programs	http://www1.nyc.gov/site/internationalbusiness/programs/programs.page
DR681	N/A	City of New York	Smart Cities & Clean Tech Programs	http://www1.nyc.gov/site/internationalbusiness/programs/smart-cities-and-clean-tech-programs.page
DR682	N/A	City of New York	Technology and Media Programs	http://www1.nyc.gov/site/internationalbusiness/programs/technology-and-media-programs.page
DR683	N/A	City of New York	NYCEDC and the Mayor's Office of Media and Entertainment Announce Plan for VR/AR Lab	http://www1.nyc.gov/site/mome/news/121416-vr-lab.page
DR684	N/A	City of New York	Digital Vans	http://www1.nyc.gov/site/nycha/residents/digital-van.page
DR685	N/A	City of New York	Open Data for All New Yorkers	https://data.cityofnewyork.us/
DR686	N/A	City of New York	311 Service Requests from 2010 to Present	https://data.cityofnewyork.us/Social-Services/311-Service-Requests-from-2010-to-Present/erm2-nwe9
DR687	N/A	City of New York	Approved Link NYC Kiosk Locations	https://data.cityofnewyork.us/Social-Services/Approved-Link-NYC-Kiosk-Locations/gsr2-xq9e

DR688	N/A	City of New York	LinkNYC Locations	https://data.cityofnewyork.us/Social-Services/LinkNYC-Locations/s4kf-3yrf
DR689	N/A	City of New York	LinkNYC New Site Permit Applications	https://data.cityofnewyork.us/Social-Services/LinkNYC-New-Site-Permit-Applications/xp25-gxux
DR690	N/A	City of New York	NYC Developer Portal Is...	https://developer.cityofnewyork.us/
DR691	N/A	GitHub	City of New York: Geoclient Geocoder	https://github.com/cityofnewyork/geoclient
DR692	N/A	GitHub	City of New York: NYC Planimetric Database	https://github.com/CityOfNewYork/nyc-planimetrics/blob/master/Capture_Rules.md
DR693	N/A	City of New York	NYC Open Data: Home	https://opendata.cityofnewyork.us/
DR694	N/A	City of New York	NYC Open Data: Data	https://opendata.cityofnewyork.us/data/
DR695	N/A	City of New York	NYC Open Data: How To	https://opendata.cityofnewyork.us/how-to/
DR696	N/A	City of New York	NYC Open Data: Laws and Reports	https://opendata.cityofnewyork.us/open-data-law/
DR697	N/A	City of New York	NYC Open Data: Overview	https://opendata.cityofnewyork.us/overview/
DR698	N/A	Transit Wireless	Transit Wireless: About	https://transitwireless.com/about-us/
DR699	N/A	City of New York	Job Posting Notice	https://www1.nyc.gov/assets/doitt/downloads/jobs/333313-Cyber-Command-Urban-Tech-Security-Researcher.pdf
DR700	N/A	City of New York	Job Posting Notice	https://www1.nyc.gov/assets/doitt/downloads/jobs/333803-Cyber-Command-Urban-Tech-Arch.pdf

Continued

TABLE C.1 Digital records collected during the search phase—cont'd

ID	Date	Producer	Title	Source
DR701	N/A	City of New York	Application Development Guidelines	https://www1.nyc.gov/assets/doitt/downloads/pdf/application_development_guidelines_public.pdf
DR702	N/A	City of New York	Intra-City Agreement Between the New York City Department of Health and Mental Hygiene and the New York City Department of Information Technology and Telecommunications	https://www1.nyc.gov/assets/doitt/downloads/pdf/dohmh_agreement.pdf
DR703	N/A	City of New York	LinkNYC: Memorandum of Understanding	https://www1.nyc.gov/assets/doitt/downloads/pdf/LinkNYC-Siting-MOU-With-BPs.pdf
DR704	N/A	City of New York	Franchise Agreement Between The City of New York and Transit Wireless, LLC	https://www1.nyc.gov/assets/doitt/downloads/pdf/LLC_Franchise_Agreement_Executed.pdf
DR705	N/A	City of New York	CityBridge, LLC Franchise Agreement. Appendix A: Investigation Clause	https://www1.nyc.gov/assets/doitt/downloads/pdf/Proposed-PCS-Franchise-Appendix-A-Investigation-Clause.pdf
DR706	N/A	City of New York	CityBridge, LLC Franchise Agreement. Appendix B: MacBride Principles Provisions for New York City Contractors	https://www1.nyc.gov/assets/doitt/downloads/pdf/Proposed-PCS-Franchise-Appendix-B-MacBride-Principles.pdf
DR707	N/A	City of New York	CityBridge, LLC Franchise Agreement. Appendix C: Certification by Broker	https://www1.nyc.gov/assets/doitt/downloads/pdf/Proposed-PCS-Franchise-Appendix-C-Certification-by-Broker.pdf
DR708	N/A	City of New York	CityBridge, LLC Franchise Agreement. Appendix D: Initial Members of Franchisee	https://www1.nyc.gov/assets/doitt/downloads/pdf/Proposed-PCS-Franchise-Appendix-D-Initial-Members-of-Franchisee.pdf

DR709	N/A	City of New York	CityBridge, LLC Franchise Agreement. Appendix E: Permitted Transfers	https://www1.nyc.gov/assets/doitt/downloads/pdf/Proposed-PCS-Franchise-Appendix-E-Permitted-Transfers.pdf
DR710	N/A	City of New York	CityBridge, LLC Franchise Agreement. Appendix F: Franchisee Lender Provisions	https://www1.nyc.gov/assets/doitt/downloads/pdf/Proposed-PCS-Franchise-Appendix-F-Franchisee-Lender-Provisions.pdf
DR711	N/A	City of New York	CityBridge, LLC Franchise Agreement. Exhibit 1: Minimum Terms of Services	https://www1.nyc.gov/assets/doitt/downloads/pdf/Proposed-PCS-Franchise-Exhibit-1-Terms-of-Service.pdf
DR712	N/A	City of New York	CityBridge, LLC Franchise Agreement. Exhibit 2: CityBridge Privacy Policy	https://www1.nyc.gov/assets/doitt/downloads/pdf/Proposed-PCS-Franchise-Exhibit-2-CityBridge-Privacy-Policy.pdf
DR713	N/A	City of New York	CityBridge, LLC Franchise Agreement. Exhibit 3: Service Level Agreement and Schedule of Liquidated Damages	https://www1.nyc.gov/assets/doitt/downloads/pdf/Proposed-PCS-Franchise-Exhibit-3-Service-Level-Agreement-and-Liquidated-Damages-Table.pdf
DR714	N/A	City of New York	CityBridge, LLC Franchise Agreement. Exhibit 4: Siting Criteria	https://www1.nyc.gov/assets/doitt/downloads/pdf/Proposed-PCS-Franchise-Exhibit-4-Siting-Criteria.pdf
DR715	N/A	City of New York	CityBridge, LLC Franchise Agreement. Exhibit 5: Structure Designs	https://www1.nyc.gov/assets/doitt/downloads/pdf/Proposed-PCS-Franchise-Exhibit-5-Structure-Designs.pdf
DR716	N/A	City of New York	DoITT 3 Tier Architectural Standard	https://www1.nyc.gov/assets/doitt/downloads/pdf/three_tier_architecture_public.pdf

Continued

TABLE C.1 Digital records collected during the search phase—cont'd

ID	Date	Producer	Title	Source
DR717	N/A	City of New York	Engage NYC: Social Media for Nonprofits Conference	https://www1.nyc.gov/nyc-resources/nonprofits-social-media-toolkit.page
DR718	N/A	City of New York	NYC DoITT: Interagency MOUs	https://www1.nyc.gov/site/doitt/about/agency-mous.page
DR719	N/A	City of New York	NYC DoITT: Agency Rules	https://www1.nyc.gov/site/doitt/about/agency-rules.page
DR720	N/A	City of New York	NYC DoITT: Commissioner's Bio	https://www1.nyc.gov/site/doitt/about/commissioners-bio.page
DR721	N/A	City of New York	NYC DoITT: Community Partnerships	https://www1.nyc.gov/site/doitt/about/community-partnerships.page
DR722	N/A	City of New York	NYC DoITT: Divisions	https://www1.nyc.gov/site/doitt/about/divisions.page
DR723	N/A	City of New York	NYC DoITT: 2012 Excellence in Technology Award Program Winners	https://www1.nyc.gov/site/doitt/about/etapw.page
DR724	N/A	City of New York	NYC DoITT: DoITT's Security Cloud, Chief Information Security Officer Receives 2012 InformationWeek Government IT Innovators Award	https://www1.nyc.gov/site/doitt/about/it-innovators.page
DR725	N/A	City of New York	NYC DoITT: IT Policy & Governance	https://www1.nyc.gov/site/doitt/about/it-policy-governance.page
DR726	N/A	City of New York	NYC DoITT: Language Gateway and Access Plan	https://www1.nyc.gov/site/doitt/about/language-access-plan.page

DR727	N/A	City of New York	NYC DoITT: Legislative & Regulatory Filings Archive	https://www1.nyc.gov/site/doitt/about/legislative-regulatory-filings-archive.page
DR728	N/A	City of New York	NYU Tandon and New York City Cyber Command Launch New York Cyber Fellows Master's Degree Program	https://www1.nyc.gov/site/doitt/about/press-releases/nyu-nyc-cyber-command.page
DR729	N/A	City of New York	NYC DoITT: Reports & Presentations	https://www1.nyc.gov/site/doitt/about/reports-presentations.page
DR730	N/A	City of New York	NYC DoITT: 10 Points of Change	https://www1.nyc.gov/site/doitt/about/strategic-plan.page
DR731	N/A	City of New York	NYC DoITT: Testimonies	https://www1.nyc.gov/site/doitt/about/testimonies.page
DR732	N/A	City of New York	NYC DoITT: What We Do	https://www1.nyc.gov/site/doitt/about/what-we-do.page
DR733	N/A	City of New York	NYC DoITT: Who We Are	https://www1.nyc.gov/site/doitt/about/who-we-are.page
DR734	N/A	City of New York	NYC DoITT: CityNet	https://www1.nyc.gov/site/doitt/agencies/citynet.page
DR735	N/A	City of New York	NYC DoITT: Citywide Data Center	https://www1.nyc.gov/site/doitt/agencies/citywide-data-center.page
DR736	N/A	City of New York	NYC DoITT: Citywide Radio Network	https://www1.nyc.gov/site/doitt/agencies/citywide-radio-network.page
DR737	N/A	City of New York	NYC DoITT: Citywide Service Desk	https://www1.nyc.gov/site/doitt/agencies/citywide-service-desk.page

Continued

TABLE C.1 Digital records collected during the search phase—cont'd

ID	Date	Producer	Title	Source
DR738	N/A	City of New York	NYC DoITT: For Agencies	https://www1.nyc.gov/site/doitt/agencies/for-agencies.page
DR739	N/A	City of New York	NYC DoITT: IT Operations Center	https://www1.nyc.gov/site/doitt/agencies/it-operations-center.page
DR740	N/A	City of New York	NYC DoITT: IT Security	https://www1.nyc.gov/site/doitt/agencies/it-security.page
DR741	N/A	City of New York	NYC DoITT: NYCWiN	https://www1.nyc.gov/site/doitt/agencies/nycwin.page
DR742	N/A	City of New York	NYC DoITT: Cable Renewal Comments	https://www1.nyc.gov/site/doitt/business/cable-renewal-comments.page
DR743	N/A	City of New York	NYC DoITT: Cable TV Franchises	https://www1.nyc.gov/site/doitt/business/cable-tv-franchises.page
DR744	N/A	City of New York	NYC DoITT: Cable TV Pedestals	https://www1.nyc.gov/site/doitt/business/cable-tv-pedestals.page
DR745	N/A	City of New York	NYC DoITT: Contractual Authority & Adding Additional Terms	https://www1.nyc.gov/site/doitt/business/contractual-authority-adding-additional-terms.page
DR746	N/A	City of New York	NYC DoITT: Franchise Process	https://www1.nyc.gov/site/doitt/business/franchise-process.page
DR747	N/A	City of New York	NYC DoITT: Information Services Franchises	https://www1.nyc.gov/site/doitt/business/information-services-franchises.page

DR748	N/A	City of New York	NYC DoITT: Cybersecurity Requirements for Vendors & Contractors	https://www1.nyc.gov/site/doitt/business/it-security-requirements-vendors-contractors.page
DR749	N/A	City of New York	NYC DoITT: LinkNYC Franchises	https://www1.nyc.gov/site/doitt/business/linknyc-franchises.page
DR750	N/A	City of New York	NYC DoITT: Microtrenching Application Form	https://www1.nyc.gov/site/doitt/business/microtrenching-application-form.page
DR751	N/A	City of New York	NYC DoITT: Microtrenching	https://www1.nyc.gov/site/doitt/business/microtrenching.page
DR752	N/A	City of New York	NYC DoITT: Mobile Subway Stations Franchises	https://www1.nyc.gov/site/doitt/business/mobile-subway-stations-franchises.page
DR753	N/A	City of New York	NYC DoITT: Mobile Telecom Franchises	https://www1.nyc.gov/site/doitt/business/mobile-telecom-franchises.page
DR754	N/A	City of New York	NYC DoITT: Mobile Telecommunication Franchises - PIN: 8582018FRANCH1	https://www1.nyc.gov/site/doitt/business/mobile-telecommunications-franchises-download.page
DR755	N/A	City of New York	NYC DoITT: Open Business Opportunities	https://www1.nyc.gov/site/doitt/business/open-business-opportunities.page
DR756	N/A	City of New York	NYC DoITT: Pedestal Installation Form	https://www1.nyc.gov/site/doitt/business/pedestal-installation.page
DR757	N/A	City of New York	NYC DoITT: Recently Closed Solicitations	https://www1.nyc.gov/site/doitt/business/recently-closed-solicitations.page
DR758	N/A	City of New York	NYC DoITT: Technical Vendor Resources	https://www1.nyc.gov/site/doitt/business/technical-vendor-resources.page

Continued

TABLE C.1 Digital records collected during the search phase—cont'd

ID	Date	Producer	Title	Source
DR759	N/A	City of New York	NYC DoITT: Broadband Access	https://www1.nyc.gov/site/doitt/initiatives/broadband-access.page
DR760	N/A	City of New York	NYC DoITT: Broadband Deployment	https://www1.nyc.gov/site/doitt/initiatives/broadband-deployment.page
DR761	N/A	City of New York	NYC DoITT: Broadband	https://www1.nyc.gov/site/doitt/initiatives/broadband.page
DR762	N/A	City of New York	NYC DoITT: LinkNYC	https://www1.nyc.gov/site/doitt/initiatives/linknyc.page
DR763	N/A	City of New York	NYC DoITT: NYC TLD	https://www1.nyc.gov/site/doitt/initiatives/nyc-tld.page
DR764	N/A	City of New York	NYC DoITT: Read the Open Data Law	https://www1.nyc.gov/site/doitt/initiatives/open-data-law.page
DR765	N/A	City of New York	NYC DoITT: Open Data	https://www1.nyc.gov/site/doitt/initiatives/open-data.page
DR766	N/A	City of New York	NYC DoITT: Resiliency	https://www1.nyc.gov/site/doitt/initiatives/resiliency.page
DR767	N/A	City of New York	NYC DoITT: Cable TV	https://www1.nyc.gov/site/doitt/residents/cable-tv.page
DR768	N/A	City of New York	NYC DoITT: GIS & Mapping	https://www1.nyc.gov/site/doitt/residents/gis-mapping.page

DR769	N/A	City of New York	NYC DoITT: NYC.gov	https://www1.nyc.gov/site/doitt/residents/nyc-gov.page
DR770	N/A	City of New York	NYC DoITT: Pay Phones	https://www1.nyc.gov/site/doitt/residents/pay-phones.page
DR771	N/A	City of New York	Apply for a Neighborhoods.nyc Domain	https://www1.nyc.gov/site/forward/initiatives/dotnyc/domain-requests.page
DR772	N/A	City of New York	.nyc Documentation	https://www1.nyc.gov/site/forward/initiatives/dotnyc/dotnycdocs.page
DR773	N/A	City of New York	Introducing .nyc	https://www1.nyc.gov/site/forward/initiatives/dotnyc/nyc.page
DR774	N/A	City of New York	Public Interest Proposals for .nyc Domains	https://www1.nyc.gov/site/forward/initiatives/dotnyc/public-interest-proposals.page
DR775	N/A	City of New York	NYC International Business: Welcome to NYC	https://www1.nyc.gov/site/internationalbusiness/index.page
DR776	N/A	City of New York	NYC International Business: Additional Industries	https://www1.nyc.gov/site/internationalbusiness/industries/additional-industries.page
DR777	N/A	City of New York	NYC International Business: Fashion Industry	https://www1.nyc.gov/site/internationalbusiness/industries/fashion-industry.page
DR778	N/A	City of New York	NYC International Business: Finance Industry	https://www1.nyc.gov/site/internationalbusiness/industries/finance-industry.page
DR779	N/A	City of New York	NYC International Business: Food and Beverage Industry	https://www1.nyc.gov/site/internationalbusiness/industries/food-and-beverage-industry.page

Continued

TABLE C.1 Digital records collected during the search phase—cont'd

ID	Date	Producer	Title	Source
DR780	N/A	City of New York	NYC International Business: Industries	https://www1.nyc.gov/site/internationalbusiness/industries/industries.page
DR781	N/A	City of New York	NYC International Business: Life Sciences Industry	https://www1.nyc.gov/site/internationalbusiness/industries/life-sciences-industry.page
DR782	N/A	City of New York	NYC International Business: Technology and Media Industry	https://www1.nyc.gov/site/internationalbusiness/industries/technology-and-media-industry.page
DR783	N/A	City of New York	NYC International Business: Programs for Any Industry	https://www1.nyc.gov/site/internationalbusiness/programs/programs-for-any-industry.page
DR784	N/A	City of New York	NYC International Business: Programs	https://www1.nyc.gov/site/internationalbusiness/programs/programs.page
DR785	N/A	City of New York	NYC International Business: Smart Cities & Clean Tech Programs	https://www1.nyc.gov/site/internationalbusiness/programs/smart-cities-and-clean-tech-programs.page
DR786	N/A	City of New York	NYC International Business: Technology and Media Programs	https://www1.nyc.gov/site/internationalbusiness/programs/technology-and-media-programs.page
DR787	N/A	City of New York	About the Procurement Policy Board (PPB)	https://www1.nyc.gov/site/mocs/legal-forms/about-procurement-policy-board-ppb.page
DR788	N/A	City of New York	NYCEDC and the Mayor's Office of Media and Entertainment Announce Plan for VR/AR Lab	https://www1.nyc.gov/site/mome/news/121416-vr-lab.page
DR789	N/A	City of New York	Neighborhood Challenge	https://www1.nyc.gov/site/sbs/neighborhoods/neighborhood-challenge.page

DR790	N/A	Medium	NYC BigApps	http://www.bigapps.nyc/
DR791	N/A	Medium	NYC BigApps: Challenges	http://www.bigapps.nyc/challenges/
DR792	N/A	Medium	NYC BigApps: Workshops	http://www.bigapps.nyc/workshops/
DR793	N/A	City of New York	NYC OpenData Technical Standards Manual (TSM): City Policies	http://cityofnewyork.github.io/opendatatsm/citypolicies.html
DR794	N/A	City of New York	NYC OpenData Technical Standards Manual (TSM): Background	http://cityofnewyork.github.io/opendatatsm/background.html
DR795	N/A	City of New York	NYC OpenData Technical Standards Manual (TSM): City Standards	http://cityofnewyork.github.io/opendatatsm/citystandards.html
DR796	N/A	City of New York	NYC OpenData Technical Standards Manual (TSM): City Guidelines	http://cityofnewyork.github.io/opendatatsm/cityguidelines.html
DR797	N/A	City of New York	NYC OpenData Technical Standards Manual (TSM): Public Policies	http://cityofnewyork.github.io/opendatatsm/publicpolicies.html
DR798	N/A	City of New York	Procurement Policy Board (PPB) Rules	https://www1.nyc.gov/site/mocs/legal-forms/procurement-policy-board-ppb-rules.page
DR799	N/A	CityBridge	LinkNYC: Press Kit	https://www.link.nyc/presskit.html
DR800	N/A	City of New York	NYC International Business: Fashion Programs	https://www1.nyc.gov/site/internationalbusiness/programs/fashion-programs.page
DR801	N/A	City of New York	NYC International Business: Finance Industry Programs	https://www1.nyc.gov/site/internationalbusiness/programs/finance-industry-programs.page

Continued

TABLE C.1 Digital records collected during the search phase—cont'd

ID	Date	Producer	Title	Source
DR802	N/A	City of New York	NYC International Business: Food, Beverage & Retail Programs	https://www1.nyc.gov/site/internationalbusiness/programs/food-beverage-and-retail-programs.page
DR803	N/A	City of New York	NYC International Business: Industrial & Manufacturing Programs	https://www1.nyc.gov/site/internationalbusiness/programs/industrial-manufacturing-programs.page
DR804	N/A	City of New York	NYC International Business: Life Sciences and Healthcare Programs	https://www1.nyc.gov/site/internationalbusiness/programs/life-sciences-programs.page
DR805	N/A	City of New York	Media Labs	https://www.nycgovparks.org/facilities/media-labs
DR806	N/A	City of New York	TechOpps	https://www.nycgovparks.org/programs/media/techopps
DR807	N/A	City of New York	UrbanTech NYC: About	http://www.urbantechnyc.com/about/
DR808	N/A	City of New York	UrbanTech NYC: Initiatives	http://www.urbantechnyc.com/initiatives/
DR809	N/A	City of New York	OneNYC: Initiatives	https://onenyc.cityofnewyork.us/wp-content/uploads/2018/04/OneNYC-Initiatives-1.pdf
DR810	N/A	City of New York	NYC Analytics: About the Office of Data Analytics	https://www1.nyc.gov/site/analytics/about/about-office-data-analytics.page
DR811	N/A	City of New York	NYC Analytics: Initiatives	https://www1.nyc.gov/site/analytics/initiatives/initiatives.page
DR812	N/A	City of New York	NYC Analytics: Supporting Operations	https://www1.nyc.gov/site/analytics/initiatives/supporting-operations.page

DR813	N/A	City of New York	NYC Analytics: Citywide Data Sharing	https://www1.nyc.gov/site/analytics/initiatives/citywide-data-sharing.page
DR814	N/A	City of New York	NYC Analytics: Disaster Response and Resiliency	https://www1.nyc.gov/site/analytics/initiatives/disaster-response-resiliency.page
DR815	N/A	City of New York	NYC Analytics: Economic Development	https://www1.nyc.gov/site/analytics/initiatives/economic-development.page
DR816	N/A	City of New York	NYC Analytics: Open Data	https://www1.nyc.gov/site/analytics/initiatives/open-data.page
DR817	N/A	Georgetown Climate Center	PlaNYC 2030—A Greener Greater New York	http://www.adaptationclearinghouse.org/resources/planyc-2030-a-greener-greater-new-york.html
DR818	N/A	City of New York	NYC Readiness Challenge	https://www1.nyc.gov/assets/em/downloads/pdf/NYC_Readiness_Challenge_Summary.pdf
DR819	N/A	City of New York	NYC BigApps	https://www.nycedc.com/program/nyc-bigapps
DR820	N/A	City of New York	NYC Open Data: Welcome to the NYC Open Data Project Gallery!	https://opendata.cityofnewyork.us/projects/
DR821	N/A	City of New York	NYC Open Data: 311 Data & Life In NYC	https://opendata.cityofnewyork.us/projects/311-data-life-in-nyc/
DR822	N/A	City of New York	NYC Open Data: Keeping Track Online	https://opendata.cityofnewyork.us/projects/keeping-track-online-map-community-resources/
DR823	N/A	City of New York	NYC Open Data: What We Learned from Open Data on Bullying and Harassment in NYC Schools	https://opendata.cityofnewyork.us/projects/what-we-learned-from-open-data-on-bullying-and-harassment-in-nyc-schools/

Continued

TABLE C.1 Digital records collected during the search phase—cont'd

ID	Date	Producer	Title	Source
DR824	N/A	City of New York	NYC Open Data: CityGram.NYC	https://opendata.cityofnewyork.us/projects/citygram-nyc/
DR825	N/A	City of New York	NYC Open Data: BoardStat	https://opendata.cityofnewyork.us/projects/boardstat/
DR826	N/A	City of New York	NYC Open Data: NYC High School AP Exam Comparison: 2010 & 2012	https://opendata.cityofnewyork.us/projects/nyc-high-school-ap-exam-comparison-2010-2012/
DR827	N/A	City of New York	NYC Open Data: Stop, Question, and Frisk Visualized	https://opendata.cityofnewyork.us/projects/stop-question-and-frisk-visualized/
DR828	N/A	City of New York	NYC Open Data: NYC Data Explorer	https://opendata.cityofnewyork.us/projects/nyc-data-explorer/
DR829	N/A	City of New York	NYC Open Data: Open Sewer Atlas NYC	https://opendata.cityofnewyork.us/projects/open-sewer-atlas-nyc/
DR830	N/A	City of New York	NYC Open Data: Automatic Reconstruction of Immersive Urban Environments	https://opendata.cityofnewyork.us/projects/automatic-reconstruction-of-immersive-urban-environments/
DR831	N/A	City of New York	NYC Open Data: JailVizNYC	https://opendata.cityofnewyork.us/projects/jailviznyc/
DR832	N/A	City of New York	NYC Open Data: An Interactive Visualization of NYC Street Trees	https://opendata.cityofnewyork.us/projects/an-interactive-visualization-of-nyc-street-trees-contest-winner/

DR833	N/A	City of New York	NYC Open Data: Plan(t)wise	https://opendata.cityofnewyork.us/projects/plantwise-planning-a-green-canopy-over-the-big-apple-contest-winner/
DR834	N/A	City of New York	NYC Open Data: myPB.community	https://opendata.cityofnewyork.us/projects/mypb-community-contest-winner/
DR835	N/A	City of New York	NYC Open Data: Five Communities of Williamsburg	https://opendata.cityofnewyork.us/projects/five-communities-of-williamsburg/
DR836	N/A	City of New York	NYC Open Data: Introduction to Choropleth Maps	https://opendata.cityofnewyork.us/projects/introduction-to-choropleth-maps/
DR837	N/A	City of New York	NYC Open Data: Rentlogic	https://opendata.cityofnewyork.us/projects/rentlogic/
DR838	N/A	City of New York	NYC Open Data: Customizing Zoning Maps	https://opendata.cityofnewyork.us/projects/customizing-zoning-maps/
DR839	N/A	City of New York	NYC Open Data: After the Pride Parade	https://opendata.cityofnewyork.us/projects/after-the-pride-parade/
DR840	N/A	City of New York	NYPD: Crime Statistics	https://www1.nyc.gov/site/nypd/stats/crime-statistics/crime-statistics-landing.page
DR841	N/A	Open NY Community	Commission on Public Information and Communication	http://datanyc.org/nycgov/commission-on-public-information-and-communication/
DR842	N/A	City of New York	NY Tech Meetup	https://www.digital.nyc/startups/ny-tech-meetup
DR843	N/A	WeWork Companies	NY Tech Meetup	https://www.meetup.com/ny-tech/

Continued

TABLE C.1 Digital records collected during the search phase—cont'd

ID	Date	Producer	Title	Source
DR844	N/A	Crunchbase	Internet Week New York	https://www.crunchbase.com/organization/internet-week-new-york#section-overview
DR845	N/A	Sandia Corporation	Brooklyn Army Terminal Smart Grid Demonstration Project—New York City Economic Development Corporation	https://www.energystorageexchange.org/projects/1219
DR846	N/A	City of New York	Applied Sciences NYC	https://www.nycedc.com/project/applied-sciences-nyc
DR847	N/A	City of New York	Checkbook NYC	https://www.checkbooknyc.com/spending_landing/yeartype/B/year/120

Appendix D

See Table D.1.

TABLE D.1 New York City's smart city development strategy: collaborative environment

Entity ID code	Name	Category	Number of activities	Degree of centrality
1	3 Black Cats Café and Cakery	IND	1	41
2	3i Infotech	IND	1	1
3	3M	IND	1	13
4	3rd Ward	IND	2	42
5	About.com	IND	1	52
6	Accellion	IND	1	27
7	Adobe	IND	2	23
8	Aecom	IND	1	5
9	Albany County	GOV	1	3
10	Alcoa	IND	1	3
11	Alfresco Software	IND	1	16
12	Ali Forney Center	CIV	1	1
13	All Things Digital	OTH	2	15
14	Alldayeveryday	IND	1	28
15	Alliance for a Greater New York	IND	1	13
16	Alliance for Downtown New York	IND	2	55
17	Alliance for the Arts	CIV	1	13
18	Amazon	IND	2	42
19	America Online (AOL)	IND	1	23

Continued

TABLE D.1 New York City's smart city development strategy: collaborative environment—cont'd

Entity		Category	Number of activities	Degree of centrality
ID code	Name			
20	American Society of Heating, Refrigerating and Air-Conditioning Engineers (ASHRAE)	IND	1	23
21	Amherst College	RES	1	16
22	Antenna Design	IND	2	34
23	Anthony E. Meyer Family Foundation	CIV	1	16
24	Apple	IND	1	1
25	AppNexus	IND	2	80
26	Appnovation	IND	1	34
27	Association for a Better New York	IND	1	12
28	Association for Energy Affordability	IND	1	23
29	Association for High School Innovation	RES	1	13
30	Association of Energy Engineers	IND	1	23
31	AT&T	IND	3	5
32	Avangrid	IND	1	16
33	BakerHostetler	IND	1	34
34	Barrel	IND	1	28
35	Bed-Stuy Campaign Against Hunger	CIV	1	41
36	Belmont Business Improvement District	IND	1	2
37	BetaNYC	CIV	7	64
38	Betaworks	IND	5	46
39	BIAS Corporation	IND	1	13
40	Big Brothers Big Sisters of America	CIV	1	34

TABLE D.1 New York City's smart city development strategy: collaborative environment—cont'd

Entity				
ID code	Name	Category	Number of activities	Degree of centrality
41	Bigbelly	IND	1	3
42	Bitly	IND	1	25
43	BKLYN	IND	1	34
44	Bloc Bully IT Solutions	IND	1	53
45	Bloom Energy	IND	1	16
46	BMC Software	IND	1	1
47	BMW	IND	7	80
48	Booth Ferris Foundation	CIV	1	16
49	BoxGroup	IND	1	25
50	Brattle Group	IND	1	11
51	Breaking Ground	CIV	1	41
52	Brocade Creations	IND	1	13
53	Brookdale University Hospital Medical Center	IND	1	41
54	Brooklyn Academy of Music	IND	2	55
55	Brooklyn Beta	RES	1	5
56	Brooklyn Chamber of Commerce	IND	1	53
57	Brooklyn Community Foundation	CIV	1	53
58	Brooklyn Community Services	CIV	1	41
59	Brooklyn Neighborhood Improvement Association	CIV	1	41
60	Brownsville Collective	OTH	1	41

Continued

TABLE D.1 New York City's smart city development strategy: collaborative environment—cont'd

Entity		Category	Number of activities	Degree of centrality
ID code	Name			
61	Brownsville Community Development Corporation	CIV	1	41
62	Brownsville Community Farm	CIV	1	41
63	Brownsville Community Justice Center	CIV	5	90
64	Brownsville Heritage House	CIV	1	41
65	Brownsville Houses Resident Association	CIV	1	41
66	Brownsville Think Tank Matters	CIV	1	41
67	Building and Construction Trades Council of Greater New York	IND	1	30
68	Building Owners and Managers Association of New York	IND	1	12
69	Bureau Blank	IND	1	34
70	BuroHappold Engineering	IND	1	11
71	Butler Family Fund	CIV	1	53
72	Cablevision Systems	IND	4	37
73	CAMBA	CIV	1	41
74	Cambridge Solutions	IND	1	1
75	Capital One	IND	2	64
76	Carbon Calculated	IND	1	25
77	CareerBuilder	IND	1	25
78	Carnegie Corporation of New York	CIV	1	16

TABLE D.1 New York City's smart city development strategy: collaborative environment—cont'd

Entity ID code	Name	Category	Number of activities	Degree of centrality
79	Carnegie Mellon University	RES	1	7
80	CartoDB	IND	2	69
81	Case Foundation	CIV	1	5
82	Catholic Charities Brooklyn and Queens	CIV	1	41
83	Center for Court Innovation	CIV	1	53
84	Center for NYC Neighborhoods	CIV	1	23
85	Center on Reinventing Public Education	RES	1	16
86	Central Brooklyn Economic Development Corporation	CIV	2	4
87	CenturyLink	IND	3	39
88	CEO Works	IND	1	25
89	CEOs for Cities	GOV	1	5
90	CFI Group	IND	1	2
91	Charles and Mildred Schnurmacher Foundation	CIV	1	53
92	Charles River Associates	IND	1	5
93	Cheng Solutions	IND	1	11
94	Chinatown Partnership	IND	1	0
95	Chinese-American Planning Council	CIV	1	1
96	Cisco Systems	IND	3	48
97	Citigroup	IND	2	6
98	Citizens	CIV	267	211

Continued

TABLE D.1 New York City's smart city development strategy: collaborative environment—cont'd

Entity		Category	Number of activities	Degree of centrality
ID code	Name			
99	Citizens Committee for New York City	CIV	1	2
100	Citizens Union	CIV	4	17
101	City National Bank	IND	1	3
102	City of Barcelona	GOV	2	3
103	City of Boston	GOV	1	3
104	City of Chicago	GOV	1	5
105	City of Los Angeles	GOV	2	7
106	City of Miami	GOV	1	3
107	City of New York	GOV	627	497
108	City of San Francisco	GOV	1	5
109	City of Seattle	GOV	1	5
110	City Parks Foundation	CIV	1	41
111	City University of New York	RES	14	167
112	Civic Hall	IND	2	50
113	Clarkson University	RES	1	16
114	Clever	IND	1	16
115	Closed Loop Fund	IND	1	23
116	Columbia University	RES	6	42
117	Comark	IND	2	34
118	Common Cause	CIV	3	15
119	Common Sense Media	CIV	2	21
120	Community By Design	IND	1	34
121	Community Education Council 23	GOV	1	41
122	Community Service Society of New York	CIV	1	30
123	Community Solutions	CIV	2	90

TABLE D.1 New York City's smart city development strategy: collaborative environment—cont'd

Entity ID code	Name	Category	Number of activities	Degree of centrality
124	Commvault	IND	1	13
125	Computers for Youth Foundation	RES	2	21
126	Con Edison	IND	5	36
127	Conductor	IND	1	28
128	Connectivity for the arts	IND	1	28
129	Control Group	IND	3	50
130	Cornell University	RES	1	2
131	Couch White	IND	1	5
132	Crisp Media	IND	1	28
133	Crown Castle	IND	1	27
134	CSC State and Local Solutions	IND	1	21
135	CSRA Inc.	IND	1	16
136	CSRHub	IND	1	52
137	CVenture	IND	1	11
138	DataSphere	IND	1	52
139	DecisionDesk	IND	1	28
140	Dell	IND	3	48
141	Deloitte	IND	2	29
142	Democracy Works	CIV	1	52
143	Design Trust for Public Space	CIV	1	23
144	Dev Bootcamp	RES	1	4
145	Devpost	IND	5	56
146	DFJ Gotham Ventures	IND	4	34
147	Dharam Consulting	IND	1	11
148	Diploma Plus	RES	1	13

Continued

TABLE D.1 New York City's smart city development strategy: collaborative environment—cont'd

Entity		Category	Number of activities	Degree of centrality
ID code	Name			
149	Direct Energy	IND	1	16
150	DonorsChoose	CIV	1	25
151	Doris Duke Charitable Foundation	CIV	1	53
152	DoSomething	CIV	2	47
153	Downtown Brooklyn Partnership	IND	2	6
154	Dream Big Foundation	CIV	3	92
155	DUMBO Improvement District	IND	1	1
156	DynTek	IND	3	45
157	East Harlem Business Capital Corporation	IND	2	6
158	East Village Independent Merchants Association	IND	1	0
159	eBay	IND	1	25
160	EdSurge	IND	1	16
161	EDVenture	IND	3	17
162	Elastic	IND	1	27
163	Embedly	IND	1	52
164	Emerson	IND	1	13
165	Empire State Development Corporation	GOV	2	21
166	Enigma	IND	1	52
167	Environmental Defense Fund	CIV	2	48
168	eRepublic	IND	1	3
169	Ericsson	IND	1	16
170	Esri	IND	1	34

TABLE D.1 New York City's smart city development strategy: collaborative environment—cont'd

Entity		Category	Number of activities	Degree of centrality
ID code	Name			
171	Etsy	IND	1	25
172	Facebook	IND	3	28
173	Falchi Building	IND	1	52
174	Family Services Network of New York	CIV	1	41
175	Federal Government of the United States	GOV	14	148
176	Federation of Protestant Welfare Agencies	CIV	1	30
177	Fira de Barcelona	IND	1	2
178	FireEye	IND	1	13
179	First Republic Bank	IND	1	34
180	First Round Capital	IND	1	5
181	FirstBuild	IND	1	52
182	FirstMark Capital	IND	5	34
183	Flatiron 23rd Street Partnership	IND	1	5
184	Ford Foundation	CIV	2	62
185	ForeScout Technologies	IND	1	16
186	Fortinet	IND	1	27
187	Foursquare	IND	6	79
188	Fragomen LLP	IND	1	0
189	Friends of Brownsville Parks	CIV	1	41
190	Friends of The High Line	CIV	1	23
191	Frog Design	IND	1	15
192	Fuhrman Family Foundation	CIV	1	4

Continued

TABLE D.1 New York City's smart city development strategy: collaborative environment—cont'd

Entity		Category	Number of activities	Degree of centrality
ID code	Name			
193	Full Spectrum of NY	IND	1	30
194	FWD	CIV	1	34
195	FXFOWLE Architects	IND	1	15
196	General Assembly	RES	6	116
197	General Code	IND	2	37
198	General Dynamics Information Technology	IND	1	27
199	General Electric	IND	1	52
200	Gilt	IND	1	11
201	GitHub	IND	1	52
202	Gladstein, Neandross and Associates	IND	1	11
203	Glenmore Plaza Resident Association	CIV	1	41
204	Good Shepherd Services	CIV	2	14
205	Google	IND	10	125
206	Government Technology	OTH	7	54
207	GovLab	RES	1	52
208	GOWEX	IND	1	5
209	Grand Central Tech	IND	1	23
210	Grand Street Business Improvement District	IND	1	0
211	Grant Associates	IND	1	53
212	Greater New York Hospital Association	IND	1	30
213	Greater Ridgewood Youth Council	CIV	1	1
214	Green City Force	CIV	1	53

TABLE D.1 New York City's smart city development strategy: collaborative environment—cont'd

Entity				
ID code	Name	Category	Number of activities	Degree of centrality
215	Green Spaces NY	IND	1	28
216	GuideStar	IND	1	53
217	Harlem Children's Zone	CIV	1	4
218	Harman International Industries	IND	1	21
219	Haystack Partners	IND	1	1
220	HDR	IND	1	11
221	HeartShare Human Services of New York	CIV	1	1
222	Heat Seek NYC	IND	1	34
223	Hewlett Packard Enterprise	IND	1	13
224	Howard Houses Resident Association	CIV	1	41
225	HR&A Advisors	IND	1	52
226	Hudson River Foundation	RES	1	23
227	Huffington Post	OTH	2	69
228	HUGE	IND	3	54
229	Human Services Council	CIV	1	30
230	Hunch	IND	2	15
231	IBM	IND	11	74
232	IDEO	IND	2	35
233	iGiveMore	IND	1	13
234	Indeed	IND	1	25
235	Independent Consultant	IND	1	30
236	Indian Institute of Technology Bombay	RES	1	7

Continued

TABLE D.1 New York City's smart city development strategy: collaborative environment—cont'd

Entity		Category	Number of activities	Degree of centrality
ID code	Name			
237	Industry City	IND	1	52
238	Infor	IND	2	29
239	Information Builders	IND	1	13
240	Intel	IND	1	11
241	International Academy of Digital Arts and Sciences (IADAS)	OTH	9	2
242	Internet Corporation for Assigned Names and Numbers	OTH	1	2
243	Intersection	IND	1	34
244	Isabahlia Ladies of Elegance Foundation	CIV	1	41
245	James Weldon Johnson Community Centers	CIV	1	1
246	Jamestown	IND	1	12
247	Jasmine Universe	IND	1	16
248	Jeremiah Program	IND	1	41
249	Jewish Community Center	CIV	1	1
250	JKMuir	IND	1	11
251	Jobs for the Future	CIV	1	13
252	John and James Knight Foundation	CIV	1	5
253	Journelle	IND	1	28
254	JPMorgan Chase	IND	1	4
255	Junction International	IND	1	13
256	Juniper Networks	IND	1	13
257	JustFix.nyc	CIV	1	34
258	Kaiser Permanente	IND	1	53
259	Kickstarter	IND	1	28

TABLE D.1 New York City's smart city development strategy: collaborative environment—cont'd

Entity		Category	Number of activities	Degree of centrality
ID code	Name			
260	Kodak	IND	1	13
261	KPMG	IND	2	21
262	Krossover	IND	1	28
263	League of Women Voters of the City of New York	CIV	3	15
264	LearningTimes	IND	1	2
265	Legal Services NYC	CIV	1	53
266	Lehman College	RES	1	52
267	Lenovo	IND	1	11
268	Lexent Metro Connect	IND	1	1
269	LGBT Community Center	CIV	1	1
270	LifeSize	IND	1	13
271	Lily Auchincloss Foundation	CIV	1	53
272	Lingo Service Translations	IND	1	5
273	LinkUp	IND	2	69
274	littleBits Electronics	IND	1	52
275	Local Development Corporation of East New York	CIV	3	46
276	Local Initiatives Support Corporation	CIV	1	53
277	Local Projects	IND	1	5
278	LocalResponse	IND	1	28
279	Long Island City Partnership	IND	1	0
280	Lookbooks	IND	1	28

Continued

TABLE D.1 New York City's smart city development strategy: collaborative environment—cont'd

Entity		Category	Number of activities	Degree of centrality
ID code	Name			
281	Lower Manhattan Development Corporation	GOV	1	9
282	M&T Bank	IND	1	53
283	MacArthur Foundation	CIV	1	53
284	Made in Brownsville	CIV	1	53
285	Madison Avenue Business Improvement District	IND	1	0
286	Mahalo.com	OTH	1	11
287	Manhattan Chamber of Commerce	IND	1	0
288	Mapbox	IND	2	53
289	Mashable	OTH	1	3
290	Mastercard	IND	1	52
291	MAXIMUS	IND	1	53
292	McAfee	IND	7	38
293	McKinsey & Company	IND	1	5
294	McKissack & McKissack	IND	1	30
295	Metro Fiber	IND	1	1
296	Microsoft	IND	10	89
297	Mobilitie	IND	1	1
298	Motorola	IND	1	2
299	Mouse	RES	3	12
300	Museum of the Moving Image	OTH	1	52
301	Mutual Housing Association of New York	CIV	1	41
302	Myrtle Avenue Brooklyn Partnership	IND	1	0

TABLE D.1 New York City's smart city development strategy: collaborative environment—cont'd

Entity				
ID code	Name	Category	Number of activities	Degree of centrality
303	National Academy of Sciences	RES	1	9
304	National Grid	IND	2	35
305	Natural Areas Conservancy	RES	2	6
306	Natural Resources Defense Council	CIV	1	23
307	Nehemiah Economic Development Inc	IND	1	41
308	Neighborhood Trust	IND	1	53
309	NetApp	IND	3	16
310	Neustar	IND	2	14
311	New Visions for Public Schools	RES	1	13
312	New York Building Congress	IND	1	30
313	New York City Brownfield Partnership	IND	1	23
314	New York City Central Labor Council	IND	1	30
315	New York City Energy Efficiency Corporation	IND	2	6
316	New York City Workforce Funders	OTH	1	4
317	New York Civil Liberties Union	CIV	3	15
318	New York Community Trust	CIV	1	4
319	New York Harbor School	RES	1	23
320	New York Housing Conference	CIV	1	23

Continued

TABLE D.1 New York City's smart city development strategy: collaborative environment—cont'd

Entity		Category	Number of activities	Degree of centrality
ID code	Name			
321	New York Immigration Coalition	CIV	1	34
322	New York Independent System Operator	IND	1	23
323	New York Law School	RES	1	15
324	New York League of Conservation Voters	CIV	1	30
325	New York Public Interest Research Group	CIV	3	15
326	New York Restoration Project	CIV	1	23
327	New York Road Runners	CIV	1	53
328	New York University	RES	14	152
329	New Yorkers for Parks	CIV	1	53
330	Next Jump	IND	1	14
331	NextG Networks of NY	IND	1	1
332	Nomi	IND	1	52
333	Northrop Grumman	IND	4	2
334	Northwell Health	IND	1	9
335	Northwest Bronx Community and Clergy Coalition	CIV	1	0
336	Novelty Crystal	IND	1	28
337	Npower	IND	1	1
338	Nutanix	IND	1	16
339	NY Tech Alliance	IND	11	122
340	NY/NJ Baykeeper	CIV	1	23

TABLE D.1 New York City's smart city development strategy: collaborative environment—cont'd

Entity		Category	Number of activities	Degree of centrality
ID code	Name			
341	NYS Health Foundation	CIV	1	53
342	O'Reilly Media	OTH	3	5
343	Ocean Hill-Brownsville Coalition of Young Professionals	CIV	1	41
344	Ocean Hill-Brownsville Neighborhood Improvement Association	CIV	1	53
345	Octopart	IND	1	52
346	Older Adults Technology Services	IND	2	2
347	Ontodia	IND	2	52
348	OpenPlans	CIV	3	15
349	OpenStreetMap Foundation	CIV	1	2
350	Opportunities for a Better Tomorrow	RES	2	76
351	Optical Communications Group	IND	1	4
352	Oracle Corporation	IND	4	54
353	Our Lady of Mercy	CIV	1	41
354	Overture	OTH	1	52
355	Palo Alto Networks	IND	1	16
356	Parse	IND	1	52
357	Participatory Budgeting Project	IND	1	23
358	Partnership for New York City	IND	1	30
359	PayByPhone	IND	1	2

Continued

TABLE D.1 New York City's smart city development strategy: collaborative environment—cont'd

Entity				
ID code	Name	Category	Number of activities	Degree of centrality
360	Pegasystems	IND	1	13
361	Penn South Social Services	CIV	1	1
362	Pentagram	IND	3	94
363	People's Production House	IND	1	1
364	Pia Car and Limo	IND	1	5
365	Pitkin Avenue Business Improvement District	IND	2	90
366	Pivot3	IND	1	21
367	Police Athletic League	CIV	2	42
368	Port Authority of New York and New Jersey	GOV	5	31
369	Productivity Apex Inc.	IND	1	11
370	Progress Playbook	IND	1	53
371	Public Works Partners	IND	1	53
372	PublicSway	OTH	1	0
373	Pure Energy Partners	IND	1	23
374	Pure Storage	IND	1	27
375	Purelements	IND	1	41
376	Purpose	IND	1	34
377	Pushd	IND	1	28
378	PricewaterhouseCoopers (PwC)	IND	1	13
379	Qualcomm	IND	2	34
380	Queens Economic Development Corporation	IND	2	6
381	Quirky	IND	1	15
382	R/GA	IND	1	23

TABLE D.1 New York City's smart city development strategy: collaborative environment—cont'd

Entity		Category	Number of activities	Degree of centrality
ID code	Name			
383	RCN Telecom Services, LLC	IND	1	4
384	Real Estate Board of New York	IND	3	59
385	Reboot	IND	1	1
386	Red Hat	IND	1	27
387	Red Hook Initiative	CIV	1	1
388	RedLand Strategies, Inc.	IND	1	27
389	Regional Plan Association	CIV	1	30
390	Reinvent Albany	CIV	3	15
391	Reliance Globalcom	IND	1	4
392	Reserve	IND	1	34
393	Resource Recycling Systems	IND	1	11
394	RiseBoro Community Partnership	CIV	1	53
395	Robert Wood Johnson Foundation	CIV	1	53
396	Robin Hood Foundation	CIV	4	141
397	Rockaway Business Alliance	IND	1	0
398	Rockaway Development and Revitalization Corporation	CIV	1	1
399	Rockefeller Brothers Fund	CIV	1	30
400	RRE Ventures	IND	2	15
401	RSA Security	IND	1	27

Continued

TABLE D.1 New York City's smart city development strategy: collaborative environment—cont'd

Entity		Category	Number of activities	Degree of centrality
ID code	Name			
402	Rudin Management	IND	1	12
403	RXR Realty	IND	1	12
404	Sabaoth Group	IND	1	41
405	Sage Group	CIV	1	34
406	Sage and Coombe Architects	IND	1	15
407	Salesforce.com	IND	2	37
408	Sam Schwartz Engineering	IND	1	11
409	SAP	IND	1	16
410	SapientRazorfish	IND	1	52
411	SCAN New York	CIV	1	1
412	SCAPE Landscape Architecture	IND	1	30
413	Schneider Electric	IND	1	13
414	School of Visual Arts	RES	1	15
415	SCO Family of Services	CIV	1	53
416	Seaport District NYC	IND	1	23
417	SeatGeek	IND	1	52
418	Second Nature	RES	2	21
419	SeeMe	IND	1	28
420	Selfhelp Community Services, Inc.	CIV	1	3
421	ServiceNow	IND	2	37
422	Shapeways	IND	1	28
423	Shoot HR	IND	1	28
424	Shorenstein	IND	1	12
425	Simply Hired, Inc.	IND	1	25
426	Simpson Thacher and Bartlett LLP	IND	1	30

TABLE D.1 New York City's smart city development strategy: collaborative environment—cont'd

Entity ID code	Name	Category	Number of activities	Degree of centrality
427	Skillsoft	IND	1	4
428	Sky Packets	IND	1	4
429	Smarter Grid Solutions	IND	1	16
430	Socrata	IND	5	64
431	Socratic Labs	OTH	1	16
432	Software House International	IND	2	37
433	Soho Strut	IND	1	1
434	Solar One	IND	1	6
435	Songza	IND	1	52
436	Soofa	IND	1	1
437	SoTechie Spaces	IND	1	28
438	Splunk	IND	1	13
439	St. Mark's Avenue Block Association	CIV	1	41
440	StartUp Box	IND	1	15
441	Staten Island Economic Development Corporation	IND	1	0
442	Stealth Communications Services	IND	1	1
443	Stella and Charles Guttman Foundation	CIV	1	53
444	Stony Brook University	RES	1	16
445	Sunlight Foundation	CIV	1	4
446	Sunnyside Community Services	CIV	1	1
447	Superflex	IND	1	28
448	Symantec Corporation	IND	1	27

Continued

TABLE D.1 New York City's smart city development strategy: collaborative environment—cont'd

Entity		Category	Number of activities	Degree of centrality
ID code	Name			
449	Talking Alternative	IND	1	28
450	Technical Machine	IND	1	52
451	Technion—Israel Institute of Technology	RES	1	2
452	TechStars	IND	1	14
453	Tehuti Ma'at Garden	CIV	1	41
454	Telecommunications Industry Association	IND	1	12
455	Temboo	IND	1	28
456	Tesla, Inc.	IND	1	16
457	The Advisory Board Company	RES	1	4
458	The Bridge Fund of New York	CIV	1	53
459	The California Endowment	IND	1	53
460	The Diller–von Furstenberg Family Foundation	CIV	1	16
461	The District of Columbia	GOV	1	5
462	The Feil Organization	IND	1	12
463	The Holiday Inn Manhattan View	IND	1	28
464	The HOPE Program	CIV	1	53
465	The Jacob and Valeria Langeloth Foundation	CIV	1	53
466	The Kinnon Group	IND	1	53
467	The Knowledge House	CIV	1	34
468	The Kresge Foundation	CIV	1	53
469	The Made in NY Media Center	IND	1	52

TABLE D.1 New York City's smart city development strategy: collaborative environment—cont'd

Entity ID code	Name	Category	Number of activities	Degree of centrality
470	The Millennial Solution	IND	1	27
471	The Municipal Art Society of New York	CIV	1	53
472	The Nemours Foundation	CIV	1	53
473	The New School	RES	1	15
474	New York State	GOV	22	223
475	The New York Times	OTH	1	52
476	The Noguchi Museum	OTH	1	30
477	The Rockefeller Foundation	CIV	2	34
478	The Trust for Public Land	CIV	1	23
479	The University of Chicago	RES	1	13
480	The University of Warwick	RES	1	7
481	Tides	IND	1	53
482	Tilden Houses Resident Association	CIV	1	41
483	Time Warner Cable	IND	24	57
484	Times Square Alliance	IND	1	3
485	Tishman Speyer	IND	1	12
486	Titan	IND	3	35
487	Transit Wireless	IND	2	34
488	Transportation Alternatives	CIV	2	65
489	True Sound Lounge	IND	1	28
490	Tumbador Chocolate	IND	1	28

Continued

TABLE D.1 New York City's smart city development strategy: collaborative environment—cont'd

Entity				
ID code	Name	Category	Number of activities	Degree of centrality
491	Tumblr	IND	2	6
492	Twilio	IND	1	52
493	Twitter	IND	2	9
494	US Green Building Council	IND	1	23
495	UBM	IND	1	13
496	Union Square Ventures	IND	4	34
497	United Federal Data of New York	OTH	1	1
498	United For Brownsville	CIV	1	53
499	United Way of New York City	CIV	1	1
500	University of Toronto	RES	1	7
501	UPROSE	CIV	1	30
502	Urban Strategies	IND	1	41
503	Urban.us	IND	1	23
504	Van Dyke Houses Residents Association	CIV	1	41
505	Van Wagner	IND	1	2
506	Veritas	IND	1	21
507	Verizon	IND	6	65
508	Vertical Lessons	IND	1	16
509	Vizalytics Technology	IND	1	1
510	Vonage	IND	1	5
511	W.K. Kellogg Foundation	CIV	1	53
512	Wayside Outreach Development	CIV	1	41
513	WE ACT for Environmental Justice	CIV	1	30

TABLE D.1 New York City's smart city development strategy: collaborative environment—cont'd

Entity				
ID code	Name	Category	Number of activities	Degree of centrality
514	We Run Brownsville	CIV	1	41
515	Wells Fargo	IND	1	27
516	West Brighton Community Local Development Corporation	CIV	2	6
517	Westchester Square Business Improvement District	IND	1	30
518	WeWork	IND	1	52
519	Wi-Fi Salon	IND	1	1
520	Women's City Club of New York	CIV	3	15
521	Women's Housing and Economic Development Corporation	IND	2	6
522	Woodside On the Move	CIV	1	1
523	Workday	IND	2	37
524	Workforce Opportunity Services	CIV	1	25
525	World Young Women's Christian Association	CIV	1	1
526	Xchange Telecom	IND	1	1
527	Xerox Corporation	IND	1	13
528	XO Group Inc.	IND	1	52
529	Yahoo!	IND	2	70
530	Yelp	IND	2	69
531	Zayo Group	IND	1	4
532	ZenFi Networks	IND	2	1

IND, industry; *RES*, research; *GOV*, government; *CIV*, civil society; *OTH*, others.

Index

Note: Page numbers followed by *f* indicate figures and *t* indicate tables.

E

F

G

H

I

K

L

M

N

O